lonely planet

Thailand's Islands & Beaches

Bangkok p50

Ko Chang & the Eastern Seaboard p94

Hua Hin & the Upper Gulf p137

Phuket & the Northern Andaman Coast p241

Ko Samui & the Lower Gulf p170

Ko Phi-Phi & the Southern Andaman Coast p301

THIS EDITION WRITTEN AND RESEARCHED BY

Celeste Brash,
Aust[illegible] ...[illegible]nick

PLAN YOUR TRIP

GEORGETTE DOUWMA/GETTY IMAGES ©

DIVING & SNORKELLING, P39

DAVID HENLEY/GETTY IMAGES ©

ANG THONG MARINE NATIONAL PARK, P224

ON THE ROAD

Contents

UNDERSTAND

SURVIVAL GUIDE

SPECIAL FEATURES

Welcome to Thailand's Islands & Beaches

Bays of peach-tinged sand, hammocks swinging between palm trees, castle-like karsts emerging from the deep; these dreams of a tropical paradise become reality along southern Thailand's coasts.

Splendid Beaches

Thailand's beaches are legendary: tall palms angle over pearlescent sand, coral gardens flourish in the shallow seas and beach parties are liberally lubricated with alcohol and fun. With two long coastlines and jungle-topped islands anchored in azure waters, Thailand is a getaway for the hedonist and the hermit, the prince and the pauper. Scale the sheer sea cliffs of Krabi, cavort with gentle whale sharks at pinnacles off Ko Tao and Ko Pha-Ngan, toe the curling tide alongside gypsy fishermen in Trang, gorge on seafood in Hua Hin or relish perfectly practised butler service at your luxury digs in Phuket. The adventure awaits.

Hot & Spicy

The beaches may bring you to Thailand, but it's the food that will lure you back. Enjoyed around the world, Thai cuisine expresses fundamental aspects of Thai culture: it is generous and warm, outgoing and nuanced, refreshing and relaxed. And it is much more delicious in its native setting. Thai dishes rely on fresh and local ingredients, from pungent lemon grass and searing chillies to plump seafood and crispy fried chicken. With a tropical abundance, the varied national menu is built around the four fundamental flavours: spicy, sweet, salty and sour.

Local Smiles

Whether it's the glimmering eye of the meditative *wâi* (palms-together Thai greeting) or the mirthful smirk of passers-by, it's hard not to be charmed by the Land of Smiles. The moniker is not only apt but also well earned. Thailand has long been Southeast Asia's mama-san, inviting foreigners from near and far to indulge in the kingdom's natural splendours. This recipe is perfected along the beaches and islands where a heady mix of seascapes, limestone towers and equatorial sunshine provides the perfect backdrop to expertly run resorts catering to whimsy with a desire to please.

Mean Massages

You asked for this. The view may be of white sands and blue waters but as your massage therapist squeezes the stress from your back with an exceptionally strong fist, twists your body until you let out a small yelp, then cracks your finger joints, you begin to question your sanity. But, when they're done, a smile spreads over your face, your shoulders drop and you feel more at one with the tides, the breeze wafting through the palms and the cold Singha awaiting you.

Why I Love Thailand's Islands & Beaches

By Celeste Brash, Author

When I think of southern Thailand all the colours in my mind go electric. The sun reflecting off the white sand, beyond-blue water and the green jungles make everything surreal, a cinematographer's interpretation of a tropical dream. No matter how many times I return to this region, I'm always stunned by the beauty and I gorge myself on delicious food; the temples ease my soul and the locals make me smile. Who wouldn't love it here? My favourite moments are always off the tourist trail where nature and local culture still reign.

For more about our authors, see page 448

Above: Hat Mae Nam, Ko Samui (p171)

Thailand's Islands & Beaches

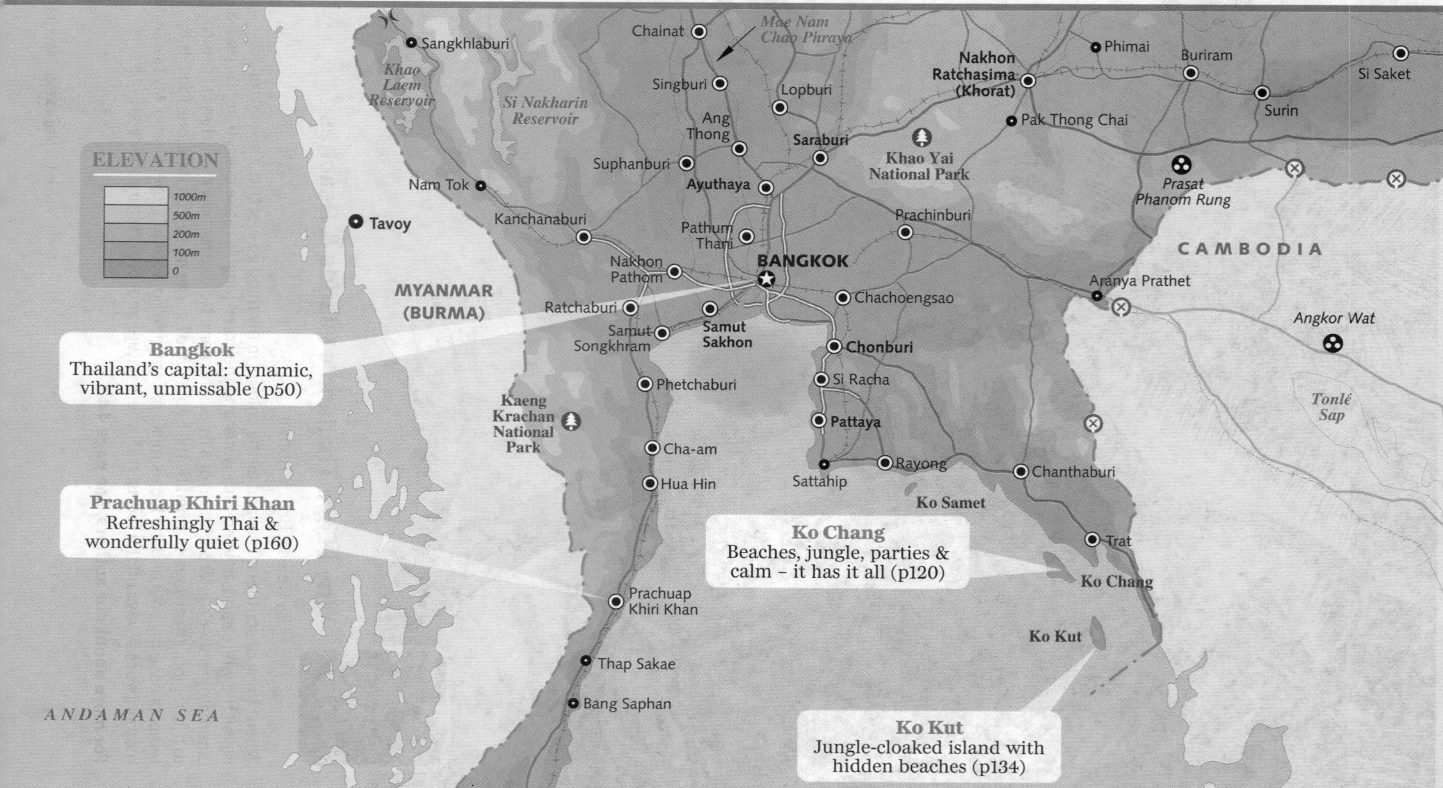

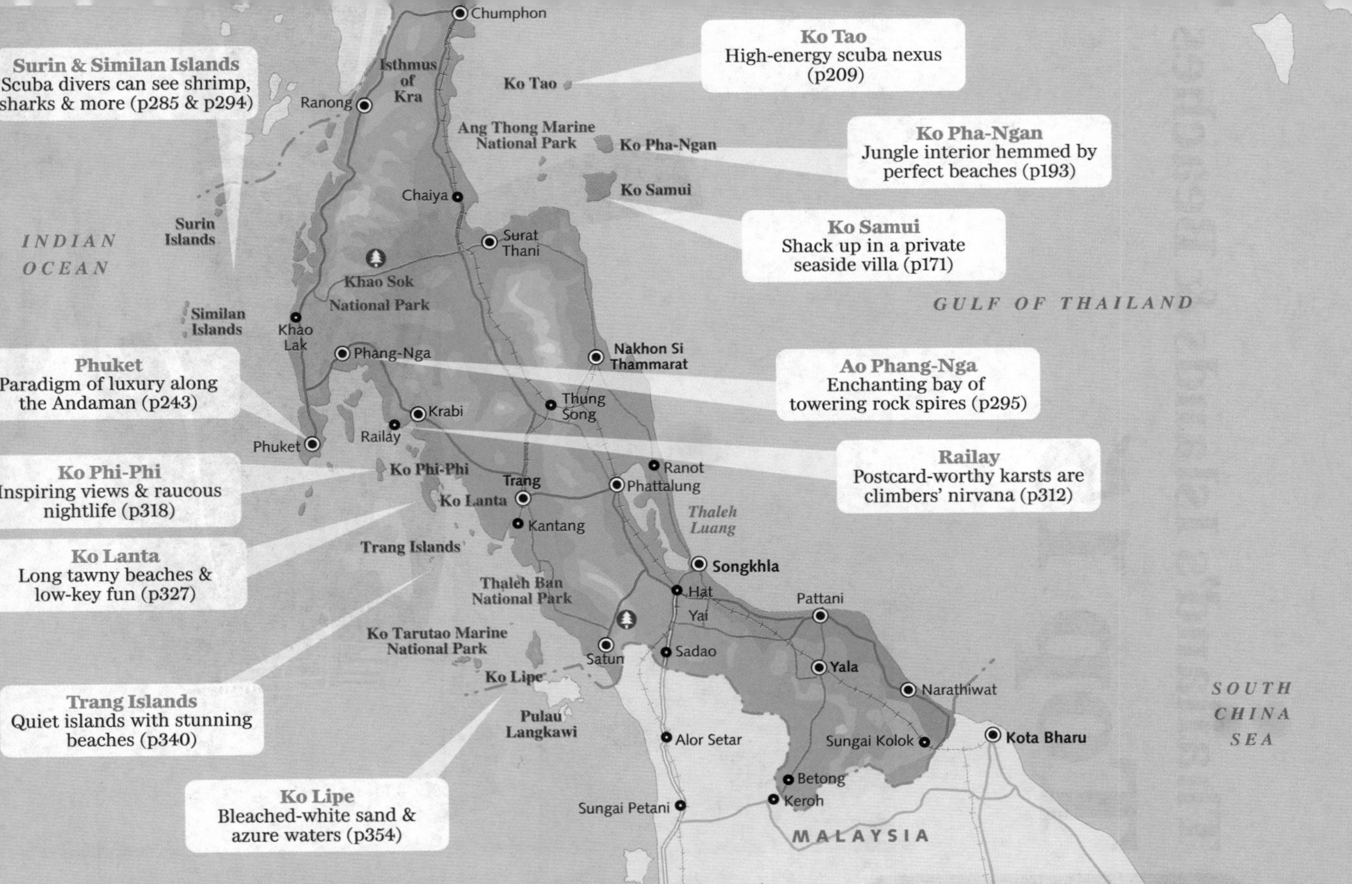

Surin & Similan Islands
Scuba divers can see shrimp, sharks & more (p285 & p294)
Ko Tao
High-energy scuba nexus (p209)
Ko Pha-Ngan
Jungle interior hemmed by perfect beaches (p193)
Ko Samui
Shack up in a private seaside villa (p171)
Phuket
Paradigm of luxury along the Andaman (p243)
Ao Phang-Nga
Enchanting bay of towering rock spires (p295)
Ko Phi-Phi
Inspiring views & raucous nightlife (p318)
Railay
Postcard-worthy karsts are climbers' nirvana (p312)
Ko Lanta
Long tawny beaches & low-key fun (p327)
Trang Islands
Quiet islands with stunning beaches (p340)
Ko Lipe
Bleached-white sand & azure waters (p354)
Chumphon
Isthmus of Kra
Ranong
Ko Tao
Ang Thong Marine National Park
Ko Pha-Ngan
Ko Samui
Chaiya
Surat Thani
INDIAN OCEAN
Surin Islands
Khao Sok National Park
Similan Islands
Khao Lak
Phang-Nga
Nakhon Si Thammarat
GULF OF THAILAND
Thung Song
Krabi
Railay
Phuket
Ko Phi-Phi
Ranot
Trang
Phattalung
Ko Lanta
Kantang
Thaleh Luang
Trang Islands
Songkhla
Hat Yai
Thaleh Ban National Park
Pattani
Ko Tarutao Marine National Park
Satun
Sadao
Yala
Ko Lipe
Narathiwat
SOUTH CHINA SEA
Pulau Langkawi
Alor Setar
Sungai Kolok
Kota Bharu
Betong
Sungai Petani
Keroh
MALAYSIA

Thailand's Islands & Beaches Top 15

1

Trang Islands

1 The early morning sun casts honeylike shadows across another deep-green isle rising out of the blue. The warm wind ruffles your hair and all you can hear is the motor of the long-tail boat. The whole scene is framed by a weathered boat bow decorated in colourful bands of cloth. Your next island-hopping destination is that white beach in the distance – one of many to explore, hike and snorkel – but the boat ride is so extraordinarily gorgeous, it's as enjoyable as being at your destination in the Trang Islands (p340). Below left: Long-tail boats, Ko Ngai (p341), Trang Islands

Ko Tao

2 The dive-master's island, Ko Tao (p209) is the cheapest and easiest spot to learn how to strap on a tank and dive into the deep. The water is warm and gentle, and the submarine spectacles are not to be missed. Just offshore, scenic rocky coves and coral reefs frequented by all sorts of fish provide a snorkelling 'aperitif'. Ko Tao's small size means you can explore all of its jungle nooks and crannies, and find a sandy niche to call your own. Below: Scuba diver, Ko Tao

ERIC PHAN-KIM/GETTY IMAGES ©

2

BLAKE KENT/GETTY IMAGES ©

STEVE MACAULAY/GETTY IMAGES ©

Railay

3 Whether you're a pro or have never grabbed a notch hole in your life, the rock-climbing scene at Railay (p312) will get you scrambling skywards with joy. With about 500 bolted routes of limestone walls overlooking some of the world's most spectacular scenery – think vertical grey spires decorated in greenery surrounded by crystalline sea and white beaches – even the shortest jaunt guarantees thrills. Seasoned climbers could stay for months. For even more adventure, try deep-water soloing where the climb ends with a splash in the water below. Above left: Rock climber, Railay

Ko Kut

4 Thailand's large island frontier, Ko Kut (p134) is a verdant canvas of dense jungle hemmed by pristine beaches – perfect for uninterrupted afternoons of sun worship and calm evenings accented by the meditative hum of the cicada. Although Ko Kut's topography is similar to many of the other islands in the kingdom, with rainforest and waterfalls hidden deep within, its location at the tip of the Ko Chang archipelago means that the coastal waters glimmer with a unique emerald tint.

Ko Pha-Ngan

5 Famous for its debauched Full Moon Parties and all-night techno fun, Ko Pha-Ngan (p193) has graduated from a sleepy bohemian island to full-on attraction for all types of travellers. The beach shanties are becoming more boutique, so comfort seekers and families have an alternative to Ko Samui. And on the northern and eastern coasts, hammock hangers can still escape enough to feel like a modern castaway (a well-fed one, of course). Just offshore is Sail Rock, one of the gulf's best dive sites. Above right: Full Moon Party, Hat Rin, Ko Pha-Ngan

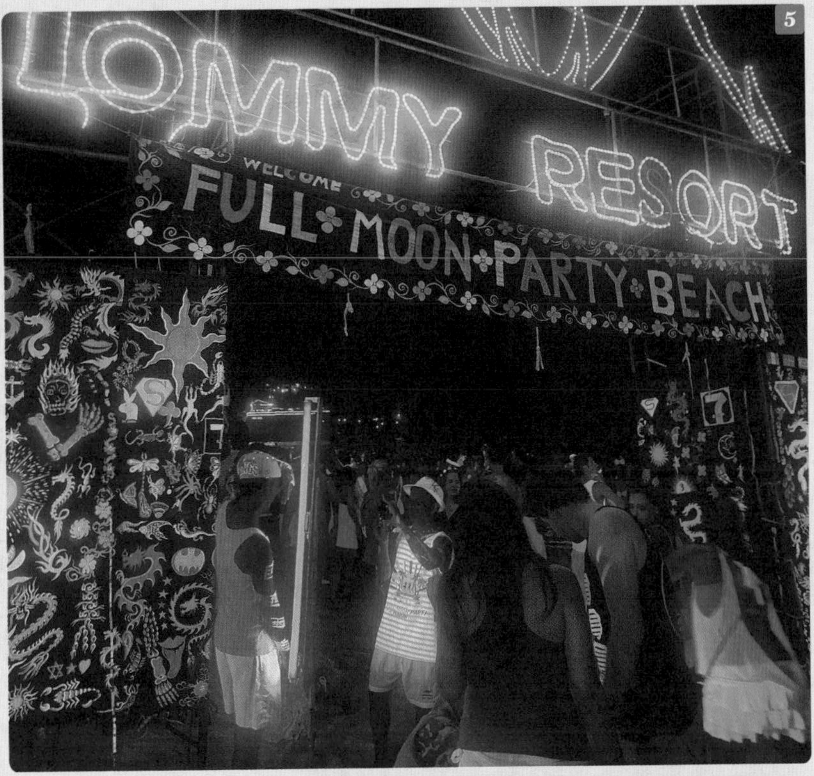

STEPHEN J BOITANO/GETTY IMAGES ©

Phuket

6 Known mostly for its excellent-value luxury resorts and Patong's hedonism, there's a lot more to Phuket (p243) than the brochures tell you. Head to Phuket Town for some gorgeous restored heritage Sino-Portugese architecture, hike the steamy jungles of Khao Phra Thaew Royal Wildlife & Forest Reserve, take a cooking class, go diving or learn to surf during low season. For beach-side lounging away from the Phuket buzz, try the northern beaches like Hat Nai Thon or to the south at Laem Phanwa.

Right: Luxury accommodation, Phuket

KEVIN MILLER/GETTY IMAGES ©

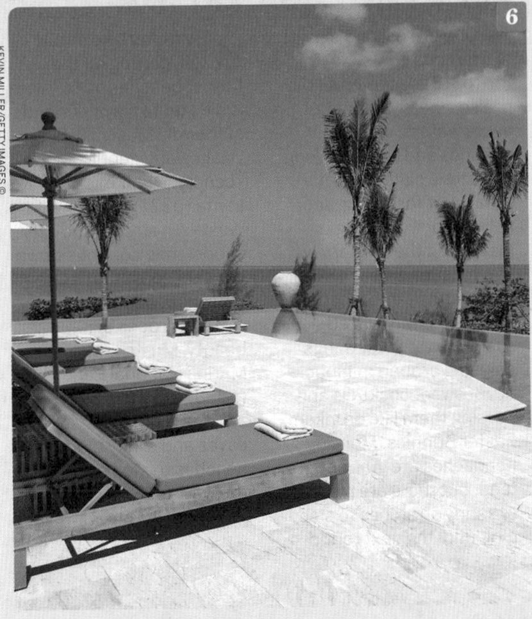

NORBERT HOHN/GETTY IMAGES ©

MICHAEL ZEGERS/GETTY IMAGES ©

Ko Phi-Phi

7 One of Thailand's most famous spots, Ko Phi-Phi (p318) deserves all the praise it gets. Stunning azure waters, gorgeous beaches and breath-taking limestone cliffs make it a great spot for diving, snorkelling, rock climbing or just ogling the scenery as you toast on a beach. After dark, it turns into a hedonistic mess, with dazed-eyed twenty-somethings carrying around minibuckets of sweet cocktails and nursing them like drunken Easter Bunnies. Morning headaches are guaranteed, but there are plenty of sandy stretches to sleep it off until the next round.

Ko Lanta

8 By motorbike or túk-túk, getting off the tourist beaches of Ko Lanta is a ticket to a wonderland of friendly Muslim fishing villages and gentle jungle scenery. Don't miss Ban Ko Lanta (p327) with its Wild West–era streets and arty shops, then continue down the east coast that's been little influenced by tourism. For a dose of natural beauty, Mu Ko Lanta Marine National Park (p333) is hard to beat – and there are plenty of caves and slinky blonde beaches to stop at along the way. Top right: Ao Kantiang (p333), Ko Lanta

Ko Chang

9 The rugged landscape of Ko Chang (p120) conceals some of Southeast Asia's best-preserved wilderness. The island's craggy mountainous interior is home to a veritable Jurassic Park of flora and fauna; the hills are cut with rivers and waterfalls. The abounding biodiversity includes exotic reptiles, colourful birds and even some friendly elephants, and plenty of guides are available to help you find them. Although developers have snared all of the attractive beachfront real estate there are some sand-fringed nooks in the east and south that feel decidedly off the beaten path. Above: Bungalows, Ko Chang

Ko Lipe

10 Hat Pattaya on Ko Lipe (p354) is a perfect arc of the whitest white sand with long-tails bobbing in its azure bay, busy seafood barbecues spread out on the foreshore and fit folks playing volleyball through the day. Quieter Sunrise Beach is more golden and stretches on till it curves at the sight of majestic Ko Adang across the blue. If you tire of one beach, it's a short walk over the small hill to the other, or explore trails for more hidden swathes of sand.

Ao Phang-Nga

11 While other visitors squeeze onto speedboats to get blurry glimpses of Ao Phang-Nga National Park's (p296) spectacular limestone tower–studded bay, sea-kayakers get to enjoy it in slow silence. Cavort with flying lizards, banded sea snakes or helmeted hornbills. Glide past rock art inside sea caves, picnic on secluded beaches and swim in silky water. Yes, a few boats will whiz by, but for the most part you'll just enjoy the music of your paddle rippling through the water. At nightfall, become enchanted with the bay's famed bioluminescence.

10

11

Ko Samui

12 Eager to please, Samui (p171) is a civilised beach-resort island for the vacationing masses, many of whom fly in and out having made hardly any contact with the local culture. Reserve a resort, then let them do the thinking for you. If this sounds boring, there are still sleepy spits to the south and west, reminiscent of Samui's old moniker, 'Coconut Island', that are easy to get to. Explore the thriving health scene with yoga, meditation and detox retreats to enhance your relaxation. Below: Hat Mae Nam, Ko Samui

Ko Ratanakosin, Bangkok

13 The artificial island of Ko Ratanakosin (p54) is the birthplace of modern Bangkok but it's also among the city's most atmospheric 'hoods. Home to the bulk of Bangkok's must-see sights, such as the Emerald Buddha, Wat Phra Kaew and Wat Pho, Ko Ratanakosin also holds several low-key treasures, including the hectic amulet market and the delightful Museum of Siam. Approach it via a scenic trip on the Chao Phraya Express Boat, then link the sights on foot for an atmospheric walking tour. Below: Buddha statues, Wat Pho (p54)

12

13

14

WU NORBERT/GETTY IMAGES ©

15

MONTHON WA/GETTY IMAGES ©

Richelieu Rock

14 The world-renowned dive sites dotting the crystal seas of the Surin and Similan Islands Marine National Parks are some of the best spots in the country to strap on a scuba mask and dive deep. The ultimate prize, however, is distant Richelieu Rock (p286), accessible only to those who venture north towards the so-called Burma Banks on a live-aboard diving trip. The horseshoe-shaped outcrop acts as a feeding station luring manta rays and whale sharks. Top: A diver and a whale shark near Richelieu Rock

Prachuap Khiri Khan

15 A delightful throwback to the time when Thailand's beaches were crowd-free and fishing boats rather than jet skis bobbed on the waves, Prachuap (p160) is set around a series of beautiful bays and surrounded by karst outcrops and fine beaches. Nightlife means a leisurely drink overlooking the ocean, and the seafood is some of Thailand's tastiest and cheapest. Best of all, Prachuap is so laid-back that almost everyone who visits ends up staying far longer than they anticipated. Above: Fishing boats at sunrise, Prachuap Khiri Khan

Need to Know

For more information, see Survival Guide (p405)

Currency
Thai baht (B)

Language
Thai

Visas
Thirty-day visas for international air arrivals; 15-day visas at land borders; 60-day visas from a Thai consulate before leaving home.

Money
ATMs are widespread and charge a 150B foreign-account fee. Visa and MasterCard accepted at upmarket establishments.

Mobile Phones
Thailand is on a GSM network; inexpensive prepaid SIM cards are available. Bangkok and the more populated islands have 4G.

Time
GMT/UTC plus seven hours.

When to Go

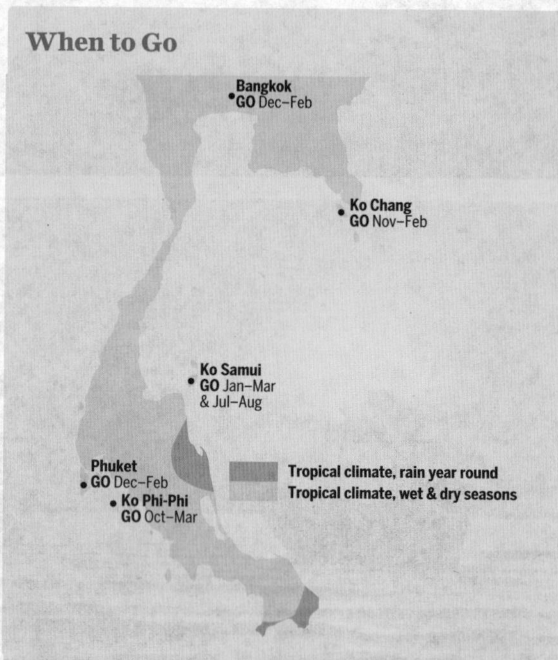

High Season (Nov–Mar)

➡ A cool and dry season follows the monsoons, meaning the landscape is lush and temperatures are comfortable.

➡ Western Christmas and New Year's holidays bring crowds and inflated rates to the beaches.

Shoulder Season (Apr–Jun)

➡ April, May and June are generally very hot and dry, but the sea breeze provides plenty of natural air-con.

Low Season (Jul–Oct)

➡ The Andaman and gulf coasts take turns being pummelled by monsoon rains.

➡ Weather is generally favourable along the southern gulf in July and August.

➡ Some islands shut down and boats are limited during stormy weather.

Websites

Tourism Authority of Thailand (TAT; www.tourismthailand.org) National tourism department.

Thaivisa (www.thaivisa.com) Expat site.

Lonely Planet (www.lonelyplanet.com/thailand) Country profile and what to do and see.

Bangkok Post (www.bangkokpost.com) English-language daily newspaper.

Thai Language (www.thai-language.com) Online dictionary and Thai tutorials.

Thai Travel Blogs (www.thaitravelblogs.com) Thailand-based travel blogger.

Important Numbers

Thailand country code	☎66
Emergency	☎191
International access codes	☎001, ☎007, ☎008, ☎009 (various service providers)
Operator-assisted international calls	☎100
Tourist police	☎1155

Exchange Rates

Australia	A$1	30B
Canada	C$1	30B
China	Y10	51B
Euro zone	€1	43B
Japan	¥100	32B
New Zealand	NZ$1	26B
Russia	R10	10B
UK	£1	50B
USA	US$1	31B

For current exchange rates see www.xe.com.

Your Daily Costs

Budget: Less than 2000B

- Basic guesthouse room: 400–1000B
- Market and street-stall meals: 40-100B
- One or two evening drinks: 60-300B
- Mix of walking and public transport: 10-200B

Midrange: 2000–5000B

- Flashpacker guesthouse or midrange hotel room: 1000–3000B
- Western lunches and seafood dinners: 150-300B
- Several evening beers: 250B
- Motorbike hire: 150-250B

Top end: Over 5000B

- Boutique hotel room: 3000B and beyond
- Fine dining: 250B and up
- Private tours: from 2000B
- Car hire: from 800B per day

Opening Hours

Opening hours vary, especially in more remote places where businesses open and close at whim.

Banks 9.30am-3.30pm Mon-Fri

Restaurants 10am-10pm

Bars and Clubs 8pm-2am

Government Offices 8.30am-4.30pm Mon-Fri

Shops 9am-6pm daily

Arriving in Thailand

Suvarnabhumi International Airport

Airport Bus Every hour from 6.10am to 9pm (150B).

Airport Rail Link Local service (45B, 30 minutes) to Phaya Thai station; express service (150B, 15 minutes) to Makkasan station.

Taxi Meter taxis 220B to 380B plus 50B airport surcharge and tolls; about an hour to the city.

Don Muang International Airport

Bus One to two hours to Th Khao San (18B).

Shuttle to BTS Shuttles every 20 minutes (20 minutes, 30B) between airport and Mo Chit BTS station.

Train Every one to 1½ hours to Hualamphong train station from 4am to 9.30pm.

Taxi Meter taxis 200B to 220B plus 50B airport surcharge and tolls; 30 minutes to one hour to the city.

Getting Around

Planes, trains, buses and boats easily whisk you to the south. Or you can fly directly to Phuket or Ko Samui from a variety of international destinations rather than connecting through Bangkok.

Air Increasing numbers of flights and destinations, but can be expensive.

Bus & minivan Lots of options, cheap and efficient.

Train Inexpensive and comfortable, but frequent breakdowns make them less reliable than buses.

Boat Everything from big, slow ferries to the bigger islands to fast, private long-tails or flashy speedboats for day trips.

For much more on **getting around**, see p420

First Time Thailand

For more information, see Survival Guide (p405)

Checklist

- Make sure your passport is valid for at least six months.
- Inform your debit/credit card company of your travels.
- Visit the Thai consulate for a tourist visa for stays of more than 30 days.
- Organise travel insurance and diver's insurance.
- Check baggage restrictions. Get plane seat assignments online if possible.
- Visit the doctor for a check-up and medical clearance if you intend to go scuba diving.

What to Pack

- Thai phrasebook
- Power converter
- Waterproof sunscreen
- Mosquito repellent with DEET
- Anti-itch cream (for sandfly bites)
- Light, long-sleeve shirt
- Breathable pants
- Hat
- Sunglasses
- Comfortable sandals
- Torch/headlamp

Top Tips for Your Trip

- If you rent a vehicle, take pictures of it before you drive it. This may help shield you from the rife rental scam of accusing tourists of scratching or damaging already beat-up vehicles.
- If booking online make sure you know exactly where your hotel is located. Many 'great deals' end up being out in the middle of nowhere. Pay upfront for as few nights as possible so you can leave without having to haggle your money back.
- Don't lose your cool even in the most difficult situations. Thais greatly respect a 'cool heart', and shouting or anger will only escalate a situation, usually not to your benefit.
- Relax and smile! If you go with the flow it's unlikely you'll have any of the above problems.

What to Wear

Light, loose-fitting clothes will prove the most comfortable in the tropical heat throughout the year. Bring one reasonably warm sweater for the odd cool evening (or the blasting air-con on the plane). To visit temples, you will need shirts with long sleeves and full-length pants. While sandals are definitely the way to go, you should bring one pair of good shoes for the occasional night out in Bangkok or Phuket.

Sleeping

Outside of high season only the most popular resorts need to be booked in advance. At this time of year walk-in or call-in prices are cheaper than what you'll find online.

- **Resorts** Range from villas with their own swimming pools and butlers to ageing shacks cooled by sea breezes.
- **Guesthouses** Are becoming fewer in number as resorts take over. Those remaining often have few amenities but low price tags and plenty of authenticity.

Money

Paying for your food, drinks, entertainment and souvenirs is usually easier with cash than cards. Most midrange and top-end hotels take credit cards, as will most diving outfits, but expect to pay a 'processing fee' (of 2% to 3%) when you swipe your Visa or MasterCard (the preferred cards).

Withdrawing money usually includes a 150B withdrawal fee. You'll find ATMs at (or near) almost all 7-Elevens. Smaller islands have limited to no withdrawal facilities.

For more information, see p413.

Bargaining

➡ When to bargain

Bargaining forms the crux of almost any commercial interaction in Thailand. There are no set rules. If you're purchasing something, it's best to buy in bulk – the more T-shirts you buy, the lower the price will go. Keep it lighthearted.

➡ When not to bargain

You shouldn't bargain in restaurants, 7-Elevens and petrol stations. Don't haggle for a better price at a high-end hotel, though bargaining is fair game at most beach establishments.

Tipping

Tipping is not generally expected in Thailand. The exception is loose change from a large restaurant bill.

Etiquette

The best way to win over the Thais is to smile – any visible anger or arguing is embarrassing; the locals call this 'loss of face'. Never disrespect the royal family with disparaging remarks, and also treat objects depicting the king (like money) with respect.

➡ Temples

When visiting a temple, dress neatly and conservatively with shoulders to knees covered. It's expected that you remove all footwear. When sitting, keep your feet pointed away from any Buddha images. Women should never touch a monk or a monk's belongings.

➡ At the beach

Avoid public nudity; in fact, most Thais will swim fully clothed. Away from the sand, men should wear shirts and women should be appropriately dressed (no bikinis).

Language

Don't know a lick of Thai? In most places, you won't need to. Bus drivers, market vendors and even taxi drivers tend to know at least basic English. In small, less touristy towns, it helps to know how to order food and count in Thai. With a few phrases, you'll be rewarded with big grins.

Thais have their own script, which turns Westerners into illiterates. Street signs are always transliterated into English, but there is no standard system so spellings vary widely and confusingly.

What's New

Fast Flying to the Islands

The new airport scheduled to open on Ko Pha-Ngan in late 2014 will further decrease the time it takes to get to Thailand's most popular white beaches and azure waters. Meanwhile, more and more international flights are servicing Phuket and Ko Samui directly and increasing numbers of domestic flights are available to Chumphon, Krabi and Trang.

HTMS Chang Wreck Diving

Sunk on purpose in 2012 to create an artificial reef, this 100m Thai naval vessel is attracting fish and scuba divers to the coast of Ban Bang Bao, Ko Chang. (p125)

Whale Shark Sightings Made Easier

Get on the Ace Marine Expeditions limited 'whaleshark watch list' (on Ko Tao) to be whisked out to look for – and hopefully dive with – the amazing creatures. (p175)

Suay Cooking School & Restaurant

Learn to cook with Noy Tammasak, one of Phuket's best chefs. Otherwise, dine at the Phuket Town restaurant for sublime fusion fare. (p247)

Evolving Bangkok Nightlife

Yay for non-dirty nightlife options in the city. Start in a bar perched on a skyscraper, throw down a few roadside beers and finish up at a basement-level live music pub. (p81)

Kiteboarding Mania

Kiteboarding Asia claims that Ko Samui is the best place in the country to learn the sport, but most of the new schools are opening on Phuket. (p176)

Chalong Bay Rum

New rum distillery using Thai sugarcane on Phuket. Tour the factory and imbibe a cocktail. (p258)

Dorm Beds A-Go-Go in Hat Rin

A slew of very cramped, rudimentary dorms have popped up all over town. Who needs sleep anyway? (p197)

Fun Flashpacking in BKK

Flashpacker pads continue to multiply in Bangkok and new hostels are combining high-tech dorm beds, publike communal areas and loads of fun activities. (p72)

Ko Samet Oil Spill

In July 2013 Thailand suffered its fourth-largest oil spill, off Ko Samet. The clean-up has been massive but it may be inadvisable to swim off Ao Prao or Ko Si Chang for some time. (p111)

For more recommendations and reviews, see lonelyplanet.com/thailand

If You Like...

Beautiful Beaches

From intimate coves to sandy coastlines, Thailand's beaches include some of the most gorgeous on Earth. Gone are the days of having paradise to yourself, but the scenery is sublime.

Ko Kut Kilometres of unpopulated sand arc around lonely Ko Kut, while Hat Khlong Chao is the *crème de la crème* of dreamy beaches. (p134)

Ko Pha-Ngan The original beach bum island hosts boisterous Full Moon Parties on Hat Rin and plenty of hammock-hanging on the Northern Beaches. (p193)

Ko Lipe Crystal-white sand beckons the click of a camera on Hat Pattaya. (p354)

Similan Islands Just as stunning above the sea as below it. Strewn boulders punctuate the pearly white and deep blue vistas. (p294)

Thai Food

Street stalls spring up wherever there are appetites, night markets serve everyone dinner, and family restaurants deliver colourful plates of traditional recipes.

Bangkok The best place in the country and with the most variety – from street stall *pat tai* to the finest Thai food in the world. (p78)

Hua Hin Seafood meets a night market geared towards Thai tourists. Amazing crab curry, mussel omelettes and giant prawns. (p153)

Trang The mother of Andaman Coast night markets cooks up weird stuff like crickets, plus easy-to-down dishes like fresh, spicy salads. (p339)

Phuket Town Fantastic-value fusion and classy Thai fare served in luscious restored heritage buildings. Great street and market food, too. (p251)

Five-Star Pampering

No one does luxury better than Thailand. The country's larger islands boast some of the finest five-star properties that the world has to offer (and some are surprisingly inexpensive).

Phuket Enjoy a parade of upmarket accommodation such as **Pullman** (p275) along the silky western sands of Phuket. Even if you're not overnighting, it's worth coming by for cocktails.

Ko Samui Samui knows how to blend posh digs with quiet seclusion – the northern beaches in particular offer a private paradise to those who open their wallets. (p176)

Bangkok Intense competition among hotels has kept prices low in the capital, so splurge on a fancy crash pad like **Siam Heritage** (p75) at one of the city's luxury headliners.

Hat Pakarang and Hat Bang Sak Adjacent to the diving town of Khao Lak, here you'll find five-star properties such as **Sarojin** (p290) that are easier on the wallet than nearby Phuket picks.

Adventure Sports

Get the blood pumping with one of Thailand's many adventure activities. Sure, there's plenty of scuba diving, but you'll find just as many thrills without strapping on a tank.

Rock climbing in Railay The Andaman's signature limestone

IF YOU LIKE...NIGHTLIFE

A night in Bangkok is a must. You're also apt to find plenty of boozing down in Phuket and Ko Samui, and don't forget the veritable beeline of backpackers who move between Ko Pha-Ngan and Ko Phi-Phi.

outcrops come to a dramatic climax in Railay – look up high and spot hundreds of dangling climbers. (p314)

Kiteboarding off Phuket, Ko Samui & Hua Hin Steady winds and shallow waters make these coasts a great place to learn this increasingly popular sport. (p243, p176 and p150)

Sea kayaking in Phang-Nga Gaze towards the heavens from your kayak as jagged stone pierces the clouds above. (p244)

Ziplining in Phuket Go gibbon-style through a vast acreage of palm trees and swing through the canopy, catching glimpses of the secreted forest below. (p243)

Basic Beach Shacks

Though their numbers are dwindling, there are still cheap, beach-side bungalows in Thailand with little more than a terrace, bed, cold shower and mosquito net.

Ko Pha-Ngan Things may be moving upscale, but Ko Pha-Ngan still has myriad nooks such as Chalok Lam that have yet to see any sign of true development. (p193)

Ko Wai Gaze from your bungalow at **Ko Wai Paradise** (p132) as day trippers depart at sunset, on this fleck of a white sand isle in the Ko Chang Archipelago.

Little Ko Chang Ao Yai (p283), a beachy slice of jungle-clad hippy-dom near the Myanmar border, has been slow to change and has many return visitors (don't confuse it with Ko Chang on the gulf coast).

Bang Saphan Yai Tucked along the mainland's overlooked upper gulf region, Bang Saphan Yai basks in its back-to-Thai life-style – there are bamboo huts aplenty like **Roytawan** (p165).

GLENN VAN DER KNIJFF/GETTY IMAGES ©

JOHN HARPER/GETTY IMAGES ©

(Top) Sea kayakers, Ao Phang-Nga National Marine Park (p296)
(Bottom) Kiteboarder, Hat Kata (p259)

Month by Month

TOP EVENTS

Songkran, April

Loi Krathong, November

Full Moon Party, Monthly

Vegetarian Festival, October

HM the King's Birthday, December

January

The weather is cool and dry in Thailand, ushering in the peak tourist season when Europeans escape dreary winter weather.

Chinese New Year

Thais with Chinese ancestry celebrate the Chinese lunar new year (dates vary) with a week of house-cleaning and fireworks. Phuket, Bangkok and Pattaya all host citywide festivities, but in general Chinese New Year *(drùt jeen)* is a family event.

February

Still in the high season swing, snowbirds flock to Thailand for sun and fun.

Makha Bucha

Makha Bucha *(mah·ká boo·chah)* falls on the full moon of the third lunar month and commemorates Buddha preaching to 1250 enlightened monks who came to hear him 'without prior summons'. This public holiday is mainly a day for temple visits.

March

Hot and dry season approaches. The winds kick up, ushering in kite-flying and kiteboarding season. This is Thailand's semester break, and students head out on sightseeing trips.

Golden Mango Season

Luscious, ripe mangoes come into season from March to June and are sliced before your eyes, packed in containers with sticky rice and accompanied with a sweet sauce.

Pattaya International Music Festival

Pattaya showcases pop and rock bands from across Asia at this free music event, attracting busloads of Bangkok university students. (p103)

April

Hot, dry weather sweeps across the land as the tourist season winds down, except for one last hurrah during Songkran. Make reservations well in advance since the whole country is on the move for this holiday.

Songkran

Thailand's traditional new year (mid-April) starts with morning visits to the temple. Afterwards everyone loads up their water guns and heads out to the streets for battle: water is thrown and sprayed from roving commandos at targets both willing and unwilling.

May

Leading up to the rainy season, festivals encourage plentiful rains and bountiful harvests. This is an underappreciated shoulder season when prices are lower and tourists are few.

Royal Ploughing Ceremony

This ceremony employs astrology and ancient Brahman rituals to kick off the rice-planting season. Sacred oxen are hitched to a wooden plough and part the ground of Sanam Luang in Bangkok. The ritual was revived in the 1960s by the king.

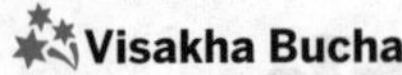

Visakha Bucha

The holy day of Visakha Bucha *(wí·săh·kà boo·chah,* on the 15th day of the waxing moon in the sixth lunar month, commemorates the date of the Buddha's birth, enlightenment and *parinibbana* (passing away).

June

In some parts of the region, the rainy season is merely an afternoon shower, leaving the rest of the day for music and merriment.

Hua Hin Jazz Festival

Jazz groups descend on this royal retreat for a musical homage to the king, an accomplished jazz saxophonist and composer. Sometimes held in May. (p151)

July

With the start of the rainy season, the religious community and attendant festivals prepare for Buddhist Lent, a period of reflection and meditation.

Asanha Bucha

The full moon of the eighth lunar month commemorates Buddha's first sermon. The day after this begins Khao Phansaa, also called Buddhist Lent.

Khao Phansaa

Buddhist Lent (the first day of the waning moon in the eighth lunar month) is the traditional time for men to enter the monkhood and monks typically retreat inside the monastery for a period. During Khao Phansaa, worshippers make offerings to the temples and attend ordinations.

August

Overcast skies and daily showers mark the middle of the rainy season. The rain just adds to the ever-present humidity.

HM the Queen's Birthday

The Thai Queen's Birthday (12 August) is a public holiday and national mother's day. In Bangkok, the day is marked with cultural displays along Th Ratchadamnoen and Sanam Luang.

October

Religious preparations for the end of the rainy season and the end of Buddhist Lent begin. The monsoons are reaching the finish line (in most of the country).

Ork Phansa

The end of Buddhist Lent (three lunar months after Khao Phansaa) is followed by the *gà·tĭn* ceremony, in which new robes are given to monks by merit-makers.

Vegetarian Festival

The Vegetarian Festival is a holiday from meat taken for nine days (during the ninth lunar month) in adherence with Chinese Buddhist beliefs of mind and body purification. In Phuket the festival can turn extreme, with entranced marchers transforming themselves into human shish kebabs. (p252)

November

The cool, dry season has arrived and if you get here early enough, you'll beat the tourist crowds. The landscape is lush: perfect for trekking and waterfall-spotting.

Loi Krathong

Loi Krathong is celebrated on the first full moon of the 12th lunar month. The festival thanks the river goddess for providing life to the fields and forests, and asks for forgiveness. Origami-like boats made from banana leaves are set adrift on the country's waterways.

December

The peak of the tourist season has returned with fair skies and a holiday mood.

HM the King's Birthday

Honouring the king's birthday on 5 December, this public holiday hosts parades and merit-making events; it is also recognised as national father's day. Th Ratchadamnoen Klang in Bangkok is decorated with lights and regalia. Everyone wears pink shirts, pink being the colour associated with the monarchy.

Above: Thai women enjoying Songkran (p23)

MATTEO COLOMBO/GETTY IMAGES ©

Plan Your Trip
Itineraries

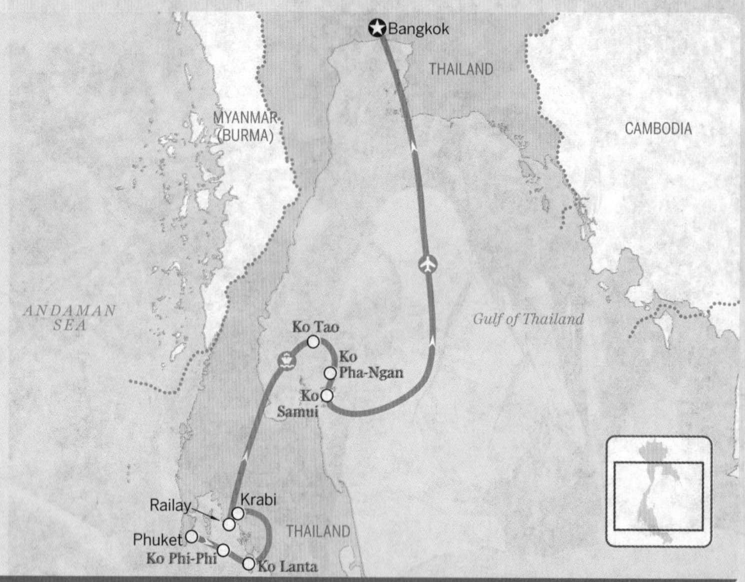

Essential Islands & Beaches

Consider this the itinerary for the uninitiated, and what a warm welcome you'll receive. Flying directly to the islands either internationally or from Bangkok will save you about a day's worth of travel at either end, so decide what's more valuable to you: beach time or money.

Do not pass 'Go', do not collect $200, just head directly to **Phuket** and pick a beach from which to recover from jet lag for a day or two before starting your journey down one of the finest stretches of coastline in the world. Party-goers should base themselves in lively, sleaze-tinged Patong and lovers of quiet should consider the northern beaches, but there's a perfect seaside ambience for everyone on this huge island. For variety, Phuket Town brims with gorgeous, heritage Sino-Portuguese architecture. Once the first stages of relaxation have set in, hop on a boat over to **Ko Phi-Phi** and join the legions of bucket-wielding backpackers as they sit in the soft sands of the island's signature hourglass bays, or take a boat to the quieter east side of the island. Soak in the beauty of this place for two days until taking another

A woman on a long-tail boat, Ko Phi-Phi Leh (p327)

boat to **Ko Lanta**, with its flat vistas of tawny shoreline and lapping waves. Park yourself on the sand for a couple of days or rent a motorbike to tour the less touristed parts of this Muslim fishing island. Take a bus and boat combo to **Krabi** where you'll enjoy the craggy spires of stone in **Railay**, a rock climber's paradise with some of the most awesome beaches and sea views on the planet.

Then it's time to switch coasts overland to choose one or two of the gulf's triad of idyllic islands – dive-centric **Ko Tao**, lazy, lie-in-the-sun **Ko Pha-Ngan** and luxury-focused **Ko Samui** – for around five days before your flight out. If you're up for some serious partying, try to arrange your visit to coincide with Ko Pha-Ngan's notorious Full Moon Party, which comes roaring to life roughly once a month on the south-eastern shore.

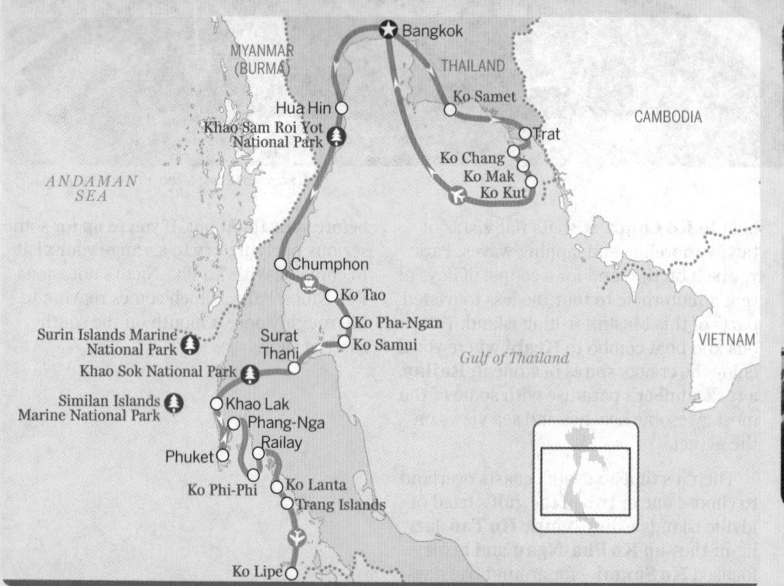
Bangkok
MYANMAR (BURMA)
THAILAND
Ko Samet
CAMBODIA
Hua Hin
Khao Sam Roi Yot National Park
Trat
Ko Chang
Ko Mak
Ko Kut
ANDAMAN SEA
Chumphon
Ko Tao
Ko Pha-Ngan
Surin Islands Marine National Park
Surat Thani
Ko Samui
VIETNAM
Gulf of Thailand
Khao Sok National Park
Similan Islands Marine National Park
Khao Lak
Phang-Nga
Railay
Phuket
Ko Phi-Phi
Ko Lanta
Trang Islands
Ko Lipe

FOLLOW ME AT/GETTY IMAGES ©

The Full Monty

A month, you say? This is not just any old beach trip, but is enough time to really get to know southern Thailand's islands, beaches and jungle-clad parks.

Start your journey in Thailand's capital, **Bangkok**, before heading south. Your first stop is beach-laden **Ko Samet**, where Bangkokians and expats let loose on weekends. Follow the coast to sleepy **Trat** then hop on a boat for one of the Ko Chang archipelago's many islands. Ride elephants and hike the interior of jungle-topped **Ko Chang**, the largest and most developed island in the region. Hop over to flat but beachy **Ko Mak** or rugged **Ko Kut**. Next, backtrack by making your way to **Hua Hin**, the king's preferred holiday destination and home to a thriving local and expat scene with seafood markets and charming shanty piers. Hike the craggy hills of quiet **Khao Sam Roi Yot National Park** before making your way out to **Ko Tao**. Strap on your tank and dive with the fish below before moving over to **Ko Pha-Ngan** for some subdued beachside relaxing. **Ko Samui**, next door, offers a bit more variety and has a magical stash of holiday fodder to suit every budget and desire.

Swap coasts with a stop in **Khao Sok National Park**, known to be one of the oldest stretches of jungle in the world. Depending on how much time you have, take either a day trip or live-aboard diving excursion in **Khao Lak** to explore the diving treasures of the **Surin Islands** and **Similan Islands Marine National Parks**. Travel down the coast to **Phuket** and sample Thailand's finest iteration of luxury hospitality. Paddle around the majestic limestone islets of quiet **Phang-Nga** then sleep beneath the ethereal crags of **Ko Phi-Phi** after a spirited evening (no pun intended) of beach dancing and fire twirling. Scale the stone towers of **Railay** next door, zoom around the flat tracts of land on mellowed-out **Ko Lanta**, then hop on a boat bound for the **Trang Islands** – paradise found. One last archipelago awaits those who travel further south towards the Malaysian border – **Ko Lipe** is the island of choice for those looking for stunning beaches with a fun, social vibe.

MATTEO COLOMBO/GETTY IMAGES ©

Top: Khao Sok National Park (p288)
Bottom: Ko Ngai (p341), Trang Islands

Off The Beaten Track: Thailand's Islands & Beaches

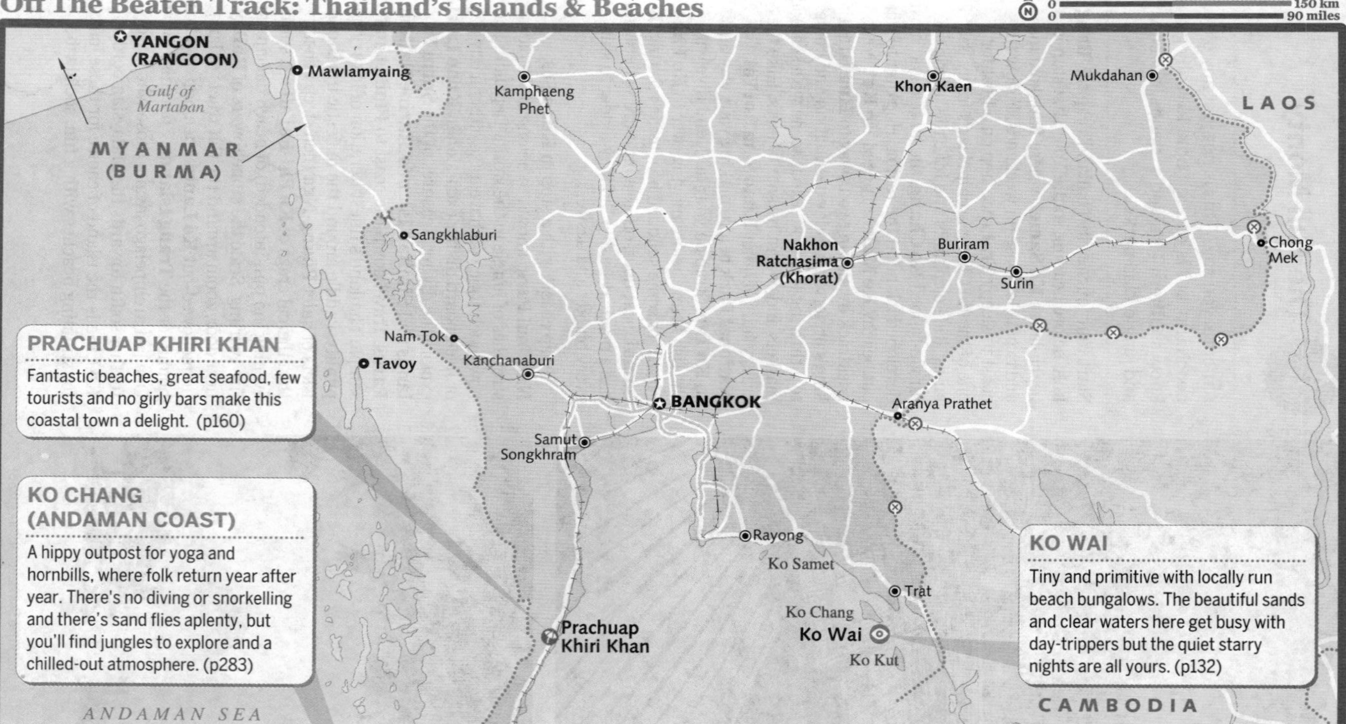

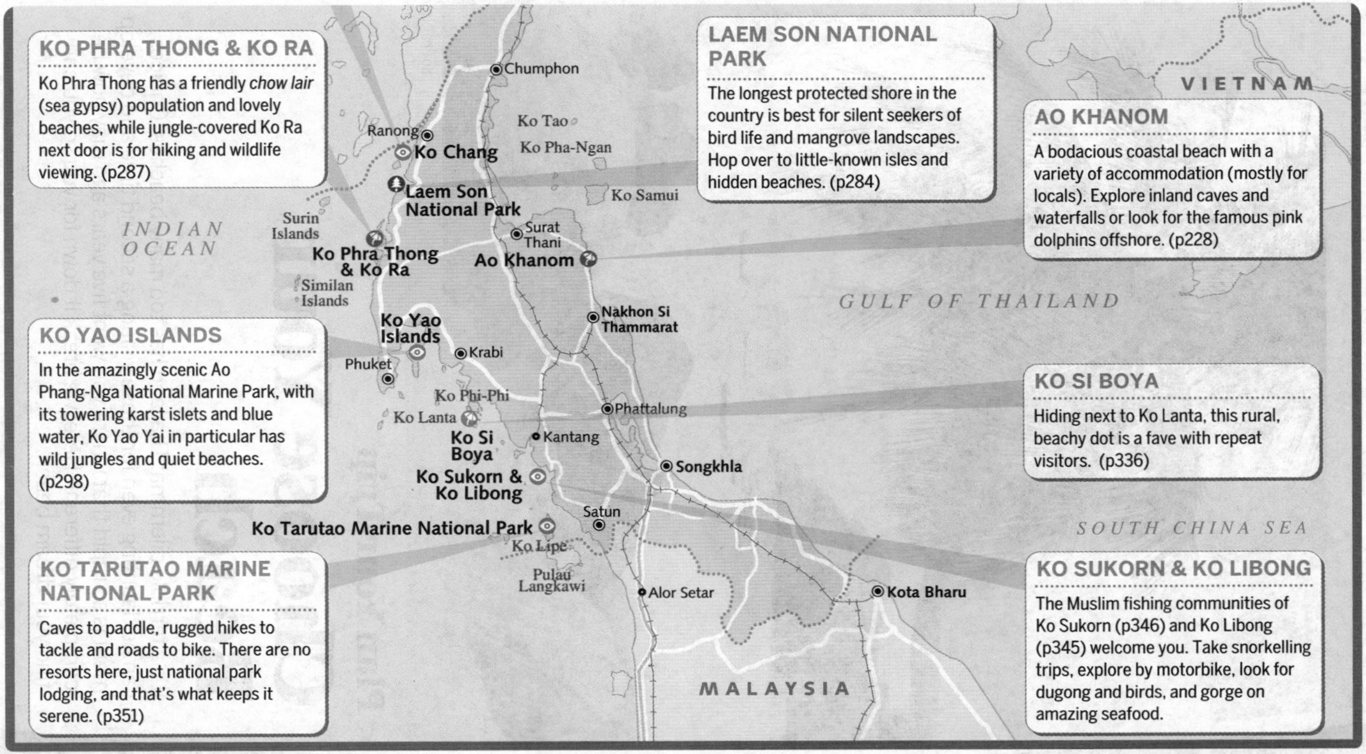

KO PHRA THONG & KO RA

Ko Phra Thong has a friendly *chow lair* (sea gypsy) population and lovely beaches, while jungle-covered Ko Ra next door is for hiking and wildlife viewing. (p287)

LAEM SON NATIONAL PARK

The longest protected shore in the country is best for silent seekers of bird life and mangrove landscapes. Hop over to little-known isles and hidden beaches. (p284)

AO KHANOM

A bodacious coastal beach with a variety of accommodation (mostly for locals). Explore inland caves and waterfalls or look for the famous pink dolphins offshore. (p228)

KO YAO ISLANDS

In the amazingly scenic Ao Phang-Nga National Marine Park, with its towering karst islets and blue water, Ko Yao Yai in particular has wild jungles and quiet beaches. (p298)

KO SI BOYA

Hiding next to Ko Lanta, this rural, beachy dot is a fave with repeat visitors. (p336)

KO TARUTAO MARINE NATIONAL PARK

Caves to paddle, rugged hikes to tackle and roads to bike. There are no resorts here, just national park lodging, and that's what keeps it serene. (p351)

KO SUKORN & KO LIBONG

The Muslim fishing communities of Ko Sukorn (p346) and Ko Libong (p345) welcome you. Take snorkelling trips, explore by motorbike, look for dugong and birds, and gorge on amazing seafood.

Ko Pha-Ngan (p193)

Choose Your Beach

It's a terrible dilemma: Thailand has too many beaches. Choices can be daunting even for those visiting a second time and development is so rapid that where you went five years ago may now be completely different. Here, we break it down for you so you can find your dream beach.

SEEN BY TOBFL / GETTY IMAGES ©

Best Beaches for...

Peace–Action Balance

Ko Mak Beach bar scene, explore-ably flat and tonnes of beach.

Ko Phayam Bike back roads to empty beaches or to parties.

Hat Mae Nam Quiet Ko Samui beach close to lots of action.

Ko Bulon Leh Chilled-out vibe but lots to do.

Kids

Dolphin Bay Low-key scenic bay close to Bangkok.

Hua Hin Mainland resort with a long gulf-side coastline.

Ko Ngai (Trang Islands) Shallow Andaman bay with coral reefs.

Ko Lanta Build sandcastles all day on this Andaman package-tour island.

Local Culture

Ko Yao Noi Thai-Muslim fishing island with beautiful karst scenery.

Ko Sukorn Agricultural and fishing gem filled with mangroves and water buffalo.

Ko Phra Thong Look for rare orchids with *chow lair.*

Hua Hin Recreate with middle-class Thais in this urban beach getaway.

Quick & Easy Access from Bangkok

Nowadays the closest beaches to Bangkok aren't necessarily the quickest and easiest to get to. There are international flights direct to Phuket and Ko Samui that allow you to skip the big city altogether, and flights from Bangkok (and some Southeast Asian countries) can shuttle you to several southern towns with ease.

If you don't want or can't afford to fly, but are still short on time, the closest beach island to Bangkok is Ko Samet (count on around four hours total travel time) while the closest beach resort is Pattaya (1½ hours). The next-closest stops by land are the beach towns of Cha-am (2½ hours) and Hua Hin (three hours). It takes around six hours to get to Ko Chang which beats the minimum of 10 hours to reach the lower gulf islands. If you're in a hurry and want to take the bus, anywhere on the Andaman Coast is not your best choice.

To Party Or Not To Party

Where

A big percentage of travellers to southern Thailand want to party. If there are buckets of sugary cocktails and cheap beer, hordes or revellers will turn up and give the night their all. For other visitors, this sounds like a complete nightmare.

Luckily it's as easy to escape the madness as it is to join in. The main party zones are well known to be just that. Anywhere you go that's not a major tourist enclave will have peace and quiet on offer. Small towns will have zero nightlife and a few beaches sit somewhere in between where you can have a nice sunset drink or maybe stay out till midnight at small, fun bars.

The Girly Bar Issue

Bangkok, Pattaya and Phuket are the capitals of push-up bras and 'hello meesta', while Hat Lamai on Ko Samui is the centre of this small universe in the lower gulf islands. Islands like Ko Samet and Ko Chang and mid-sized towns such as Hat Yai and Ao Nang have small enclaves of questionable massage parlors and bars with the telltale pole dancer silhouette on the sign, but it won't be in your face. Smaller islands and towns will be clear of this sort of thing, at least on the surface.

Your Party Level

Level One: Dead Calm Surin & Similan Islands, Laem Son National Park, Hat Pak Meng & Hat Chang Lang

Level Two: A Flicker of Light Ko Tarutao, Ko Libong, Prachuap Khiri Khan

Level Three: There's a Bar Ko Yao Islands, Ao Khanom, Ko Kut

Level Four: Maybe a Few Bars Hat Khao Lak, Ko Muk, Ao Thong Nai Pan (Pha-Ngan)

Choose your own Beach Adventure

How far will you travel to find your perfect beach? Pick a starting point based on your travel priorities, then fill in the blanks.

Start

Seeking popular Hotspots

I'll take a one-hour flight or the night train from Bangkok, but I don't want to spend an entire day travelling.

When it comes to accommodation, I tend to pick...

...backpacker digs.

...something family-friendly or luxurious.

Scuba diving...

...sounds great.

...is not for me.

My top activity is...

...relaxing on a beach.

...rock climbing.

I prefer my beaches...

...long, tawny and family-friendly.

...for long walks and beautiful sunsets.

...bright white and fronted by blue water.

The perfect resort...

...is on a quieter beach with a youthful vibe.

...has an international standard of excellence.

Ko Lanta p327

Hua Hin p146

Ko Tao p209

Railay p312

Ko Samui p171

Phuket p243

Ko Chang (Andaman Coast) p283

Trang Islands p341

Easy access from Bangkok

Start

No planes or night trains. I'll only travel a few hours from Bangkok.

I'd prefer an island with plenty of...

...activities and mingling. → Ko Chang (Gulf Coast) p120

...solitude. → Ko Kut p134

I want to meet...

...other families. → Ko Samet p108

...weekending locals.

...Thai seafood enthusiasts.

I plan to...

...party. → Ko Phi-Phi p318

...spend some time haggling at the markets. → Hat Khao Lak p290

I consider myself...

...athletic and social.

...a party animal.

...very laid-back.

Beach parties and booze buckets...

...are annoying. → Ko Phayam p281

...sound like a blast! → Ko Pha-Ngan p193

Far-flung Paradises

Start

Planes, trains and automobiles. I'll do anything to reach my dream vacation spot.

When I'm not lying in my hammock, I'm...

...biking back roads

...swimming with fish.

...lying in the sun. → Ko Bulon Leh p350

I also want to...

...party and eat seafood on the beach. → Ko Lipe p354

...renew my visa.

...putter between karsts on long-tail boats.

Level Five: Easy to Find a Drink Hua Hin, Bo Phut (Samui), Ao Nang

Level Six: There's A Beach Bar Scene Ko Mak, Ko Phayam, Railay

Level Seven: Magic Milkshake Anyone? Ko Lanta, Ko Chang, Ban Tai (Pha-Ngan)

Level Eight: I Forget What Eight Was For Hat Lamai (Samui), Ko Lipe, Ko Samet

Level Nine: What Happened Last Night? Hat Chaweng (Samui), Pattaya, Ko Tao

Level Ten: Don't Tell Me What Happened Last Night Patong (Phuket), Ko Phi-Phi, Hat Rin (Ko Pha-Ngan)

Resort Town Personalities

The personality of a Thai resort town depends a lot on the prices. In places where midrange options dominate, you'll usually find package tourists, rows of beach loungers and umbrellas along the beach, and plenty of big boats full of snorkelling tours.

At upscale places things settle down. The ritzier beaches of Phuket like Surin and Ao Ban Tao are among the quieter on the island yet still have plenty of dining and cocktail options. Ko Kut off the eastern seaboard has lovely resorts on some of the country's most unspoiled beaches, while the more secluded beaches of northeastern Ko Samui have some of the most luxurious resorts in Thailand. Once you go very high end, privacy and seclusion become a bigger part of the picture.

There are a few remaining beach huts that are often found on some of the country's most secluded beaches. See our Off The Beaten Track feature for details.

Activities

Diving & Snorkelling

The Andaman Coast and Ko Tao in the lower gulf have the best undersea views in the country. Islands like Ko Samui and Ko Lanta that don't have great snorkelling from the beach will have snorkelling tours to nearby sites.

Climbing

Railay is the best-known place to climb in southern Thailand; it has the best set up for beginners and a fun scene. Ko Phi-Phi has some great climbing options, and there are more off-the-beaten-path climbing options around Krabi. The Ko Yao islands are slowly getting bolted and offer horizons to more seasoned climbers.

Hiking

The mainland national parks like Khao Sok have the most jungle walking opportunities, but more forested islands such as Ko Chang, Ko Pha-Ngan and Phuket have great hiking.

Culture

For a taste of authentic Thai culture, head to Trang, Surat Thani or Songkhla, to lesser known islands like Ko Si Chang or Ko Sukorn, or to the south coast of Ko Samui or the east coast of Ko Lanta. But even tourist central Patong or Ko Phi-Phi can give you a taste of what's beyond resort land, just by eating at food stalls and talking to the owners, smiling a lot and being open to interactions with locals.

WHEN TO GO

REGION	JAN-MAR	APR-JUN	JUL-SEP	OCT-DEC
Bangkok	Hotter towards March	Hot and humid rainy season	Cooler towards December	
Eastern Seaboard	Peak season; thins towards March	Rainy season begins in May	Some islands close for the monsoon	Cooler weather; low hotel rates
Southern Gulf	Hot and dry	Hot and dry	Occasional rains and strong winds	Occasional rains and strong winds
Lower Gulf	Clear and sunny	Hot and dry	Clear and sunny	Monsoon and rough waters
Northern Andaman	High season; high prices	Fringe season with iffy weather	Rainy season and surf season	High season picks up again
Southern Andaman	High season	Monsoons usually begin in May	Some resorts close for rainy season	Crowds return with the sun

OVERVIEW OF THAILAND'S ISLANDS & BEACHES

BEACHES	PACKAGE, HIGH-END TOURISTS	BACK-PACKERS	FAMILIES	PARTIES	DIVING & SNORKELLING	PER
Ko Chang & the Eastern Seaboard						
Ko Samet	✓	✓	✓	✓		P… f…
Ko Chang	✓	✓	✓	✓	✓	… beaches, jungle …
Ko Wai		✓	✓		✓	Primitive day-tripper, deserted in the evening
Ko Mak	✓	✓	✓			Mediocre beaches, great island vibe
Ko Kut	✓	✓	✓			Pretty semi-developed island, great for solitude
Hua Hin & the Upper Gulf						
Hua Hin	✓	✓	✓			International resort, easy access to Bangkok
Pranburi & Around	✓		✓			Quiet and close to Bangkok
Ban Krut			✓			Low-key and popular with Thais
Bang Saphan Yai		✓	✓			Cheap mainland beach
Ko Samui & the Lower Gulf						
Ko Samui	✓	✓	✓	✓		International resort for social beach-goers
Ko Pha-Ngan	✓	✓	✓	✓	✓	Popular beach, with boozy Hat Rin
Ko Tao	✓	✓	✓	✓	✓	Dive schools galore
Ang Thong		✓	✓			Gorgeous karst scenery, rustic
Ao Khanom		✓	✓			Quiet, little known
Phuket & the Andaman Coast						
Ko Chang (Ranong)		✓	✓		✓	Rustic
Ko Phayam		✓	✓			Quiet, little known
Surin & Similan Islands			✓		✓	Dive sites accessed by live-aboards
Ko Yao	✓	✓	✓			Poor beaches but nice vibe, great scenery
Phuket	✓	✓	✓	✓	✓	International resort for social beach-goers
Ao Nang	✓	✓	✓		✓	Touristy, close to Railay
Railay	✓	✓	✓			Rock-climbing centre
Ko Phi-Phi	✓	✓		✓	✓	Pretty party island
Ko Jum	✓	✓	✓			Mediocre beach, nice island vibe
Ko Lanta	✓	✓	✓		✓	Emerging package tourist scene
Trang Islands	✓	✓	✓		✓	Ko Ngai good for kids
Ko Bulon Leh		✓	✓		✓	Pretty beaches, little known
Ko Tarutao		✓	✓			Semi-developed national park
Ko Lipe	✓	✓	✓	✓	✓	Hot spot, handy for visa runs
Ko Adang		✓			✓	Popular with day-trippers

SCOTT DARSNEY/GETTY IMAGES ©

Top: Ko Lipe (p354)
Bottom: Rock-climbing in Railay (p312)

A diver off the coast of Ko Tao (p209)

Plan Your Trip

Diving & Snorkelling

Those who have explored the deep undoubtedly agree with Jacques Cousteau: 'the sea, once it casts its spell, holds one in its net of wonder forever'. When Mr Cousteau sang those praises, he may have been talking about Thailand, as he was the discoverer of several sites frequented by divers and snorkellers today.

Diving & Snorkelling Lowdown

Best Places to Learn

Ko Tao Fantastic dive energy and scores of shallow dive sites sometimes visited by whale sharks. This is the best (and cheapest) place in Thailand to lose your scuba virginity. Sail Rock (closer to Ko Pha-Ngan) and Chumphon Pinnacle are the star sites. (p195)

Best Live-Aboards

Khao Lak The gateway to the Surin and Similan Islands. Explore the myriad dive sites on a live-aboard trip and check out Richelieu Rock – a stunning diving spot discovered by Jacques Cousteau. (p286)

Best Marine Life

Ko Lanta/Ko Phi-Phi Don A top spot for plenty of fish, recurrent visits by manta rays and the odd whale shark. Try the submerged pinnacles at Hin Daeng and Hin Muang. (p318)

Best Snorkelling

Ko Phi-Phi Has made a triumphant comeback after the tsunami, with loads of shimmering reefs. Ko Mai Phai and Ko Nok are great snorkelling spots (p319), while Hin Bida and Ko Bida Nok are the local diving faves. (p318)

Diving

For the beginner through to the pro, Thailand has some of the most affordable, accessible and stunning diving in the world.

Planning Your Trip

The monsoon rains and peak tourist season are two factors determining when to go and which islands and beaches to pick. The severity of the rainy weather varies between seasons and coasts, and there are dry and wet microclimates as well.

When to Go

Generally speaking, the Gulf of Thailand has a year-round dive season, while the Andaman Coast has optimal diving conditions between December and April. In the Ko Chang archipelago, November to early May is the ideal season. Try to avoid the monsoon and rainy seasons.

December–February Days are mostly rain-free and under the waves you'll find a conglomeration of large pelagics at the feeding stations along the Andaman Coast.

April–June Along the gulf things are pretty quiet at this time, and the weather holds out nicely, allowing for good visibility underwater.

June–September The monsoon rains arrive on the Andaman Coast, some hotels shut down and boat travel can be interrupted by storms.

October–December The gulf coast bears the brunt of its rainy season during this period.

Pre-Booking

It is not necessary to pre-book any diving excursions in Thailand unless you plan on doing a live-aboard up to the Surin and Similan Islands Marine National Parks.

Costs

Diving in Thailand is significantly cheaper than in most other nations around the world. A 10-dive package goes for around 7000B to 12,000B on the more affordable beaches. Day-trip prices largely depend on how far the boat will travel as petrol prices are at a premium. Figure around 2500B for a day trip from Ko Pha-Ngan and up to around 6000B for a trip out to Hin Daeng and Hin Muang from Ko Lanta.

Where to Dive

Thailand's coastal topography sits at the junction of two distinct oceanic zones – the Andaman waters wash in from the west, while the gulf coast draws its waters from the islands of Indonesia and the South China Sea.

Diving the Andaman

When the weather is right, the Andaman Sea has some of the finest diving in Southeast Asia. Many would argue that the Andaman has better diving than the gulf, but this is mostly attributed to excellent visibility during the few months of favourable sea conditions. Over the last several years coral bleaching has been an issue and you'll encounter less of this around more remote sites like Richelieu Rock.

Exploring the Gulf

The best part about diving in the Gulf of Thailand is that sea conditions are generally favourable throughout the year. The southwestern gulf coast has the finest diving spots, near the islands of Ko Tao and Ko Pha-Ngan. Pattaya, just a quick two-hour hop from the Bangkok bustle, offers a few memorable dives as well, including a couple of wrecks. On the far eastern side of the coast, the Ko Chang archipelago provides for some pleasant scuba possibilities, although choppy seas limit the season to between November and May.

Safe Diving

Before You Dive

Before embarking on a scuba-diving trip, carefully consider the following points to ensure a safe and enjoyable experience:

➡ Ensure you're healthy and feel comfortable diving. Make sure to be very hydrated on the days you dive.

➡ Remember that your last dive should be completed 24 hours before you fly. It is, however, fine to dive soon after arriving by air.

➡ Make sure your insurance policy covers diving injuries. If it doesn't, purchase additional coverage at www.diversalertnetwork.org.

Decompression Chambers

For the amount of diving occurring in Thailand, the kingdom has a surprisingly limited number of medical facilities dedicated to diving accidents.

JASON EDWARDS/GETTY IMAGES ©

Marine life, Ko Phi-Phi Don (p318)

Decompression (hyperbaric) chambers can be found at most major hubs, including Bangkok, Ko Samui, Pattaya and Phuket. Ko Tao has an emergency chamber – most injuries are dealt with on Ko Samui. Injured divers out of Khao Lak are generally rushed south to Phuket (about an hour away). We advise you to ask your operator of choice about the nearest chamber. Also, make sure there is an emergency supply of oxygen on your dive boat.

Coursework

Thailand is one of the best places in the world to learn how to dive. If you are looking for the best bang for your baht, we recommend getting certified on Ko Tao, where coursework starts at 9000B to 10,000B depending on the type of licence you receive. Beyond Ko Tao, there are plenty of places to get certified, though you're looking at an extra 3000B to 6000B for your Open Water certificate. Ko Pha-Ngan, Ko Phi-Phi, Khao Lak and Ko Lanta round out Thailand's top five places to learn to dive.

WHALE SHARKS

The elusive whale shark – the largest fish in the sea – has a giant mouth that can measure about 2m wide (so just imagine how big their bodies are!) Don't worry: they are filter feeders, which means they mostly feed on plankton, krill and other tiny organisms. Usually these gentle creatures gravitate towards submerged pinnacles. They often hang out at a site for several days before continuing on, so if rumours are flying around about a recent sighting, strap on your scuba gear and hit the high seas.

Tropical fish, Similan Islands Marine National Park (p294)

Live-Aboards

The live-aboard industry has been steadily growing in Thailand over the past 20 years. Most live-aboards are based out of Khao Lak, just north of Phuket on the Andaman Coast. These live-aboard excursions are all-inclusive (lodging on the boat, food, scuba gear, guides) and vary in length from two to five nights. Note that there are no diving live-aboards in the gulf.

Freediving

Freediving is a type of underwater exploration where a diver goes below the waves with a single breath hold and no scuba or snorkelling gear. Currently, one of the top spots to try this sport is on Ko Tao in the southern gulf. Beginner courses (usually two days of diving) cost around 5000B.

For more information on freediving check out **AIDA International** (International Association for Development of Apnea; www.aidainternational.org) and **CMAS** (World Underwater Federation; www.cmas.org).

Technical Diving

Often called tec diving by those in the industry, technical diving is an advanced type of scuba diving involving additional equipment and, most notably, a tank of mixed breathing gases to allow for deeper dives. Technical diving is often taken on as a recreational sport for those interested in exploring deep wrecks and caves.

Underwater caving has really taken off in recent years, and there are several operators on Ko Tao that offer one-day/one-night trips out to the submerged grottoes in Khao Sok National Park (p288).

Snorkelling

Many islands, including the Trang island chain, Ko Tao, Ko Pha-Ngan, Ko Phi-Phi and the islands in the Ko Chang archipelago, have phenomenal snorkelling spots right offshore.

Snorkelling in Maya Bay, Ko Phi-Phi (p318)

Tours

Many tour offices and dive operators offer snorkelling trips. Expect to pay between 500B and 1200B for a day trip depending on how far you travel. Often a snorkelling component is tied into larger day trips that take in virgin islands and kayaking too.

High-end excursions usually use fancy speedboats and expensive equipment, while cheaper deals tend to focus more on the social aspect of the trip, taking customers to so-so reefs.

On Your Own

Orchestrating your own snorkelling adventure is a cinch – there are loads of resorts and dive shops spread throughout Thailand's islands and beaches that rent out gear for 100B to 200B per day. If you plan on snorkelling under your own steam, it is best to follow the same simple rules that you would for scuba:

- Bring a buddy with you.
- Don't go without a guide if you're an unsure swimmer, or are unsure of rip tides.
- Let someone on land know that you are going snorkelling, just in case something happens to you and your buddy.
- Keep an eye out above water to make sure you're not swimming too far out.

Preserving Thailand's Reefs

Thailand's underwater kingdom is incredibly fragile and it's worth taking some time to educate yourself on responsible practices while you're visiting. Here are a few of the more important sustainable practices, but this is by no means an exhaustive list.

- Whether on an island or in a boat, take all litter with you – even biodegradable material like apple cores – and dispose of it back on the mainland.
- Remember that it is an offence to damage or remove coral in marine parks.
- Don't touch or harass marine animals.
- Never rest or stand on coral because touching or walking on it will damage it. It can also cause some nasty cuts.
- Ensure that no equipment is dragging over the reef.
- If you're snorkelling (and especially if you are a beginner), practise your technique away from coral until you've mastered control in the water.
- Hire a wetsuit rather than slathering on sunscreen, which can damage the reef.
- Watch where your fins are – try not to stir up sediment or disturb coral.
- Do not enter the water near a dugong, including when swimming or diving.
- Do not take any shells home with you – it's illegal.

A teenager jumps into Thailand's welcoming waters

Travel with Children

Thais are serious 'cute' connoisseurs and exotic-looking foreign children rank higher on their adorable meter than stuffed animals and fluffy dogs. Children are instant celebrities and attract almost paparazzi-like attention. Older kids get less of this but will revel in the sandy beaches and warm water.

DENNIE CODY/GETTY IMAGES ©

Best Regions for Kids

Ko Samui & the Lower Gulf

Older children can strap on a mask and snorkel Ko Tao without worry. Ko Samui's northern beaches and Ko Pha-Ngan's north and eastern beaches are popular with toddlers, while Hat Chaweng appeals to older kids. (p170)

Phuket & the Northern Andaman Coast

Phuket has amusements galore, but steer clear of the Patong party scene. (p241)

Ko Phi-Phi & the Southern Andaman Coast

Ko Lanta has long stretches of beach with mellow surf and elephant rides in the interior while the Trang Islands offer peaceful sands and easy swimming. (p301)

Ko Chang & the Eastern Seaboard

Shallow seas are kind to young swimmers and low evening tides make for good beachcombing. Older kids will like the interior jungle, elephant camp (p123) and mangrove kayaking (p123).

Hua Hin & the Upper Gulf

Hua Hin has a long sandy coastline and hillside temples for monkey spotting. Phetchaburi's cave temples (p141) often deliver a bat sighting. Ban Krut and Bang Saphan Yai are very casual.

Thailand for Children

Babies do surprisingly well with their new-found stardom. If you've got a babe in arms, food vendors will often offer to hold the child while you eat, taking the child for a brief stroll to visit the other vendors.

At a certain age, kids develop stranger anxiety, which doesn't mix well with the Thai passion for children. For the preschool set, who are becoming self-conscious but still have major cute quotient, we recommend sticking to tourist centres instead of trotting off to far-flung places where foreigners, especially children, will attract too much attention.

To smooth out the usual road bumps of dragging children from place to place, check out Lonely Planet's *Travel with Children,* which contains useful advice with a focus on travel in developing countries.

Children's Highlights

Of the many destinations in Thailand, children will especially enjoy the beaches, as most are shallow, gentle bays good for beginner swimmers. Please, however, be aware of rip tides and take all sea-related warnings with the utmost seriousness. Many of the beach resorts, such as Phuket and Ko Chang, also have wildlife encounters, waterfall spotting and organised water sports ideal for children aged six years and older.

Bangkok is great fun for those in awe of construction sites: the city is filled with cranes, jackhammers and concrete-pouring trucks. Then there's the above-ground Skytrain and shopping malls complete with escalators (a preschool favourite). The city's immense shopping options will appeal to tweens and teens.

Kids on a train kick might like an overnight journey. They can walk around on the train and they're assigned the lower sleeping berths with views of the stations.

Temples can be engaging places for children. Some of the forested temples have resident monkeys and cave shrines. Merit-making at a Buddhist temple is surprisingly kid-friendly – there's the burning joss sticks, the bowing in front of the Buddha and the rubbing of gold leaf on the central image. Most temples also have a fortune-telling area, where you shake a bamboo container until a numbered stick falls out. The number corresponds to a printed fortune.

Planning & Practicalities

- Child-safety seats for cars, high chairs in restaurants, nappy-changing facilities in public restrooms are virtually nonexistent. Parents will have to be resourceful in seeking out substitutes, or follow the example of Thai families (holding smaller children on their laps).

➡ Baby formula and nappies (diapers) are available at minimarkets and 7-Elevens in larger towns and cities, but sizes are usually small, smaller and smallish. If your kid wears size 3 or larger, head to Tesco Lotus, Big C or Tops Market stores. Nappy rash cream is sold at pharmacies.

➡ Thailand's footpaths are often too crowded to push a pram. Opt for a compact umbrella stroller that can squeeze past the fire hydrant and the mango cart and that can be folded up and thrown in a túk-túk. A baby pack is also useful but make sure that the child's head doesn't sit higher than yours: there are lots of hanging obstacles poised at forehead level.

Eating with Kids

Dining with children, particularly with infants, in Thailand is a liberating experience as the Thais are so fond of kids. Take it for granted that your babies will be fawned over, played with and, more often than not, carried around by restaurant wait staff. Regard this as a much-deserved break, not to mention a bit of free cultural exposure.

Because much of Thai food is so spicy, there is an entire art devoted to ordering 'safe' dishes for children, and the vast majority of Thai kitchens are more than willing to oblige.

In general Thai children don't start to eat spicy food until primary school. Before then they seemingly survive on *kôw něe·o* (sticky rice) and jelly snacks. Other kid-friendly meals include chicken in all its nonspicy permutations – *gài yâhng* (grilled chicken), *gài tôrt* (fried chicken) and *gài pàt mét má·môo·ang* (chicken stir-fried with cashew nuts) – as well as *kài jee·o* (Thai-style omelette). Mild options include *kôw man gài* (Hainanese chicken rice).

Girl looking at Buddha statues, Wat Pho (p54), Bangkok

Health & Safety

For the most part parents needn't worry too much about health concerns, although a few ground rules (such as regular hand washing) can head off potential medical problems. In particular:

➡ Children should be warned not to play with animals as rabies is relatively common in Thailand and many dogs are better at barking and eating garbage than being pets.

➡ Mosquito bites often leave big welts on children. If your child is bitten, there are a variety of locally produced balms that can reduce swelling and itching. All the usual health precautions apply.

Regions at a Glance

Bangkok

Culture/History
Food
Nightlife

Classic Siam

Once a show of strength after the devastating war with Burma, Bangkok's royal Buddhist temples are now both national pilgrimage sites and fabulous displays of classical art and architecture.

More is Better

This multiwatt megacity peddles excess, from skyscrapers and luxe malls to the never-ending traffic jams and after-hours clubs. Food is everywhere, and shopping flourishes in crisp modern centres and humble streetside markets.

Toast the Stars

The quintessential night out in Bangkok is still a plastic table and plenty of sweating Beer Chang, but this aspirational city capitalises on its skyscraper towers with half a dozen rooftop bars. Music clubs and entertainment zones lure the young and hip.

p50

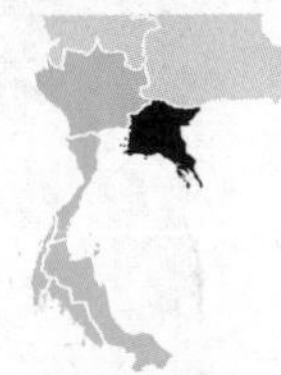

Ko Chang & the Eastern Seaboard

Beaches
Diving
Small Towns

A Cluster of Islands

Ko Chang has jungles and party animals, Ko Mak boasts a laid-back island vibe and little Ko Wai has the prettiest views you'll ever seen. There are easy transport connections between them.

Wrecks & Reefs

It may not compare with further south, but a wreck and coral banks make this a worthy region to blow bubbles.

Provincial Prominence

The eastern seaboard's small towns include Chanthaburi, famous for a weekend gem market, and Trat, a transit link to Ko Chang. These provincial towns are charming for their ordinariness and a middle-class prosperity that is not found on the islands.

p94

Hua Hin & the Upper Gulf

Culture/History
Beaches
Food

Royal Coast

Thai kings escaped Bangkok's stifling climate in Hua Hin, and modern Bangkokians follow suit, touring the historic hilltop palace and cave shrines. The region's coastline is long, inviting and not nearly as crowded as other resort areas.

Surf & Turf

Little Prachuap Khiri Khan has stunning karst scenery, and Hua Hin and Phetchaburi boast atmospheric shophouse districts indicative of Thailand's coast settled by Chinese merchants.

Southern Seafood

Some of the most authentic southern seafood is found along this coast, which caters more to Thai tourists. Get ready for a fire in your belly.

p137

Ko Samui & the Lower Gulf

Beaches
Diving
Nightlife

Bronzing Bodies

Ko Pha-Ngan's lay-about vibe remains while professional Ko Samui caters to international tastes and active vacationers. A day-trip dreamboat, stunning limestone Ang Thong Marine National Park juts out of azure seas.

Diver Down

With warm gentle seas and wallet-friendly prices, Ko Tao remains one of the world's best places to learn how to dive. Just offshore are snorkelling points that make fish-spotting fun and easy.

Full Moon Fiesta

The biggest party in Thailand happens once a month on Ko Pha-Ngan. Be prepared for booze buckets, neon paint and very little sleep.

p170

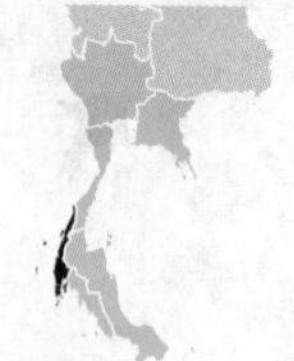

Phuket & the Northern Andaman Coast

Resorts
Diving
Nightlife

Luxury Villas

Thailand's leading international beach destination excels in comfort. Resorts specialise in design and pampering, and the convenience of an airport delivers visitors from sky to shore faster.

Cousteau Territory

Big fish, pristine coral, clear waters – diving and snorkelling sites orbit the world-renowned Similan and Surin Islands. Most visitors pack a snorkel set in their day bags for impromptu sessions. Hop on a live-aboard and cavort with manta rays and whale sharks at Richelieu Rock.

Patong Party

Flickering neon and short skirts abound in this city of sin at the south end of Phuket.

p241

Ko Phi-Phi & the Southern Andaman Coast

Diving
Food
Culture

Under the Sea

The undersea pinnacles at Hin Muang and Hin Daeng, accessed from Ko Lanta, are quietly world class. Ko Phi-Phi also has some of the finest snorkelling in the kingdom – don't miss an early morning session with docile reef sharks.

To Market

Trang and Krabi have great night markets – browse for perfect noodles, grilled fish or spicy salads. On islands, barbecues and iceboats filled with the day's catch take pride of place.

Muslim Seafarers

Head to Ko Libong and Ko Sukorn to experience Muslim life based around agriculture and fishing boats. Dress conservatively away from resorts.

p301

On the Road

Bangkok

Includes ➡

Best Places to Eat

- nahm (p80)
- Krua Apsorn (p78)
- Eat Me (p80)
- Jay Fai (p79)

Best Places to Stay

- Siam Heritage (p75)
- AriyasomVilla (p77)
- Metropolitan by COMO (p76)
- Bangkok Tree House (p77)
- Lamphu Treehouse (p72)
- Loy La Long (p74)

Why Go?

If all you want to do is kick back on a beach, Bangkok might seem like a transit burden full of concrete towers instead of palm trees. But it's shockingly easy to succumb to Bangkok's conveniences, sophistication and fast pace.

This big, crowded, polluted and seemingly chaotic Asian megacity is many things to many people, but no one calls it boring. For the visitor, the impact is immediate. Everywhere you look the streets and waterways are alive with commuters. School kids run without sweating, smiling vendors create mouth-watering food in push-away kitchens, and monks rub bare shoulders with businessmen in air-conditioned malls. Throw in Bangkok's unique mix of the historic and contemporary, dangerously appealing shopping and some of the most delicious and best-value eating on earth, and we're certain that you'll find the City of Angels more than just a junction.

When to Go

- The World Meteorological Organisation rates Bangkok as one of the hottest cities in the world. There's very little fluctuation in the temperature, and the average high sways between a sweat-inducing 32°C and a stifling 34°C.
- The rainy season runs from approximately May to October, when the city receives as much as 300mm of rain a month.
- Virtually the only break from the relentless heat and humidity comes during Bangkok's winter, a few weeks of relative coolness in December/January.

History

Now the centre of government and culture in Thailand, Bangkok was a historical miracle during a time of turmoil. Following the fall of Ayuthaya in 1767, the kingdom fractured into competing forces, from which General Taksin emerged as a decisive unifier. He established his base in Thonburi, on the western bank of Mae Nam Chao Phraya (Chao Phraya River), a convenient location for sea trade from the Gulf of Thailand. Taksin proved more of a military strategist than a popular ruler. He was later deposed by another important military general, Chao Phraya Chakri, who in 1782 moved the capital across the river to a more defensible location in anticipation of a Burmese attack. The succession of his son in 1809 established the present-day royal dynasty, and Chao Phraya Chakri is referred to as Rama I.

Court officials envisioned the new capital as a resurrected Ayuthaya, complete with an island district (Ko Ratanakosin) carved out of the swampland and cradling the royal court (the Grand Palace) and a temple to the auspicious Emerald Buddha (Wat Phra Kaew). The emerging city, which was encircled by a thick wall, was filled with stilt and floating houses ideally adapted to seasonal flooding.

Modernity came to the capital in the late 19th century as European aesthetics and technologies filtered east. During the reigns of Rama IV (King Mongkut; r 1851–68) and Rama V (King Chulalongkorn; r 1868–1910), Bangkok received its first paved road (Th Charoen Krung, formerly known as New Road) and a new royal district (Dusit) styled after European palaces.

Bangkok was still a gangly town when soldiers from the American war in Vietnam came to rest and relax in the city's go-go bars and brothels. It wasn't until the boom years of the 1980s and 1990s that Bangkok exploded into a fully fledged metropolis crowded with hulking skyscrapers and an endless spill of concrete that gobbled up rice paddies and green space. The city's extravagant tastes were soon tamed by the 1997 economic meltdown, the effects of which can still be seen in the numerous half-built skyscrapers. Nearly two decades later, many of these still exist, but they are becoming increasingly obscured behind a modern public transport system and the seemingly endless high-rise condos and vast glass-fronted mega-malls that have come to define the Bangkok of today.

Sights

Thailand's islands and beaches are not particularly well stocked with traditional Thai 'sights', so it's well worth taking in a few while you're in Bangkok.

Keep in mind that Thai temples are sacred places, and visitors should dress and behave

BANGKOK IN...

One Day

Get up as early as you can and take the **Chao Phraya Express Boat** (p71) to Tha Chang to explore the museums and temples of **Ko Ratanakosin** (p54), followed by lunch in **Banglamphu** (p78). After freshening up, gain a new perspective on Bangkok with sunset cocktails at one of the city's **rooftop bars** (p82), followed by an upscale Thai dinner at **nahm** (p80) or **Bo.lan** (p81).

Two Days

Allow the BTS to whisk you to various **shopping** (p85) destinations in central Bangkok and a visit to **Jim Thompson House**, (p60) punctuated by lunch at one of the city's **food courts** (p80). Wrap up the daylight hours with a **traditional Thai massage** (p67). Then work off those calories at the nightclubs of **RCA** (p83).

Three Days

Spend a day at **Chatuchak Weekend Market** (p87), or if it's a weekday, enrol in a **cooking school** (p69). Unwind by bumping to a DJ set at **Cosmic Café** (p84) or swaying to live folk music at **Raintree** (p85).

Four Days

Take the MRT to **Chinatown** (p59) for bustling markets and for some of the city's best old-school street food. Contrast this with an evening of bar-hopping along **Thanon Sukhumvit** (p82).

Bangkok Highlights

1. Basking in the glow of all that gold at **Wat Phra Kaew & Grand Palace** (p54)
2. Taking in the immense Buddha statue at **Wat Pho** (p54)
3. Skipping between sightseeing spots on a cruise of **Bangkok's canals** (p71)
4. Encountering the best of Thai architecture and artwork at **Jim Thompson House** (p60)
5. Burning baht at **Chatuchak Weekend Market** (p87)
6. Learning to make authentic Thai dishes at one of Bangkok's **cooking schools** (p69)
7. Toasting the stars and the twinkling skyscraper lights

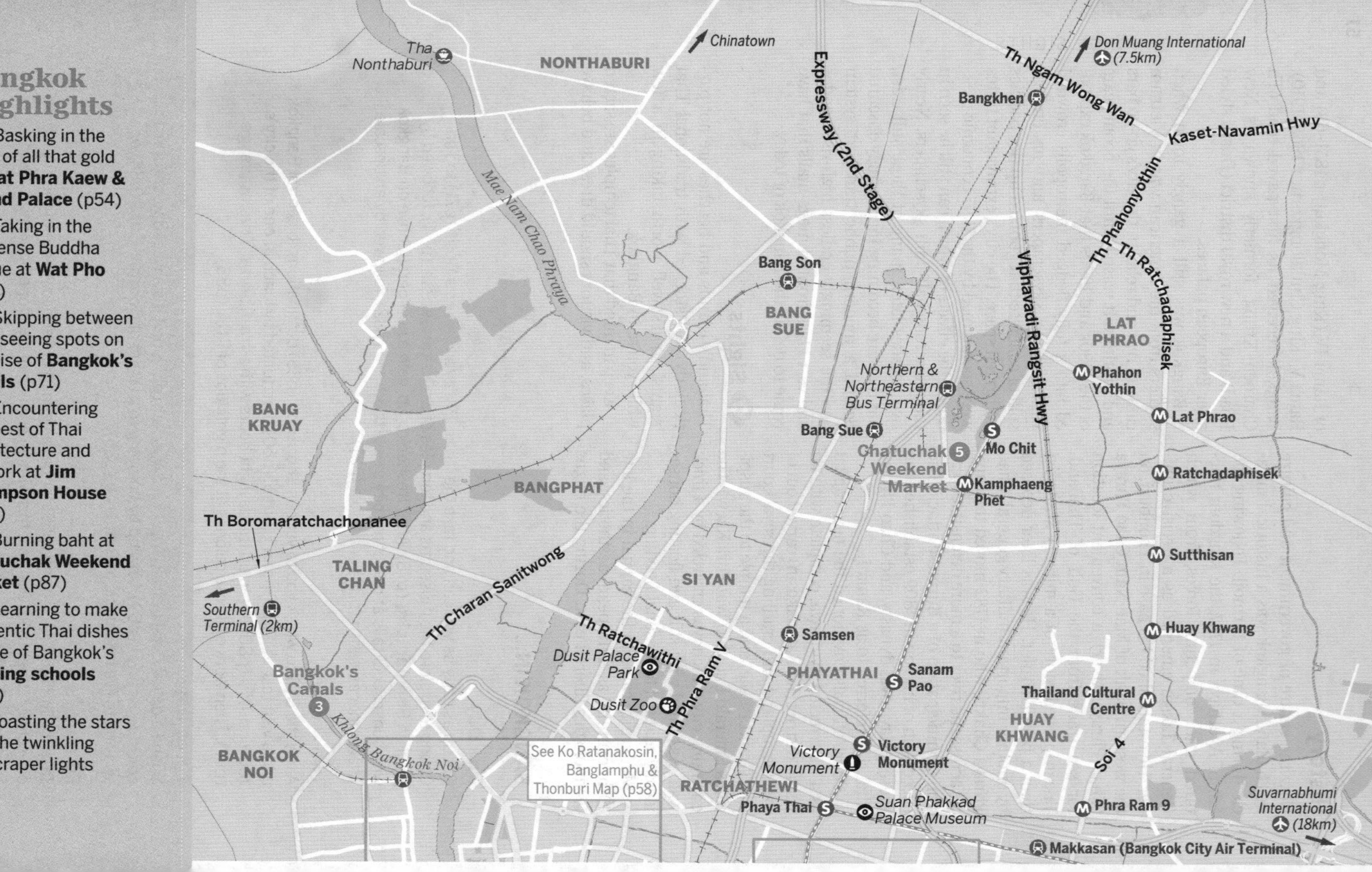

atop one of the city's **rooftop bars** (p82)

8 Being blissfully pounded into submission at one of Bangkok's terrific-value **Thai massage centres** (p67)

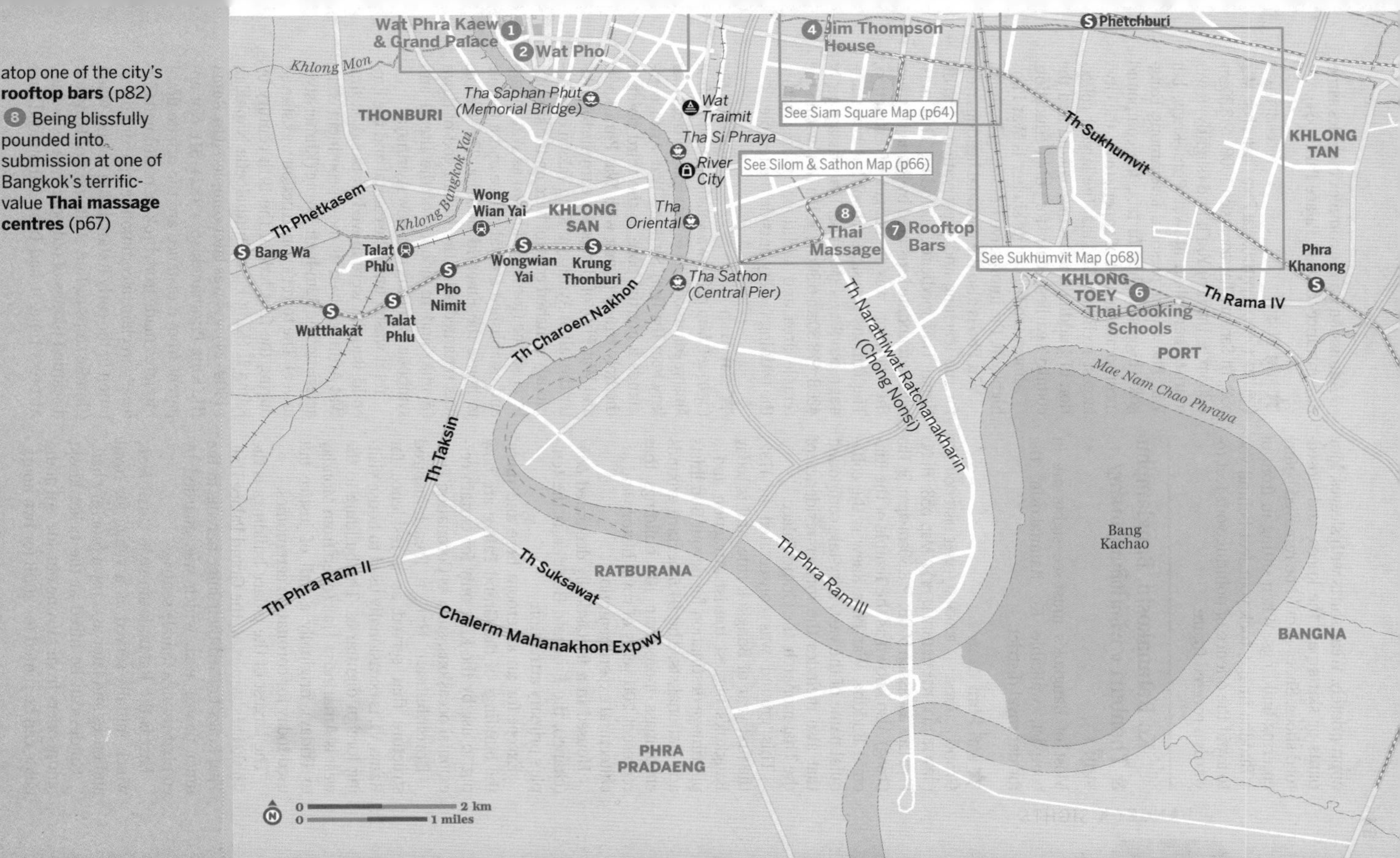

appropriately. Wear shirts with sleeves, long pants or skirts past the knees, and closed-toed shoes. Shoes should be removed before entering buildings. When sitting in front of a Buddha image, tuck your feet behind you to avoid the offence of pointing your feet towards a revered figure.

Ko Ratanakosin, Banglamphu & Thonburi เกาะรัตนโกสินทร์/บางลำพู/ธนบุรี

Most of Bangkok's must-see sights are in compact, walkable Ko Ratanakosin, the former royal district.

★ Wat Phra Kaew & Grand Palace BUDDHIST TEMPLE, HISTORICAL SITE

(วัดพระแก้ว, พระบรมมหาราชวัง; Map p58; Th Na Phra Lan; admission 500B; 8.30am-4pm; Tha Chang) Also known as the Temple of the Emerald Buddha, Wat Phra Kaew is the colloquial name of the vast, fairy-tale compound that also includes the former residence of the Thai monarch, the Grand Palace.

This ground was consecrated in 1782, the first year of Bangkok rule, and is today Bangkok's biggest tourist attraction and a pilgrimage destination for devout Buddhists and nationalists. The 94.5-hectare grounds encompass more than 100 buildings that represent 200 years of royal history and architectural experimentation.

Housed in a fantastically decorated *bòht* (chapel), the **Emerald Buddha** is the temple's primary attraction.

Except for an anteroom here and there, the buildings of the Grand Palace are now put to use by the king only for certain ceremonial occasions, such as Coronation Day. **Borombhiman Hall**, a French-inspired structure that served as a residence for Rama VI, is occasionally used to house visiting foreign dignitaries. The building to the west is **Amarindra Hall** (open from Monday to Friday), originally a hall of justice but used today for coronation ceremonies.

The largest of the palace buildings is the **Chakri Mahaprasat**, the Grand Palace Hall. Thai kings housed their huge harems in the inner palace area, which was guarded by combat-trained female sentries.

Last is the Ratanakosin-style **Dusit Hall**, which initially served as a venue for royal audiences and later as a royal funerary hall.

Guides can be hired at the ticket kiosk; ignore offers from anyone outside. An audio guide can be rented for 200B for two hours.

Admission for the complex includes same-day entrance to Dusit Palace Park (p64).

★ Wat Pho BUDDHIST TEMPLE

(วัดโพธิ์ (วัดพระเชตุพน), Wat Phra Chetuphon; Map p58; Th Sanam Chai; admission 100B; 8.30am-6.30pm; Tha Tien) You'll find (slightly) fewer tourists here than at Wat Phra Kaew, but Wat Pho is our personal fave among Bangkok's biggest sights. In fact, the compound incorporates a host of superlatives: the city's largest reclining Buddha, the largest collection of Buddha images in Thailand and the country's earliest centre for public education.

Almost too big for its shelter is Wat Pho's highlight, the impressive **Reclining Buddha**.

Wat Pho is also the national headquarters for the teaching and preservation of traditional Thai medicine, including Thai massage, a mandate legislated by Rama III when the tradition was in danger of extinction. The famous massage school has two **massage pavilions** (Map p58; Thai massage per hr 420B; 8.30am-6.30pm; Tha Tien) within the temple area and additional rooms within the training facility outside the temple.

★ Wat Arun BUDDHIST TEMPLE

(วัดอรุณฯ; Map p58; www.watarun.net; off Th Arun Amarin; admission 50B; 8am-6pm; cross-river ferry from Tha Tien) Striking Wat Arun commands a martial pose as the third point in the holy trinity (along with Wat Phra Kaew and Wat Pho) of Bangkok's early history. After the fall of Ayuthaya, King Taksin ceremoniously clinched control here on the site of a local shrine (formerly known as Wat Jaeng) and established a royal palace and a temple to house the Emerald Buddha. The temple was renamed after the Indian god of dawn (Aruna) and in honour of the literal and symbolic founding of a new Ayuthaya.

Yet it wasn't until the capital and the Emerald Buddha were moved to Bangkok that Wat Arun received its most prominent characteristic: the 82m-high *Ƀrang* (Khmer-style tower). The tower's construction was started during the first half of the 19th century by Rama II (King Phraphutthaloetla Naphalai; r 1809–24) and was later completed by Rama III (King Phranangklao; r 1824–51). Not apparent from a distance are the ornate floral **mosaics** made from broken, multihued Chinese porcelain, a common temple ornamentation in the early Ratanakosin period, when Chinese ships calling at the port of Bangkok discarded tonnes of old porcelain as ballast. At press time, it had been announced that the *brang* would be closed for as long as three years due to renovation. Visitors can enter the compound, but cannot, as in previous years, climb the tower.

Also worth a look is the interior of the *bòht*. The main Buddha image is said to have been designed by Rama II. The **murals** date from the reign of Rama V; particularly impressive is one that depicts Prince Siddhartha encountering examples of birth, old age, sickness and death outside his palace walls, an experience that led him to abandon the worldly life. The ashes of Rama II are interred in the base of the presiding Buddha image.

Cross-river ferries run from Tha Tien to Wat Arun every few minutes from 6am to 8pm (3B).

National Museum MUSEUM

(พิพิธภัณฑสถานแห่งชาติ; Map p58; 4 Th Na Phra That; admission 200B; 9am-4pm Wed-Sun; Tha Chang) Often touted as Southeast Asia's biggest museum, Thailand's National Museum is home to an impressive collection

BANGKOK FOR CHILDREN

There aren't a whole lot of attractions in Bangkok meant directly to appeal to the little ones, but there's no lack of locals willing to provide attention. The website www.bangkok.com/kids has an excellent spread of things to do for kids, and www.bambiweb.org is a useful resource for parents of young children in Bangkok.

Kid-Friendly Museums

Although not specifically child-targeted, the Museum of Siam (p58) has lots of interactive exhibits that will appeal to children.

Outside of town, Ancient City (p61) recreates Thailand's most famous monuments. They're linked by bicycle paths and were practically built for being climbed on.

Parks

★**Lumphini Park** (สวนลุมพินี; Map p66; bounded by Th Sarasin, Th Phra Ram IV, Th Witthayu (Wireless Rd) & Th Ratchadamri; 4.30am-9pm; M Lumphini exit 3, Si Lom exit 1, S Sala Daeng exit 3, Ratchadamri exit 2) FREE is a trusty ally in the cool hours of the morning and evening for kite-flying (during February and March) as well as for stretching the legs and lungs. Nearby, kids can view lethal snakes become reluctant altruists at the adjacent antivenin-producing **Queen Saovabha Memorial Institute snake farm** (สถานเสาวภา; Map p66; cnr Th Phra Ram IV & Th Henri Dunant; adult/child 200/50B; 9.30am-3.30pm Mon-Fri, to 1pm Sat & Sun; M Si Lom exit 1, S Sala Daeng exit 3).

Rainy-Day Fun

MBK Center (p85) and Siam Paragon (p86) have bowling alleys to keep the older ones occupied. Siam Discovery Center has a branch of **Madame Tussaud's** (Map p64; www.madametussauds.com/Bangkok/en/; 6th fl; adult/child 800/600B; 10am-8pm; S Siam exit 1).

Krung Sri IMAX (Map p64; 0 2129 4631; www.majorcineplex.com/en/cinema/paragon-cineplex/; 5th fl, Siam Paragon, 991/1 Th Phra Ram I; tickets 250-1200B; S Siam exits 3 & 5) screens special-effects versions of Hollywood action flicks and nature features.

Bangkok's biggest indoor playground is **Fun-arium** (Map p68; 0 2665 6555; www.funarium.co.th; 111/1 Soi 26, Th Sukhumvit; admission 110-320B; 9am-7pm; S Phrom Phong exit 1 & taxi). Slightly older kids can land a plane, record an album, or, er, perform a root canal at **KidZania** (Map p64; 0 2683 1888; bangkok.kidzania.com/en/; 5th fl, Siam Paragon, 991/1 Th Phra Ram I; adult/child 650/400B; 10am-5pm Mon-Fri, 10am-3pm & 4-9pm Sat & Sun; S Siam exits 3 & 5), a new and impressive learn-and-play centre.

Zoos & Animals

Dusit Zoo (สวนสัตว์ดุสิต (เขาดิน); Th Ratchawithi; adult/child 100/50B; 8am-6pm; S Phaya Thai exit 3 & taxi) covers 19 hectares with caged exhibits of more than 300 mammals, 200 reptiles and 800 birds, including relatively rare indigenous species such as banteng, gaur, serow and some rhinoceros. There are shady grounds plus a lake in the centre with paddleboats for hire and a small children's playground.

A massive underwater world has been recreated at the Siam Ocean World (p86) shopping-centre aquarium.

Wat Phra Kaew & Grand Palace

EXPLORE BANGKOK'S PREMIER MONUMENTS TO RELIGION AND REGENCY

This tour can be covered in a couple of hours. The first area tourists enter is the Buddhist temple compound generally referred to as Wat Phra Kaew. A covered walkway surrounds the area, the inner walls of which are decorated with the **murals of the *Ramakian*** 1 and 2. Originally painted during the reign of Rama I (r 1782-1809), the murals, which depict the Hindu epic the *Ramayana*, span 178 panels that describe the struggles of Rama to rescue his kidnapped wife, Sita.

After taking in the story, pass through one of the gateways guarded by ***yaksha*** 3 to the inner compound. The most important structure here is the ***bòht*, or ordination hall** 4, which houses the eponymous **Emerald Buddha** 5.

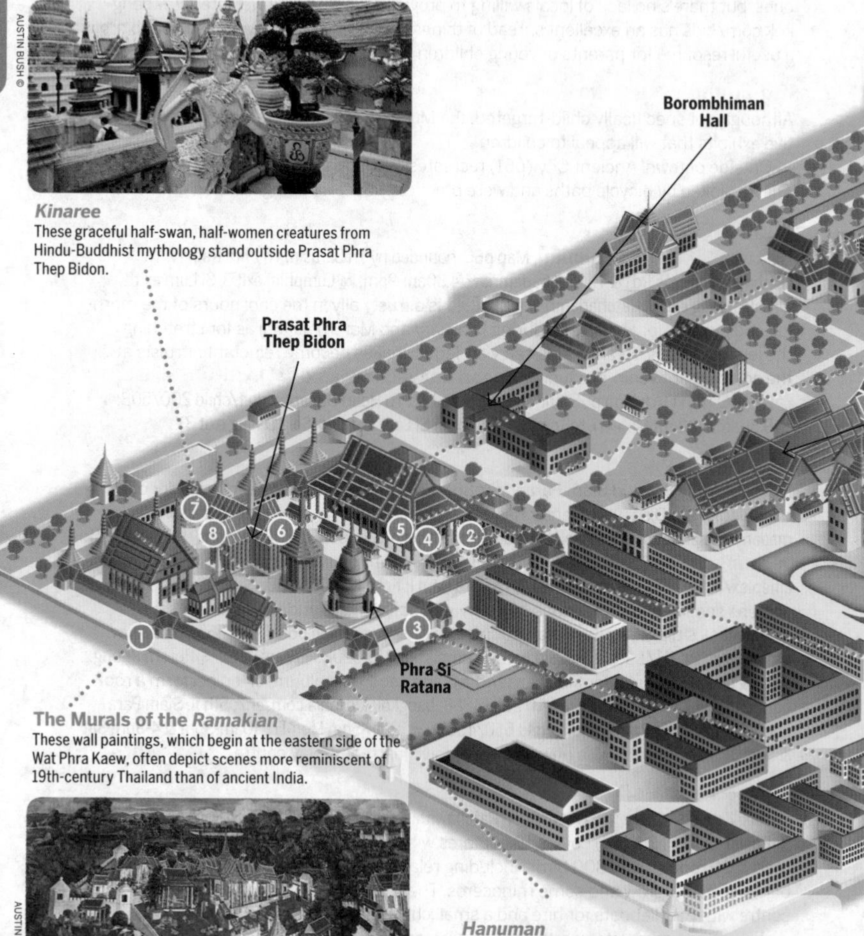

Kinaree
These graceful half-swan, half-women creatures from Hindu-Buddhist mythology stand outside Prasat Phra Thep Bidon.

The Murals of the *Ramakian*
These wall paintings, which begin at the eastern side of the Wat Phra Kaew, often depict scenes more reminiscent of 19th-century Thailand than of ancient India.

Hanuman
Rows of these mischievous monkey deities from Hindu mythology appear to support the lower levels of two small *chedi* near Prasat Phra Thep Bidon.

Head east to the so-called Upper Terrace, an elevated area home to the **spires of the three primary *chedi*** (6). The middle structure, Phra Mondop, is used to house Buddhist manuscripts. This area is also home to several of Wat Phra Kaew's noteworthy mythical beings, including beckoning ***kinaree*** (7) and several grimacing **Hanuman** (8).

Proceed through the western gate to the compound known as the Grand Palace. Few of the buildings here are open to the public. The most noteworthy structure is **Chakri Mahaprasat** (9). Built in 1882, the exterior of the hall is a unique blend of western and traditional Thai architecture.

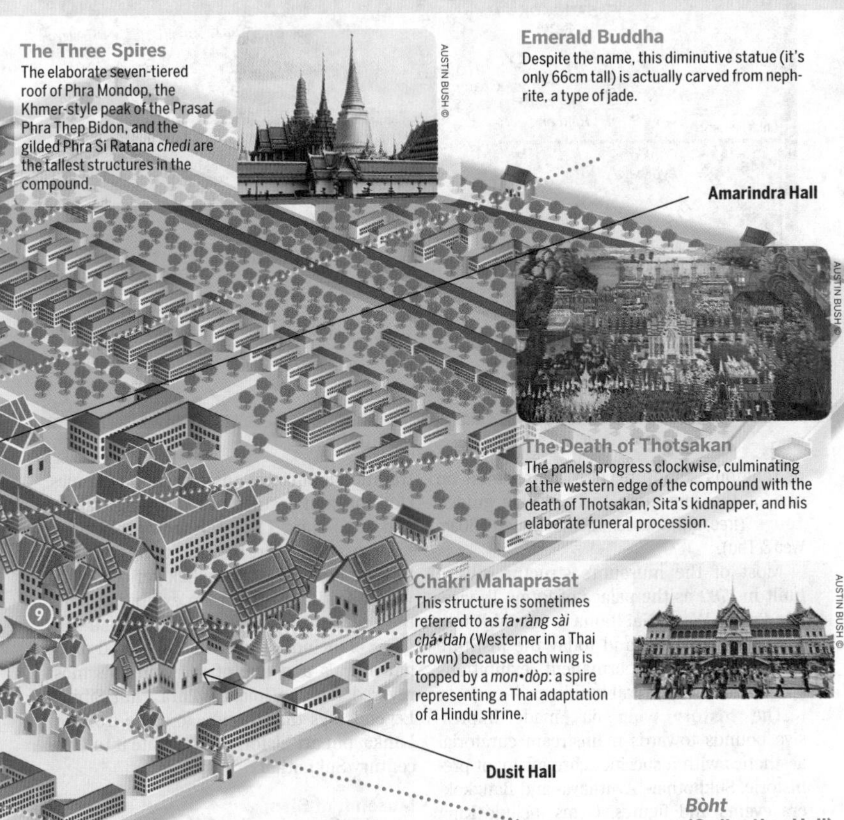

***Bòht* (Ordination Hall)**
This structure is an early example of the Ratanakosin school of architecture, which combines traditional stylistic holdovers from Ayuthaya along with more modern touches from China and the West.

Yaksha
Each entrance to the Wat Phra Kaew compound is watched over by a pair of vigilant and enormous *yaksha*, ogres or giants from Hindu mythology.

AUSTIN BUSH ©

Ko Ratanakosin, Banglamphu & Thonburi

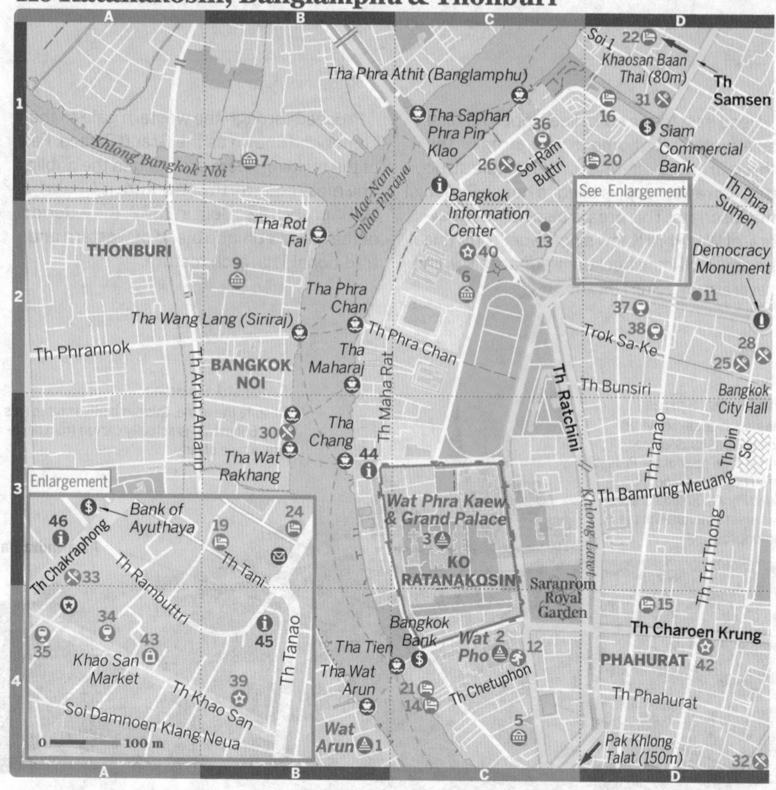

of religious sculpture, best appreciated on one of the museum's twice-weekly guided **tours** (free with museum admission; ⌚9.30am Wed & Thu).

Most of the museum's structures were built in 1782 as the palace of Rama I's viceroy, Prince Wang Na. Rama V turned it into a museum in 1874, and today the institute consists of three permanent exhibitions spread out over several buildings.

The **history wing** has made impressive bounds towards mainstream curatorial aesthetics with a succinct chronology of prehistoric, Sukhothai-, Ayuthaya- and Bangkok-era events and figures. Gems include King Ramkamhaeng's inscribed stone pillar, said to be the oldest record of Thai writing; King Taksin's throne; the Rama V section; and the screening of a movie about Rama VII (King Prajadhipok; r 1925–35), *The Magic Ring*.

The **decorative arts and ethnology exhibit** covers every possible handicraft: traditional musical instruments, ceramics, clothing and textiles, woodcarving, regalia and weaponry. The **archaeology and art history wing** has exhibits ranging from prehistoric times to the Bangkok period.

In addition to the main exhibition halls, the **Buddhaisawan (Phutthaisawan) Chapel** includes some well-preserved original murals and one of the country's most revered Buddha images, Phra Phut Sihing. Legend says that the image came from Sri Lanka, but art historians attribute it to 13th-century Sukhothai.

Museum of Siam MUSEUM

(สถาบันพิพิธภัณฑ์การเรียนรู้แห่งชาติ; Map p58; www.museumsiam.com; Th Maha Rat; admission 300B; ⌚10am-6pm Tue-Sun; Tha Tien) This fun museum employs a variety of media to explore the origins of the Thai people and their culture. Housed in a European-style 19th-century building that was once the Ministry of Commerce, the exhibits are

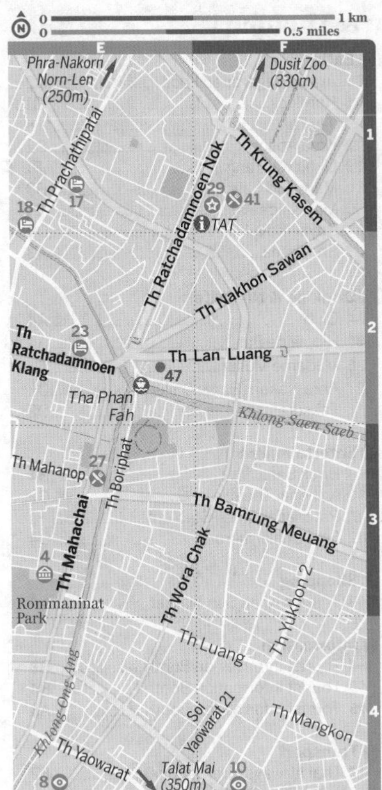

presented in an engaging, interactive fashion not often found in Thailand. They are also refreshingly balanced and entertaining, with galleries dealing with a range of questions about the origins of the nation and its people.

Each room has an informative narrated video started by a sensory detector, keeping waiting to a minimum. An Ayuthaya-era battle game, a room full of traditional Thai toys and a street vending cart where you can be photographed pretending to whip up a pan of *pàt tai* (fried noodles) will keep kids interested for at least an hour, and adults for longer. Check out the attached shop for some innovative gift ideas.

Chinatown & Phahurat เยาวราช/พาหุรัด

Gold shops, towering neon signs and shopfronts spilling out onto the sidewalk – welcome to Chinatown (also known as Yaowarat). The neighbourhood's energy is at once exhilarating and exhausting, and it's fun to explore at night when it's lit up like a Christmas tree and there's lots of street food for sale.

Just west is Phahurat, Bangkok's Little India: a seemingly endless bazaar uniting flamboyant Bollywood fabric, photogenic vendors selling *paan* (betel nut for chewing) and shops stocked with delicious northern Indian-style sweets.

★ Wat Traimit BUDDHIST TEMPLE

(วัดไตรมิตร, Temple of the Golden Buddha; Th Mitthaphap (Th Traimit); admission 40B; 8am-5pm; Tha Ratchawong, Hua Lamphong exit 1) The attraction at Wat Traimit is undoubtedly the impressive 3m-tall, 5.5-tonne, solid-gold Buddha image, which gleams like, well, gold. Sculpted in the graceful Sukhothai style, the image was 'discovered' some 40 years ago beneath a stucco or plaster exterior when it fell from a crane while being moved to a new building within the temple compound. It has been theorised that the covering was added to protect it from marauding hordes, either during the late Sukhothai period or later in the Ayuthaya period when the city was under siege by the Burmese. The temple itself is said to date from the early 13th century.

Donations and a constant flow of tourists have proved profitable, and the statue is now housed in an imposing four-storey marble structure. The 2nd floor of the building is home to the **Phra Buddha Maha Suwanna Patimakorn Exhibition** (admission 100B; 8am-5pm Tue-Sun), which has exhibits on how the statue was made, discovered and came to arrive at its current home, while the 3rd floor houses the **Yaowarat Chinatown Heritage Center** (admission 100B; 8am-5pm Tue-Sun), a small but engaging museum with multimedia exhibits on the history of Bangkok's Chinatown and its residents.

Talat Mai MARKET

(ตลาดใหม่; Soi 6 (Trok Itsaranuphap), Th Yaowarat; 6am-6pm; Tha Ratchawong, Hua Lamphong exit 1 & taxi) With nearly two centuries of history under its belt, 'New Market' is no longer an entirely accurate name for this strip of commerce. Essentially it's a narrow covered alleyway between tall buildings, but even if you're not interested in food the hectic atmosphere and exotic sights and smells combine to create something of a surreal sensory experience.

Ko Ratanakosin, Banglamphu & Thonburi

Top Sights
1 Wat Arun ... B4
2 Wat Pho ... C4
3 Wat Phra Kaew & Grand Palace ... C3

Sights
4 Corrections Museum ... E3
5 Museum of Siam ... C4
6 National Museum ... C2
7 Royal Barges National Museum ... B1
8 Sampeng Lane ... E4
9 Songkran Niyomsane Forensic Medicine Museum & Parasite Museum ... B2
10 Wat Mangkon Kamalawat ... F4

Activities, Courses & Tours
11 Grasshopper Adventures ... D2
12 Massage Pavilions ... C4
13 Sor Vorapin Gym ... C2

Sleeping
14 Arun Residence ... C4
15 Feung Nakorn Balcony ... D4
16 Fortville Guesthouse ... D1
17 Hotel Dé Moc ... E1
18 Lamphu Treehouse ... E1
19 NapPark Hostel ... B3
20 Rambuttri Village Inn ... D1
21 Sala ... C4
22 Sam Sen Sam Place ... D1
23 Sourire ... E2
24 Suneta Hostel Khaosan ... B3

Eating
25 Arawy Vegetarian Food ... D2
26 Hemlock ... C1
27 Jay Fai ... E3
28 Krua Apsorn ... D2
29 Likhit Kai Yang ... F1
30 Mangkud Cafe ... B3
31 May Kaidee's ... D1
32 Royal India ... D4
33 Shoshana ... A3

Drinking & Nightlife
34 Club ... A4
35 Hippie de Bar ... A4
36 Madame Musur ... C1
37 Phra Nakorn Bar & Gallery ... D2
38 Taksura ... D2

Entertainment
39 Brick Bar ... B4
40 National Theatre ... C2
41 Ratchadamnoen Stadium ... F1
42 Sala Chalermkrung ... D4

Shopping
43 Thanon Khao San Market ... A4

Information
44 Tourist Information Booth ... B3
45 Tourist Information Booth ... B4
46 Tourist Information Booth ... A3

Transport
47 Thai Airways International ... E2

Wat Mangkon Kamalawat BUDDHIST TEMPLE
(วัดมังกรกมลาวาส; Map p58; cnr Th Charoen Krung & Th Mangkon; 6am-6pm; Tha Ratchawong, M Hua Lamphong exit 1 & taxi) FREE Clouds of incense and the sounds of chanting form the backdrop at this Chinese-style Mahayana Buddhist temple. Dating back to 1871, it's the largest and most important religious structure in the area.

Siam Square

★ **Jim Thompson House** HISTORICAL BUILDING
(Map p64; www.jimthompsonhouse.com; 6 Soi Kasem San 2; adult/child 100/50B; 9am-5pm, compulsory tours in English & French every 20min; klorng boat to Tha Saphan Hua Chang, S National Stadium exit 1) This jungly compound is the former home of the eponymous American silk entrepreneur and art collector. Born in Delaware in 1906, Thompson briefly served in the Office of Strategic Services (the forerunner of the CIA) in Thailand during WWII. Settling in Bangkok after the war, his neighbours' handmade silk caught his eye and piqued his business sense; he sent samples to fashion houses in Milan, London and Paris, gradually building a steady worldwide clientele.

In addition to textiles, Thompson also collected parts of various derelict Thai homes and had them reassembled in their current location in 1959. Some of the homes were brought from the old royal capital of Ayuthaya; others were pulled down and floated across the canal from Baan Krua, including the first building you enter on the tour. One striking departure from tradition is the way each wall has its exterior side facing the house's interior, thus exposing the wall's bracing system. His small but splendid Asian art collection and his personal belongings are also on display in the main house.

Thompson's story doesn't end with his informal reign as Bangkok's best-adapted foreigner. While he was out for an afternoon walk in the Cameron Highlands of western Malaysia in 1967, Thompson mysteriously disappeared. That same year his sister was murdered in the USA, fuelling various conspiracy theories. Was it communist spies? Business rivals? Or a man-eating tiger? Although the mystery has never been solved, evidence revealed by American journalist Joshua Kurlantzick in his profile of Thompson, *The Ideal Man,* suggests that the vocal anti-American stance Thompson took later in his life may have made him a potential target of suppression by the CIA.

Beware of dapper touts in soi near the Thompson house who will tell you it is closed and try to haul you off on a dodgy buying spree.

Erawan Shrine MONUMENT
(ศาลพระพรหม; Map p64; cnr Th Ratchadamri & Th Ploenchit; 6am-11pm; S Chit Lom exit 8) FREE
The Erawan Shrine was originally built in 1956 as something of a last-ditch effort to end a string of misfortunes that occurred during the construction of the hotel, at that time known as the Erawan Hotel. After several incidents ranging from injured construction workers to the sinking of a ship carrying marble for the hotel, a Brahmin priest was consulted. Since the hotel was to be named after the elephant escort of Indra in Hindu mythology, the priest determined that Erawan required a passenger, and suggested it be that of Lord Brahma. A statue was built, and lo and behold, the misfortunes miraculously ended.

Although the original Erawan Hotel was demolished in 1987, the shrine still exists, and today remains an important place of pilgrimage for Thais, particularly those in need of some material assistance. Those making a wish from the statue should ideally come between 7am and 8am, or 7pm and 8pm, and should offer a specific list of items that includes candles, incense, sugar cane or bananas, all of which are almost exclusively given in multiples of seven. Particularly popular are teak elephants, the money gained through the purchase of which is donated to a charity run by the current hotel, the Grand Hyatt Erawan. And as the tourist brochures

OFF THE BEATEN TRACK

BIZARRE BANGKOK MUSEUMS

If looking at stuffed tigers and Buddha statues just isn't doing it for you, then consider a visit to one of these quirky institutions.

➜ **Songkran Niyomsane Forensic Medicine Museum & Parasite Museum** (พิพิธภัณฑ์นิติเวชศาสตร์สงกรานต์นิยมเสน; Map p58; 2nd fl, Adulyadejvikrom Bldg, Siriraj Hospital; admission 40B; 9am-4pm Mon-Sat; Tha Wang Lang (Siriraj)) This gory institution contains the various appendages and remnants of famous murders, including the bloodied T-shirt from a victim who was stabbed to death with a dildo. If you're still with us at this point, you'll probably also enjoy the adjacent **Parasite Museum**. The easiest way to reach the museum is by taking the river-crossing ferry to Tha Wang Lang (on the Thonburi side) from Tha Chang. At the exit of the pier, turn right to enter Siriraj Hospital, and follow the green signs.

➜ **Ancient City** (เมืองโบราณ, Muang Boran; www.ancientcity.com; 296/1 Th Sukhumvit, Samut Prakan; adult/child 500/250B; 8am-5pm) Claiming to be the largest open-air museum in the world, the site covers more than 80 hectares of peaceful countryside littered with 109 scaled-down facsimiles of many of the kingdom's most famous monuments. It's an excellent place to explore by bicycle (per day 50B), as it is usually quiet and never crowded. Ancient City lies outside Samut Prakan, which is accessible via air-conditioned bus 511 from Bearing BTS station at the east end of Th Sukhumvit. Upon reaching the bus terminal at Pak Nam, board minibus 36, which passes the entrance to Ancient City.

➜ **Corrections Museum** (พิพิธภัณฑ์ราชทัณฑ์; Map p58; 436 Th Mahachai; admission free; 9am-4pm Mon-Fri; 508, klorng taxi to Tha Phan Fah) Learn about the painful world of Thai-style punishment at what's left of this former jail. Life-sized models re-enact a variety of horrendous executions and punishments, encouraging most visitors to remain law-abiding citizens for the remainder of their visit.

Wat Pho

A WALK THROUGH THE BIG BUDDHAS OF WAT PHO

The logical starting place is the main *wí•hăhn* (sanctuary), home to Wat Pho's centrepiece, the immense **Reclining Buddha** ❶. Apart from its huge size, note the **mother-of-pearl inlays** ❷ on the soles of the statue's feet. The interior walls of the *wí•hăhn* are covered with murals depicting previous lives of the Buddha, and along the south side of the structure are 108 bronze monk bowls; for 20B you can buy 108 coins, each of which is dropped in a bowl for good luck.

Exit the *wí•hăhn* and head east via the two **stone giants** ❸ who guard the gateway to the rest of the compound. Directly south of these are the four towering **royal *chedi*** ❹.

Continue east, passing through two consecutive **galleries of Buddha**

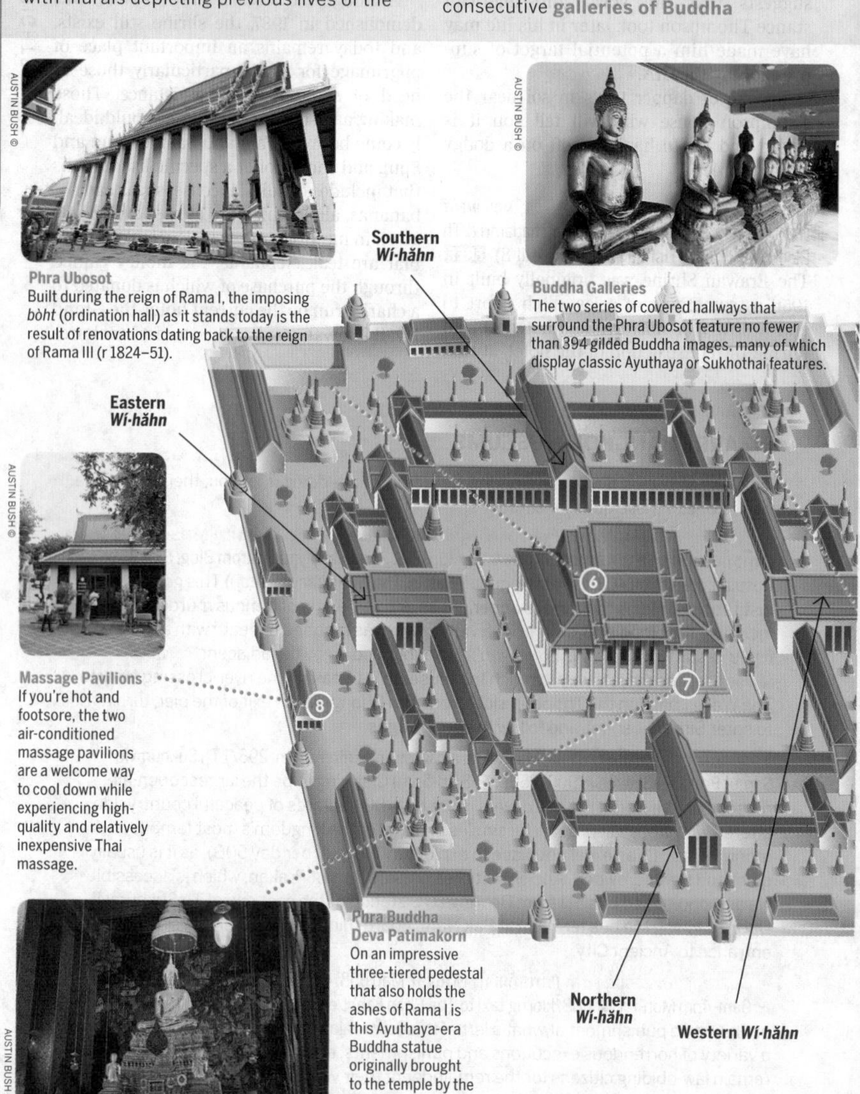

Phra Ubosot
Built during the reign of Rama I, the imposing *bòht* (ordination hall) as it stands today is the result of renovations dating back to the reign of Rama III (r 1824–51).

Buddha Galleries
The two series of covered hallways that surround the Phra Ubosot feature no fewer than 394 gilded Buddha images, many of which display classic Ayuthaya or Sukhothai features.

Massage Pavilions
If you're hot and footsore, the two air-conditioned massage pavilions are a welcome way to cool down while experiencing high-quality and relatively inexpensive Thai massage.

Phra Buddha Deva Patimakorn
On an impressive three-tiered pedestal that also holds the ashes of Rama I is this Ayuthaya-era Buddha statue originally brought to the temple by the monarch.

statues 5 linking four *wí•hăhn*, two of which contain notable Sukhothai-era Buddha statues; these comprise the exterior of **Phra Ubosot** 6, the immense ordination hall that is Wat Pho's second-most noteworthy structure. The base of the building is surrounded by bas-relief inscriptions, and inside is the notable Buddha statue, **Phra Buddha Deva Patimakorn** 7.

Wat Pho is often referred to as Thailand's first university, a tradition that continues today in an associated traditional Thai medicine school and, at the compound's eastern extent, two **massage pavilions** 8.

Interspersed throughout the eastern half of the compound are several additional minor *chedi* and rock gardens.

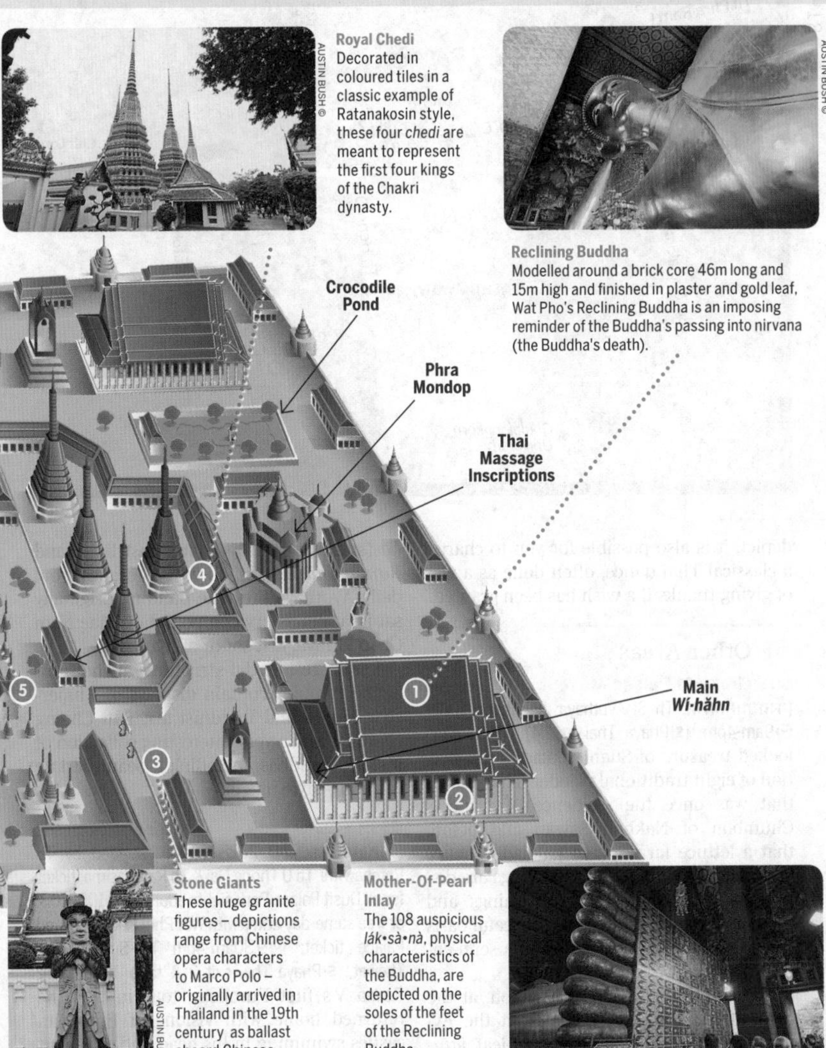

Royal Chedi
Decorated in coloured tiles in a classic example of Ratanakosin style, these four *chedi* are meant to represent the first four kings of the Chakri dynasty.

Reclining Buddha
Modelled around a brick core 46m long and 15m high and finished in plaster and gold leaf, Wat Pho's Reclining Buddha is an imposing reminder of the Buddha's passing into nirvana (the Buddha's death).

Stone Giants
These huge granite figures – depictions range from Chinese opera characters to Marco Polo – originally arrived in Thailand in the 19th century as ballast aboard Chinese junks.

Mother-Of-Pearl Inlay
The 108 auspicious *lák•sà•nà*, physical characteristics of the Buddha, are depicted on the soles of the feet of the Reclining Buddha.

Siam Square

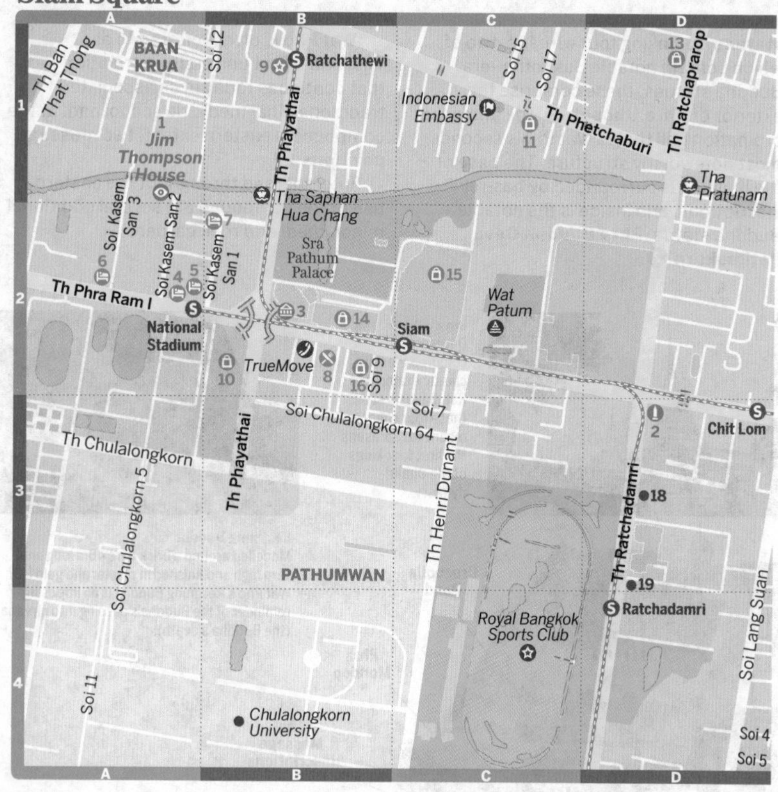

depict, it is also possible for you to charter a classical Thai dance, often done as a way of giving thanks if a wish has been granted.

Other Areas

Suan Pakkad Palace Museum MUSEUM
(วังสวนผักกาด; Th Si Ayuthaya; admission 100B; 9am-4pm; Phaya Thai exit 4) The overlooked treasure of Suan Pakkad is a collection of eight traditional wooden Thai houses that was once the residence of Princess Chumbon of Nakhon Sawan and before that a lettuce farm ('suan pakkad')– hence the name. Within the stilt buildings are displays of art, antiques and furnishings, and the landscaped grounds are a peaceful oasis complete with ducks, swans and a semi-enclosed garden.

The diminutive Lacquer Pavilion, at the back of the complex, dates from the Ayuthaya period and features gold-leaf *jataka* (stories of the Buddha's past lives) and *Ramayana* murals, as well as scenes from daily Ayuthaya life. The building originally sat in a monastery compound on Mae Nam Chao Phraya, just south of Ayuthaya.

Larger residential structures at the front of the complex contain displays of Khmer-style Hindu and Buddhist art, Ban Chiang ceramics and a very interesting collection of historic Buddhas, including a beautiful late U Thong–style image.

Dusit Palace Park MUSEUM, HISTORICAL SITE
(วังสวนดุสิต; 0 2628 6300; bounded by Th Ratchawithi, Th U Thong Nai & Th Ratchasima; ticket for all Dusit Palace Park sights adult/child 100/20B, or free same-day entry with Wat Phra Kaew & Grand Palace ticket; 9.30am-4pm Tue-Sun; Tha Thewet, Phaya Thai exit 2 & taxi) Following Rama V's first European tour in 1897, he returned home with visions of European castles swimming in his head and set about transforming these styles into a uniquely

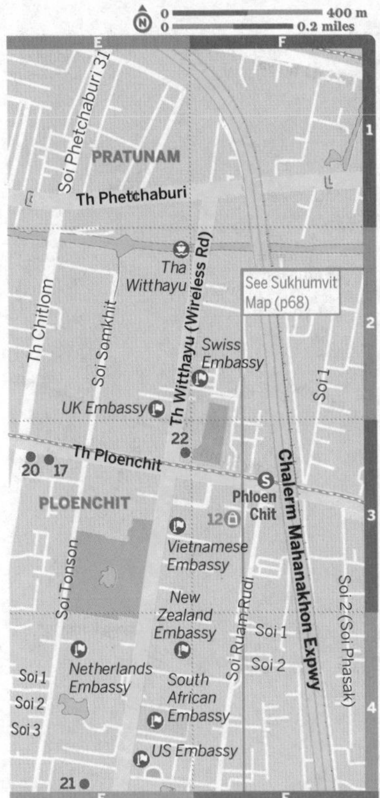

Thai expression, today's Dusit Palace Park. The royal palace, throne hall and minor palaces for extended family were all moved here from Ko Ratanakosin, and today this complex holds a house museum and other cultural collections.

Originally constructed on Ko Si Chang in 1868 and moved to the present site in 1910, **Vimanmek Teak Mansion** (☎0 2628 6300; Th Ratchawithi, Dusit Palace Park; ⊙9.30am-4pm Tue-Sun, last entry 3.15pm) contains 81 rooms, halls and anterooms, and is said to be the world's largest golden-teak building, allegedly built without the use of a single nail. The mansion was the first permanent building on the Dusit Palace grounds, and served as Rama V's residence in the early 1900s. The interior of the mansion contains various personal effects of the king and a treasure trove of early Ratanakosin art objects and antiques. Compulsory tours (in English) leave every half-hour between 9.45am and 3.15pm, and last about an hour.

The nearby **Ancient Cloth Museum** (☎0 2628 6300; Th Ratchawithi, Dusit Palace Park; ⊙9.30am-4pm Tue-Sun) presents a beautiful collection of traditional silks and cottons that make up the royal cloth collection.

Originally built as a throne hall for Rama V in 1904, the smaller **Abhisek Dusit Throne Hall** (☎0 2628 6300; Th Ratchawithi, Dusit Palace Park; ⊙9.30am-4pm Tue-Sun) is typical of the finer architecture of the era. Victorian-influenced gingerbread architecture

Siam Square

Top Sights
1 Jim Thompson House A1

Sights
2 Erawan Shrine D3
3 Madame Tussaud's B2
Siam Ocean World .... (see 15)

Activities, Courses & Tours
KidZania .... (see 15)

Sleeping
4 Lub*d A2
5 Reno Hotel A2
6 Siam@Siam A2
7 Wendy House B2

Eating
Food Republic .... (see 14)
Gourmet Paradise .... (see 15)
8 Koko B2
MBK Food Island .... (see 10)

Entertainment
Krung Sri IMAX .... (see 15)
Paragon Cineplex .... (see 15)
9 Playhouse Theater Cabaret B1

Shopping
10 MBK Center B2
11 Pantip Plaza C1
12 Pinky Tailors F3
13 Pratunam Market D1
14 Siam Center & Siam Discovery Center B2
15 Siam Paragon C2
16 Siam Square B2

Transport
17 Cathay Pacific Airways E3
18 China Airlines D3
19 Japan Airlines D3
20 Malaysia Airlines E3
21 United Airlines E4
22 Vietnam Airlines E3

Silom & Sathon

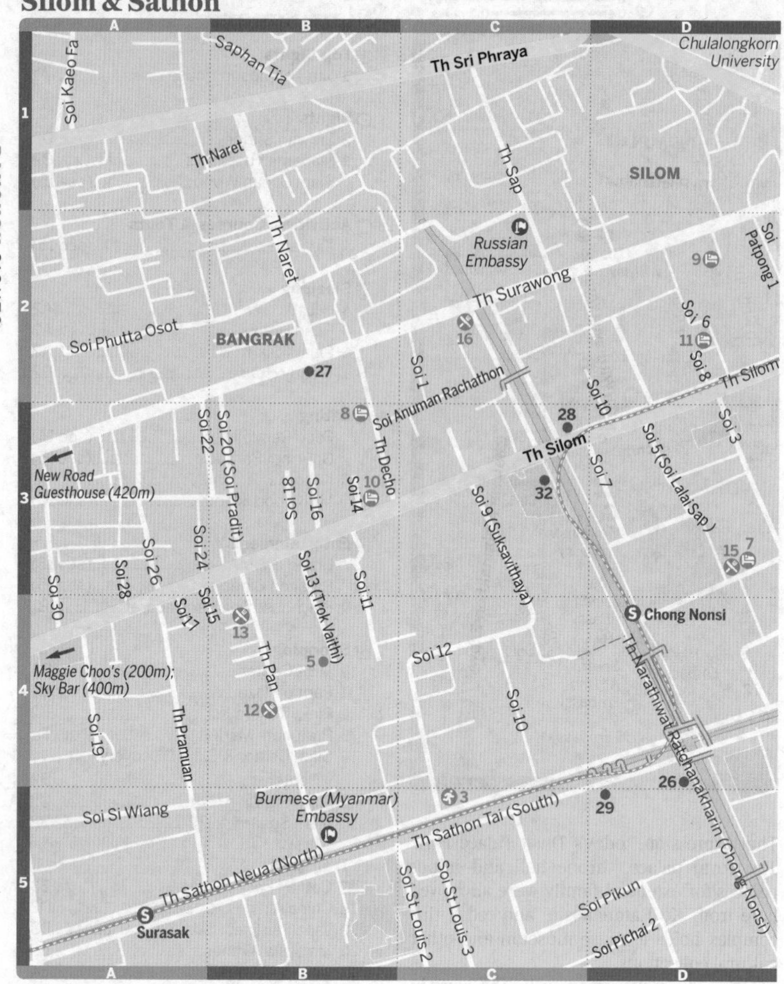

and Moorish porticoes blend to create a striking and distinctly Thai exterior. The structure itself is more interesting than the display of regional handiwork crafted by members of the Promotion of Supplementary Occupations & Related Techniques (Support) foundation, an organisation sponsored by Queen Sirikit.

Near the Th U Thong Nai entrance, two large stables that once housed three white elephants – animals whose auspicious albinism automatically make them crown property – are now the **Royal Thai Elephant Museum** (☎0 2628 6300; Th Ratchawithi, Dusit Palace Park; ⏲9.30am-4pm Tue-Sun). One of the structures contains artefacts and photos outlining the importance of elephants in Thai history and explaining their various rankings according to physical characteristics. The second stable holds a sculptural representation of a living royal white elephant. Draped in royal vestments, the statue is more or less treated as a shrine by the visiting Thai public.

Because this is royal property, visitors should wear long pants (no capri pants) or long skirts and shirts with sleeves.

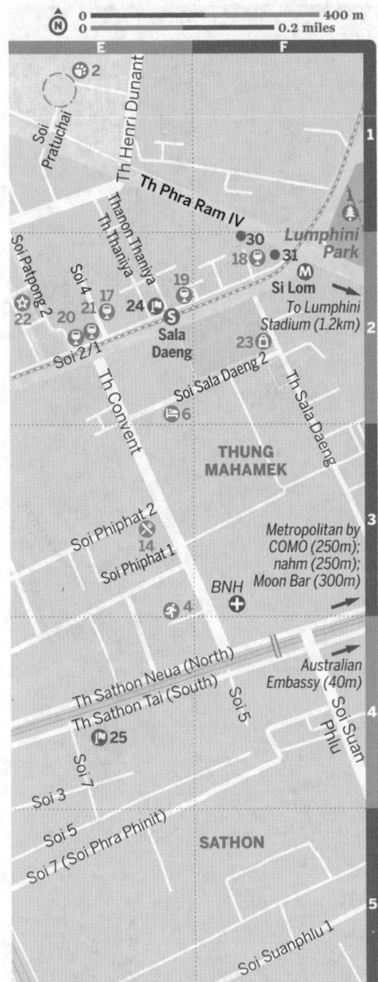

Silom & Sathon

Top Sights

1 Lumphini Park F1

Sights

2 Queen Saovabha Memorial Institute E1

Activities, Courses & Tours

3 Health Land C5
4 Ruen-Nuad Massage Studio E3
5 Silom Thai Cooking School B4

Sleeping

6 Bangkok Christian Guest House E2
7 Glow Trinity Silom D3
8 Lub*d B3
9 Siam Heritage D2
10 Silom Art Hostel B3
11 Smile Society D2

Eating

12 Bonita Cafe & Social Club B4
13 Chennai Kitchen B4
14 Eat Me E3
15 FooDie D3
16 Somboon Seafood C2

Drinking & Nightlife

17 Balcony E2
18 DJ Station F2
19 G.O.D E2
20 Tapas Room E2
21 Telephone Pub E2

Entertainment

22 Patpong E2

Shopping

23 July F2

Information

24 Irish Honorary Consulate E2
25 Singaporean Embassy E4

Transport

26 Air Canada D4
27 Air China B2
28 Air New Zealand C3
British Airways .... (see 30)
29 Nok Air D5
30 Qantas Airways F2
31 Singapore Airlines F2
32 Thai Airways International C3

Activities

For a crash course in Thai massage, see p401.

Ruen-Nuad Massage Studio THAI MASSAGE

(Map p66; 0 2632 2662; 42 Th Convent; Thai massage per hr 350B; 10am-9pm; M Si Lom exit 2, S Sala Daeng exit 2) Set in a refurbished wooden house, this charming place successfully avoids both the tackiness and New Agedness that characterise many Bangkok massage joints. Prices are approachable, too.

Health Land THAI MASSAGE

(www.healthlandspa.com; Thai massage 2hr 500B; 9am-midnight) A winning formula of affordable prices, expert treatments and pleasant facilities has created a small empire of Health Land centres with branches at **Ekamai** (Map p68; 0 2392 2233; 96/1 Soi Ekamai 10; S Ekkamai exit 2 & taxi), **Sathon** (Map p66; 0 2637 8883; 120 Th Sathon Neua (North); S Surasak

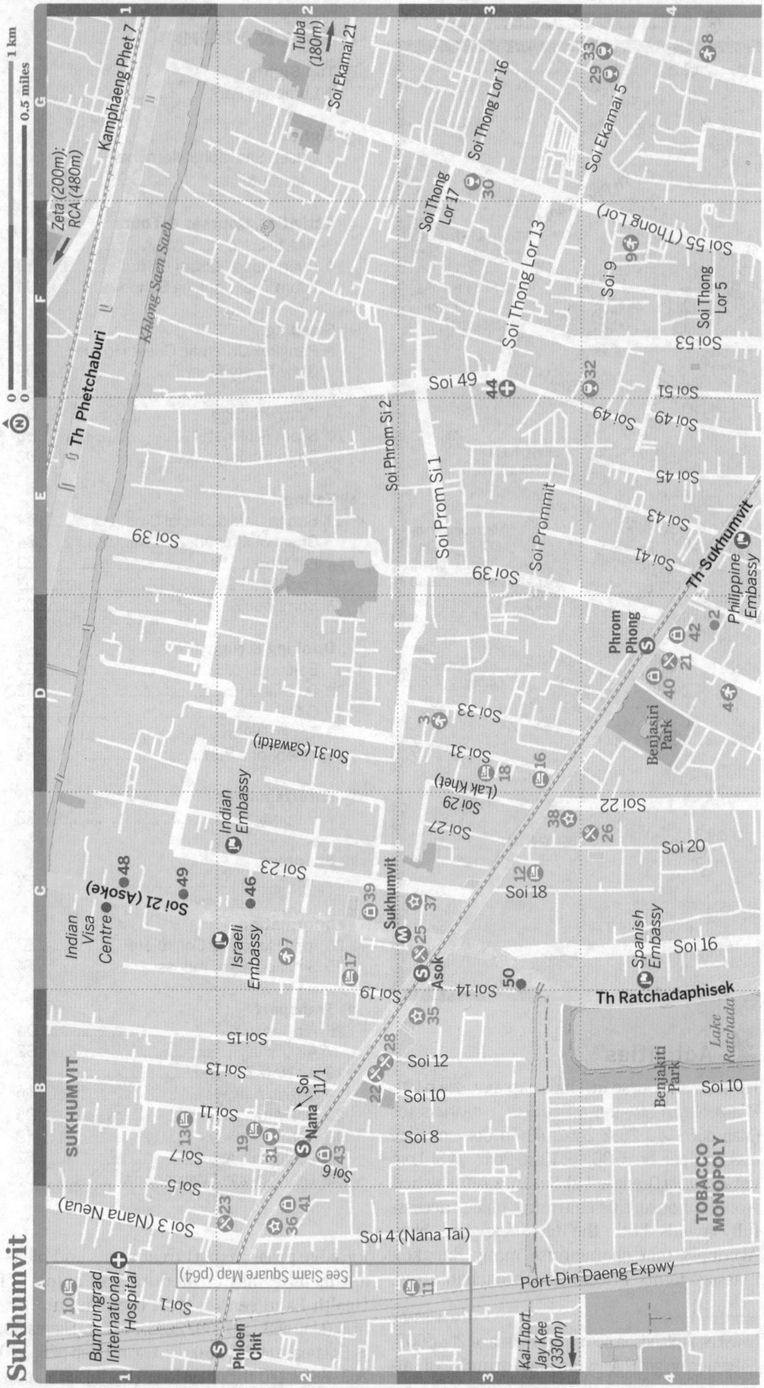

Sukhumvit

0 1 km
0 0.5 miles
A B C D E F G
1 2 3 4
SUKHUMVIT
Bumrungrad International Hospital
Phloen Chit
See Siam Square Map (p64)
Soi 1
Soi 3 (Nana Neua)
Soi 5
Soi 7
Soi 11
Soi 13
Soi 15
Soi 19
Soi 21 (Asoke)
Soi 23
Soi 27
Soi 29 (Lak Khet)
Soi 31
Soi 31 (Sawatdi)
Soi 33
Soi 39
Soi 41
Soi 43
Soi 45
Soi 49
Soi 51
Soi 53
Soi 55 (Thong Lor)
Soi 4 (Nana Tai)
Soi 6
Soi 8
Soi 10
Soi 11/1
Soi 12
Soi 14
Soi 16
Soi 18
Soi 20
Soi 22
Nana
Asok
Sukhumvit
Phrom Phong
Indian Visa Centre
Israeli Embassy
Indian Embassy
Spanish Embassy
Philippine Embassy
Th Phetchaburi
Kamphaeng Phet 7
Khlong Saen Saeb
Zeta (200m); RCA (480m)
Tuba (180m)
Soi Ekamai 21
Soi Ekamai 5
Soi Phrom Si 2
Soi Prom Si 1
Soi Prommit
Soi Thong Lor 17
Soi Thong Lor 16
Soi Thong Lor 13
Soi Thong Lor 5
Soi 9
Th Sukhumvit
Th Ratchadaphisek
Benjasiri Park
Benjakiti Park
Lake Ratchada
TOBACCO MONOPOLY
Port-Din Daeng Expwy
Kai Thort Jay Kee (330m)
10 11 13 19 31 23 36 41 43 22 28 17 7 46 48 49 39 35 25 37 50 12 18 16 38 26 3 40 21 42 2 4 44 32 30 9 29 33 8

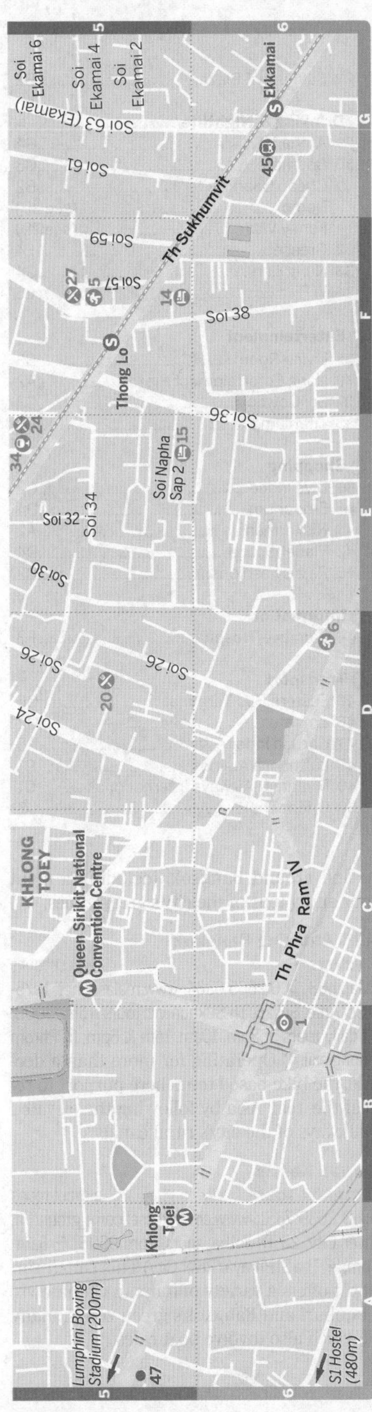

exit 3) and **Sukhumvit** (Map p68; ☎0 2261 1110; 55/5 Soi 21 (Asoke), Th Sukhumvit; MSukhumvit exit 1, S Asok exit 5).

Asia Herb Association THAI MASSAGE
(www.asiaherbassociation.com; Thai massage per hr 400B, Thai massage with herbal compress 1½hr 900B; ⊙9am-midnight) With outposts at **Phrom Phong** (Map p68; ☎0 2261 7401; 33/1 Soi 24, Th Sukhumvit; S Phrom Phong exit 4), **Sawadee** (Map p68; ☎0 2261 2201; 20/1 Soi 31 (Sawatdi), Th Sukhumvit; S Phrom Phong exit 5) and **Thong Lor** (Map p68; ☎0 2392 3631; 58/19-25 Soi 55 (Thong Lor), Th Sukhumvit; S Thong Lo exit 3), this Japanese-owned chain specialises in massage using *ǝrà·kóp* (traditional Thai herbal compresses).

Courses

Helping Hands COOKING
(☎08 4901 8717; www.cookingwithpoo.com; 1200B; ⊙lessons 8.30am-1pm) This popular cookery course was started by a native of Khlong Toey's slums and is held in her neighbourhood. Courses, which must be booked in advance, span four dishes and include a visit to Khlong Toey Market and transport to and from **Emporium** (Map p68; www.emporiumthailand.com; cnr Soi 24 & Th Sukhumvit; ⊙10am-10pm; S Phrom Phong exit 2).

Silom Thai Cooking School COOKING
(Map p66; ☎08 4726 5669; www.bangkokthaicooking.com; 68 Soi 13, Th Silom; 1000B; ⊙lessons 9am-12.30pm, 1.40-5.30pm & 6-9pm; S Chong Nonsi exit 3) The facilities are basic, but Silom crams a visit to a local market and instruction of five to six dishes into 3½ hours, making it the best bang for your baht. Located at the very end of Soi 13, Th Silom – follow the signs.

Sor Vorapin Gym THAI BOXING
(Map p58; ☎0 2282 3551; www.thaiboxings.com; 13 Th Kasab; per session/month 500/9000B; ⊙lessons 7.30-9.30am & 3-5pm; Tha Phra Athit (Banglamphu)) Specialising in training foreign students of both genders, this gym is sweating distance from Th Khao San.

Tours

If you're not travelling with a group but would like a guide, recommended outfits include the following:

Tour With Tong GUIDED TOUR
(☎08 1835 0240; www.tourwithtong.com; day tour from 1500B) Guided tours in and around Bangkok.

Sukhumvit

Sights
1 Khlong Toey Market B6

Activities, Courses & Tours
2 ABC Amazing Bangkok Cyclists D4
3 Asia Herb Association D3
4 Asia Herb Association D4
5 Asia Herb Association F5
6 Fun-arium D6
7 Health Land C2
8 Health Land G4
9 Wild Animal Rescue Foundation of Thailand F4

Sleeping
10 AriyasomVilla A1
11 Atlanta A3
12 Baan Sukhumvit C3
13 Federal Hotel B1
14 HI-Sukhumvit F5
15 Napa Place E5
16 S31 ..... D3
17 Sacha's Hotel Uno C2
18 Seven D3
19 Suk 11 ..... B2

Eating
20 Bo.lan D5
21 Imoya D4
22 Myeong Ga B2
23 Nasir Al-Masri A2
24 Opposite Mess Hall E5
25 Pier 21 ..... C3
26 Saras C4
27 Soul Food Mahanakorn F5
28 Sukhumvit Plaza B2

Drinking & Nightlife
29 Arena 10 ..... G4
30 Badmotel G3
31 Cheap Charlie's B2
Demo ..... (see 29)
Funky Villa ..... (see 29)
32 Grease F4
33 Nung-Len G4
34 WTF E5

Entertainment
35 Living Room B3
36 Nana Entertainment Plaza A2
37 Soi Cowboy C3
38 Titanium C3

Shopping
39 Dive Indeed C2
40 Emporium D4
41 Nickermann's A2
42 Planet Scuba D4
43 Raja's Fashions B2

Information
44 Samitivej Hospital F3

Transport
45 Eastern Bus Terminal G6
46 Emirates C2
47 Garuda Indonesia A5
48 Lufthansa Airlines C1
49 Myanmar Airways International C1
50 Orient Thai C3

Thai Private Tour Guide GUIDED TOUR
(☎08 9661 6706, 08 9822 1798; www.thaitourguide.com; day tour from 2000B) Ms Pu and TJ get good reviews.

Bangkok Private Tours WALKING TOUR
(www.bangkokprivatetours.com; half-/full-day walking tour 4700/6000B) Customised walking tours of the city.

Bicycle Tours

Although some cycling tours tackle Bangkok's urban neighbourhoods, most take advantage of the nearby lush, undeveloped district to the south known as Phra Pradaeng.

Grasshopper Adventures BICYCLE TOURS
(Map p58; ☎0 2280 0832; www.grasshopperadventures.com; 57 Th Ratchadamnoen Klang; half-day tours from 1100B, full-day tours from 1600B; ⌚9am-6pm; klorng boat to Tha Phan Fah) This lauded outfit runs a variety of bicycle tours in and around Bangkok, including a night tour and a tour of the city's green zones.

ABC Amazing Bangkok Cyclists BICYCLE TOURS
(Map p68; ☎0 2665 6364; www.realasia.net; 10/5-7 Soi Aree, Soi 26, Th Sukhumvit; tours from 1300B; ⌚daily tours at 8am, 10am, 1pm & 6pm; S Phrom Phong exit 4) Operating for more than a decade, the bike-based tours here purport to reveal the 'real' Asia by following the elevated walkways of the city's rural canals.

Co van Kessel Bangkok Tours BICYCLE TOURS
(☎0 2639 7351; www.covankessel.com; ground fl, River City, 23 Th Yotha; tours from 950B; ⌚6am-7pm; Tha Si Phraya/River City) This Dutch-run outfit offers a variety of tours in Chinatown, Thonburi and Bangkok's green zones, many of which also involve boat rides.

River & Canal Trips

Glimpses of Bangkok's past as the 'Venice of the East' are still possible today, even though the motor vehicle has long since become the city's conveyance of choice.

The most obvious way to get between riverside attractions is the **Chao Phraya Express Boat** (0 2623 6001; www.chaophrayaexpressboat.com). See p92 for more information about Bangkok's commuter boats.

Long-tail boats are Bangkok icons and can be chartered for tours of the Thonburi *klorng* (canals; also spelled *khlong*); see the boxed text below for details.

Dinner Cruises

Perfect for romancing couples or subdued families, dinner cruises glide along Mae Nam Chao Phraya, basking in the twinkling city lights at night, far away from the heat, bustle and noise of town. Cruises range from down-home to sophisticated, but the food generally ranges from mediocre to forgettable.

The vast majority of cruises depart from, or very near, the pier at **River City** (www.rivercity.co.th; 23 Th Yotha; 10am-10pm; Tha Si Phraya/River City or shopping centre shuttle boat from Tha Sathon (Central Pier)).

Loy Nava DINNER CRUISE
(0 2437 4932; www.loynava.com; from 1648B; cruises 6-8pm & 8.10-10.10pm) Operating since 1970, and quite possibly the original Bangkok dinner cruise. A vegetarian menu is available.

Wan Fah DINNER CRUISE
(0 2622 7657; www.wanfah.in.th/eng/dinner; 1300B; cruise 7-9pm) The buxom wooden boats here are more intimate than most. Dinner options include a standard or seafood set menu.

White Orchid DINNER CRUISE
(0 2476 5207; www.thairivercruise.com; 1400B; cruise 7.45-9.45pm) One of the larger boats; entertainment here is provided by *gà·teu·i* (transgendered people; also spelt *kathoey*) performers.

Festivals & Events

In addition to the national holidays, there's always something going on in Bangkok. Many Thai holidays are based on the lunar calendar, which varies year to year, so check the website of **TAT** (Tourism Authority of Thailand; Map p58; www.tourismthailand.org) or the Bangkok Information Center (p89) for exact dates.

Chinese New Year NEW YEAR
(Jan or Feb) Thai-Chinese celebrate the lunar New Year with a week of housecleaning, lion dances and fireworks. Most festivities centre on Chinatown. Dates vary.

Songkran NEW YEAR
(mid-Apr) The celebration of the Thai New Year has morphed into a water war with high-powered water guns and water balloons being launched at suspecting and unsuspecting participants. The most intense water battles take place on Th Khao San.

DON'T MISS

EXPLORING BANGKOK'S CANALS

For an up-close view of the city's famed canals, long-tail boats are available for hire at Tha Chang, Tha Tien, Tha Oriental and Tha Phra Athit (Tha Banglamphu). Prices at Tha Chang are the highest and allow little room for negotiation, but you stand the least chance of being taken for a ride or hit with tips and other unexpected fees.

Trips explore the Thonburi canals **Khlong Bangkok Noi** and, further south, **Khlong Mon**, taking in the **Royal Barges National Museum** (พิพิธภัณฑสถานแห่งชาติ เรือพระราชพิธี (เรือพระที่นั่ง); Map p58; Khlong Bangkok Noi or 80/1 Th Arun Amarin; admission 100B, camera/video 100/200B; 9am-5pm; Tha Saphan Phra Pin Klao), Wat Arun (p54) and a riverside temple with fish feeding. Longer trips diverge into **Khlong Bangkok Yai**, further south, which offers more typical canal scenery, including orchid farms. On weekends, you have the option of visiting the **Taling Chan floating market** (ตลาดน้ำตลิ่งชัน; Khlong Bangkok Noi, Thonburi; 7am-4pm Sat & Sun). However, to actually disembark and explore any of these sights, the most common tour of one hour (1000B, up to eight people) is simply not enough time and you'll most likely need 1½ (1300B) or two hours (1500B).

Vegetarian Festival FOOD
(⏲ Sep or Oct) A 10-day Chinese-Buddhist festival wheels out yellow-bannered streetside vendors serving meatless meals. The greatest concentration of vendors is found in Chinatown. Dates vary.

Loi Krathong FULL MOON
(www.loikrathong.net/en; ⏲ early Nov) A beautiful national festival where, on the night of the full moon, small lotus-shaped boats made of banana leaf and containing a lit candle are set adrift on Mae Nam Chao Phraya.

King's Birthday ROYAL EVENT
(⏲ 5 Dec) Locals celebrate their monarch's birthday with lots of parades and fireworks.

Sleeping

At first glance, deciding where to lay your head in Bangkok appears an insurmountable task – there are countless hotels in virtually every corner of this sprawling city.

Making the job slightly easier is the fact that where you stay is largely determined by your budget. Banglamphu and the tourist ghetto of Th Khao San still hold the bulk of Bangkok's budget accommodation, although the downside is that it can be difficult to get to other parts of town. Cheap rooms are also available around lower Th Sukhumvit, although you'll have to put up with sex tourists and touts. Chinatown also has its share of hotels in this category.

Those willing to spend a bit more can consider staying in 'downtown' Bangkok. Both Th Sukhumvit and Th Silom have solid midrange options, typically within walking distance of the BTS or MRT. The soi opposite the National Stadium, near Siam Sq, have some good budget/midrange options, and have the benefit of being close to the BTS.

Upper Sukhumvit is home to many of Bangkok's boutique and upscale designer hotels. And the city's most legendary luxury hotels are largely found along the riverside near Th Silom.

Ko Ratanakosin, Banglamphu & Thonburi

Fortville Guesthouse HOTEL $
(Map p58; ☎0 2282 3932; www.fortvilleguesthouse.com; 9 Th Phra Sumen; r 790-1120B; ❄@📶; ⛴Tha Phra Athit (Banglamphu)) The rooms here are stylishly minimal, and the more expensive ones include perks such as fridge, balcony and five hours of free wi-fi.

Rambuttri Village Inn HOSTEL $$
(Map p58; ☎0 2282 9162; www.rambuttrivillage.com; 95 Soi Ram Buttri; r incl breakfast 1030-1600B; ❄📶🏊; ⛴Tha Phra Athit (Banglamphu)) If you're willing to subject yourself to the relentless gauntlet of tailors along the path approaching it ('Excuse me, suit?'), this plain and busy place has an abundance of good-value rooms and a rooftop pool.

★ **Lamphu Treehouse** HOTEL $$
(Map p58; ☎0 2282 0991; www.lamphutreehotel.com; 155 Wanchat Bridge, off Th Prachathipatai; r incl breakfast 1450-2500B, ste incl breakfast 3600-4900B; ❄@📶🏊; ⛴Tha Phan Fah) Despite the name, this attractive midranger has its feet firmly on land and, as such, represents great value. The rooms, panelled in wood and decorated with subtle Thai accents, are attractive and inviting, and the rooftop bar, pool, internet, restaurant and quiet canal-side location ensure that you may never feel the need to leave.

Feung Nakorn Balcony HOTEL $$
(Map p58; ☎0 2622 1100; www.feungnakorn.com; 125 Th Fuang Nakhon; dm 600B, r 1650B, ste 2000-3000B; ❄@📶; ⛴klorng boat to Tha Phan Fah) Located in a former school, the 42 rooms here surround an inviting garden courtyard and are generally large, bright and cheery. Amenities such as a free minibar, safe and flat-screen TV are standard, and the hotel has a quiet and secluded location away from the strip, with capable staff. Rates include breakfast. A charming and inviting, if not extremely great-value, place to stay.

Sam Sen Sam Place GUESTHOUSE $$
(Map p58; ☎0 2628 7067; www.samsensam.com; 48 Soi 3, Th Samsen; r incl breakfast 590-2500B; ❄@📶; ⛴Tha Phra Athit (Banglamphu)) One of the homiest places around, this colourful, refurbished antique villa gets glowing reports about its friendly service and quiet location. Note that the cheapest rooms are fan-cooled and share a bathroom.

Sourire HOTEL $$
(Map p58; ☎0 2280 2180; www.sourirebangkok.com; Soi Chao Phraya Si Phiphat; r incl breakfast 1500-3500B; ❄@📶; ⛴Tha Phan Fah) More home than hotel, the 38 rooms here exude a calming, matronly feel. Soft lighting, comfortable, sturdy wood furniture and the friendly, aged owners round out the pack-

age. To reach the hotel, follow Soi Chao Phraya Si Phiphat to the end and knock on the tall brown wooden door immediately on your left.

Hotel Dé Moc HOTEL $$
(Map p58; ☎0 2282 2831; www.hoteldemoc.com; 78 Th Prachathipatai; r incl breakfast 2549-2804B; ❄@📶🏊; ⛴Tha Phan Fah) The rooms at this

BATHROOMLESS IN BANGKOK

If you don't require your own en suite bathroom, Bangkok has heaps of options, ranging from high-tech dorm beds in a brand-new hostel to private bedrooms in an antique wooden house. Some of our picks:

➡ ★ **Lub*d** (Map p64; ☎0 2634 7999; siamsquare.lubd.com; Th Phra Ram I; dm 750B, r 1800-2400B; ❄@📶; Ⓢ National Stadium exit 1) The title is a play on the Thai *làp dee*, meaning 'sleep well', but the fun atmosphere here might make you want to stay up all night. There's an inviting communal area stocked with games and a bar, and thoughtful facilities ranging from washing machines to a theatre room. If this one's full, there's another **branch** (Map p66; ☎0 2634 7999; silom.lubd.com; 4 Th Decho; dm 550-650B, r 1400-1800B; ❄@📶; Ⓢ Chong Nonsi exit 2) just off Th Silom.

➡ **NapPark Hostel** (Map p58; ☎0 2282 2324; www.nappark.com; 5 Th Tani; dm 570-750B; ❄@📶; ⛴Tha Phra Athit (Banglamphu)) This well-run hostel features dorm rooms of various sizes, all of which boast podlike beds outfitted with power points, mini-TV, reading lamp and wi-fi. Free bicycles and hypersocial communal areas ensure you may not actually get the chance to plug in.

➡ **Khaosan Baan Thai** (☎0 2628 5559; www.khaosanbaanthai.com; 11/1 Soi 3, Th Samsen; r incl breakfast 390-730B; ❄@📶; ⛴Tha Phra Athit (Banglamphu)) This tiny wooden house holds 10 rooms decked out in cheery pastels and hand-painted bunny pictures. Half of the rooms are fan-cooled, and most are little more than a mattress on the floor, but warm service and an authentic homestay vibe compensate for this.

➡ **Silom Art Hostel** (Map p66; ☎0 2635 8070; www.silomarthostel.com; 198/19-22 Soi 14, Th Silom; dm 400-550B, r 1200-1500B; ❄@📶; Ⓢ Chong Nonsi exit 3) Quirky, artsy, bright and fun, Silom Art Hostel combines recycled materials, bizarre furnishings and colourful kitsch to arrive at a hostel that's quite unlike anywhere else in town. It's not all about style though: beds and rooms are functional and comfortable, and share clean bathrooms and appealing communal areas.

➡ **Saphaipae** (☎0 2238 2322; www.saphaipae.com; 35 Th Surasak; dm 400-550B, r 1800-2500B; ❄@📶; Ⓢ Surasak exit 1) The bright colours, chunky furnishings and bold murals in the lobby of this new hostel give it the vibe of a day-care centre for travellers – a feel that continues through to the playful communal areas and rooms. Dorms and rooms are well-equipped, and there's heaps of useful travel resources and facilities.

➡ **Suneta Hostel Khaosan** (Map p58; ☎0 2629 0150; www.sunetahostel.com; 209-211 Th Kraisi; dm incl breakfast 440-590B, r incl breakfast 900-1090B; ❄@📶; ⛴Tha Phra Athit (Banglamphu)) This young hostel is getting rave reviews for its retro-themed design, comfy dorms and friendly service.

➡ **S1 Hostel** (☎0 2679 7777; www.facebook.com/S1hostelBangkok; 35/1-4 Soi Ngam Duphli; dm 330-380B, r 700-1300B; ❄@📶; Ⓜ Lumphini exit 1) A huge new hostel with dorm beds and private rooms decked out in a simple yet attractive primary colour scheme. A host of facilities (laundry, kitchen, rooftop garden) and a convenient location near the MRT make it great value.

➡ **HI-Sukhumvit** (Map p68; ☎0 2391 9338; www.hisukhumvit.com; 23 Soi 38, Th Sukhumvit; dm incl breakfast 350B, r incl breakfast 690-1590B; ❄@📶; Ⓢ Thong Lo exit 4) The dorms here are admittedly rather plain, but clean bathrooms and a location in a quiet residential area with easy access to street food make it comfortable and convenient.

➡ **New Road Guesthouse** (☎0 2630 9371; www.newroadguesthouse.com; 1216/1 Th Charoen Krung; dm 250B, r 550-1600B; ❄@📶; ⛴Tha Oriental) The fan-cooled dorms here, among the cheapest accommodation in all of Bangkok, are clean and welcoming.

THINKING AHEAD

The rates listed in this chapter are high-season rack rates; ie the highest price a hotel will generally charge for a room. However, there's no reason you should be paying this much, especially if you know ahead of time when you'll be in town. Booking rooms online can lead to savings of at least 20%, and often more, at many of Bangkok's leading hotels. This can be done directly through the hotel websites or by sites such as **Lonely Planet's Hotels & Hostels** (www.hotels.lonelyplanet.com), which features thorough reviews from authors and traveller feedback, and a booking facility.

1960s-era hotel feel spacious, with high ceilings and generous windows, although the furnishings, like the exterior, are stuck in the previous century. The grounds include an inviting and retro-feeling pool and cafe, and complimentary transport to Th Khao San and free bike rental are thoughtful perks. Hefty online discounts are available.

★ Arun Residence HOTEL $$$
(Map p58; ☎0 2221 9158; www.arunresidence.com; 36-38 Soi Pratu Nokyung; r incl breakfast 4000-4200B, ste incl breakfast 5800B; ❄@📶; ⛴Tha Tien) Although strategically located across from Wat Arun, this multilevel wooden house on the river is about much more than just brilliant views. The six rooms here manage to feel both homey and stylish, some being tall and loftlike, while others join two rooms (the best is the top-floor Arun Suite, with its own balcony). There are also inviting communal areas, including a library, rooftop bar and restaurant. Reservations essential.

Sala Rattanakosin HOTEL $$$
(Map p58; ☎0 2622 1388; www.salaresorts.com/rattanakosin; Soi Tha Tian; r incl breakfast 3100-4900B, ste incl breakfast 9,000B; ❄@📶; ⛴Tha Tien) This new riverside place boasts a sleek, modernist feel – an intriguing contrast with the former warehouse it's located in. The 17 rooms, decked out in black and white, and boasting open-plan bathrooms and big windows looking out on the river and Wat Arun, aren't particularly huge, but will satisfy the fashion-conscious.

Chinatown & Phahurat

Siam Classic GUESTHOUSE $
(☎0 2639 6363; 336/10 Trok Chalong Krung; r incl breakfast 500-1200B; ❄@📶; MHua Lamphong exit 1) The rooms here don't include much furniture, but a genuine effort has been made at making them feel comfortable, tidy and even a bit stylish. An inviting ground-floor communal area encourages meeting and chatting, and the whole place exudes a welcoming homestay vibe.

@Hua Lamphong HOSTEL $
(☎0 2639 1925; www.at-hualamphong.com; 326/1 Th Phra Ram IV; dm 400-450B, r 690-950B; ❄@📶; ⛴Tha Ratchawong, MHua Lamphong) Plain-yet-clean dorm beds and rooms can be found at this new-feeling hostel across the street from the train station.

★ Loy La Long HOTEL $$
(☎0 2639 1390; www.loylalong.com; 1620/2 Th Songwat; dm incl breakfast 1300B, r incl breakfast 2100-4000B; ❄@📶; ⛴Tha Ratchawong, MHua Lamphong exit 1 & taxi) Rustic, retro and charming; the six rooms in this 100-year-old wooden house have heaps of personality. And united by breezy, inviting nooks and crannies and a unique location elevated over Mae Nam Chao Phraya, the whole place boasts a hidden, almost secret feel. The only downside is finding it; to get there, proceed to Th Songwat and cut directly through Wat Patumkongka Rachaworawiharn to the river.

Siam Square

Reno Hotel HOTEL $$
(Map p64; ☎0 2215 0026; www.renohotel.co.th; 40 Soi Kasem San 1; r incl breakfast 1590-2390B; ❄@📶🏊; SNational Stadium exit 1) The rooms here are relatively large, if somewhat dark, and reflect the renovations evident in the lobby and exterior. But the cafe and pool of this Vietnam War–era hotel cling to the past.

Wendy House HOSTEL $$
(Map p64; ☎0 2214 1149; www.wendyguesthouse.com; 36/2 Soi Kasem San 1; r incl breakfast 1100-1490B; ❄@📶; SNational Stadium exit 1) Basic but clean and relatively well-stocked (TV, fridge) rooms for this price range.

Siam@Siam HOTEL $$$
(Map p64; ☎0 2217 3000; www.siamatsiam.com; 865 Th Phra Ram I; r incl breakfast 7000-11,200B; ❄@📶🏊; SNational Stadium exit 1) A seemingly random mishmash of colours and

industrial/recycled materials results in a style one could only describe as 'junkyard chic' – but in a good way, of course. The rooms, which largely continue the theme, are between the 14th and 24th floors, and offer terrific city views. There's a spa, a rooftop restaurant and a pool on the 11th floor.

Silom & Sathon

Smile Society HOTEL $$

(Map p66; ☎08 1343 1754, 08 1442 5800; www.smilesocietyhostel.com; 30/3-4 Soi 6, Th Silom; dm incl breakfast 420B, r incl breakfast 900-1880B; ❄@📶; Ⓜ Si Lom exit 2, Ⓢ Sala Daeng exit 1) Part boutique, part hostel, this four-storey shophouse combines small but comfortable and well-equipped rooms and dorms with spotless shared bathrooms. A central location, a communal area with TV and free computers, and helpful, English-speaking staff are additional perks.

Glow Trinity Silom HOTEL $$

(Map p66; ☎0 2231 5050; www.zinchospitality.com/glowbyzinc/silom; 150 Soi Phiphat 2; r incl breakfast 1900-2600B, ste incl breakfast 3600B; ❄@📶🏊; Ⓢ Chong Nonsi exit 2) A sophisticated-feeling hotel at a midrange price, Glow has contemporary, tech-equipped rooms and great service, and pool and fitness can be accessed next door. The suites aren't worth the extra baht unless you really need a bit more space and a bigger TV.

Bangkok Christian Guest House HOTEL $$

(Map p66; ☎0 2233 2206; www.bcgh.org; 123 Soi Sala Daeng 2; r incl breakfast 1100-2860B; ❄📶; Ⓜ Si Lom exit 2, Ⓢ Sala Daeng exit 2) This somewhat institutional-feeling guesthouse is a wise choice for families on a budget, as some rooms have as many as five beds and there's a 2nd-floor children's play area.

★ **Siam Heritage** HOTEL $$$

(Map p66; ☎0 2353 6101; www.thesiamheritage.com; 115/1 Th Surawong; incl breakfast r 2900B, ste 4000-9300B; ❄@📶🏊; Ⓜ Si Lom exit 2, Ⓢ Sala Daeng exit 1) Tucked off busy Th Surawong, this classy boutique hotel oozes with homey Thai charm – probably because the owners also live in the same building. The 73 rooms are decked out in silk and dark woods with classy design touches and thoughtful amenities. There's an inviting rooftop garden/pool/spa, and it's all cared for by a team of charming and professional staff. Highly recommended.

LATE-NIGHT TOUCHDOWN

A lot of nail-biting anxiety is expended on international flights arriving in Bangkok around midnight. Will there be taxis into town? Will there be available rooms? Will my family ever hear from me again? Soothe those nagging voices with the knowledge that most international flights arrive late and that Bangkok is an accommodating place. Yes, there are taxis and even an express train service that runs until midnight.

If you haven't already made hotel reservations, a good area to look for a bed is lower Sukhumvit – it's right off the expressway and hotels around Soi Nana such as **Federal Hotel** (Map p68; ☎0 2253 0175; www.federalbangkok.com; 27 Soi 11, Th Sukhumvit; r incl breakfast 1400-1600B; ❄@📶🏊; Ⓢ Nana exit 4) are used to lots of late-night traffic and won't break the bank. Or you could go to Th Khao San, which stays up late, is full of hotels and guesthouses, and sees a near-continuous supply of 'fresh-off-the-birds' just like you.

If, for some reason, you can't stray too far from the airport, these places provide a more than adequate roof.

Suvarnabhumi International Airport

➡ **Grand Inn Come Hotel** (☎0 2738 8189; www.grandinncome-hotel.com; 99 Moo 6, Th Kingkaew; r 1400-2300B, ste 4500-5000B; ❄@📶) Solid midranger 10km west of the airport, with airport shuttle and self-professed 'lively' karaoke bar.

➡ **Novotel Suvarnabhumi Airport Hotel** (☎0 2131 1111; www.novotelairportbkk.com; r incl breakfast 7301-9216B, ste incl breakfast 10,174B; ❄@📶) With 600-plus luxurious rooms in the airport compound.

Don Muang International Airport

➡ **Amari Airport Hotel** (☎0 2566 1020; www.amari.com/donmuang; 333 Th Choet Wutthakat; r 1750-2150B, ste 3150B; ❄@📶🏊) Directly opposite the airport.

COMMON BANGKOK SCAMS

Commit these classic rip-offs to memory and join us in our ongoing crusade to outsmart Bangkok's crafty scam artists.

- **Closed today** Ignore any 'friendly' local who tells you an attraction is closed for a Buddhist holiday or for cleaning. These are set-ups for trips to a bogus gem sale.
- **Túk-túk rides for 10B** Say goodbye to your day's itinerary if you climb aboard this ubiquitous scam. These alleged 'tours' bypass all the sights and instead cruise to all the fly-by-night gem and tailor shops that pay commissions.
- **Flat-fare taxi ride** Flatly refuse any driver who quotes a flat fare (usually between 100B and 150B for in-town destinations), which will usually be three times more expensive than the reasonable meter rate. Walking beyond the tourist area will usually help in finding an honest driver.
- **Tourist buses to the south** On the long journey south, well-organised and connected thieves have hours to comb through your bags, breaking into (and later resealing) locked bags, searching through hiding places and stealing credit cards, electronics and even toiletries. This scam has been running for years but is easy to avoid simply by carrying valuables with you on the bus.
- **Friendly strangers** Be wary of smartly dressed men who approach you asking where you're from and where you're going. Their opening gambit is usually followed with: 'Ah, my son/daughter is studying at university in (your city)' – they seem to have an encyclopaedic knowledge of major universities. As the tourist authorities here pointed out, this sort of behaviour is out of character for Thais and should be treated with suspicion.

★ Metropolitan by COMO HOTEL $$$

(☎0 2625 3333; www.comohotels.com/metropolitanbangkok; 27 Th Sathon Tai (South); r incl breakfast 9220-11,220B, ste incl breakfast 12,200-78,720B; ; M Lumphini exit 2) The exterior of Bangkok's former YMCA has changed relatively little, but a peek inside reveals one of the city's sleekest, sexiest hotels. A recent renovation has all 171 rooms looking better than ever in striking tones of black, white and yellow. The 'City' rooms tend to feel a bit tight, while the two-storey penthouse suites feel like small homes.

Sukhumvit

Suk 11 HOTEL $

(Map p68; ☎0 2253 5927; www.suk11.com; 1/33 Soi 11, Th Sukhumvit; r incl breakfast 500-1600B; ; S Nana exit 3) Extremely well run and equally popular, this rustic guesthouse is an oasis of woods and greenery in the urban jungle that is Th Sukhumvit. The basic rooms are clean and comfy, if a bit dark, and the cheapest ones share bathrooms. Although the building holds nearly 70 rooms, you'll still need to book at least two weeks ahead.

Atlanta HOTEL $

(Map p68; ☎0 2252 1650; www.theatlantahotelbangkok.com; 78 Soi 2, Th Sukhumvit; r incl breakfast 690-800B, ste incl breakfast 950-1950B; ; S Nana exit 2) Defiantly antiquated and equal parts frumpy and grumpy, this crumbling gem has changed very little since its construction in 1952. The opulent lobby stands in stark contrast to the simple rooms, and the frantic anti-sex tourist tone can be rather disturbing, but the inviting pool (allegedly the country's first hotel pool) and delightful restaurant (for guests only) are enough incentive to get past these.

Napa Place HOTEL $$

(Map p68; ☎0 2661 5525; www.napaplace.com; 11/3 Soi Napha Sap 2; r incl breakfast 2200-2400B, ste incl breakfast 3400-4100B; ; S Thong Lo exit 2) Hidden in the confines of a typical Bangkok urban compound is what must be the city's homiest accommodation. The 12 expansive rooms have been decorated with dark woods from the family's former business and light brown cloths from the hands of Thai weavers, and the cosy communal areas couldn't be much different from the suburban living room you grew up in.

Sacha's Hotel Uno HOTEL $$

(Map p68; ☎0 2651 2180; www.sachas.hotel-uno.com; 28/19 Soi 19, Th Sukhumvit; r incl breakfast 1800-2300B; ; M Sukhumvit exit 1, S Asok exit 1) Soi 19 and around are home to a handful of good-value, stylish hotels that barely edge into the midrange category, including Uno, surprisingly sophisticated for this price range. Its 56 rooms are comfortable and equally well equipped for work or play.

Baan Sukhumvit HOTEL $$

(Map p68; 0 2258 5630; www.baansukhumvit.com; 392/38-39 Soi 20, Th Sukhumvit; r incl breakfast 1440-1540B; ; M Sukhumvit exit 1, S Asok exit 1) One of a handful of midrangers located on this small side street off Soi 20, Baan Sukhumvit's 12 rooms exude a homey, cosy atmosphere. A newer branch is around the corner on Soi 18.

★ **Ariyasom Villa** HOTEL $$$

(Map p68; 0 2254 8880; www.ariyasom.com; 65 Soi 1, Th Sukhumvit; r incl breakfast 5353-11,682B; ; S Phloen Chit exit 3) Located at the end of Soi 1 behind a virtual wall of frangipani, this renovated 1940s-era villa is one of Bangkok's worst-kept accommodation secrets. If you can score a reservation, you'll be privy to one of 24 spacious rooms, meticulously outfitted with thoughtful Thai design touches and beautiful antique furniture. There's a spa and an inviting tropical pool, and breakfast is vegetarian and served in the villa's stunning glass-encased dining room.

Seven HOTEL $$$

(Map p68; 0 2662 0951; www.sleepatseven.com; 3/15 Soi 31, Th Sukhumvit; r incl breakfast 4708-7062B; ; S Phrom Phong exit 5) This tiny hotel somehow manages to be chic and homey, stylish and comfortable, Thai and international all at the same time. Each of the five rooms is decked out in a different colour that corresponds to Thai astrology, and thoughtful amenities and friendly service abound.

S31 HOTEL $$$

(Map p68; 0 2260 1111; www.s31hotel.com; 545 Soi 31, Th Sukhumvit; r incl breakfast 4000B, ste incl breakfast 7000-60,000B; ; S Phrom Phong exit 5) The bold patterns and graphics of its interior and exterior make the S31 a fun, young-feeling choice. Thoughtful touches such as kitchenettes with large fridge, super-huge beds and free courses (cooking, Thai boxing and yoga) prove that the style also has substance. Branches can also be found on Soi 15 and Soi 33.

Other Areas

The following hotels lie outside our neat neighbourhood designations, so they require a little more effort to reach. This also means that they tend to be located in less hectic parts of the city, perfect for those who'd rather not stay in the thick of it.

If you need to stay near one of Bangkok's two airports, check the accommodation options on p75.

★ **Phra-Nakorn Norn-Len** HOTEL $$

(0 2628 8188; www.phranakorn-nornlen.com; 46 Soi Thewet 1; r incl breakfast 1800-3600B; ; Tha Thewet) Set in an expansive garden compound decorated like the Bangkok of yesteryear, this bright and cheery hotel is an atmospheric if not necessarily stupendous-value place to stay. The 31 rooms are attractively furnished with old-timey antiques and wall paintings, and there's massage and endless opportunities for peaceful relaxing.

Mystic Place HOTEL $$

(0 2270 3344; www.mysticplacebkk.com; 224/5-9 Th Pradiphat; r incl breakfast 1530-1870B; ; S Saphan Khwai exit 2 & taxi) This hotel unites 36 rooms, each of which is individually and playfully designed. One of the rooms we checked out combined a chair upholstered with stuffed animals and walls covered with graffiti, while another was swathed in eye-contorting op art. Heaps of fun and perpetually popular, so be sure to book ahead.

Swan Hotel HOTEL $$

(0 2235 9271; www.swanhotelbkk.com; 31 Soi 36, Th Charoen Krung; r incl breakfast 1200-2000B; ; Tha Oriental) The 1960s-era furnishings date this classic Bangkok hotel despite recent renovations. But the rooms are airy and virtually spotless, and the antiquated vibe provides the Swan, in particular its pool, with a funky, retro feel.

★ **Bangkok Tree House** HOTEL $$$

(08 1453 1100; www.bangkoktreehouse.com; near Wat Bang Nam Pheung Nork; bungalow incl breakfast 6000-10,000B; ; S Bang Na exit 2 & taxi) The 12 multilevel bungalows here are stylishly sculpted from sustainable and recycled materials, resulting in a vibe that calls to mind a sophisticated, eco-friendly summer camp. Thoughtful amenities include en suite computers equipped with movies, free mobile phone and bicycle use, and free ice cream.

To get to Bangkok Tree House, take the BTS to Bang Na and jump in a taxi for the short ride to the pier at Wat Bang Nam Pheung Nork. From there, take the river-crossing ferry (4B, from 5am to 9.30pm), and continue by motorcycle taxi (10B) or on foot (call in advance for directions).

Mandarin Oriental HOTEL $$$
(☎0 2659 9000; www.mandarinoriental.com; 48 Soi 40, Th Charoen Krung; r incl breakfast 15,150-30,000B, ste incl breakfast 27,500-160,000B; ; Tha Oriental, or hotel shuttle boat from Tha Sathon (Central Pier)) For the true Bangkok experience, a stay at this grand old riverside hotel is a must. The majority of rooms are in the modern and recently refurbished New Wing, but we prefer the old-world ambience of the Garden and Authors' Wings. The hotel is also home to one of the region's most acclaimed spas, a legendary fine dining restaurant and a cooking school.

Shangri-La Hotel HOTEL $$$
(☎0 2236 7777; www.shangri-la.com; 89 Soi 42/1 (Soi Wat Suan Phlu); r incl breakfast 7600-11,300B, ste incl breakfast 12,800-120,000B; ; S Saphan Taksin exit 1) A recent facelift has the longstanding Shangri-La looking better than ever. And a convenient location near the BTS, generous rates, a resortlike riverside atmosphere and ample activities and amenities make it a smart choice for families.

Eating

Nowhere else is the Thai reverence for food more evident than in Bangkok. The city's characteristic scent is a unique blend of noodle stall and car exhaust, and in certain parts of town, restaurants appear to form the majority of businesses, typically flanked by street-side hawker stalls and mobile snack vendors. Because of this obsession with eating, and because much of the food served at Thailand's beaches and islands is modified for foreigners, Bangkok is the ideal place to dig into the real deal. For more information on Thai food, see p386.

Ko Ratanakosin, Banglamphu & Thonburi

Likhit Kai Yang NORTHEASTERN THAI $
(Map p58; off Th Ratchadamnoen Nok; mains 30-150B; 10am-10pm; ; klorng boat to Tha Phan Fah) Located just behind Ratchadamoen Stadium (avoid the rather grotty branch directly next door to the stadium), this decades-old restaurant is where locals come for a quick northeastern Thai–style meal before a Thai boxing match. The friendly English-speaking owner will coach you through the ordering process, but don't miss the herbal grilled chicken.

★**Krua Apsorn** THAI $$
(Map p58; www.kruaapsorn.com; Th Din So; mains 65-350B; 10.30am-8pm Mon-Sat; ; klorng boat to Tha Phan Fah) This homey dining room has served members of the Thai royal family

VEGGING OUT IN BANGKOK

Vegetarianism is a growing trend among urban Thais, but meat-free restaurants are still generally few and far between.

Banglamphu has the greatest concentration of vegetarian-friendly restaurants, thanks to the preponderance of nonmeat-eating *fa·ràng* (foreigners). In this part of town, there's longstanding **Arawy Vegetarian Food** (Map p58; 152 Th Din So; mains 20-40B; 7am-8.30pm; ; Tha Phan Fah) and **May Kaidee's** (Map p58; www.maykaidee.com; 33 Th Samsen; mains 50-100B; 9am-10pm; ; Tha Phra Athit (Banglamphu)), the latter with a vegetarian cookery school. Restaurants such as Shoshana (p79) and **Hemlock** (Map p58; 56 Th Phra Athit; mains 60-220B; 4pm-midnight Mon-Sat; ; Tha Phra Athit (Banglamphu)) have lots of meat-free options.

Elsewhere in Bangkok, **Anotai** (976/17 Soi Rama 9 Hospital, Th Phra Ram IX; mains 150-300B; 10am-9pm Thu-Tue; ; M Phra Ram 9 exit 3 & taxi), **Baan Suan Pai** (Banana Family Park, Th Phahonyothin; mains 15-30B; 7am-3pm; ; S Ari exit 1), **Bonita Cafe & Social Club** (Map p66; 56/3 Th Pan; mains 160-250B; 11am-10pm Wed-Mon; ; S Surasak exit 3), **Chennai Kitchen** (Map p66; 10 Th Pan; mains 70-150B; 10am-3pm & 6-9pm; ; S Surasak exit 3) and Saras (p81) are all vegetarian-specific restaurants. As well, **Koko** (Map p64; 262/2 Soi 3, Siam Sq; mains 70-220B; 11am-9pm; ; S Siam exit 2), Opposite Mess Hall (p81) and stall C8 at the **MBK Food Island** (Map p64; 6th fl, MBK Center, cnr Th Phra Ram I & Th Phayathai; mains 35-150B; 10am-10pm; ; S National Stadium exit 4) all offer a generous selection of meat-free menu items.

During the Vegetarian Festival (p72) in October, the whole city goes mad for tofu. Stalls and restaurants indicate their nonmeat menu with yellow banners; Chinatown has the highest concentration of stalls.

and, back in 2006, was recognised as Bangkok's Best Restaurant by the *Bangkok Post*. Must-eat dishes include mussels fried with fresh herbs, the decadent crab fried in yellow chilli oil and the *tortilla Española*-like crab omelette.

Shoshana ISRAELI **$$**
(Map p58; 88 Th Chakraphong; mains 70-240B; 10am-midnight; ; Tha Phra Athit (Banglamphu)) Although prices have gone up slightly since it opened back in 1982, Shoshana still puts together a cheap and tasty Israeli meal. Feel safe ordering anything deep-fried – they do an excellent job of it – and don't miss the deliciously garlicky eggplant dip.

Mangkud Cafe THAI **$$**
(Club Arts; Map p58; www.clubartsgallery.com; Soi Wat Rakhang; mains 100-350B; 11am-10pm Tue-Thu, to 11pm Fri-Sun; ; cross-river ferry from Tha Chang) Mangkud is probably the most sophisticated place to eat on the Thonburi side of Mae Nam Chao Phraya. The river views and breezes are unparalleled, and the upscale-ish herb-heavy Thai dishes are clever and tasty; try the 'watermelon with dried fish', a traditional sweet-savoury snack. Look for the sign that says Club Arts.

★ **Jay Fai** THAI **$$$**
(Map p58; 327 Th Mahachai; mains from 400B; 3pm-2am Tue-Sun; klorng boat to Tha Phan Fah) You wouldn't think so by looking at her bare-bones dining room, but Jay Fai is known far and wide for serving Bangkok's most expensive – and arguably most delicious – *pàt kêe mow* (drunkard's noodles). The price is justified by the copious fresh seafood, as well as Jay Fai's special frying style that results in a virtually oil-free finished product.

Chinatown & Phahurat

Samsara JAPANESE, THAI **$$**
(1612 Th Songwat; mains 110-320B; 4pm-midnight Tue-Thu, to 1am Fri-Sun; ; Tha Ratchawong, M Hua Lamphong exit 1 & taxi) Combining Thai-Japanese dishes, Belgian beers and a retro/artsy atmosphere, Samsara is easily Chinatown's most eclectic place to eat. It's also very tasty, and the generous riverside breezes and views round out the package. The restaurant is at the end of tiny Soi Khang Wat Pathum Khongkha, just west of the temple of the same name.

> **DAY OFF**
>
> Fans of street food be forewarned that all of Bangkok's stalls close on Monday for compulsory street cleaning (the results of which are never entirely evident come Tuesday morning). If you happen to be in the city on this day, take advantage of the lull to visit one of the city's upscale hotel restaurants, which virtually never close.

Thanon Phadungdao Seafood Stalls THAI **$$**
(cnr Th Phadungdao & Th Yaowarat; mains 100-600B; 4pm-midnight Tue-Sun; Tha Ratchawong, M Hua Lamphong exit 1 & taxi) After sunset, two opposing open-air restaurants – each of which claims to be the original – become a culinary train wreck of outdoor barbecues, screaming staff, iced seafood trays and messy sidewalk seating. True, the vast majority of diners are foreign tourists, but this has little impact on the cheerful setting, the fun experience and the cheap bill.

Royal India INDIAN **$$**
(Map p58; 392/1 Th Chakraphet; mains 70-195B; 10am-10pm; ; Tha Saphan Phut (Memorial Bridge)) Yes, we're aware that this hole in the wall has been in every edition of our guide since the beginning, but after all these years it's still the most reliable place to eat in Bangkok's Little India. Try any of the delicious breads or rich curries, and don't forget to finish with a homemade Punjabi sweet.

Siam Square

Kai Thort Jay Kee THAI **$$**
(Soi Polo Fried Chicken; 137/1-3 Soi Sanam Khlii (Soi Polo); mains 40-280B; 11am-9pm; ; M Lumphini exit 3) Although the *sôm·đam* (spicy green papaya salad), sticky rice and *lâhp* (a minced meat 'salad') give the impression of a northeastern Thai–style eatery, the restaurant's namesake deep-fried chicken is more southern in origin. Regardless, smothered in a thick layer of crispy deep-fried garlic, it is none other than a truly Bangkok experience.

Silom & Sathon

FooDie THAI **$$**
(Map p66; Soi Phiphat 2; mains 80-150B; 11am-11pm; ; S Chong Nonsi exit 2) The recently renovated FooDie has an interesting menu

of hard-to-find central- and southern-style Thai dishes. Highlights include the *yam sôm oh* (a spicy/sour/sweet salad of pomelo) and the spicy *prík kĭng Ɓlah dùk foo* (catfish fried in a curry paste until crispy).

★ nahm
THAI $$$

(☎0 2625 3388; www.comohotels.com/metropolitanbangkok/dining/nahm; ground fl, Metropolitan Hotel, 27 Th Sathon Tai (South); set lunch 1100B, set dinner 2000B, mains 180-700B; ⊙noon-2pm Mon-Fri, 7-10.30pm daily; ❄; Ⓜ Lumphini exit 2) Australian chef/author David Thompson is behind what is quite possibly the best Thai restaurant in Bangkok. Using ancient cookbooks as his inspiration, Thompson has given new life to previously extinct and exotic-sounding dishes such as 'smoked fish curry with prawns, chicken livers, cockles and black pepper'. Dinner takes the form of a multicourse set meal, while lunch emphasises *kà·nŏm jeen* (thin rice noodles served with curries).

If you're expecting bland, gentrified Thai food meant for non-Thais, prepare to be disappointed. Reservations recommended.

★ Eat Me
INTERNATIONAL $$$

(Map p66; ☎0 2238 0931; www.eatmerestaurant.com; Soi Phiphat 2; mains 340-1350B; ⊙3pm-1am; ❄🍷; Ⓜ Si Lom exit 2, Ⓢ Sala Daeng exit 2) The dishes at this longstanding restaurant, with descriptions like 'fig & blue cheese ravioli w/ walnuts, rosemary and brown butter', or 'beef cheek tagine w/ saffron and dates', may sound all over the map or perhaps somewhat pretentious, but they're actually just plain tasty. A buzzy, casual-yet-sophisticated atmosphere, good cocktails and a handsome wine list, as well as some of Bangkok's best desserts are additional reasons why this is one of our favourite places to dine.

Somboon Seafood
THAI $$$

(Map p66; ☎0 2233 3104; www.somboonseafood.com; cnr Th Surawong & Th Narathiwat Ratchanakharin (Chong Nonsi); mains 120-900B; ⊙4-11.30pm; ❄; Ⓢ Chong Nonsi exit 3) Holy seafood factory: ascending the many staircases to a free table might make you nervous about the quality of so much quantity. But Somboon's legendary 'fried curry crab' will leave you messy and full. Dainty eaters can opt for the slightly more surgical pursuit of devouring a whole fried fish.

Sukhumvit

Imoya
JAPANESE $

(Map p68; 3rd fl, Terminal Shop Cabin, 2/17-19 Soi 24, Th Sukhumvit; mains 40-400B; ⊙6pm-midnight; ❄; Ⓢ Phrom Phong exit 4) A visit to this well-hidden Japanese restaurant, with its antique ads, wood panelling, wall of sake bottles and stuck-in-time prices, is like taking a trip in a time machine.

DON'T MISS

BANGKOK'S BEST FOOD COURTS

Every Bangkok mall worth its escalators has some sort of food court. They are a great way to dip your toe in the sea of Thai food as they're generally cheap, clean, air-conditioned and have English-language menus. At most, paying is done by exchanging cash for vouchers or a temporary credit card at one of several counters; your change is refunded at the same desk.

➡ **MBK Food Island** (p78) The granddaddy of the genre offers tens of vendors selling dishes from virtually every corner of Thailand and beyond.

➡ **Gourmet Paradise** (Map p64; ground fl, Siam Paragon, 991/1 Th Phra Ram I; mains 35-500B; ⊙10am-10pm; ❄; Ⓢ Siam exits 3 & 5) The perpetually busy Gourmet Paradise unites international fast-food chains, domestic restaurants and food court–style stalls, with a particular emphasis on the sweet stuff.

➡ **Food Republic** (Map p64; 4th fl, Siam Center, cnr Th Phra Ram I & Th Phayathai; mains 30-200B; ⊙10am-10pm; ❄🍷; Ⓢ Siam exit 1) The city's newest food court has a good mix of Thai and international (mostly Asian) outlets, all in an open, contemporary-feeling locale.

➡ **Pier 21** (Map p68; 5th fl, Terminal 21, cnr Th Sukhumvit & Soi 21 (Asoke); mains 39-200B; ⊙10am-10pm; ❄🍷; Ⓜ Sukhumvit exit 3, Ⓢ Asok exit 3) Ascend a seemingly endless number of escalators to arrive at this expansive food court cobbled together from famous vendors across the city. The selection is vast and the dishes exceedingly cheap, even by Thai standards.

Saras INDIAN $

(Map p68; www.saras.co.th; Soi 20, Th Sukhumvit; mains 90-200B; 8.30am-10.30pm; ; M Sukhumvit exit 2, S Asok exit 4) Describing your restaurant as a 'fast-food feast' may not be the cleverest PR move we've ever encountered, but it's a spot-on description of this Indian restaurant. Order at the counter to be rewarded with crispy *dosai*, meat-free regional set meals or rich curries (dishes are brought to your table).

Nasir Al-Masri MIDDLE EASTERN $$

(Map p68; 4/6 Soi 3/1, Th Sukhumvit; mains 160-370B; 24hr; ; S Nana exit 1) One of several Middle Eastern restaurants on Soi 3/1, Nasir Al-Masri is easily recognisable by its floor-to-ceiling stainless steel 'theme'. Middle Eastern food generally means meat, meat and more meat, but there are also several delicious vegie-based *mezze*.

Soul Food Mahanakorn THAI $$

(Map p68; 0 2714 7708; www.soulfoodmahanakorn.com; 56/10 Soi 55 (Thong Lor), Th Sukhumvit; mains 220-300B; 5.30pm-midnight; ; S Thong Lo exit 3) Soul Food gets its buzz from its dual nature as both an inviting restaurant – the menu spans tasty interpretations of rustic Thai dishes – and a bar serving deliciously boozy, Thai-influenced cocktails. Reservations recommended.

Bo.lan THAI $$$

(Map p68; 0 2260 2962; www.bolan.co.th; 42 Soi Rongnarong Phichai Songkhram, Soi 26, Th Sukhumvit; set dinner 1980B; 6pm-midnight Tue-Sun; ; S Phrom Phong exit 4) Upscale Thai is often more garnish than flavour, but Bo.lan, started up by two former chefs of London's Michelin-starred nahm, is the exception. Bo and Dylan (Bo.lan, a play on words that also means 'ancient') take a scholarly approach to Thai cuisine, and generous set meals featuring full flavoured Thai dishes are the results of this tuition. Reservations recommended.

Sukhumvit Plaza KOREAN $$$

(Korean Town; Map p68; Soi 12, Th Sukhumvit; mains 200-1000B; 11am-10pm; ; M Sukhumvit exit 3, S Asok exit 2) Known around Bangkok as 'Korean Town', this multistorey complex is the city's best destination for authentic 'Seoul' food. Expat Koreans swear by **Myeong Ga** (Map p68; mains 200-950B; 11am-10pm Tue-Sun, 4-10pm Mon) on the ground floor, although there are slightly cheaper places in the complex as well.

Opposite Mess Hall INTERNATIONAL $$$

(Map p68; www.oppositebangkok.com; 2nd fl, 27/2 Soi 51, Th Sukhumvit; mains 220-650B; 6-11pm Tue-Sun; ; S Thong Lo exit 1) Much like the dishes served there (eg 'savoury duck waffle, leg confit, pate, crispy skin & picalily relish'), Opposite can be a bit hard to categorise. But, really, how can you go wrong with a cosy space, food using great local ingredients, and excellent cocktails? There's a menu, but the best strategy is to see what the ever-changing blackboard has to offer.

Drinking & Nightlife

Bangkok's bar scene is notably legendary and, well, justifiably infamous. But if you ask us, it gets insufficient credit for its diversity. A drink in Bangkok can mean sweaty bottles of Singha at a roadside table or a cocktail crafted by a Swedish mixologist in a themed den, or just about anything in between. Formerly, Thais and foreigners watered at different holes, but in recent years these paths have begun to cross, resulting in yet another element of variety. The official closing time for most bars is 1am.

Bangkok's nightclub scene is similarly diverse, yet fickle as a ripe mango, and that really fun disco you found on your last trip three years ago is most likely history today. To find out what is going on when you're in town, check listings rag *BK* or the *Bangkok Post's* Friday supplement, *Guru*. Don't even think about showing up before 11pm, and always bring ID. Most clubs close at 2am.

Ko Ratanakosin, Banglamphu & Thonburi

Madame Musur BAR

(Map p58; 41 Soi Ram Buttri; 8am-1am; Tha Phra Athit (Banglamphu)) Saving you the trip north to Pai, Madame Musur combines the vibes of northern Thailand and Th Khao San all in one convenient locale. Serving a short menu of northern Thai dishes (including what some consider to be one of the city's better bowls of *kôw soy* – a northern-style curry noodle soup), it's also not a bad place to eat.

Hippie de Bar BAR

(Map p58; www.facebook.com/hippie.debar; 46 Th Khao San; 6pm-2am; Tha Phra Athit (Banglamphu)) Popular with the domestic crowd, Hippie boasts a Thai retro theme and several levels of fun, both indoor and outdoor.

DON'T MISS

UP ON THE ROOF

In previous years, Bangkok's rooftop bars were largely the realm of well-heeled tourists, but now they comprise a diverse spread, with options ranging from scruffy to formal. Our faves:

➜ ★ **Moon Bar** (www.banyantree.com; 61st fl, Banyan Tree Hotel, 21/100 Th Sathon (South) Tai; ⏲5pm-1am; Ⓜ Lumphini exit 2) Precariously perched on top of 61 floors of skyscraper, Moon Bar offers a heart-stopping bird's-eye view of central Bangkok. Things can get a bit crowded here come sunset, so be sure to show up a bit early to snag the best seats. Note that Moon Bar does not allow entry to those wearing shorts or sandals.

➜ **River Vibe** (8th fl, River View Guest House, 768 Soi Phanurangsi, Th Songwat; ⏲7.30-11pm; ⛴ Tha Marine Department, Ⓜ Hua Lamphong exit 1 & taxi) Can't afford the drinks and/or have objections to the dress code at Bangkok's other rooftop bars? Slap on some shorts and head to the top floor of this guesthouse; the casual vibe and stunning river views will hardly feel like a compromise.

➜ **Phra Nakorn Bar & Gallery** (Map p58; 58/2 Soi Damnoen Klang Tai; ⏲5pm-1am; ⛴ klorng boat to Tha Phan Fah) In addition to charming views of old Bangkok, the breezy rooftop of this artsy bar also offers cheap and tasty Thai food.

➜ **Sky Bar** (www.lebua.com/sky-bar; 63rd fl, State Tower, 1055 Th Silom; ⏲6pm-1am; Ⓢ Saphan Taksin exit 3) Descend the sweeping stairs like a Hollywood diva to the precipice bar of this rooftop restaurant – allegedly the world's highest open-air bar. But leave your shorts and sandals at home.

There's also food, pool tables and a more sophisticated soundtrack than most.

Club NIGHTCLUB

(Map p58; www.theclubkhaosan.com; 123 Th Khao San; ⏲10pm-3am; ⛴ Tha Phra Athit (Banglamphu)) This cavernlike dance hall hosts a fun mix of locals and backpackers.

Taksura BAR

(Map p58; 156/1 Th Tanao; ⏲5pm-1am; ⛴ Tha Phan Fah) There's little to indicate the location of this seemingly abandoned century-old mansion in the heart of old Bangkok, which is all the better, according to the cool uni-artsy crowd who frequent the place.

Silom & Sathon

Tapas Room NIGHTCLUB

(Map p66; 114/17-18 Soi 4, Th Silom; admission 100B; ⏲9pm-2am; Ⓜ Si Lom exit 2, Ⓢ Sala Daeng exit 1) You won't find gazpacho here, but the name is an accurate indicator of the Spanish/Moroccan-inspired vibe of this multilevel den. Come from Wednesday to Saturday when the combination of DJs and live percussion brings the body count to critical level.

Maggie Choo's BAR

(www.facebook.com/maggiechoos; basement, Novotel Bangkok Fenix Silom, 320 Th Silom; ⏲6.30pm-1.30am; Ⓢ Surasak exit 1) A former bank vault with a Chinatown opium den vibe; secret passageways; women lounging in silk dresses; with all this going on, it's easy to forget that Maggie Choo's is actually a bar. But creative yet expensive house cocktails, and a crowd that blends selfie-snapping locals and curious tourists, are reminders of this.

Sukhumvit

★ **WTF** BAR

(Map p68; www.wtfbangkok.com; 7 Soi 51, Th Sukhumvit; ⏲6pm-1am Tue-Sun; Ⓢ Thong Lo exit 3) No, not that WTF; Wonderful Thai Friendship combines a bar and an art gallery in one attractive package. Throw in some of Bangkok's best cocktails, delicious Spanish-influenced bar snacks and a friendly, artsy clientele and as far as we're concerned, you've got Bangkok's best bar.

Badmotel BAR

(Map p68; www.facebook.com/badmotel; Soi 55 (Thong Lor), Th Sukhumvit; ⏲5pm-1.30am; Ⓢ Thong Lo exit 3 & taxi) The new Badmotel blends the modern and the kitschy, the cosmopolitan and the Thai, in a way that has struck a (admittedly detached) nerve among Bangkok hipsters. This is manifest in drinks that combine Hale's Blue Boy, a Thai childhood drink staple, with rum, and bar snacks such as 'naam prik ong' a northern-style dip, here served with pappadam.

Tuba BAR

(34 Room 11-12 A, Soi Ekamai 21, Soi 63 (Ekamai), Th Sukhumvit; ⏲11am-2am; S Ekkamai exit 1 & taxi) Part showroom for over-the-top vintage furniture, part restaurant, part friendly local boozer, this bar certainly doesn't lack in quirk, nor fun. Indulge in a whole bottle (they'll hold onto it if you don't finish it) and don't miss the delicious chicken wings.

Grease NIGHTCLUB

(Map p68; www.greasebangkok.com; 46/12 Soi 49, Th Sukhumvit; ⏲6pm-4am Mon-Sat; S Phrom Phong exit 3 & taxi) Bangkok's newest, hottest club is also one of its biggest – you could get lost in the four floors of dining venues, lounges and dance floors here.

Cheap Charlie's BAR

(Map p68; Soi 11, Th Sukhumvit; ⏲4.30-11.45pm Mon-Sat; S Nana exit 3) There's never enough seating, and the design concept is best classified as 'junkyard', but on most nights this chummy open-air beer corner is a great place to meet everybody from package tourists to resident English teachers.

Arena 10 NIGHTCLUB

(Map p68; cnr Soi Ekamai 5 & Soi 63 (Ekamai), Th Sukhumvit; S Ekkamai exit 2 & taxi) This entertainment zone is the destination of choice for Bangkok's young and beautiful – for the moment at least. **Demo** (Map p68; www.facebook.com/demobangkok; admission free; ⏲6pm-2am; S Ekkamai exit 2 & taxi) combines blasting beats and a NYC warehouse vibe, while **Funky Villa** (Map p68; www.facebook.com/funkyvillabkk; ⏲7pm-2am; S Ekkamai exit 2 & taxi), with its outdoor seating and Top 40 soundtrack, is more chilled. Fridays and Saturdays see a 400B entrance fee for foreigners.

Nung-Len NIGHTCLUB

(Map p68; www.nunglen.net; 217 Soi 63 (Ekamai), Th Sukhumvit; ⏲6pm-1am Mon-Sat; S Ekkamai exit 1 & taxi) Young, loud and Thai, Nung-Len (literally 'sit and chill') is a ridiculously popular den of dance tunes, live music and uni students on popular Th Ekamai. Make sure you get in before 10pm or you won't get in at all.

Other Areas

RCA NIGHTCLUB

(Royal City Avenue; Royal City Ave, off Th Phra Ram IX; M Phra Ram 9 exit 3 & taxi) Formerly a bastion of the teen scene, this Vegas-like strip has finally graduated from high school to become Bangkok's premier clubbing zone, although it must be said that its Top 40 roots still show. **Slim/Fix** (www.facebook.com/slimbkk; Royal City Ave, off Th Phra Ram IX; ⏲8pm-2am; M Phra Ram 9 exit 3 & taxi) and **Route 66** (www.route66club.com; 29/33-48 Royal City Ave (RCA),

GAY & LESBIAN BANGKOK

Bangkok is so gay it makes San Francisco look like rural Texas. The website Utopia (p412) is an evergreen crash course in Bangkok's gay scene, while local listings mags such as BK (p88) can point you in the direction of the bars and clubs that are hot when you're in town. The **Lesbian Guide to Bangkok** (www.bangkoklesbian.com) is the only English-language tracker of the lesbian scene.

Lower Th Silom is Bangkok's unofficial gaybourhood, and highlights include tiny Soi 2, which is lined with dance clubs such as **DJ Station** (Map p66; www.dj-station.com; 8/6-8 Soi 2, Th Silom; admission from 100B; ⏲10.30pm-3am; M Si Lom exit 2, S Sala Daeng exit 1), the busiest and arguably most famous gay nightclub in Thailand. Virtually next door is Soi 2/1 where bars like **G.O.D** (Guys on Display; Map p66; Soi 2/1; admission 280B; ⏲8pm-late; M Si Lom exit 2, S Sala Daeng exit 1) are not averse to a little shirtless dancing. A more casual scene is found on Soi 4, home to longstanding streetside bars **Balcony** (Map p66; www.balconypub.com; 86-88 Soi 4, Th Silom; ⏲5.30pm-1am; 📶; M Si Lom exit 2, S Sala Daeng exit 1) and **Telephone** (Map p66; www.telephonepub.com; 114/11-13 Soi 4, Th Silom; ⏲6pm-1am; 📶; M Si Lom exit 2, S Sala Daeng exit 1).

Further out of town are a couple of smaller gay scenes, including the strip of mostly Thai-frequented bars along Th Kamphaengphet such as **Fake Club** (www.facebook.com/fakeclub.bangkok; Th Kamphaengphet; ⏲8pm-2am; M Kamphaeng Phet exit 1); the slightly seedier knot of bars along Soi 8, Th Ratchada, including the infamous **G-Star** (Soi 8, Th Ratchadaphisek; ⏲8pm-1am; S Phra Ram 9 exit 3); and at RCA, the new, sleek **Castro** (www.facebook.com/Castro.rca.bangkok; Block C, RCA, off Th Phra Ram IX; ⏲9.30pm-4.30am; M Phra Ram 9 exit 3 & taxi).

off Th Phra Ram IX; ⌚8pm-2am; Ⓜ Phra Ram 9 exit 3 & taxi) are the big hitters here, and foreigners must pay a 300B entry fee on Fridays and Saturdays.

Viva & Aviv BAR
(www.vivaaviv.com; ground fl, River City, 23 Th Yotha; ⌚11am-midnight; river ferry Tha Si Phraya/River City or shopping centre shuttle boat from Tha Sathon (Central Pier)) An enviable riverside location, casual open-air seating and a funky atmosphere make this restaurant-ish bar a contender for Bangkok's best sunset cocktail destination. Expect a pun-heavy menu (sample item: 'I focaccia name') of pizzas, meaty snacks and salads that really is no joke.

☆ Entertainment

Shame on you if you find yourself bored in Bangkok. And even more shame if you think the only entertainment options involve the word 'go-go'. Nowadays Bangkok's nightlife is as diverse as that of virtually any modern city.

Gà·teu·i Cabaret

Over the last few years, *gà·teu·i* (transgendered people; also spelt *kathoey*) cabaret has emerged to become a staple of the Bangkok tourist circuit. **Calypso Bangkok** (☎0 2688 1415; www.calypsocabaret.com; Asiatique, Soi 72-76, Th Charoen Krung; admission 1200B; ⌚show times 8.15pm & 9.45pm; shuttle ferry from Tha Sathon (Central Pier)), **Mambo Cabaret** (☎0 2294 7381; www.mambocabaret.com; 59/28 Yannawa Tat Mai; tickets 800-1000B; ⌚show times 7.15pm & 8.30pm; Ⓢ Chong Nonsi exit 2 taxi) and **Playhouse Theater Cabaret** (Map p64; ☎0 2215 0571; www.playhousethailand.com; basement, Asia Hotel, 296 Th Phayathai; admission 1200B; ⌚show times 8.15pm & 9.45pm; Ⓢ Ratchathewi exit 1) host choreographed stage shows featuring Broadway high kicks and lip-synched pop tunes by the most well-endowed dudes you'll find anywhere.

Go-Go Bars

Although technically illegal, prostitution is fully 'out' in Bangkok, and the influence of organised crime and healthy kickbacks mean that it will be a long while before the existing laws are ever enforced. Yet, despite the image presented by much of the Western media, the underlying atmosphere of Bangkok's red-light districts is not necessarily one of illicitness and exploitation (although these do inevitably exist), but rather an aura of tackiness and boredom.

Patpong (Map p66; Soi Patpong 1 & 2, Th Silom; ⌚4pm-2am; Ⓜ Si Lom exit 2, Ⓢ Sala Daeng exit 1), arguably one of the world's most famous red-light districts, earned its notoriety during the 1980s for its wild sex shows involving everything from ping-pong balls to razors to midgets on motorbikes. Today it is more of a circus for curious spectators than sexual deviants. These days, **Soi Cowboy** (Map p68; btwn Soi 21 (Asoke) & Soi 23, Th Sukhumvit; ⌚4pm-2am; Ⓜ Sukhumvit exit 2, Ⓢ Asok exit 3) and **Nana Entertainment Plaza** (Map p68; Soi 4 (Nana Tai), Th Sukhumvit; ⌚4pm-2am; Ⓢ Nana exit 2) are the real scenes of sex for hire.

Live Music

Music is an essential element of a Thai night out, and just about every pub has a house band. For the most part this means perky Thai pop covers or tired international standards (if you've left town without having heard a live version of *Hotel California*, you haven't really been to Bangkok), but an increasing number of places are starting to deviate from the norm with quirky bands and performances.

★ **Brick Bar** LIVE MUSIC
(Map p58; www.brickbarkhaosan.com; basement, Buddy Lodge, 265 Th Khao San; admission 100B; ⌚8pm-2am; Tha Phra Athit (Banglamphu)) This cavelike pub hosts a nightly revolving cast of live music for an almost exclusively Thai crowd. Come at midnight, wedge yourself into a table a few inches from the horn section, and lose it to Teddy Ska, one of the most energetic live acts in town.

Cosmic Café LIVE MUSIC
(www.facebook.com/cosmiccafe.bkk; Block C, Royal City Ave (RCA), off Th Phra Ram IX; ⌚8pm-2am Mon-Sat; Ⓜ Phra Ram 9 exit 3 & taxi) Blessedly more low-key than most places on RCA, Cosmic calls itself a cafe but looks like a bar, and in recent years has become one of Bangkok's better destinations for live music. Despite the identity crisis, it's a fun place to drink, rock to live music and meet Thai-style.

Titanium LIVE MUSIC
(Map p68; www.titaniumbangkok.com; 2/30 Soi 22, Th Sukhumvit; ⌚8pm-1am; Ⓢ Phrom Phong exit 6) Some come to this slightly cheesy 'ice bar' for the chill and the flavoured vodka, but we come for Unicorn, the all-female house band.

Living Room LIVE MUSIC
(Map p68; ☎0 2649 8888; www.sheratongrandesukhumvit.com/en/thelivingroom; Level 1, Sheraton Grande Sukhumvit, 250 Th Sukhumvit; ⏱6pm-midnight; Ⓜ Sukhumvit exit 3, Ⓢ Asok exit 2) Don't let looks deceive you; every night at 8pm this seemingly bland hotel lounge transforms into the city's best venue for live jazz. Contact ahead of time to see which sax master or hide hitter is currently in town.

Raintree LIVE MUSIC
(116/63-64 Th Rang Nam; ⏱8pm-2am; Ⓢ Victory Monument exit 2) This rustic pub is one of the few remaining places in town to hear 'songs for life', Thai folk music with roots in the communist insurgency of the 1960s and 1970s.

Thai Boxing (Moo·ay tai)

Thai boxing's best of the best fight it out at Bangkok's two boxing stadiums: **Lumpinee Boxing Stadium** (www.muaythailumpinee.net/en/index.php; Th Ramintra; tickets 3rd class/2nd class/ringside 1000/2000/3000B; Ⓜ Chatuchak Park exit 2 & taxi, Ⓢ Mo Chit exit 3 & taxi) and **Ratchadamnoen Stadium** (Map p58; off Th Ratchadamnoen Nok; tickets 3rd class/2nd class/ringside 1000/1500/2000B; ⛴ klorng boat to Tha Phan Fah, Ⓢ Phaya Thai exit 3 & taxi). You'll note that tickets are not cheap, and these prices are exponentially more than what Thais pay. To add insult to injury, the inflated price offers no special service or seating, and at Ratchadamnoen Stadium foreigners are sometimes corralled into an area with an obstructed view. As long as you are mentally prepared for the financial jabs from the promoters, you'll be better prepared to enjoy the real fight.

Fights are held throughout the week, alternating between the two stadiums. Ratchadamnoen hosts the matches on Monday, Wednesday, Thursday and Sunday at 6pm, while Lumpinee hosts matches on Tuesday and Friday at 6.30pm and Saturday at 4pm and 8.30pm. There is a total of eight to 10 fights of five rounds apiece. The stadiums don't usually fill up until the main events, which normally start around 8pm or 9pm.

Traditional Arts

Sala Chalermkrung THEATRE
(Map p58; ☎0 2222 0434; www.salachalermkrung.com; 66 Th Charoen Krung; tickets 800-1200B; ⏱shows 7.30pm Thu & Fri; ⛴ Tha Saphan Phut (Memorial Bridge), Ⓜ Hua Lamphong exit 1 & taxi) In a Thai art deco building at the edge of the Chinatown-Phahurat district, this theatre provides a striking venue for *kŏhn* (masked dance-drama based on stories from the *Ramakian,* the Thai version of the *Ramayana*). Performances are held every Thursday and Friday and last about two hours plus intermission. The theatre requests that patrons dress respectfully, which means no shorts, tank tops or sandals.

National Theatre THEATRE
(Map p58; ☎0 2224 1342; 2 Th Ratchini; tickets 60-100B; ⛴ Tha Chang) Performances of *kŏhn* are held here at 2pm on the first and second Sundays of the month from January to March and July to September, and *lá·kon,* Thai dance-dramas, are held at 2pm on the first and second Sundays of the month from April to June and October to December.

Shopping

Welcome to a true buyer's market. Home to one of the world's largest outdoor markets, numerous giant upscale malls, and sidewalk-clogging bazaars on nearly every street, it's impossible not to be awed by the sheer amount of commerce in Bangkok. However, despite the apparent scope and variety, Bangkok really excels in one area when it comes to shopping: cheap stuff. Although luxury items and brand names are indeed available in Bangkok, prices are high, and you'll find much better deals at online warehouses in the US or bargain-basement sales in Hong Kong. Ceramics, dirt-cheap T-shirts, fabric, Asian knick-knackery and, yes, if you can deal with the guilt, pirated items, are Bangkok's bargains.

Shopping Centres

Bangkok may be crowded and polluted, but its department stores are modern oases of order. They're also downright frigid, and Sunday afternoons see a significant part of Bangkok's population crowding into the city's indoor malls to escape the heat.

★**MBK Center** SHOPPING CENTRE
(Map p64; www.mbk-center.com; cnr Th Phra Ram I & Th Phayathai; ⏱10am-10pm; Ⓢ National Stadium exit 4) This colossal mall has become a tourist destination in its own right. Swedish and other languages can be heard as much as Thai, and on any given weekend half of Bangkok can be found here combing through an inexhaustible range of small stalls and shops.

MBK is the cheapest place to buy mobile phones and accessories (4th floor) and

ONE NIGHT IN BANGKOK... IS NOT ENOUGH TO HAVE A SUIT MADE

Many tourists arrive in Bangkok with the notion of getting clothes custom-tailored at a bargain price, which is entirely possible. Prices are almost always lower than what you'd pay at home, but common scams ranging from commission-hungry túk-túk (pronounced *đúk đúk)* drivers to shoddy workmanship and inferior fabrics make bespoke tailoring in Bangkok a potentially disappointing investment. To maximise your chances of walking away feeling (and looking) good, read on...

➡ **You get what you pay for** If you sign up for a suit, two pants, two shirts and a tie, with a silk sarong thrown in for US$169 (a very popular offer in Bangkok), the chances are it will look and fit like a sub-US$200 wardrobe.

➡ **Have a good idea of what you want** If it's a suit you're after, should it be single- or double-breasted? How many buttons? What style trousers? Of course, if you have no idea then the tailor will be more than happy to advise.

➡ **Set aside a week to get clothes tailored** Shirts and trousers can often be turned around in 48 hours or less with only one fitting, but no matter what a tailor may tell you, it takes more than one and often more than two fittings to create a good suit. Any tailor who can sew your order in less than 24 hours should be treated with caution.

Reputable tailors include:

➡ **Pinky Tailors** (Map p64; www.pinkytailor.com; 888/40 Mahatun Plaza, Th Ploenchit; ⏲10am-7pm Mon-Sat; Ⓢ Phloen Chit exits 2 & 4) Custom-made shirts and suit jackets have been Mr Pinky's speciality for more than three decades. Located behind the Mahatun Building.

➡ **July** (Map p66; ☎0 2233 0171; www.julytailor.com; 30/6 Th Sala Daeng; ⏲9am-7pm; Ⓜ Si Lom exit 2, Ⓢ Sala Daeng exit 4) Tailor to Thailand's royalty and elite alike, the suits here don't come cheap and the cuts can be somewhat conservative, but the quality is unsurpassed.

➡ **Raja's Fashions** (Map p68; ☎0 2253 8379; www.rajasfashions.com; 160/1 Th Sukhumvit; ⏲10am-8pm Mon-Sat; Ⓢ Nana exit 4) One of Bangkok's more famous tailors, Raja's gets a mixed bag of reviews, but the majority swear by the service and quality.

➡ **Nickermann's** (Map p68; ☎0 2252 6682; www.nickermanns.net; basement, Landmark Hotel, 138 Th Sukhumvit; ⏲10am-8.30pm Mon-Sat, noon-6pm Sun; Ⓢ Nana exit 2) Corporate ladies rave about Nickermann's tailor-made power suits: pants and jackets that suit curves and busts. Formal ball gowns are another area of expertise.

name-brand knock-offs (nearly every other floor). It's also one of the better places in Bangkok to stock up on camera gear (ground floor and 5th floor), and the expansive food court (6th floor) is one of the best in town.

★ **Siam Square** SHOPPING CENTRE
(Map p64; Th Phra Ram I; ⏲11am-9pm; Ⓢ Siam exits 2, 4 & 6) This open-air shopping zone is ground zero for teenage culture in Bangkok. Pop music blares out of tinny speakers, and gangs of hipsters in various costumes ricochet between fast-food restaurant, and closet-sized boutiques. It's a great place to pick up designs you're guaranteed not to find anywhere else, though most outfits require a barely-there waist.

Siam Paragon SHOPPING CENTRE
(Map p64; www.siamparagon.co.th; 991/1 Th Phra Ram I; ⏲10am-10pm; Ⓢ Siam exits 3 & 5) The biggest and glitziest of Bangkok's shopping malls, Siam Paragon is more of an urban park than a shopping centre. Astronomically luxe brands occupy most floors, but there's also **Siam Ocean World** (สยามโอเชี่ยนเวิร์ล; Map p64; www.siamoceanworld.com; basement, Siam Paragon, 991/1 Th Phra Ram I; adult/child 900/700B; ⏲10am-9pm; Ⓢ Siam exits 3 & 5), **Paragon Cineplex** (Map p64; ☎0 2129 4635; www.paragoncineplex.com; 5th fl, Siam Paragon, 991/1 Th Phra Ram I; Ⓢ Siam exits 3 & 5), a huge basement-level food court, and on the 3rd floor **Kinokuniya**, Thailand's largest English-language bookstore.

Siam Center & Siam Discovery Center SHOPPING CENTRE
(Map p64; cnr Th Phra Ram I & Th Phayathai, Siam Sq; ⏲10am-9pm; S Siam exit 1) Siam Discovery Center excels in home decor, with the whole 3rd floor devoted to Asian-minimalist styles and jewel-toned fabrics; we love the earthy, Thai-influenced designs at **Doi Tung**. The attached Siam Center has gone under the redesign knife for a younger, hipper look. Youth fashion is its new focus, and several local labels, ranging from **anr** to **senada***, are on the 2nd floor.

Pantip Plaza SHOPPING CENTRE
(Map p64; 604 Th Phetchaburi; ⏲10am-9pm; S Ratchathewi exit 4) Pantip is five storeys of computer and software stores ranging from legit to flea market. Many locals come here to buy 'pirated' software and computer peripherals, but the crowds and touts ('DVD sex? DVD sex?') make it among the more tedious shopping experiences in town.

Markets

Although air-conditioned malls have better PR departments, open-air markets are the true face of commercial Bangkok, and are where you'll find the best bargains.

★**Chatuchak Weekend Market** MARKET
(ตลาดนัดจตุจักร, Talat Nat Jatujak; www.chatuchak.org; Th Phahonyothin; ⏲9am-6pm Sat & Sun; M Chatuchak Park exit 1, Kamphaeng Phet exits 1 & 2, S Mo Chit exit 1) The mother of all markets sprawls over a huge area with 15,000 stalls and an estimated 200,000 visitors a day. Everything is sold here, from snakes to handicrafts to aisles and aisles of clothes. Plan to spend a full day, as there's plenty to see, do and buy (if you see something you like, buy it, as you probably won't find your way back). But come early, ideally around 9am to 10am, to beat the crowds and the heat.

There is an information centre and a bank with ATMs and foreign-exchange booths at the Chatuchak Park offices, near the northern end of the market's Soi 1, Soi 2 and Soi 3. Schematic maps and toilets are located throughout the market.

There are a few vendors out on weekday mornings, and a daily vegetable, plant and flower market opposite the market's southern side. One section of the latter, known as the **Or Tor Kor Market** (องค์กรตลาดเพื่อเกษตรกร (ตลาด อ.ต.ก.); Th Kamphaengphet; ⏲8am-6pm; M Kamphaeng Phet exit 3), is Bangkok's most upscale fresh market, which sells

OFF THE BEATEN TRACK

MARKETS AS SIGHTS?

Even if you don't have a shopping list, several of Bangkok's markets are well worth a visit. Here are some of our favourites:

➡ **Talat Rot Fai** (ตลาดรถไฟ; www.facebook.com/taradrodfi; Soi 51, Th Srinakharin; ⏲6pm-midnight Wed & Fri-Sun; S Udom Suk exit 2 & taxi) This night market is all about the retro, from antique enamel platters to secondhand Vespas. With mobile snack vendors, VW van–based bars and even a few land-bound pubs, it's also much more than just a shopping destination.

➡ **Pak Khlong Talat** (ปากคลองตลาด, Flower Market; Th Chakraphet; ⏲24hr; ⛴ Tha Saphan Phut (Memorial Bridge)) Every night this market near Mae Nam Chao Phraya becomes the city's largest depot for wholesale flowers. Arrive as late as you're willing to stay up, and be sure to take a camera, as the technicolour blur of roses, lotuses and daisies on the move is a sight worth capturing.

➡ **Sampeng Lane** (สำเพ็ง; Map p58; Soi Wanit 1 (Sampeng Lane); ⏲8am-6pm; ⛴ Tha Ratchawong, M Hua Lamphong exit 1 & taxi) This crowded wholesale market runs roughly parallel to Th Yaowarat, bisecting the two districts of Chinatown and Phahurat. Pick up the narrow artery from Th Ratchawong and follow it through its many manifestations – from handbags, homewares, hair decorations, stickers, Japanese-animation gear and plastic beeping key chains.

➡ **Khlong Toey Market** (ตลาดคลองเตย; Map p68; cnr Th Ratchadaphisek & Th Phra Ram IV; ⏲5-10am; M Khlong Toei exit 1) This wholesale market, one of the city's largest, is the origin of many of the meals you'll eat during your stay in Bangkok. Get there early, and although some corners of the market can't exactly be described as photogenic, bring a camera to capture the stacks of durians and the cheery fishmongers.

fantastically gargantuan fruit and seafood, and has a decent food court as well.

Asiatique MARKET
(www.thaiasiatique.com; Soi 72-76, Th Charoen Krung; 4-11pm; shuttle boat from Tha Sathon (Central Pier)) At press time Bangkok's buzziest market, Asiatique takes the form of rows of open-air warehouses of commerce next to Mae Nam Chao Phraya. At this slightly more upscale version of Chatuchak Market, shoppers can expect clothing, handicrafts, souvenirs and quite a few dining and drinking venues. To get here, take one of the frequent shuttle boats from Tha Sathon (Central Pier) between 4pm and 11.30pm.

Thanon Khao San Market SOUVENIRS
(Map p58; Th Khao San; 10am-midnight; Tha Phra Athit (Banglamphu)) The main guesthouse strip in Banglamphu is a day-and-night shopping bazaar for serious baht pinchers, with cheap T-shirts, 'bootleg' CDs, wooden elephants, hemp clothing, fisherman pants and other goods that make backpackers go ga-ga.

Pratunam Market CLOTHING
(Map p64; cnr Th Phetchaburi & Th Ratchaprarop; 10am-10pm; klorng boat to Tha Pratunam, S Ratchathewi exit 4) The city's biggest wholesale clothing market, Pratunam is a tight warren of stalls trickling deep into the block. In addition to cheap T-shirts and jeans, luggage, bulk toiletries and souvenirs are also available.

Scuba-Diving Supplies

Most of Bangkok's dive shops are located around Th Sukhumvit.

Dive Indeed SCUBA-DIVING SUPPLIES
(Map p68; 0 2665 7471; www.diveindeed.com; 14/2 Soi 21 (Asoke), Th Sukhumvit; 11am-7pm Mon-Sat; M Sukhumvit exit 2, S Asok exit 3)

Dive Supply SCUBA-DIVING SUPPLIES
(0 2354 4815; www.divesupply.com; 457/4 Th Si Ayuthaya; 11am-7.30pm Tue-Sat; S Phaya Thai exit 4)

Planet Scuba SCUBA-DIVING SUPPLIES
(Map p68; 0 2261 4412; www.planetscuba.net; 666 Th Sukhumvit; 10am-8pm Mon Sat, 11am-6pm Sun; S Phrom Phong exit 4)

Information

EMERGENCY

If you have a medical emergency and need an ambulance, contact the hospitals listed below. In case of a police or safety issue, contact the following emergency services:

Fire (199) You're unlikely to find an English-speaker at this number, so it's best to use the default 191 emergency number.

Police (191)

Tourist Police (24hr hotline 1155) The best way to deal with most problems requiring police (usually a rip-off or theft) is to contact the tourist police, who are used to dealing with foreigners and can be very helpful in cases of arrest. Although they typically have no jurisdiction over the kinds of cases handled by regular cops, they should be able to help with translation, contacting your embassy and/or arranging a police report you can take to your insurer.

INTERNET & TELEPHONE ACCESS

There's no shortage of internet cafes in Bangkok competing to offer the cheapest and fastest connection. Rates vary depending on the concentration and affluence of net-heads – Banglamphu is cheaper than Sukhumvit or Silom, with rates as low as 15B per hour. Many internet shops have Skype and headsets so that international calls can be made for the price of surfing the web.

A convenient place to take care of your communication needs in the centre of Bangkok is the **TrueMove Shop** (Map p64; www.truemove.com; Soi 2, Siam Sq; 7am-10pm; S Siam exit 4). It has high-speed internet computers equipped with Skype, sells phones and mobile subscriptions, and can also provide information on city-wide wi-fi access for computers and phones.

Wi-fi, provided mostly free of charge, is becoming more and more ubiquitous around Bangkok and is available at more businesses and public hot spots than we have space to list here. For relatively authoritative lists of wi-fi hot spots in Bangkok, go to www.bkkpages.com (under 'Directory') or www.stickmanweekly.com/WiFi/BangkokFreeWirelessInternetWiFi.htm.

MEDIA

Daily newspapers are available at streetside newsagents. Monthly magazines are available in most bookstores.

Bangkok 101 (www.bangkok101.com) A monthly city primer with photo essays and reviews of sights, restaurants and entertainment.

Bangkok Post (www.bangkokpost.com) The leading English-language daily with Friday and weekend supplements covering city events.

BK (www.bk.asia-city.com) Free weekly listings mag for the young and hip.

Nation (www.nationmultimedia.com) English-language daily with a heavy focus on business.

MEDICAL SERVICES

Thanks to its high standard of hospital care, Bangkok is fast becoming a destination for medical tourists shopping for more affordable dental check-ups, elective surgery and cosmetic procedures. Pharmacists (chemists) throughout the city can diagnose and treat most minor ailments (Bangkok belly, sinus and skin infections etc).

The following hospitals offer 24-hour emergency services, and the numbers below should be contacted if you need an ambulance or immediate medical attention.

BNH (Map p66; ☎0 2686 2700; www.bnhhospital.com; 9 Th Convent; M Si Lom exit 2, S Sala Daeng exit 2)

Bumrungrad International Hospital (Map p68; ☎0 2667 1000; www.bumrungrad.com; 33 Soi 3, Th Sukhumvit; S Phloen Chit exit 3)

Samitivej Hospital (Map p68; ☎0 2711 8000; www.samitivejhospitals.com; 133 Soi 49, Th Sukhumvit; S Phrom Phong exit 3 & taxi)

MONEY

Regular bank hours in Bangkok are generally 8.30am to 3.30pm, although branches in busy areas and shopping malls are open later. ATMs are common in all areas of the city. Many Thai banks also have currency-exchange bureaus; there are also exchange desks within eyeshot of most tourist areas. Go to 7-Eleven shops or other reputable places to break 1000B bills; don't expect a vendor or taxi to be able to change a bill 500B or larger.

POST

Main Post Office (☎0 2233 1050; Th Charoen Krung; ⊙8am-8pm Mon-Fri, to 1pm Sat & Sun; Tha Oriental) Near Soi 35, Th Charoen Krung, services include poste restante and packaging within the main building. Branch post offices throughout the city also offer poste restante and parcel services.

TOILETS

Public toilets in Bangkok are few and far between and your best bet is to head for a shopping centre, fast-food restaurant, or our favourite, a luxury hotel (just waltz in as if you're staying there). Shopping centres might charge 2B to 5B for a visit; some newer shopping centres have toilets for the disabled. Despite what you'll hear, squat toilets are a dying breed in Bangkok.

TOURIST INFORMATION

Official tourist offices distribute maps, brochures and advice on sights and activities. Some private travel agencies incorporate elements of the official national tourism organisation name (Tourism Authority of Thailand; TAT) into their own name to mislead tourists.

Bangkok Information Center (Map p58; ☎0 2225 7612-4; www.bangkoktourist.com; 17/1 Th Phra Athit; ⊙9am-7pm Mon-Fri, 9am-5pm Sat-Sun; Tha Phra Athit (Banglamphu)) City-specific tourism office that provides maps, brochures and directions. They also operate 26 sporadically staffed tourist information booths (⊙9am-5pm Mon-Sat) in touristed areas.

Tourism Authority of Thailand (TAT; ☎nationwide call centre 1672; www.tourismthailand.org) Head Office (☎0 2250 5500; 1600 Th Phetchaburi Tat Mai; ⊙8.30am-4.30pm; M Phetchaburi exit 2); Banglamphu (☎0 2283 1500; cnr Th Ratchadamnoen Nork & Th Chakrapatdipong; ⊙8.30am-4.30pm; Tha Phan Fah); Suvarnabhumi International Airport (☎0 2134 0040; 2nd fl, btwn Gates 2 & 5, Suvarnabhumi International Airport; ⊙24hr).

Getting There & Away

Bangkok is Thailand's undisputed transportation hub, and a huge and growing number of domestic air routes, convenient and modern buses, and a reliable and comprehensive train network mean that getting to just about any of the country's beachy destinations is a snap.

AIR

Bangkok has two airports. **Suvarnabhumi International Airport** (☎0 2132 1888; www.suvarnabhumiairport.com), 30km east of central Bangkok, began commercial international and domestic service in 2006. The airport's name is pronounced *sù·wan·ná·poom*, and it inherited the airport code (BKK) previously used by the old airport at Don Muang. The airport website has real-time details of arrivals and departures. Bangkok's former international and domestic **Don Muang International Airport** (p420), 25km north of central Bangkok, was retired from commercial service in September 2006, only to reopen later as Bangkok's de-facto budget hub.

Airlines operating domestic routes to Thailand's islands and beaches include:

Air Asia (☎0 2515 9999; www.airasia.com) Flies between Don Muang International Airport and domestic destinations including Hat Yai, Krabi, Nakhon Si Thammarat, Narathiwat, Phuket, Surat Thani and Trang.

Air Asia has 'service centres' on Thanon Khao San, Thanon Phra Ram I and Thanon Sukhumvit.

Bangkok Airways Head Office (☎0 2270 6699; 99 Moo 14, Th Viphawadee; ⊙8am-5.30pm Mon-Fri; S Mo Chit exit 1 & taxi) Flies from Suvarnabhumi International Airport to Ko Samui, Krabi, Pattaya, Phuket and Trat.

Happy Air (☎0 2134 8000; www.happyair.co.th; Room T1-112, Suvarnabhumi International Airport) Flies between Suvarnabhumi International Airport and Chumphon and Ranong.

Nok Air (Map p66; ☎0 2900 9955; 17th fl, Rajanakarn Bldg, 183 Th Sathon Tai (South); S Chong Nonsi exit 1) Flies from Don Muang International Airport to Hat Yai, Nakhon Si Thammarat, Narathiwat, Phuket, Surat Thani and Trang.

TRANSPORT TO/FROM BANGKOK

The following shows travel times and costs to Thailand's most popular beach and island destinations. Several airlines now offer air-bus-boat links to various islands, although we've not included this below; for more detailed information, be sure to refer to the Getting There & Away chapter of your specific destination.

DESTINATION	AIR	BUS	TRAIN
Chumphon	from 2200B; 70min; 3 daily (from Don Muang & Suvarnabhumi)	380B; 7hr; 9pm (from Southern Bus Terminal)	192-1194B; 10hr; 10 departures 8.05am-10.50pm
Hat Yai	from 1700B; 1½hr; 17 daily (from Don Muang); 3010B; 1½hr; 4 daily (from Suvarnabhumi)	581-1162B; 13hr; hourly 5-8am & 3-9pm (from Southern Bus Terminal)	259-1590B; 12-15hr; 6 departures 1-10.40pm
Khao Lak	see Phuket	1011B; 12hr; 8pm (from Southern Bus Terminal)	–
Ko Chang	see Trat	see Trat	–
Ko Lipe	–	612-787B; 12½-14hr; 7am & 5-6.45pm (from Southern Bus Terminal)	
Ko Pha-Ngan	see Chumphon, Ko Samui or Surat Thani	see Chumphon or Surat Thani	see Chumphon or Surat Thani
Ko Phi-Phi	see Krabi or Phuket	see Krabi or Phuket	–
Ko Samet	–	220B; 4hr; frequent departures 7am-6.30pm (from Eastern Bus Terminal to Ban Phe)	–
Ko Samui	3300B; 1½hr; 19 daily (from Suvarnabhumi)	458-916B; 12hr; every 30min 7-8am & 6-8.30pm (not incl ferry transfer; from Southern Bus Terminal)	–
Ko Tao	see Chumphon, Ko Samui or Surat Thani	see Chumphon or Surat Thani	see Chumphon or Surat Thani
Krabi	1500-7760B; 1hr 25min-1hr 45min; frequent (from Don Muang & Suvarnabhumi)	666-1000B; 12hr; 6-7.30pm (from Southern Bus Terminal)	–
Phuket	3033B; 75min; 9 daily (from Don Muang); 3780-5480B; 75min; frequent daily (from Suvarnabhumi)	529-1058B; 12-15hr; hourly 5-9pm & 3-9pm (from Southern Bus Terminal)	–
Surat Thani	from 1400B; 75min; frequent departures daily (from Don Muang & Suvarnabhumi)	413-826B; 12hr; 23 departures 6.30am-9pm	217-1379B; 12hr; 10 departures 8.05am-10.50pm (to Phun Phin)
Trat	2550B; 1hr; 3 departures daily (from Suvarnabhumi International Airport)	248-275B; 5½hr; frequent 4-9.45am (from Eastern Bus Terminal); 272B; 6hr; 5 departures 11.30am-11.30pm (from Northern & Northeastern Bus Terminal)	–
Trang	from 1600B; 1hr 20min; 3 departures daily (from Don Muang International Airport)	667-1057B; 11½hr; 7am & frequent 5-7.30pm	

Orient Thai (Map p68; ☎0 2229 4260; 18 Th Ratchadaphisek; ⊙8.30am-6pm Mon-Fri; M Sukhumvit exit 3, S Asok exit 4) Flies from Don Muang International Airport to Phuket.

Solar Air (☎0 2535 2448; 1st fl, Don Muang International Airport) Flies from Don Muang International Airport to Chumphon.

Thai Airways International (THAI; ☎nationwide call centre 0 2356 1111; www.thaiairways.com) Banglamphu (p421) Silom (Map p66; ☎0 2288 7000; 485 Th Silom; ⊙8am-5pm Mon-Sat; S Chong Nonsi exit 3) Suvarnabhumi International Airport (☎0 2134 5483; 4th fl) Flies between Suvarnabhumi and Hat Yai, Ko Samui, Krabi, Phuket and Surat Thani.

BUS

Bangkok has three main bus terminals – two of which are an inconvenient distance from the centre of the city – and a terminal at the public transport centre at Suvarnabhumi International Airport with inter-provincial departures.

For long-distance journeys to popular tourist destinations it is advisable to buy tickets directly from the bus companies at the bus stations, rather than through travel agents in tourist centres such as Th Khao San.

Eastern Bus Terminal (Ekamai; Map p68; ☎0 2391 2504; Soi 40, Th Sukhumvit; S Ekkamai exit 2) The departure point for buses to Pattaya, Rayong, Chanthaburi and other points east. Most people call it *sà·tăh·nee èk·gà·mai* (Ekamai station). It's near the Ekkamai BTS station.

Southern Bus Terminal (Sai Tai Mai; ☎0 2894 6122; Th Boromaratchachonanee) The city's newest terminal lies a long way west of the centre of Bangkok. Commonly called *săi đâi mài*, it's among the more pleasant and orderly in the country. The easiest way to reach the station is by taxi, or you can take bus 79, 159, 201 or 516 from Th Ratchadamnoen Klang, or bus 40 or a minivan from the Victory Monument.

Northern & Northeastern Bus Terminal (Mo Chit; ☎for northeastern routes 0 2936 2852, ext 602/605, for northern routes 0 2936 2841, ext 325/614; Th Kamphaeng Phet; M Kamphaeng Phet exit 1 & taxi, S Mo Chit exit 3 & taxi) Located just north of Chatuchak Park, this hectic bus station is also commonly called *kŏn sòng mŏr chít* (Mo Chit station) – not to be confused with Mo Chit BTS station. Buses depart from here for all northern and northeastern destinations.

Suvarnabhumi Public Transport Centre (☎0 2132 1888; Suvarnabhumi Airport) Located 3km from Suvarnabhumi International Airport, this terminal has relatively frequent departures to points east including Chanthaburi, Ko Chang, Pattaya, Rayong and Trat. It can be reached from the airport by a free shuttle bus.

TRAIN

Hualamphong Train Station (☎0 2220 4334, nationwide call centre 1690; www.railway.co.th; off Th Phra Ram IV; M Hua Lamphong exit 2) Hualamphong is the terminus for the main rail services to the south and east.

Bookings can be made in person at the advance booking office (just follow the signs; open from 8.30am to 4pm). From 5am to 8.30am and 4pm to 11pm, advance bookings can also be made at windows 2 to 11. You can obtain a train timetable from the information window. Ignore smiling 'information' staff who try to direct all arrivals to outside travel agencies.

Hualamphong has the following services: shower room, mailing centre, luggage storage, cafes and food courts. To get to the station from Sukhumvit take the MRT to the Hua Lamphong stop. From western points (Banglamphu, Thewet), take bus 53.

Getting Around

Although Bangkok's rush-hour traffic is the stuff of nightmares, seemingly random acts of gridlock can impede even the shortest trip, any day, any time. If it's an option, going by river, canal or BTS/MRT is always the best choice; otherwise assume a 45-minute journey for most outings.

TO/FROM THE AIRPORT

Bangkok is served by two airports; the vast majority of flights are out of Suvarnabhumi International Airport, while the budget airlines operate out of Don Muang International Airport. If you need to transfer between the two, pencil in *at least* an hour, as the two airports are at opposite ends of town. Minivans run between the two airports from 5.30am to 5pm (50B).

Suvarnabhumi International Airport

The following ground transport options leave directly from the Suvarnabhumi terminal to in-town destinations: metered taxis, hotel limousines, airport rail link, private vehicles and some minivans.

Airport Rail Link The elevated train service linking central Bangkok and Suvarnabhumi International Airport is comprised of a local service, which makes six stops before terminating at Phaya Thai station (45B, 30 minutes, every 15 minutes from 6am to midnight), connected by a walkway to BTS at Phaya Thai station, and an express service that runs, without stops, between Phaya Thai and Makkasan stations and the airport (90B, 15 to 17 minutes, hourly from 6am to midnight). Makkasan, also known as Bangkok City Air Terminal, is a short walk from MRT Phetchaburi, and if you arrive at least three hours before your departure, also has check-in facilities for passengers on Thai Airways International flights departing between

MINIVANS TO/FROM BANGKOK

Privately run minivans, called *rót đôo*, are a fast and relatively comfortable way to get between Bangkok and its neighbouring provinces. Minivans bound for a number of destinations wait at various points around the **Victory Monument** (อนุสาวรีย์ชัย; cnr Th Ratchawithi & Th Phayathai; 24hr; Victory Monument).

DESTINATION	COST	DURATION	FREQUENCY
Cha-am	160B	2½hr	every 30min, 5am-7pm
Chanthaburi	200B	3hr	hourly, 6am-7.30pm
Hua Hin	180B	3hr	every 30min, 5am-7pm
Pattaya	100B	2hr	every 40min, 5.30am-8pm
Phetchaburi	100B	2hr	every 45min, 6.15am-8pm
Southern Bus Terminal	35B	20min	frequent, 8am-8pm
Suvarnabhumi International Airport	40B	30min	every 30min, 5am-9pm

7am and 9pm. Both train lines run from 6am to midnight.

The Airport Rail Link is on floor B1 of Suvarnabhumi International Airport.

Bus & Minivan The public-transport centre is 3km from Suvarnabhumi and includes a public bus terminal, metered taxi stand and long-term parking. A free airport shuttle bus running both an ordinary and express route connects the transport centre with the passenger terminals. Lines that city-bound tourists are likely to use include bus 554, which stops across from Don Muang International Airport (34B, runs 24 hours), and minivan lines 551 to Victory Monument BTS station (40B, frequent from 5am to 10pm) and 552 to On Nut BTS station (25B, frequent from 5am to 10pm). From these points, you can continue on public transport or by taxi to your hotel. There are also buses and minivans to destinations south and east including Chanthaburi, Hua Hin, Ko Chang, Ko Samet, Pattaya and Trat.

Relatively frequent minivans to Don Muang International Airport wait on floor 1, outside door 8 (50B, 40 minutes, from 5.30am to 5pm).

From town, you can take the BTS to On Nut, then from near the market entrance opposite Tesco Lotus take minivan 552 (25B, frequent from 5am to 10pm), or BTS to Victory Monument, then the minivan to Suvarnabhumi (40B, 30 minutes, every 30 minutes from 5am to 9pm).

Taxi As you exit the terminal, ignore the touts and all the signs pointing you to overpriced 'official airport taxis'; instead, descend to floor 1 to join the generally fast-moving queue for a public taxi. Cabs booked through these desks should always use their meter, but they often try their luck so insist by saying, 'Meter, please'. Toll charges (paid by the passengers) vary between 25B and 60B. Note also that there's an additional 50B surcharge added to all fares departing from the airport, payable directly to the driver.

Don Muang International Airport

Bus & Minivan From outside the arrivals hall, there are two airport bus lines from Don Muang: A1 makes stops at BTS Mo Chit and the Northern and Northeastern Bus Terminal (30B, hourly from 9am to midnight); A2 makes stops at BTS Mo Chit and BTS Victory Monument (30B, hourly from 9am to midnight).

Relatively frequent minivans also departing from outside the arrivals hall link Don Muang International Airport and Suvarnabhumi International Airport (50B, 40 minutes, from 5.30am to 5pm).

Public buses stop on the highway in front of the airport. Lines include 29, with a stop at Victory Monument BTS station before terminating at Hualamphong Train Station (runs 24 hours); 59, with a stop near Th Khao San (runs 24 hours); line 538, stopping at Victory Monument BTS station (4am to 10pm); and line 555, bound for Suvarnabhumi International Airport (4am to 11pm); fares are approximately 30B.

Taxi As at Suvarnabhumi, public taxis leave from outside the arrivals hall and there is a 50B airport charge added to the meter fare.

Train The walkway that crosses from the airport to the Amari Airport Hotel also provides access to Don Muang train station, which has trains to Hualamphong Train Station every one to 1½ hours from 4am to 11.30am and then roughly every hour from 2pm to 9.30pm (5B to 10B).

BOAT

Once the city's dominant form of transport, public boats still survive along the mighty Mae Nam Chao Phraya and on a few interior *klorng*.

Canal Routes

Canal taxi boats run along Khlong Saen Saeb (Banglamphu to Ramkhamhaeng) and are an easy way to get from Banglamphu to Jim Thompson House, the Siam Square shopping centres (get off at Tha Saphan Hua Chang for both), and other points further east along Sukhumvit – after a mandatory change of boat at Tha Pratunam. Fares range from 10B to 20B and boats run from approximately 5.30am to 8.30pm (to 7pm on weekends and holidays).

River Routes

Chao Phraya Express Boat (p71) provides one of the city's most scenic (and efficient) transport options, running passenger boats along Mae Nam Chao Phraya to destinations both south and north of Bangkok. The central pier is known varyingly as Tha Sathon and Saphan Taksin, and connects to the Saphan Taksin BTS station, at the southern end of the city. Visitors are most likely to go northwards, to the stops designated with an N prefix.

Tickets range from 10B to 40B and are generally purchased on board the boat, although some larger stations have ticket booths. Either way, hold on to your ticket as proof of purchase. Boats generally run from 6am to 7pm.

The company operates express (indicated by an orange, yellow or green flag), local (without a flag) and tourist boat (blue flag) services. During rush hour, pay close attention to the flag colours to avoid an unwanted journey to a foreign province. Ask for one of the route maps provided at some of the larger piers.

River Crossing Boats

There are also flat-bottomed cross-river ferries that connect Thonburi and Bangkok. These piers are usually next door to Chao Phraya Express Boat piers, cost 3B per crossing and run from approximately 7am to 7pm.

BTS & MRT

The elevated **BTS** (☎0 2617 7300; www.bts.co.th), also known as the Skytrain, spans two lines that whisk you through 'new' Bangkok (Th Silom, Th Sukhumvit and Siam Sq). The interchange is at Siam station, and trains run frequently from 6am to midnight. Fares range from 15B to 42B, or 130B for a one-day pass. Most ticket machines only accept coins, but change is available at the information booths.

Bangkok's **MRT** (www.bangkokmetro.co.th) or metro is helpful for people staying in the Th Sukhumvit or Th Silom area to reach the train station at Hualamphong. Otherwise the system is mainly a suburban commuter line. Fares cost 16B to 40B, or 120B for a one-day pass. The trains run frequently from 6am to midnight.

BUS

The city's public bus system is operated by **Bangkok Mass Transit Authority** (☎0 2246 0973; www.bmta.co.th); the website is a great source of information on all bus routes, but this doesn't really help the fact that Bangkok's bus system is confusing and generally lacks English. If you're determined, or are pinching pennies, fares for ordinary (fan) buses start at 7B and air-conditioned buses at 10B. Smaller privately operated green buses cost 5B.

Most of the bus lines run between 5am and 10pm or 11pm, except for the 'all-night' buses, which run from 3am or 4am to midmorning.

MOTORCYCLE TAXI

Forming the backdrop of modern Bangkok, teams of cheeky, numbered and vested motorcycle-taxi drivers can be found at the end of just about every long street. A ride to the end *(sùt soy)* or mouth *(Ъàhk soy)* of an average soi usually costs 10B to 15B. Longer journeys should be negotiated in advance, and can range from 20B to 100B.

TAXI

Although many first-time visitors are hesitant to use them, in general, Bangkok's taxis are new and spacious and the drivers are courteous and helpful, making them an excellent way to get around. Flag fares start at 35B and fares to most places within central Bangkok cost 60B to 80B. Freeway tolls – 25B to 60B depending on where you start – must be paid by the passenger.

Taxi Radio (☎1681; www.taxiradio.co.th) and other 24-hour 'phone-a-cab' services are available for 20B above the metered fare. Taxis are usually plentiful except during peak commute hours, when bars are closing (1am to 2am), or when it is raining and your destination requires sitting in too much traffic.

TÚK-TÚK

A ride on Thailand's most emblematic three-wheeled vehicle is an experience particularly sought after by new arrivals, but it only takes a few seconds to realise that most foreigners are too tall to see anything beyond the low-slung roof.

Túk-túk drivers also have a knack for smelling crisp bills and can potentially take you and your wallet far away from your desired destination. In particular, beware of drivers who offer to take you on a sightseeing tour for 10B or 20B – it's a touting scheme designed to pressure you into purchasing overpriced goods. A short trip on a túk-túk will cost at least 60B.

Ko Chang & the Eastern Seaboard

Includes ➡

Best Places to Eat

- Mum Aroi (p105)
- Phu-Talay (p130)
- Norng Bua (p130)
- Cool Corner Cafe (p119)
- Pan & David Restaurant (p100)

Best Places to Stay

- Keereeta Resort (p127)
- Bann Makok (p135)
- Rabbit Resort (p104)
- Koh Chang Sea Hut (p129)
- Tok's (p110)

Why Go?

Bangkok Thais have long escaped the urban grind with weekend escapes to the eastern seaboard. Some of the country's first beach resorts sprang up here, starting a trend that has been replicated wherever sand meets sea. As the country has industrialised, only a few beaches within reach of the capital, such as Ko Samet's, remain spectacular specimens. Further afield, Ko Chang and its sister islands offer a more 'tropical' ambience, but are far from undiscovered.

Just beyond the foothills and the curving coastline is Cambodia, and the east coast provides a cultural link between the two countries. Many of the mainland Thai towns were at some point occupied by the French during the shifting border days of the colonial era. Travellers who take the time to explore these lesser-known spots will find remnants of Old Siam, tasty market meals and an easy-going prosperity that defines ordinary Thai life in this region.

When to Go

➡ The best time to visit is the end of the rainy season (usually around November) but before the start of high season (December to March) when the weather is cool, the landscape green and rates reasonable. Peak season on Ko Chang is the Christmas and New Year holiday period. Crowds thin in March, the start of the hot season.

➡ The rainy season runs from May to October. A few businesses on Ko Chang close and the nearby islands of Ko Kut, Ko Mak and Ko Wai go into hibernation with many places shut. Your best monsoon bet is Ko Samet, which enjoys its own micro-climate and stays relatively dry.

Si Racha

ศรีราชา

POP 68,292

A subdued seaside town, Si Racha is a mix of a traditional fishing village and modern industry. Waterfront condo towers eclipse a labyrinth of rickety piers, while the container ships docking at the Laem Chabang port share the shipping channels with wooden, multicoloured fishing boats.

Thai towns are adept at disguising themselves so that they resemble each other. Si Racha, though, is more international than most, thanks to the Japanese car manufacturers based nearby. There are many sushi joints here, as well as Japanese-style bars, and on weekends the impeccably maintained health park is full of Japanese expats jogging and throwing baseballs around.

But Si Racha is most attractive for what it doesn't have; there are no girlie bars or traffic jams and precious few foreign visitors, allowing you to enjoy a taste of small town Thai life.

Best of all, Si Racha is the gateway to the peaceful little island of Ko Si Chang. Once a royal retreat, the island feels like an extended fishing village, only with a palace and some impressive temples scattered around it.

Sights

Si Racha's attractions are limited, but the town itself makes for a pleasant stroll.

Ko Loi ISLAND

This small rocky island is connected to the mainland by a long jetty at the northern end of Si Racha's waterfront and lauded as a local highlight. It has a festival atmosphere centred around a **Thai-Chinese temple** (daylight hours), decorated by a couple of giant ponds with turtles of every size, from tiny hatchlings to seen-it-all-before seniors. This is also where you can catch the boat to Ko Si Chang.

Health Park GARDEN

The town's waterfront Health Park is possibly one of the best-maintained municipal parks in the country. There are sea breezes, a playground, a shady coffee shop with wi-fi, a jogging track and a lot of evening activity.

Sleeping

The most authentic (read: basic) places to stay are the wooden hotels on the piers.

Samchai HOTEL $

(0 3831 1800; Soi 10, Th Jermjompol; r 350B;) More comfortable than other pier options, this place seems to ramble forever. The rooms are functional, but clean and acceptable.

Siriwatana Hotel HOTEL $

(0 3831 1037; Soi Siriwatana, Th Jermjompol; r 200B) This wooden stilt hotel sits above the sea – in fact, you can look straight through the squat toilet's hole to the ocean. It's very simple and very cheap.

Seaview Sriracha Hotel HOTEL $$

(0 3831 9000; 50-54 Th Jermjompol; r 990-1900B; @) Rooms are large and comfortable; try to score one at the back for views of the sea and piers and to avoid traffic noise.

Eating & Drinking

Unsurprisingly, Si Racha is famous for its seafood and you have the choice of eating it both Thai- and Japanese-style.

Ko Loi Seafood Stalls SEAFOOD $

(dishes 40-160B; 10am-9pm) Perched on the Ko Loi jetty, these humble spots specialise in fresh seafood. There is no English menu, so just point and pick.

Night Square MARKET $

(Th Jermjompol & Th Si Racha Nakorn; dishes from 50B; 5pm) This evening market is small, but big enough to feed a street-stall appetite.

Moom Aroy SEAFOOD $$

(Soi 8, Th Jermjompol; dishes 60-420B; 11am-10pm) Moom Aroy delivers on its name, which means 'delicious corner'. This is *the* place to enjoy a Si Racha seafood meal with views of the pier and squid rigs. It is north of town; turn left at Samitivet Sriracha Hospital and look for the tank with the 2m fish out front.

Asami Sriracha JAPANESE $$

(Th Jermjompol; sushi from 80B, sashimi from 140B; 11am-11pm;) Authentic and popular eatery that sees a lot of expat Japanese customers. The sushi is as fresh as possible, and there are also ramen and teppanyaki dishes here.

Bang Saen SEAFOOD $$

(dishes 150-350B; 11am-10pm) Do as the Thais do and judge your beach by its seafood restaurants. This resort, 18km north of town, isn't good for swimming but weekending Bangkokians and local university students love it for its food and views. You'll need private transport to reach it.

Ko Chang & the Eastern Seaboard Highlights

1. Beachcombing and jungle trekking on **Ko Chang** (p120)
2. Floating the day away on the crystalline waters of **Ko Kut** (p134)
3. Swimming with the fishes in the gin-clear coves of **Ko Wai** (p132)
4. Cove-hopping on pretty **Ko Samet** (p108), so close to Bangkok but so far away
5. Strolling the old city and watching the gem traders in **Chanthaburi** (p113)
6. Kicking back in **Trat's** (p116) atmospheric wooden shophouse quarter
7. Avoiding Bangkok's hustle and bustle with a day trip to peaceful **Ko Si Chang** (p99) and a layover in **Si Racha** (p95)
8. Admiring the modern masterpiece of Pattaya's **Sanctuary of Truth** (p101), an elaborately carved testament to the artistry of Buddhism and Hinduism
9. Dining on seafood beside the sea everywhere – the principal reason Thais travel to the beach

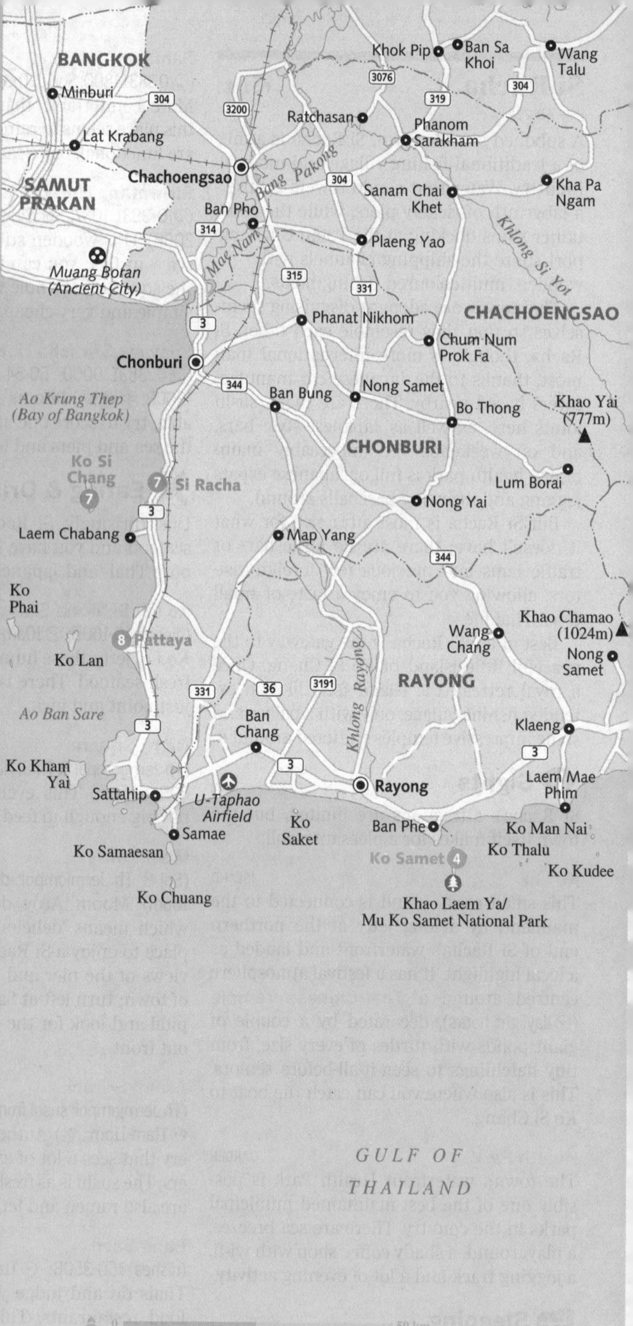

BANGKOK
Minburi
Lat Krabang
SAMUT PRAKAN
Muang Boran (Ancient City)
Chachoengsao
Ban Pho
Mae Nam Bang Pakong
Khok Pip
Ban Sa Khoi
Wang Talu
Ratchasan
Phanom Sarakham
Sanam Chai Khet
Kha Pa Ngam
Plaeng Yao
Khlong Si Yot
CHACHOENGSAO
Phanat Nikhom
Chum Num Prok Fa
Chonburi
Ao Krung Thep (Bay of Bangkok)
Ban Bung
Nong Samet
Bo Thong
Khao Yai (777m)
CHONBURI
Ko Si Chang
Si Racha
Lum Borai
Nong Yai
Laem Chabang
Map Yang
Ko Phai
Pattaya
Ko Lan
Khao Chamao (1024m)
Wang Chang
Nong Samet
Khlong Rayong
RAYONG
Ao Ban Sare
Ban Chang
Klaeng
Ko Kham Yai
Sattahip
U-Taphao Airfield
Rayong
Laem Mae Phim
Samae
Ko Saket
Ban Phe
Ko Man Nai
Ko Samaesan
Ko Samet
Ko Thalu
Ko Kudee
Ko Chuang
Khao Laem Ya/ Mu Ko Samet National Park
GULF OF THAILAND
0 50 km
0 25 miles
3076 304 319 3200 304 314 315 331 3 344 3 344 331 36 3191 3 3 3

Sa Kaew
Lam Prachin buri
Watthana Nakhon
Huay Jot
Sai Yoi
Khao Chakan
Aranya Prathet
Ang Sila
Non Mak Mun
Poipet
CAMBODIA
Sisophon
Sai Diaw
Non Sao-Eh
Khlong Hat
Khao Takrup (660m)
Wang Mai
Khao Daeng
Thun Khanan
CHANTHABURI
Tamun
Khao Soi Dao Nua (1566m)
Battambang
Pung Ngon
Nong Chek Soi
Takra
Ban Pakard
Psar Pruhm
Khao Chamao/ Khao Wong National Park
Khao Khitchakut National Park
Pong Nam Ron
Pailin
Si Yaek Kong Din
Nong Khla
Makham
Ban Pa-Ah
Tha Mai
5 Chanthaburi
Chang Thun
Nam Tok Phlio National Park
Nong Sii
Laem Sadet
Ta Chalap
Chak Yai
Laem Singh
Khlung
Pong
Dan Chumpon
Laem Ko Proet
Tha Chot
TRAT
CAMBODIA
Trat 6
Bang Kradan
Ban Noen Sung
Laem Muang
Laem Ngop
Ao Trat
Tha Sen
1 Ko Chang
Laem Sok
Mu Ko Chang National Marine Park
Mai Rut
Ko Wai 3
Ko Kradat
Ko Mak
Ko Rayang
Khlong Yai
Ko Mai Si
2 Ko Kut
Hat Lek
Krong Koh Kong
348
33
317
3395
3395
317
317
3
3157
3159
3271
3156
3
318

Si Racha

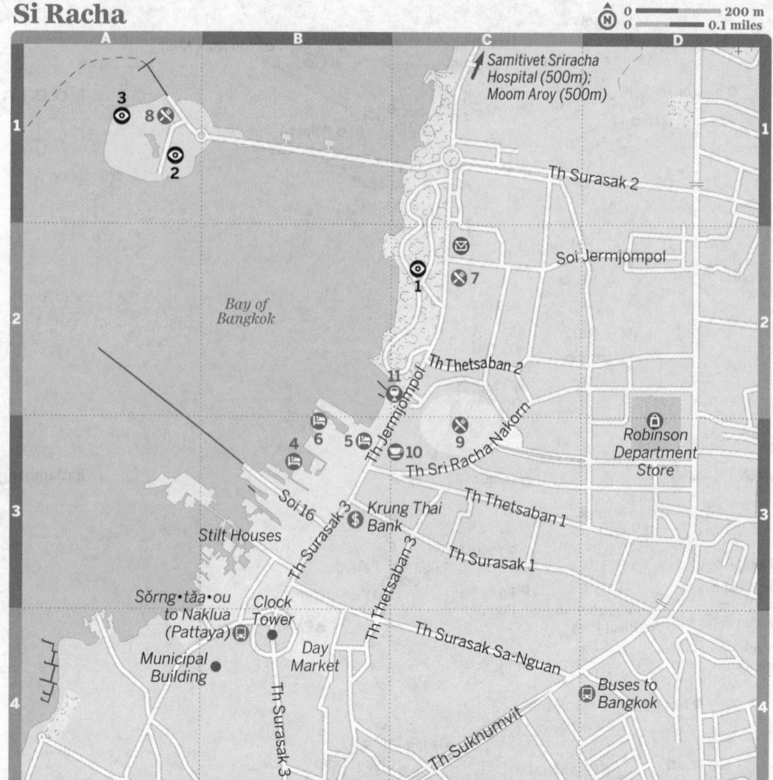

Si Racha

Sights

Sleeping

Eating

Drinking & Nightlife

Coffee Tree CAFE
(Th Jermjompol; ⌚7am-7pm; 📶) Cute cafe that caters to Si Racha's student hipsters. It offers coffee, juices and tea, as well as snacks.

Pop Pub BAR
(Th Jermjompol; dishes 60-220B; ⌚5-11pm) More like 'Rock', this waterfront beer-hall-meets-live music venue boasts a menu ranging from salty snacks to full meals and plenty of liquid sustenance.

Information

Krung Thai Bank (cnr Th Surasak 1 & Th Jermjompol) Has an ATM and exchange facilities.

Post Office (Th Jermjompol) A few blocks north of the Krung Thai Bank.

Samitivet Sriracha Hospital (☎0 3832 4111; Soi 8, Th Jermjompol) Regarded as Si Racha's best.

CHILI SAUCE BY ANY OTHER NAME

Judging by the phenomenal popularity of Sriracha Hot Chili sauce in the USA, you'd expect the eponymous town to be a veritable sauce temple. But no one in the town of Si Racha seems to know much about the sauce, much less that US haute cuisine chefs are using it on everything from cocktails to marinades and that food magazines are profiling it alongside truffle oil as a must-have condiment. Curiously, the culinary world also mispronounces the name of the sauce: Sriracha, an alternative spelling of 'Si Racha', is pronounced 'see-rach-ah' not 'sir-rach-ah'.

There's a good explanation for all this: the stuff sold in the US was actually invented on home soil. A Vietnamese immigrant living in a Los Angeles suburb concocted a chilli sauce to accompany noodles based on his memory of Vietnamese hot sauces. His first batches were sold out of his car but eventually his business grew into the Huy Fong Foods company.

Today, the company's distinctive rooster logo bottles are distributed in the US and Australia, but not in any Asian countries, according to a company spokesperson. But every now and then you might spot it at a Thai noodle shop. How this US-born, Thai-named, Vietnamese-inspired sauce got here, Huy Fong Foods does not know.

But that doesn't mean Thailand doesn't have its own version of a vinegar-based chilli sauce *(nám prík sěe rah·chah)*. In fact, many believe that the condiment must have originated in Si Racha and then migrated across Asia while undergoing various permutations. In Thailand, Si Racha–style sauces, including such popular brands as Golden Mountain or Sriraja Panich, are used with *kài jee·o* (omelette) and *hǒy tôrt* (fried mussel omelette) and tend to be sweeter and of a thinner consistency than the rooster brand.

Getting There & Around

Si Racha doesn't have a consolidated bus station but all buses stop on Th Sukhumvit (Hwy 3) by Robinson Department Store, or the nearby IT Mall (Tuk Com).

Buses heading north to Bangkok's bus terminals (88B to 97B, two hours) pass by every 30 minutes or so until late. There are also seven buses daily to Suvarnabhumi International Airport (200B, two hours) from an office beside the IT Mall.

Minivans stop in front of Robinson's and have frequent services to Bangkok's various bus stations (100B to 120B, two hours) and Victory Monument (100B, two hours). They head south to Pattaya (40B, 45 minutes) often, too.

White *sǒrng·tăa·ou* (passenger pick-up trucks) leave from near Si Racha's clock tower to Pattaya's Naklua market (25B, 45 minutes).

One daily train from Bangkok's Hua Lamphong station stops at Si Racha (30B, three hours). Si Racha's train station is 3km east of the waterfront.

Motorbike taxis zip around town for 20B to 30B.

Ko Si Chang เกาะสีชัง

POP 5012

Once a royal beach retreat, Ko Si Chang has a fishing village atmosphere and enough attractions to make it a decent day's excursion from Si Racha, or an overnight stop for those who want to chill out. It gets busier at weekends, when Bangkok Thais come to eat seafood, pose in front of the sea and make merit at the local temples.

Sights

Phra Chudadhut Palace HISTORICAL SITE

(9am-5pm Tue-Sun) FREE This former royal palace was used by Rama V (King Chulalongkorn) over the summer months, but was abandoned when the French briefly occupied the island in 1893. The main throne hall – a magnificent golden teak structure known as Vimanmek Teak Mansion – was moved to Bangkok in 1910. What's left are subdued Victorian-style buildings set in gardenlike grounds.

Ruen Vadhana and Ruen Mai Rim Talay contain historical displays about the king's visits to the island and his public works programs, including a lecture to the local people on Western tea parties. Up the hill is Wat Asadang Khanimit, a temple containing a small, consecrated chamber where Rama V used to meditate. The Buddha image inside was fashioned more than 50 years ago by a local monk. Nearby is a stone outcrop wrapped in holy cloth, called Bell Rock because it rings like a bell when struck.

As this was a palace, proper attire is technically required (legs and arms should be covered) but the rules aren't enforced here. While some desultory renovations are going on, there is a rather melancholy air to the place and it is far less well-maintained than most royal properties.

Cholatassathan Museum AQUARIUM
(admission by donation; ⏲9am-5pm Tue-Sun) This aquarium has a few marine exhibits and a dash of English-language signage. It's fun to watch the Thais gazing at the outdoor tank and discussing which animals are delicious to eat. The Aquatic Resources Research Institute conducts coral research here.

San Jao Phaw Khao Yai TEMPLE
(⏲daylight hours) FREE The most imposing sight on the island, this ornate Chinese temple dates back to the days when Chinese traders anchored in the sheltered waters. During Chinese New Year in February, the island is overrun with tourists from mainland China. There are also shrine caves, multiple platforms and a good view of the ocean. It's east of town.

Wat Tham Yai Phrik TEMPLE
(วัดถ้ำยายปริก; donation appreciated; ⏲dawn-dusk) This Buddhist monastery is built around several meditation caves running into the island's central limestone ridge and offers fine views from its hilltop *chedi* (stupa). Monks and *mâa chee* (nuns) from across Thailand come to take advantage of the caves' peaceful environment. Someone is usually around to give informal tours and talk about Buddhism; meditation retreats can also be arranged.

Hat Tham Phang BEACH
On the southwest side of the island, Hat Tham Phang (Fallen Cave Beach) is the only sandy beach on the island. You can hire kayaks and there is deckchair and umbrella rental. Swimming here isn't recommended, although the Thais plunge in.

Activities

Several locals run **snorkelling** trips to nearby Koh Khang Khao (Bat Island). Ask at Pan & David Restaurant for details.

Kayaks are available for rent (150B per hour) on Hat Tham Phang. It's a nice paddle down the coast to Koh Khang Khao.

Sleeping & Eating

There are a smattering of guesthouses and homestays on the island, as well as a fair few restaurants specialising in seafood.

Charlie's Bungalows GUESTOUSE $$
(☎08 5191 3863; www.kosichang.net; Th Makham Thaew; r 1000-1100B; ❄📶) Bright, fresh, all-white bungalows set around a garden. All come with TVs and DVD players. Friendly and helpful staff. Book ahead at weekends and public holidays.

Lek Tha Wang SEAFOOD $
(dishes 35-420B; ⏲10.30am-9pm) This famous, if ramshackle, open-air restaurant is where Thais go to eat conch and other shellfish. For the rest of us, there's always *dôm yam gûng* (spicy and sour prawn soup) and fried fish.

★**Pan & David Restaurant** INTERNATIONAL-THAI $$
(☎0 3821 6629; 167 Mu 3 Th Makham Thaew; dishes 60-440B; ⏲8am-10pm) With free-range chicken, homemade ice cream, a reasonable wine list and excellent Thai dishes, you can't go wrong here. Phoning ahead for a booking at weekends is recommended. The restaurant is 200m from the palace.

Information

The island's one small settlement faces the mainland and is the terminus for the ferry. A bumpy road network links the village with all the other sights.

Kasikornbank (99/12 Th Atsadang) Has an ATM and exchange facilities.

Pan & David's Ko Si Chang (www.koh-sichang.com) An excellent source of local information.

Post Office (Th Atsadang) Near the pier.

Getting There & Around

Boats to Ko Si Chang leave hourly 7am to 8pm from the Ko Loi jetty in Si Racha (one way 50B, 45 minutes). From Ko Si Chang boats shuttle back hourly 6am to 7pm. Boats leave promptly.

Motorbike taxis wait at the pier and will take you anywhere for 30B to 60B.

Motorbikes are available to rent on the pier (250B per day, 80B hourly).

Pattaya พัทยา

POP 215,888

Synonymous with sex tourism, Pattaya is unapologetic about its bread-and-butter industry. Go-go clubs, massage parlours and girlie bars occupy block after block of the central city, making Bangkok's red-light districts look small and provincial. But walking the same streets as the stiletto-wearing ladyboys are ever-increasing numbers of Russian tourists and Chinese tour groups. More than anything, Pattaya today is a schizophrenic experience: part package holiday destination; part prostitution central.

During the day, the city is slightly less seedy as the beach gets crowded out and jet skis and speed boats bounce across the waves. A fair few Thais, too, have adopted Pattaya as a weekend getaway, drawn by the excellent seafood and lower prices than elsewhere on the eastern seaboard. But not even the most enthusiatic Pattaya promoter could claim that the city has changed too much from its original incarnation as an anything-goes sin city for GIs on R & R from the Vietnam War.

The city is built around **Ao Pattaya**, a wide crescent-shaped bay that was one of Thailand's first beach resorts in the 1960s. The surrounding area is now Thailand's manufacturing base, transforming the bay from fishing area and swimming pool into an industrial port. Some provincial Thais still swim here but we don't think you should as the water is dirty. The oceanfront promenade does, however, provide a scenic stroll under shady trees and a lovely coastal view.

Optimists claim that Hat Jomtien, south of the centre, is a family-friendly scene. True, there are fewer girlie bars and the beach is nicer, but Jomtien is about two decades away from being retro and there's a preponderance of mediocre hotels and restaurants. North Pattaya (Pattaya Neua) is fashioning itself as a mini-Bangkok with modern condo towers and respectable corporate hotels. North of the city is **Naklua**, which is glossier than Jomtien and a little more promising for Pattaya's alternative tourists.

Sights & Activities

Sanctuary of Truth MONUMENT

(ปราสาทสัจธรรม; ☎0 3836 7229; www.sanctuaryoftruth.com; 206/2 Th Naklua; adult/child 500/250B; ⏲8am-6pm) Made entirely of wood (no metal nails) and commanding a celestial view of the ocean, the Sanctuary of Truth is best described as a visionary environment: part art installation, religious shrine and cultural monument. Constructed in four wings dedicated to Thai, Khmer, Chinese and Indian religious iconography, the architecture and setting is impressive.

The ornate temple-like complex was conceived by Lek Viriyaphant, a Thai millionaire who spent his fortune on this and other heritage projects (such as Ancient City near Bangkok) that revived and preserved ancient building techniques and architecture in danger of extinction. In this case, the building will continue to support hand-hewn woodworking skills because it has been under construction for 30 years and still isn't finished.

Every centimetre of the 20-storey-tall building is covered with wood carvings of Hindu and Buddhist gods and goddesses – an artistic consolidation of centuries of religious myths under one unifying roof for greater spiritual enlightenment. For non-Buddhists the experience may be more educational than transcendent as much of the symbolism will be unfamiliar.

Compulsory tours are led through the building every half hour. Thai dancing is on display at 11.30am and 3.30pm. Motorcycle taxis can be hired from Pattaya for 50B to 70B. The sanctuary is 1km down Soi 12 off Th Naklua, about 3km from the centre of town.

Anek Kusala Sala (Viharn Sien) MUSEUM

(อเนกกุศลศาลา (วิหารเซียน); ☎0 3823 5250; off Th Sukhumvit; admission 50B; ⏲9am-5pm) A popular stop for tour groups, this museum contains more than 300 very impressive pieces of Chinese artwork, mainly bronze and brass statues depicting historical figures as well as Buddhist, Confucian and Taoist deities. Founded by Sa-nga Kulkobkiat, a Thai national who grew up in China, the museum was intended as a friendship-building project between the two countries.

The 1st floor is a crowded pavilion of Chinese immortals, from Pangu, the cosmic giant, to Guan Yin, the goddess of mercy. The 2nd-floor terrace is the museum's most dramatic, with larger-than-life-sized statues of Shaolin monks depicting different martial arts poses. Nearby, is a touching collection of daily life statues (a fortune teller, dress maker, liquor seller) that visitors place 1 baht coins on.

Pattaya & Naklua

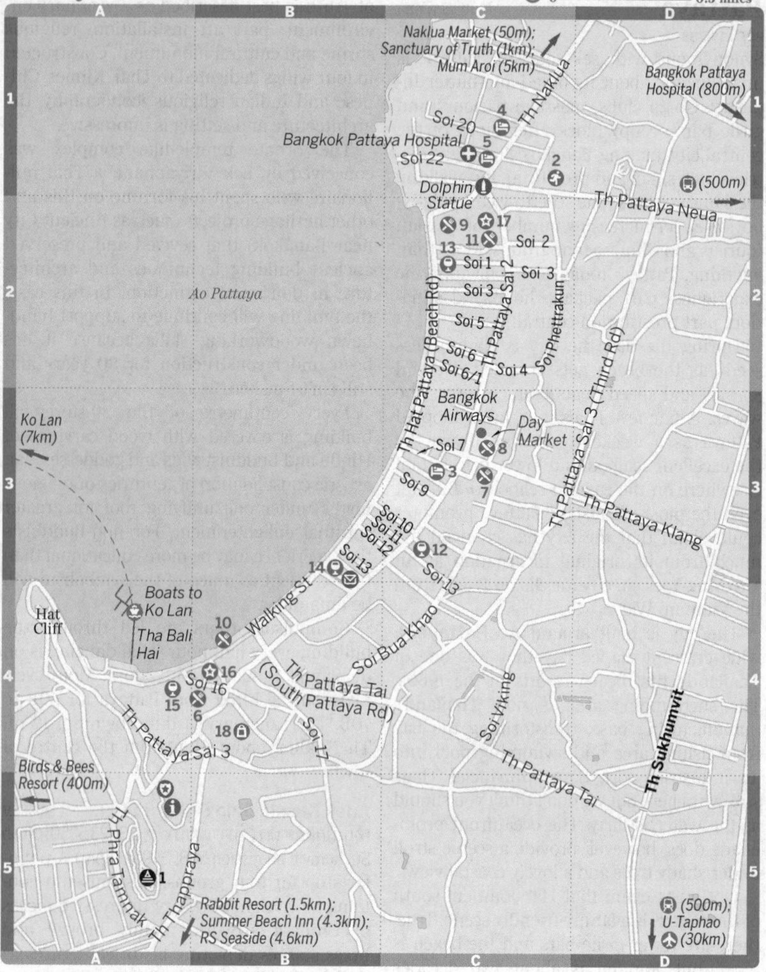

The museum is 16km south of central Pattaya; take Th Sukhumvit to the turn-off for Wat Yan Sangwararam. There is a Pattaya–Sattahip *sŏrng·tăa·ou* (25B) that will take you to the turn-off; from there you can hire a motorcycle the remaining 3km to the museum (50B) but finding a ride back to the main road is difficult. You can either negotiate with the driver to wait or come with your own transport.

Hat Ko Lan BEACH

(เกาะล้าน) Day-trippers flock to this small island, 7km offshore of central Pattaya. On weekends, its five beaches are crowded and the aquamarine sea is busy with banana boats and other marine merriment. Overcrowded ferries leave Pattaya's Bali Hai pier (30B, five daily departures) at the southern end of Walking St. The last boat back from Ko Lan is at 6pm.

Khao Phra Tamnak BUDDHIST SITE

(เขาพระตำหนัก; daylight hours) FREE A giant golden Buddha sits atop this forested hill between Jomtien and South Pattaya, proof perhaps that religion has not forsaken this modern-day Gomorrah. The serene Buddha

Pattaya & Naklua

figure of Wat Phra Yai dates back to when Pattaya was a small fishing village, long before mini-skirts, high heels and happy hours arrived. You can walk here from the southern end of Walking St.

Flight of the Gibbon ZIP LINING
(08 9970 5511; www.treetopasia.com; tours from 3000B) This zip-line course extends 3km with 26 platforms through the forest canopy of Khao Kheeo Open Safari in Chonburi, 50 minutes from Pattaya. It is an all-day tour with additional add-on activities, like a jungle obstacle course and a visit to the neighbouring animal zoo. Children 1m tall can do the zip line independently, while nippers can ride tandem with adults.

Fairtex Sports Club FITNESS, MOO·AY TAI
(0 3825 3888; www.fairtex-muaythai.com; 179/185-212 Th Pattaya Neua; per session 800-1200B) Burned-out professionals, martial arts fans and adventurous athletes flock to this resort-style sports camp for *moo·ay tai* (Thai boxing; also spelled *muay thai*) training and a sweat-inducing vacation. Accommodation packages are available and use of the club's pool and other sports facilities are included.

Fairtex has been training *moo·ay tai* fighters for 40 years. In 2005, the company opened this sports club to provide Western-style comfort for international visitors interested in fighting and fitness courses.

Daily sessions include pad work, sparring and clinching, exercise drills and body sculpting work. There are also occasional brushes with fame: domestically famous *moo·ay tai* champions and international mixed martial arts fighters also train here.

Festivals

Pattaya International Music Festival MUSIC
(www.pattayamusicfest.com; mid-Mar) In mid-March, Pattaya's oceanfront esplanade is transformed into an outdoor concert venue running for three days of live music. Local musicians, as well as bands from across Asia, take to the stages playing everything from hip-hop to rock.

Sleeping

If you're an 'alternative' Pattaya tourist (meaning you aren't a sex tourist or a package tourist), then you can avoid staying in central Pattaya and opt instead for Naklua, Jomtien or parts of Pattaya Neua. Even if you have no desire to visit Pattaya, you might consider an overnight here if you're transiting to Suvarnabhumi International Airport, 110km away, and don't want to layover in Bangkok.

RS Seaside HOTEL $
(0 3823 1867; www.rs-seaside.com; Th Hat Jomtien; r 660-1400B;) Opposite the beach and popular with Thais, RS has small-ish rooms but remains a good-value spot in the package-tour part of town. Two breakfasts are included in the room rate.

Bella Vista HOTEL $
(0 3836 2132; www.eastinypattaya.com; 217/29 Moo 9 Th Pattaya Beach, Soi 7 ; r 750-900B;) If you want to stay in the belly of the beast, then the Bella Vista is a comfortable and reasonably priced place to rest your head. Solid rooms, pleasant staff.

CHARITY SQUAD

A natural counterpoint to the city's prominent debauchery is the city's solid network of charitable organisations. Among the many benevolent servants in Pattaya, Father Ray Brennan, an American priest with the Redemptorist Order who died in 2003, established a lasting and inspiring legacy that today includes six charitable programs under the umbrella of the Redemptorist Foundation. He also founded the Pattaya Orphanage and School for the Deaf, both of which are now operated by the Catholic diocese. All of them succeed thanks to the generosity of benefactors and volunteers.

Pattaya Orphanage (0 3842 3468; www.thepattayaorphanage.org; Th Sukhumvit, North Pattaya) was founded in the 1970s when Father Ray was given a baby by a parishioner who could not care for the child. This first child led to many more as word spread that the priest could care for the unintended consequences of the US military presence in the area during the Vietnam War. Today the orphanage cares for children orphaned by modern misfortunes (poverty, drug abuse, HIV/AIDS) and helps find adoptive parents. Those interested in helping the orphanage can sponsor a meal, donate useful items and volunteer for an extended period of time.

Redemptorist Foundation (0 3871 6628; www.fr-ray.org) operates schools for the blind and disabled and a home and drop-in centre for street children, many of whom may be involved in Pattaya's child-sex industry. The foundation also runs a day-care centre for children of labourers who would otherwise accompany their parents to dangerous work sites. Volunteers rotate through the different centres, teaching English, playing with the children and leading art projects. A six-month commitment is required; contact the foundation for a volunteer handbook that outlines the application process.

If you don't have the time to commit to volunteering, stop by **Thais 4 Life** (www.thais4life.com; Soi Yen Sabai Condotel, Th Phra Tamnak; noon-6pm Mon-Sat), a charity bookstore whose proceeds go to medical treatments for destitute patients, orphanages and school uniform scholarships.

Garden Lodge Hotel HOTEL **$$**
(0 3842 9109; www.gardenlodgepattaya.net; cnr Soi 20 & Th Naklua; r 1250-2500B;) Rather old-fashioned rooms, but they're a good size and come with balconies, set around a landscaped garden and large swimming pool.

Summer Beach Inn HOTEL **$$**
(0 3823 1777; Th Hat Jomtien; r 700-900B;) Uninspired but fair-enough rooms in an anonymous high-rise hotel far from Pattaya's vice.

★ **Rabbit Resort** HOTEL **$$$**
(0 3825 1730; www.rabbitresort.com; Hat Dongtan; r 3700-11,000B;) Rabbit Resort has stunning, stylish and secluded bungalows and villas that showcase Thai design and art, all set in beachfront forest hidden between Jomtien and Pattaya Tai. There are no rabbits here, but it's a perfect choice for families with a couple of swimming pools and easy beach access.

Birds & Bees Resort HOTEL **$$$**
(0 3825 0556; www.cabbagesandcondoms.co.th; Soi 4, Th Phra Tamnak; r 2000-12,000B;) Retreat into a tropical garden resort bisected by meandering paths and decorated with tongue-in-cheek artwork. The cheaper rooms are a little drab for the price, but there's a semi-private beach and an incongruous wholesomeness for a resort affiliated with PDA, the Thai family planning NGO that promotes condom use.

Woodlands Resort HOTEL **$$$**
(0 3842 1707; www.woodland-resort.com; cnr Soi 22, 164/1 Th Naklua; r 2500-5200B;) A surprisingly affordable quality resort, marred only by the 300B per day fee for wi-fi; Woodlands Resort is low-key and professional with light, airy rooms, a tropical garden and two swimming pools.

Eating

Pattaya is a package holiday town, so there are a lot of overpriced, mediocre restaurants. But the seafood is always good.

Leng Kee THAI-CHINESE **$**
(Th Pattaya Klang; dishes 100-300B; 24hr) Pattaya has a thriving Chinatown run by families who expertly balance their Thai

and Chinese heritage. Leng Kee specialises in duck dishes, but is city-renowned during Chinese New Year when the menu goes vegetarian and includes golden good-luck noodles.

Mae Sai Tong THAI $

(Th Pattaya Klang; dishes 50B) Next to the day market, a fine spot for cheap fried rice and noodle dishes, this stand is famous for selling *kôw nĕe·o má·môo·ang* (ripe mango with sticky rice) all year round. Everyone else has to wait for the hot-dry season to compete.

★Mum Aroi THAI $$

(0 3822 3252; 83/4 Soi 4, Th Naklua; dishes 180-380B; 5-10pm) 'Delicious corner' is a contemporary glass-and-concrete restaurant perched beside the sea in the fishing village end of Naklua. Old fishing boats sit marooned offshore and crisp ocean breezes envelop diners as they greedily devour fantastic Thai food. Try *sôm·đam Ƀoo* (spicy papaya salad with crab) and *Ƀlah mèuk nêung ma-now* (squid steamed in lime juice). You'll need to charter a baht bus to get here (one way 100B).

Nang Nual THAI $$

(0 3842 8478; Walking St; dishes 80-500B; 11am-11pm) Pattaya's most famous seafood restaurant now spreads across both sides of Walking St. The dishes are pleasant, if not spectacular, and the fish are all on display. The section of the restaurant on the waterfront has an outdoor deck offering bay views.

Abu Saeed MIDDLE EASTERN $$

(363/13 Soi 16, off Walking St; dishes 60-300B; 8am-midnight) Soi 16 is Pattaya's Arab quarter, home to shisha cafes and authentic Middle Eastern cuisine. This long-established, alcohol-free place is always busy. The house speciality is couscous royale and the menu ranges across the Middle East.

Ban Amphur THAI $$

(dishes 100-380B; 11am-11pm) This fishing village 15km south of Pattaya is a dinner destination for Thais. A half-dozen seafood restaurants line the beach road and some are so large the waiters use walkie-talkies. Pick one that doesn't seem lonely or overwhelmed and order all the seafood specialities. You'll have to hire transport to get here.

Sketch Book Art Cafe INTERNATIONAL-THAI $$

(Th Tha Phraya; dishes 90-640B; 8am-11pm;) A cool, surprising place to find in Jomtien. There's a pleasant garden, while inside the walls are covered with paintings by customers; kids will like it. Decent steaks, as well as Western and Thai faves. They sell art supplies, too.

La Baguette BAKERY $$

(0 3842 1707; 164/1 Th Naklua; dishes 210-360B; 8am-midnight;) This posh cafe is a favourite of upmarket Thais. Great salads, yummy pastries and crepes and lots of coffee options.

PATTAYA – GLOBAL RETIREMENT HOME

Pattaya! The very name conjures up images of aged sex tourists walking seedy streets lined with scantily clad women trying to entice them into beer bars and go-go shows.

Yet, despite the very obvious sex industry here, there's no question that Pattaya is Thailand's only truly international city after Bangkok. From its beginnings as a quiet fishing village transformed by the arrival of US servicemen on leave from the Vietnam War, to the booming metropolis it is now, Pattaya has always attracted visitors from all over the world.

Russians and Chinese are a huge presence, but there's also a thriving Arab community centred around Soi 16 at the south end of Walking St. In contrast, Naklua is home to many Germans and Scandinavians.

In their wake have come increasing numbers of shops offering specialist services and goods for foreigners, whether it's South American coffee or French cheese.

It's the presence of those amenities, as well as the climate and cheap cost of living compared to the West, that has helped turn sleazy Pattaya into one of the world's most popular retirement havens.

Accurate figures are hard to come by, but it's likely that over 50,000 foreigners call Pattaya home now, with many more spending part of the year here. And as the city continues to adapt to their presence, those numbers are set to increase.

Traktirr Zaharovna RUSSIAN $$

(Th Pattaya Sai btwn Soi 1 & 2; dishes 120-400B; 11am-midnight) With so many Russians in Pattaya now, there are a growing number of places offering food from the old country. This one is Russian-run and serves up classic dishes like borscht, as well as a good range of salads.

Mantra INTERNATIONAL $$$

(0 3842 9591; Th Hat Pattaya; dishes 160-1240B; 5pm-midnight Mon-Sat, 11am-2pm & 5pm-midnight Sun;) Industrial cool and rather posh for Pattaya, Mantra is fun even if you can only afford a classy cocktail (from 180B). The menu combines Japanese, Thai and Western dishes and it's a popular spot for Sunday brunch.

Drinking & Nightlife

Despite the profusion of identikit beer bars, there are still some good places for a no-strings-attached drink.

Hopf Brew House BAR

(0 3871 0650; 219 Th Hat Pattaya; beers from 90B; 3pm-late) Moodily authentic in dark wood, the Hopf Brew House gets packed at weekends when there is live music. Beers and pizza (from 160B) are brewed and wood-fired on-site.

Green Bottle BAR

(0 3842 9675; 216/6-20 Th Pattaya Sai 2; beers from 65B) Cheap beer, pool and sport on the TV at this laid-back, dressed-down, wood-themed bar.

Gulliver's BAR

(0 3871 0641; Th Hat Pattaya; beers from 90B; 3pm-2am) The neo-colonial facade belies the sports bar inside. There are lots of screens for watching the football.

BYPASSING BANGKOK

An expanding network of bus and minivan services now connects the eastern seaboard with Suvarnabhumi airport, meaning that you don't have to transit through Bangkok for a flight arrival or departure. This is especially alluring to winter-weary visitors eager to reach a beach fast. Ko Samet is the closest prettiest beach to the airport and its southeastern beaches are serene enough for honeymooners. From the airport bus terminal, check the schedule for Rayong-bound buses and then catch a *sŏrng·tăa·ou* to reach the ferry pier to Ko Samet.

Lima Lima NIGHTCLUB

(Walking St; 7pm-late) International DJs, sometimes, and a mix of Russian and Western tourists, locals and expats. Free entry but the drinks are pricey.

Entertainment

Tiffany's THEATRE

(0 3842 1700; www.tiffany-show.co.th; 464 Th Pattaya Sai 2; admission 800-1200B; 6pm, 7.30pm & 9pm) Family-friendly ladyboy show (lots of sequins, satin and sentimental songs) and madly popular with Chinese tour groups and Russians.

Blues Factory LIVE MUSIC

(0 3830 0180; www.thebluesfactorypattaya.com; Soi Lucky Star, Walking St; 8.30pm-late) Classic rock (think '70s Americana) is performed every night at this long-running venue.

Information

DANGERS & ANNOYANCES

So many people are so drunk in this town that all sorts of mayhem ensues (fighting, pickpocketing and reckless driving) after dark. Keep your wits about you and leave the passport and credit cards at your hotel.

EMERGENCY

Tourist Police (emergency 1155; tourist@police.go.th) The head office is beside the Tourism Authority of Thailand office on Th Phra Tamnak with police boxes along Pattaya and Jomtien beaches.

MEDIA

Pattaya Mail (www.pattayamail.com) is the city's English-language weekly. **Pattaya One** (www.pattayaone.net) is a website that offers an intriguing insight into the darker side of the city.

MEDICAL SERVICES

Bangkok Pattaya Hospital (0 3842 9999; www.bph.co.th; 301 Th Sukhumvit, Naklua; 24hr) For first-class health care.

MONEY

There are banks and ATMs throughout the city.

POST

Post Office (Soi 13/2, Th Pattaya Sai 2)

TOURIST INFORMATION

Tourism Authority of Thailand (TAT; 0 3842 8750; 609 Th Phra Tamnak; 8.30am-4.30pm) Located at the northwestern edge of Rama IX Park. The helpful staff have brochures and maps.

Getting There & Away

Pattaya's airport is **U-Taphao Airfield** (☎ 0 3824 5599), 33km south of town. **Bangkok Airways** (☎ 0 3841 2382; www.bangkokair.com; 179/85-212 Th Pattaya Sai 2) flies from here.

The main bus station is on Th Pattaya Neua.

Minivans heading north to Bangkok leave from the corner of Th Sukhumvit and Th Pattaya Klang.

Pattaya Train Station (☎ 0 3842 9285) is off Th Sukhumvit south of town.

Getting Around

Locally known as 'baht buses', *sŏrng·tăa·ou* do a loop along the major roads; just hop on and pay 10B when you get off. If you're going all the way to or from Jomtien to Naklua, you might have to change vehicles at the dolphin roundabout in Pattaya Neua and the price goes up to 20B. Baht buses run to the bus station from the dolphin roundabout as well. If you're going further afield, you can charter a baht bus; establish the price beforehand.

Motorbikes can be hired around town for 200B a day.

Rayong & Ban Phe ระยอง/บ้านเพ

POP 106,737/16,717

You're most likely to transit through these towns en route to Ko Samet. Rayong has frequent bus connections to elsewhere and the little port of Ban Phe has ferry services to Ko Samet. Blue *sŏrng·tăa·ou* link the two towns (25B, 45 minutes, every 15 minutes).

Sleeping

Rayong President Hotel HOTEL $

(☎ 0 3861 1307; www.rayongpresident.com; Th Sukhumvit, Rayong; d & tw 400B; ❄ wi-fi) From the bus station, cross to the other side of Th Sukhumvit and walk to the right. The hotel is down a side street that starts next to the Siam Commercial Bank; look for the sign.

Christie's Guesthouse GUESTHOUSE $

(☎ 0 3865 1976; 280/92 Soi 1, Ban Phe; r 600B; ❄ wi-fi) Christie's is a comfortable place near the pier if you need a room, meal or a book.

Getting There & Away

Minivans from Rayong's bus station go to Bangkok's eastern (Ekamai) and northern (Mo Chit)

TRANSPORT TO/FROM PATTAYA

DESTINATION	BUS	MINIVAN	TRAIN	AIR
Bangkok's Eastern Bus Terminal	124B; 2hr; every 30min 4.30am-11pm	40B; 2hr; frequent		
Bangkok Suvarnabhumi International Airport	250B; 2hr; 7 daily 6pm-7pm	140B; 2hr; frequent		
Bangkok Northern Bus Terminal	133B; 2½hr; every 30min 4.30am-9pm	140B; 2½hr; frequent		
Bangkok Southern Bus Terminal	124B; 2½hr; hourly 6am-6.30pm			
Bangkok Hua Lamphong		38B; 3½hr; 1 daily		
Ko Chang		300B; 3½hr; 3 daily		
Ko Samet		200B; 2hr; 4 daily		
Ko Samui				from 3890B; 13½hr; daily
Phuket				from 2590B; 14hr; daily
Rayong	90B; 1½hr; frequent	100B; 1½hr; frequent		
Si Racha	40B; 45min; frequent	40B; 50min; frequent	30B; 1¼hr; 1 daily	

BEACH ADMISSION FEE

Ko Samet is part of the Mu Ko Samet National Park and charges all visitors an entrance fee (adult/child 200/100B) upon arrival. If you can prove that you live and work in Thailand, you'll get in for 40B, the price Thais pay. The fee is collected at the national parks office (p113) in Hat Sai Kaew; *sǒrng·tǎa·ou* from the pier will stop at the gates for payment. Hold on to your ticket for later inspections.

bus terminals, as well as Suvarnabhumi Airport (160B, 3½ hours, frequently 5am to 8pm).

There are also minivans to Chanthaburi (120B, 2½ hours, frequent) and Pattaya (100B, 1½ hours, frequent).

Buses from Ban Phe's bus station (near Tha Thetsaban) go to/from Bangkok's Eastern (Ekamai) station (173B, four hours, hourly 6am to 6pm).

Ban Phe also has minivan services to Laem Ngop for boats to Ko Chang (300B, four hours, three daily), Pattaya (230B, two hours, three daily) and Bangkok's Victory Monument (250B, four hours, hourly 7am to 6pm).

There are also boats to/from Ko Samet.

Ko Samet เกาะเสม็ด

An idyll island, Ko Samet bobs in the sea with a whole lot of scenery: small sandy bays bathed by clear aquamarine water. You'll have to share all this prettiness with other beach lovers as it's an easy weekend escape from Bangkok, as well as a major package-tour destination.

But considering its proximity and popularity, Ko Samet is surprisingly underdeveloped with a thick jungle interior crouching beside the low-rise hotels. There are, though, plans in place to redevelop the main street that runs from the pier to Hat Sai Kaew, so expect some changes. The interior road around the island remains rutted and largely unpaved, however most beach-hopping is done the old-fashioned way, by foot along wooded trails skirting the coastline.

Sights & Activities

On some islands you beach-hop, but on Ko Samet you cove-hop. The coastal footpath traverses rocky headlands, cicada-serenaded forests and one stunning bay after another. The mood becomes successively more mellow the further south you go.

Hat Sai Kaew BEACH

Starting in the island's northeastern corner, Hat Sai Kaew, or 'Diamond Sand', is the island's widest and whitest stretch of sand, as well as its busiest beach. With sunbathers, sarong-sellers, speedboats, jet-skis, resorts and restaurants galore, the people-watching here is part of the appeal. At night, the scene is equally rambunctious with late-night parties and karaoke sessions.

At the southern end of Hat Sai Kaew are the prince and **mermaid statues** that memorialise Samet's literary role in *Phra Aphaimani,* the great Thai epic by Sunthorn Phu. The story follows the travails of a prince exiled to an undersea kingdom ruled by a lovesick female giant (who has her own lonely statue in Hat Puak Tian in Phetchaburi). A mermaid aids the prince in his escape to Ko Samet, where he defeats the giant by playing a magic flute.

Ao Hin Khok & Ao Phai BEACH

Less frenetic than their northern neighbour, Ao Hin Khok and Ao Phai are two gorgeous bays separated by rocky headlands. The crowd here tends to be younger and more stylish than the tour groups who gather in Hat Sai Kaew; these two beaches are the traditional backpacker party centres of the island.

Ao Phutsa (Ao Tub Tim) BEACH

Further still is wide and sandy Ao Phutsa (Ao Tub Tim), a favourite for solitude seekers, families and couples who need access to 'civilisation' but not a lot of other stimulation.

Ao Wong Deuan BEACH

A smaller sister to Hat Sai Kaew, Ao Wong Deuan is a lovely crescent-shaped bay. Busy at the weekends, it's much more relaxed during the week.

Ao Thian BEACH

Ao Thian (Candlelight Beach) is punctuated by big boulders that shelter small sandy spots creating a castaway ambience. More developed than it once was, it's still one of Samet's most easy-going beaches and is deliciously lonely on weekdays. On weekends, Bangkok university students serenade the stars with all-night guitar sessions.

Ko Samet

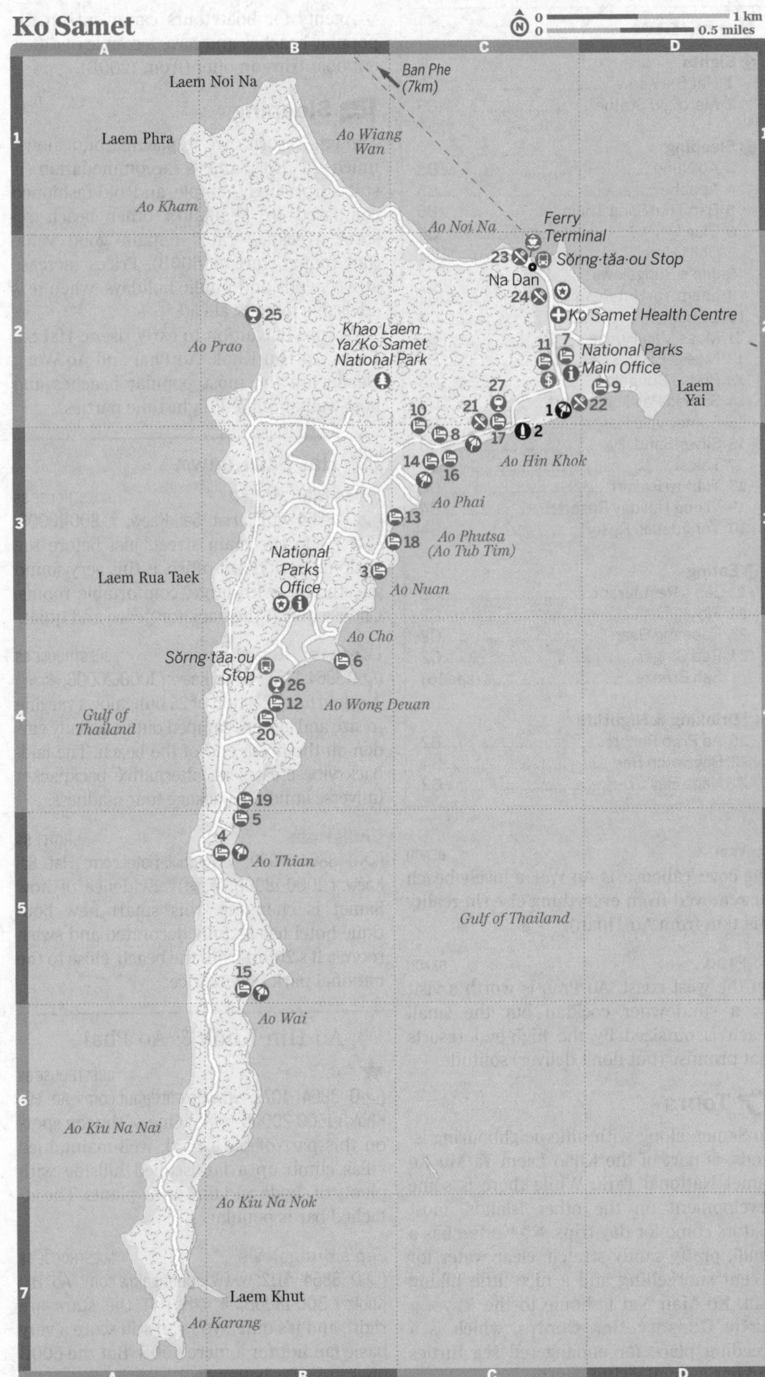
0 1 km
0 0.5 miles
Ban Phe (7km)
Laem Noi Na
Laem Phra
Ao Wiang Wan
Ao Kham
Ao Noi Na
Ferry Terminal
23
Sŏrng·tăa·ou Stop
Na Dan
24
Ko Samet Health Centre
25
Ao Prao
Khao Laem Ya/Ko Samet National Park
7
11
National Parks Main Office
9
Laem Yai
27
10
21
1
22
8
17
2
Ao Hin Khok
14
16
Ao Phai
13
18
Ao Phutsa (Ao Tub Tim)
National Parks Office
3
Laem Rua Taek
Ao Nuan
Ao Cho
Sŏrng·tăa·ou Stop
6
26
12
Ao Wong Deuan
Gulf of Thailand
20
19
5
4
Ao Thian
Gulf of Thailand
15
Ao Wai
Ao Kiu Na Nai
Ao Kiu Na Nok
Laem Khut
Ao Karang

Ko Samet

Sights

1 Hat Sai Kaew C2
2 Mermaid Statue C3

Sleeping

3 Ao Nuan B3
4 Apache B5
5 Ban Thai Sang Thain B5
6 Blue Sky B4
7 Chilli Hotel C2
8 Jep's Bungalows C3
9 Laem Yai Hut Resort D2
10 Le Blanc C3
11 Moss Man House C2
12 Nice & Easy B4
13 Pudsa Bungalow C3
14 Samed Pavilion Resort C3
15 Samet Ville Resort B5
16 Silver Sand C3
17 Tok's C2
18 Tubtim Resort C3
19 Viking Holiday Resort B4
20 Vongdeuan Resort B4

Eating

21 Jep's Restaurant C2
22 Ploy C2
23 Rabeang Baan C2
24 Red Ginger C2
Sea Breeze .... (see 16)

Drinking & Nightlife

25 Ao Prao Resort B2
26 Baywatch Bar B4
27 Naga Bar C2

Ao Wai BEACH
The cove 'caboose' is Ao Wai, a lovely beach far removed from everything else (in reality it is 1km from Ao Thian).

Ao Prao BEACH
On the west coast, Ao Prao is worth a visit for a sundowner cocktail but the small beach is outsized by the high-end resorts that promise (but don't deliver) solitude.

Tours

Ko Samet, along with nine neighbouring islands, is part of the Khao Laem Ya/Mu Ko Samet National Park. While there is some development on the other islands, most visitors come for day trips. **Ko Kudee** has a small, pretty sandy stretch, clear water for decent snorkelling and a nice little hiking trail. Ko Man Nai is home to the **Rayong Turtle Conservation Centre**, which is a breeding place for endangered sea turtles and has a small visitor centre.

Agents for boat tours camp out on the popular beaches and have a couple of different boat trips on offer (from 1200B).

Sleeping

Though resorts are replacing bungalows, much of Ko Samet's accommodation is still surprisingly simple and old-fashioned compared to Thailand's other beach resorts. Weekday rates remain good value (fan rooms start at 600B). Prices increase at weekends and public holidays, when it is advisable to book ahead.

A word of caution to early risers: Hat Sai Kaew, Ao Hin Khok, Ao Phai and Ao Wong Deuan are the most popular beaches and host well-amplified night-time parties.

Hat Sai Kaew

Moss Man House GUESTHOUSE $$
(0 3864 4017; Hat Sai Kaew; r 800-1000B;) On the main street, just before the national park ticket office, is this very sound guesthouse, with large, comfortable rooms. Choose one at the back for peace and quiet.

Laem Yai Hut Resort GUESTHOUSE $$
(0 3864 4282; Hat Sai Kaew; r 1000-2000B;) A colourful collection of 25 bungalows varying in size and age are camped out in a shady garden on the north end of the beach. The laid-back vibe creates an alternative backpacker universe amid the package tour madness.

Chilli Hotel HOTEL $$
(0 3864 4039; www.chilli-hotel.com; Hat Sai Kaew; r 1000-1800B;) Evidence of how Samet is changing, this smart new boutique hotel has artfully decorated and swish rooms. It's 200m from the beach, close to the national park ticket office.

Ao Hin Khok & Ao Phai

★ **Tok's** GUESTHOUSE $$
(0 3864 4073; www.tok-littlehut.com; Ao Hin Khok; r 1500-2000B;) One of the top spots on this part of the island, well-maintained villas climb up a landscaped hillside with plenty of shade and flowering plants. The attached bar is popular.

Jep's Bungalows GUESTHOUSE $$
(0 3864 4112; www.jepbungalow.com; Ao Hin Khok; r 300-1800B; @) If the stars are right, and it's quiet, you can still score a very basic fan hut for a mere 300B. But the 600B ones are a far better deal.

Le Blanc GUESTHOUSE $$
(0 3861 1646; www.leblancsamed.com; Ao Hin Khok; r 1500-2500B;) Formerly known as Ao Pai, this place has gone upmarket and re-branded itself with smart, all-white bungalows. They're perched amid trees and there's enough space between them for proper privacy.

Silver Sand HOTEL $$
(0 3864 4300; www.silversandsamed.com; Ao Phai; r 2000-4000B;) An expanding empire, Silver Sand is a mini-resort, complete with bar, restaurant and shops. It's a little impersonal but the rooms are flashpacker quality and on a super strip of beach.

Samed Pavilion Resort HOTEL $$$
(0 3864 4420; www.samedpavilionresort.com; Ao Phai; r 3000-5000B;) Part of the Jep family (the posh branch), this new-ish boutique resort comes with all the trimmings and has elegant, sizeable rooms.

Ao Phutsa & Ao Nuan

Tubtim Resort HOTEL $$
(0 3864 4025; www.tubtimresort.com; Ao Phutsa; r 600-3600B;) Well-organised place with great, nightly barbecues and a range of solid, spacious bungalows of varying quality all close to the same dreamy beach. It's popular with upmarket Thais.

Ao Nuan GUESTHOUSE $$
(Ao Nuan; r 600-2500B;) The inventor of chillaxin' on Ko Samet, quirky Ao Nuan has both very simple wooden bungalows and a few posh ones with air-con and sea views. No reservations. Nor is there any internet access; you hang out in the attached restaurant and talk to people. Old school!

Pudsa Bungalow GUESTHOUSE $$
(0 3864 4030; Ao Phutsa; r 600-1700B;) The nicer bungalows with beach views are trimmed with driftwood, and look their age now, but this is still a good place to kick back and listen to the sound of the sea.

Ao Wong Deuan & Ao Thian (Candlelight Beach)

Ferries run between Ao Wong Deuan and Ban Phe (140B return), with increased services at the weekend.

To get to Ao Thian, catch a ferry to Ao Wong Deuan and walk south over the headland. It's also a quick walk from here to the west side of the island – look for the marked trail on Ao Thian.

Blue Sky GUESTHOUSE $
(08 9936 0842; Ao Wong Deuan; r 800-1200B;) A rare budget spot on Ao Wong Deuan, Blue Sky has beaten-up bungalows set on a rocky headland. Though we love cheapies, budgeteers will get better value on other beaches.

Apache GUESTHOUSE $
(08 1452 9472; www.apachesamed.com; Ao Thian; r 800-1300B;) Still one of the most chilled spots on Samet, Apache's bungalows have seen better days but are good enough. The bar/restaurant is popular with people who like to roll their own cigarettes.

Nice & Easy HOTEL $$
(0 3864 4370; nice.easy_samed.island@hotmail.com; Ao Wong Deuan; r 1200-2000B;) As the name suggests, a very amenable place with comfortable, modern and big bungalows set around a garden behind the beach. A decent deal for this part of Samet.

Viking Holiday Resort HOTEL $$
(0 3864 4353; www.sametvikingresort.com; Ao Thian; r 1200-2000B;) Ao Thian's most upscale spot with comfortable, if not very modern, rooms. There are only nine of them so book ahead. Pleasant staff and OK restaurant.

AO PRAO OIL SPILL

In late July 2013, the east coast of Ko Samet was severely affected by the fourth-largest oil spill in Thailand's history. Around 50,000 litres of crude oil gushed out of a pipeline operated by PTT Global Chemical, a subsidiary of Thailand's largest energy company, into the Gulf of Thailand close to Samet.

Worst hit was the beach of Ao Prao, where an estimated 20% of the oil ended up. After a massive clean-up operation, the beach has been restored to its usual, sandy state. Less certain, though, is the condition of the ocean, with reports in the Thai media stating that the number of fish being caught in the area has plummeted since the spill.

For now, we don't advise swimming off Ao Prao. But check with the locals to ascertain the current situation.

GETTING TO CAMBODIA: BAN PAKARD TO PSAR PRUHM

Getting to the Border Minivans (☎08 1949 0455) depart from a stop across the river from River Guest House in Chanthaburi to Ban Pakard/Pong Nam Ron (150B, 1½ hours, two daily).

At the Border This is a far less busy and more pleasant crossing than Poipet further north. You need a passport photo and US$20 for the visa fee.

Moving On Hop on a motorbike taxi to Pailin. From there, you can catch frequent shared taxis ($5 per person, 1½ hours) to scenic Battambang. After that, you can move on to Siem Reap by boat, or Phnom Penh by bus.

Ban Thai Sang Thain HOTEL $$
(☎08 1305 9408; www.bathaisangthain.com; Ao Thian; r 1000-2000B; ❄📶) Think of traditional Thai architecture with a tree-house twist and you'll sum up this family-run place, which offers rooms rather than bungalows. It's slap in the centre of the beach.

Vongdeuan Resort HOTEL $$$
(☎0 3864 4171; www.vongdeuan.com; Ao Wong Deuan; r 2500-4500B; ❄📶🏊) This sprawling resort occupies much of the southern part of Ao Wong Deuan with its gardenlike setting. Popular with families and efficiently run, the smart bungalows come with the best bathrooms in this part of the world.

Ao Wai

Ao Wai is about 1km from Ao Thian but can be reached from Ban Phe by chartered speedboat.

Samet Ville Resort HOTEL $$$
(☎0 3865 1682; www.sametvilleresort.com; Ao Wai; r 1080-4500B; ❄📶) Under a forest canopy, it's a case of 'spot the sky' at the only resort at this secluded bay. It is an unpretentious place with a range of rooms and cottages that suit most budgets. Plus, the beach is great.

Eating

Most hotels and guesthouses have restaurants that moonlight as bars after sunset. The food and the service won't blow you away, but there aren't many alternatives. Nightly beach barbecues are an island favourite but pick one that looks professionally run and popular. There are cheapie Thai places in town.

Rabeang Baan THAI $
(Na Dan; dishes 70-120B; ⏰8am-10pm) Right by the ferry terminal, this spot has food so good you'll forget you have to leave the island. It's busier at lunch than dinner.

Jep's Restaurant INTERNATIONAL $
(Ao Hin Khok; mains 60-150B; ⏰7am-11pm) Canopied by the branches of an arching tree decorated with lights, this pretty place does a little of everything. It's right on the beach.

Red Ginger INTERNATIONAL-THAI $$
(Na dan; dishes 125-285B; ⏰11am-10pm) Small but select menu of the French-Canadian chef's favourite dishes at this atmospheric eatery in between the pier and Hat Saw Kaew. Good salads, great oven-baked ribs. There's Thai food, too.

Sea Breeze SEAFOOD $$
(Ao Phai; dishes 80-500B; ⏰11am-11pm) Appropriately named: you can dine on a wide range of seafood right on Ao Phai's pretty beach here. There's some Western food on the menu as well.

Ploy SEAFOOD $$
(Hat Sai Kaew; dishes 50-400B; ⏰11am-11pm) Long-established, massive operation that's packed most nights with Thais crunching crabs and lobster. Huge array of dishes and a humming bar too.

Drinking & Nightlife

On weekends, Ko Samet is a boisterous night-owl with provincial tour groups crooning away on karaoke machines or the young ones slurping down beer and buckets to a techno beat. The bar scene changes depending on who is around but there is usually a crowd on Hat Sai Khao, Ao Hin Khok, Ao Phai and Ao Wong Deuan.

Baywatch Bar BAR
(Ao Wong Deuan; beers from 80B) A good spot for after-dark beach-gazing, with a fun crowd and strong cocktails.

Naga Bar BAR
(Ao Hin Khok; beers from 70B) This busy beachfront bar comes with a *moo·ay tai* ring, although the days of drunk foreigners getting battered by the locals are long gone. Instead, you get DJs and lots of whisky and vodka/Red Bull buckets.

Ao Prao Resort BAR
(Ao Prao; drinks from 90B;) On the sunset-side of the island, there's a lovely sea-view restaurant perfect for a sundowner. You'll need private transport to reach it.

Information

There are several ATMs on Ko Samet, including those near the Na Dan pier, Ao Wong Deuan and Ao Thian.

Ko Samet Health Centre (0 3861 1123; 8.30am-9pm Mon-Fri, 8.30am-4.30pm Sat & Sun) On the main road between Na Dan and Hat Sai Kaew. On-call mobile numbers are posted for after-hours emergencies.

National Parks Main Office (btwn Na Dan & Hat Sai Kaew; sunrise-sunset) Has another office on Ao Wong Deuan.

Police Station (1155) On the main road between Na Dan and Hat Sai Kaew. There's a substation on Ao Wong Deuan.

Getting There & Away

Ko Samet is accessed via the mainland piers in Ban Phe. There are dozens of piers each used by different ferry companies, but they all charge the same fares (one way/return 70/100B, 40 minutes, hourly 8am to 5pm) and dock at Na Dan, the main pier on Ko Samet. The last boat back to the mainland leaves at 6pm.

If you're staying at Ao Wong Deuan or further south, catch a ferry from the mainland directly to the beach (one way/return 90/140B, one hour, three daily departures).

Speedboats charge 200B one way and will drop you at the beach of your choice, but they only leave when they have enough passengers.

Getting Around

Ko Samet's small size makes it a great place to explore on foot. A network of dirt roads connects most of the western side of the island.

Green *sŏrng·tăa·ou* meet arriving boats at the pier and provide drop-offs at the various beaches (100B to 400B, depending on the beach). The same fares apply no matter how many people are on board.

You can rent motorcycles nearly everywhere along the northern half of the island. Expect to pay 300B per day. The dirt roads are rough and hazardous, and larger vehicles can leave behind blinding dust clouds. Test the brakes before you drive off and exercise caution.

Chanthaburi จันทบุรี

POP 99,819

Chanthaburi is proof that all that glitters is not gold. Here, gemstones do the sparkling, attracting international traders, including many South Asians, dealing in sapphires, rubies, emeralds, agate and jade. Thanks to the gem market and Chanthaburi's multicultural history (French, Vietnamese and Chinese), the so-called 'City of the Moon' is surprisingly diverse for a regional Thai town. It's well worth visiting for an appreciation of the economic and religious sanctuary Thailand has long provided in the region.

WORTH A TRIP

NATIONAL PARKS NEAR CHANTHABURI

Two small national parks are easily reached from Chanthaburi, and make good day trips. Both are malarial, so take the usual precautions.

Khao Khitchakut National Park (อุทยานแห่งชาติเขาคิชฌกูฏ; 0 3945 2074; admission 200B; 6am-6pm) is 28km northeast of town. The cascade of **Nam Tok Krathing** is the main attraction; though it is only worth a visit just after the rainy season.

To get to Khao Khitchakut, take a *sŏrng·tăa·ou* from next to the post office, near the northern side of the market in Chanthaburi (35B, 45 minutes). The *sŏrng·tăa·ou* stops 1km from the park headquarters on Rte 3249, from which point you'll have to walk. Returning transport is scarce so expect to wait or hitch.

Nam Tok Phlio National Park (อุทยานแหง่ ชาติน้ำตกพลิ้ว; 0 3943 4528; admission 200B; 8.30am-4.30pm), off Hwy 3, is 14km to the southeast of Chanthaburi and is much more popular. A pleasant, 1km nature trail loops around the waterfalls, which teem with soro brook carp. To get to the park, catch a *sŏrng·tăa·ou* from the northern side of the market in Chanthaburi to the park entrance (50B, 30 minutes). You'll get dropped off about 1km from the entrance.

Accommodation is available at both parks; book with the **park reservation system** (0 2562 0760; www.dnp.go.th).

Chanthaburi

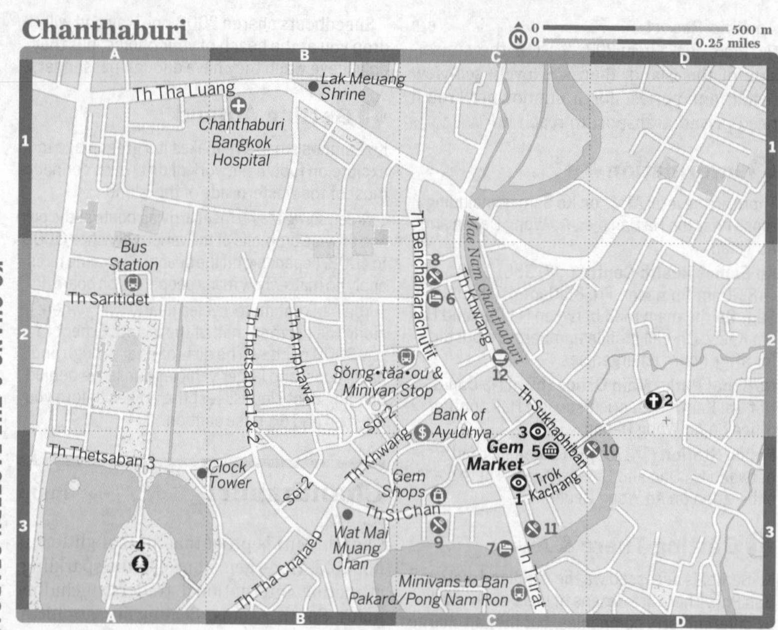

The old city (also known as the Chantaboon Waterfront Community) is the best place to chart the course of immigration and international involvement in the city. The Vietnamese began arriving in the 19th century when Christian refugees escaped religious and political persecution in Cochin China (southern Vietnam). A second wave of Vietnamese refugees followed in the 1920s and 1940s, fleeing French rule, and a third arrived after the 1975 communist takeover of southern Vietnam. The French occupied Chanthaburi from 1893 to 1905, a consequence of a dispute over the border between Siam and Indochina.

Sights & Activities

★Gem Market MARKET

(ตลาดพลอย; Th Si Chan & Trok Kachang; Fri, Sat & Sun) On weekends, the streets and side streets near Th Si Chan (or 'Gem Rd') overflow with the banter and intrigue of the hard sell. Incongruously humble considering the value of the commodities on offer, people cluster around makeshift tables or even a trader's outstretched palm, examining small piles of unset stones.

In the more formal shops, hard-eyed staff examine the gemstones under magnifying glasses looking for quality and authenticity. Buying and selling gems here is not recommended for the uninitiated, but it is a fascinating glimpse at a relatively private trade.

In the hills surrounding Chanthaburi, several sapphire and ruby mines once supplied the palace with fine ornaments prior to the mid-19th century when the mines were developed into commercial operations by Shan (Burmese) traders. These days, locally mined gems are of inferior international quality but the resourceful Chanthaburi traders roam the globe acquiring precious and semi-precious stones, which are in turn traded here to other globetrotters.

The last remaining mine in the area is **Khao Phloi Waen**, 6km from town, which is famous locally for its 'Mekong Whiskey' yellow-coloured sapphire.

Chantaboon Waterfront Community HISTORICAL SITE

(Th Sukhaphiban) Along the banks of Mae Nam Chanthaburi is a 1km stretch of old wooden houses that are valiantly being preserved. It makes for an atmospheric stroll with a typical Thai twist: food features more prominently than facts. Stop by the **Learning House** (08 1945 5761; 9am-5pm), which displays historic photos, paintings and architectural drawings that reveal the community's history.

Of especial interest are the drawings of the homes' beautifully carved ventilation panels. Much of the community's immigrant past is revealed in these unique panels: there are carvings of Chinese characters and even French fleurs-de-lis.

Farmers and merchants first settled on the fertile river banks some 300 years ago, establishing the area as an agricultural trading post. Chinese traders and economic migrants sought refuge here, thus diversifying the local population. Vietnamese Catholics fled from religious persecution in their home country. And before long the different groups had intermarried until everyone claimed a little bit of each culture.

Today, the older generation remains in the rickety old houses but increasing numbers of domestic tourists are coming for weekend outings to eat Chinese, Thai and Vietnamese specialities and listen to all the old stories.

Cathedral CHURCH

(east bank of Mae Nam Chanthaburi; ⏲daylight hours) This French-style cathedral, across a footbridge from Th Sukhaphiban, is the town's architectural highlight. A small missionary chapel was built here in 1711, when Vietnamese Catholics and a French priest arrived. The original has undergone four reconstructions between 1712 and 1906 and is now the largest building of its kind in Thailand.

Chanthaburi

Top Sights

1 Gem Market C3

Sights

2 Cathedral D2
3 Chantaboon Waterfront Community C2
4 King Taksin Park A3
5 Learning House C3

Sleeping

6 Kasemsarn Hotel C2
7 River Guest House C3

Eating

8 Chanthorn Phochana C2
9 Muslim Restaurant C3
10 Seafood Noodle Shop D3
11 Sony Yaday C3

Drinking & Nightlife

12 Sweet Moon C2

King Taksin Park PARK

(สวนสาธารณะสมเด็จพระเจ้าตากสิน; Th Tha Chalaep; ⏲daylight hours) The town's main oasis is filled with picnicking families and joggers. It's a pleasant spot for an evening stroll.

Festivals

Fruit Festival FOOD

(⏲May or Jun) At the end of May, or beginning of June, Chanthaburi's annual fruit

LIVING WITH HISTORY

Pratapan Chatmalai is the community leader of the Chantaboon Waterfront Community Association. She grew up here and fondly remembers Chantaboon's tight-knit community of culturally diverse people. Today, she works to save the stories and the character of this community in Chanthaburi.

What Does Your Organisation Do?

Now this community is a 'grandma' city. The old city is losing life and the young people have moved away. I want to keep the culture for the next generation to learn about and I'm trying to help the people in the area have a good life. We run the Learning House so that people can come look at the daily life of the past.

What Do You Recommend Tourists See or Do in the Old City?

There is unique history and lifestyle of the past here. Come look at the cathedral, Chinese shrines and old houses. Each house is different and mixes Thai, Chinese and Western styles. Eat at the local restaurants. There are seafood noodles, old-style ice cream and dim sum. If you get tired, you can have a massage in an old Thai-style house.

What Is Your Favourite Part of the Old City?

I love the whole place because it is a living museum and I can walk along and talk to the people about the past and make them happy.

As told to China Williams

festival is a great opportunity to sample the region's superb produce, especially rambutans, mangosteens and the ever-pungent durian.

Sleeping

Accommodation can get busy at weekends when the gem traders are in town.

River Guest House HOTEL $
(0 3932 8211; 3/5-8 Th Si Chan; r 190-490B;) Lumpy beds, boxlike rooms and tiny bathrooms, but this is as good as it gets in the budget range. The relaxed outdoor terrace is a plus. Try to score a room away from the highway.

Kasemsarn Hotel HOTEL $$
(0 3931 1100; www.hotelkasemsarn.com; 98/1 Th Benchamarachutit ; r 1300-4300B;) Good enough for visiting Bangkokians, Kasemsarn has modern rooms and friendly staff. Discounts of 30% are standard during the week.

Eating & Drinking

Seafood Noodle Shop THAI $
(Th Sukhaphiban; dishes 50-70B; 10.30am-9pm) The old city, along Mae Nam Chanthaburi, is where you'll find most sightseeing Thais eating this Chanthaburi variation of the basic rice-noodle theme; nearby are other homemade snacks.

Muslim Restaurant MUSLIM-THAI $
(08 1353 5174; cnr Soi 4, Th Si Chan; dishes 40-200B; 9.30am-9pm) Run by Thai Muslims, this place has excellent paratha, biryani, curries and chai tea. Most dishes are under 100B.

Sony Yaday INDIAN $
(Th Si Chan; dishes 50-100B; 8am-10pm;) Hole-in-the-wall Muslim vegetarian restaurant patronised by visiting South Asian gem traders.

Chanthorn Phochana THAI-CHINESE $$
(0 3931 2339; 102/5-8 Th Benchamarachutit; dishes 80-300B; 8am-10pm) The Thai-Chinese menu includes such specialities as stir-fried papaya and mangosteen wine. The soft-shell crab with black pepper is delicious. Pick up a bag of local durian chips (tastier than you think) for your next bus ride.

Sweet Moon CAFE
(Th Sukhaphibon; coffee from 35B;) Cool spot to sip a coffee or a fruit juice right by the river. Decent cakes, too.

Information

Banks with change facilities and ATMs can be found across town.

Bank of Ayudhya (Th Khwang)

Chanthaburi Bangkok Hospital (0 3935 1467; Th Tha Luang; 6am-9pm) Part of the Bangkok group; handles emergencies.

Getting There & Around

Chanthaburi's bus station is west of the river. Minivans leave from near the market.

Motorbike taxis charge 20B to 30B for trips around town.

Trat ตราด

POP 21,590

A major transit point for Ko Chang and coastal Cambodia, Trat's provincial charms are underappreciated. The guesthouse neighbourhood occupies an atmospheric wooden shophouse district, bisected by winding sois and filled with typical Thai street life: kids riding bikes, housewives running errands, small businesses selling trinkets and necessities. Since your destination is still far away, stay a little longer and enjoy all the things you can't get on the islands: fresh, affordable fruit, tasty noodles and tonnes of people-watching.

TRANSPORT TO/FROM CHANTHABURI

DESTINATION	BUS	MINIVAN
Bangkok Eastern (Ekamai) Bus Terminal	250B; 4hr; 25 daily	
Bangkok Northern (Mo Chit) Bus Terminal	214B; 4hr; 2 daily	
Khorat	292B; 4hr; hourly	
Rayong		100B; 2½hr; frequent
Sa Kaew	150B; 2hr; hourly	
Trat	74B; 1hr; every 30min	70B; 50min; frequent

Trat's signature product is a medicinal herbal oil (known in Thai as *nám·man lĕu·ang*), touted as a remedy for everything from arthritis to bug bites and available at local pharmacies. It's produced by resident Mae Ang-Ki (Somthawin Pasananon), using a secret pharmaceutical recipe that has been handed down through her Chinese-Thai family for generations. It's said that if you leave Trat without a couple of bottles of *nám·man lĕu·ang*, then you really haven't been here.

Sights

One booming business in the city is **swiftlet farming**. Walk down Th Lak Meuang and you'll soon figure out that the top floors of a shophouse have been purposefully converted into a nesting site for a flock of birds who produce the edible nests considered a delicacy among the Chinese. Swiflets' nests were quite rare (and expensive) because they were only harvested from precipitous sea caves by trained, daring climbers. But in the 1990s, entrepreneurs figured out how to replicate the cave atmosphere in multistorey shophouses and the business has become a key operation throughout Southeast Asia and here in Trat. Now many municipalities are dealing with the noise pollution of these moneymakers; have a listen for yourself.

Indoor Market MARKET
The indoor market sprawls east from Th Sukhumvit to Th Tat Mai and has a little bit of everything, especially all the things that you forgot to pack. Without really noticing the difference you will stumble upon the **day market**, selling fresh fruit, vegetables and takeaway food.

Sleeping

Trat has many budget hotels housed in traditional wooden houses on and around Th Thana Charoen.

Ban Jaidee Guest House GUESTHOUSE $
(☎08 3589 0839; banjaideehouse@yahoo.com; 6 Th Chaimongkol; r 200B; 🛜) In a charming neighbourhood, this relaxed traditional wooden house has simple rooms with shared bathrooms (hot-water showers). Paintings and objets d'art made by the artistically inclined owners decorate the common spaces. It's very popular and booking ahead is essential.

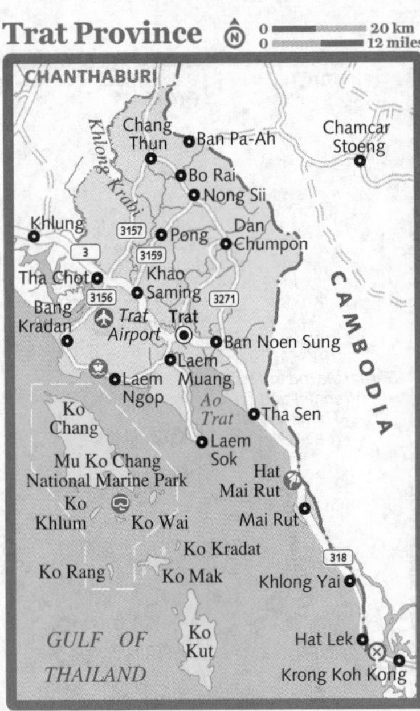

Pop Guest House GUESTHOUSE $
(☎0 3951 2392; 1/1 Th Thana Charoen; r 150-600B; ❄@🛜) The owner isn't the most popular man in Trat, thanks to his aggressive touting for guests which puts some travellers off, but Pop is an efficient and expanding – if bland – operation. There are many rooms here, all well-maintained, and the restaurant is OK, too.

NP Guest House GUESTHOUSE $
(☎0 3951 2270; Soi Yai On; r 150-400; ❄🛜) Tucked down a quiet soi running between Th Lak Meuang and Th Thana Charoen, this newcomer offers simple rooms with a few nice, decorative touches. The cheapest rooms have shared bathrooms.

Orchid GUESTHOUSE $
(☎0 3953 0474; orchidguesthouse@gmail.com; 92 Th Lak Meuang; r 150-600B; ❄🛜) Big, slightly battered rooms in a house with a large garden. The cheapest rooms are fan-only and share bathrooms. The excessively laid-back owner sometimes opens her attached restaurant, which serves rather good pizzas.

Trat

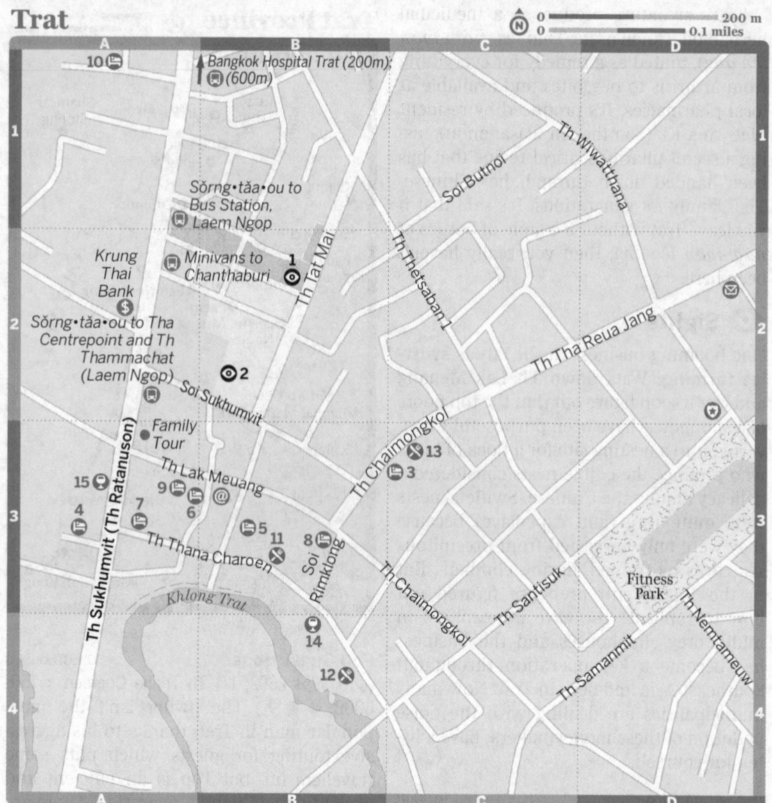

Trat

Sights

1 Day Market ...B2
2 Indoor Market ...B2

Sleeping

3 Ban Jaidee Guest House ...C3
4 Garden Guest House ...A3
5 NP Guest House ...B3
6 Orchid ...A3
7 Pop Guest House ...A3
8 Rimklong ...B3
9 Sawadee ...A3
10 Trat Center Hotel ...A1

Eating

11 Cool Corner Cafe ...B3
12 Pier 112 ...B4
13 Story House ...C3

Drinking & Nightlife

14 Cafe Oscar ...B4
15 Gru ...A3

Sawadee GUESTHOUSE $
(☎0 3953 0063; sawadee_23000@hotmail.com; 94 Th Lak Meuang; r 100-300B;) Located above an internet cafe in a converted shophouse, this simple family-run place has boxlike fan rooms with shared bathrooms.

Garden Guest House GUESTHOUSE $
(☎0 3952 1018; 87/1 Th Sukhumvit; r 150-350B) A cheerful grandmotherly type runs this guesthouse festooned with flowers and the flotsam of Thai life. Of the eight basic rooms, only one has a private bathroom.

Rimklong HOTEL $$
(☎0 3952 3388; soirimklong@hotmail.co.th; 194 Th Lak Meuang; r 800-900B;) Trat's only boutique hotel occupies both ends of the soi. Rooms are bright and welcoming, if a little small. There's a pleasant, attached cafe.

Trat Center Hotel HOTEL $$
(☎0 3953 1234; www.tratcenterhotel.com; 45/65 Th Tasaban 5; r 900B;) Spotless, modern rooms with comfy beds at this decent mid-range option. It's a 10-minute walk north of the day market.

Eating & Drinking

Trat is all about market eating: head to the day market on Th Tat Mai for *gah·faa bo·hrahn* (ancient coffee), the indoor market for lunchtime noodles, or the night market for a stir-fried dinner. Food stalls line Th Sukhumvit come nightfall.

★**Cool Corner Cafe** INTERNATIONAL-THAI $
(☎08 4159 2030; 49-51 Th Thana Charoen; dishes 60-160B; ⏰8am-10pm) Run by Khun Morn, a modern Renaissance woman (writer, artist and traveller) from Bangkok, Cool Corner is an anchor for Trat's expats. The cafe has a degree of sophistication that you don't usually find in provincial towns and serves up a great mix of Thai and Western dishes with an Indian influence, as well as beers, coffee and lassies.

Story House INTERNATIONAL-THAI $
(61-65 Th Chaimongkol; dishes 50-150B; ⏰9.30am-9.30pm) Bright and cheerful restaurant serving up Thai and Western classics, as well as sandwiches. It makes for a good coffee/smoothie stop as well.

Pier 112 THAI $$
(132/1 Th Thana Charoen; dishes 80-250B; ⏰10.30am-10.30pm;) Large selection of vegetarian dishes here, as well as reliable curries, and you can eat outside in a plant-festooned garden.

Cafe Oscar BAR
(Th Thana Charoen; beers from 55B; ⏰9am-2am) A very eclectic crew of locals and expats gather at this cubbyhole corner bar, with wooden furniture and a retro 1970s and '80s soundtrack. In low season, it opens in the evening only.

Gru BAR
(Th Sukhumvit; beers from 75B; ⏰6pm-late) Key local hang-out that sees few foreigners, with live music most nights and football on the TV at weekends.

Information

Th Sukhumvit runs through town, though it's often referred to as Th Ratanuson.

Bangkok Hospital Trat (☎0 3953 2735; www.bangkoktrathospital.com; 376 Moo 2, Th Sukhumvit; ⏰24hr) Best health care in the region. It's 400m north of the town centre.

Krung Thai Bank (Th Sukhumvit) Has an ATM and currency-exchange facilities.

Police Station (☎1155; cnr Th Santisuk & Th Wiwatthana) A short walk from Trat's centre.

Post Office (Th Tha Reua Jang) East of Trat's commercial centre.

Sawadee@Cafe Net (☎0 3952 0075; Th Lak Meuang; per min 1B; ⏰10am-10pm)

Trat Map (www.Tratmap.com) An online directory of businesses and attractions in Trat.

TRANSPORT TO/FROM TRAT

DESTINATION	BUS	MINIVAN	AIR
Bangkok Suvarnabhumi International Airport	272B; 5-6hr; 5 daily		from 2550B; 1hr; 3 daily
Bangkok Eastern (Ekamai) Bus Terminal	265B; 5hr; 17 daily		
Bangkok Northern (Mo Chit) Bus Terminal	272B; 5-6hr; 5 daily		
Chanthaburi	80B; 1hr; hourly 7.30am-11.30pm	70B; 50min; frequent 5am-7pm	
Hat Lek (for Cambodia)		120B; 1½hr; hourly 5am-6pm	
Pattaya	245B; 4hr; 1 daily	300B; 3½hr; hourly 7am-4pm	
Rayong/Ban Phe (for Ko Samet)		200B; 2½hr; hourly 5am-7pm	

WORTH A TRIP

SCRATCHING THE BEACH ITCH

If you're going through coastal withdrawal, the sliver of Trat Province that extends southeast towards Cambodia is fringed by sandy beaches. One of the easiest beaches to reach is **Hat Mai Rut**, roughly halfway between Trat and the border crossing of Hat Lek. Nearby is a traditional fishing village filled with colourful wooden boats and the sights and smells of a small-scale industry carried on by generations of families. **Mairood Resort** (☎08 9841 4858; www.mairood-resort.com; Km 53; r from 1300B ; ❄@🏊) is a lovely spot to stay overnight, with slick cottages by the sea and in the mangroves.

You can get to Hat Mai Rut from the Trat bus station via Hat Lek–bound *sǒrng·tǎa·ou*. The resort is 3km from the Km 53 highway marker.

Getting There & Around

Trat's bus station is 2km out of town.

Minivans leave from various points along Th Sukhumvit. **Family Tour** (☎08 1940 7380; Th Sukhumvit cnr Th Lak Meuang) has minivans to Bangkok's Victory Monument and northern (Mo Chit) bus terminal.

The three piers that handle boat traffic to Ko Chang, Ko Kut, Ko Mak and Ko Wai are located in Laem Ngop, about 30km southwest of Trat. For prices and departure times to the islands, see the section for each island.

Sǒrng·tǎa·ou to Laem Ngop and the piers (50B per person for six passengers, 200B for the whole vehicle, 35 to 50 minutes) leave from Th Sukhumvit just past the market.

Bangkok Airways (☎Trat airport 0 3955 1654/5, in Bangkok 0 2265 5555; www.bangkokair.com) operates flights from the airport, which is 40km from town. Taxis to Trat cost a ridiculous 600B.

Motorbike taxis charge 20B to 30B for local hops.

Motorbikes can be rented for 200B a day along Th Sukhumvit near the guesthouse area.

Ko Chang เกาะช้าง

POP 7033

With steep, jungle-covered peaks, picturesque Ko Chang (Elephant Island) retains its remote and rugged spirit despite its current status as a package-tour resort akin to Phuket. The island's swathes of sand are girl-next-door pretty but not beauty-queen gorgeous. What it lacks in sand, it makes up for in an unlikely combination: accessible wilderness with a thriving party scene. Convenient forays into a verdant jungle or underwater coral gardens can be enthusiastically toasted at one of Lonely Beach's many beer and bucket parties.

A little more than a decade ago, Ko Chang didn't have 24-hour electricity, was still considered malarial, had few paved roads and only a handful of motorised vehicles. Today, it is still a slog to get here, but there is a constant migration of visitors: Russian package tourists, Cambodia-bound backpackers and beach-hopping couples funnelling through to more remote islands in the Mu Ko Chang National Marine Park. Along the populous west coast are virtual mini-cities with a standard of living that has noticeably outpaced the island's infrastructure, a common problem on many Thai islands. Ko Chang struggles to provide decent sanitation and

KO CHANG IN...

Four Days

Lie on the beach, rotate your body and repeat, with occasional forays into the ocean. Do this until you get sunburned or bored and then rouse yourself out of your sun-induced stupor to explore the island. Do a **day hike** (p124) through the jungle or view the island from aboard a **kayak** (p123). Catch a *sǒrng·tǎa·ou* to **Ban Bang Bao** for lunch or an early dinner and work off your meal with some souvenir shopping. The next day rent a motorbike and explore the **east coast** (p123).

One Week

Migrate to the nearby islands of **Ko Wai** (p132) or **Ko Kut** (p134) for a little sightseeing, or devote a day or two giving back to the island by volunteering at **Koh Chang Animal Project**.

Ko Chang

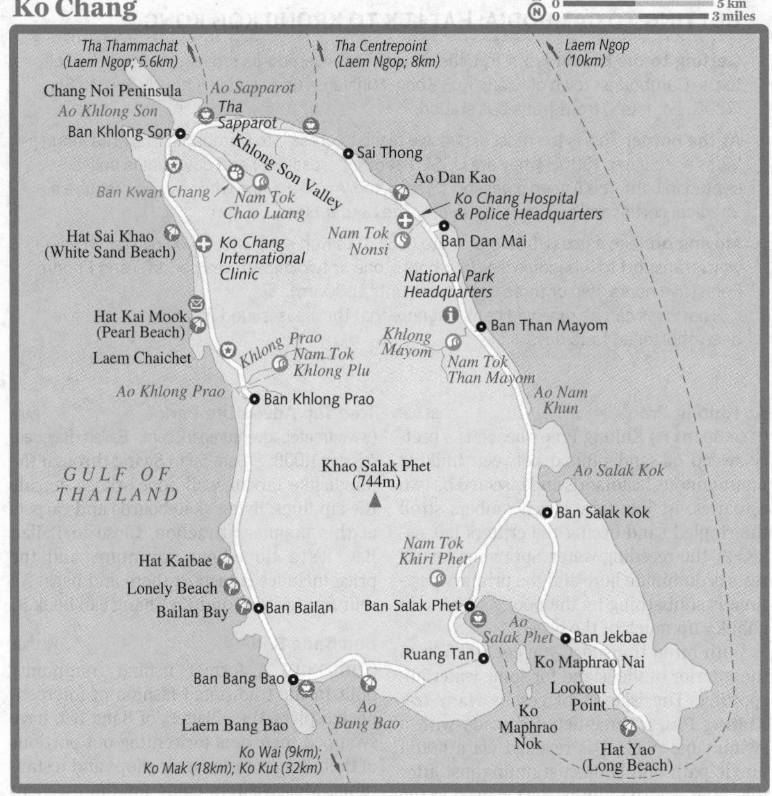

alternative means of transport to an ever-expanding nonresident population.

Sights

Although Thailand's second-largest island has accelerated into the modern world with some understandable growing pains, Ko Chang still has tropically hued seas, critter-filled jungles and a variety of water sports for athletic beach bums.

West Coast

The west coast has the island's widest and sandiest beaches and the greatest amount of development. Frequent public *sŏrng·tăa·ou* make beach-hopping easy and affordable. It is a good idea to bring swim shoes, especially for children, as many of the beaches are rocky in spots. These shallow, gentle seas are great for inexperienced swimmers, but be careful of riptides during storms and the rainy season (May to September).

Hat Sai Khao BEACH

(หาดทรายขาว, White Sand Beach) The longest, most luxurious stretch of sand on the island is packed with package-tour hotels and serious sunbathers. Finding a towel's-worth of sand can be tough during the high season; try the more low-key backpacker area in the far northern section of the beach. Along the main road, the village is busy and brash – but comes with all the necessary amenities.

Hat Kai Mook BEACH

(หาดไข่มุก, Pearl Beach) The pearls here are large pebbles that pack the shore and culminate in fish-friendly headlands. Swimming and sunbathing are out but there's good snorkelling.

GETTING TO CAMBODIA: HAT LEK TO KRONG KOH KONG

Getting to the border From Trat, the closest Thai–Cambodia crossing is from Hat Lek to the Cambodian town of Krong Koh Kong. Minivans run to Hat Lek hourly 5am to 6pm (120B, 1½ hours) from Trat's bus station.

At the border This is the most expensive place to cross into Cambodia from Thailand. Visas are a steep 1500B (they are US$20 at other crossings) and payment is only accepted in baht. You'll need a passport photo, too. Avoid anyone who says you require a 'medical certificate' or other paperwork. The border closes at 8pm.

Moving on Take a taxi (US$10) or moto (US$3) to Koh Kong where you can catch onward transport to Sihanoukville (four hours, one or two departures per day) and Phonm Penh (five hours, two or three departures until 11.30am).

Thai visas can be renewed here, but note that the visas issued at land borders have been shortened to 15 days.

Ao Khlong Prao BEACH
(อ่าวคลองพร้าว) Khlong Prao's beach is a pretty sweep of sand pinned between hulking mountainous headlands and bisected by two estuaries. At low tide, beachcombers stroll the rippled sand eyeing the critters left naked by the receding water. Sprawling luxury resorts dominate here and the primary pastime is sunbathing by the pool, as high tide gobbles up much of the beach.

With hired transport, you can head in to the interior of the island for some waterfall-spotting. The island's biggest is **Nam Tok Khlong Plu**, a three-tiered cascade with a swimmable pool. It is reached via a 600m jungle path and is most stunning just after the rainy season months. Best viewed in the morning before the crowds arrive.

Hat Kaibae BEACH
(หาดไก่แบ้) A companion beach to Khlong Prao, Hat Kaibae is a good spot for families and thirty-something couples. A slim strip of sand unfurls around an island-dotted bay far enough removed from the package tour scene that you'll feel self-righteously independent. There's kayaking to the outlying island and low tide provides hours of beachcombing.

Lonely Beach BEACH
There's nothing very lonely about this beach anymore, especially not in high season. Ko Chang's backpacker enclave is the most social place on the island come nightfall, when the music is loud, the drinks strong and the young crowd have shaken off the previous night's hangovers. The beach itself is a bit scruffy, but still a decent strip of sand.

Tree Top Adventure Park PARK
(www.treetopadventurepark.com; Bailan Bay; admission 1100B; ⏲9am-5pm) Swing through the jungle like Tarzan, walk rope bridges, or ride the zip lines, flying skateboards and carpets at this popular attraction. Close to Bailan Bay, it's a three-hour adventure, and the price includes transport there and back. All tour agencies around Ko Chang can book it.

Ban Bang Bao VILLAGE
(บ้านบางเบ้า) A former fishing community built in the traditional fashion of interconnected piers, the villagers of Bang Bao have swapped their nets for renting out portions of their homes to souvenir shops and restaurants. Most visitors come for the excellent seafood and a bit of shopping.

While Bang Bao isn't a very traditional experience, the commercialisation of Bang Bao has been done the Thai way. It's much like a mainland market, with every possible space dedicated to selling something. Follow the pier all the way to the end, though, and you'll find a big blue ocean and boats waiting to take you past the horizon. There are some fine places to stay here, but if you're heading back up the coast, finish your visit before sunset, as taxis become scarcer and more expensive after dark.

Hat Khlong Kloi BEACH
At the eastern end of Ao Bang Bao, Khlong Kloi is a sandy beach that feels a lot like a secret though there are other people here and all the requisite amenities (beer, fruit, food, massage) and a few guesthouses if you want the place to yourself. You'll need private transport to get out here.

Northern Interior

Ko Chang's mountainous interior is mostly protected as a national park. The forest is lush and alive with wildlife and threaded by silvery waterfalls.

Ban Kwan Chang ELEPHANT CAMP
(บ้านควาญช้าง; ☎08 1919 3995; changtone@yahoo.com; ⏰8am-5pm) In a beautiful forested setting, this is the best of the three elephant camps on the island; deeper in the jungle and you get more time riding the beasts. Tours range from 1½ to three hours (500/900B) and involve feeding, bathing and riding a pachyderm. Transport to and from the camp is included in the price. Be sure to apply mozzie spray.

Pittaya Homkrailas is the camp owner, a well-regarded conservation enthusiast who works to preserve a humane relationship between the elephant and mahout. His interest in environmental and community issues also includes efforts to preserve the southeastern mangroves in Ao Salak Kok on the island's east coast.

East Coast

The east coast is still peaceful and undeveloped, mainly undulating hills of coconut and palm trees and low-key fishing villages that have resisted the resort rush of the west coast. You'll need private transport to explore this lost coast of scenic bays and mangrove forests.

Nam Tok Than Mayom WATERFALL
(น้ำตกธารมะยม; park fee 200B; ⏰8am-5pm) A series of three falls along the stream of Khlong Mayom can be reached via the park office near Tha Than Mayom. The view from the top is superb and nearby there are inscribed stones bearing the initials of Rama V, Rama VI and Rama VII.

Ao Salak Kok MANGROVE BAY
(อ่าวสลักคอก) From a developers' perspective, this thick tangle of mangroves is an unprofitable wasteland. But the local population of fisherfolk recognises that its beauty and profit are in its environmental fertility. Mangroves are the ocean's nurseries, fostering the next generation of marine species, as well as resident birds and crustaceans, and this bay is now Ko Chang's prime ecotourism site.

Villagers, working in conjunction with Khun Pittaya, of Ban Kwan Chang elephant camp, operate an award-winning program to preserve the environment and the traditional way of life. They rent kayaks through the Salak Kok Kayak Station and run an affiliated restaurant.

Ban Salak Phet VILLAGE
(บ้านสลักเพชร) In the southeast pocket of the island is Ban Salak Phet, a surprisingly bustling community of fisherfolk and merchants plus lots of bike-riding kids and yawning dogs. This is what most of Ko Chang looked like less than a generation ago. Most visitors come for the seafood restaurants, or to cruise the lonely byways for a secluded beach.

Beyond the commercial heart of the village is **Ao Salak Phet**, a beautiful blue bay serenely guarded by humpbacked islands.

Nam Tok Khiri Phet WATERFALL
(น้ำตกคีรีเพชร) This small waterfall, 2km from Ban Salak Phet, is a 15-minute walk from the road and rewards you with a small, deep plunge pool. It's usually less crowded than many of the larger falls and is easily reached if you're in the neighbourhood of Ao Salak Phet.

Activities

Kayaking

Ko Chang cuts an impressive and heroic profile when viewed from the sea aboard a kayak. The water is generally calm and offshore islands provide a paddling destination that is closer than the horizon. Most hotels rent open-top kayaks (from 300B per day) that are convenient for near-shore outings and noncommittal kayakers.

KayakChang KAYAKING
(☎0 3955 2000; www.kayakchang.com; Amari Emerald Cove Resort, Khlong Prao) For more serious paddlers, KayakChang rents high-end, closed-top kayaks (from 1000B per day) that handle better and travel faster. They also lead one-day and multiday trips (from 2200B) to other islands in the archipelago.

Salak Kok Kayak Station KAYAKING
(☎08 1919 3995; kayak rentals per hr 100B) On the east side of the island, explore the mangrove swamps of Ao Salak Kok, while supporting an award-winning eco-tour program. Salak Kok Kayak Station rents self-guided kayaks and is a village-work project designed to promote tourism without affecting the traditional

way of life. They can also help arrange village homestays and hiking tours.

Hiking

Ko Chang is unusual for a Thai island in that is has a well-developed trekking scene. The island is blessed with lush forests filled with birds, monkeys, lizards and beautiful flowers. Best of all there are a handful of guides who know and love the forest and can speak English so that it can be shared with tourists.

Mr Tan from **Evolution Tour** (☎0 3955 7078; www.evolutiontour.com) or Lek from **Jungle Way** (☎08 9247 3161; www.jungleway.com) lead one-day treks (700B to 1400B) through Khlong Son Valley. The trip works up a sweat and then rewards with a waterfall swim and a stop at the Ban Kwan Chang elephant camp organisations. Multiday trips can be arranged through both. Mr Tan also has family-friendly treks and a hike that heads west from Khlong Son to Hat Sai Khao.

Koh Chang Trekking HIKING, BIRDWATCHING
(☎08 1588 3324; www.kohchangtrekking.info) Bird-watchers should contact Koh Chang Trekking which runs one- and two-day trips (1200B to 1500B) into Mu Ko Chang National Marine Park and hikes to the top of Khao Chom Prasat, two nearby rocky tipped peaks. Prices are for a group of four people.

Salak Phet Kayak Station HIKING
(☎08 7834 9489; from 1500B) Guides overnight treks on Khao Salak Phet, Ko Chang's highest peak, which rises 744m into the heavens and provides a sunrise and sunset view. This is one of the few places in Thailand where you can combine such serious exertion with a coastal landscape; you can choose to sleep in a tent or under the stars.

NATIONAL PARK STATUS

Some areas of Ko Chang are protected and maintained as part of the Mu Ko Chang National Marine Park. Conservation efforts are a bit haphazard, but you will be required to pay a 200B park entrance fee when visiting some of the waterfalls (entrance fees are stated in the reviews and payable at the site). **National Park headquarters** (☎0 3955 5080; Ban Than Mayom; ⏲8am-5pm) is on the eastern side of the island near Nam Tok Than Mayom.

Be aware also that nudity and topless sunbathing are forbidden by law in Mu Ko Chang National Marine Park; this includes all beaches on Ko Chang, Ko Kut, Ko Mak and Ko Wai.

Volunteering

Koh Chang Animal Project VOLUNTEERING
(☎08 9042 2347; www.kohchanganimalproject.org; Ban Khlong Son) Abused, injured or abandoned animals receive medical care and refuge at this nonprofit centre, established in 2002 by American Lisa McAlonie. The centre also works with local people on spaying, neutering and general veterinarian services, and Lisa is well-known to concerned pet owners and flea-ridden dogs on the island. Volunteers, especially travelling vets and vet nurses, are welcome to donate a bit of TLC and elbow grease for the cause. Call to make an appointment. Most *sŏrng·tăa·ou* drivers know how to get here; tell them you're going to 'Ban Lisa' (Lisa's House) in Khlong Son.

Massage

Sima Massage MASSAGE
(☎08 1489 5171; main road, Khlong Prao; massage per hr 250B; ⏲8am-10pm) Across from Tropicana Resort, and regarded by locals as the best massage on the island – quite an accolade in a place where a massage is easier to find than a 7-Eleven.

Bailan Herbal Sauna SAUNA
(☎0 3955 8077; www.bailan-kohchang.com; Ban Bailan; sauna from 250B; ⏲3-9pm) Sweating on purpose might seem like a free and unintended consequence of tropical living but, just south of Lonely Beach, Bailan continues an old-fashioned Southeast Asian tradition of the village sauna. Set amid lush greenery, the earthen huts are heated with a health-promoting stew of herbs. There's also massage, facial treatments and a post-steam juice bar.

Courses

Break up your lazy days with classes designed to enhance mind and body. Khlong Prao hosts a well-regarded culinary school. Classes are typically four to five hours, include a market tour and cost 1200B per person; book ahead.

Koh Chang Thai Cookery School COOKING
(☎0 3955 7243; Blue Lagoon Bungalows, Khlong Prao) Slices, dices and sautées in a shady open-air kitchen beside the estuary.

DON'T MISS

DIVING & SNORKELLING

The dive sites near Ko Chang offer a variety of coral, fish and beginner-friendly shallow waters on par with other Gulf of Thailand dive sites.

The seamounts off the southern tip of the island within the Mu Ko Chang National Marine Park are reached within a 30-minute cruise. Popular spots include **Hin Luk Bat** and **Hin Rap**, rocky, coral-encrusted seamounts with depths of around 18m to 20m. These are havens for schooling fish and some turtles.

By far the most pristine diving in the area is around **Ko Rang** (boat from Ko Chang), an uninhabited island protected from fishing by its marine park status. Visibility here is much better than near Ko Chang and averages between 10m and 20m. Everyone's favourite dive is **Hin Gadeng**, spectacular rock pinnacles with coral visible to around 28m. On the eastern side of Ko Rang, **Hin Kuak Maa** (also known as Three Finger Reef) is another top dive spot and is home to a coral-encrusted wall sloping from 2m to 14m and attracting swarms of marine life.

Ko Yak, **Ko Tong Lang** and **Ko Laun** are shallow dives perfect for both beginners and advanced divers. These small rocky islands can be circumnavigated and have lots of coral, schooling fish, puffer fish, morays, barracuda, rays and the occasional turtle.

About 7km offshore from Ban Bang Bao (p122) there's a popular dive to the wreck of the **HTMS Chang**, a 100m-long former Thai naval vessel which was purposely sunk in 2012 to form an artifical reef and now sits 30m beneath the surface.

Reef-fringed **Ko Wai** features a good variety of colourful hard and soft corals and is great for snorkelling. It is a popular day-tripping island but has simple overnight accommodation for more alone time with the reef.

The snorkelling on **Ko Mak** is not as good as elsewhere, but the island offers some decent dives even if the reefs don't see as many fish.

One-day diving trips typically start at 2500B. PADI Open Water certification costs 14,500B per person. Many dive shops remain open during the rainy season (June to September) but visibility and sea conditions are generally poor. The following are recommended dive operators:

- **BB Divers** (☎0 3955 8040; www.bbdivers.com) Based at Bang Bao with branches in Lonely Beach, Khlong Prao and Hat Sai Khao, as well as outposts on Ko Kut and Ko Wai (high season only).
- **Lonely Beach Divers** (☎08 0619 0704; www.lonelybeachdivers.com) Operating out of Lonely Beach, this place offers multilingual instructors.
- **Paradise Divers** (☎08 7144 5945) Branches on Ko Mak and Ko Kut.

Sleeping

Ko Chang's package-tour industry has distorted accommodation pricing. In general, rates have risen while quality has not, partly because hotels catering to group tours are guaranteed occupancy and don't have to maintain standards to woo repeat visitors or walk-ins. There is also a lot of copy-cat pricing giving value-oriented visitors little to choose from.

A few places close down during the wet season (April to October) and rates drop precipitously. Consider booking ahead and shopping for online discounts during peak season (November to March), weekends and holidays.

On the west coast, Lonely Beach is still the best budget option, Hat Kai Bae is the best-value option and Hat Sai Khao is the most overpriced; you will also find accommodation on the east coast at Ao Salak Kok and Ao Dan Kao.

Hat Sai Khao

The island's prettiest beach is also its most expensive. The northern and southern extremities have some budget and midrange options worth considering if you need proximity to the finest sand. There's a groovy backpacker enclave north of KC Grande Resort accessible only via the beach. There are more further north.

At the southern end, you can find some good-value budget and midrange places but this end of the beach is rocky and lacking sand during high tide.

If you want to splash out, don't do it on Hat Sai Khao where good money will be wasted.

Independent Bo's GUESTHOUSE $
(☎08 5283 5581; Hat Sai Khao; r 400-850B; ❄📶) Despite the eccentric Scottish owner (no reservations accepted here) this place on the jungle hillside exudes a creative, hippy-ish vibe that Ko Chang used to be famous for. Each bungalow is funky and different.

Starbeach Bungalows GUESTHOUSE $
(☎09 2575 7238; Hat Sai Khao; bungalows 700B; 📶) Ramshackle in appearance, the simple bungalows here wind up the hillside and are solid enough. You're very close to the prime part of the beach.

Arunee Resort GUESTHOUSE $
(☎0 3955 1075; aruneeresorttour@hotmail.com; Hat Sai Khao; r 250-500B; 📶) Digs don't come much cheaper than this anywhere on the island, and you're a 50m walk from the beach. But, the rooms are basic and cramped. Strong wi-fi signal, though.

Rock Sand Beach Resort GUESTHOUSE $$
(☎08 4781 0550; www.rocksand-resort.com; r 550-3750B; ❄📶) Touting itself as a flashpacker destination, this place isn't really a resort. But the sea-view rooms are decent and come wth shared balconies. Cheaper rooms are plainer. Be prepared to wade here when it's high tide.

Sai Khao Inn GUESTHOUSE $$
(☎0 3955 1584; www.saikhaoinn.com; r 1200-1800B; ❄📶) A garden setting on the interior side of the road and good value in the land of resorts, Sai Khao Inn has a little bit of everything – bungalows on stilts and more ordinary rooms. It's up an alley off the main road.

Koh Chang Hut Hotel HOTEL $$
(☎08 9831 4851; www.kohchanghut.com; r 450-1800B; ❄📶) At the southern end of the beach, this cliff-side hotel was being extensively refurbished at the time of writing. A pleasant, breezy spot, you're within walking distance of the beach without spending a lot of baht. The cheaper street-side rooms are noisier.

Palm Garden Hotel HOTEL $$
(☎0 3955 1095; www.15palms.com; r 1200-1500B; ❄📶) Across the road from the attached beachfront restaurant are plain-ish but clean midrange rooms very close to the most popular part of the beach. You have to use the wi-fi in the restaurant.

Keereeelé HOTEL $$
(☎0 3955 1285; www.keereeele.com; r 2200-2600B; ❄📶🏊) An excess of 'e's in the name doesn't detract from the merits of this multistorey hotel on the interior side of the road. The rooms are modern and comfortable with beds raised off the floor Chinese-style. Some have views of the mountains behind. The beach is 300m away.

Ao Khlong Prao

Ao Khlong Prao is dominated by high-end resorts, with just a few budget spots peppered in between. There are a handful of cheapies on the main road that are within walking distance to the beach, though traffic can be treacherous and noisy.

Tiger Huts GUESTHOUSE $
(☎08 4109 9660; Ao Khlong Prao; r 300-600B) Basic wooden huts, rock-hard beds and cold-water showers, but this is the prettiest part of the beach. You'll need the attached restaurant; it's over 1km to the main road from here.

Blue Lagoon Bungalows GUESTHOUSE $$
(☎0 3955 7243; www.kohchangbluelagoon.com; Ao Khlong Prao; r 650-1300B; ❄📶) An exceedingly friendly garden spot with a range of bungalows to suit different budgets beside a peaceful estuary. A wooden walkway leads to the beach. All sorts of amenities, including yoga, cooking school, kids' playground and activities, are on offer, too.

Lin Bungalow GUESTHOUSE $$
(☎08 4120 1483; lin.bungalow@gmail.com; r 1300B; ❄📶) Ten sturdy and sizeable bungalows right on the beach. A good midrange choice.

Baan Rim Nam GUESTHOUSE $$
(☎08 7005 8575; www.iamkohchang.com; r 1200-1600B; ❄📶) Converted fisherman's-house-turned-guesthouse teeters over a mangrove-lined river; kayaks and dialled-in advice free of charge.

Sofia Resort HOTEL $$
(☎08 1191 9205; www.jussinhotel.com; r 790-1190B; ❄📶🏊) Great price for the comfort factor, but not a lot of character to the rooms and the location is on the main road without direct beach access.

★Keereeta Resort GUESTHOUSE $$$
(☎0 3955 1304; www.keereeta.com; r 3500B; ❄📶) Only five very special rooms here; all individually colour-themed, huge, secluded and oh so stylish. Free kayaks for guests to paddle to the beach or the restaurants opposite. Book ahead.

Aana HOTEL $$$
(☎0 3955 1137; www.aanaresort.com; r 3500-6500B; ❄@🏊) Private villas perch prettily above the forest and Khlong Prao, kayaking distance from the beach. The cheaper rooms are a little faded for the price.

Hat Kaibae

Hat Kaibae has some of the island's best variety of accommodation, from boutique hotels to budget huts and midrange bungalows. The trade-off is that the beach is only sandy in parts.

Porn's Bungalows GUESTHOUSE $
(☎08 0613 9266; www.pornsbungalows-kohchang.com; Hat Kaibae; r 550-1500B) Very chilled spot at the far western end of the beach. All bungalows are fan-only. The 900B beachfront bungalows are a great deal.

Buzza's Bungalows GUESTHOUSE $
(☎08 7823 6674; Hat Kaibae; r 400-450B; 📶) Simple fan-only bungalows with porches that face each other, creating a laid-back travellers ambience. However, this is the rocky part of the beach.

KB Resort HOTEL $$
(☎0 3955 7125; www.kbresort.com; r 1250-5000B; ❄@📶🏊) Lemon-yellow bungalows have cheery bathrooms and pose peacefully beside the sea. Listen to the gentle lapping surf while the kids construct mega-cities in the sand. The fan bungalows are overpriced. Sleepy staff.

Kaibae Hut Resort HOTEL $$
(☎08 1862 8426; www.kaibaehutresort.com; r 700-2500B; ❄📶) Sprawling across a scenic stretch of beach, Kaibae Hut has a variety of lodging options – slightly worn fan huts, fancier concrete bungalows and modern hotel-style rooms. A large open-air restaurant fires up nightly barbecues and there's plenty of room for free-ranging kids.

Garden Resort HOTEL $$
(☎0 3955 7260; www.gardenresortkohchang.com; r 2200-2600B; ❄@📶🏊) On the interior side of the main road, Garden Resort has large and well-kept bungalows blossoming in a shady garden with a salt-water swimming pool. A sandy stretch of beach is 150m away.

GajaPuri Resort & Spa HOTEL $$$
(☎0 3969 6918; www.gajapuri.com; r 4350-19,000B; ❄📶🏊) Polished wooden cottages gleam with quintessential Thai touches so that you have a sense of place and pampering. Oversized beds with crisp linens, sun-drenched reading decks and a pretty beach are even more luxurious if you score an online discount.

Lonely Beach

A backpacker party fave, Lonely Beach is one of the cheapest places to sleep on the island, though oceanfront living has mostly moved upmarket, pushing the penny-pinchers into the interior village. If you've been flashpackerised, there are several creative midrangers that will save you from carbon-copy resorts. This end of the island is less developed and the jungle broods just over the squatty commercial strip.

Little Eden GUESTHOUSE $
(☎08 4867 7459; www.littleedenkohchang.com; Lonely Beach; r 600-1100B; ❄📶) Fifteen bungalows here, all connected by an intricate series of wooden walkways, and a decent size with better bathrooms than the price indicates. Pleasant communal area and staff.

Siam Hut GUESTHOUSE $
(☎0 3961 9012; Lonely Beach; r 480-680B; ❄📶) Raucous, a bit random and party central for backpackers. This is the only budget option right on the sandy stretch of the beach. Small-ish wooden huts, but then you won't be spending much time in them.

Paradise Cottages HOTEL $
(☎08 1773 9337; www.paradisecottagekochang.com; Lonely Beach; r 400-1000B; ❄📶) Stylishly minimalist rooms and a mellow atmosphere with hammocks for guests to swing their worries away. It's oceanfront, but the beach is too rocky for swimming.

KLKL Hostel GUESTHOUSE $
(☎08 3088 3808; r 500-700B; ❄@📶🏊) Not a true hostel – no dorms here. Instead, rather pleasant blue-, green- and pink-themed rooms at a reasonable price. Cheaper rooms are fan only, but all have hot water.

Oasis Bungalows GUESTHOUSE $$
(08 1721 2547; www.oasis-kohchang.com; r 500-1300B;) Sitting up a steep hill that offers sea views, Oasis has roomy, midrange bungalows in a pretty fruit and flower garden. But even the cheaper, fan bungalows come with cute outdoor bathrooms. It's a fair walk to the beach from here.

Warapura Resort HOTEL $$
(0 3955 8123; www.warapuraresort.com; r 1400-3300B;) Chic for relatively cheap prices, Warapura has a collection of adorable cottages tucked in between the village and a mangrove beach. The oceanfront pool is perfect for people who would rather gaze at the ocean than frolic in it.

Lonely Beach Resort GUESTHOUSE $$
(08 1279 5120; www.lonelybeach.net; r 1300B;) The bungalows here slope downhill amid a leafy garden. They're plain but a good size and comfortable enough. The attached restaurant is a bizarre, albeit tasty, mix of Danish and Thai dishes.

Ban Bang Bao

Despite its touristy veneer, Ban Bang Bao is still a charming place to stay for folks who pre-

GETTING TO CAMBODIA: ARANYA PRATHET TO POIPET

Getting to the Border The easiest way to get from Bangkok to Siem Reap overland is the direct bus departing from the Northern (Mo Chit) Bus Terminal. The through-service bus trips sold on Th Khao San and elsewhere in Bangkok seem cheap and convenient, but they haven't been nicknamed 'scam buses' for nothing, and you will be most likely hassled and ripped off, often quite aggressively.

If you choose to do it in stages (much cheaper than the direct Mo Chit bus), you can get from Bangkok to the border town of Aranya Prathet (aka Aran) by bus from Mo Chit, by bus or minivan from the Eastern (Ekamai) Bus Terminal, by bus from Suvarnabhumi International Airport bus station, by minivan from Victory Monument or by 3rd-class train (only the 5.55am departure will get you there early enough to reach Siem Reap the same day) from Hualamphong. Aran also has bus service about every one or two hours from other cities in the area including Khorat, Surin and Chanthaburi. All minivans, plus some buses, go all the way to the Rong Kluea Market next to the border, so there's no need to stop in Aranya Prathet city. Otherwise, you'll need to take a *sŏrng·tăa·ou* (15B), motorcycle taxi (60B) or túk-túk (pronounced *đúk đúk;* 80B) the final 7km to the border.

At the Border The border is open 7am to 8pm daily. There are many persistent scammers on the Thai side trying to get you to buy your Cambodia visa through them, but no matter what they might tell you, there's absolutely no good reason to get visas anywhere except the border. Buying them elsewhere costs more and takes longer. Don't even show your passport to anyone before you reach Thai immigration and don't change money.

After getting stamped out of Thailand – an easy and completely straightforward process – follow the throng to Cambodian immigration and find the 'Visa on Arrival' sign if you don't already have a visa. Weekday mornings you might finish everything in 10 to 20 minutes, but if you arrive after midday it could take an hour or more. Weekends and holidays, when many Thais arrive to gamble and foreign workers do visa runs, are also very busy. You will probably be offered the opportunity to pay a special 'VIP fee' (aka a bribe) of 200B to jump to the front of the queue. You will almost certainly be asked to pay another small bribe, which will be called a 'stamping' or 'overtime' fee. You should refuse, though doing so might mean you have to wait a few extra minutes.

Moving On There are frequent buses and share taxis from Poipet to Siem Reap along a good sealed road from the main bus station, which is about 1km away (2000r by motorcycle taxi) around the main market, one block north of Canadia Bank off NH5. Poipet also has a second 'international' bus station 9km east of town where tickets cost double and which is only used by uninformed or gullible foreigners who get swept into the free shuttle that takes travellers out there. Lonely Planet's *Cambodia* guide has full details for travel on this side of the border.

fer scenery to swimming. Accommodation is mainly converted pier houses overlooking the sea with easy access to inter-island ferries. Daytime transport to a swimmable beach is regular thanks to the steady arrival and departure of day-trippers. Night owls should either hire a motorbike or stay elsewhere, as *sŏrng·tăa·ou* become rare and expensive after dinnertime.

Bang Bao Paradise GUESTHOUSE $
(☎08 8838 0040; r 500-700B; ❄) Six mini-huts perched over the water, all in bright, fresh colours and all sharing bathrooms.

Bang Bao Cliff Cottage GUESTHOUSE $
(☎08 5904 6706; www.cliff-cottage.com; r 400-1200B; ❄📶) Partially hidden on a verdant hillside west of the pier are a few dozen simple thatch huts overlooking a rocky cove. Most have sea views and a couple offer spectacular vistas. The cheaper rooms share bathrooms.

★Koh Chang Sea Hut HOTEL $$
(☎08 1285 0570; www.kohchang-seahut.com; r 2500B; ❄📶) With seven luxurious bungalows built on the edge of Bang Bao's pier, this is one of Ko Chang's most unusual places to stay, offering near panoramic views of the bay. Each bungalow is surrounded by a private deck where breakfast is served. There are five rooms here, too.

Buddha View GUESTHOUSE $$
(☎0 3955 8157; www.thebuddhaview.com; Ban Bang Bao; r 800-1200B; 🚭❄📶) Swish pier guesthouse popular with Bangkok Thais. Only seven thoughtfully designed rooms, four of which come with private bathrooms. The restaurant is also excellent.

Nirvana HOTEL $$$
(☎0 3955 8061; www.nirvanakohchang.com; r 2500-8500B; ❄📶🏊) Super-deluxe, Balinese-style bungalows hidden away on a rocky, jungle-filled peninsula. Come to get away from it all, including everything else on the island, and to enjoy the stunning sea views. The adjacent beach is scenic but not swimmable.

Northern Interior & East Coast

The northern and eastern part of the island is less developed than the west coast and much more isolated. You'll need your own transport and maybe even a posse not to feel lonely out here, but you'll be rewarded with a quieter, calmer experience.

Jungle Way GUESTHOUSE $
(☎08 9247 3161; www.jungleway.com; Khlong Son Valley; r 300-500B) Ko Chang's un-sung attribute is its jungle interior and the English-speaking guides who grew up playing in it. Lek, a local guide, and his family run this friendly guesthouse, deep in the woods and beside a babbling brook. Bungalows are simple but adequate and the on-site restaurant will keep you well fed. Free pier pick-up.

Souk GUESTHOUSE $$
(☎08 1553 3194; www.thesoukkohchang.com; Ao Dan Kao; r 700B; ❄@📶) This cool spot has seven pop-art bungalows at a pleasant price. There are lots of chill-out spaces and an open-deck restaurant and cocktail bar, just in front of the red-sand beach. There's good snorkelling 150m offshore and free kayaks.

Amber Sands HOTEL $$
(☎0 3958 6177; www.ambersandsbeachresort.com; Ao Dan Kao; r 1800-4250B; ❄@📶🏊) Sandwiched between mangroves and a quiet red-sand beach, Amber Sands has smart bungalows and great sea views. The location feels a world away but it is only 15 minutes from the pier. Closes low season.

Spa Koh Chang Resort HOTEL $$$
(☎0 3955 3091; www.thespakohchang.com; Ao Salak Kok; r 3178-4060B; ❄📶🏊) In a lush garden setting embraced by the bay's mangrove forests, this spa resort specialises in all the popular health treatments (yoga, meditation, fasting etc) that burned-out professionals need. Elegantly decorated bungalows scramble up a flower-filled hillside providing a peaceful getaway for some quality 'me' time. No beach access.

Eating & Drinking

Virtually all of the island's accommodation has attached restaurants with adequate but not outstanding fare. Parties abound on the beaches and range from the older, more restrained scene on Hat Sai Khao, to the younger and sloppier fiestas on Lonely Beach.

West Coast

Porn's Bungalows Restaurant THAI $
(Hat Kaibae; dishes 80-180B; ⏲11am-11pm) This laid-back, dark-wood restaurant is the quintessential beachside lounge. Great barbecue. Feel free to have your drinks out-size your meal and don't worry about dressing for dinner.

Nid's Kitchen THAI $
(nidkitchen@hotmail.com; Hat Kaibae; dishes 50-150B; 6pm-midnight) Nid's does all the Thai standards like a wok wizard in a hut festooned with rasta imagery. Equally fine for a drink or three.

Baan Mai THAI $
(dishes 50-160B; 9am-11pm) Extensive Thai menu, with a vague Chinese influence, at this two-floor converted house that sits in a strategic spot on the main road through Lonely Beach.

Magic Garden THAI $
(0 3955 8027; Lonely Beach; dishes 60-220B; 11am-late) Still a popular Lonely Beach hang-out, but better for a drink than a meal. The menu covers Thai and Western standards.

★Norng Bua THAI $$
(Hat Sai Khao; dishes 40-300B; 8am-11pm) Once a stir-fry hut, now a fully fledged restaurant that makes everything fast and fresh and with chillies and fish sauce (praise the culinary gods). Always crowded with visiting Thais, a good sign indeed.

★Phu-Talay SEAFOOD $$
(Khlong Prao; 100-320B; 10am-10pm) Cute, homey feel at this wooden-floored, blue and white decorated place perched over the lagoon. Sensible menu of Ko Chang classics (lots of fish) and far more reasonably priced than many other seafood places.

Oodie's Place INTERNATIONAL-THAI $$
(0 3955 1193; Hat Sai Khao; dishes 80-390B; 11am-midnight) Local musician Oodie runs a nicely diverse operation with excellent French food, tasty Thai specialities and live music from 10pm. After all these years, it is still beloved by expats.

Ruan Thai SEAFOOD $$
(Ban Bang Bao; dishes 80-400B; 9.30am-10pm) It's about as fresh as it gets (note your future dinner greeting you in tanks as you enter) and the portions are large. The doting service is beyond excellent – they'll even help you crack your crabs.

Ton Sai THAI $$
(Khlong Prao; dishes 80-350B; 11am-10pm) A favourite of locals, visiting Thais and foreigners, paintings adorn this hut of a restaurant. A mix of well-prepared, creative Thai and Western dishes are on the menu. Closed low season.

Saffron on the Sea THAI $$
(0 3955 1253; Hat Kai Mook; dishes 120-350B; 8am-10pm;) Owned by an arty escapee from Bangkok, this friendly boutique hotel has a generous portion of oceanfront dining and a relaxed, romantic atmosphere. All the Thai dishes are prepared in the island style, more sweet than spicy.

Iyara Seafood SEAFOOD $$
(0 3955 1353; Khlong Prao; dishes 180-1250B; 11am-10pm) Iyara isn't your standard island seafood warehouse: after dining in the lovely bamboo pavilion, guests are invited to kayak along the nearby estuary.

Chowlay SEAFOOD $$
(Ban Bang Bao; dishes 100-450B; 10am-10pm) Fine bay views at this pier restaurant and enough fresh fish to start your own aquarium.

Kaotha INTERNATIONAL-THAI $$
(Lonely Beach; dishes 50-300B; 9am-midnight;) One of the hot spots on the Lonely Beach dining scene, with an excellent selection of pizzas and nice and spicy Thai dishes, this airy venue is a popular hang-out for coffee, too. There's live music on Saturdays.

KaTi Culinary THAI $$
(08 1903 0408; Khlong Prao; dishes 120-550B; 11am-10pm) Seafood, and a few Isan dishes and their famous, homemade curry sauce. The menu features creative smoothies, such as lychee, lemon and peppermint, and there's a kid's menu as well.

Invito Al Cibo ITALIAN $$$
(0 3955 1326; Koh Chang Hut, Hat Sai Khao; dishes 190-609B; 11am-11pm) Popular with *fa•ràng* visitors who come for the top pizzas, homemade pasta and stunning sea views.

Northern Interior & East Coast

Blues Blues Restaurant THAI $
(08 5839 3524; Ban Khlong Son; dishes 40-150B; 10am-9pm) Through the green screen of tropical plants is an arty stir-fry hut that is beloved for expertise, efficiency and economy. The owner's delicate watercolour paintings are on display too. Take the road to Ban Kwan Chang and it's 600m ahead on the right.

Jungle Way Restaurant THAI $
(08 9247 3161; Ban Khlong Son; dishes 70-120B; 8am-9pm;) Enjoy the natural setting and home-style cooking of this guesthouse res-

taurant. Meal preparation takes a leisurely pace so climb up to the elevated wildlife-viewing platform to spot some jungle creatures while the wok is sizzling.

Paradise Behind the Sea Restaurant THAI **$$**
(☎08 1900 2388; Ban Hat Sai Daeng; dishes 120-320B; ⏰10am-10pm) If you're cruising the east coast for scenery, stop in for a view and a meal at this cliff-side restaurant. Vietnamese and Thai dishes crowd the tables and cool breezes provide refreshment. In Thai, it's called 'Lang Talay'.

Information

DANGERS & ANNOYANCES

It is not recommended to drive between Ban Khlong Son south to Hat Sai Khao, as the road is steep and treacherous with several hairpin turns. There are mud slides and poor conditions during storms. If you do rent a motorbike, stick to the west coast beaches and take care when travelling between Hat Kaibae and Lonely Beach. Wear protective clothing when riding or driving a motorcycle.

The police conduct regular drug raids on the island's accommodation. If you get caught with narcotics, you could face heavy fines or imprisonment.

Be aware of the cheap minibus tickets from Siem Reap to Ko Chang; these usually involve some sort of time- and money-wasting commission scam.

Ko Chang is considered a low-risk malarial zone, meaning that liberal use of mosquito repellent is probably an adequate precaution.

EMERGENCY

Police Station (☎0 3958 6191; Ban Dan Mai)

Tourist Police Office (☎1155) Based north of Ban Khlong Prao. Also has smaller police boxes in Hat Sai Khao and Hat Kaibae.

MEDICAL SERVICES

Bang Bao Health Centre (☎0 3955 8088; Ban Bang Bao; ⏰8.30am-6pm) For the basics.

Ko Chang Hospital (☎0 3952 1657; Ban Dan Mai) Public hospital with a good reputation and affordably priced care; south of the ferry terminal.

Ko Chang International Clinic (☎0 3955 1151; Hat Sai Khao; ⏰24hr) Related to the Bangkok Hospital Group; accepts most health insurances and has expensive rates.

MONEY

There are banks with ATMs and exchange facilities along all the west coast beaches.

POST

Ko Chang Post Office (☎0 3955 1240; Hat Sai Khao) At the far southern end of Hat Sai Khao.

TOURIST INFORMATION

The free magazine **Koh Chang Guide** (www.koh-chang-guide.com) is widely available on the island and has handy beach maps.

The comprehensive website **I Am Koh Chang** (www.iamkohchang.com) is a labour of love by an irreverent Brit living on the island. It's jam-packed with opinion and information.

Getting There & Away

Whether originating from Bangkok or Cambodia, it is an all-day haul to reach Ko Chang.

Ferries from the mainland leave from either Tha Thammachat, operated by **Koh Chang Ferry** (☎0 3955 5188), or Tha Centrepoint (Laem Ngop) with **Centrepoint Ferry** (☎0 3953 8196). Boats from Tha Thammachat arrive at Tha Sapparot; Centrepoint ferries at a pier down the road.

The inter-island ferry **Bang Bao Boats** (www.bangbaoboat.com) connects Ko Chang with Ko Mak, Ko Kut and Ko Wai during the high season. The boats leave from Bang Bao in the southwest of the island.

TRANSPORT TO/FROM KO CHANG

ORIGIN	DESTINATION	BOAT	BUS
Bangkok Eastern (Ekamai) Bus Terminal	Tha Thammachat		275B; 7hr; 3 daily
Ko Chang	Ko Kut	900B; 5hr; 1 daily	
Ko Chang	Ko Mak	550B; 2hr; 1 daily	
Ko Chang	Ko Wai	300B; 1hr; 1 daily	
Ko Chang	Bangkok Airport		550B; 6-7hr; 3 daily
Tha Centrepoint	Ko Chang	80B; 45min; hourly 6.30am-7pm	
Tha Thammachat	Ko Chang	80B; 30min; every 30min 6.30am-7pm	

Speedboats travel between the islands during high season.

It's possible to go direct to and from Ko Chang from both Bangkok's Eastern (Ekamai) bus terminal and Bangkok's Suvaranabhumi International Airport, via Chanthaburi and Trat.

Getting Around

Shared *sŏrng·tăa·ou* meet arriving boats to shuttle passengers to the various beaches (Hat Sai Khao 100B, Khlong Prao 150B and Lonely Beach 200B). Hops between neighbouring beaches range from 50B to 200B but prices rise dramatically after dark, when it can cost 500B to travel to Bang Bao to Hat Sai Khao.

Motorbikes can be hired from 200B per day. Ko Chang's hilly and winding roads are quite dangerous; make sure the bike is in good working order. Remember that if you crash, you'll be paying for the bike repairs as well as your medical bills.

Ko Wai เกาะหวาย

Stunning Ko Wai is teensy and primitive, but endowed with gin-clear waters, excellent coral reefs for snorkelling and a handsome view across to Ko Chang. Expect to share the bulk of your afternoons with day-trippers but have the remainder of your time in peace.

Most bungalows close during the May-to-September low season when seas are rough and flooding is common.

Sleeping

Good Feeling GUESTHOUSE $
(☎08 1850 3410; r 400-500B) Twelve wooden bungalows, all but one with private bathroom, spread out along a rocky headland interspersed with private, sandy coves.

Ko Wai Paradise GUESTHOUSE $
(☎08 1762 2548; r 300-500B) Simple wooden bungalows (with shared bathrooms and no electricity) on a postcard-perfect beach. You'll share the coral out front with day-trippers.

Grandma Hut GUESTHOUSE $
(☎08 1841 3011; r 350-500B) On the rocky northeastern tip of the island is this basic and remote place; speedboat operators know it by the nearby bay of Ao Yai Ma.

Ko Wai Pakarang GUESTHOUSE $$
(☎08 4113 8946; www.kohwaipakarang.com; r 600-2200B; ❄@📶) Wooden and concrete bungalows, the cheaper ones fan-only, an OK attached restaurant and helpful, English-speaking staff.

Koh Wai Beach Resort HOTEL $$$
(☎08 1306 4053; www.kohwaibeachresort.com; r 2100-5400B; ❄📶) Upscale collection of spacious bungalows with all mod cons just a few steps from the beach and on the southern side of the island.

Getting There & Around

Boats will drop you off at the nearest pier to your guesthouse; otherwise you'll have to walk 15 to 30 minutes along a narrow forest trail.

Bang Bao Boat (www.bangbaoboat.com) is the archipelago's inter-island ferry running a daily loop from Ko Chang to Ko Kut. Boats depart Ko Chang at 9am and arrive at Ko Wai (one way 300B, one hour) and continue on to Ko Mak (one way 400B, one hour) and Ko Kut (700B, three hours).

During high season, speedboats run from Ko Wai to the following destinations:

SPEEDBOAT TRANSPORT FROM KO WAI

DESTINATION	PRICE	DURATION	FREQUENCY
Ko Chang	one way 400B	15min	2 daily
Ko Kut	one way 800B	1hr	2 daily
Ko Mak	one way 450B	30min	2 daily
Laem Ngop	450B	2-3hr	1 daily

Ko Mak เกาะหมาก

Little Ko Mak measures only 16 sq km and doesn't have speeding traffic, wall-to-wall development, noisy beer bars or crowded beaches. The palm-fringed bays are bathed by gently lapping water and there's a relaxed vibe. But Ko Mak is not destined for island super-stardom: the interior is a utilitarian landscape of coconut and rubber plantations and reports of sand flies make visitors a little nervous. The vast majority of tourists are Scandinavian and German families, but a growing number of independent travellers congregate here, too.

Visiting the island is easier in the high season; during the low season (May to September) many boats stop running and bungalow operations wind down. Storms also deposit uninvited litter on the exposed southern beaches.

Sights & Activities

The best beach on the island is **Ao Pra** in the west, but it's completely undeveloped and hard to reach. For now, swimming and beach strolling are best on the northwestern bay of **Ao Suan Yai**, which is a wide arc of sand and looking-glass-clear water that gets fewer sand flies than the beaches on the southern side of the island. It is easily accessible by bicycle or motorbike if you stay elsewhere.

Offshore is **Ko Kham**, a private island that was sold in 2008 for a reported 200 million baht. It used to be a popular day-trippers' beach but is currently being developed into a superluxury resort.

Koh Mak Divers DIVING
(08 3297 7724; www.kohmakdivers.com; dive trips from 2400B) Koh Mak Divers runs dive trips to the Mu Ko Chang National Marine Park, about 45 minutes away.

Sleeping & Eating

Most budget guesthouses are on Ao Khao, a decent strip of sand on the southwestern side of the island, while the resorts sprawl on the more scenic northwestern bay of Ao Suan Yai.

There are a handful of family-run restaurants on the main road between Monkey Island and Makathanee Resort. And if you feel like a journey, use a meal or a sundowner as an excuse to explore different bays.

Koh Mak Cottage GUESTHOUSE $
(08 1910 2723; Ao Khao; r 400-500B; @) Eighteen small and rustic bungalows. No frills, but you're right on the beach.

Monkey Island GUESTHOUSE $$
(08 5389 0949; www.monkeyislandkohmak.com; Ao Khao; r 350-2000B; @) The troop leader of guesthouses, Monkey Island has earthen or wooden bungalows in three creatively named models – Baboon, Chimpanzee and Gorilla – with various amenities (shared or private bathroom or private deck). All have fun design touches and the hip restaurant does respectable Thai cuisine in a leisurely fashion. In true Thai beach style, the affiliated bar rouses the dead with its nightly parties.

Bann Chailay GUESTHOUSE $$
(08 0101 4763; Ao Khao; r 800-1600B;) A cross between a homestay and a guesthouse, you can stay in bungalows on the beach, or rooms in the family house at this friendly place at the eastern, less busy, end of Ao Khao. Fine for barbecues on the beach, too.

Makathanee Resort HOTEL $$
(08 7600 00374; www.makathanee.com; Ao Khao; r 1500-5200B;) Floor-to-ceiling windows are open to sea views in these plush bungalows, which have deliciously soft mattresses and lots of breathing room. Behind them are rooms in a hotel block, some of which offer sea views. Kayaks for rent (400B per day) and professional service.

Baan Koh Mak GUESTHOUSE $$
(08 9895 7592; www.baan-koh-mak.com; Ao Khao; r 1000-1900B;) Bright and funky, Baan Koh Mak provides a respectable flashpacker abode with colourful paint jobs and soft mattresses.

Ao Kao Resort GUESTHOUSE $$
(08 3152 6564; www.aokaoresort.com; Ao Khao; r 2500-3000B;) In a pretty crook of the bay, Ao Kao has an assortment of stylish bungalows. Opt for a traditional Thai-style house complete with carved wood flourishes and handsome balconies. Families congregate here as there is front-yard swimming and the rocky headland harbours sea creatures.

Lazy Day Resort GUESTHOUSE $$
(08 1882 4002; www.kohmaklazyday.com; r 2250-2700B;) This professionally run operation has big bungalows stationed around an attractive garden; rates include breakfast.

Koh Mak Resort HOTEL $$$
(0 3950 1013; www.kohmakresort.com; Ao Suan Yai; r 2800-6800B;) A self-contained resort, with restaurants, a direct speedboat to and

SPEEDBOAT TRANSPORT FROM KO MAK

DESTINATION	PRICE	DURATION	FREQUENCY
Ko Chang	one way 600B	45min	3 daily
Ko Kut	one way 500B	45min	2 daily
Ko Wai	one way 400B	30min	2 daily
Laem Ngop (mainland pier)	one way 500B	1hr	4 daily

from the mainland (450B), and an amenable bar. The best bungalows come with Jacuzzis and they line a stretch of pretty beach.

Information

There are no banks or ATMs on the island, so stock up on cash before visiting.

Ball's Cafe (☎08 1925 6591; Ao Nid Pier; ⊙9am-6pm) Has internet access, travel agent and coffee shop. Khun Ball is an active island promoter and runs www.kohmak.com as well as environmental initiatives.

Ko Mak Health Centre (☎08 9403 5986; ⊙8.30am-4.30pm) Can handle basic first-aid emergencies and illnesses. It's on the cross-island road near Ao Nid Pier.

Police (☎0 3952 5741) Near the health centre.

Getting There & Around

Speedboats (450B one way, 50 minutes) arrive at the pier on Ao Suan Yai or at Makathanee Resort on Ao Khao.

A fast speedboat instead of a ferry now runs to Ao Nid (450B one way, four daily, 50 minutes), the main port on the eastern side of the island. There are only two boats daily in low season. Guesthouses and hotels pick people up free of charge.

Bang Bao Boat (www.bangbaoboat.com) is the archipelago's inter-island ferry running a daily loop from Ko Chang to Ko Kut. Boats depart Ko Chang at 9am and arrive at Ko Mak (one way 400B, 1½ to two hours) and continue on to Ko Kut (one way 300B, one to two hours, departs 1pm). In the opposite direction, you can catch it to Ko Wai (one way 300B, 45 minutes) and Ko Chang (400B, 2½ hours).

In high season, speedboats run from Ko Mak to various destinations. Once on the island, you can pedal (40B per hour) or motorbike (200B per day) your way around.

Ko Kut เกาะกูด

All the paradise descriptions apply to Ko Kut: the beaches are graceful arcs of sand, the water clear, coconut palms outnumber buildings, and a secluded, unhurried atmosphere embraces you upon arrival. Far less busy than Ko Chang, there's nothing in the form of nightlife, or even dining really, but those are the reasons for visiting.

Half as big as Ko Chang and the fourth-largest island in Thailand, Ko Kut (also known as Koh Kood) has long been the domain of package-tour resorts and a seclusion-seeking elite. But the island is becoming more egalitarian and independent travellers, especially families and couples, will find home sweet home here.

Sights & Activities

Beaches BEACHES

White sand beaches with gorgeous aquamarine water are strewn along the western side of the island. **Hat Khlong Chao** is the island's best and could easily compete with Samui's Hat Chaweng in a beach beauty contest. **Ao Noi** is a pretty boulder-strewn beach with a steep drop-off and steady waves for strong swimmers. **Ao Prao** is another lovely sweep of sand.

There is no public transport on Ko Kut but you can rent motorbikes for exploring the west coast beaches. Traffic is minimal and the road is mostly paved from Khlong Hin in the southwest to Ao Noi in the northeast.

With its quiet rocky coves and mangrove estuaries, Ko Kut is great for **snorkelling** and **kayaking**. Most resorts have equipment on offer.

Nam Tok Khlong Chao WATERFALL

Two waterfalls on the island make good short hiking destinations. The larger and more popular Nam Tok Khlong Chao is wide and pretty with a massive plunge pool. It's a quick jungle walk to the base, or you can kayak up Khlong Chao. Further north is **Nam Tok Khlong Yai Ki**, which is smaller but also has a large pool to cool off in.

Sleeping & Eating

During low season (May to September) many boats stop running and bungalow operations wind down. On weekends and holidays during the high season, vacationing Thais fill the resorts. Call ahead during busy periods so you can be dropped off at the appropriate pier by the speedboat operators.

You can scrimp your way into the neighbourhood of beautiful Hat Khlong Chao by staying at one of the village guesthouses, which are a five- to 15-minute walk to the beach. Families might like the midrange and budget options on Ao Ngam Kho, which has a small sandy section in the far northern corner of the bay, though the rest is an old coral reef and very rocky. Bring swim shoes.

Ao Ngam Khao is also a popular spot for independent travellers, thanks to its good choice of accommodation options.

If you're itching to splurge, Ko Kut is the place to do it.

Cozy House GUESTHOUSE $

(☎08 5101 4838; www.kohkoodcozy.com; Khlong Yai; r 250-600B; ❄📶) The go-to place for backpackers, Cozy is just a 10-minute walk from delightful Hat Khlong Yai. There are cheap and cheerful rooms with shared bathrooms, or more comfortable wooden bungalows.

Koh Kood Ngamkho Resort GUESTHOUSE $
(☎08 1825 7076; www.kohkood-ngamkho.com; Ao Ngam Kho; r 750B; @ 📶) One the best budget options around. Agreeably rustic huts perch on a forested hillside over a reasonable beach. Some are bigger than others. They rent kayaks (250B per day) and the restaurant is fabulous.

Happy Days Guesthouse GUESTHOUSE $
(☎08 7144 5945; www.kohkood-happydays.com; r 450-750B; ❄ 📶) Laidback joint halfway between Hat Khlong Yao and Ao Ngam Khao. Rooms are spread over two floors, there are hammocks to swing in, lots of dogs and a couple of resident monkeys.

Koh Kood Boutique House HOTEL $$
(☎08 4524 4321; www.kohkoodboutiquehouse.com; Ao Prao; r 1200-2800B; ❄ 📶) Almost at the southernmost point of the island is this secluded, very peaceful hotel that was converted from two traditional houses on stilts. Reservations are required.

Dusita HOTEL $$
(☎08 1707 4546; Ao Ngam Kho; r 1290-2190B; ❄) Justifiably popular with families, whose kids can run wild in the huge oceanfront garden. For everyone else, solid well-spaced-out bungalows provide a perfect retreat from the real world. Closed low season.

Siam Beach GUESTHOUSE $$
(☎08 4332 0788; www.siambeachkohkood.net; Ao Bang Bao; r 1400-2000B; ❄ @ 📶) With a monopoly on the sandiest part of the beach, Siam Beach has adequate, if unremarkable, bungalows. But location is what you get.

Mark House Bungalows GUESTHOUSE $$
(☎08 6133 0402; www.markhousebungalow.com; Ban Khlong Chao; r 1200B; ❄ 📶) Right behind the beachside resorts, Mark House is the closest cheapie to the beach. The bungalows sit beside the canal and it feels like you're halfway through a nap all the time you stay here.

★**Bann Makok** HOTEL $$$
(☎08 1643 9488; www.bannmakok.com; Khlong Yai Ki; r 2800-4000B; ❄ @ 📶) Be the envy of the speedboat patrons when you get dropped off at this boutique hotel tucked into the mangroves. Recycled timbers painted in vintage colours have been constructed into a maze of eight rooms designed to look like a traditional pier fishing village. Common decks and reading nooks provide a peaceful space to listen to birdsong or get lost in a book.

Tinkerbell Resort HOTEL $$$
(☎08 1826 1188; www.tinkerbellresort.com; Hat Khlong Chao; r 9900B; ❄ @ 📶 🏊) Natural materials, like towering bamboo privacy fences and thatched roof villas, blend this resort seamlessly into the landscape. The bungalows are smack dab on the prettiest beach you've ever seen; the rooms behind come with plunge pools. The bar is a great spot for a sundowner. Expect 40% discounts in low season.

Homefood Restaurant THAI $$
(Khlong Yai; dishes 60-350B; ⊙8.30am-9.30pm; 📶) A few independent restaurants are scattered across the island. This is the most pleasant of them; family-run with an outdoor eating area and an alluring selection of seafood and salads, as well as Western breakfasts.

ℹ Information

There are no banks or ATMs, though major resorts can exchange money. A small **hospital** (☎0 3952 5748; ⊙8.30am-4.30pm) can handle minor emergencies and is located inland at Ban Khlong Hin Dam. The **police station** (☎0 3952 5741) is nearby. Almost all hotels and guesthouses have wi-fi now.

ℹ Getting There & Around

Ko Kut is accessible from the mainland pier of Laem Sok, 22km southeast of Trat, the nearest bus transfer point.

Koh Kood Princess (☎08 6126 7860; www.kohkoodprincess.com) runs an air-con boat (one way 350B, one daily, one hour 40 minutes) that docks at Ao Salad, in the northeastern corner of the island. There's free land transfer on your arrival.

Speedboats also make the crossing to/from Laem Sok (one way 600B, 1½ hours) during high season and will drop you off at your hotel's pier.

Bang Bao Boat (www.bangbaoboat.com) is the archipelago's inter-island ferry running a daily loop from Ko Chang, departing at 9am, to Ko Kut (one way 900B, five to six hours). In the opposite direction, you can catch it to Ko Mak (one way 300B, one to two hours) and Ko Wai (one way 400B, 2½ hours).

Ko Kut's roads are steep, ruling out renting a push bike unless you are a champion cyclist. Motorbikes can be rented for 250B per day.

Hua Hin & the Upper Gulf

Includes ➡

Best Places to Eat

- Rang Yen Garden (p145)
- Hua Hin Koti (p154)
- Prikhorm (p168)
- Rim Lom (p163)
- Rabieng Rim Nam (p142)

Best Places to Stay

- Baan Bayan (p152)
- Brassiere Beach (p158)
- Away Hua Hin (p157)
- NaNa Chart Baan Krut (p165)
- House 73 (p162)

Why Go?

Known as the 'royal' coast, the upper gulf has long been the favoured playground of the Bangkok monarchy and elite. Every Thai king from Rama IV on has found an agreeable spot to build a royal getaway. Today, domestic tourists flock to this coast in the same pursuit of leisure, as well as to pay homage to the revered kings whose summer palaces are now open to the public.

Culture meets the coast here, with historic sites, national parks and long sandy beaches ideal for swimming all an easy commute from Bangkok. And while Thais have long known of the region's delights, increasing numbers of Western travellers are now falling for the combination of an unspoiled coastline and the easy pace of provincial life on offer. There's little diving or snorkelling, but kiteboarders will be in paradise as this region is by far the best place in Thailand to jump the waves.

When to Go

- The best time to visit is during the hot and dry season (February to June). From July to October (southwest monsoon) and October to January (northeast monsoon) there is occasional rain and strong winds; but the region tends to stay drier than the rest of the country because of a geographic anomaly.
- During stormy periods, jellyfish are often carried close to shore making swimming hazardous. The Thais get around this by swimming fully clothed.

Hua Hin & the Upper Gulf Highlights

1. Motorcycling between curvaceous bays and limestone peaks in **Prachuap Khiri Khan** (p160)
2. Strolling the long blonde coastline of **Hua Hin** (p146) dotted with wave-jumping kiteboarders
3. Eating and shopping (and eating some more) at Hua Hin's **night market** (p153)
4. Escaping into the depths of **Kaeng Krachan National Park** (p143) and spotting gibbons and wild elephants
5. Being a beach bum on laid-back **Hat Thung Wua Laen** (p166)
6. Exploring the hilltop palace and underground caves, while dodging monkeys, in **Phetchaburi** (p139)
7. Making the popular pilgrimage to **Khao Sam Roi Yot National Park** (p158) to see the illuminated cave shrine of Tham Phraya Nakhon
8. Letting the kids run around all day in their bathing suits at **Dolphin Bay** (p137)

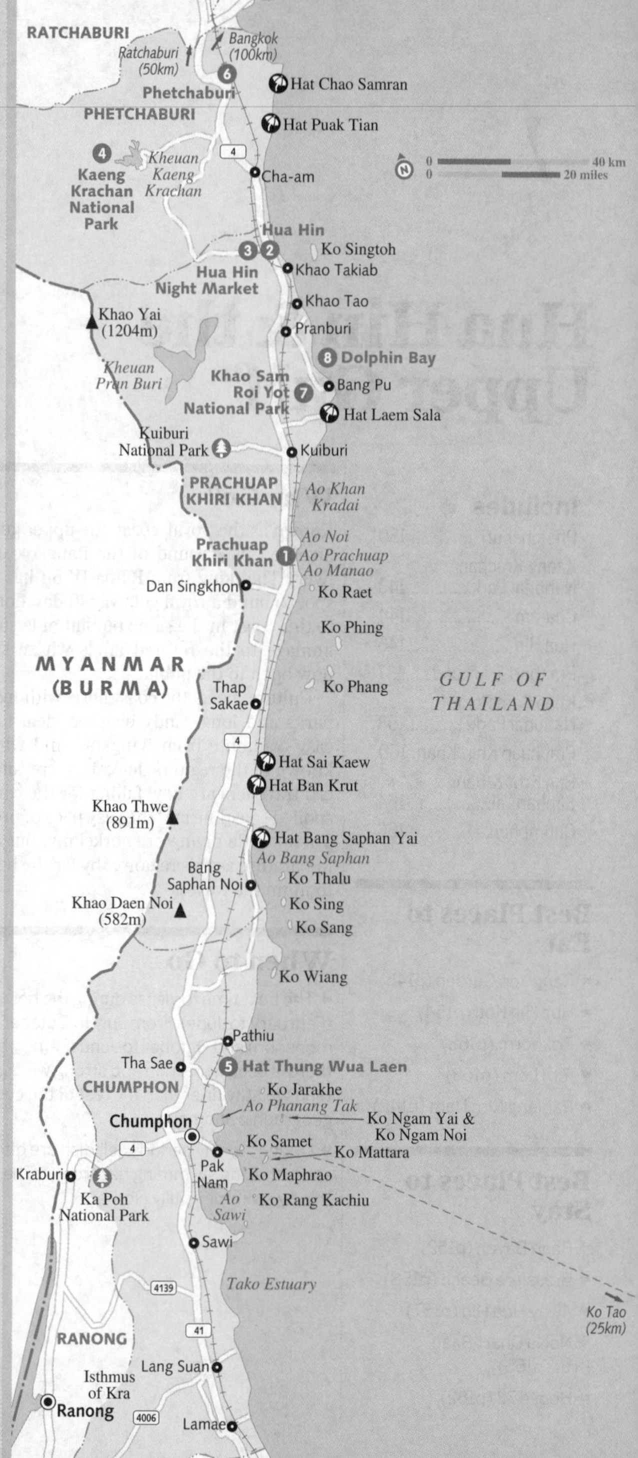

Phetchaburi (Phetburi)

เพชรบุรี

POP 46,600

An easy escape from Bangkok, Phetchaburi should be on every cultural traveller's itinerary. It has temples and palaces, outlying jungles and cave shrines, as well as easy access to the coast. Best of all, Phetchaburi remains a sleepy provincial town, complete with markets and old teak shophouses. Relatively few foreigners make it here; instead it is visiting groups of Thai students who can be found touring the sites and working up the courage to say 'hello' to any wandering Westerners.

Historically, Phetchaburi is a visible timeline of kingdoms that have migrated across Southeast Asia. During the 11th century the Khmer empire settled in, although their control was relatively short-lived. As Khmer power diminished, Phetchaburi became a strategic royal fort during the Thai-based Sukhothai and Ayuthaya kingdoms. During the stable Ayuthaya period, the upper gulf flourished and Phetchaburi thrived as a 17th-century trading post between Myanmar and Ayuthaya. The town is often referred to as a 'Living Ayuthaya', since the equivalent of the many relics that were destroyed in the former kingdom's capital are still intact here.

Sights & Activities

For such a small town, Phetchaburi has enough historic temples to keep anyone busy for the day.

Phra Nakhon Khiri Historical Park HISTORICAL SITE

(อุทยานประวัติศาสตร์พระนครคีรี; ☎0 3240 1006; admission 150B, tram return adult/child 40B/free; ⏲8.30am-4.30pm, tram 8.30am-4.30pm) This national historical park sits regally atop Khao Wang (Palace Hill) surveying the city with subdued opulence. Rama IV (King Mongkut) built the palace, in a mix of European and Chinese styles, and surrounding temples in 1859 as a retreat from Bangkok. The hilltop location allowed the king to pursue his interest in astronomy and stargazing.

Each breezy hall of the palace is furnished with royal belongings. Cobblestone paths lead from the palace through the forested hill to three summits, each topped by a *chedi* (stupa). The white spire of **Phra That Chom Phet** skewers the sky and can be spotted from the city below.

There are two entrances to the site. The front entrance is across from Th Ratwithi and involves a strenuous footpath that passes a troop of unpredictable monkeys. The back entrance is on the opposite side of the hill and has a **tram** that glides up and down the summit. This place is a popular school-group outing, and you'll be as much a photo-op as the historic buildings.

A **Monday night market** lines the street in front of Khao Wang with the usual food and clothing stalls.

Wat Mahathat Worawihan BUDDHIST TEMPLE

(วัดมหาธาตุวรวิหาร; Th Damnoen Kasem) FREE Centrally located, gleaming white Wat Mahathat is a lovely example of an everyday temple with as much hustle and bustle as the busy commercial district around it. The showpiece is a five-tiered Khmer-style *prang* (stupa) decorated in stucco relief, a speciality of Phetchaburi's local artisans, while inside the main *wí·hăhn* (shrine hall or sanctuary) are contemporary murals.

The tempo of the temple is further heightened with the steady beat from traditional musicians and dancers who perform for merit-making services.

After visiting here, follow Th Suwanmunee through the old teak-house district filled with the smells of incense from religious paraphernalia shops.

Tham Khao Luang CAVE

(ถ้ำเขาหลวง; ⏲8am-6pm) FREE About 4km north of town is Tham Khao Luang, a dramatic stalactite-stuffed chamber that is one of Thailand's most impressive cave shrines and a favourite of Rama IV. Accessed via a steep set of stairs, its central Buddha figure is often illuminated with a heavenly glow when sunlight filters in through the heart-shaped skylight.

At the opposite end of the chamber are a row of sitting Buddhas casting repetitive shadows on the undulating cavern wall.

PHETCHABURI SIGHTSEEING

Some of the city's best sights are outside town, but don't let the distance deter you. Hire a *sŏrng·tăa·ou* (passenger pick-up truck) for the day (usually around 500B) to hit all the highlights. Alternatively, you can rent a motorbike (200B to 300B) or a bicycle (100B).

Phetchaburi (Phetburi)

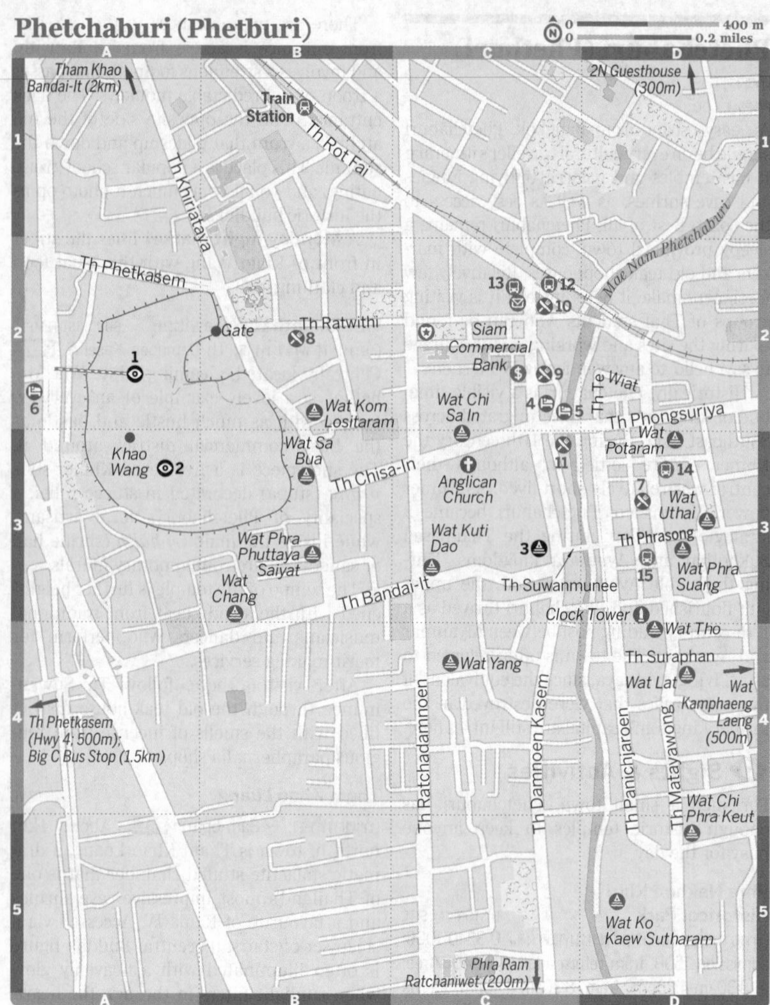

The story is that Rama IV built the stone gate that separates the main chamber from a second chamber as a security measure for a couple who once lived in the cave. A figure of a prostrate body in the third chamber is said to represent the cycle of life and death but it hasn't experienced a peaceful resting place as bandits destroyed much of it in search of hidden treasures. Deeper in the cave is supposedly a rock formation that looks like Christ on the cross but our literal eyes couldn't spot it. (Thais are especially imaginative at spotting familiar forms in cave stalactites.)

Around the entrance to the cave you'll meet brazen monkeys looking for handouts. Guides lurk in the car park, but they're not essential and aren't always forthcoming about their fees (usually 100B per person). You'll need to arrange transport here from town (around 150B round-trip).

Phra Ram Ratchaniwet HISTORICAL SITE
(พระรามราชนิเวศน์; ☎0 3242 8083; Ban Peun Palace; admission 50B; ⊙8.30am-4.30pm Mon-Fri) An incredible art nouveau creation, construction of this elegant summer palace began in 1910 at the behest of Rama V (who

Phetchaburi (Phetburi)

Sights

1 Phra Nakhon Khiri Historical Park....A2
2 Phra That Chom Phet....A3
3 Wat Mahathat Worawihan....C3

Sleeping

4 J.J. Home....C2
5 Sabaidee Resort....C2
6 Sun Hotel....A2

Eating

7 Day Market....D3
8 Jek Meng....B2
9 Ne & Nal....C2
10 Night Market....C2
11 Rabieng Rim Nam....C3

Transport

12 Air-con Buses to Bangkok....C2
13 Minivans to Bangkok....C2
14 Ordinary Buses to Cha-am & Hua Hin....D3
15 Sŏrng·tăa·ou to Kaeng Krachan National Park....D3

died just after the project was started). Designed by German architects, who used the opportunity to showcase contemporary design innovations, inside there are spacious sun-drenched rooms decorated with exquisite glazed tiles, stained glass, parquet floors and plenty of wrought-iron details.

While the structure is typical of early 20th century Thailand, a period that saw a local passion for erecting European-style buildings in an effort to keep up with the 'modern' architecture of Thailand's colonised neighbours, the scale of the palace is impressive. Check out the double-spiral staircase, which provides a classic debutante's debut, and the state-of-the-art, for the time, personal bathroom of the king. The palace is on a military base 1km south of town; you may be required to show your passport.

Wat Kamphaeng Laeng BUDDHIST TEMPLE

(วัดกำแพงแลง; Th Phokarang) FREE A 12th-century remnant of the time when the Angkor (Khmer) kingdom stretched from present-day Cambodia all the way to the Malay peninsula, this ancient and once ornate shrine was originally Hindu before Thailand's conversion to Buddhism. There is one intact sanctuary, flanked by two smaller shrines and crumbling sandstone walls, making for intriguing photo opportunities.

Tham Khao Bandai-It CAVE

(ถ้ำเขาบันไดอิฐ; donation appreciated; 9am-4pm) This hillside monastery, 2km west of town, sprawls through several large caverns converted into simple Buddha shrines and meditation rooms. English-speaking guides (tip appreciated) lead tours, mainly as a precaution against the monkeys. One cavern contains a significant population of bats, and guides will instruct you not to look up with your mouth open (a good rule for everyday life).

Hat Puak Tian BEACH

(หาดปึกเตียน) Locals come to this dark-sands beach, 20km southeast of Phetchaburi and famed for its role in Thai literature, on weekends to eat seafood and frolic in the surf. You'll need private transport to get here.

The beach is mentioned in the Thai epic poem *Phra Aphaimani,* written by Sunthorn Phu. A partially submerged statue of a giant woman standing offshore with an outstretched hand and a forlorn expression depicts a character from the poem who disguised herself as a beautiful temptress to win the love of the hero and imprison him on this beach. But he discovers her treachery (and her true ugliness) and with the help of a mermaid escapes to Ko Samet (which has nicer beaches so maybe he was onto something).

Festivals & Events

Phra Nakhon Khiri Fair CULTURAL

(Apr) Centred on Khao Wang, this provincial-style celebration takes place in early April and lasts nine days. Phra Nakhon Khiri is festooned with lights, there are traditional dance performances, craft and food displays and a beauty contest.

Sleeping

Once bereft of guesthouses, Phetchaburi's accommodation options have improved significantly in the last couple of years. But there aren't many places, so it's worth booking ahead, especially in high season.

2N Guesthouse GUESTHOUSE $

(0 3240 1309; two_nguesthouse@hotmail.com; 98/3 Moo 2, Tambol Bankoom; d & tw 580B;) There are only six big and bright rooms, all with small balconies. The friendly staff are a solid source of information and they offer free pick-ups and bicycles.

Sabaidee Resort GUESTHOUSE $
(☎0 3240 0194; sabai2505@gmail.com; 65-67 Th Klongkrachang; r 250-500B; ❄@📶) Basic but well-kept bungalows and rooms, some fan only and all with shared bathrooms, set around a small garden. Pleasant staff and a popular spot for breakfast.

J.J. Home GUESTHOUSE $
(☎08 1880 9286; a.sirapassorn@hotmail.com; 2 Th Chisa-In; r 200-500B; ❄📶) By the road, so a little noisy, but the rooms here are spacious and clean and a decent deal. The more expensive options have private bathrooms and air-con.

Sun Hotel HOTEL $$
(☎0 3240 1000; www.sunhotelthailand.com; 43/33 Soi Phetkasem; r 900-1150B; ❄@📶) The only realistic midrange option in town, the Sun Hotel sits opposite the back entrance to Phra Nakhon Khiri. It has large, modern but uninspired rooms with professional staff. There's a pleasant cafe downstairs and you can rent bikes for 20B per hour.

Eating

Surrounded by palm sugar plantations, Phetchaburi is famous for Thai sweets, including *kà·nŏm môr gaang* (egg custard) and the various 'golden' desserts made from egg yolks to portend good fortune. Nearby fruit orchards produce refreshingly aromatic *chom·pôo Phet* (Phetchaburi rose apple), pineapples and golden bananas.

★**Rabieng Rim Nam** INTERNATIONAL-THAI $
(☎0 3242 5707; 1 Th Chisa-In; dishes 45-80B; ⏲7am-10pm; 📶) This riverside restaurant serves up terrific food and the English-speaking owner is a fount of tourist information. The affiliated guesthouse has a few run-down but bearable rooms, all with shared bathrooms.

Jek Meng THAI $
(www.jekmeng-noodle.com; 85 Th Ratwithi; dishes 50-150B; ⏲7am-5pm) A cut above your average hole-in-the-wall joint, you can find curries and dumplings here, as well as fried rice and noodles. It's opposite the Shell petrol station. Look for the black-and-white checked tablecloths.

Ne & Nal THAI $
(Th Damnoen Kasem; dishes 40-60B; ⏲8am-5pm) Great slow-cooked soups in claypots are the signature dishes at this casual place. The *gŏo·ay đĕe·o gài* (chicken noodles) comes southern style with a whole chicken drumstick.

Night Market THAI $
(Th Ratwithi; ⏲4pm-10pm) Big and bustling from the late afternoon, head here for all the standard Thai fast food favourites and decent barbecue.

Day Market THAI $
(⏲6am-6pm) A good spot for people-watching, the day market, north of the clock tower, has food stalls on the perimeter serving the usual noodle dishes as well as specialities such as *kà·nŏm jeen tôrt man* (thin noodles with fried spicy fishcake) and the hot-season favourite *kôw châa pét·bù·ree* (moist chilled rice served with sweetmeats).

MONKEY BUSINESS

Phetchaburi is full of macaque monkeys who know no shame or fear. Having once just congregated on Khao Wang (Palace Hill), they have now spread to the surrounding streets, as well as to the road leading to Tham Khao Luang. There they lurk by food stands, or eye up pedestrians as potential mugging victims. These apes love plastic bags – regarding them as a signal that you are carrying food – so be wary about displaying them. Keep a tight hold on camera bags too. Above all, don't feed or bait the monkeys. They do bite.

Information

There's no formal information source in town, but 2N Guesthouse and Rabieng Rim Nam are both good for traveller tips.

Main Post Office (cnr Th Ratwithi & Th Damnoen Kasem)

Police Station (☎0 3242 5500; Th Ratwithi) Near the intersection of Th Ratchadamnoen.

Siam Commercial Bank (2 Th Damnoen Kasem) Other nearby banks also offer foreign exchange and ATMs.

Getting There & Away

The stop for buses to Bangkok is at the back of the night market. Across the street is a minivan stop with services to Bangkok. Minivans for Kaen Krachan National Park also leave from opposite the night market.

Ordinary buses to Cha-am and Hua Hin stop in town near Th Matayawong.

Most southbound air-conditioned buses and minivans stop out of town on Th Phetkasem in

TRANSPORT TO/FROM PHETCHABURI

DESTINATION	BUS	MINIVAN	TRAIN
Bangkok Hua Lamphong			84-388B; 3-4hr; 12 daily 1.53am-4.47pm
Bangkok southern bus terminal	120B; 2-3hr; 8.30am & 10.30am	100B; 2hr; hourly 7am-6pm	
Bangkok Victory Monument		100B; 2hr; every 45min 5am-6pm	
Chaam from Th Matayawong	30B; 40min; frequent		
Hua Hin from Th Matayawong	40B; 1½ hours; frequent		12 daily
Kaeng Krachan National Park		100B; 1hr; hourly 6.30am-6pm	

front of the Big C department store. Destinations include Cha-am and Hua Hin. Motorcycle taxis await and can take you into town for around 50B.

Frequent rail services run to/from Bangkok's Hua Lamphong station. Fares vary depending on the train and class.

Getting Around

Motorcycle taxis go anywhere in the town centre for 40B to 50B. *Sŏrng·tăa·ou* (pick-up trucks) cost about the same. It's a 20-minute walk (1km) from the train station to the town centre.

Rabieng Rim Nam restaurant hires out bicycles (100B per day) and motorbikes (200B to 300B per day).

Kaeng Krachan National Park

อุทยานแห่งชาติแก่งกระจาน

Wake to an eerie symphony of gibbon calls as the early morning mist hangs limply above the forest canopy. Hike through lush forests in search of elephant herds and other wildlife at the communal watering holes. Or sweat through your clothes as you summit the park's highest peak. At 3000 sq km, Thailand's largest **national park** (☎0 3245 9293; www.dnp.go.th; admission 200B; ⊙visitors centre 8.30am-4.30pm) is surprisingly close to civilisation but shelters an intense tangle of wilderness that sees few tourists. Two rivers (Mae Nam Phetchaburi and Mae Nam Pranburi), a large lake and abundant rainfall keep the place green year-round. Animal life is prolific and includes wild elephants, deer, gibbons, boars, dusky langurs and wild cattle.

This park also occupies an interesting, overlapping biozone for birds as the southernmost spot for the northern species and the northernmost for the southern species. There are about 400 species of birds, including hornbills as well as pheasants and other ground dwellers.

Activities

Hiking is the best way to explore the park. Most of the trails are signed and branch off the main road. The **Nam Tok Tho Thip** trail starts at the Km 36 marker and continues for 4km to an 18-tiered waterfall. **Phanoen Thung** (1112m) is the park's highest point and can be summited via a 6km hike that starts at the Km 27 marker. Note that most trails, including the one to Phanoen Thung, are closed during the rainy season (August to October).

The twin waterfalls of **Pa La-U Yai** and **Pa La-U Noi** in the southern section of the park are popular with day-trippers on tours from Hua Hin and stay open in the rainy season, when they are in full flow. It's also possible to organise mountain biking in the park from Hua Hin.

Tourist infrastructure in Kaeng Krachan is somewhat limited and the roads can be rough. The park rangers can help arrange camping-gear rental, food and transport. There are crowds on weekends and holidays but weekdays should be people free. The best months to visit are between November and April.

Sleeping & Eating

There are various **bungalows** (☎0 2562 0760; www.dnp.go.th/parkreserve; bungalows from 1200B) within the park, mainly near the reservoir. These sleep from four to six people and are simple affairs with fans and fridges. There are also **campsites** (per person 60-90B), including a pleasant grassy one near the reservoir at the visitors centre, and a modest restaurant. Tents can be rented at the visitors centre. Bear in mind that you can't stay overnight during the rainy season.

On the road leading to the park entrance are several simple resorts and bungalows. About 3.5km before reaching the visitors centre, **A&B Bungalows** (☎08 9891 2328; r from 700B) is scenic and popular with bird-watching groups. There is a good restaurant here that can provide you with a packed lunch.

Getting There & Away

Kaeng Krachan is 52km southwest of Phetcha buri, with the southern edge of the park 35km from Hua Hin. If you have your own vehicle, drive 20km south from Phetchaburi on Hwy 4 to the town of Tha Yang. Turn right (west) and after 38km you'll reach the visitors centre. You use the same access road from Tha Yang if coming south from Hua Hin.

You can also reach the park by **minivan** (☎08 9231 5810; one-way 100B; hourly 6.30am-6pm) from Phetchaburi. Alternatively you can catch a *sŏrng·tăa·ou* (80B, 1½ hours, 6am to 2pm) from Phetchaburi (near the clock tower) to the village of Ban Kaeng Krachan, 4km before the park. From the village, you can charter transport to the park. You can also hire your own *sŏrng·tăa·ou* all the way to the park; expect to pay around 1500B for the return trip.

Minivan tours also operate from Hua Hin.

Cha-am

ชะอำ

POP 72,341

Cheap and cheerful Cha-am has long been a popular beach getaway for working-class families and Bangkok students. On weekends and public holidays, neon-painted buses (called '*chor ching cha*'), their sound systems pumping, deliver groups of holidaymakers. It is a very Thai-style beach party with eating and drinking marathons held around umbrella-shaded beach chairs and tables. Entertainment is provided by the banana boats that zip back and forth, eventually making a final jack-knife turn that throws the passengers into the sea. Applause and giggles usually follow from the beachside audience.

Cha-am doesn't see many foreigners; visitors are usually older Europeans who winter here instead of more expensive Hua Hin. And there are even fewer bathing suits on display as most Thais frolic in the ocean fully clothed. This isn't the spot to meet a lot of young travellers or even a good option for families of young children who might be overwhelmed by paparazzi-like Thais in holiday mode. But for everyone else, Cha-am's beach is long, wide and sandy, the grey-blue water is clean and calm, the seafood is superb, the people-watching entertaining and the prices are some of the most affordable anywhere on the coast.

Festivals & Events

Crab Festival FOOD

(⏲Feb) In February, Cha-am celebrates one of its local marine delicacies: blue crabs. Food stalls, concerts, and lots of neon turn the beachfront into a pedestrian party.

Gin Hoy, Do Nok, Tuk Meuk FOOD

(⏲Sep) You really can do it all at this annual festival held in September. The English translation means 'Eat Shellfish, Watch Birds, Catch Squid' and is a catchy slogan for all of Cha-am's local attractions and fishing traditions. Mainly it is a food festival showcasing a variety of shellfish but there are also bird-watching events at nearby sanctuaries and squid-fishing demonstrations.

Sleeping

Cha-am has two basic types of accommodation: hotels along the beach road (Th Ruamjit) and more expensive 'condotel' developments (condominiums with a kitchen and operating under a rental program). Expect a discount on posted rates for weekday stays. For guesthouses, head to Soi 1 North off Th Ruamjit or raucous Soi Bus Station, a few hundred metres south of Soi 1 North.

The northern end of the beach (known as Long Beach) has a wider, blonder strip of sand and sees more foreign tourists, while the southern end is more Thai. Th Narathip divides the beach into north and south and the soi off Th Ruamjit are numbered in ascending order in both directions from this intersection.

Charlie House GUESTHOUSE $

(☎0 3243 3799; www.charlie-chaam.com; 241/60-61, Soi 1 North, Th Ruamjit; r 650-800B; ❄📶) This

ANIMAL ENCOUNTERS

Modern sensibilities have turned away from circuslike animal attractions but many well-intentioned animal lovers curious to see Thailand's iconic creatures (such as elephants, monkeys and tigers) unwittingly contribute to an industry that is poorly regulated and exploitative. Animals are often illegally captured from the wild and disfigured to be less dangerous (tigers often have their claws and teeth removed), they are acquired as pets and then neglected or inhumanely confined, or abandoned when they are too sick or infirm to work.

Wildlife Friends Foundation Thailand runs a **wildlife rescue centre** (☎0 3245 8135; www.wfft.org; Wat Khao Luk Chang), 35km northwest of Cha-am, that adopts and cares for abused and abandoned animals. Most of these animals are creatures that can't return to the wild due to injuries or lack of survival skills. The centre cares for 400 animals, including bears, tigers, gibbons, macaques, loris and birds. There is also an affiliated elephant rescue program that buys and shelters animals being used as street beggars.

The centre offers a **full access tour** (5000B for six people) that introduces the animals and discusses their rescue histories. The tour includes a visit with the elephants (but no rides are offered) and hotel transfer from Hua Hin or Cha-am.

Those looking for a more intimate connection with the animals can volunteer to help at the centre. An average day could involve chopping fruits and vegetables to feed sun bears, cleaning enclosures and rowing out to the gibbon islands with a daily meal. Volunteers are required to stay a minimum of one week and have to make a compulsory donation (from US$455/14,368B) to the centre. Contact the centre or visit the **volunteer website** (www.wildlifevolunteer.org) for details.

cheery place boasts a lime-green lobby and modern, comfortable and colourful rooms. Don't confuse it with the institutional Charlie Place or Charlie TV on the same soi.

Cha-am Mathong Guesthouse GUESTHOUSE $
(☎0 3247 2528; www.chaammathong.com; 263/47-48 Th Ruamjit; r 600-700B; ❄📶) No frills here, but the rooms are clean and you're right across from the beach. Better rooms have sea views and small balconies. The attached restaurant does brisk business during the day.

Sala Thai Guest House GUESTHOUSE $
(☎0 3243 3505; www.guesthousesalathai.com; Soi 1 North, Th Ruamjit; r 600-800B; ❄📶) Run by two slightly grumpy ladies (their bark is worse than their bite), this place has a cool wooden exterior and large rooms. Not much English spoken.

Baan Pantai Resort HOTEL $$
(☎0 3243 3111; www.baanpantai.com; 247/58 Th Ruamjit; r from 2000B; 🚭❄📶🏊) Rather more upmarket than most hotels in Cha-am, this family-friendly place has a huge pool and small fitness centre. It's in the heart of all the action, but the rooms towards the back are quiet.

Eating

From your beach chair you can wave down the itinerant vendors selling barbecued and fried seafood, or order from the many nearby beachfront restaurants. At the far northern end of the beach, seafood restaurants with reasonable prices can be found at the fishing pier. There's also a large night market on Th Narathip close to the train station.

★**Rang Yen Garden** THAI $
(☎0 3247 1267; 259/40 Th Ruamjit; dishes 60-180B; ⏰11am-10pm Nov-Apr) This lush garden restaurant is a cosy and friendly spot to feel at home after a day of feeling like a foreigner. It serves up Thai favourites and is only open in the high season.

Didine INTERNATIONAL-THAI $$
(Soi Bus Station, Th Ruamjit; dishes 80-350B; ⏰10am-11pm; 📶) There are two chefs here, one French, one Thai, and the menu spans continental Europe, as well as offering a very solid selection of seafood and local favourites.

Bella Pizza ITALIAN $$
(☎0 3247 0980; 328/19 Th Nongjiang; pizzas from 155B; ⏰4pm-midnight) Now relocated to the southern end of town, this popular pizza place has a large, quiet outdoor terrace. Thai food is on offer as well and they deliver free if you're feeling lazy.

Information

Phetkasem Hwy runs through Cha-am's busy town centre, which is about 1km away from the beach. The town centre is where you'll find the main bus stop, banks, the main post office, an outdoor market and the train station.

You'll find plenty of banks along Th Ruamjit with ATMs and exchange services.

Only Chaam (www.onlychaam.com) An online blog and website about visiting Cha-am.

Post Office (Th Ruamjit) On the main beach strip.

Tourism Authority of Thailand (TAT; ☎0 3247 1005; tatphet@tat.or.th; 500/51 Th Phetkasem; ⌚8.30am-4.30pm) On Phetkasem Hwy, 500m south of town. The staff speak good English.

Getting There & Away

Buses stop on Phetkasem Hwy near the 7-Eleven store at the intersection of Th Narathip. Frequent bus services operating to/from Cha-am include to Bangkok, Phetchaburi and Hua Hin.

Minivans to Bangkok's Victory Monument leave from Soi Bus Station, in between Th Ruamjit and Th Chao Lay. Buses to Bangkok's southern bus terminal also leave from Soi Bus Station. Other minivan destinations include Hua Hin and Phetchaburi. A private taxi to Hua Hin will cost 500B.

The **train station** (Th Narathip) is west of Phetkasem Hwy. From Bangkok's Hua Lamphong station trains go to Cha-am and continue on to Hua Hin. Note that Cha-am is listed in the timetable only in Thai as 'Ban Cha-am'.

Getting Around

From the city centre to the beach it's a quick motorcycle ride (40B). Some drivers may try to take you to hotels that offer commissions instead of the one you requested.

You can hire motorcycles for 200B to 300B per day all along Th Ruamjit. Cruisy bicycles are available everywhere for 20B per hour or 100B per day, and are a good way to get around.

Hua Hin หัวหิน

POP 98,896

Thailand's original beach resort is no palm-fringed castaway island and, arguably, is better for it. Instead, it is a delightful mix of city and sea with a cosmopolitan ambience, lively markets, tasty street eats, long beaches and fully functional city services (meaning no septic streams bisect the beach like those *other* places).

Hua Hin traces its aristocratic roots to the 1920s when Rama VI (King Vajiravudh) and Rama VII (King Prajadhipok) built summer residences here to escape Bangkok's stifling climate. The more famous of the two is **Phra Ratchawang Klai Kangwon** (Far from Worries Palace), 3km north of town, which is still a royal residence today and so poetically named that Thais often invoke it as a city slogan. Rama VII's endorsement of Hua Hin and the construction of the southern railway made the town *the* place to be for Thai nobility, who built their own summer residences beside the sea.

In the 1980s, the luxury hotel group Sofitel renovated the town's grand dame hotel and foreign tourists started arriving. Today, all the international hotel chains have properties in Hua Hin, and a growing number of wealthy expats retire to the nearby housing estates and condominiums. Middle-class and high-society Thais from Bangkok swoop into town on weekends, making parts of the city look a lot like upper Sukhumvit.

There's a lot of money swirling around but because this is a bustling Thai town, seafood is plentiful and affordable, there's cheap public transport for beach-hopping and it takes a lot less effort (and money) to get here from Bangkok than to the southern islands. So, stop wasting your time elsewhere and grab a spot on the beach!

TRANSPORT TO/FROM CHA-AM

DESTINATION	BUS	MINIVAN	TRAIN
Bangkok Hua Lamphong			40-90B; 4½hr; 4.55am & 2.33pm daily
Bangkok southern bus terminal	150B; 3hr; frequent	160B; 2½hr; hourly 7am-6pm	
Bangkok Victory Monument		160B; 2½hr; every 30min 7am-6.30pm	
Hua Hin	30B; 30min; frequent	40B; frequent	30-40B; 1½hr; 2 daily
Phetchaburi	30B; 40min; frequent	50B; frequent	20-30B; 1hr; 3 daily

Sights

The city's beaches are numerous, wide and long; swimming is safe, and Hua Hin continues to enjoy some of the peninsula's driest weather. During stormy weather, watch out for jellyfish.

Hua Hin Town เมืองหัวหิน

A former fishing village, Hua Hin town retains its roots with an old teak shophouse district bisected by narrow soi, pier houses that have been converted into restaurants or guesthouses and a busy fishing pier still in use today. South of the harbour is a rocky headland that inspired the name 'Hua Hin', meaning 'Stone Head'. In the commercial heart are busy markets and all the modern conveniences you forgot to pack.

Hat Hua Hin BEACH

(หาดหัวหิน; public access via eastern end of Th Damnoen Kasem) When viewed from the main public entrance, Hua Hin's beach is a pleasant but not stunning stretch of sand punctuated by round, smooth boulders. Don't be dismayed; this is the people-watching spot. If you're after swimming and sunbathing continue south where the sand is a fine white powder and the sea a calm grey-green.

The 5km-long beach stretches to a Buddha-adorned headland (Khao Takiab). The north end is where Thais come to photograph their friends wading ankle-deep in the sea, and pony rides are offered to anyone standing still. Further south, resort towers rather than coconut trees line the interior of the beach, but that's a minor distraction if you're splashing around in the surf. Access roads lead to Th Phetkasem, where you can catch a green *sŏrng·tăa·ou* back to town.

Hua Hin Train Station HISTORICAL SITE

(สถานีรถไฟหัวหิน; Th Liap Thang Rot Fai) An iconic piece of local architecture, the red-and-white pavilion that sits beside Hua Hin's train station once served as the royal waiting room during Rama VI's reign. Cutting the journey time from Bangkok to a mere four hours, the arrival of the railway made Hua Hin a tourist destination for the Bangkok-based monarchy and the city's elite.

One hundred years later even speeding minivan drivers fuelled by energy drinks can't do it much quicker.

North Hua Hin

The summer residences of the royal family and minor nobility dot the coast northwards from Hua Hin's fishing pier towards Cha-am.

Hat Hua Hin Neua BEACH

(หาดหัวหินเหนือ; North Hua Hin Beach; ⏲ grounds 5.30-7.30am & 4-7pm) While the northern end of Hua Hin's beach is not its most spectacular section, it is lined with genteel Thai-Victorian garden estates bestowed with ocean-inspired names such as 'Listening to the Sea House'. The current monarchy's palace lies about 3km north of town but visitors are only allowed on the **grounds** (ID required).

There are public access paths to the beach off Th Naebkehardt. On weekends, Th Naebkehardt is the preferred getaway for Bangkok Thais, some of whom still summer in the old-fashioned residences while others come to dine in the houses that have been converted into restaurants (p153).

Plearn Wan NOTABLE BUILDING

(เพลินวาน; ☎0 3252 0311; www.plearnwan.com; Th Phetkasem btwn Soi 38 & Soi 40; ⏲9am-9pm) FREE As much an art installation as a commercial enterprise, Plearn Wan is a vintage village containing stylised versions of the old-fashioned shophouses which once occupied the Thai-Chinese districts of Bangkok and Hua Hin. There's a pharmacy selling (well actually displaying) roots, powders and other concoctions that Thai grandmothers once used, as well as music and clothes stores.

It would be a tourist trap if it charged an admission fee but the mostly Thai visitors just wander the grounds snapping photos without making any impulse purchases. If you want to support this bit of nostalgia, there are retro souvenirs and snack shops.

Phra Ratchaniwet Mrigadayavan HISTORICAL SITE

(พระราชนิเวศน์มฤคทายวัน; ☎0 3250 8443; admission 30B; ⏲8.30am-4pm) With a breezy seaside location 12km north of Hua Hin, this summer palace was built in 1923 during the reign of Rama VI. Set in a beautiful garden with statuesque trees and stunning sea views, it's a series of interlinked teak houses with tall shuttered windows and patterned fretwork built upon stilts forming a shaded ground-level boardwalk.

Hua Hin

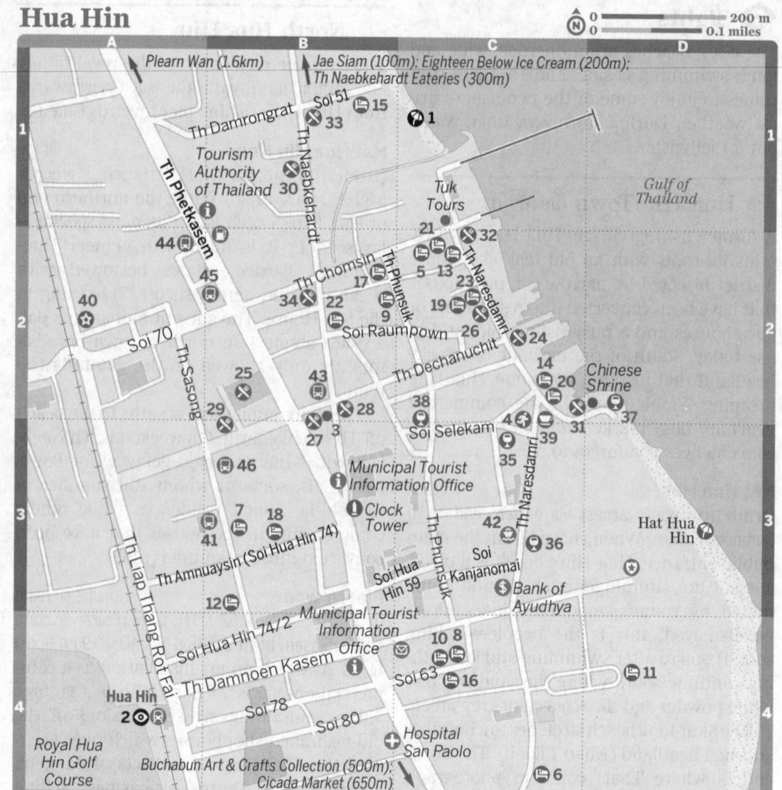

The functional but elegant style of the palace was a result of Rama VI suffering from rheumatoid arthritis; the court's Italian architect designed it to maximise air circulation and make the most of the seaside location. There's not a huge amount to see (a small selection of royal photos is on display), but it's a tranquil spot and Thais flock here to pay their respects.

The palace is within the grounds of Camp Rama VI, a military base, and you may need to show ID. It is easiest to get here with private transport but you can also catch a Hua Hin to Cha-am bus and ask to be dropped off opposite the camp's front gate. Motorcycle taxis are sometimes waiting to take you the remaining 2km. As this is a royal palace, legs and arms should be covered, otherwise you'll be given a sarong-like garment to hide your limbs.

Inland from Hua Hin

Baan Silapin ART GALLERY

(บ้านศิลปิน; ☎0 3253 4830; www.huahinartistvillage.com; Th Hua Hin-Pa Lu-U; art classes adult/child 150/100B; ⏰10am-5pm Tue-Sun, art classes 9.30-11.30am) Local painter Tawee Kasengam established this artist collective in a shady grove 4km west of Th Phetkasem. The galleries and studio spaces showcase the works of 19 artists, many of whom opted out of Bangkok's fast-paced art world in favour of Hua Hin's more relaxed atmosphere and scenic landscape of mountains and sea.

There are rotating exhibitions, while outlying clay huts shelter the playful sculptures. **Art classes** are available for adults on Tuesday and Thursday and for kids on Saturday.

Hua Hin Hills Vineyard VINEYARD

(ไร่องุ่นหัวหินฮิลล์ วินยาร์ด; ☎08 1701 0222; www.huahinhillsvineyard.com; Th Hua Hin-Pa Lu-U; vine-

Hua Hin

Sights
1 Hat Hua Hin C1
2 Hua Hin Train Station A4

Activities, Courses & Tours
3 Hua Hin Adventure Tour B2
4 Hua Hin Golf Centre C2

Sleeping
5 Baan Chalelarn Hotel C2
6 Baan Laksasubha C4
7 Baan Manthana B3
8 Baan Oum-or Hotel C4
9 Baan Tawee Suk B2
10 Ban Somboon C4
11 Centara Grand Resort and Villas D4
12 Euro-Hua Hin City Hotel YHA B3
13 Fat Cat Guesthouse C2
14 Fulay Guesthouse C2
15 Green Gallery B1
16 Hotel Alley C4
17 King's Home B2
18 My Place Hua Hin B3
19 Pattana Guest House C2
20 Sirima C2
21 Tai Tai Guest House C2
22 Tong-Mee House B2
23 Victor Guest House C2

Eating
24 Chaolay C2
25 Chatchai Market B2
26 Cool Breeze C2
27 Hua Hin Koti B3
28 Jek Pia Coffeeshop B2
29 Night Market B3
30 Ratama B1
31 Sadko C2
32 Sang Thai Restaurant C2
33 Sôm·đam Stand B1
34 Thanon Chomsin Food Stalls B2

Drinking & Nightlife
35 El Murphy's Mexican Grill & Steakhouse C3
36 Mai Tai Cocktail & Beer Garden C3
37 No Name Bar D2
38 O'Neill's Irish Pub C2
39 World News Coffee C2

Entertainment
40 Bang Bar A2

Transport
41 Air-con Buses to Bangkok B3
42 Lomprayah Office C3
43 Minivans to Bangkok B2
44 Minivans to Bangkok's Victory Monument A2
45 Ordinary Buses to Phetchaburi & Cha-am B2
46 Sŏrng·tăa·ou to Khao Takiab; bus to Pranburi B3

yard tour 1500-2100B, wine tasting 3 glasses 290B; 9am-7pm) Part of the New Latitudes wine movement (p154), this vineyard is nestled in a scenic mountain valley 45km west of Hua Hin. The loamy sand and slate soil feeds several Rhone grape varieties that are used in its Monsoon Valley wine label. Daily **vineyard tours** start at 1500B, including return transport, wine and a three-course meal. Alternatively you can just do the **wine tasting**.

There is also a pétanque course, mountain-biking trails and the picturesque **Sala Wine Bar & Bistro** (dishes from 300B; 11am-6.30pm).

A vineyard shuttle leaves the affiliated **Hua Hin Hills Wine Cellar store** (0 3252 6351; Market Village, Th Phetkasem, South Hua Hin) at 10.30am and 3pm and returns at 1.30pm and 6pm; a return ticket is 300B.

Khao Takiab เขาตะเกียบ

About 7km south of Hua Hin, Monumental Chopstick Mountain guards the southern end of Hua Hin beach and is adorned with a giant standing Buddha. Atop the 272m mountain is a Thai-Chinese temple (**Wat Khao Lat**) and many resident monkeys who are not to be trusted – but the views are great.

On the southern side of Khao Takiab is **Suan Son Pradipath** (Sea Pine Garden), a muddy beach maintained by the army and popular with weekending Thais. Green *sŏrng·tăa·ou* go all the way from Hua Hin to Khao Takiab village, where you'll find loads of simple Thai eateries serving fish straight off the fishing boats that dock here.

The nearby **Cicada Market** (Th Phetkasem; dishes 45-120B; 4-11pm Fri & Sat, 4-10pm Sun) hosts lots of outdoor food stalls at the weekend and is a pleasant, mellow spot with live music from 7pm. It's just before Khao Takiab on the left-hand side of the road. You can catch a green *sŏrng·tăa·ou* (20B, from 6am to 9pm) from Hua Hin's night market; a hired túk-túk (pronounced *đúk đúk;* motorised three-wheeled taxi) will cost 150B one-way.

Activities

With nine courses scattered around its environs, Hua Hin continues to be an international and domestic golfing destination.

Cycling is a scenic and affordable option for touring Hua Hin's outlying attractions, especially since hiring a taxi to cover the same ground is ridiculously expensive. Don't be spooked by the busy thoroughfares; there are plenty of quiet byways where you can enjoy the scenery.

Kiteboarders flock to Hua Hin for the strong winds that blow almost all year round.

Kiteboarding Asia KITEBOARDING
(☎08 1591 4593; www.kiteboardingasia.com; South Hua Hin; beginner courses 11,000B) This long-established company operates three beach-side shops that rent kite-boarding equipment and offer lessons. The three-day introductory course teaches beginners the physical mechanics of the sport, and the instructor recommends newbies come when the winds are blowing from the southeast (January to March) and the sea is less choppy.

Hua Hin Golf Centre GOLF
(☎0 3253 0476; www.huahingolf.com; Th Selakam; ⏰noon-9pm) The friendly staff at this pro shop can steer you to the most affordable, well-maintained courses where the monkeys won't try to run off with your balls. The company also organises golf tours and rents sets of clubs (500B to 700B per day).

Black Mountain Golf Course GOLF
(☎0 3261 8666; www.bmghuahin.com; green fees 2100-3600B) The most popular course in Hua Hin, and one that has hosted Asian PGA tournaments. About 10km west of Hua Hin, its 18 holes are carved out of jungle and an old pineapple plantation and it retains some natural creeks as water hazards.

Tours

There are many travel agencies in town offering day trips to nearby national parks. Unless you're in a group, you may have to wait until enough people sign up for the trip of your choice.

Hua Hin Adventure Tour ADVENTURE TOURS
(☎0 3253 0314; www.huahinadventuretour.com; 69/8 Th Naebkehardt) Hua Hin Adventure Tour offers somewhat more active excursions including kayaking trips in the Khao Sam Roi Yot National Park and mountain biking in Kaeng Krachan National Park.

Hua Hin Bike Tours CYCLING
(☎08 1173 4469; www.huahinbiketours.com; 15/120 Th Phetkasem btwn Soi 27 & 29; tours 1500-2750B) A husband-and-wife team operates this cycling company that leads half-, full- and multiday tours to a variety of attractions in and around Hua Hin. Pedal to the Hua Hin Hills Vineyard for some well-earned refreshment, tour the coastal byways south of Hua Hin, or ride among the limestone mountains of Khao Sam Roi Yot National Park. They also rent premium bicycles (500B per day) for independent cyclists and can

KITE CRAZY

Adding to the beauty of Hua Hin's beach are the kiteboarders flying and jumping above the ocean. Hua Hin is Thailand's kiteboarding, or kitesurfing, capital, blessed with strong, gusty winds, shallow water and a long, long beach off which to practise your moves.

From here down to Pranburi, the winds blow from the northeast October to December, and then from the southeast January to May: perfect for kitesurfing. Even during the May to October rainy season, there are plenty of days when the wind is fine for taking to the waves. In fact, this stretch of coast is so good for kiteboarding that Hua Hin hosted the Kiteboarding World Cup in 2010.

This is also the best place in Thailand to learn how to kiteboard, with a number of schools in Hua Hin offering tuition. After three days with them, you can be leaping into the air too. The schools also cater for more advanced students, and you can qualify as an instructor here as well.

But if you prefer to stay on the ground while flying a kite, then check out the **Hua Hin International Kite Festival**. Staged every two years in March, 12km north of town at the Rama VI military base, it's a chance to see stunt kiters in action, as well as kites of every conceivable size and colour.

recommend routes. The same couple also leads long-distance charity and corporate bike tours across Thailand; visit the parent company **Tour de Asia** (www.tourdeasia.org) for more information.

Courses

Buchabun Art & Crafts Collection COOKING (08 1572 3805; www.thai-cookingcourse.com; 19/95 Th Phetkasem; courses 1500B) Aspiring chefs should sign up for a half-day Thai cooking class that includes a market visit and recipe book. The course runs only if there are a minimum of four people.

Festivals & Events

King's Cup Elephant Polo Tournament CULTURAL (Aug & Sep) Polo with a Thai twist, this annual tournament involving elephant mounts instead of horses takes place on the scenic grounds of the Anantara Hua Hin resort in late August and early September. It might not be as fast-paced as its British cousin but it is a charitable event that raises money for elephant-welfare issues.

Hua Hin Jazz Festival MUSIC (May or Jun) In honour of the king's personal interest in the genre, the city that hosts royal getaways also hosts an annual jazz festival featuring Thai and international performers. All events are free and usually occur in May or June.

Fringe Festival THEATRE (Jan-Mar) Organised by the Patravadi Theatre, a renowned avant-garde performance space in Bangkok, this modern arts festival is held at its sister location, **Vic Hua Hin** (0 3282 7814; www.vichuahin.com; 62/70 Soi Hua Na Nong Khae, South Hua Hin). Running from January to March, there are a host of dance, music and comedy performances from local and international artists as well as multinational collaborations.

Sleeping

Most budget and midrange options are in town occupying multistorey buildings in the old shophouse district. It is an atmospheric setting with cheap tasty food nearby but you'll have to 'commute' to the beach, either by walking to north Hat Hua Hin (best at low tide) or catching a *sŏrng·tăa·ou* to the southern end of Hat Hua Hin.

The top-end options are beachfront resorts sprawling south from the Sofitel. All the international brands have a presence in Hua Hin but we've only listed special local options for a more intimate experience.

Hua Hin Town

Victor Guest House GUESTHOUSE $ (0 3251 1564; victorguesthouse@gmail.com; 60 Th Naresdamri; r 390-790B;) Popular with both Thais and foreigners, this new-ish guesthouse has solid rooms, a small garden and a central location. Helpful staff and a good source of travel tips.

Fulay Guesthouse GUESTHOUSE $ (0 3251 3145; www.fulayhuahin.net; 110/1 Th Naresdamri; r 550-900B;) With the waves crashing underneath and the floorboards creaking, this is a fine old-school pier guesthouse. Good beds, OK bathrooms and flowering plants in the common area.

Pattana Guest House GUESTHOUSE $ (0 3251 3393; 52 Th Naresdamri; r 390-590B;) Located in a simple teak house tucked away down a soi. There's a lovely garden here filled with little reading nooks. The rooms are small and basic, but the more expensive ones have private bathroom.

Euro-Hua Hin City Hotel YHA HOSTEL $ (0 3251 3130; www.huahineuro.com; 5/15 Th Sasong; r 179-999B;) Some dorms are fan-only, all are cramped and it feels a tad institutional, but the price is right for Hua Hin and the staff are helpful. The private rooms are sizeable, though the bathrooms could do with an overhaul. Add 50B to these prices if you don't belong to HI. It's off the road; look for the sign.

Sirima GUESTHOUSE $ (0 3251 1060; www.sirimaguesthouse.blogspot.com; Th Naresdamri; r 450-1000B;) A classic pier guesthouse, Sirima has a pretty exterior with lots of polished wood and a common deck overlooking the water. The cheaper rooms are small and fan-only but good value for Hua Hin.

Tong-Mee House GUESTHOUSE $$ (0 3253 0725; tongmeehuahin@hotmail.com; 1 Soi Raumpown, Th Naebkehardt; r 550-950B;) Hidden away in a quiet residential soi, this smart guesthouse has cosy and clean rooms with balconies. Book ahead here.

King's Home GUESTHOUSE $$ (08 9052 0490; huahinkingshome@gmail.com; off Th Phunsuk; 550-1200;)

Family-run guesthouse with loads of character; it's crammed with antiques and artefacts from the owners' travels across Southeast Asia. Decent-sized rooms, and it even has a small splash pool out back. It gets a lot of repeat guests, which says it all.

Baan Chalelarn Hotel HOTEL $$
(☎0 3253 1288; www.chalelarnhotel.com; 11 Th Chomsin; r 1200-1600B;) Chalelarn has a beautiful lobby with wooden floors, while the 12 big rooms are equipped with king-size beds. Verandahs and breakfast are all part of the perks. Book ahead here.

Tai Tai Guest House GUESTHOUSE $$
(☎0 3251 2891; 1/8 Th Chomsin; r 800B;) Formerly known as the Supasuda, the large rooms come with excellent beds, mermaid murals and hot showers. The more expensive ones have verandahs and a bit of road noise. There's a cosy communal roof terrace.

Fat Cat Guesthouse GUESTHOUSE $$
(☎08 6206 2455; www.thefatcathuahin.com; 8/3 Th Naresdamri; r 300-950B;) The air-con rooms for 650B are a great deal and go quick. The cheaper rooms with fan occupy a separate building and some have fantastic views of the city. They do a decent breakast.

Ban Somboon GUESTHOUSE $$
(☎0 3251 1538; www.baansomboon.com; 13/4 Soi Hua Hin 63, Th Phetkasem; r 900-1000B;) With family photos decorating the walls and a compact garden, this place on a very quiet centrally located soi is like staying at your favourite Thai auntie's house. The rooms, though, are showing their age and could do with an upgrade.

Hotel Alley HOTEL $$
(☎0 3251 1787; www.hotelalleyhuahin.com; 13/5 Soi Hua Hin 63, Th Phetkasem; r 1200-1400B;) New hotel in a quiet soi with spacious rooms decorated in pastel colours. Most have balconies and breakfast is included.

Baan Oum-or Hotel HOTEL $$
(☎08 1944 9390; baan_oum-or@hotmail.com; 77/18-19 Soi 63, Th Phetkasem; r 1000-1200B;) The rooms are big and bright, and there are only seven of them so book ahead.

Baan Manthana HOTEL $$
(☎0 3251 4223; www.manthanahouse.com; 24/10 Th Sasong; r 800-1200B;) With three separate wings, there's always space here even during public holidays. Rooms are anonymous but comfortable and proper-sized and there's a pool too. The rooms at the back are quieter.

Baan Tawee Suk GUESTHOUSE $$
(☎08 9459 2618; 43/8 Th Phunsuk; r 800-1000B;) This efficient guesthouse has clean and modern rooms on both sides of the soi. They are cramped, so leave the super-sized luggage at home.

My Place Hua Hin HOTEL $$$
(☎0 3251 4111; www.myplacehuahin.com; 17 Th Amnuaysin, Th Phetkasem; r 1850-6500B;) A smart, amiable and efficient place in the heart of the city with stylish, good-sized rooms that qualify it for boutique status. There's a rooftop swimming pool.

Hua Hin Beaches

Rahmahyah Hotel GUESTHOUSE $$
(☎0 3253 2106; Rahmahyah@yahoo.co.uk; 113/10 Soi Hua Hin 67, Th Phetkasem, South Hua Hin; r 800-1200B;) Across the street from Market Village, about 1km south of town, is a small guesthouse enclave tucked between the high-end resorts, with beach access. The Rahmahyah is the best of the bunch with clean, functional rooms. Guests can use the communal swimming pool opposite.

★**Baan Bayan** HOTEL $$$
(☎0 3253 3540; www.baanbayan.com; 119 Th Phetkasem, South Hua Hin; r 3300-9000B;) A colonial beach house built in the early 20th century, Baan Bayan is perfect for travellers seeking a luxury experience without the overkill of a big resort. Airy, high-ceilinged rooms, attentive staff – and the location is absolute beachfront.

Green Gallery HOTEL $$$
(☎0 3253 0487; www.greenhuahin.com; 3/1 Soi Hua Hin 51, Th Naebkehardt, North Hua Hin; r 2500-8500B;) As cute as candy, this small hotel occupies a converted colonial-style beach house that was once the vacation home of a princess. Individually decorated rooms reflect a hip artiness that defines urban Thai style. The attached restaurant is recommended.

Baan Laksasubha HOTEL $$$
(☎0 3251 4525; www.baanlaksasubha.com; Th 53/7 Naresdamri; r 2999-13,275B;) Sixteen much-in-demand cottages are on offer at this petite resort, owned by a Bangkok aristocrat. The decor is crisp and subdued, meandering garden paths lead to the beach

and there's a dedicated kid's room with toys and books. The taxi drivers will understand you better if you say 'baan lak-su-pah'.

Centara Grand Resort and Villas HOTEL $$$
(☎0 3251 2021; www.centarahotelsresorts.com; 1 Th Damnoen Kasem; r 7600-27,000B;) The historic Railway Hotel, Hua Hin's first seaside hotel, still has a colonial vibe but has been restored to world-class levels. Fantastic grounds, great pool, beach access, huge rooms, many restaurants and super-smooth staff.

Veranda Lodge HOTEL $$$
(☎0 3253 3678; www.verandalodge.com; 113 Soi Hua Hin 67, Th Phetkasem, South Hua Hin; r 3400-5500B;) Beachfront without the whopping price tag, the garden bungalows are very pleasant; the rooms are a little plain for the price. Noisy parrots live next to the lobby.

Eating

Night Market THAI $
(Th Dechanuchit btwn Th Phetkasem & Th Sasong; dishes from 50B; 5pm-midnight) An attraction that rivals the beach, Hua Hin's night market tops locals' lists of favourite spots to eat. Ice-packed displays of spiny lobsters and king prawns appeal to the big spenders but the simple stir-fry stalls are just as tasty. Try *pàt pŏng gà·rèe Ъoo* (crab curry), *gûng tôrt* (fried shrimp) and *hŏy tôrt* (fried mussel omelette). In between, souvenir stalls cater to the Thai favourite digestive activity: shopping.

Jek Pia Coffeeshop THAI $
(51/6 Th Dechanuchit; dishes 80-160B; 9am-1pm & 5.30-8.30pm) More than just a coffee shop, this 50-year-old restaurant is a culinary destination specialising in an extensive array of stir-fried seafood dishes. It's wildly popular with the locals and they stick rigidly to their serving hours; get here after 7.30pm and you won't be able to order.

Thanon Chomsin Food Stalls THAI $
(cnr Th Chomsin & Th Naebkehardt; dishes 30-40B; 9am-9pm) If you're after 100% authentic eats, check out the food stalls that congregate at this popular lunch corner. Though the setting is humble, Thais are fastidious eaters and use a fork (or their fingers with a pinch of *kôw nĕe·o*) to remove the meat from the bones of *gài tôrt* (fried chicken) rather than putting teeth directly to flesh.

Chatchai Market THAI $
(Th Phetkasem; dishes from 30B; daylight hours) The city's day market resides in a historic

WEEKENDS EATING WITH BANGKOK'S THAIS

On weekends, a different kind of tidal system occurs in Hua Hin. Bangkok professionals flow in, filling up hotels and restaurants on Th Naebkehardt, washing over the night market or crowding into nightclubs. And then come Sunday they clog the roadways heading north, obeying the pull of the upcoming work week.

Their presence is so pronounced that there is an irresistible urge to join them. And because of restaurant features on Thai TV or food magazines, everyone goes to the same places. So don your designer sunglasses and elbow your way to a table at one of these popular spots in North Hua Hin:

➡ **Sôm·đam Stand** (Th Naebkehardt; dishes 25-70B; 10am-2pm) Across from Iammeuang Hotel is a *sôm·đam* stand that easily wipes out the country's supply of green papayas in one weekend. Great grilled chicken too. On the other side of the road are other food stalls.

➡ **Eighteen Below Ice Cream** (Th Naebkehardt; ice cream from 69B; 11am-5pm, closed Tue) At the end of the road behind Baan Talay Chine Hotel, this gourmet ice-cream shop is run by a trained chef and specialises in rich and creamy flavours.

➡ **Ratama** (12/10 Th Naebkehardt; dishes 50-390B; 10am-10pm) New spot for visiting hipsters, with a menu that runs from simple noodle dishes to great, spicy seafood curries. If you're feeling very Thai, go for the hot and sour chicken-feet soup.

➡ **Jae Siam** (Th Naebkehardt; dishes 35-60B; 9am-10pm) If you've lost track of the days of the week, cruise by this open-air noodle shop, just before the Evergreen Hotel, where Hua Hin civil servants pack in on weekdays and Bangkok Thais come on weekends. The shop is famous for *gŏo·ay đĕe·o mŏo đŭn* (stewed pork noodles) and *gŏo·ay đĕe·o gài đŭn* (stewed chicken noodles).

building built in 1926 with a distinctive seven-eaved roof in honour of Rama VII. There are the usual market refreshments: morning vendors selling *ɓah·tôrng·gŏh* (Chinese-style doughnuts) and *gah·faa boh·rahn* (ancient-style coffee spiked with sweetened condensed milk); as well as all-day noodles with freshly made wontons; and the full assortment of fresh tropical fruit.

★Hua Hin Koti THAI $$
(☎0 3251 1252; 16/1 Th Dechanuchit; dishes 120-300B; ⏲11am-10pm) Across from the night market, this Thai-Chinese restaurant is a national culinary luminary. Thais adore the fried crab balls, while foreigners swoon over *đôm yam gûng* (shrimp soup with lemon grass). And everyone loves the spicy seafood salad *(yam tá-lair)* and deep-fried fish with ginger. Be prepared to queue for a table.

Sang Thai Restaurant SEAFOOD $$
(Th Naresdamri; dishes 100-300B; ⏲10am-11pm) One of many beloved pier-side restaurants, Sang Thai is a Hua Hin institution and a massive operation. There's a vast choice of seafood housed in giant tanks awaiting your decision. You can eat very well for not much, or spend lots.

Chaolay SEAFOOD $$
(15 Th Naresdamri; dishes 100-700B; ⏲10.30am-11pm) Another Hua Hin old-time pier restaurant and always busy. There's a big open kitchen on the ground floor enabling you to see the chefs preparing your seafood selection. Ascend the stairs to find a table.

Cool Breeze MEDITERRANEAN $$
(62 Th Naresdamri; tapas from 100B; ⏲11am-midnight) Popular tapas joint spread over two floors. Decent wine list and an amiable spot for a drink.

Sadko RUSSIAN $$
(Th Naresdamri; dishes 100-300B; ⏲9am-11pm, closed Sun) More and more Russians are visiting Hua Hin, and this friendly place caters to them with authentic dishes cooked by a Russian chef. Top dumplings and borscht, and vodka as well. Good for a Western or Russian breakfast (pancakes and sour cream) too.

Drinking & Entertainment

Drinking destinations in Hua Hin are stuck in a time warp: sports bars or hostess bars – and sometimes you can't tell the difference. But the onslaught of weekending Bangkok Thais has kicked up the sophistication factor.

No Name Bar BAR
(Th Naresdamri) Past the Chinese shrine that sits on the rocky headland is this cliff-side bar. It feels miles away from the lurid and loud hostess bars and is perfect for a chilled beer; sit and listen to the waves slapping against the rocks below.

NEW ATTITUDES TOWARDS WINE

Common wisdom would tell you that tasty wine grapes don't grow alongside coconut trees. But advances in plant sciences and a global palate for wines has ushered in the geographic experiment dubbed New Latitude Wines, produced from grapes grown outside the traditional 30- to 50-degree parallels.

The New Latitudes' main challenge is to replicate the wine-producing grapes' preferred climate as best as possible. That means introducing a false dormancy or winter period through pruning, regulated irrigation and companion planting of grasses to prevent soil loss during the rainy season. If you're familiar with viticulture in the Old World, you'll be shocked to see all the cultivation rules Thai vineyards successfully break.

Wine experts have yet to crown a New Latitude that surpasses the grand dames, but they do fill a local niche. Siam Winery, the parent company of Hua Hin Hills Vineyard (p148), aims to produce wines that pair with the complex flavours of Thai food. The vineyard grows columbard, chenin blanc, muscat, shiraz and sangiovese grapes, among others, and typically the citrus-leaning whites are a refreshing complement to the fireworks of most Thai dishes.

Because of the hot climate, a wine drinker's palate is often altered. The thinner wines produced in Thailand tend to have a more satisfying effect than the bold chewy reds that pair well with a chilly spring day. Drinking red wine in Thailand has always been a challenge because the heat turns otherwise leathery notes straight into vinegar. To counteract the tropical factor, break yet another wine rule and chill reds in the refrigerator to replicate 'cellar' temperature as close as possible.

Mai Tai Cocktail & Beer Garden BAR
(33/12 Th Naresdamri) Recession-era prices are on tap at this convivial, always crowded outdoor terrace made for people-watching and beer-drinking.

O'Neill's Irish Pub BAR
(5 Th Phunsuk) Reasonably authentic for being so far from the Blarney Stone, O'Neill's has a pool table and a fine wooden bar to sit around. Cheap draught specials and live sport on several TVs.

World News Coffee CAFE
(130/2 Th Naresdamri; coffee from 90B, sandwiches from 180B; ⌚8am-11pm) This Starbucks-esque cafe serves many varieties of coffee and tea, as well as Western breakfasts, hefty sandwiches and tasty bagels, You can surf the web for 150B per hour. Wi-fi is free if you spend over 300B. Otherwise, it's 75B for 30 minutes.

El Murphy's Mexican Grill & Steakhouse BAR
(25 Soi Selakam, Th Phunsuk) Every sports bar has an international gimmick and this comfy spot marries Mexico and Ireland. There's a big menu, live music sometimes and a pleasant vibe, although the beers aren't cheap.

Bang Bar LIVE MUSIC
(Th Liap Thang Rot Fai) North of Soi 70 along Railway Road are a string of Thai music bars, nearly all foreigner-free. This one stays packed into the early hours, with rotating singers and bands.

Information

EMERGENCY

Tourist Police (☎0 3251 5995; Th Damnoen Kasem) At the eastern end of the street.

INTERNET ACCESS

Internet access is available all over Hua Hin, in guesthouses and cafes.

MEDICAL SERVICES

Bangkok Hospital Hua Hin (☎0 3261 6800; www.bangkokhospital.com/huahin; Th Phetkasem btwn Soi Hua Hin 94 & 106) The latest outpost of the luxury hospital chain; it's in South Hua Hin.

Hospital San Paolo (☎0 3253 2576; 222 Th Phetkasem) Just south of town with emergency facilities.

MONEY

There are exchange booths and ATMs on Th Naresdamri and banks on Th Phetkasem.

POST & TELEPHONE

Main Post Office (Th Damnoen Kasem)

TOURIST INFORMATION

Municipal Tourist Information Office (☎0 3251 1047; cnr Th Phetkasem & Th Damnoen Kasem; ⌚8.30am-4.30pm Mon-Fri) Provides maps and information about Hua Hin. There's another branch (☎0 3252 2797; Th Naebkehardt; ⌚9am-7.30pm Mon-Fri, 9.30am-5pm Sat & Sun) near the clock tower.

Tourism Authority of Thailand (TAT; ☎0 3251 3885; 39/4 Th Phetkasem; ⌚8.30am-4.30pm) Staff here speak English and are quite helpful; the office is north of town near Soi Hua Hin 70.

TRAVEL AGENCIES

Tuk Tours (☎0 3251 4281; www.tuktours.com; 2/1 Th Chomsin) Helpful, no-pressure place that can book activities and transport all around Thailand.

WEBSITES

Hua Hin Observer (www.observergroup.net) An online expat-published magazine.

Tourism Hua Hin (www.tourismhuahin.com) A cursory intro to the city with a good rundown on the outlying area.

Getting There & Away

The **airport** (www.huahinairport.com) is 6km north of town, but only has charter services through **Nok Mini** (☎0 2641 4190; www.nokair.com).

Hua Hin's **long-distance bus station** (Th Phetkasem btwn Soi Hua Hin 94 & 98) is south of town and goes to Chiang Mai, Prachuap Khiri Khan, Phuket, Surat Thani and Ubon Ratchathani. Buses to Bangkok leave from a bus company's in-town **office** (Th Sasong), near the night market. Buses to Bangkok Suvarnabhumi International Airport leave from the long-distance bus station.

Ordinary buses depart from north of the market on Th Phetkasem, and destinations include Cha-am and Phetchaburi.

Lomprayah offers a bus-boat combination from Hua Hin to Ko Tao (1000B, 8½ hours, one morning and one night departure).

Minivans go to Bangkok's Sai Tai Mai (southern) bus terminal and Victory Monument. A direct service to Victory Monument leaves from an office on the corner of Th Phetkasem and Th Chomsin.

There are frequent trains running to/from Bangkok's Hua Lamphong station and other stations on the southern railway line (see table p156).

TRANSPORT TO/FROM HUA HIN

DESTINATION	BUS	MINIVAN	TRAIN	AIR
Bangkok Don Muang Airport				from 1500B Nok Air; 1hr; 3 weekly
Bangkok Hua Lamphong			44-421B; 5-6hr; 13 daily 12.45am-4.01pm	
Bangkok southern bus terminal	175B; 4½hr; 8 daily 3am-9pm			
Bangkok Suvarnabhumi Airport	305B; 5hr; 6 daily 7am-6pm			
Bangkok Victory Monument		180B; 4hr; every 30min 6am-7pm		
Cha-am	30B; 30min; frequent		20-30B; 2 daily	
Chiang Mai	851B; 12hr; 3 daily 8am, 5pm & 6pm			
Ko Tao	1000B; 8½hr; 1 daily			
Phetchaburi	40B; 1½hr; frequent		30-40B; 12 daily	
Phuket	823B; 9-10hr; 3 nightly			
Surat Thani	413-829B; 7-8hr; 4 daily			
Ubon Ratchathani	1005B; 13hr; 3 nightly			

Getting Around

Green *sŏrng·tăa·ou* depart from the corner of Th Sasong & Th Dechanuchit, near the night market and travel south on Th Phetkasem to Khao Takiab (20B). Pranburi-bound buses (20B) depart from the same stop.

Túk-túk fares in Hua Hin are outrageous and start at a whopping 100B and barely budge from there. Motorcycle taxis are much more reasonable (40B to 50B) for short hops.

Motorcycles (250B to 500B per day) can be hired from shops on Th Damnoen Kasem and Th Chomsin. **Thai Rent A Car** (☎0 2737 8888; www.thairentacar.com) is a professional car-rental agency with competitive prices, a well-maintained fleet and hotel drop-offs.

Hua Hin to Pranburi

South of Hua Hin are a series of beaches framed by dramatic headlands that make great day trips when Hua Hin beach feels too urban.

Hat Khao Tao หาดเขาเต่า

About 13km south of Hua Hin, a barely inhabited beach stretches several kilometres south from Khao Takiab to Khao Tao (Turtle Mountain). It's far quieter and less-developed than Hua Hin's beach: there are no high-rises, no beach chairs, no sarong sellers and no horseback riders.

The mountain has a sprawling temple dedicated to almost every imaginable deity: Buddha, Guan Yin (Chinese goddess of Mercy), Vishnu and even the Thai kings. Follow the trail towards the oceanfront to hike up to the Buddha on the hill.

To get here, take a Pranburi-bound bus from Hua Hin and ask to be dropped off at the turn-off for Khao Tao (20B); a motorbike taxi can take you to the temple (20B). A motorbike from Hua Hin will cost 200B one-way. Return transport is rare; you can walk or flag down a ride as people are usually coming and going from the temple.

Hat Sai Noi หาดทรายน้อย

About 20km south of Hua Hin, a scenic cove, Hat Sai Noi, drops off quickly into the sea, providing a rare opportunity for deep-water swimming. Mostly patronised by Thais, nearby are all the amenities: simple seafood restaurants and even small guesthouses.

For ideal seclusion, come on a weekday. The beach is south of Khao Tao on a lovely road that passes a reservoir and is lined with bougainvillea and limestone cliffs. To get there take a Pranburi-bound bus from Hua Hin and ask to be dropped off at the turn-off for Khao Tao (20B); then ask a motorcycle taxi to take you to Hat Sai Noi (60B). Getting back to the highway will be difficult but inquire at one of the restaurants for assistance.

Pranburi & Around

POP 75,571

Continuing along the highway south from Hua Hin leads to the country 'suburb' of Pranburi district, which has become the in-the-know coastal alternative for Bangkok Thais. Ever-more popular, some even go so far as to call it the 'Thai Riveria'. Yet locally the fishing village and nearby beaches are known by a more humble name: **Pak Nam Pran** (mouth of the Pranburi River), which designates its geographic location only.

A coastal road separates a string of small villa-style resorts, and an increasing number of condo developments, from the beach. With each successive rainy season, the ocean claims more sand than its fair share and a breakwater is being constructed along parts of the coastline. Since most of the visitors are Thai, the disappearing beach is of minor consequence. Instead, most domestic tourists come for sea views and the village's primary product: dried squid. Every morning, the squid boats dock in the river, unload their catch and begin the process of sun-drying. It is a pungent but interesting affair with large drying racks spread out across town.

Bordering the river is an extensive mangrove forest, protected by the **Pranburi Forest Park** (☎0 3262 1608) FREE. Within the park is a wooden walkway that explores the mangroves from the perspective of a mud-dweller, a sea-pine lined beach and accommodation facilities. The park also offers boat trips along the river and small canals.

The coastal road provides a pleasant trip to **Khao Kalok** (Skull Mountain), a mammoth headland that shelters a beautiful bay on the southern side. This southern beach is wide and sandy and far removed from the hubbub of Hua Hin and even from Pak Nam Pran for that matter, though it does get busy on weekends. Lazing along this stretch are several secluded boutique resorts that are ideal for honeymooners or folks looking to 'get away from it all' without having to go too far.

The next southern bay is often called **Dolphin Bay**, because of the seasonal visit from bottlenose dolphins and finless porpoise from February to May. Sculpted, jungle-covered islands sit scenically offshore and the beach is a lovely, wide strip of powdery sand. This area is a family favourite because the resorts are value-oriented, traffic is minimal and nightlife is nonexistent. You're also a few kilometres from the northern entrance to Khao Sam Roi Yot National Park.

Sleeping & Eating

It is mainly high-end here but not all of the beach resorts earn the price tag so be discerning when making online reservations for places not listed below. That said, this area has some of the best seaside boutique hotels in Thailand, making it a fine place to splash out.

Beach House GUESTHOUSE $$
(☎08 7164 6307; karl@beachhousepranburi.com; Pak Nam Pran; r 700-1200B;) One of the cheapest options around, this affable, English-run guesthouse has comfortable, decent-sized rooms. It caters mainly to young kiteboarders; you can learn to kitesurf here and the wind is as good, if not better, than Hua Hin.

Palm Beach Resort & Hotel HOTEL $$
(☎0 3263 1304; www.palmbeachpranburi.com; Pak Nam Pran; r 1800-2500B;) Right by the beach. Although the spacious rooms are a little under-maintained, the staff are nice and breakfast is included.

★ **Away Hua Hin** HOTEL $$$
(☎08 9144 6833; www.away-huahin.com; south of Khao Kalok; r 3500-4500B;) A boutique resort without pretence, and one of the more affordable in the area, seven antique teak houses have been transported to this coastal patch of paradise and outfitted with large comfy beds and stylish bathrooms.

The amiable owners, a Thai-Australian family, set a homey mood where breakfast is enjoyed at a common table in the 'big' house providing instant camaraderie. Some villas offer extreme privacy while others accommodate families. The beach is just across the road.

South of Hua Hin

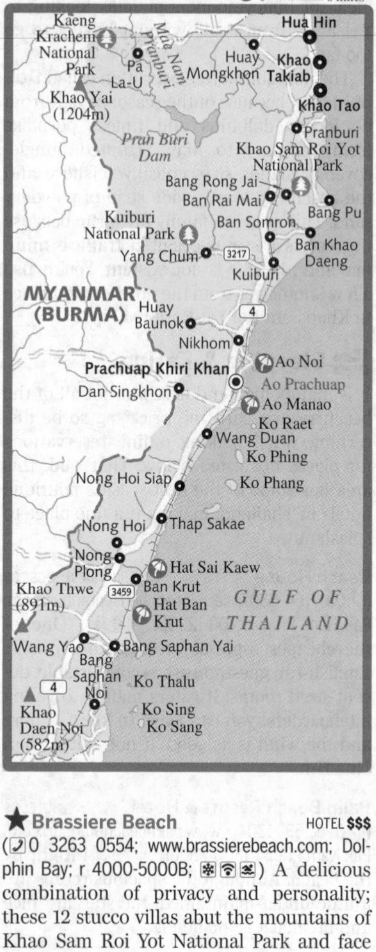

★ **Brassiere Beach** HOTEL $$$
(☎0 3263 0554; www.brassierebeach.com; Dolphin Bay; r 4000-5000B; ❄📶🏊) A delicious combination of privacy and personality; these 12 stucco villas abut the mountains of Khao Sam Roi Yot National Park and face a secluded beach, 100m from the nearest paved road. The rooms have an uncluttered Spanish colonial feel, some with roof decks and most with open-air showers. You might mispronounce its name, but Brassiere Beach deserves your support.

La a natu Bed & Bakery HOTEL $$$
(☎0 3268 9941; www.laanatu.com; south of Khao Kalok; r 4488-15,888B; ❄📶🏊) Turning the humble Thai rice village into a luxury experience is all the rage in the boutique hotel world but La a natu does it with more panache than most. The thatched roof villas growing on stilts from cultivated rice paddies have rounded modern corners and a Flintstone-esque playfulness to their design. Each villa is extremely private but evocative of traditional rustic lifestyles with living quarters on the ground floor and often steep, ladderlike stairs leading to the sleeping area. And then there's the semi-private beach right on your doorstep.

Dolphin Bay Resort HOTEL $$$
(☎0 3255 9333; www.dolphinbayresort.com; Dolphin Bay; r 1790-14,300B; ❄@📶🏊) The resort that defined Dolphin Bay as a family-friendly retreat offers a low-key holiday camp ambience with a variety of standard-issue, value-oriented bungalows and apartments, as well as a few very expensive ones. The grounds are large enough for kids to roam safely, there are two big pools and there's a great sandy beach opposite.

Khao Kalok Restaurant THAI $$
(dishes 80-300B; ⏰11am-10pm) At the southern base of the mountain, this open-air restaurant provides a front-row view of the moored fishing boats. Tasty dishes, like *gaang kĕe·o wăhn* (green curry), *Ъlah mèuk gà·prow* (squid stir-fried with basil) and even the standard *pàt pàk roo·am* (stir-fried vegetables) arrive at a leisurely pace.

ℹ Getting There & Around

Pranburi is about 35km south of Hua Hin and accessible by ordinary bus from Hua Hin's night market (20B). You'll be dropped off on the highway where you can catch a *sŏrng·tăa·ou* to Pak Nam Pran.

There is also a minivan service from Bangkok's Victory Monument to Pranburi (200B); if you're going to Dolphin Bay (sometimes referred to as Khao Sam Roi Yot Beach), you'll have to negotiate an additional fare with the driver (usually 100B).

If you want to explore the area, you'll need to rent a motorbike; public transport isn't an option.

Khao Sam Roi Yot National Park

อุทยานแห่งชาติเขาสามร้อยยอด

Towering limestone outcrops form a rocky jigsaw-puzzled landscape at this 98-sq-km **park** (☎0 3282 1568; www.dnp.go.th; adult/child 200/100B), which means Three Hundred Mountain Peaks. There are also caves, beaches and coastal marshlands to explore for outdoor enthusiasts and bird-watchers.

With its proximity to Hua Hin, the park is well travelled by day-trippers and contains a mix of public conservation land and private shrimp farms, so don't come expecting remote virgin territory.

Rama IV and a large entourage of Thai and European guests came here on 18 August 1868 to see a total solar eclipse (apparently predicted by the monarch himself) and to enjoy a feast prepared by a French chef. Two months later the king died from malaria, contracted from mosquito bites inflicted here. Today the risk of malaria in the park is low but the mosquitoes can be pesky, especially during the rainy season.

The **Khao Daeng Visitors Centre** in the southern end of the park has the largest collection of tourist information, and English-speaking rangers. Maps are handed out at the entrance gates.

Travel agencies in Hua Hin run day trips to the park. Hua Hin Bike Tours (p150) offers cycling and hiking tours.

Sights & Activities

Maps provided at the park checkpoints are often in Thai. The following sites are listed in geographical order from north to south.

Tham Kaew — CAVE

(ถ้ำแก้ว) Tham Kaew is a series of underground chambers and narrow passageways accessed by a steep scramble 128m up the mountain. It's not a popular stop, even though the stalactites and limestone formations here glitter with calcite crystals (hence the cave's name, 'Jewel Cave'). You can hire lamps from the booth at the footpath's entrance. The path can be slippery and dangerous.

Tham Phraya Nakhon & Hat Laem Sala — CAVE

(ถ้ำพระยานคร/หาดแหลมศาลา) The park's most-visited attraction is this revered cave sheltering a royal *săh·lah* (meeting hall; often spelled *sala*) built for Rama V in 1890 that is often bathed in streams of light. It's accessed via a walking trail from the picturesque sandy beach of **Hat Laem Sala**, flanked on three sides by limestone hills and casuarinas.

The beach hosts a small visitors centre, restaurant, bungalows and campsites. The cave trail is 450m long and is steep, rocky and at times slick so don't wear your ballet flats. Once there you'll find two large caverns with sinkholes – the meeting hall is the second of the two.

Reaching Laem Sala requires alternative travel since there is no road connection. It is reached by boat from Bang Pu (300B return), which sits beachfront from the turn-off from Tham Kaew. Alternatively, you can follow the steep footpath from Bang Pu for a 20-minute hike to the beach.

Tham Sai — CAVE

(ถ้ำไทร) Sitting at the end of a 280m hillside trail, Tham Sai features a large single cavern filled with stalactites and stalagmites. Be careful of steep drop-offs inside and slippery footings. Usually, only more adventurous types undertake this one. Villagers rent out lamps near the cave mouth. It is just north of Hat Sam Phraya.

Hat Sam Phraya — BEACH

(หาดสามพระยา) This shady casuarina-lined beach is about 1km long and is a pleasant stop for a swim after a sweaty hike. There is a restaurant and toilets.

Khao Daeng — HIKING

(เขาแดง) The turn-off to the trail winds through towering mountains promising a rewarding hike. The 30-minute steep trail that leads to the top of Khao Daeng delivers

BIRDS OF A FEATHER

At the intersection of the East Asian and Australian migration routes, Thung Sam Roi Yot National Park is home to as many as 300 migratory and resident bird species, including yellow bitterns, cinnamon bitterns, purple swamp hens, water rails, ruddy-breasted crakes, bronze-winged jacanas, grey herons, painted storks, whistling ducks, spotted eagles and black-headed ibises. The park is one of only two places in the country where the purple heron breeds.

Waterfowl are most commonly seen in the cool season from November to March. The birds come from as far as Siberia, China and northern Europe to winter here. Common places for bird-watchers are the Mangrove Centre, Khlong Khao Daeng and even some of the beaches.

Thai Birding (www.thaibirding.com) provides more in-depth information about the park's bird species and where to spot them.

WORTH A TRIP

WHERE THE ELEPHANTS ARE

Want to see herds of wild elephants enjoying an evening bath surrounded by the sounds of the jungle? Although urbanised Thailand seems hundreds of kilometres away from such a natural state, **Kuiburi National Park** (☎0 3264 6292; Hwy 3217; adult/child 200/100B), southwest of Khao Sam Roi Yot National Park, shelters one of the country's largest herds of wild elephants (estimated at 230 animals). The park provides an important habitat link between the rugged Myanmar border and Kaeng Krachan National Park, forming one of the largest intact forest tracts in Southeast Asia. The herds can frequently be found bathing at the watering ponds near the Pa Yang substation, which is equipped with wildlife-viewing platforms.

Trekking and elephant-spotting tours include English-speaking guides and transport and can be arranged through the park headquarters.

Bungalow **accommodation** (☎0 2562 0760; www.dnp.th.go/parkreserve; bungalows 1800B) is available for overnight stays with advance reservations.

spectacular views of limestone cliffs against a jagged coastline.

Khlong Khao Daeng BIRD WATCHING

(คลองเขาแดง) You can hire a boat at Wat Khao Daeng for a cruise (500B, 50 minutes) along the canal in the morning or afternoon. Before heading out, chat with your prospective guide to see how well they speak English. Better guides will know the English names of common waterfowl and point them out to you.

Thung Sam Roi Yot BIRD WATCHING

(ทุ่งสามร้อยยอด) The country's largest freshwater marsh is recognised as a natural treasure and provides an important habitat for songbirds and water birds, amphibians and other wetland species. It sits in the western corner of the park accessible from Hwy 4 (Th Phetkasem) at the Km 275.6 marker; hold on to your entrance fee ticket to avoid having to pay again.

Mangrove Walk NATURE TRAIL

Located behind the visitors centre in the southern end of the park is a 900m wooden boardwalk that circumnavigates a mangrove swamp popular for bird-watching and crab spotting. There are guides for hire from the centre, depending on availability and English-language skills.

Sleeping & Eating

There are private resorts within 4km of the park at Dolphin Bay.

National Parks Department CAMPING GROUND $

(☎0 2562 0760; www.dnp.go.th/parkreserve; tent sites 160-225B, bungalows at visitors centre 1200-1400B, bungalows at Hat Laem Sala 1600-3000B) The National Parks Department hires out bungalows (sleeping up to six people) at Hat Laem Sala and at the visitors centre; advance reservations are required. You can pitch a tent at campsites near the Khao Daeng viewpoint, Hat Laem Sala or Hat Sam Phraya. There are basic restaurants at all these locations.

Getting There & Away

The park is about 40km south of Hua Hin, and best visited by vehicle. There are two main entrances into the park. The turn-off for the northern entrance is at Km 256 marker on Hwy 4 (Th Phetkasem). The southern entrance is off the Km 286.5 marker.

If there's a group of you, a taxi from Hua Hin is 1800B return. You can also come on day tours from there. Alternatively, you can catch a minivan from Bangkok's Victory Monument to Pranburi (200B) and then hire a motorcycle to tour the park independently. You can also negotiate with the minivan driver to drop you off at the entrance to the park but then you won't have transport into the park.

Prachuap Khiri Khan

ประจวบคีรีขันธ์

POP 86,870

A sleepy seaside town, Prachuap Khiri Khan is a delightfully relaxed place; one of the real jewels of this part of Thailand. The broad bay is a tropical blue punctuated by bobbing fishing boats and there are tremendous beaches close by, all overlooked by honeycombed limestone mountains – scenery that you usually have to travel to the southern Andaman to find.

In recent years, expats have discovered Prachuap's charms and begun defecting here from the overdeveloped Samui archipelago. But their numbers are still small, leaving plenty of room on the beaches, at the hilltop temples and the many excellent seafood restaurants.

Sights & Activities

Khao Chong Krajok VIEWPOINT

(เขาช่องกระจก) At the northern end of town, Khao Chong Krajok ('Mirror Tunnel Mountain', so named for the mountain-side hole that seemingly reflects the sky) provides a beloved Prachuap tradition: climbing to the **temple** at the top, dodging ill-behaved monkeys and enjoying a cascading view of a curlicue coastline.

A long flight of stairs soiled by the partly wild monkeys leads to a mountaintop temple established by Rama VI. From here there are perfect views of the town and the bay and even the border with Myanmar, just 11km away. Don't bring food, drink or plastic bags with you as the monkeys will assume it is a prize worth having.

Ao Prachuap BAY

(อ่าวประจวบ) The town's crowning feature is Ao Prachuap (Prachuap Bay), a gracefully curving bay outlined by an oceanfront esplanade. In the cool hours of the morning and evening, locals run, shuffle or promenade along this route enjoying the ocean breezes and sea music.

On Friday and Saturday evenings, the esplanade hosts a **Walking Street market**, selling food, souvenirs and clothes.

North of Khao Chong Krajok, just over the bridge, the bay stretches peacefully to a toothy mountain scraper with less commercial activity than its in-town counterpart. There is a good sandy beach here though it does lack privacy due to its proximity to passing motorists. Nonetheless, weekending Thais often visit because there is no breakwater and it is a pleasant beachcombing spot. At the far northern end is a traditional fishing village decorated with colourful wooden trawlers and a visible sense of a hard-working life.

Wat Ao Noi BUDDHIST TEMPLE

(วัดอ่าวน้อย) From Ao Prachuap, follow the coastal road 8km north as it skirts through the fishing village to reach this beautiful teak temple that straddles two bays (Ao Noi and Ao Khan Kradai). Limestone mountains

Prachuap Khiri Khan

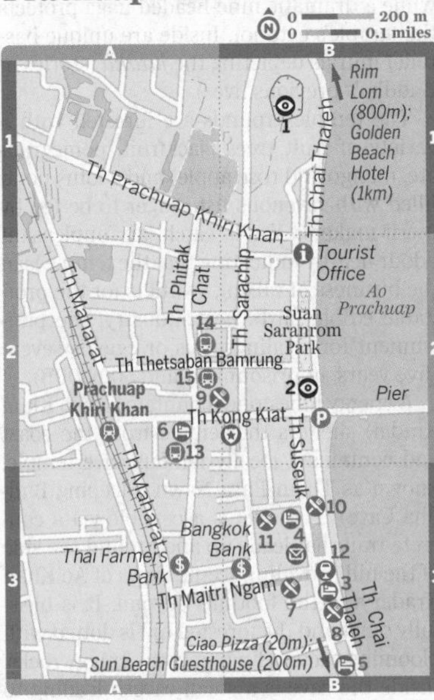

Prachuap Khiri Khan

Sights

1 Khao Chong Krajok B1
2 Weekend Walking Street/Market B2

Sleeping

3 House 73 .... B3
4 Maggie's Homestay B3
5 Prachuap Beach Hotel B3
6 Yuttichai Hotel A2

Eating

7 Day Market B3
8 Ma Prow B3
9 Night Market A2
10 Phloen Samut B3
11 Suan Krua B3

Drinking & Nightlife

12 Jim's Bar & Restaurant B3

Transport

13 Air-con Buses to Hua Hin, Cha-am, Phetchaburi & Bangkok A2
14 Minivans to Ban Krut, Bang Saphan Yai & Chumphon A2
15 Minivans to Hua Hin & Bangkok A2

pose photogenically in the background, while a dramatic nine-headed naga protects the temple's exterior. Inside are unique bas-relief murals depicting the *jataka* (stories of Buddha's previous lives).

The temple grounds are forested with a variety of fruit trees (jackfruit, pomegranate, mango and rose apple) and a lotus pond filled with ravenous fish, eager to be fed by merit-makers. You'll catch an unpleasant odour nearby indicating that the temple is in the business of raising swiftlets for the profitable edible bird's nest industry; the punishment for stealing nests or eggs is severe (five years' imprisonment and 500,000B).

A craggy limestone mountain (Khao Khan Kradai) shelters the temple from the coast and contains a locally famous cave temple, known as Tham Phra Nawn (Sleeping Buddha Cave). The cave is accessible via a concrete trail that leads up and around the side of the hill providing scenic views of Ao Khan Kradai and the foothills beyond. It is blissfully quiet and the forested hill is dotted with blooming cactus clinging to the craggy rocks. Inside the cave is a small cavern leading to a larger one that contains the eponymous reclining Buddha. If you have a torch (flashlight) you can proceed to a larger second chamber also containing Buddha images.

Ao Manao SWIMMING

(อ่าวมะนาว) On weekends, locals head to Ao Manao, 4km south of town, an island-dotted bay ringed by a clean sandy beach. It is within Wing 5 of a Thai air-force base and each and every week the beach is given a military-grade clean up.

There are the usual beach amenities: a restaurant and beach chairs, umbrellas and inner tubes for hire. En route to the beach you'll pass Thailand's Top Guns relaxing on a nearby golf course and driving range. You enter the base through a checkpoint on Th Suseuk from town; you may need to show your passport. The beach closes at 8pm.

PRACHUAP KHIRI KHAN IN WORLD WAR II

Prachuap, and specifically Ao Manao, was one of seven points on the gulf coast where Japanese troops landed on 8 December 1941 during their invasion of Thailand. The air-force base at Ao Manao was the site of fierce skirmishes, with the Japanese unable to capture it until the Thai government ordered its soldiers to stop fighting as an armistice had been arranged.

Several street names around town refer to that time, such as Phithak Chat (Defend Country), Salachip (Sacrifice Life) and Suseuk (Fight Battle), and an annual memorial service commemorates the soldiers and civilians who died in the battle.

Sleeping

There are a number of oceanfront options, ranging from guesthouses to hotels. It's rare that you can't find a cosy spot to lay your head.

In Town

Maggie's Homestay GUESTHOUSE $

(08 7597 9720; 5 Soi Tampramuk; r 180-550B;) In the old-fashioned backpacker tradition, lovely owner Maggie oversees an eclectic collection of travellers who call her house home. Comfortable rooms, all with shared bathrooms, occupy a converted house with a shady garden and shared kitchen facilities.

Yuttichai Hotel GUESTHOUSE $

(0 3261 1055; 115 Th Kong Kiat; r 160-350B;) Yuttichai has simple budget rooms (with cold-water showers) close to the train station. The cheapest rooms are cell-like and share OK bathrooms. Their old-school Thai-Chinese cafe is decent and patronised by the local fuzz.

★ **House 73** GUESTHOUSE $$

(08 6046 3923; www.house73prachuab.com; 73 Th Suseuk; r 800-1300B;) Lovingly designed to within an inch of its life, this modernist boutique guesthouse is the most eye-catching building in town. There are only four big rooms here, all painted in pastel colours, with huge beds. There's a communal lounge and, best of all, a fantastic roof terrace with commanding views across the bay.

Sun Beach Guesthouse GUESTHOUSE $$

(0 3260 4770; www.sunbeach-guesthouse.com; 160 Th Chai Thaleh; r 700-1100B;) With hotel amenities and guesthouse hospitality, Sun Beach is a superb midranger. Its neo-classical styling and bright-yellow paint liven things up, while the rooms are super-clean and come with large verandahs.

WORTH A TRIP

DAN SINGKHON BORDER MARKET

A mere 12km southwest of Prachuap Khiri Khan is the Myanmar border town of Dan Singkhon. Once a strategic military point, Dan Singkhon now hosts a lively border **market** beloved by locals for its many bargains.

Beginning at dawn on Saturday mornings, locals from Myanmar appear from a bend in the road just beyond the checkpoint, pushing handcarts piled high with the usual trinkets, market goods and plants. Short-term tourists might be befuddled as to what will fit in a suitcase, but locals and expats make frequent buying trips here for orchids, the market's speciality, and hardwood furniture. Even if you come to window-shop, the market has a festive vibe, with music blaring, colourful umbrellas lining the road and thatched 'sales booths' hidden under palms. You'll need to arrive well before noon to enjoy it, as the market closes at midday.

To get to Dan Singkhon from Prachuap Khiri Khan with your own vehicle, head south on Hwy 4. After several kilometres you'll see a sign for Dan Singkhon; from there head west about 15km to reach the border.

Prachuap Beach Hotel HOTEL $$
(☎0 3260 1288; www.prachuapbeach.com; 123 Th Suseuk; r 700-1200B; ❄📶) Crisp white linens and modern, comfortable rooms at this multi-storey number. One side has fabulous sea views, while the other has decent, though not exciting, mountain views.

Out of Town

Natural Home GUESTHOUSE $
(☎0 3260 2082; 149-151 Th Suanson; r 250-600B; ❄📶) About 1km north of town, these small bungalows (with closetlike bathrooms and cold-water showers) are simple, but you are right across the road from Ao Prachuap's beach. Pleasant staff.

Aow Noi Sea View HOTEL $$
(☎0 3260 4440; www.aownoiseaview.com; Ao Noi; r 800-1200B; ❄📶) North of town, this secluded three-storey hotel is Prachuap's best beachfront choice. With pretty Ao Noi beach at your doorstep, you'll enjoy sea breezes, spacious rooms with balconies and a homey ambience.

Golden Beach Hotel HOTEL $$
(☎0 3260 1626; www.goldenbeachprachuap.com; 113-115 Th Suanson; r 500-1000B; ❄📶) A comfortable midrange option opposite Ao Prachuap's beach, and a decent deal these days for a sea view. The rooms are plain and a little old-fashioned, but clean.

Eating & Drinking

Restaurants in Prachuap are cheap and offer excellent seafood, while Western dishes are popping up more frequently. The **day market** (Th Maitri Ngam; ⏲daylight hours) is the place to get pineapples fresh from the orchards; ask the vendor to cut it for you. The **night market** (Th Kong Kiat; ⏲5-9pm) is small and has the usual stir-fry stalls.

Suan Krua VEGETARIAN $
(Soi Tampramuk; dishes 20-60B; ⏲6.30am-3pm; 🖉) Super vegetarian, buffet-style eatery. Choose from an array of dishes, but they go fast and then it shuts. Be here promptly and with an appetite.

★**Rim Lom** SEAFOOD $$
(5 Th Suanson; dishes 120-290B; ⏲10am-10pm) Still the go-to place in town for the locals, the *pàt pǒng gà·rèe Ƅoo* (crab curry) comes with big chunks of sweet crab meat and the *yam ta-lair* (seafood salad) is spicy and zesty. It's 200m past the bridge on the left.

Phloen Samut SEAFOOD $$
(44 Th Chai Thaleh; dishes 120-250B; ⏲10am-10pm) One of a few seafood restaurants along the promenade, Phloen Samut is a big, bustling operation. The dishes are tasty, especially if you can handle spicy.

Ma Prow INTERNATIONAL-THAI $$
(48 Th Chai Thaleh; dishes 120-395B; ⏲10am-10pm) An airy wooden pavilion, Ma Prow is more foreigner-orientated than other places on the promenade. This is the best option in town if you're craving a steak rather than seafood, although the tamarind fish here goes down a treat.

Ciao Pizza ITALIAN $$
(Th Suseuk; pizzas from 170B; ⏲11am-10pm) Italian-owned, come here for fine pizzas,

homemade pasta and gelato, as well as fresh bread baked daily and a takeaway selection of cheese, sausage and salami.

Jim's Bar & Restaurant BAR
(53 Th Chai Thaleh; beers from 60B; ⏲4pm-1am) Prachuap is an early to bed town, but at Jim's you can sip a libation till late while gazing out at the winking lights of the fishing boats in the bay.

Information

Bangkok Bank (cnr Th Maitri Ngam & Th Sarachip)

Police Station (Th Kong Kiat) Just west of Th Sarachip.

Post Office (cnr Th Maitri Ngam & Th Suseuk)

Thai Farmers Bank (Th Phitak Chat) Just north of Th Maitri Ngam.

Tourist Office (☎0 3261 1491; Th Chai Thaleh; ⏲8.30am-4.30pm) At the northern end of town. The staff speak English and are helpful.

Getting There & Away

Seven air-conditioned buses run daily to Bangkok's southern terminal from Th Phitak Chat. Buses also leave from here for Ban Krut and Bang Saphan Yai.

Minivans leave from the corner of Th Thetsaban Bamrung and Th Phitak Chat

Long-distance buses to southern destinations (such as Phuket and Krabi) stop at the new bus station, 2km northwest of town on the main highway; motorcycle taxis will take you for 40B to 50B.

The train station is on Th Maharat; there are frequent services to/from Bangkok.

Getting Around

Prachuap is small enough to get around on foot, but you can hop on a motorcycle taxi for 30B. A bike to Ao Noi and Ao Manao is 100B to 150B.

You can hire motorbikes for 250B per day. The roads in the area are very good and it's a great way to see the surrounding beaches.

Ban Krut & Bang Saphan Yai บ้านกรูด/บางสะพานใหญ่

POP 4275/ 68,344

What a nice surprise to find these lovely, low-key beaches (80km to 100km south of Prachuap Khiri Khan, respectively) so close to civilisation, yet so bucolic. Dusk falls softly through the coconut trees and the sea is a crystalline blue lapping at a long sandy coastline. No high-rises, no late-night discos and no speeding traffic to distract you from a serious regimen of reading, swimming, eating and biking.

Although both beaches are pleasantly subdued, they are also well known to Thais. Ban Krut, in particular, hosts bus tours as well as weekending families. During the week you'll have the beaches largely to yourself and a few long-tail boats.

Check out the websites **Ban Krut Info** (www.bankrutinfo.com) and **Bang Saphan Guide** (www.bangsaphanguide.com) for local information on the area.

Sights & Activities

Ban Krut is divided into two beaches by a temple-topped headland. To the north is **Hat Sai Kaew**, which is remote and private with only a few resorts in between a lot of

TRANSPORT TO/FROM PRACHUAP KHIRI KHAN

DESTINATION	BUS	MINIVAN	TRAIN
Ban Krut		70B; 1hr; hourly 6am-5pm	1 daily
Bang Saphan Yai		80B; 1½hr; hourly 6am-5pm	8 daily
Bangkok Hua Lamphong			168-455B; 7-8hr; 8 daily 2.41am-11.26pm
Bangkok southern bus terminal	200B; 6-7hr; 7 daily 9am-1am	200B; 5-6hr; hourly 7am-5pm	
Bangkok Victory Monument		240B; 6hr; hourly 6am-5pm	
Cha-am		120B; 2hr; hourly 6am-5pm	1 daily
Hua Hin		80B; 1½hr; hourly 6am-5pm	8 daily
Phetchaburi		150B; 3hr; hourly 6am-5pm	8 daily

jungle. To the south is **Hat Ban Krut**, with a string of bungalow-style resorts and restaurants sitting opposite the beach. Both are golden-sand beaches with clear, calm water but Hat Ban Krut is more social and developed (you'll find ATMs here) and easier to get around without private transport.

Bang Saphan Yai, 20km south of Ban Krut, fits that most famous beach cliché: it is Thailand 15 years ago before pool villas and package tourists pushed out all the beach bums. Once you settle into a simple beachfront hut, you probably won't need shoes and the days will just melt away. Islands off the coast, including **Ko Thalu** and **Ko Sing**, offer good **snorkelling** and **diving** from the end of January to mid-May.

Sleeping & Eating

Ban Krut

You'll struggle to find true budget options here, but if you visit on a weekday you should secure a discount. In Hat Ban Krut, bicycles (100B per day) and motorcycles (300B per day) can be hired to run errands in town, and most accommodation options arrange snorkelling trips to nearby islands. If you stay in Hat Sai Kaew you'll need private transport.

★ **NaNa Chart Baan Krut** HOTEL $$
(☎0 3269 5525; www.thailandhostel.com; 123 Th Ban Krut-Kohktahom; dm 400B, r 600-2900B; ❄@📶≋) Technically it is a hostel – and it does have dorms – but NaNa Chart easily qualifies as a resort with a variety of bungalows on a barely inhabited, superb stretch of beach. The cheapest are wooden huts with fans, while the ritzy beachfront ones have all the mod cons. The resort caters to large groups so expect some company at peak times; in low season it's much quieter. Hostel members receive discounted rates.

Proud Thai Beach Resort GUESTHOUSE $$
(☎08 9682 4484; www.proudthairesort.com; Hat Ban Krut; r 800-1200B; ❄📶) Well-maintained bungalows in a flower-filled garden have porches, and morning coffee delivered by the affable owner. Prices rise at weekends and on public holidays.

Bayview Beach Resort HOTEL $$$
(☎0 3269 5566; www.bayviewbeachresort.com; Hat Ban Krut; r 1600-5400B; ❄📶≋) A great choice for families, Bayview has handsome bungalows with large verandahs amid shady grounds. There's a beachside pool and a kid-friendly wading pool as well as a small playground. The resort also offers snorkelling and diving trips and rents kayaks and bikes.

Kasama's Pizza ITALIAN $$
(Hat Ban Krut; pizza from 180B; ⏲7.30am-11pm, closed Thu; 📶) Substantial, succulent baguettes (from 90B) for beach-snacking, and it's fine for breakfast or a New York-style pizza in the evening.

Bang Saphan Yai

The beach is 6km south of the town of Bang Saphan Yai. It's not as idyllic a strip of sand as Ban Krut, but there's both budget accommodation and high-end pool villas here. Walk north of the Why Not Bar for the cheaper places.

Roytawan GUESTHOUSE $
(☎08 7670 8943; Hat Bang Saphan Yai; r from 300B) Smack dab on the beach, this bare-bones operation is run by a friendly local Muslim family. The bungalows are simple but adequate and the resident roosters kindly sleep until daybreak. The restaurant is fab too.

Suan Luang Resort GUESTHOUSE $
(☎0 3269 1663; www.suanluangresort.com; Hat Bang Saphan Yai; bungalows 480-680B; ❄📶) Run by a laid-back family, Suan Long is the most professional of the guesthouses with rustic wooden bungalows set around an interior garden. The air-con ones are a big step up from the fan rooms, but you're 700m from the beach. The excellent restaurant serves Thai and French food, and motorbikes are available for rent (300B per day).

Patty Hut GUESTHOUSE $
(☎08 6171 1907; Hat Bang Saphan Yai; r 300-700B) The most basic option (mattress on the floor, fan and cold-water showers), but you're just 300m from the beach.

Coral Hotel HOTEL $$$
(☎0 3281 7121; www.coral-hotel.com; Hat Bang Saphan Yai; r 2385-6890B; ❄@📶≋) Catering mostly to French tourists – the restaurant is decent – this upmarket hotel is right on the beach and has all the resort amenities, including organised diving and snorkelling tours. The tastefully decorated rooms are very comfortable and the pool is big.

Getting There & Around

Public transport is either nonexistent or limited. When booking transport, don't confuse Bang Saphan Yai with Bang Saphan Noi, which is a fishermen's village 15km further south.

From Bangkok's southern (Sai Tai Mai) terminal buses go to Bang Saphan Yai (275B, hourly, six hours); in Bangkok, use **Bangsaphan Tour** (08 7829 7752).

Frequent minivans run from Prachuap Khiri Khan to Ban Krut (70B) and Bang Saphan Yai (80B). Most minivans to Ban Krut will stop on the highway, a 100B motorbike ride from the beach.

Many seasoned visitors prefer to take the train for closer proximity to the beaches. There are several daily options but the sprinter train (special express No 43) is one of the fastest. It leaves Bangkok's Hua Lamphong station at 8.05am and arrives in Ban Krut (445B) at 1.07pm and Bang Saphan Yai (450B) at 1.20pm. You can also hop on an afternoon train to Chumphon with plenty of time to spare before the ferry to Ko Tao.

A motorcycle taxi from town to Bang Saphan Yai is 70B. Talk to your hotel or guesthouse about arranging transport back to town for your onward travel.

Chumphon

ชุมพร

POP 55,835

A transit town funnelling travellers to and from Ko Tao or westwards to Ranong or Phuket, Chumphon is also where the south of Thailand starts proper; Muslim headscarves are a common sight here.

While there's not a lot to do while you wait for your ferry, there's good seafood in town and the surrounding beaches are great places to step off the backpacker bandwagon for a few days. **Hat Thung Wua Laen** (15km north of town) is an excellent beach with plenty of traveller amenities and during the week you'll have it mostly to yourself.

For a transit hub, Chumphon is surprisingly unconsolidated: the main bus station and piers for boats to Ko Tao, Ko Samui and Ko Pha-Ngan are some distance from town. Travel agencies and guesthouses can book tickets, provide timetables and point you to the right bus stop; fortunately agents in Chumphon are a dedicated lot.

Festivals & Events

Chumphon Marine Festival CULTURAL

(Mar) Normally held in mid-March, Hat Thung Wua Laen hosts a variety of events including folk-art exhibits, shadow-puppet performances and a food display.

Chumphon Traditional Boat Race CULTURAL

(Oct) To mark the end of Buddhist Lent in October (Ork Phansaa), traditional long-tail boats race each other on the Mae Nam Lang Suan (Lang Suan River), about 60km south of Chumphon. Other merit-making activities coincide with the festival.

Sleeping

As most people overnighting in Chumphon are backpackers, accommodation is priced accordingly. Th Tha Taphao is the local Th Khao San, with many guesthouses and travel agencies.

★ **Suda Guest House** GUESTHOUSE $

(08 0144 2079; 8 Soi Sala Daeng 3; r 250-650B;) Suda, the friendly English-speaking owner, maintains her impeccable standards with six rooms, all with wooden floors and a few nice touches that you wouldn't expect for the price. It's very popular so phone ahead.

Salsa Hostel HOSTEL $

(0 7750 5005; www.salsachumphon.com; 25/42 Th Krom Luang Chumphon; dm/d 230/700B;) Helpful hostel (the owner speaks good English) with cramped but clean and modern dorms. The private rooms are big and bright, even if they are overpriced for this town.

Fame Guest House GUESTHOUSE $

(0 7757 1077; 188/20-21 Th Sala Daeng; r 200-300B;) A *fa·ràng* (Westerner) depot, Fame does a little bit of everything, from providing basic but OK rooms to booking tickets and renting motorbikes. The attached restaurant is a key backpacker hang-out, staying open until midnight and offering a wide range of Thai, Indian and Western food.

San Tavee New Rest House GUESTHOUSE $

(0 7750 2147; 4 Soi Sala Daeng 3; r 250-300B) Only four rooms, all with shared bathrooms. They're small, well-kept and set around a garden. It feels more like a homestay than a guesthouse.

View Resort BUNGALOW $

(0 7756 0214; Hat Thung Wua Laen; r 650-1100B;) Sleepy bungalow operation outside town that's right on the beach. The restaurant is pretty good too.

Chumphon

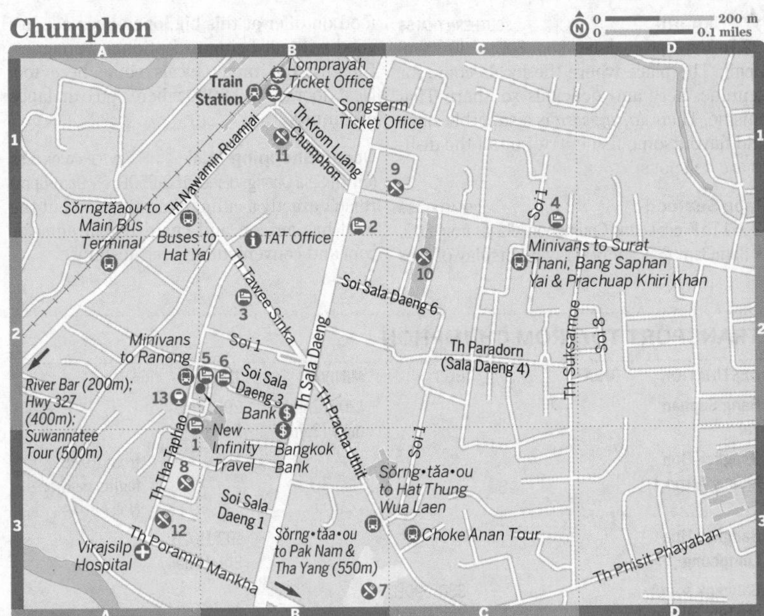

Chumphon Gardens Hotel HOTEL **$$**
(☎0 7750 6888; www.chumphongarden.com; 66/1 Th Tha Taphao; r 730B; ❄📶) Sports a 1970s-style design but has large, comfortable rooms and the bathrooms are a cut above the local competition.

Morakot Hotel HOTEL **$$**
(☎0 7750 2999; www.morakothotel.com; 102-112 Th Tawee Sinka; r 490-890B; ❄📶) Spread across two buildings, the rooms here are characterless but modern and clean, making it a solid midrange option.

Chumphon Cabana Resort & Diving Centre HOTEL **$$$**
(☎0 7756 0245; www.cabana.co.th; Hat Thung Wua Laen; r 1650-3000B; ❄📶) The most pleasant resort on the beach, despite the rather plain bungalows, Chumphon Cabana has done a great job upgrading its environmental profile. Inspired by the King's environmental sustainability speech, the owner reconfigured the resort to look to the past for instructions on how to be green. Now, the grounds are devoted to raising the resort's own food with rice fields, hydroponic vegetable gardens and a chicken farm. Waste water is recycled through water- hyacinth ponds. If you don't stay here, at least try the homegrown food at **Rabieng Talay**, the resort's affiliated restaurant.

Chumphon

Sleeping
1 Chumphon Gardens Hotel A2
2 Fame Guest House B1
3 Morakot Hotel B2
4 Salsa Hostel C1
5 San Tavee New Rest House B2
6 Suda Guest House B2

Eating
7 Day Market B3
8 Day Market A3
9 Night Market C1
10 Ocean Shopping Mall C2
11 Papa Seafood B1
12 Prikhorm A3

Drinking & Nightlife
13 Farang Bar A2

Eating & Drinking

Chumphon's **night market** (Th Krom Luang Chumphon) is excellent, with a huge variety of food options and good people-watching. There are **day markets** along **Th Tha Taphao** (Th Tha Taphao) and **Th Pracha Uthit** (Th Pracha Uthit), and Th Sala Daeng and Th Pracha Uthit are both lined with hole-in-the-wall noodle joints.

★Prikhorm SOUTHERN THAI $$
(32 Th Tha Taphao; dishes from 80B; ⏲10.30am-11pm) The place where the locals come for genuine, fiery and delicious southern Thai cuisine. Their *gaang som* is a superbly spicy and flavoursome fish curry, but all the dishes are delicious.

Papa Seafood SEAFOOD $$
(2-2/1 Th Krom Luang Chumphon; dishes from 80B; ⏲3pm-3am; 📶) There's a wide display of seafood on offer at this big, open-air place; it's good without being exceptional. Foreigner-friendly, but many locals come here too. Next door is Papa 2000 where you can dance off dinner.

Ocean Shopping Mall INTERNATIONAL $$
(off Th Sala Daeng; dishes 150-250B; ⏲ 9am-8pm) It isn't exactly a culinary destination but the mall has air-con and chain restaurants for cool and convenient layover noshing.

TRANSPORT TO/FROM CHUMPHON

DESTINATION	BOAT	BUS	MINIVAN	TRAIN	AIR
Bang Saphan Yai			120B; 2hr; 1 daily (2pm)	20B; 2hr; 12 daily	
Bangkok Don Muang Airport					from 1674B; 2 flights daily on Nok Air
Bangkok Hua Lamphong				192-1162B; 8hr; 11 daily	
Bangkok southern bus terminal		380-590B; 8hr; 11 daily			
Hat Yai		400B; 4 daily; 7hr		6 daily	
Ko Pha-Ngan via Lomprayah	1000B; 3¼hr; 2 daily (7am & 1pm)				
Ko Pha-Ngan via Songserm	900B; 5½hr; 1 daily (7am)				
Ko Samui via Lomprayah	1100B; 4½hr; 2 daily (7am & 1pm)				
Ko Samui via Songserm	1000B; 7hr; 1 daily (7am)				
Ko Tao via car ferry	400B; 6hr; 1 daily (11pm Mon-Sat)				
Ko Tao via Lomprayah	600B; 1½hr; 2 daily (7am & 1pm)				
Ko Tao via slow boat	250B; 6hr; 1 daily (midnight)				
Ko Tao via Songserm	500B; 3hr; 1 daily (7am)				
Phetchaburi		210B; 5 daily; 6hr		11 daily	
Phuket		350B; 4 daily; 3½hr			
Prachuap Khiri Khan			180B; 1 daily (3pm); 4hr	10 daily	
Ranong		120B; 4 daily; 2½hr	130B; frequent; 2hr		
Surat Thani			170B; hourly 6am-5pm; 3hr	12 daily	

River BAR

(4/9 Th Poramin Mankha; ⌚4pm-1am; 📶) Perched over the Taphao River, this bar has live music every night. It's a fine spot for a sundowner; it gets more lively later on. The menu is a mix of classic Thai and Western dishes.

Farang Bar BAR

(☎0 7750 1003; www.farangbarchumphon.com; 69/36 Th Tha Taphao; beers from 80B; ⌚11am-midnight; 📶) An agreeable hang-out for expat English teachers and passing travellers, the Farang Bar is an easy place to while away a few hours over a drink. The menu mixes Thai and Western dishes; the local ones are better. There are also basic rooms here (250B) and day-use showers (20B).

ℹ Information

There are banks along Th Sala Daeng with exchange facilities and ATMs.

Bangkok Bank (Th Sala Daeng) Has an ATM.

Main Post Office (Th Poramin Mankha) In the southeastern part of town.

New Infinity Travel (☎0 7757 0176; 68/2 Th Tha Taphao; ⌚8am-10pm; 📶) A great travel agency with knowledgeable and friendly staff; they'll also sell you paperbacks and rent you one of four rooms (250B).

Tourism Authority of Thailand (TAT; ☎0 7750 1831; 111/11-12 Th Tawee Sinka; ⌚8.30am-4.30pm) Hands out maps and brochures but not always up-to-date on transport information.

Virajsilp Hospital (☎0 7750 3238; Th Poramin Mankha) Privately owned; handles emergencies.

ℹ Getting There & Away

Boats leave from different piers; bus transfer is sometimes included in the ticket price. Otherwise, you pay an extra 50B for transport to the pier. During low season, the car ferry and slow boat don't always run.

BOAT

You have many boat options for getting to Ko Tao, though departure times are limited to mainly morning and night. Most ticket prices include pier transfer. If you buy a combination ticket, make sure you have a ticket for both the bus and the boat.

Slow boat – the cheapest, slowest and most scenic option as everyone stretches out on the open deck of the fishing boat with the stars twinkling overhead. This boat doesn't run in rough seas or inclement weather.

Car ferry – a more comfortable ride with bunk or mattress options available on board.

Songserm (☎0 7750 6205; www.songserm-expressboat.com; ⌚9am-8pm)express boat – faster, morning option leaving from Tha Talaysub, about 10km from town, but the company has a growing reputation for being poorly organised and for not providing promised free transport into town if you are coming from the islands.The ticket office doesn't seem to open often; book tickets through guesthouses.

Lomprayah (☎0 7755 8214; www.lomprayah.com; ⌚5am-9pm) catamaran – the best and most popular bus-boat combination that leaves from Tha Tummakam, 25km from town; the ticket office is beside Chumphon train station.

BUS

The main bus terminal is on the highway, an inconvenient 16km from Chumphon. To get there you can catch a *sŏrng·tăa·ou* (50B) from Th Nawamin Ruamjai. You'll have to haggle with the opportunistic taxi drivers for night transit to/from the station; no matter what they tell you, it shouldn't cost more than 200B.

There are several in-town bus stops to save you a trip out to the main bus station. **Choke Anan Tour** (☎0 7751 1757; soi off of Th Pracha Uthit), in the centre of town, has departures to Bangkok, Phuket and Ranong. **Suwannatee Tour** (☎0 7750 4901), 700m southeast of train station road, serves Bangkok, Phetchaburi and Prachuap Khiri Khan. Buses to Hat Yai depart from near the petrol station on Th Nawamin Ruamjai.

All minivans for Surat Thani, Bang Saphan Yai and Prachuap Khiri Khan leave from the unnamed soi opposite Salsa Guesthouse.

TRAIN

There are frequent services to/from Bangkok (2nd class 292B to 382B, 3rd class 235B, 7½ hours). Overnight sleepers range from 440B to 770B.

Southbound rapid and express trains – the only trains with 1st and 2nd class – are less frequent and can be difficult to book out of Chumphon from November to February.

ℹ Getting Around

Sŏrng·tăa·ou and motorcycle taxis around town cost 40B and 20B respectively per trip. *Sŏrng·tăa·ou* to Hat Thung Wua Laen cost 30B.

Motorcycles can be rented at travel agencies and guesthouses for 200B to 350B per day.

Ko Samui & the Lower Gulf

Includes ➡

Best Places to Eat

- Dining On The Rocks (p187)
- 69 (p187)
- Ging Pagarang (p188)
- Fisherman's Restaurant (p205)
- Baraccuda (p219)

Best Places to Stay

- Six Senses Samui (p181)
- Divine Comedie (p199)
- Viewpoint Resort (p218)
- Samui-Ley (p182)
- Sanctuary (p204)

Why Go?

The Lower Gulf features Thailand's ultimate island trifecta: Ko Samui, Ko Pha-Ngan and Ko Tao. This family of spectacular islands lures millions of tourists every year with their powder-soft sands and emerald waters. Ko Samui is the oldest sibling, who has made it big. Here, high-class resorts operate with Swiss efficiency as uniformed butlers cater to every whim. Ko Pha-Ngan is the slacker middle child with tangled dreadlocks and a penchant for hammock-lazing and all-night parties. Meanwhile Ko Tao is the outdoorsy, fun-loving kid with plenty of spirit and spunk – the island specialises in high-adrenalin activities, including world-class diving and snorkelling.

The mainland coast beyond the islands sees few foreign visitors. From the pink dolphins and waterfalls of sleepy Ao Khanom to the Thai Muslim flavours of kite-flying, beach strolling Songkhla, this region will convince any naysayer that Thailand still holds a bevy of off-the-beaten-track wonders.

When to Go

- February to April celebrates endless sunshine after the monsoon rains have cleared. June to August, conveniently coinciding with the northern hemisphere's summer holidays, are among the most inviting months, with relatively short drizzle spells.
- October to December is when torrential monsoon rains rattle hot-tin roofs, and room rates drop significantly to lure optimistic beach goers.

GULF ISLANDS

Ko Samui เกาะสมุย

POP 50,000

Ko Samui is like a well-established Hollywood celebrity: she's outrageously manicured, has lovely blonde tresses and has gracefully removed all of her wrinkles without more than a peep in the tabloids. She's been in the tourism business longer than almost any other Thai island, but rather than becoming passe, she's embraced a new generation of resort goers, many of them upscale and Russian. Academy Award–winning holidays here include fine stretches of sand clogged with beach loungers, rubbish-free roads, world-class international cuisine, luxurious spas and beach bar parties for scantily clad 20-somethings that start at noon.

Behind the glossy veneer there's still a glimmer of the girl from the country. Look for steaming street-side food stalls beyond the beach, backpacker shanties plunked down on quiet stretches of sand and secreted Buddhist temples along the backstreets. It's then that you remember you're in Thailand and not a globalisation-induced trance of a Photoshopped beach vacation. To really get away, head to the south or the west of the island, where you'll find authentic Samui family-run seafood restaurants, tourist-free towns buzzing with descendents of the original Chinese merchant settlers and long stretches of refreshingly wild and shaggy coconut palms.

Sights

Ko Samui is quite large – the island's ring road is almost 100km total.

Hin-Ta & Hin-Yai LANDMARK

At the south end of **Hat Lamai**, the second-largest beach, you'll find these infamous stone formations (also known as Grandfather and Grandmother Rocks). These rocks, shaped like genitalia, provide endless mirth for giggling Thai tourists.

Ban Hua Thanon NEIGHBOURHOOD

Just beyond Hat Lamai, Hua Thanon is home to a vibrant Muslim community, and its anchorage of high-bowed fishing vessels is a veritable gallery of intricate designs.

Nam Tok Na Muang WATERFALL

At 30m, this is the tallest waterfall on Samui and lies in the centre of the island about 12km from Na Thon. The water cascades over ethereal purple rocks, and there's a great pool for swimming at the base. This is the most scenic – and somewhat less frequented – of Samui's falls.

There are two other waterfalls in the vicinity: a smaller waterfall called **Na Muang 2**, and the high drop at **Nam Tok Wang Saotong**, which, thanks to recently improved road conditions, is now accessible. These chutes are just north of the ring road near Ban Hua Thanon. There's a great fried chicken and *sôm·đam* (spicy green papaya salad)

GULF ISLANDS IN...

One Week

First, shed a tear that you have but one week to explore these idyllic islands. Then start on one of **Ko Pha-Ngan's** (p193) secluded beaches in the west or east to live out your ultimate castaway fantasies. For the second half of the week choose between partying in **Hat Rin** (p197), pampering on **Ko Samui** (p171) or diving on little **Ko Tao** (p209).

Two Weeks

Start on **Ko Tao** (p209) with a 3½-day Open Water certification course, or sign up for a few fun dives. Slide over to **Ko Pha-Ngan** (p193) and soak up the sociable vibe in party-prone Hat Rin. Then, grab a long-tail and make your way to one of the island's hidden coves for a few days of detoxing and quiet contemplation. **Ko Samui** is next. Try **Bo Phut** (p182) for boutique sleeps or live it up like a rock star on Chaweng or Choeng Mon beach. If you have time, do a day trip to **Ang Thong National Marine Park** (p224).

One Month

Follow the two-week itinerary at a more relaxed pace, infusing many extra beach-book-and-blanket days on all three islands. Be sure to plan your schedule around the Full Moon Party, which takes place at Hat Rin's Sunrise Beach on **Ko Pha-Ngan** (p193).

Ko Samui & the Lower Gulf Highlights

1. Finding Nemo in the technicolour kingdom off the coast of **Ko Tao** (p209)
2. Paddling to the hidden bleach-blonde beaches of **Ang Thong Marine National Park** (p224)
3. Stringing up a cotton hammock and toeing the curling tide along a secluded beach on **Ko Pha-Ngan** (p193)
4. Enjoying five-star international cuisine and sipping fancy sunset cocktails on **Ko Samui** (p171)
5. Joining the masses of party pilgrims and trancing the night away at the **Full Moon Party** at Hat Rin on Ko Pha-Ngan (p194)

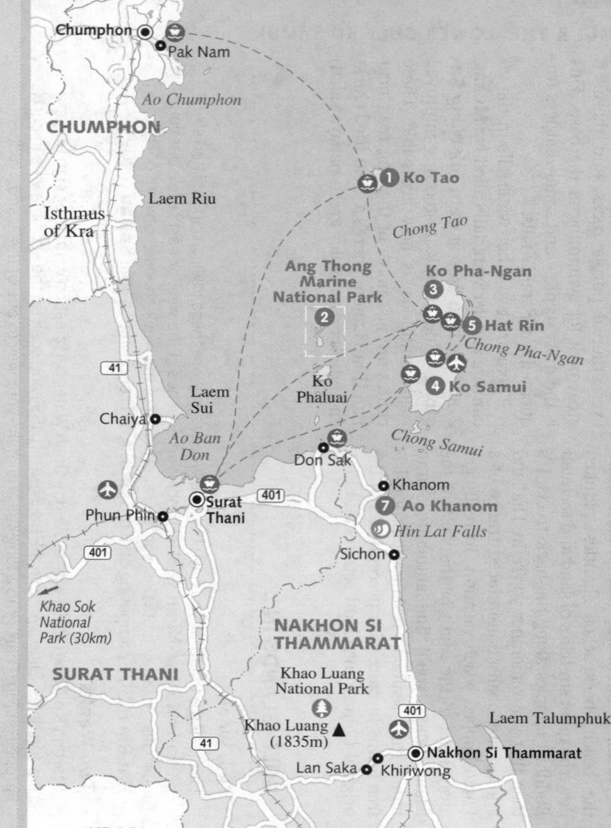

6 Savouring steaming street-stall seafood on the sands of **Songkhla** (p231)

7 Spotting elusive pink dolphins gliding along the shores of **Ao Khanom** (p228)

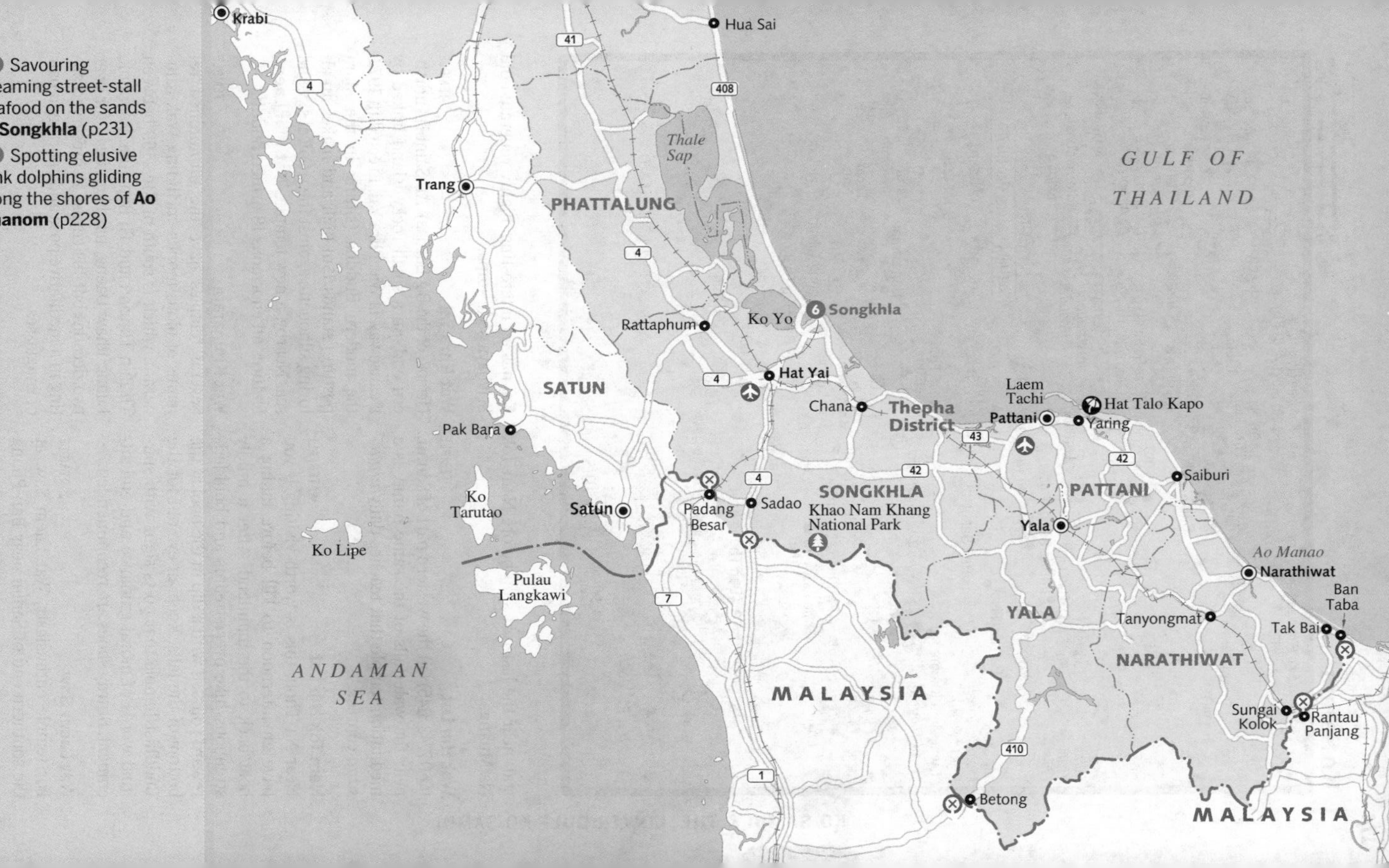

Ko Samui

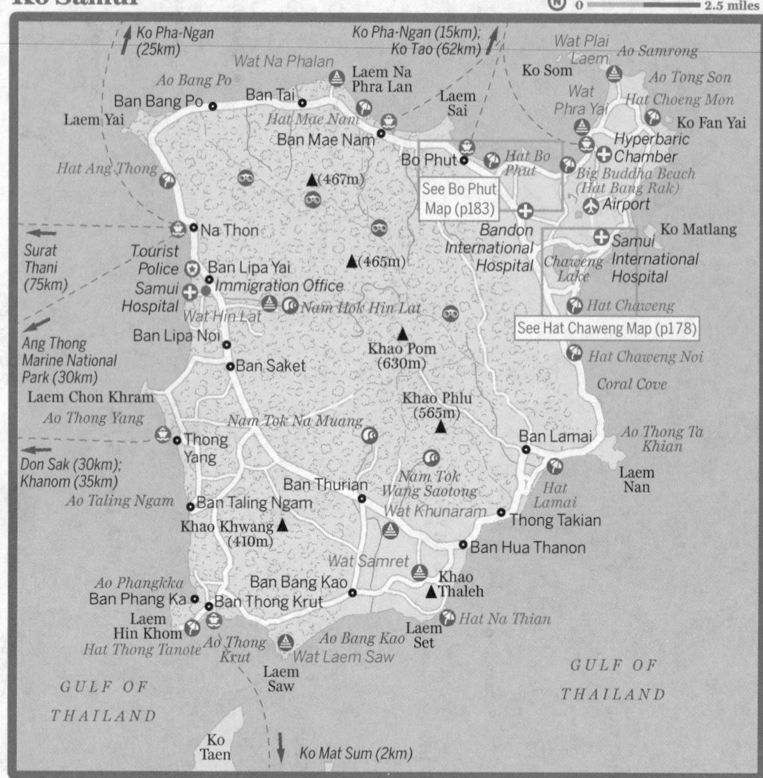

stall near the last rest stop before Nam Tok Na Muang.

Wat Hin Lat TEMPLE
(☎0 7742 3146) On the western part of Samui, near the waterfalls of the same name, is a meditation temple that teaches daily *vipassana* courses.

Nam Tok Hin Lat WATERFALL
Near Na Thon, this is worth visiting if you have an afternoon to kill before taking a boat back to the mainland. After a mildly strenuous hike over streams and boulders, reward yourself with a dip in the pool at the bottom of the falls. Keep an eye out for the Buddhist temple that posts signs with spiritual words of moral guidance and enlightenment. Sturdy shoes are recommended.

Wat Laem Saw TEMPLE
For temple enthusiasts, Wat Laem Saw, at the southern end of Samui near Ban Phang Ka, has an interesting, highly venerated old Srivijaya-style stupa.

Wat Phra Yai TEMPLE
(Temple of the Big Buddha) At Samui's northern end, on a small rocky island linked by a causeway, is Wat Phra Yai. Erected in 1972, the modern Buddha (sitting in the Mara posture) stands 15m high and makes an alluring silhouette against the tropical sky and sea. Nearby, a new temple, **Wat Plai Laem**, features an enormous 18-armed Buddha.

Wat Khunaram TEMPLE
Several temples have the mummified remains of pious monks, including Wak Khunaram, which is south of Rte 4169 between Th Ban Thurian and Th Ban Hua. Its monk, Luang Phaw Daeng, has been dead for over two decades but his corpse is preserved sitting in a meditative pose and sporting a pair of sunglasses.

Wat Samret BUDDHIST TEMPLE

At Wat Samret, near Th Ban Hua, you can see a typical Mandalay sitting Buddha carved from solid marble – a common sight in India and northern Thailand, but not so common in the south.

Activities

Ko Samui is an excellent choice for families travelling with kids as there are many activities especially geared to the little ones.

Blue Stars KAYAKING, SNORKELLING

(Map p178; ☎0 7741 3231; www.bluestars.info; Hat Chaweng; kayak & snorkelling tours 2200B) There are many choices for snorkelling and kayak tours to Ang Thong Marine National Park, but Blue Stars has the best reputation and the coolest boat. Even if you don't go with this company, don't miss taking a trip to these islands.

Naish SUP WATERSPORTS

(Map p178; ☎08 6947 7233; Hat Chaweng; SUP rental per hr/day 200/500B) Paddle it like a boat (although you're standing up) or try to surf it; popular stand up paddle boards have reached Ko Samui and you can rent them here. Take an hour-long lesson in the sandy shallows if it's your first time for 300B.

Football Golf FOOTBALL GOLF

(☎08 9771 7498; ⊙9am-6.30pm) At Hat Choeng Mon there's a strange combustion called 'football golf' where you 'putt' your football into a rubbish-bin-sized hole. It's great for the kids and each game (350B) comes with a complimentary soft drink. It's a par 66.

Magic Alambic RUM TASTING

(www.rumdistillerie.com; Ban Bang Kao; tasting shots 50-75B; ⊙noon-6pm) The only rum distillery in Thailand produces Caribbean agricole style (distilled from fresh, fermented sugar cane juice) in a variety of all natural flavours including a delectable coconut rum obtained from soaking coconut meat in the rum for several months. There's a video about the production process, a tasting area and shop in beautiful palm-shaded surrounds. It's on Samui's southern coast.

Aquapark SEA PARK

(Map p178; Hat Chaweng; hourly/half-day 200/350B; ⊙10am-6pm) Let the kids loose on these gigantic green, climbable, slip-off-able and all-around-fun inflatables (including a UFO, an iceberg climbing wall and trampolines) anchored to a corded-off area of Ao Chaweng. All participants are required to wear lifejackets. Meanwhile you can lounge on the beach and watch, or join them as many parents are enticed to do.

Coco Splash Waterpark WATER PARK

(Ban Lamai; admission 200B; ⊙10.30am-5.30pm) Kids under 10 will love this small park of fun painted concrete water slides. Towel hire is 60B and there's mediocre food available. Note that if you're planning on watching the kids and not going in the water yourself, you get in for free. Arrive after 4pm and the price drops to 60B.

Samui Dog & Cat Rescue Centre VOLUNTEERING

(Map p178; ☎0 7741 3490; www.samuidog.org; Soi 3, Chaweng Beach Rd; ⊙9am-6pm) Donations of time and/or money are hugely appreciated at the aptly named Samui Dog & Cat Rescue Centre. Volunteers are always needed to take care of the animals at either of the kennel/clinics (in Hat Chaweng and Ban Taling Ngam). Call the centre for volunteering details or swing by for additional info.

The organisation has played an integral role in keeping the island's dog population under control through an active spaying and neutering program. The centre also vaccinates dogs against rabies.

Diving

If you're serious about diving, head to Ko Tao and base yourself there for the duration of your diving adventure. If you're short on time and don't want to leave Samui, there are plenty of operators who will take you to the same dive sites (at a greater fee, of course). Try to book with a company that has its own boat (or leases a boat) – it's slightly more expensive, but you'll be glad you did it. Companies without boats often shuttle divers on the passenger catamaran to Ko Tao, where you board a second boat to reach your dive site. These trips are arduous, meal-less and rather impersonal.

Certification courses tend to be twice as expensive on Ko Samui as they are on Ko Tao, due largely to use of extra petrol, since tiny Tao is significantly closer to the preferred diving locations. You'll spend between 14,000B and 22,000B on an Open Water certification, and figure on between 4500B and 6200B for a diving day trip including two dives, depending on the location of the site.

Ko Samui's hyperbaric chamber is at Big Buddha Beach (Hat Bang Rak).

WORTH A TRIP

KO TAH

Tired of tours and busy beaches? For the intrepid DIY traveller there's no better way to spend a day on Ko Samui than with a trip to the white sands of Ko Tah. Hire a long-tail boat from the boatmen who beach their boats alongside the strip of seafood restaurants on Hat Thong Tanote on Ko Samui's south coast; a boat for up to six people should cost 1500B to 2000B for a four-hour trip. The island itself is only about 15 minutes from Ko Samui. While the snorkelling isn't that great, the white-sand beach is empty aside from the occasional visit by charter boats and local fishermen, and the views and swimming are sublime.

100 Degrees East DIVING
(☎0 7742 5936; www.100degreeseast.com; Hat Bang Rak) Highly recommended.

Samui Planet Scuba DIVING
(SIDS; Map p178; ☎0 7723 1606; samuiplanetscuba@planetscuba.net; Hat Chaweng)

Spas & Yoga

Competition for Samui's five-star accommodation is fierce, which means that the spas are of the highest calibre. For top-notch pampering, try the spa at Anantara (p182) in Bo Phut, or the Hideaway Spa at the Six Senses Samui (p181). The Spa Resort (p180) in Lamai is the island's original health destination, and is still known for its effective 'clean me out' fasting regime.

Yoga Thailand YOGA, SPA
(☎0 7792 0090; www.yoga-thailand.com; Phang Ka; retreats around €840) Secreted away along the southern shores, Yoga Thailand is ushering in a new era of therapeutic holidaying with its state-of-the-art facilities and dedicated team of trainers. Accommodation is in a comfy apartment block up the street while yoga studios, wellness centres and a breezy cafe sit calmly along the shore.

Tamarind Retreat THAI MASSAGE
(☎0 7723 0571; www.tamarindretreat.com) Tucked far away from the beach within a silent coconut-palm plantation, Tamarind's small collection of villas and massage studios is seamlessly incorporated into nature: some have granite boulders built into walls and floors, while others offer private ponds or creative outdoor baths.

Absolute Sanctuary YOGA, SPA
(☎0 7760 1190; www.absolutesanctuary.com) What was once a friendly yoga studio has blossomed into a gargantuan wellness complex featuring plenty of accommodation and an exhaustive menu of detox and wellness programs. Located a few kilometres north of Chaweng.

Courses

Samui Institute of Thai Culinary Arts COOKING
(SITCA; Map p178; ☎0 7741 3434; www.sitca.net; Hat Chaweng; one-day course 1950B) If you're contemplating a Thai cooking course, SITCA is the place to do it. It has daily Thai-cooking classes and courses in the aristocratic Thai art of carving fruits and vegetables into intricate floral designs. Lunchtime classes begin at 11am, while dinner starts at 4pm (both are three-hour courses with three or more dishes).

Included is an excellent tutorial about procuring ingredients in your home country. Of course, you get to eat your projects, and you can even invite a friend along for the meal. Complimentary DVDs with Thai cooking instruction are also available so you can practise at home.

Lamai Muay Thai Camp THAI BOXING
(☎08 7082 6970; www.lamaimuaythaicamp.com; 82/2 Moo3, Lamai; 1-day/1-week training sessions 250/1250B; ⏲7am-8pm) The island's best *moo·ay tai* (also spelt *muay thai*) training (best for the seriously serious) is at this place catering to beginners as well as those wanting to hone their skills. There's also a well-equipped gym for boxers and non-boxers who want to up their fitness levels.

Kiteboarding Asia KITEBOARDING
(☎08 3643 1627; www.kiteboardingasia.com; 1-/3-day courses 4000/11,000B) With two locations – one on Hua Thanon in the south of the island for May to October winds and the other at Na Thon on the west side for November to March winds – this pro place will get you kitesurfing on flat shallow water. The instructors here claim that Ko Samui is the best place in the country to learn the sport.

Sleeping

The island's array of sleeping options is overwhelming. If you're looking to splurge, there is definitely no shortage of top-end resorts sporting extravagant bungalows, charming spas, private infinity pools and first-class dining. Bo Phut, on the island's northern coast, has a charming collection of boutique lodging – the perfect choice for midrange travellers. Backpack-toting tourists will have to look a little harder, but budget digs do pop up once in a while along all of the island's beaches.

Most visitors arrive having prebooked their resort but outside of peak season most midrange and budget places offer discounted walk-in rates equal or better to what you'll find online. Calling around in advance rather than surfing the web is the best way to find a deal if you don't want to schlep your stuff on foot from place to place. We've compiled a list of our favourite places to stay but the following inventory is by no means exhaustive.

Private villa services have become quite popular in recent years; www.gosamuivillas.com is a good place to book the luxury variety.

Hat Chaweng

Busy, bodaciously flaxen Chaweng is packed wall-to-wall with every level of accommodation from cheap backpacker pads advertised with cardboard signs (some as low as 300B for a double) to futuristic villas with private swimming pools – and these might be just across the street from each other. The northern half of the beach is the biggest party zone and resorts in this region will be in earshot of the thumping bass emanating from Ark Bar at the centre of it all. If you're hoping for early nights, pick a resort near the southern half of the beach or bring earplugs.

Lucky Mother GUESTHOUSE $

(Map p178; ☎0 7723 0931; 60 Moo 2; r & bungalows 800-1500B;) First, let's take a moment to giggle at the name. OK now let's appreciate the action-filled beachfront location, clean, bright, polished cement detailed rooms and popular bar out front that's prime for mingling with your toes in the sand. In all it's a great deal if you avoid the sour lemons on staff.

P Chaweng HOTEL $

(Map p178; ☎0 7723 0684; r from 600B, ste 1000B;) Off the main drag and a short walk to the beach, this vine-covered cheapie has extra-clean, pink-tiled or wood-floored spacious rooms, all decked out with air-con, hot water, TVs and fridges. It's a 10-minute walk to the bar zone and not particularly hip, but good luck finding a better room in the area for this price.

Loft Samui HOSTEL $

(Map p178; ☎0 7741 3420; www.theloftsmaui.com; r 700-1500B;) The row house doubles and deluxe rooms in the new building have a warm, butter-yellow, near-Mexican style, but avoid the darker, mustier bungalows across from reception. All walls are thin and despite the distance from the 'scene' (about 10 minutes' walking) this place is popular with partiers, so bring earplugs if you're an early sleeper.

Queen Boutique Resort HOTEL $

(Map p178; ☎0 7741 3148; queensamui@yahoo.com; r 700-1500B;) The Queen offers up boutique sleeps at backpacker prices. Reception is friendly and the clean well-equipped (with air-con, TVs and DVD) rooms get style points from colourful throw pillows and modern Asian art on the walls. However, most are boxy and many of them windowless.

Pott Guesthouse GUESTHOUSE $

(Map p178; r fan/air-con 300/500B;) The big, bright cement rooms all with attached hot-water bathrooms in this nondescript apartment block are a steal. Reception is at an unnamed restaurant on the main drag across the alley.

Akwa GUESTHOUSE $

(Map p178; ☎08 4660 0551; www.akwaguesthouse.com; r from 700B;) Akwa has a few funky rooms decorated with bright colours but there's little natural light and everything is a bit past its prime. There's no shortage of character, however, with teddy bears adorning each bed, quirky bookshelves stocked with DVDs and cartoon paintings all over.

Samui Hostel HOSTEL $

(Map p178; ☎08 9874 3737; dm 200B;) It doesn't look like much from the front, but the three dorm rooms here are surprisingly spic and span and each has its own hot water bathroom and air-conditioning. The staff are sweet too.

★ Jungle Club BUNGALOW $$

(☎08 1894 2327; www.jungleclubsamui.com; huts 800-1800B, houses 2700-4500B;) The perilous drive up the slithering road is totally worthwhile once you take in the

Hat Chaweng

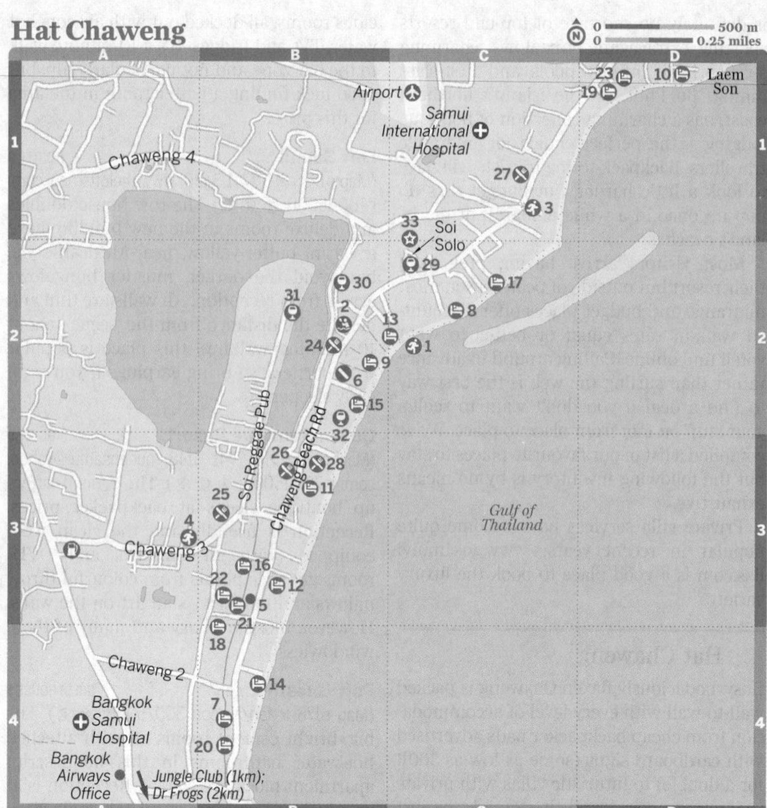

incredible views from the top. This isolated mountain getaway is a huge hit among locals and tourists alike. There's a relaxed back-to-nature vibe – guests chill around the stunning horizon pool or catnap under the canopied roofs of an open-air *săh·lah* (often spelt as *sala*).

Call ahead for a pick-up – you don't want to spend your precious jungle vacation in a body cast.

Chaweng Garden Beach RESORT **$$**
(Map p178; 0 7796 0394; www.chawenggarden.com; r 2300-9500B;) There's a large variety of room types here from rather bland standards to a private beachfront pool villa. The best value is found in those such as the modern Asian-inspired 'Shinto' rooms and polished wood bungalows. The whole place is hidden in foliage and serviced by an extra-smiley staff.

Pandora Boutique Hotel RESORT **$$**
(Map p178; 0 7741 3801; www.pandora-samui.com; r 2940-4470B;) As adorable as it is memorable, Pandora looks like it just fell out of a comic book – maybe *Tintin and the Mystery of Surprisingly Cheap Accommodation in Chaweng*? Rooms are outfitted with cheerful pastels, wooden mouldings and the occasional stone feature. It's about a five-minute walk to the beach.

Tango Beach Resort RESORT **$$**
(Map p178; 0 7742 2470; www.tangobeachsamui.com; r 1700-7400B;) Tango features a string of bungalows arranged along a teak boardwalk that meanders away from an excellent but busy stretch of beach. The dark tinted windows make the place look a little tacky from the outside (and the 1980s-era pool doesn't help) but bright paint and wood floors make the rooms feel fresh.

Hat Chaweng

Activities, Courses & Tours

1 Aquapark ... C2
2 Blue Stars ... B2
3 Naish SUP ... C1
4 Samui Dog & Cat Rescue Centre ... A3
5 Samui Institute of Thai Culinary Arts ... B3
6 Samui Planet Scuba ... B2

Sleeping

7 Akwa ... B4
8 Ark Bar ... C2
9 Baan Chaweng Beach Resort ... B2
10 Baan Haad Ngam ... D1
11 Buri Rasa Village ... B3
12 Centara Grand ... B3
13 Chaweng Garden Beach ... C2
14 Kirikayan Boutique Resort ... B4
15 Library ... B2
16 Loft Samui ... B3
17 Lucky Mother ... C2
18 P Chaweng ... B4
19 Pandora Boutique Hotel ... D1
20 Pott Guesthouse ... B4
21 Queen Boutique Resort ... B3
22 Samui Hostel ... B3
23 Tango Beach Resort ... D1

Eating

24 Khaosan Restaurant & Bakery ... B2
25 Laem Din Market ... B3
26 Ninja Crepes ... B3
Page ... (see 15)
27 Prego ... C1
28 Wave Samui ... B3

Drinking & Nightlife

Ark Bar ... (see 8)
29 Bar Solo ... C2
30 Green Mango ... B2
31 Reggae Pub ... B2
32 Tropical Murphy's Irish ... B2

Entertainment

33 Moulin Rouge ... C1

Ark Bar RESORT **$$**
(Map p178; ☎0 7742 2047; www.ark-bar.com; r 1630-4200B; ❄☜≋) You'll find two of every party animal at Ark Bar – frat boys, chilled-out hippies, teenagers, 40-somethings and so on. Contemporary, brightly painted rooms are staggering distance from the bar that pumps out techno all day and well into the night. Beds are hard but chances are you'll be too drunk to care.

★**Library** RESORT **$$$**
(Map p178; ☎0 7742 2767; www.thelibrary.name; r from 9140B; ❄@☜≋) This library is too cool for school. The entire resort is a sparkling white mirage accented with black trimming and slatted curtains. Besides the futuristic iMac computer in each page (rooms are 'pages' here), our favourite feature is the large monochromatic wall art – it glows brightly in the evening and you can adjust the colour to your mood.

Life-size statues are engaged in the act of reading, and if you too feel inclined to pick up a book, the on-site library houses an impressive assortment of colourful art and design books. The large rectangular pool is not to be missed – it's tiled in piercing shades of red, making the term 'bloodbath' suddenly seem appealing. It has an on-site restaurant (p186).

Buri Rasa Village RESORT **$$$**
(Map p178; ☎0 7723 0222; samui.burirasa.com; r 4900-6900B; ❄☜≋) Thai-style wooden doors lead to private villa patios and simple yet elegant rooms. This Zen-feeling place is beautifully landscaped with palms and frangipani, central, well-priced and on a good stretch of busy beach, but the real reason to stay here is the bend-over-backwards friendly and helpful service.

Baan Haad Ngam RESORT **$$$**
(Map p178; ☎0 7723 1500; www.baanhaadngam.com; bungalows 6250-14,000B; ❄@☜≋) Classy yet simple lime green rooms and villas are tucked into a veritable botanical garden cut with mini waterfalls and streams that lead to a small infinity pool that gazes over aqua sea. Its best asset, however, is its location, close to the action yet quiet and private.

Kirikayan Boutique Resort RESORT **$$$**
(Map p178; ☎0 7733 2299; www.kirikayan.com; r from 6840B; ❄@☜≋) Simple whites, lacquered teak and blazing red accents set the colour scheme at this small, hip address along Hat Chaweng's southern sands. Wander past thick palm trunks and sky-scraping foliage to find the relaxing pool deck at the back.

Centara Grand RESORT **$$$**
(Map p178; ☎0 7723 0500; www.centralhotelsresorts.com; r 8900-21,500B; ❄@☜≋) Centara is a massive, manicured compound in the heart of Hat Chaweng, but the palm-filled property is so large you can safely escape the street-side bustle. Rooms are found in

a hotel-like building that is conspicuously Western in theme and decor. Babysitting and family-friendly services abound. Check online for big discounts out of high season.

Baan Chaweng Beach Resort RESORT $$$
(Map p178; ☎0 7742 2403; www.baanchawengbeachresort.com; bungalows 4500-13,600B;) A bit of luxury without the hefty bill, Baan Chaweng draws in families and retiree bargain-seekers who roast themselves on loungers along the lovely beach. The immaculate rooms are painted in various shades of peach and pear, with teak furnishings that feel both modern and traditional.

Hat Lamai

The central, powdery white area of Hat Lamai is packed with an amazing quantity of sunburned souls lounging on beach chairs, but head to the grainier northern or southern extremities and things get much quieter. Ban Lamai runs back from the main beach area. Unlike Hat Chaweng, the main party in Lamai takes place off the beach so the sand here is generally free of a dance-beat soundtrack. However, the party scene that is here, mostly along the town's main drag and its smaller arteries, is of the seedier bar-girl-oriented variety.

Beer's House BUNGALOW $
(☎0 7723 0467; 161/4 Moo 4, Lamai North; bungalows 600-700B, r 1000B) One of the last of a dying breed on Ko Samui, this old-school-backpacker, low-key village of coconut bark huts sits right on a beautiful, sandy beach. Some huts have a communal toilet, but all have plenty of room to sling a hammock and laze the day away.

If the huts are too basic for you, check out the plain air-con rooms at Beer & Wine's Hut, across the road and away from the beach.

Amarina Residence HOTEL $
(www.amarinaresidence.com; r 900-1200B;) A two-minute walk to the beach, this excellent-value small hotel has two storeys of big, tastefully furnished, tiled rooms encircling the lobby and an incongruous dipping pool.

New Hut BUNGALOW $
(☎0 7723 0437; newhutlamai@yahoo.co.th; Lamai North; huts 300-500B;) A-frame huts right on the beach all share a big, clean block of bathrooms. There's a lively restaurant, friendly staff and one of the most simple and happy backpacker vibes on the island.

Spa Resort BUNGALOW $$
(☎0 7723 0855; www.spasamui.com; Lamai North; bungalows 1000-3500B;) Programs at this practical, not glamorous spa include colonics, massage, aqua detox, hypnotherapy and yoga, just to name a few. The bathrooms leave a bit to be desired, but (colonics aside) who needs a toilet when you're doing a week-long fast? Accommodation books up quickly. Nonguests are welcome to partake in the programs and dine at the excellent (and healthy) restaurant.

★**Rocky Resort** RESORT $$$
(☎0 7741 8367; www.rockyresort.com; Hua Thanon; r 6800-11,800B;) Our favourite spot in Lamai (well, actually just south of Lamai), Rocky finds the right balance between an upmarket ambience and unpretentious, sociable atmosphere. During the quieter months the prices are a steal, since ocean views abound, and each room is furnished with beautiful Thai-inspired furniture that seamlessly incorporates a modern twist.

The pool has been carved in between a collection of boulders mimicking the rocky beach nearby (hence the name).

Banyan Tree Koh Samui RESORT $$$
(☎0 7791 5333; www.banyantree.com/en/samui/overview; villas from 23,300B;) Occupying an entire bay, this sprawling over-the-top luxury delight encompasses dozens of pool villas hoisted above the foliage by spiderlike stilts. Golf carts zip around the grounds carrying jet-setters between the myriad dining venues and the gargantuan spa (which sports a relaxing rainforest simulator).

Samui Jasmine Resort RESORT $$$
(☎0 7723 2446; 131/8 Moo 3, Lamai; r & bungalows 4600-12,000B;) Smack dab in the middle of Hat Lamai, varnished-teak yet frilly Samui Jasmine is a great deal. Go for the lower-priced rooms – most have excellent views of the ocean and the crystal-coloured lap pool.

Choeng Mon

Choeng Mon is actually an area that holds several beaches that span the northeastern nub of the island. Samrong and Ton Son to the north are home to small communities and some of the most luxurious resorts in the world. Those with mortal budgets tend to stay on the beach at Choeng Mon proper whose perfect (although busy) half-moon of sand is considered by many to be the most beautiful beach on the island.

Ô Soleil BUNGALOW $

(☎0 7742 5232; osoleilbungalow@yahoo.fr; Choeng Mon; r fan/air-con from 500/700B; ❄📶) Located in a sea of luxury resorts, Thai-Belgian family-run stalwart Ô Soleil offers a welcome scatter of budget concrete bungalows and semidetached rooms extending inland from a gorgeous stretch of sand. As long as your expectations keep in line with what you're paying, this simple place will charm you.

Honey Resort RESORT $$

(☎0 7742 7094; www.samuihoney.com; Choeng Mon; r 3500-6500B; ❄📶🏊) At the quieter southern part of the beach, this small resort (with an equally small pool) isn't anything that special but it's nicer than some of the other mediocre offerings in this price range on this beach. Expect classic Zen-style rooms with black and white decor.

★**Six Senses Samui** RESORT $$$

(☎0 7724 5678; www.sixsenses.com/hideaway-samui/index.php; Samrong; bungalows from 13,000B; ❄@📶🏊) This hidden bamboo paradise is worth the once-in-a-lifetime splurge. Set along a rugged promontory, Six Senses strikes the perfect balance between opulence and rustic charm, and defines the term 'barefoot elegance'. Most of the villas have stunning concrete plunge pools and offer magnificent views of the silent bay below.

The regal, semi-outdoor bathrooms give the phrase 'royal flush' a whole new meaning. Beige golf buggies move guests between their hidden cottages and the stunning amenities strewn around the property – including a world-class spa and two excellent restaurants.

Tongsai Bay RESORT $$$

(☎0 7724 5480, 0 7724 5500; www.tongsaibay.co.th; Tong Son; ste 9800-34,000B; ❄📶🏊) For serious pampering, head to this secluded luxury gem. Expansive and impeccably maintained, the hilly grounds make the cluster of bungalows look more like a small village. All the extra-swanky split-level suites have day-bed rest areas, gorgeous romantic decor, stunning views, large terraces and creatively placed bathtubs (you'll see).

Facilities include salt- and freshwater pools, a tennis court, the requisite spa, a dessert shop and also several restaurants.

Sala Samui RESORT $$$

(☎0 7724 5888; www.salasamui.com; Choeng Mon; r 6200B, villas 8400-20,100B; ❄@📶🏊) Is the hefty price tag worth it? Definitely. The dreamy, modern design scheme is exquisite – clean whites and lacquered teaks are lavish throughout, while subtle turquoise accents draw on the colour of each villa's private plunge pool. It feels like a surreal white dream of a futuristic regal Asia.

Big Buddha Beach (Hat Bang Rak)

This area gets its moniker from the huge golden Buddha that acts as overlord from the small nearby quasi-island of Ko Fan. The western half of the beach is by far the best with its relatively empty stretch of white sand although the main road runs just parallel so parts of the beach is buzzed by traffic. The closer you get to the busy pier areas, the coarser and browner the sand becomes and the murkier the water. Big Buddha Beach's proximity to the airport means some noise overhead but quick and cheap taxi rides if you're flying in or out.

Secret Garden Bungalows BUNGALOW $$

(☎tel, info 0 7724 5255; www.secretgarden.co.th; bungalows 750-1600B; ❄📶) The deals here are no secret, so book in advance. This UK-run establishment has an excellent beach restaurant and bar and well-equipped, good-value yet simple bungalows in the eponymous garden. There's live music on Sundays when locals, expats and tourists come to chill out and imbibe, but it's fairly subdued the rest of the time.

★**Scent** RESORT $$$

(☎0 7796 0123; www.thescenthotel.com; ste 8500-10,500B) Find a taste (and scent if you light your complimentary incense) of *Indochine* at this resort that recreates the elegance of 1940s and '50s colonial Asia. The tall grey concrete structure is cut by elongated teak framed windows and surrounds a courtyard swimming pool and ornamental trees and plants.

Guests choose between European, Chinese or Thai-Chinese style rooms but all are spacious and decorated with tasteful opulence. Catch a classic film in the 'tea foyer' to really get into the old time groove.

Prana RESORT $$$
(☎0 7724 6362; www.pranaresorts.com; r 6650-13,100B; ❄🛜🏊) Sharp lines, polished cement and a skinny, rectangular infinity pool overlooking white sand make this place feel like the love child of an urban-chic upstairs lounge and a cushion-clad beach pad. Sophisticated bright rooms, a luxurious beachside spa and excellent service seal the deal.

Bo Phut

And now for something completely different. Bo Phut's Fisherman's Village is a collection of narrow Chinese shophouses that have been transformed into some of the island's best trendy (and often midrange) boutique hotels and eateries. The beach along most of this stretch, particularly the eastern part, is slim and coarse but it becomes whiter and lusher further west. The combination of pretty beach and gussied-up old village is beguiling.

Khuntai GUESTHOUSE $
(Map p183; ☎0 7724 5118; r fan/air-con 600/750B; ❄🛜) A block away from the beach, right in the Fisherman's Village, Khuntai's massive 2nd-floor fan rooms are drenched in afternoon sunshine and sea breezes. All rooms have hot-water bathrooms, fridges and TVs. It's a local family run place with plenty of heart.

★**Samui-Ley** GUESTHOUSE $$
(Map p183; ☎0 7724 5647; samuileyhouse@gmail.com; r 2300-2500B; ❄🛜) This tiny boutique guesthouse is shabby chic at its finest. Stylishly kistch wallpaper is paired with white walls, rag-woven rugs, paint-chipped furniture and retro Asian advert posters as well as modern art, checked and striped paint and more. Although it sounds headache-inducing, in fact the effect is soothing, especially with all the light pouring in from the sea-view terraces.

It's very laid-back and not a top choice for luxury hounds, but we love it.

Hacienda GUESTHOUSE $$
(Map p183; ☎0 7724 5943; www.samui-hacienda.com; r 1000-3400B, f 3300-3900B; ❄🛜🏊) Polished terracotta and rounded archways give the entrance a Spanish mission motif. Similar decor permeates the adorable rooms, which sport touches such as pebbled bathroom walls and translucent bamboo lamps. Hacienda Suites, the overflow property a few doors down, holds the cheaper 'eco' rooms which are minuscule and mostly windowless, but still clean and comfortable. The tiny rooftop pool has gorgeous ocean views.

The Lodge HOTEL $$
(Map p183; ☎0 7742 5337; www.lodgesamui.com; r 2300-3000B; ❄🛜) The Lodge feels like a colonial hunting chalet with pale walls and dark wooden beams jutting across the ceiling, except it all looks out over blue-green sea. Each of the eight rooms has scores of wall hangings and a private balcony overlooking the beach; the 'pent-huts' on the top floor are particularly spacious.

You're really in the heart of the Fisherman's Village making this a lively spot but somehow still intimate. It's extremely popular so reservations are a must.

Eden BUNGALOW $$
(Map p183; ☎0 7742 7645; www.edenbungalows.com; bungalows 1500-1900B; ❄🛜🏊) Eden is an exceptional find. The 10 bungalows and five rooms are all tucked away in a gorgeous tangle of garden with a small pool at its centre. Cheaper options are fairly plain but an upgrade gets you a stylish suite with yellow walls and naturalistic wood furniture. It's about a two-minute walk to the beach.

Cocooning HOTEL $$
(Map p183; ☎08 5781 4107; cocooning.samui@hotmail.com; r/ste 1000/1800B; ❄🛜🏊) New owners have spiffed up this small hotel with teak windows aplenty, which let in lovely muted light. Decor is a tasteful mix of Thai and a touch of Ikea thanks to the Swedish half of the British/Swede ownership. Service is exceptionally friendly and you'll find yourself making friends around the little green plunge pool. The beach is but a skip away.

★**Anantara** RESORT $$$
(Map p183; ☎0 7742 8300; samui.anantara.com; r 5300-18,600B; ❄@🛜🏊) Anantara's stunning palanquin entrance satisfies fantasies of a far-flung oriental kingdom. Clay and copper statues of grimacing jungle creatures abound on the property's wild acreage, while guests savour wild teas in an open-air pagoda, swim in the lagoonlike infinity-edged swimming pool or indulge in a relaxing spa treatment.

The new wing of adjacent whitewashed villas brings the resort up to another level of opulence and the whole place was upgraded in 2013.

Bo Phut

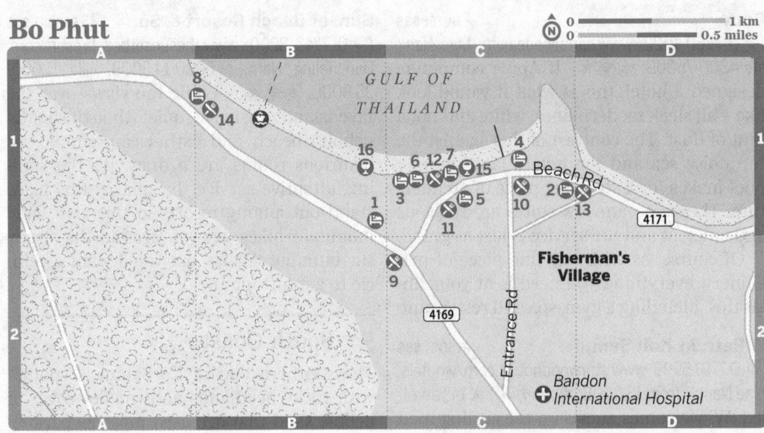

Bo Phut

Sleeping

1 Anantara ... B1
2 Cocooning ... C1
3 Eden ... C1
4 Hacienda ... C1
5 Khuntai ... C1
6 Samui-Ley ... C1
7 The Lodge ... C1
8 Zazen ... B1

Eating

9 69 ... C2
10 Karma Sutra ... C1
11 Shack Bar & Grill ... C1
12 Starfish & Coffee ... C1
13 The Hut ... D1
14 Zazen ... B1

Drinking & Nightlife

15 Billabong Surf Club ... C1
16 Coco Tam's ... B1

Zazen RESORT $$$

(Map p183; ☎0 7742 5085; www.samuizazen.com; r 6160-17,200B;) Welcome to one of the boutique-iest boutique resorts on Samui – every inch of this charming getaway has been thoughtfully and creatively designed. It's 'Asian minimalism meets modern rococo' with a scarlet accent wall, terracotta goddesses, a dash of feng shui and a generous smattering of good taste.

Guests relax poolside or on loungers gently shaded by canvas parasols on the very best stretch of this beach. Even better, the service is as luxe as the setting.

Mae Nam & Bang Po

Mae Nam's slim stretch of white that slopes down to a calm, swimmable aqua sea is one of the island's prettiest. It's popular with families and older couples, that give it a quiet yet still vibrant ambience perfect for reading under the shade of a palm tree, sleeping and indulging in beach massages. Bang Po, just around the tiny peninsula, is even quieter.

Shangri-la BUNGALOW $

(☎0 7742 5189; Mae Nam; bungalows fan/air-con from 500/1300B;) A backpacker's Shangri La indeed – these are some of the cheapest huts around and they're on a sublime part of the beach. Grounds are sparsely landscaped but the basic concrete bungalows, all with attached bathrooms (only air-con rooms have hot water), are well-kept and the staff is pleasant.

Coco Palm Resort BUNGALOW $$

(☎0 7742 5095; www.cocopalmbeachresort.com; Mae Nam; bungalows 2500-9000B;) The huge array of bungalows at Coco Palm have been crafted with hard wood, bamboo and rattan touches. A rectangular pool is the centrepiece along the beach, and the price is right for a resortlike atmosphere. The cheapest choices are the furthest from the beach but even these are comfy and pleasant.

Code HOTEL $$$

(☎0 7760 2122; www.samuicode.com; Mae Nam; ste 4300-7500B; ❄📶≋) If Apple computers designed a hotel, this is what it would look like – all sleek modern lines, white and not a hint of dust. The contrast of this against the turquoise sea and the hotel's large infinity pool makes for a stunning piece of architecture. The all-ocean-view suites are spacious and efficient and the service is just as grand.

Of course, as with any fine piece of machinery, everything you need is at your fingertips, including a gym, spa and restaurant.

W Retreat Koh Samui RESORT $$$

(☎0 7791 5999; www.starwoodhotels.com/whotels; Mae Nam; r from 13,000B; ❄@📶≋) A bejewelled 'W' welcomes guests on the curling road to the lobby, and upon arrival jaws immediate drop while staring out over the glittering infinity pools and endless horizon. The trademark 'W glam' is palpable throughout the resort, which does its darnedest to fuse an urban vibe with tropical serenity. Do note that this hotel is on a hill and not on a beach.

Napasai By Orient Express RESORT $$$

(☎0 7742 9200; www.napasai.com; Bang Po; r from 9100B; ❄@📶≋) Gorgeously manicured grounds welcome weary travellers as they glide past grazing water buffalo and groundsmen donning cream-coloured pith helmets. A generous smattering of villas dot the expansive landscape – all sport traditional Thai-style decorations, from the intricately carved wooden ornamentation to streamers of luscious local silks.

West Coast

Largely the domain of Thai tourists, Samui's west coast has skinny beaches of grainy sand but the sunsets, sandy-bottom blue seas and views out to the Five Islands and the shadowy greens of the mainland more than make up for this. It's a welcome escape from the east-side bustle.

Am Samui BUNGALOW $$

(☎0 7723 5165; www.amsamuiresort.com; Taling Ngam; bungalows 1600-6000B; ❄📶≋) Cast modesty aside, spread your curtains wide, and welcome sunshine and sea views in through your floor-to-ceiling windows. Getting out of the main tourist areas to this private beach with fantastic sunset views means your baht goes miles further in terms of room quality. Expect quiet nights and a less manicured beach.

Sunset Beach Resort & Spa RESORT $$$

(☎0 7742 8200; www.thesunsetbeachresort.com; Ban Taling Nam; r 6000-14,300B, villa 11,000-35,800B; ❄📶≋) While the views over the Five Islands at sunset, quiet (though slightly pebbly) beach and extra-clean, simple yet luxurious rooms are a draw, it's the smiling, attentive service that makes this place stand out among resorts in this area. Free mountain bikes get you around the sleepy surrounding village, but you'll want a vehicle to get further afield.

South Coast

The southern end of Ko Samui is spotted with rocky headlands and smaller coves of pebble sand that are used more as parking lots for Thai fishing boats than for lounge chairs. It's a great area to take a leisurely cycle through coconut palm groves and small Thai villages that aren't ruled by tourism.

Easy Time BUNGALOW $$

(☎0 7792 0110; www.easytimesamui.com; Phang Ka; villas 2100-3850B; ❄@📶≋) Safely tucked away from the throngs of tourists, this little haven – nestled a few minutes' walk to the beach around a serene swimming pool – doesn't have well-oiled service so be prepared to be master of your own off-the-beaten-path getaway. Duplex villa units and a chic dining space create an elegant mood that is refreshingly unpretentious.

Elements RESORT $$$

(☎0 7791 4678; www.elements-koh-samui.com; Phang Ka; r 8000-21,500B; ❄@📶≋) Peaceful Elements occupies a lonely strand of palm-studded sand with views of the stunning Five Islands, and is the perfect place for a meditative retreat or quiet couples romantic getaway. Chic rooms are arranged in condo-like blocks while hidden villas dot the path down to the oceanside lounge area. Free kayaks and bikes plus excellent service add to the calm.

We were quoted walk-in rates over 50% below the rack rates we list above, so call ahead and try your luck.

Eating

If you thought it was hard to pick a place to sleep, the island has even more options when it comes to dining. From roasted crickets to beluga caviar, Samui's got it and is not afraid to flaunt it.

SALT AND SPICE IN SOUTHERN THAI CUISINE

Don't say we didn't warn you: southern Thai cooking is undoubtedly the spiciest regional cooking style in a land of spicy regional cuisines. The food of Thailand's southern provinces also tends to be very salty, and seafood, not surprisingly, plays an important role, ranging from fresh fish that is grilled or added to soups, to pickled or fermented fish served as sauces or condiments.

Two of the principal crops in the south are coconuts and cashews, both of which find their way into a variety of dishes. In addition to these, southern Thais love their greens, and nearly every meal is accompanied by a platter of fresh herbs and veggies and a spicy 'dip' of shrimp paste, chillies, garlic and lime.

Dishes you are likely to come across in southern Thailand include the following:

➡ *Gaang đai ƀlah* – An intensely spicy and salty curry that includes đai ƀlah (salted fish stomach); much tastier than it sounds.

➡ *Gaang sôm* – Known as *gaang lěu·ang* (yellow curry) in central Thailand, this sour/spicy soup gets its hue from the liberal use of turmeric, a root commonly used in southern Thai cooking.

➡ *Gài tôrt hàht yài* – The famous deep-fried chicken from the town of Hat Yai gets its rich flavour from a marinade containing dried spices.

➡ *Kà·nŏm jeen nám yah* – This dish of thin rice noodles served with a fiery currylike sauce is always accompanied by a tray of fresh vegetables and herbs.

➡ *Kôo·a glîng* – Minced meat fried with a fiery curry paste is a southern staple.

➡ *Kôw yam* – A popular breakfast, this dish includes rice topped with sliced herbs, bean sprouts, dried prawns, toasted coconut and powdered red chilli, served with a sour/sweet fish-based sauce.

➡ *Pàt sà·đor* – This popular stir-fry of 'stink beans' with shrimp, garlic, chillies and shrimp paste is both pungent and spicy.

Influenced by the mainland, Samui is peppered with *kôw gaang* (rice and curry) shops, usually just a wooden shack displaying large metal pots of southern Thai-style curries. Folks pull up on their motorcycles, lift up the lids to survey the vibrantly coloured contents, and pick one for lunch. *Kôw gaang* shops are easily found along the Ring Rd (Rte 4169) and sell out of the good stuff by 1pm. Any build-up of local motorcycles is usually a sign of a good meal in progress.

The upmarket choices are even more numerous and although Samui's swank dining scene is laden with Italian options, visitors will have no problem finding flavours from around the globe. Lured by high salaries and spectacular weather, world-class chefs regularly make an appearance on the island.

Hat Chaweng

Dozens of the restaurants on the 'strip' serve a mixed bag of local bites, international cuisine and greasy fast food. For the best ambience head to the beach, where many bungalow operators set up tables on the sand and have glittery fairy lights at night.

Laem Din Market MARKET $

(Map p178; dishes from 35B; ⏰4am-6pm, night market 6pm-2am) A busy day market, Laem Din is packed with stalls that sell fresh fruits, vegetables and meats and stock local Thai kitchens. Pick up a kilo of sweet green oranges or wander the stalls trying to spot the ingredients in last night's curry. For dinner, come to the adjacent night market and sample the tasty southern-style fried chicken and curries.

Ninja Crepes THAI $

(Map p178; dishes from 75B; ⏰11am-midnight) Even though this basic food hall gets packed nightly and the multiple woks at the centre work double-time to keep the pace, the owners welcome and chat with nearly every one of their customers; it's a miracle of friendly service. The food, from Thai seafood and classics to sweet and savoury pancakes, is a delectable bargain.

Khaosan Restaurant & Bakery INTERNATIONAL $
(Map p178; dishes from 70B; ⌚ breakfast, lunch & dinner) From *filet mignon* to flapjacks and everything in between, this chow house is popular with those looking for cheap nosh. Hang around after your meal and catch a newly released movie on the big TV. It's everything you'd expect from a place called 'Khaosan'.

Wave Samui INTERNATIONAL $
(Map p178; dishes from 60B; ⌚ breakfast, lunch & dinner;) This jack-of-all-trades (guest-house-bar-restaurant) serves honest food at honest prices and fosters a travellers' ambience with an in-house library and a popular happy hour (3pm to 7pm). Basic, cheap rooms upstairs are 350B.

Page ASIAN FUSION $$$
(Map p178; dishes 280-1650B; ⌚ breakfast, lunch & dinner) If you can't afford to stay at the ultra-swanky Library (p179), have a meal at its beachside restaurant. The food is expensive (of course) but you'll receive glances from the beach bums on the beach as they try to figure out if you're a jet-setter or movie star. Lunch is a bit more casual and affordable, but you'll miss the designer lighting effects in the evening.

Dr Frogs STEAKHOUSE $$$
(mains 220-1350B; ⌚ lunch & dinner) Perched atop a rocky overlook, Dr Frogs combines incredible ocean vistas with delicious international flavours (namely Italian and Thai favourites). Delectable steaks and crab cakes, and friendly owners, put this spot near the top of our dining list.

Prego ITALIAN $$$
(Map p178; www.prego-samui.com; mains 200-700B; ⌚ dinner) This smart ministry of culinary style serves up fine Italian cuisine in a barely there dining room of cool marble and modern geometry. Reservations are accepted for seatings at 7pm and 9pm.

Hat Lamai

As Samui's second-most populated beach, Hat Lamai has a surprisingly limited assortment of decent eateries when compared to Hat Chaweng next door. Most nights a few noodle and pancake stalls open up around the 'Lady Boxing' bars in the centre of town, and sell dishes from 50B that you can eat at outdoor plastic tables.

Hua Thanon Market MARKET $
(dishes from 30B; ⌚ 6am-6pm) Slip into the rhythm of this village market that's slightly south of Lamai; it's a window into the food ways of southern Thailand. Vendors shoo away the flies from the freshly butchered meat and housewives load bundles of vegetables into their baby-filled motorcycle baskets.

Follow the market road to the row of food shops delivering edible Muslim culture: chicken *biryani,* fiery curries or toasted rice with coconut, bean sprouts, lemon grass and dried shrimp.

Lamai Day Market MARKET $
(dishes from 30B; ⌚ 6am-8pm) Lamai's market is a hive of activity, selling food necessities and takeaway food. Visit the covered area to pick up fresh fruit or to see vendors shredding coconuts to make coconut milk. Or hunt down the ice-cream seller for home-made coconut ice cream. It's next door to a petrol station.

Radiance INTERNATIONAL $$
(meals 100-400B; ⌚ breakfast, lunch & dinner;) Even if you're not staying at the Spa, or not even a vegetarian for that matter, healthy food never tasted this good. You'll find everything from an amazing raw *thom kha* (coconut green curry soup) to chocolate smoothies that can jive with anyone's dietary restrictions. Plus the semi-outdoor Zenlike setting is relaxing without a hint of pretension.

French Bakery BAKERY $$
(set breakfasts from 120B; ⌚ breakfast & lunch) The expat's breakfast choice is away from the main zone, near Wat Lamai on Rte 4169, but it's worth the 10-minute walk. Choose from fresh bread and pastries or unusually good set breakfasts that include fresh fruit and well-cooked eggs. Wash down your meal with espressos or a selection of teas.

Rocky's INTERNATIONAL $$$
(dishes 300-950B; ⌚ lunch & dinner) Easily the top dining spot on Lamai. Try the signature beef tenderloin with blue cheese – it's like sending your taste buds on a Parisian vacation. On Tuesdays diners enjoy a special Thai-themed evening with a prepared menu of local delicacies. Rocky's is at the like-named resort just south of Lamai.

Choeng Mon & Big Buddha Beach (Hat Bang Rak)

Choeng Mon's lively main drag that runs parallel to this main northern beach has lots of eating options, although price tags are high even without the beach view. There are fewer eating options around Big Buddha Beach, west of Choeng Mon, where the setting is less glamorous, but prices are more reasonable.

BBC INTERNATIONAL **$$**

(Big Buddha Beach; dishes 70-300B; breakfast, lunch & dinner) No, this place has nothing to do with *Dr Who* – BBC stands for Big Buddha Café. It's popular with the local expats, the international menu is large and there are exquisite ocean views from the patio.

Antica Locanda ITALIAN **$$**

(www.anticasamui.com; Hat Bang Rak; dishes 170-280B; dinner) This friendly trattoria has pressed white tablecloths and caskets of Italian wine. Try the *vongole alla marinara* (clams in white wine) and don't forget to check out the succulent specials of the day.

Catcantoo WESTERN **$$**

(http://catcantoo.net; Hat Bang Rak; mains 90-350B; breakfast, lunch & dinner) Enjoy a bargain-basement breakfast (99B) in the morning, succulent ribs at noon, or shoot some pool later in the day.

★ Dining On The Rocks ASIAN FUSION **$$$**

(0 7724 5678; reservations-samui@sixsenses.com; Choeng Mon; menus from 2200B; dinner) Samui's ultimate dining experience takes place on nine cantilevered verandahs of weathered teak and bamboo that yawn over the gulf. After sunset (and wine), guests feel like they're dining on a barge set adrift on a starlit sea. Each dish on the six-course prix-fixe menu is the brainchild of the cooks who regularly experiment with taste, texture and temperature.

If you're celebrating a special occasion, you'll have to book well in advance if you want to sit at 'table 99' (the honeymooners' table) positioned on a private terrace. Dining On The Rocks is at the isolated Six Senses Samui.

Bo Phut

The Fisherman's Village is the nicest setting for a meal but you'll find heaps of cheaper options on the road leading inland towards the main road.

The Hut THAI **$**

(Map p183; mains 80-300B; dinner) You'll find basic Thai specialities at reasonable prices (for the area) as well as more expensive fresh seafood treats. If you're a fisherman this is the place to get your own catch cooked up. There are only about a dozen tables and they fill fast so get here early or late if you don't want to wait.

★ 69 THAI FUSION **$$**

(Map p183; mains 179-550B; 11am-11pm Mon-Thu, 6-11pm Fri;) Imagine the best Thai green curry you ever had stuffed inside an Indian roti and topped with fresh mango – and this is just the beginning. Vivian is a food genius who is constantly coming up with creative twists on Thai favourites and she'll even encourage you to come up with your own ideas as you order.

The roadside setting isn't the best but the decor is as *vavoom* as the food: a cabaret of sequined tablecloths, bouquets of feathers and hanging tassels.

Karma Sutra INTERNATIONAL **$$**

(Map p183; mains 180-700B; breakfast, lunch & dinner;) A haze of purples and pillows, this charming chow spot straddles the heart of Bo Phut's Fisherman's Village and serves up very good international and Thai eats. Try the Mediterranean starter plate (300B), a beautifully arranged tray of olive tapenades, marinated peppers, eggplant caviar and more.

Starfish & Coffee THAI **$$**

(Map p183; mains 150-280B; breakfast, lunch & dinner) This streamer-clad eatery was probably named after the Prince song, since we couldn't find any starfish on the menu (there's loads of coffee though). Evenings feature standard Thai fare and sunset views of rugged Ko Pha-Ngan.

Shack Bar & Grill STEAKHOUSE **$$$**

(Map p183; www.theshackgrillsamui.com; mains 450-800B; dinner) With hands-down the best steaks on the island, the Shack imports the finest cuts of meat from Australia and slathers them in a rainbow of tasty sauces from red wine to blue cheese. Booth seating and jazz over the speakers give the joint a distinctly Western vibe, though you'll find all types of diners coming here to splurge.

DON'T MISS

'WALKING STREET' NIGHT MARKETS

The most fun dining experiences on Ko Samui are on 'Walking Streets', where once (or more) per week each beach village sets up a food-filled marketplace where you can sample local delicacies at hawker stalls, shop for crafts and trinkets and mingle with tourists and locals. All the markets are on or near the host village's main drag so they're hard to miss, and they all start setting up around 4pm to 5pm and run till 11pm or midnight. If you want to avoid the crowds count on arriving before 6pm or after about 10pm.

This was the schedule at the time of research but the popularity of these markets means that some are considering opening more frequently:

- **Ban Chaweng** Every night except Friday and Sunday. This is the biggest market with tonnes of food and seating (which is still hard to nab during peak hours)
- **Ban Lamai** Sunday
- **Ban Meanam** Thursday
- **Bo Phut** Friday
- **Ban Choeng Mon** Friday

Zazen ASIAN FUSION $$$
(Map p183; dishes 540-900B, set menu from 1300B; ⏲lunch & dinner) The chef describes the food as 'organic and orgasmic', and the ambient 'yums' from elated diners confirm the latter. This romantic dining experience comes complete with ocean views, dim candle lighting and soft music. Thai dancers animate things on Thursday and Sunday nights. Reservations recommended.

Mae Nam & Bang Po

Mae Nam has tonnes of eating options from beach-side, palm-thatch and driftwood affairs serving a mix of Thai, Western and seafood dishes to classier places tucked along the inland, lily-pad pond-dotted tangle of roads. It's a lovely place to wander and find your own surprises.

Bang Po Seafood SEAFOOD $$
(Bang Po; dishes from 100B; ⏲dinner) A meal at Bang Po Seafood is a test for the taste buds. It's one of the only restaurants that serves traditional Ko Samui fare: recipes call for ingredients such as raw sea urchin roe, baby octopus, sea water, coconut and local turmeric.

Farmer INTERNATIONAL $$$
(☎0 7744 7222; Mae Nam; mains 350-1000B; ⏲lunch & dinner) Magically set in a rice field, the Farmer is a refreshing change of setting and a romantic one at that, especially when the candlelight flickers on a clear starry night. The mostly European-inspired food is tasty and well-presented and there's a free pick-up for nearby beaches since this place is far from the main tourist areas.

West & South Coasts

The quiet west coast features some of the best seafood on Samui. Na Thon has a giant **day market** on Th Thawi Ratchaphakdi – it's worth stopping by to grab some snacks before your ferry ride.

★**Ging Pagarang** SEAFOOD $
(Thong Tanote; meals from 50B; ⏲11.30am-8pm) Locals know this is one of the island's best beachside places to sample authentic Samui-style seafood. It's simple and family-run, but the food and views are extraordinary. Try the sea algae salad with crab, fried dried octopus with coconut or the spectacular fried fish or prawns with lemon grass. The English translations on the menu will keep you giggling.

About Art & Craft Café VEGETARIAN $$
(Na Thon; dishes 80-180B; ⏲breakfast & lunch;) An artistic oasis in the midst of hurried Na Thon, this cafe serves an eclectic assortment of healthy and wholesome food, gourmet coffee and, as the name states, art and craft, made by the owner and her friends. Relaxed and friendly, this is also a gathering place for Samui's dwindling population of bohemians and artists.

Five Islands SEAFOOD $$$
(www.thefiveislands.com; Taling Ngam; dishes 250-630B, tours not incl/incl meal 3500/6900B; ⏲lunch & dinner) Five Islands offers Samui's most unique (yet pricey) eating experience.

First, a long-tail boat will take you out into the turquoise sea to visit the haunting Five Sister Islands, where you'll learn about the ancient art of harvesting bird nests to make bird's-nest soup, a Chinese delicacy. When you return a deluxe meal is waiting for you on the beach.

Lunch tours departs around 10am, and the dinner programs leave around 3pm. Customers are also welcome to dine without going on the tour and vice versa.

Drinking & Nightlife

Samui's biggest party spot is, without a doubt, noisy Hat Chaweng. Lamai and Bo Phut come in second and third respectively, while the rest of the island is generally quiet, as the drinking is usually focused around self-contained resort bars.

Hat Chaweng & Lamai

Making merry in Chaweng is a piece of cake. Most places are open until 2am and there are a few places that go strong all night long. Soi Green Mango has loads of girly bars. Soi Colibri and Soi Reggae Pub are raucous as well.

Every Saturday night around dinner hours it's lady boxing time at Lamai's thus named 'Lady Boxing' bars, when two bar girls duke it out in the ring after weeks of training. The rest of the week the girls writhe and dance at these central open-air bars, which is particularly depressing when there are no clients.

Beach Republic BAR
(www.beachrepublic.com; 176/34 Moo 4, Hat Lamai) Recognised by its yawning thatch-patched awnings, Beach Republic could be the poster child of a made-for-TV, beachside, booze swilling holiday. There's a wading pool, comfy lounge chairs, an endless cocktail list and even a hotel if you never, ever want to leave the party. The Sunday brunches here are legendary.

Ark Bar BAR
(Map p178; www.ark-bar.com; Hat Chaweng) Drinks are dispensed from the multicoloured bar draped in paper lanterns, guests recline on loungers on the beach, and the party is on day and night. If you ever dreamed of being part of an MTV spring break special, well remember this *is* Thailand, but it's getting awfully similar.

Bar Solo BAR
(Map p178; Hat Chaweng) A future-fitted outdoor beer hall in an urban setting with sleek cubist decor and a cocktail list that doesn't scream holiday hayseed. The evening drink specials lure in the front-loaders preparing for a late, late night at the dance clubs on Soi Solo and Soi Green Mango.

Tropical Murphy's Irish BAR
(Map p178; Hat Chaweng) A popular *fa·ràng* (Westerner) joint, Tropical Murphy's dishes out steak-and-kidney pie, fish and chips, lamb chops and Irish stew (mains 60B to 300B). Come night-time, the live music kicks on and this place turns into the most popular Irish bar on Ko Samui (yes, there are a few).

Green Mango BAR
(Map p178; Hat Chaweng) This place is so popular it has an entire soi named after it. Samui's favourite power drinking house is very big, very loud and very *fa·ràng*. Green Mango has blazing lights, expensive drinks and masses of sweaty bodies swaying to dance music.

Reggae Pub BAR
(Map p178; Hat Chaweng) This fortress of fun sports an open-air dance floor with music spun by foreign DJs. It's a towering two-storey affair with long bars, pool tables and a live-music stage. The whole place doubles as a shrine to Bob Marley.

Northern & West Coast Beaches

Woo Bar BAR
(Mae Nam) The W Retreat's signature lobby bar gives the word 'swish' a whole new meaning with cushion-clad pods of seating plunked in the middle of an expansive infinity pool that stretches out over the infinite horizon. This is, without a doubt, the best place on Samui for a sunset cocktail. On Monday nights get two-for-the-price-of-one mojitos.

Nikki Beach BAR
(www.nikkibeach.com/kohsamui; Lipa Noi) The acclaimed luxury brand has brought its international *savoir faire* to the secluded west coast of Ko Samui. Expect everything you would from a chic address in St Barts or St Tropez: haute cuisine, chic decor and gaggles of jet-setters. Themed brunch and dinner specials keep the masses coming

POP'S CULTURE: LIFE AS A LADYBOY

Pop, age 45, is what Thais call a *gà·teu·i,* usually referred to as a 'ladyboy' in English. Thailand's transgender population is the subject of many debates and conversations, especially among tourists. Although tolerance is widespread in Buddhist Thailand, concealed homophobia prevails – for *gà·teu·i,* this can be a challenging life, with the entertainment and sex industries the only lucrative career avenues. We spent the day with Pop and got the skinny on what life was really like as a member of Thailand's oft-talked-about 'third sex'.

Let's start with a question that many tourists in Thailand would like to ask: why does there seem to be so many ga·teu·i in Thailand?

Well, that's like asking me why I am a ladyboy! I have no idea. I didn't ask to have these feelings. I think the more important thing to notice is why there are so many ladyboys in the cabaret or sex industry. First, however, let me start by staying that the word *gà·teu·i* is the informal way of saying 'person with two sexes'; the term *pôo yĭng kâhm pêt* is generally more polite. Also, *gà·teu·i* is strictly reserved for people who still have male body parts but dress as female, so I am not technically *gà·teu·i* anymore.

Most tourists think that there are tonnes of ladyboys in Thailand because they are in places that many tourists visit. Yes, some ladyboys want to be cabaret dancers, just like some women want to be cabaret dancers, but most of them don't. These types of jobs are the only ones available to ladyboys, and the pay is lousy. Life is not as 'Hollywood' for a ladyboy as it may seem on stage. Most ladyboys don't have the chance to have a job that is respected by the community. We are not allowed to become doctors or psychologists and most corporations do not allow ladyboy employees because they don't want *gà·teu·i* to be associated with their company's image. Since many of us cannot have proper jobs, many ladyboys drop out of school at a young age, and lately this educational gap in the culture has become huge. Ladyboys work in the sex industry because they aren't given the opportunity to make a lot of money doing something else. I feel like a second-class citizen; we are not allowed to use male *or* female bathrooms! I used to have to climb 14 flights of stairs to use the special ladyboys' bathroom at my old job! Also, Thai law states that my ID cards and passport must always have an 'M' for male because the definition of a female in Thailand is someone who can bear children. It's hard for me to leave the country because my passport says 'male' but I look like a female. They will never let me through security because it looks like a fraudulent passport.

How does one tell the difference between a ladyboy and a woman?

Sometimes it's really hard to tell...a ladyboy can be more beautiful than a woman! There is no set way to figure it out, unless you ask them for their ID card. These days, doctors are really starting to perfect the operations, and the operations are expensive – mine was 150,000B! I had the 'snip', then I had breast implants, my Adam's apple was shaved off, and I also had a nose job (I didn't like my old nose anyway). Other operations available include silicone implants in the hips, jaw narrowing, cheekbone shaving and chin sculpting – to make it rounder. But before anyone can have an operation, you have to have a psych evaluation. The operation was extremely painful. I spent seven days in the hospital and it took me about two months to fully recover. Younger patients tend to heal faster – I was about 40 years old when I had the operation.

What do you feel is the biggest misconception about gà·teu·i?

This is an easy question. The biggest misconception is that we are all promiscuous whores and liars. Like any human being, we are just looking for love. It is true that many ladyboys do try to trick the people around them, but this is because they are afraid of being rejected for who they really are. Also, many of them lie because they desperately want to be real women, but they will never be real women. I know that – that's why I always show the real me – I am comfortable with who I am. I wish everyone else would be too.

As told to Brandon Presser

throughout the week, and sleek bungalow accommodation is also on offer.

Coco Tam's BAR

(Map p183; Bo Phut; shisha pipes 500B) Plop yourself on a beanbag on the sand, order a giant cocktail served in a jar and take a toke on a shisha (water pipe). It's a bit pricey, but this boho, beach bum-chic spot oozes relaxation. There are fire dancers most nights.

Billabong Surf Club BAR

(Map p183; Bo Phut) Billabong's all about Aussie Rules football – it's playing on the TV and the walls are smothered with memorabilia from Down Undah. There are great views of Ko Pha-Ngan and hearty portions of ribs and chops to go with your draught beer.

☆ Entertainment

Moulin Rouge CABARET

(Map p178; Hat Chaweng) This flashy joint offers free *gà·teu·i* (ladyboys; also spelled *kàthoey*) cabaret every night at 11pm and attracts a mixed clientele of both sexes. Other ladyboys loiter out front and try to drag customers in, so to speak.

Information

DANGERS & ANNOYANCES

The rate of road accident fatalities on Ko Samui is quite high. This is mainly due to the large number of tourists who rent motorcycles only to find out that the winding roads, sudden tropical rains and frenzied traffic can be lethal. If you decide to rent a motorcycle, protect yourself by wearing a helmet, and ask for one that has a plastic visor.

Beach vendors are registered with the government and should all be wearing a numbered jacket. No peddler should cause an incessant disturbance – seek assistance if this occurs.

EMERGENCY

Tourist Police (☎0 7742 1281, emergency 1155) Based at the south of Na Thon.

IMMIGRATION

Located about 2km south of Na Thon is Ko Samui's **Immigration Office** (☎0 7742 1069; ⏲8.30am-noon & 1-4.30pm Mon-Fri). Officials here tend to issue the minimum rather than maximum visa extensions. During our visits here we've watched dozens of tourists wait through exhausting lines only to be curtly denied an extension for no particular reason. On a particularly bad day expect extensions to take the entire afternoon.

INTERNET ACCESS

There are countless places all over the island for internet access, even at the less popular beaches. Prices range from 1B to 2B per minute. Keep an eye out for restaurants that offer complimentary wi-fi service. Most accommodation offers a wi-fi connection; ironically you'll pay extra for it at high-end hotels.

MEDIA

The **Siam Map Company** (www.siammap.com) puts out quarterly booklets including a *Spa Guide, Dining Guide*, and an annual directory, which lists thousands of companies and hotels on the island. Its *Siam Map Company Samui Guide Map* is fantastic, free and easily found throughout the island. Also worth a look is the **Samui Navigator** (www.samuinavigaot.com) pamphlet. **Essential** (www.essential-samui) is a pocket-sized pamphlet focused on promoting Samui's diverse activities. **Samui Guide** (www.samuiguide.com) looks more like a magazine and features mostly restaurants and attractions.

MEDICAL SERVICES

Ko Samui has four private hospitals, all near Chaweng's Tesco-Lotus supermarket on the east coast (where most of the tourists tend to gather). The government hospital (Samui Hospital) in Na Thon has seen significant improvements in the past couple of years but the service is still a bit grim because funding is based on the number of Samui's legal residents (which doesn't take into account the many illegal Myanmar workers).

Bandon International Hospital (Map p183; ☎0 7742 5840, emergency 0 7742 5748)

Bangkok Samui Hospital (Map p178; ☎0 7742 9500, emergency 0 7742 9555) Your best bet for just about any medical problem.

Hyperbaric Chamber (☎0 7742 7427; Big Buddha Beach) The island's dive medicine specialists.

Samui International Hospital (Map p178; ☎0 7742 2272; www.sih.co.th; Hat Chaweng) Emergency ambulance service is available 24 hours and credit cards are accepted. It's near the Amari Resort in Hat Chaweng.

MONEY

Changing money isn't a problem on the east and north coasts, and in Na Thon. Multiple banks and foreign-exchange booths offer daily services and there's an ATM. You should not have to pay credit card fees as you do on neighbouring Ko Tao.

POST

In several parts of the island there are privately run post-office branches charging a small commission. You can almost always leave your stamped mail with your accommodation.

RENTAL SCAMS

Even if you escape unscathed from a motorbike riding experience (or hire a car), some shops will claim that you damaged your rental and will try to extort some serious cash. The best way to avoid this is to take copious photos of your vehicle at the time of rental, making sure the person renting you the vehicle sees you do it (they will be less likely to make false claims against you if they know you have photos). If they still make a claim against you, keep your cool. Losing your temper won't help you win the argument and could significantly escalate the problem. The situation is just as bad on Ko Pha-Ngan, a bit less so on Ko Tao.

If things get really bad call the tourist police (p191), not the regular police.

Main Post Office Near the TAT office; not always reliable.

TOURIST INFORMATION

Tourism Authority of Thailand (TAT; ☎0 7742 0504; Na Thon; ⊙8.30am-4.30pm) At the northern end of Na Thon; this office is friendly, helpful and has handy brochures and maps, although travel agents throughout the island can provide similar information.

Getting There & Away

AIR

Ko Samui's airport is in the northeast of the island near Big Buddha Beach. **Bangkok Airways** (www.bangkokair.com) operates flights roughly every 30 minutes between Samui and Bangkok's Suvarnabhumi International Airport (50 minutes). Bangkok Airways also flies direct from Samui to Phuket, Pattaya, Chiang Mai, Singapore and Hong Kong. **Firefly** (www.fireflyz.com.my) operates direct flights from Ko Samui to Kuala Lumpur's Subang airport.

There is a **Bangkok Airways Office** (Map p178; ☎0 7742 0519, 0 7742 0512) in Hat Chaweng and another at the **airport** (Map p178; ☎0 7742 5011). The first (at 6am) and last (10pm) flights of the day are always the cheapest.

During the high season, make your flight reservations far in advance as seats often sell out. If the Samui flights are full, try flying into Surat Thani from Bangkok and taking a short ferry ride to Samui instead. Flights to Surat Thani are generally cheaper than a direct flight to the island, although they are much more of a hassle.

BOAT

To reach Samui, the four main piers on the mainland are Ao Ban Don, Tha Thong, Don Sak and Khanom – Tha Thong (in central Surat) and Don Sak being the most common. On Samui, the three oft-used ports are Na Thon, Mae Nam and Big Buddha Beach. Expect complimentary taxi transfers with high-speed ferry services.

To/From the Mainland

There are frequent boat departures between Samui and the mainland. Two options are the high-speed **Lomprayah** (☎077 4277 656; www.lomprayah.com; 450B), which departs from Na Thon, and the slower, stinkier **Raja** (☎02 2768 2112; www.rajaferryport.com) car ferry (150B), which departs from Thong Yang. Ferries take one to five hours, depending on the boat. A couple of these departures can connect with the train station in Phun Phin (for a nominal extra fee). The slow night boat to Samui (200B) leaves from central Surat Thani each night at 11pm, reaching Na Thon around 5am. It returns from Na Thon at 9pm, arriving at around 3am. Watch your bags on this boat.

To/From Ko Pha-Ngan & Ko Tao

There are almost a dozen daily departures between Ko Samui and Thong Sala on the west coast of Ko Pha-Ngan and many of these continue on to Ko Tao. These leave from the Na Thon, Mae Nam or Big Buddha Beach pier, take from 20 minutes to one hour and cost 200 to 300B to Ko Pha-Ngan, depending on the boat.

To go directly to Hat Rin, the *Haad Rin Queen* goes back and forth between Hat Rin and Big Buddha Beach four times a day. The voyage takes 50 minutes and costs 200B.

Also for Hat Rin and the more remote east coast beaches of Ko Pha-Ngan, the small and rickety *Thong Nai Pan Express* runs once a day at noon from Mae Hat on Ko Samui to Hat Rin and then up the east coast, stopping at all the beaches as far as Thong Nai Pan Noi. Prices range from 200B to 400B, depending on the destination. The boat won't run in bad weather.

BUS & TRAIN

A bus-ferry combo is more convenient than a train-ferry package for getting to Ko Samui because you don't have to switch transportation in Phun Phin. However, the trains are much more comfortable and spacious – especially at night. If you prefer the train, you can get off at Chumphon and catch the Lomprayah catamaran service the rest of the way.

Several services offer these bus-boat combo tickets, the fastest and most comfortable being the Lomprayah which has two daily departures from Bangkok at 6am and 9pm and two from Samui to Bangkok at 8am and 12.30pm. The total voyage takes about 13½ hours and costs 1450B.

Getting Around

You can rent motorcycles (and bicycles) from almost every resort on the island. The going rate is 200B per day, but for longer periods try to negotiate a better rate.

Drivers of *sŏrng·tăa·ou* (pick-up trucks) love to try to overcharge you, so it's always best to ask a third party for current rates, as they can change with the season. These vehicles run regularly during daylight hours. It's about 50B to travel between beaches, and no more than 100B to travel halfway across the island. Figure about 20B for a five-minute ride on a motorcycle taxi.

Taxi service is quite chaotic due to the plethora of cabs. In the past taxi fares were unwieldy; these days prices are more standardised across the islands (though fares are still ridiculously inflated compared to Bangkok). Taxis typically charge around 500B for an airport transfer. Some Hat Chaweng travel agencies can arrange minibus taxis for less.

Ko Pha-Ngan เกาะพงัน

POP 12,500

Slacker, hippie-at-heart Ko Pha-Ngan has become so synonymous with the wild and massive Full Moon Party on Hat Rin that the rest of the island – and even Hat Rin outside of full moon week – gets forgotten. It's a strange juxtaposition where for one week the island has some 30,000 people crammed on one beach partying their minds out and then off they all go on the next boat, leaving the beaches and accommodations half empty. It's at this time that budgeting serenity seekers can retreat into a fog (perhaps with a slight herbal scent) of the backpacker days of old and nab a fan-cooled beach shack from 400B (on the northern beaches at least). This will probably change quickly with the imminent opening of the island's airport in late 2014, but for now this exceptionally gorgeous

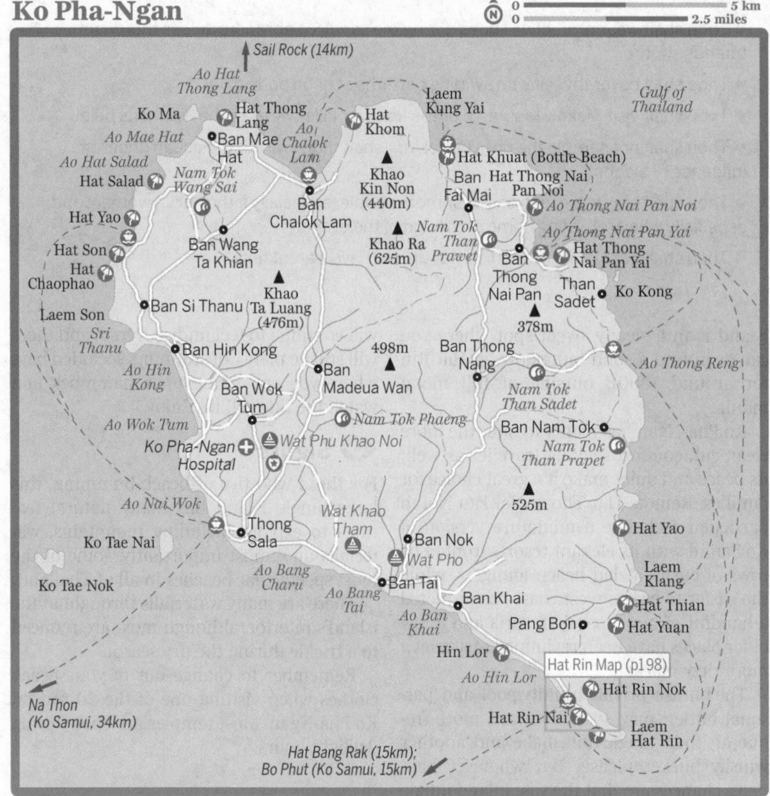

THE TEN COMMANDMENTS OF FULL MOON FUN

No one knows exactly when or how these crazy parties started – many believe they began in 1987 or 1988 as someone's 'going away party', but none of that is relevant now. Today, thousands of bodies converge monthly on the kerosene-soaked sands of Sunrise Beach for an epic trance-a-thon. Crowds can reach an outrageous 40,000 partiers during high season, while the low season still sees a respectable 5000 pilgrims.

If you can't make your trip coincide with a full moon but still want to cover yourself in fluorescent paint, fear not – enterprising locals have organised a slew of other reasons to get sloshed. There are Black Moon Parties (at Ban Khai), Half Moon Parties (at Ban Tai) and Moon-set Parties (at Hat Chaophao) just to name a few.

Some critics claim the party is starting to lose its carefree flavour, especially after increasing violence and the fact that the island's government now charges a 100B entrance fee to partygoers (the money goes towards needed beach cleaning and security). Despite changes, the night of the full moon is still the ultimate partying experience, as long as one follows the unofficial Ten Commandments of Full Moon fun:

- Thou shalt arrive in Hat Rin at least three days early to nail down accommodation during the pre-full moon rush of backpackers.
- Thou shalt double-check the party dates as sometimes they coincide with Buddhist holidays and are rescheduled.
- Thou shalt secure all valuables, especially when staying in budget bungalows.
- Thou shalt savour some delicious fried fare in Chicken Corner before the revelry begins.
- Thou shalt wear protective shoes during the sandy celebration, unless thou wants a tetanus shot.
- Thou shalt cover thyself with swirling patterns of neon body paint.
- Thou shalt visit Mellow Mountain or the Rock for killer views of the heathens below.
- Thou shalt not sample the drug buffet, nor shalt thou swim in the ocean under the influence of alcohol.
- Thou shalt stay in a group of two or more people, especially if thou art a woman, and especially when returning home at the end of the evening.
- Thou shalt party until the sun comes up and have a great time.

island is in a sleepy sweet spot where you can even find a solid bungalow on Hat Rin for around 1000B outside of full moon mania.

Ko Pha-Ngan has plenty to offer the more clean-cut, comfort-seeking traveller as well; its peace and quiet make it a great choice for families. Remote Hat Thong Nai Pan Noi in particular feels like a miniature version of Ko Samui with its elegant resorts fronted by rows of cushion-clad beach loungers, while the easier-to-access west coast has attracted a handful of new upscale resorts and a few older places have been revamped to attract a more ritzy market.

The phrase 'private infinity pool' and 'personal butler' may soon be heard more frequently than 'magic milkshake' and 'another whisky bucket please'. But whatever happens, chances are that the vast inland jungle will continue to feel undiscovered, and there will still be plenty of stunning, secluded bays where you can string up a hammock and watch the tide roll in. Enjoy.

Sights

For those who tire of beach-bumming, this large jungle island has many natural features to explore including mountains, waterfalls and, most importantly, some of the most spectacular beaches in all of Thailand.

There are many waterfalls throughout the island's interior, although most are reduced to a trickle during the dry season.

Remember to change out of your beach clothes when visiting one of the 20 wát on Ko Pha-Ngan. Most temples are open during daylight hours.

Nam Tok Than Sadet WATERFALL

These falls feature boulders carved with the royal insignia of Rama V, Rama VII and Rama IX. King Rama V enjoyed this hidden spot so much that he returned over a dozen times between 1888 and 1909. The river waters of Khlong Than Sadet are now considered sacred and used in royal ceremonies. Also near the eastern coast, **Than Prawet** is a series of chutes that snake inland for approximately 2km.

Nam Tok Phaeng WATERFALL

In the centre of the island, Nam Tok Phaeng is protected by a national park; this waterfall is a pleasant reward after a short, but rough, hike. Continue the adventure and head up to **Khao Ra**, the highest mountain on the island at 625m. Those with eagle-eyes will spot wild crocodiles, monkeys, snakes, deer and boar along the way, and the **viewpoint** from the top is spectacular – on a clear day you can see Ko Tao. Although the trek isn't arduous, it is very easy to lose one's way, and we *highly* recommend hiring an escort in Ban Madeua Wan (near the falls). The local guides have crude signs posted in front of their homes, and, if they're around, they'll take you up to the top for 500B. Most of them only speak Thai.

Hat Khuat BEACH

Also called Bottle Beach, Hat Khuat is a classic fave. Visitors flock to this shore for a relaxing day of swimming and snorkelling, and some opt to stay the night at one of the several bungalow operations along the beach. For additional seclusion, try the isolated beaches on the east coast, which include **Than Sadet**, **Hat Yuan**, **Hat Thian** and the teeny **Ao Thong Reng**. For additional enchanting beaches, consider doing a day trip to the stunning **Ang Thong Marine National Park** (p224).

Wat Phu Khao Noi BUDDHIST TEMPLE

(Map p193) The oldest temple on the island is Wat Phu Khao Noi, near the hospital in Thong Sala. While the site is open to visitors throughout the day, the monks are only around in the morning.

Wat Pho BUDDHIST TEMPLE

(Map p193; herbal sauna admission 50B; ⏲ herbal sauna 3-6pm) Wat Pho, near Ban Tai, has a **herbal sauna** accented with natural lemon grass. The **Chinese Temple** is believed to give visitors good luck. It was constructed about 20 years ago after a visiting woman had a vision of the Chinese Buddha, who instructed her to build a fire-light for the island.

Wat Khao Tham BUDDHIST TEMPLE

(Map p193) Wat Khao Tham, near Ban Tai, sits high on a hill and has resident female monks. At the temple there is a bulletin board detailing a meditation retreat taught by an American-Australian couple. For additional information, write in advance to Wat Khao Tham, PO Box 8, Ko Pha-Ngan, Surat Thani 84280.

Activities

With Ko Tao, the high-energy diving behemoth, just a few kilometres away, Ko Pha-Ngan enjoys a much quieter, more laid-back diving scene focused on fun diving rather than certifications. A recent drop in Open Water certification prices has made local prices competitive with Ko Tao. Group sizes tend to be smaller on Ko Pha-Ngan since the island has fewer divers in general.

Like the other islands in the Samui Archipelago, Pha-Ngan has several small reefs dispersed around the island. The clear favourite snorkelling spot is **Ko Ma**, a small island in the northwest connected to Ko Pha-Ngan by a charming sandbar. There are also some rock reefs of interest on the eastern side of the island.

A major perk of diving from Ko Pha-Ngan is the proximity to **Sail Rock** (Hin Bai), the best dive site in the Gulf of Thailand and a veritable beacon for whale sharks. This large pinnacle lies about 14km north of the island. An abundance of corals and large tropical fish can be seen at depths of 10m to 30m, and there's a rocky vertical swim-through called 'The Chimney'.

Dive shops on Ko Tao sometimes visit Sail Rock, however the focus tends to be more on swallow reefs (for newbie divers) and the shark-infested waters at Chumphon Pinnacle. The most popular trips departing from Ko Pha-Ngan are three-site day trips which stop at **Chumphon Pinnacle**, Sail Rock and one of the other premier sites in the area. These three-stop trips cost from around 3650B to 4000B and include a full lunch. Two-dive trips to Sail Rock will set you back around 2500B to 2800B.

Reefers, Lotus Diving and Haad Yao Divers are the main operators on the island with a solid reputation.

Hiking and snorkelling day trips to **Ang Thong Marine National Park** generally depart from Ko Samui, but recently tour operators are starting to shuttle tourists from Ko Pha-Ngan as well. Ask at your accommodation for details about boat trips as companies often come and go due to unstable petrol prices.

Many of the larger accommodation options can hook you up with a variety of aquatic equipment such as jet skis and kayaks, and the friendly staff at Backpackers Information Centre can attend to any of your other water-sports needs.

Chaloklum Diving DIVING
(☎0 7737 4025; www.chaloklum-diving.com) One of the more established dive shops on the island, these guys (based on the main drag in Ban Chalok Lam) have quality equipment and high standards in all that they do.

Reefers DIVING
(☎08 6471 4045; www.reefersdiving.com) Vic, the owner, and his gaggle of instructors are chilled and professional. Recommended.

Lotus Diving DIVING
(☎0 7737 4142; www.lotusdiving.net) This dive centre owns not one, but two beautiful boats (that's two more vessels than most of the other operations on Ko Pha-Ngan). Trips can be booked at their office in Ban Chalok Lam, or at the Backpackers Information Centre.

Haad Yao Divers DIVING
(☎08 6279 3085; www.haadyaodivers.com; Hat Yao) Established in 1997, this dive operator has garnered a strong reputation by maintaining European standards of safety and customer service.

Wake Up WAKEBOARDING
(☎08 7283 6755; www.wakeupwakeboarding.com; ⌚Jan-Oct) Jamie passes along his infinite wakeboarding wisdom to eager wannabes at his small water sports school in Chalok Lam. Fifteen minutes of 'air time' will set you back 1200B, which is excellent value considering you get one-on-one instruction. Kiteboarding, wake-skating and waterskiing sessions are also available.

Jungle Gym GYM
(Map p198; Hat Rin) One of several Thai boxing places on Ko Pha Ngan, this very conveniently located gym was one of the island's first. It also offers yoga and well-maintained fitness equipment.

Tours

Eco Nature Tour ECO TOUR
(☎08 4850 6273) This exceedingly popular oufit offers a 'best of' island trip, which includes elephant trekking, snorkelling and a visit to the Chinese temple, a stunning viewpoint and Nam Tok Phaeng. The day trip, which costs 1500B, departs at 9am and returns around 3pm. Bookings can be made at its office in Thong Sala or at the Backpackers Information Centre. **Pha-Ngan Safari** (☎08 1895 3783, 0 7737 4159) offers a similar trip for 1900B.

Sleeping

Ko Pha-Ngan's legendary history of laid-back revelry has solidified its reputation as *the* stomping ground for the gritty backpacker lifestyle. Even so, many local mainstays have recently collapsed their bamboo huts and constructed newer, sleeker accommodation aimed at the ever-growing legion of 'flashpackers'.

On other parts of the island, new tracts of land are being cleared for Samui-esque five-star resorts. But backpackers fear not; it will still be a while before the castaway lifestyle goes the way of the dodo. For now, Ko Pha-Ngan can revel in having excellent choices to suit every budget. Pha-Ngan also caters to a subculture of seclusion-seekers who crave a deserted slice of sand. The northern and eastern coasts offer just that – a place to escape.

Sleeping options start in Hat Rin, move along the southern coast, head up the west side, across the northern beaches and down the quiet eastern shore. The accommodation along the southern coast is the best bang for your baht on Ko Pha-Ngan, while the west coast is seeing a lot of development. The atmosphere here is a pleasant mix of quiet seclusion and a sociable vibe, although some of the beaches, particularly towards the south, aren't as picturesque as other parts of the island. Price tags are also higher than north or south of here.

Stretching from Chalok Lam to Thong Nai Pan, the dramatic northern coast is a wild jungle with several stunning and secluded beaches – it's the most scenic coast on the island.

The east coast is the ultimate hermit hang-out. For the most part you'll have to hire a boat to get to these beaches from Thong Sala, Chalok Lam and Hat Rin and 4WD taxis from Thong Sala are an option for the few that have dirt roads. The *Thong Nai Pan Express* boat runs daily at noon from Hat Mae Nam on Ko Samui stopping at Hat Rin and the east coast beaches as far as Thong Nai Pan Noi. The boat is a casual, rickety fishing-style vessel and won't run in rough weather.

Hat Rin

The thin peninsula of Hat Rin features three separate beaches. Beautiful blond Hat Rin Nok (Sunrise Beach) is the epicentre of full moon tomfoolery, Hat Rin Nai (Sunset Beach) is the much less impressive stretch of sand on the far side of the tiny promontory, and Hat Seekantang (also known as Hat Leela), just south of Hat Rin Nai, is a smaller, lovely white and more private beach. The three beaches are linked by Ban Hat Rin (Hat Rin Town) – a small inland collection of restaurants and bars. It takes only a few minutes to walk from one beach to another.

Hat Rin sees Thailand's greatest accommodation crunch during the full moon festivities. At this time, bungalow operations expect you to stay for a minimum number of days (usually five). If you plan to arrive the day of the party (or even the day before), we strongly suggest booking a room in advance, or else you'll probably have to sleep on the beach (which you might end up doing anyway). There's a new breed of cattle car–style dorms where a seemingly impossible number of beds are stacked and crammed into dark small rooms and shared toilets are few. These start at around 200B outside of the full moon chaos then escalate to 650B and up for party times. Even though these grim options have added a significant number of beds to the town, everything still manages to fill up. Check hostel booking websites for dorm bed availability.

Full-mooners can also stay on Ko Samui or other beaches on Ko Pha-Ngan and take speedboat shuttles to access the festivities – prices will depend on how far away you're staying but the money you'll save on staying anywhere besides Hat Rin itself will probably make it worth it. Driving on Ko Pha-Ngan during the festivities is an absolutely terrible idea and there are gory and often fatal accidents monthly.

Needless to say, the prices listed here are meaningless during periods of maximum lunar orbicularity. Expect rates to increase by 20% to 300% during full moon.

★Lighthouse Bungalows BUNGALOW $
(☎0 7737 5075; www.lighthousebungalows.com; Hat Seekantang; bungalows 500-1200B; ❄📶) This hidden, low-key collection of hip huts gathers along a sloping, bouldered terrain punctuated by towering palms. The fan options are rustic but the newest, spacious air-con bungalows are terrific value. Every option has a terrace and sweeping view of the sea plus there's a cushion-clad restaurant/common area. To get there, follow the wooden boardwalk southeast from Hat Leela.

Blue Marine BUNGALOW $
(Map p198; ☎0 7737 5079; www.bluemarinephangan.com; Hat Rin Nai; bungalows 600-1200B; ❄📶) This cluster of identical concrete bungalows with blue-tiled roofs surrounds a manicured green lawn; the best have dreamy views over the whitest and cleanest part of quiet Sunset Beach. Every unit is spacious, clean and has air-con, fridge, hot water and TV. Staff is exceptionally helpful and friendly which helps create a neighborhood vibe among guests.

Seaview Sunrise BUNGALOW $
(Map p198; www.seaviewsunrise.com; Hat Rin Nok; r 500-1400B; ❄📶) Budget full moon revellers who want to sleep inches from the tide, apply here. Some of the options back in the jungle are dark and musty but the solid, beachfront models have bright, polished wooden interiors often splashed with the occasional burst of neon paint from the ghosts of parties past.

Paradise Bungalows BUNGALOW $
(Map p198; ☎0 7737 5244; Hat Rin Nok; bungalows 650-2500B; ❄) The world-famous Full Moon Party was hatched at this scruffy batch of bungalows, and the place has been living on its fame ever since. The backpackers keep on coming to wax nostalgic, although the grounds are starting to look more like a junkyard now that the family has divvied up the land into several small 'resorts'. Paradise lost.

Same Same GUESTHOUSE $
(Map p198; ☎0 7737 5200; www.same-same.com; Ban Hat Rin; dm 500B, r 550-850B; ❄📶) A super-sociable spot for Scandinavians during the full moon madness, Same Same offers simple but bright rooms and plenty of party preparation fun.

Hat Rin

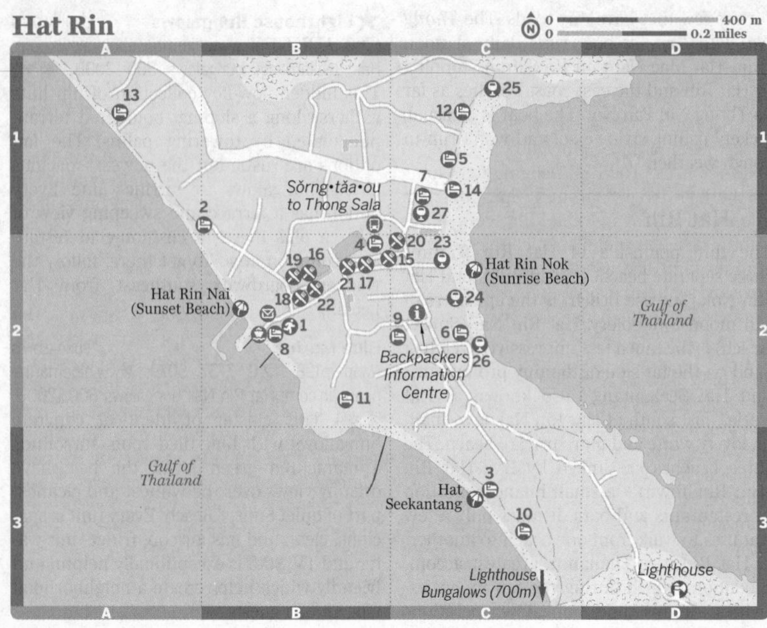

Hat Rin

Activities, Courses & Tours
1 Jungle Gym ... B2

Sleeping
2 Blue Marine ... B1
3 Cocohut Village ... C3
4 Delight ... B2
5 Palita Lodge ... C1
6 Paradise Bungalows ... C2
7 Pha-Ngan Bayshore Resort ... C1
8 Rin Beach Resort ... B2
9 Same Same ... C2
10 Sarikantang ... C3
11 Sea Breeze Bungalow ... B2
12 Seaview Sunrise ... C1
13 The Coast ... A1
14 Tommy Resort ... C1

Eating
15 Kawee ... B2
16 Lazy House ... B2
17 Little Home ... B2
18 Lucky Crab ... B2
Mama Schnitzel ... (see 20)
19 Monna Lisa ... B2
20 Mr K Thai Food ... C2
21 Nic's ... B2
22 Om Ganesh ... B2

Drinking & Nightlife
23 Cactus Bar ... C2
24 Drop-In Bar ... C2
25 Mellow Mountain ... C1
26 Rock ... C2
27 Sunrise ... C1
Tommy ... (see 14)

Cocohut Village RESORT $$
(Map p198; ☎0 7737 5368; www.cocohut.com; Hat Seekantang; bungalows 1300-12,000B;) This super-social place on a stunning stretch of sand is popular with Israelis. Plans to expand further down the beach were under way when we passed. The priciest options, including the cliff villas and beachfront bungalows, are some of the best bets in Hat Rin, while the budget choices are dark and dismal. Fantastic buffet breakfasts are included in the price.

Pha-Ngan Bayshore Resort RESORT $$
(Map p198; ☎0 7737 5227; www.phanganbayshore.com; Hat Rin Nok; r 2500-8400B;) After a much-needed overhaul in 2009, this hotel-style operation has primed itself for the ever-increasing influx of flashpackers in Hat Rin. Sweeping beach views and a giant swimming pool make Pha-Ngan Bayshore one of the top

addresses on Sunrise Beach, especially if you can nab a special promotion.

Delight GUESTHOUSE $$
(Map p198; ☎0 7737 5527; www.delightresort.com; Ban Hat Rin; r 1400-5400B; ❄☎≋) Secretly tucked behind the bright yellow Kodak sign in the centre of Hat Rin, Delight offers some of the best lodging around. Spic-and-span rooms in a Thai-style building come with subtle designer details (such as peacock murals) and are sandwiched between an inviting swimming pool and a lazy lagoon peppered with lily pads.

Tommy Resort RESORT $$
(Map p198; ☎0 7737 5215; www.phangantommyresort.com; Hat Rin Nok; r 2100-7000B; ❄☎≋) Tommy is a trendy address in the heart of Hat Rin, striking a balance between chic boutique and carefree flashpacker hang-out. The rectangular swimming pool changes things up, since every other man-made body of water on the island looks like it was manufactured at the kidney-shaped pool factory.

Palita Lodge BUNGALOW $$
(Map p198; ☎0 7737 5172; www.palitalodge.com; Hat Rin Nok; bungalows 1800-5900B; ❄☎≋) Smack in the heart of the action, Palita is a tribute to the never-ending party that is Hat Rin's Sunrise Beach. Spacious concrete bungalows look a bit ramshackle from the outside but the wooden accents and modern design elements make the interiors very comfy. It's on a beachy wedge of sand and the restaurant serves good Thai food.

Sea Breeze Bungalow BUNGALOW $$
(Map p198; ☎0 7737 5162; Ban Hat Rin; bungalows 1500-8000B; ❄☎≋) Sea Breeze gets a good report card from our readers, and we agree; the labyrinth of secluded hillside cottages is a pleasant hammocked retreat for any type of traveller. Several bungalows, poised high on stilts, deliver stunning views of Hat Rin and the sea. There's a big range of options here.

Rin Beach Resort RESORT $$
(Map p198; ☎0 7737 5112; www.rinbeachresort.com; Hat Rin Nai; bungalows 1100-8000B; ❄☎≋) Giant amphorae, spewing forth gushes of water, welcome weary travellers as they tumble off the wooden ferry. Even if you don't stay here, please take a minute to appreciate the kistch catastrophe of the candy-coloured, two-storey Spanish galleon replica bungalows along the beachfront.

Sarikantang RESORT $$$
(Map p198; ☎0 7737 5055; www.sarikantang.com; Hat Seekantang; bungalows 2500-6200B; ❄☎≋) Cream-coloured cabins, framed with teak posts and lintels, are sprinkled among swaying palms and crumbling winged statuettes on one of Hat Rin's best stretches of beach. Inside, the rooms are an Ikea chic that's not ageing well but still offers a comfy stay.

The Coast RESORT $$$
(Map p198; ☎07795 1567; www.thecoastphangan.com; Hat Rin Nai; 3500-10,000B; ❄☎≋) Yes, Hat Rin is going upscale. This dark grey, sharp-angled resort is on a slim but OK stretch of beach away from the party hub. Swanky room interiors are polished cement and beds are topped with white duvets. An infinity pool overlooks the sea and service is grand. Materials are a bit flimsy, however, and it was already showing signs of wear mere months after opening.

Ban Khai to Ban Tai

The waters at Ban Tai tend to be shallow and opaque, especially during low season, but lodging options are well-priced compared to other parts of the island, and you're not too far from Hat Rin. Like Ban Tai, Ban Khai's beaches aren't the most stunning, but the accommodation is cheap and there are beautiful views of Ang Thong Marine National Park in the distance.

These beaches are where many of the moon-but-not-full-moon parties happen so even if your resort seems quiet, there's probably some boozed-up action nearby.

Boom's Cafe Bungalows BUNGALOW $
(☎0 7723 8318; www.boomscafe.com; Ban Khai; bungalows 600-1200B; ❄) Staying at Boom's is like visiting the Thai family you never knew you had. The friendly owners lovingly tend their sandy acreage and dote on the contented clientele. No one seems to mind that there's no swimming pool, since the curling tide rolls right up to your doorstep. Boom's is at the far eastern corner of Ban Khai, near Hat Rin.

★**Divine Comedie** RESORT $$
(☎08 0885 8789; info@divine-resort.com; Ban Tai; ste 3000-4000B; ❄☎≋) A mix of 1920s sino and perhaps Mexican hacienda architecture with a colour palette that shifts from mint to ochre – it not only works, it's beguiling. Junior suites have rooftop terraces, the

elongated pool runs to the slim beach and there's an on-site restaurant serving Myanmar specialities. It's expertly run by a hip French and Corsican couple.

There's no website; contact them directly or reserve via a booking site.

Bay Lounge & Resort RESORT **$$**
(0 7737 7892; www.baylounge.com; Ban Khai; bungalows 1600-3800B;) On a private white nugget of beach sandwiched by jungle-topped boulders, this is an intimate, chic choice. Bungalows mingle with the natural surroundings yet inside look quite urban with distressed concrete and bright modern art. It's midway between Hat Rin's Full Moon Party and the Half Moon Party in Ban Khai – the resort offers transport to each.

Mac Bay BUNGALOW **$$**
(0 7723 8443; bungalows 1200-8500B;) Home to the Black Moon Party (another lunar excuse for Ko Pha-Ngan to go wild), Mac Bay is a sandy slice of Ban Khai where even the cheaper bungalows are spic and span. At beer o'clock, grab a shaded spot on the sand and watch the sun dance amorphous shadows over the distant islands of Ang Thong Marine National Park.

Milky Bay Resort RESORT **$$$**
(0 7723 8566; http://milkybaythailand.com; Ban Tai; bungalows 1800-13,200B;) Several differnt types of minimalist chic bungalows with dark-tinted glass hide in the shade of tall stands of bamboo. Wood chip paths link everything and lead to a skinny beach and somehow the ensemble is very stylish. It's a busy, well-run place.

Thong Sala

Thong Sala's beach is really just an extension of Ban Tai but the beaches are a bit wider up this way and have the advantage of being walking distance to Ko Pha-Ngan's main town, its restaurants and services.

★ **Coco Garden** BUNGALOW **$**
(08 6073 1147, 0 7737 7721; www.cocogardens.com; Thong Sala; bungalows 450-1250B;) The best budget hang-out along the southern coast, Coco Garden one-ups the nearby resorts with well-manicured grounds and sparkling bungalows. As such, it's really popular with the backpacker set and is a fun scene.

Blue Parrot BUNGALOW **$**
(0 7723 8777; www.theblueparrotphangan.com; Thong Sala; r fan/air-con 450/750B;) Two cute lines of good-sized, clean bungalows – some tiled with burnt yellow exteriors and others of grey polished cement – lead to the beach. There's a little on-site cafe that travellers say serves great Western and Thai food.

Lime n Soda RESORT **$$**
(www.limesodathailand.com; bungalows 700-4400B;) Clean and simple tiled bungalows hide in the shade of bamboo and coconut palms along a breakwater above the beach. They call themselves an 'eco resort', but it's unclear why.

Ao Nai Wok to Ao Sri Thanu

Close to Thong Sala, the resorts peppered along this breezy west-coast strip mingle with small beaches between patches of gnarled mangroves. Despite the lack of sand, the prices are cheap and the sunsets are memorable.

Chills Resort RESORT **$$**
(08 9875 2100; Ao Sri Thanu; r 1000-2500B;) Set along a stunning and secluded stretch of stony outcrops, Chills' cluster of delightfully simple-but-modern rooms all have peaceful ocean views, with windows letting in plenty of sunlight and sea breezes. It went under new management in 2013 that will hopefully improve the suffering service standards.

Shambhala Bungalow Village BUNGALOW **$$**
(08 9875 2100; www.shambhala-phangan.com; Ao Nai Wok; bungalows 850-2300B;) The owners of Shambhala have lovingly restored a batch of huts and added loads of personal touches that make this a memorable place to stay. Expect fresh linen, carved wood, artistic lighting and neatly designed bathrooms, but also isolation and a very small beach.

Loyfa Natural Resort BUNGALOW **$$**
(0 7737 7319; loyfabungalow@yahoo.com; Ao Sri Thanu; r 750B, bungalows 1300-3100B, f villas from 3825B;) Loyfa scores high marks for its friendly, French-speaking Thai staff, charming gardens and sturdy huts guarding sweeping ocean views. Modern bungalows tumble down the promontory onto an uberprivate sliver of ash-coloured sand. Cheapest rooms are in a hotel block.

Kupu Kupu Phangan Beach Villa RESORT **$$$**
(0 7737 7384; www.kupuphangan.com; Ao Nai Wok; villas from 6000B;) Opened in December 2012, this Balinese-style resort is possibly the island's most swoon-worthy, with lily ponds, tall palms, a swimming pool right off the pages of a luxury magazine and rocky boulders that meet the sea. The gorgeous wooden villas all have dipping pools and spacious, elegant interiors. They're not very private, however, and management is still finding its feet.

Hat Chaophao

Like Hat Yao up the coast, this rounded beach on the west coast is lined with a variety of bungalow operations.

Sunset Cove BUNGALOW **$$**
(0 7734 9211; www.thaisunsetcove.com; bungalows 1200-3850B;) There's a feeling of Zen symmetry among the forested assortment of boutique, but ageing bungalows; the towering bamboo shoots are evenly spaced along the cobbled paths weaving through brush and boulders. The beachside abodes are particularly elegant, sporting slatted rectangular windows and barrel-basined bathtubs.

Pha-Ngan Paragon BUNGALOW **$$$**
(08 4728 6064; www.phanganparagon.com; bungalows 2500-15,000B;) A tiny hideaway with seven rooms, the Paragon has decor that incorporates stylistic elements from ancient Khmer, India and Thailand, without forfeiting any modern amenities. The 'royal bedroom' deserves a special mention – apparently the canopied bed was imported from Kashmir.

Hat Yao & Hat Son

One of the busier beaches along the west coast, Hat Yao sports a swimmable beach, numerous resorts and a few extra services such as ATMs and convenience stores. Hat Son is a quiet, much smaller beach that feels like a big secret.

Tantawan Bungalows BUNGALOW **$**
(0 7734 9108; www.tantawanbungalow.com; Hat Son; bungalows 600-1200B;) This charming teak nest, tucked among jungle fronds, is dripping with clinking chandeliers made from peach coral and khaki-coloured seashells. It had changed management and big changes were planned when we passed.

High Life BUNGALOW **$**
(0 7734 9114; www.highlifebungalow.com; Hat Yao; fan bungalows 500B, air-con bungalows 800-2200B;) We can't decide what's more conspicuous: the dramatic ocean views from the infinity-edged swimming pool, or the blatant double entendre in the resort's name. True to its moniker, the 25 bungalows, of various shapes and sizes, sit on a palmed outcropping of granite soaring high above the cerulean sea.

Shiralea BUNGALOW **$**
(08 0719 9256; www.shiralea.com; Hat Yao; bungalows 600-1000B;) The fresh-faced poolside bungalows here are simple but the ambience, with an onsite bar with draught beer, is convivial. It's about 100m away from the beach and it fills up every few weeks with Contiki student tour groups.

Haad Son Resort & Restaurant RESORT **$$**
(0 7734 9104; www.haadson.info; Hat Son; bungalows 1000-8000B;) There's a mixed bag of rooms here from big, older wooden bungalows with terraces on the hillside to brand-new polished cement suites and rooms along the beachfront. The secluded beach setting is spectacular and is highlighted by one of the most beachy-chic restaurants on the island on a jungle- and boulder-clad peninsula overlooking the sea.

Haad Yao Bay View Resort RESORT **$$$**
(0 7734 9193; www.haadyao-bayviewresort.com; Hat Yao; r & bungalows 1500-7000B;) This conglomeration of bungalows and hotel-style accommodation looks like a tropical mirage on Hat Yao's northern headland. There's a huge array of options but our pick are the tiny but good-value rooms (from 1500B in low season) that hover right over the sea. For more luxe head up to the hillside sea-view bungalows. It's a busy, businesslike place.

Haad Yao See Through Boutique Resort HOTEL **$$**
(0 7734 9315; www.haadyao.net; Hat Yao; r 1200-3800B;) A towering polished cement double-storey complex with elongated Chinese-style wooden doors. Though the uninviting pool is hard to access and the building itself looks bizarrely placed, room interiors are comfortable and the resort has a central beachfront location.

Hat Salad

This slim, pretty beach on the northwest coast is fronted by shallow blue water – a clutch of photogenic long-tail boats tend to park at the southern end. It's slightly rustic, with local Thai fishermen coming out to throw their nets out at sunset, yet with plenty of amenities and comfortable accommodation.

Cookies Salad RESORT **$$**
(☎08 3181 7125, 0 7734 9125; www.cookiesphangan.com; bungalows 1600-5000B;) The resort with a tasty name has delicious, private Balinese-styled bungalows on a steep hill, orbiting a two-tiered lap pool tiled in various shades of blue. Shaggy thatching and dense tropical foliage give the realm a certain rustic quality, although you won't want for creature comforts. It's super friendly and books up fast.

Salad Hut BUNGALOW **$$**
(☎0 7734 9246; www.saladhut.com; bungalows 2200-5000B;) Wholly unpretentious yet sharing a beach with some distinctly upscale options, this small clutch of Thai-style bungalows sits but a stone's throw from the rolling tide. Watch the sun gently set below the waves from your lacquered teak porch.

Salad Beach Resort BUNGALOW **$$**
(☎0 7734 9149; www.phangan-saladbeachresort.com; bungalows 2000-4900B;) A full-service retreat along the sands of Salad. Room decor employs an unusual palette of colours, but the grounds are tasteful and understated – especially around the pool.

Green Papaya BUNGALOW **$$$**
(☎0 7737 4182; www.greenpapayaresort.com; bungalows 4300-8500B;) The polished wooden bungalows at Green Papaya are a clear standout along the lovely beach at Hat Salad; however, they come at quite a hefty price and you'll need a posh attitude to fit in.

Ao Mae Hat

The relatively undeveloped northwest tip of the island has excellent ocean vistas, plenty of white sand and little Ko Ma is connected to Pha-Ngan by a stunning sandbar.

Island View Cabana BUNGALOW **$**
(☎0 7737 4173; islandviewcabana@gmail.com; Ao Mae Hat; bungalows 400-1500B;) It's a bit overpriced but the bungalows here are really big, relatively new and on a truly wonderful slice of beach right at the isthmus to Ko Ma. The copious staff seem to have been trained to be exuberant although not necessarily helpful.

Mae Hat Beach View Resort BUNGALOW **$**
(☎08 9823 9756; bungalows 400-600B) Hidden behind the dune of the beach's southern end, this lost-in-time cluster of bungalows was empty when we passed save a few friendly Myanmar staff. The bamboo, fan-cooled bungalows with solid tiled floors are the perfect place to disappear into tropical mode with a good book for a few days.

Ban Chalok Lam (Chaloklum) & Hat Khom

In the north of the island, the cramped fishing village at Ban Chalok Lam is like no other place on Ko Pha-Ngan. The conglomeration of teak shanties and huts has just started to be infiltrated with the occasional (and so far welcome) European-style coffeehouse or authentic Italian restaurant. For the most part though, locals still far outnumber tourists and that's refreshing. There's not much of a beach, however.

Sŏrng·tăa·ou ply the route from here to Thong Sala for around 150B per person. There's a dirt road leading from Chalok Lam to Hat Khom, and water taxis are available to a number of beaches.

Fantasea BUNGALOW **$**
(☎08 9443 0785; www.fantasea.asia; Chalok Lam; bungalows fan/air-con 400/700B;) One of the better of a string of family-run bungalow operations along the quiet, eastern part of Chalok Lam. There's a thin beach out front with OK swimming, an elevated Thai-style restaurant area to chill out in, and you may even get a dog who sleeps on your terrace and barks at passersby.

Mandalai HOTEL **$$$**
(☎0 7737 4316; www.mymandalai.com; Chalok Lam; r 1800-5600B;) Like an ash-white Riyadh from a distant Arabian land, this small boutique hotel quietly towers over the surrounding shantytown of fishermen's huts. Floor-to-ceiling windows command views of tangerine-coloured fishing boats in the bay, and there's an intimate wading pool hidden in the inner cloister. It's all very out of place in this rickety town.

Hat Khuat (Bottle Beach)

This isolated dune in the north of the island has garnered a reputation as a low-key getaway, and has thus become quite popular. During high season, places can fill up fast so it's best to try to arrive early. Grab a long-tail taxi boat from Chalok Lam for 100B to 150B (depending on the boat's occupancy).

Smile Bungalows BUNGALOW $
(08 1956 3133; smilebeach@hotmail.com; Bottle Beach/Hat Khuat; bungalows 400-700B) At the far western corner of the beach, Smile features an assortment of wooden huts that climb up a forested hill. The two-storey bungalows (700B) are our favourite. Listen for the Bottle Beach song by Bottle Beach lover and musician John Nicholas, playing on the stereo in the loungable beach cafe.

Bottle Beach II BUNGALOW $
(0 7744 5156; Bottle Beach/Hat Khuat; bungalows 300-500B;) At the far eastern corner of the beach, this double string of very basic, turquoise bungalows is the ideal place to chill out – for as long as you can – if you don't need many creature comforts.

Thong Nai Pan

The pair of rounded bays at Thong Nai Pan, in the northeast of the island, are some of the most remote yet busy beaches on the island; Ao Thong Nai Pan Yai (*yai* means 'big') is the southern half that has some excellent budget and midrange options, and Ao Thong Nai Pan Noi (*noi* means 'little') is Pha-Ngan's most upscale beach that curves just above. Both bays are equally beautiful and great for swimming and hiking.

The road from Thong Sala to Thong Nai Pan was in the process of being widened so it could be paved when we passed. The completion will most likely increase development on these beaches.

Longtail Beach Resort BUNGALOW $
(0 7744 5018; www.longtailbeachresort.com; Thong Nai Pan; bungalows fan/air-con from 490/890B;) Tucked at the lovely southern end of the beach and effortlessly adorable, Longtail offers backpackers charming thatch-and-bamboo abodes that wind up a lush garden path. The lounge area is strewn with cushions and very busy.

Dolphin BUNGALOW $
(Thong Nai Pan; bungalows 500-1800B;) This hidden retreat gives you a chance to rough it in style. Quiet afternoons are spent lounging on the comfy cushions in one of the small pagodas hidden throughout the jungle and bungalows are quite private. Lodging is only available on a first-come, first-served basis.

Anantara Rasananda RESORT $$$
(0 7723 9555; www.rasananda.com; villas from 7500B;) Blink and you'll think you've been transported to Ko Samui. This five-star luxury resort is a sweeping sand-side property with a smattering of semi-detached villas – many with private plunge pools. A savvy mix of modern and traditional *săh·lah* styling prevails, and great Anantara management means that this high-end stalwart is here to stay.

Than Sadet

From Thong Sala a 4WD taxi leaves for Than Sadet on the east coast daily at 1pm for 200B per person. If you miss the taxi, resorts can arrange a private 4WD pick-up for 800B for the whole car. Otherwise catch the *Thong Nai Pan Express* boat from Ko Samui.

Mai Pen Rai BUNGALOW $
(0 7744 5090; www.thansadet.com; Than Sadet; bungalows 500-1200B;) This quiet, beachy bay elicits nothing but sedate smiles. Trek up to Nam Tok Than Sadet falls, hike an hour to Thong Nai Pan or explore by sea with a rented kayak. Bungalows mingle with Plaa's next door on the hilly headland, and sport panels of straw weaving with gabled roofs. Family bungalows are available for 900B and there's a friendly on-site restaurant.

Hat Thian & Hat Yuan

Both Hat Thian and Hat Yuan, near the southeastern tip of the island, have a few bungalow operations, and are quite secluded. You can walk between the two in under 10 minutes via the rocky outcrop that seperates them. Hat Yuan is the more developed beach and has the whiter, wider stretches of sand, while Hat Thain is relatively empty and is back-to-nature pretty.

To get here hire a long-tail from Hat Rin (300B to 400B for the whole boat) or organise a boat pick-up from your resort. A dirt road to Hat Yuan has been cleared for 4WDs, but is only passable in the dry season; even then the voyage by sea is much easier.

Bamboo Hut BUNGALOW $

(☎08 7888 8592; Hat Yuan; bungalows 350-1000B;) Beautifully lodged up on the bouldery outcrops that overlook Hat Yuan and back into the jungle, groovy, hippie village, Bamboo Hut is a favourite for yoga retreats and meditative relaxation. Dark wood bungalows are small and have terraces and the patrons all float around the property high on fasting.

Barcelona BUNGALOW $

(☎0 7737 5113; Hat Yuan; bungalows 400-700B) Old, rickety wood bungalows climb up the hill on stilts behind a palm garden and have good vistas. Price depends on the view, but there's not that much variation so grab a cheap one.

★ **Sanctuary** BUNGALOW $$

(☎08 1271 3614; www.thesanctuarythailand.com; Hat Thian; dm 220B, bungalows 770-6000B) A friendly forested enclave of relaxed smiles, the Sanctuary is a haven of splendid lodgings, yoga classes and detox sessions. Accommodation, in various manifestations of twigs, is scattered along a tangle of hillside jungle paths while Hat Thian is wonderfully quiet and is great for swimming. You'll want to Nama-stay forever.

Pariya Resort & Villas RESORT $$$

(☎08 7623 6678; www.pariyahaadyuan.com; Hat Yuan; villas 8000-17,000B;) The swankiest option on these beaches is found right in front of the softest sands of Hat Yuan in magestic burnt-yellow painted concrete. Octagonal, pagoda-topped bungalows are spacious yet sparsely furnished. If you can find a promotion this may be worth it but, otherwise, the resort is overpriced.

Eating

Ko Pha-Ngan is no culinary capital, especially since most visitors quickly absorb the lazy lifestyle and wind up eating at their accommodation. Those with an adventurous appetite should check out the island's centre of local commerce, Thong Sala, although there are a few surprises elsewhere as well.

Hat Rin

This bustling 'burb has the largest conglomeration of restaurants and bars on the island, yet most of them are pretty lousy. The infamous Chicken Corner is a popular intersection stocked with several faves such as **Mr K Thai Food** (Map p198; Ban Hat Rin; dishes 30-80B) and **Mama Schnitzel** (Map p198; Ban Hat Rin; dishes 40-100B), which promise to cure any case of the munchies, be it noon or midnight.

For the cheapest eats head to 'Thai Street', running roughly between Nic's and Kawee, a row of basic eateries serving noodles and curries for around 40B.

Little Home THAI $

(Map p198; Ban Hat Rin; mains from 40B; ⏰breakfast, lunch & dinner) Little Home woos the masses with cheap, flavourful Thai grub that's gobbled up with alacrity among wooden tables and flimsy plastic chairs.

★ **Kawee** THAI, FRENCH $$

(Map p198; dishes 100-350B) Calling itself an 'art-mosphere', this French-run place raises the bar for Hat Rin both with its jungle-y, dimly lit, bookstore-attached decor and its fantastic French- and Thai-inspired dishes. The *ho mok* (a savoury steamed pudding of coconut milk, curries and meat) and Kawee skewers (crispy white fish on lemon grass blades) are not to be missed.

Nic's INTERNATIONAL $$

(Map p198; Ban Hat Rin; mains 80-280B; ⏰dinner) A dizzying realm of polished concrete and coloured pillows, Nic's – at the back of Hat Rin's lake – slings tasty pizzas and tapas every evening. Slurp a Singha during the 6pm-to-8pm happy hour. New management hopes to make it shine even more.

Lazy House INTERNATIONAL $$

(Map p198; Hat Rin Nai; dishes 90-270B; ⏰lunch & dinner) Back in the day, this joint was the owner's apartment – everyone liked his cooking so much that he decided to turn the place into a restaurant and hang-out spot. Today, Lazy House is easily one of Hat Rin's best places to veg out in front of a movie with a scrumptious shepherd's pie.

Lucky Crab SEAFOOD $$

(Map p198; Hat Rin Nai; dishes 100-450B; ⏰lunch & dinner) Rows of freshly caught creatures are presented nightly atop miniature long-tail boats loaded with ice. Once you've picked your prey, grab a table inside amid dangling plants and charming stone furnishings.

Om Ganesh INDIAN $$

(Map p198; Hat Rin Nai; dishes 70-200B; ⏰breakfast, lunch & dinner) Customers meditate over curries, *biryani* rice, roti and lassis (though the local expats joke that every dish tastes the same). Platters start at 350B.

Monna Lisa ITALIAN $$
(Map p198; Hat Rin Nai; pizza & pasta from 200B; ⏲breakfast, lunch & dinner) Travellers rave about the pizza here, but we found it mediocre, so you be the judge (but definitely skip the lasagne). It's run by a team of friendly Italians and has a basic, open-air atmosphere.

Southern Beaches

On Saturday evenings from 4pm to 10pm, a side street in the eastern part of Thong Sala becomes **Walking Street** – a bustling pedestrian zone mostly filled with locals hawking their wares to other islanders. There's plenty on offer, from clothing to food. Be sure to try the delicious red pork with gravy (40B) at Lang Tang – you'll find it in glass cases next to a large English sign saying 'Numpanich'.

Night Market MARKET $
(Thong Sala; dishes 25-180B; ⏲dinner) A heady mix of steam and snacking locals, Thong Sala's night market is a must for those looking for a dose of culture while nibbling on a low-priced snack. The best place to grab some cheap grub is the stall in the far right corner with a large white banner. Hit up the vendor next door for tasty seafood platters, such as red snapper served over a bed of thick noodles. Banana pancakes and fruit smoothies abound for dessert.

Ando Loco MEXICAN $
(Ban Tai; mains from 59B; ⏲dinner) This outdoor Mexican hang-out looks like an animation cell from a vintage Hanna-Barbera cartoon, with assorted kitschy accoutrements such as papier-mâché cacti. Jibing with the look, one of its catchphrases is 'cheese on tap'. Down a super-sized margarita and show your skills on the beach volleyball court.

★**Fisherman's Restaurant** SEAFOOD $$
(☎08 4454 7240; Thong Sala; dishes 50-600B; ⏲1-10pm) Wooden tables on a sand floor look out over the sunset and a rocky pier. Lit up at night, it's one of the island's nicest settings and the food, from the addictive yellow curry crab to the massive seafood platter to share (with all assortment of critters; 800B to 900B), is as wonderful as the ambience.

★**Fabio's** ITALIAN $$
(☎08 3389 5732; Ban Khai; dishes 150-400B; ⏲1-10pm Mon-Sat) An intimate, authentic and truly delicious Italian place with golden walls, cream linens and bamboo furniture. There are only seven tables so reserve in advance. House-made delicacies like seafood risotto, pizzas and iced limoncello are as artfully presented as they are fresh and amazing. One of the island's best restaurants.

Mason's Arms BRITISH $$
(Thong Sala; mains 160-350B; ⏲lunch & dinner) Suddenly, a clunky structure emerges from the swaying palms; it's a Tudor-style manse, plucked directly from Stratford-upon-Avon and plunked down in the steamy jungle. This lodge-like lair is one blood pudding away from being an official British colony. The fish 'n' chips is a local favourite.

Other Beaches

★**Sanctuary** HEALTH FOOD $$
(Hat Thian; mains from 130B) Forget what you know about health food: the Sanctuary's restaurant proves that wholesome eats can also be delicious. Enjoy a tasty parade of plates – from Indian pakoras to crunchy Vietnamese spring rolls – as an endless playlist of music (undoubtedly the island's best) wafts overhead. Don't forget to wash it all down with a shot of neon-green wheatgrass. Yum!

★**Cucina Italiana** ITALIAN $$
(Jenny's; Chalok Lam; pizzas 180-200B; ⏲dinner) If it weren't for the sand between your toes and the long-tail boats whizzing by, you might think you had been transported to the Italian countryside. The friendly Italian chef is passionate about his food, and creates everything from his pasta to his tiramisu daily, from scratch. The rustic, thin-crust pizzas are out-of-this-world good.

Peppercorn STEAKHOUSE $$
(www.peppercornphangan.com; Hat Salad; mains 160-400B; ⏲4-10pm Mon-Sat; 🖉) Escargot and succulent steaks in a rickety jungle cottage? You bet. Peppercorn may be tucked in the brush away from the sea, but that shouldn't detract foodies from seeking out one of Pha-Ngan's best attempts at highbrow international cuisine. There's also a fine selection of very good vegetarian dishes. No artificial ingredients.

Bamboo Hut WESTERN, THAI $$
(Hat Yuan; dishes 100-300B; ⏲breakfast, lunch & dinner; 📶🖉) Lounge on a Thai-style cushion or sit at a teak table that catches sea breezes and looks over infinite blue. There are plenty of options from vegetarian specialities

and fresh juices for those coming off a fast or cleanse, to classic, very well-prepared Thai dishes with all assortment of beef, chicken and prawns.

Dolphin Bar & Cafe WESTERN, THAI $$
(Hat Thong Nai Pan Noi; dishes 80-350B; ⊙ breakfast, lunch & dinner) Fresh baked bread, mostly locally sourced produce and a healthy flair make up delicious international food enjoyed in a waterfront, old teak wood structure. There's also great coffee and cocktails.

Two Brothers SEAFOOD $$
(Chalok Lam; barbecue sets from 250B; ⊙ breakfast, lunch & dinner) One of the best of a string of Chalok Lam's seafood restaurants where fisher families serve you their bounty straight off the boats. Bamboo furniture sits on the sand and you can watch the boat action in the busy bay.

Drinking & Nightlife

Every month, on the night of the full moon, pilgrims pay tribute to the party gods with trancelike dancing, wild screaming and glow-in-the-dark body paint. The throngs of bucket-sippers and fire twirlers gather on the infamous Sunrise Beach (Hat Rin Nok) and party until the sun replaces the moon in the sky.

A few other noteworthy spots can be found around the island for those seeking something a bit mellower.

Hat Rin

Hat Rin is the beating heart of the legendary full moon fun. When the moon isn't lighting up the night sky, partygoers flock to other spots on the island's south side. Most party venues flank Hat Rin's Sunrise Beach from south to north.

Rock BAR, NIGHTCLUB
(Map p198) Great views of the party from the elevated terrace on the far south side of the beach. Also, the best cocktails in town.

Drop-In Bar BAR, NIGHTCLUB
(Map p198) This dance shack blasts the chart toppers that we all secretly love. This is one of the liveliest places and even non-full-moon nights can get boisterous.

Cactus Bar BAR, NIGHTCLUB
(Map p198) Smack in the centre of Hat Rin Nok, Cactus pumps out a healthy mix of old-school tunes, hip-hop and R&B. It's also very popular and always happening.

Sunrise BAR, NIGHTCLUB
(Map p198) A spot on the sand where trance beats shake the graffiti-ed walls.

Tommy BAR, NIGHTCLUB
(Map p198) One of Hat Rin's largest venues lures the masses with black lights and trance music blaring on the sound system. Drinks are dispensed from a large arklike bar.

Mellow Mountain BAR, NIGHTCLUB
(Map p198) Also called 'Mushy Mountain' (you'll know why when you get there), this trippy hang-out sits at the northern edge of Hat Rin Nok, delivering stellar views of the shenanigans below. One of those places you need to at least see if you're on Hat Rin.

Other Beaches

Eagle Pub BAR
(Hat Yao) At the southern end of Hat Yao, this drink-dealing shack, built right into the rock face, is tattooed with the neon graffiti of virtually every person who's passed out on the lime green patio furniture after too many caipirinhas.

Jam BAR
(www.thejamphangan.com; Hin Wong) It's DIY live music at this friendly nightspot on the west coast. Saturday nights are open mic, and the rest of the week you'll usually catch a few locals jamming on their guitars.

Pirates Bar BAR
(Hat Chaophao) This wacky drinkery is a replica of a pirate ship built into the cliffs. When you're sitting on the deck and the tide is high (and you've had a couple of drinks), you can almost believe you're out at sea. These guys host the well-attended Moon Set parties, three days before Hat Rin gets pumpin' for the full moon fun.

Flip Flop Pharmacy BAR
(Thong Nai Pan) This open-air bar on the sands of Thong Nai Pan is the area's preferred hang-out spot.

Amsterdam BAR
(Ao Plaay Laem) Near Hat Chaophao on the west coast, Amsterdam attracts tourists and locals from all over the island, who are looking for a chill spot to watch the sunset.

Information

DANGERS & ANNOYANCES

Some of your fondest vacation memories may be forged on Ko Pha-Ngan; just be mindful of the following situations that can seriously tarnish your experience.

Drugs You're relaxing on the beach when suddenly a local walks up and offers you some local herb at a ridiculously low price. 'No thanks,' you say, knowing that the penalties for drug use in Thailand are fierce. But the vendor drops his price even more and practically offers you the weed for free. Too good to be true? Obviously. As soon as you take a toke, the seller rats you out to the cops and you're whisked away to the local prison where you must pay a wallet-busting fine. This type of scenario happens all the time on Ko Pha-Ngan so it's best to avoid the call of the ganja.

Here's another important thing to remember: your travel insurance does not cover any drug-related injury or treatment. Drug-related freak-outs *do* happen – we've heard firsthand accounts of partiers slipping into extended periods of delirium. Suan Saranrom (Garden of Joys) Psychiatric Hospital in Surat Thani has to take on extra staff during full-moon and other party periods to handle the number of *fa·ràng* who freak out on magic mushrooms, acid or other abundantly available hallucinogens.

Women travellers Female travellers should be extra careful when partying on the island. We've received many reports about drug- and alcohol-related rape (and these situations are not limited to Full Moon Parties). Another disturbing problem is the unscrupulous behaviour of some of the local motorcycle taxi drivers. Several complaints have been filed about drivers groping female passengers; there are even reports of severe sexual assaults.

Motorcycles Ko Pha-Ngan has more motorcycle accidents than injuries incurred from full moon tomfoolery. Nowadays there's a system of paved roads, but much of it is a labyrinth of rutty dirt-and-mud paths. The island is also very hilly, and even if the road is paved, it can be too difficult for most to take on. The *very* steep road to Hat Rin is a perfect case in point. The island now has a special ambulance that trawls the island helping injured bikers.

EMERGENCY

Main Police Station (☎191, 0 7737 7114) Located about 2km north of Thong Sala. The police station in Hat Rin (near Hat Rin school) will not let you file a report; to do so you must go to Thong Sala. Local police have been known to charge 200B to file a report. Do not pay this – it should be free. Note that if you are arrested you do have the right to an embassy phone call; you do not have to agree to accept the 'interpreter' you are offered.

INTERNET ACCESS

Hat Rin and Thong Sala are the main centres of internet activity, but every beach with development now offers access. Rates are generally 2B per minute, with a 10B to 20B minimum and discounts if you stay on for more than an hour. Places offering a rate of 1B per minute usually have turtle-speed connections.

LAUNDRY

If you got fluorescent body paint on your clothes during your full-moon romp, don't bother sending them to the cleaners – the paint will never come out. Trust us, we've tried. For your other washing needs, there are heaps of places that will gladly wash your clothes. Prices hover around 40B per kilo, and express cleanings shouldn't be more than 60B per kilo.

MEDICAL SERVICES

Medical services can be a little crooked in Ko Pha-Ngan – expect unstable prices and underqualified doctors. Many clinics charge a 3000B entrance fee before treatment. Serious medical issues should be dealt with on nearby Ko Samui.

Ko Pha-Ngan Hospital (Map p193; ☎0 7737 7034; Thong Sala; ⏲24hr) About 2.5km north of Thong Sala; offers 24-hour emergency services.

MONEY

Thong Sala, Ko Pha-Ngan's financial 'capital', has plenty of banks, currency converters and several Western Union offices. Hat Rin has numerous ATMs and a couple of banks at the pier. There are also ATMs in Hat Yao, Chalok Lum and Thong Nai Pan.

POST

Main Post Office (⏲8.30am-4.30pm Mon-Fri, 9am-noon Sat) In Thong Sala; there's a smaller office right near the pier in Hat Rin.

TOURIST INFORMATION

There are no government-run Tourist Authority of Thailand (TAT) offices on Ko Pha-Ngan; instead tourists get their information from local travel agencies and brochures. Most agencies are clumped around Hat Rin and Thong Sala. Agents take a small commission on each sale, but collusion keeps prices relatively stable and standardised. Choose an agent you trust if you are spending a lot of money – faulty bookings do happen on Ko Pha-Ngan, especially since the island does not have a unit of tourist police.

Several mini-magazines also offer comprehensive information about the island's accommodation, restaurants, activities and Full Moon Parties. Our favourite option is the pocket-sized **Phangan Info** (www.phangan.info).

Backpackers Information Centre (Map p198; ☎0 7737 5535; www.backpackersthailand.com; Hat Rin) A must for travellers looking to book high-quality tours (diving, live-aboards, jungle safaris etc) and transport. Not just for backpackers, it's an expat-run travel agency that offers peace of mind with every purchase – travellers are provided with the mobile phone number of the owners should any problems arise. It also runs the Crystal Dive shop next door.

Backpackers Thailand (www.backpackersthailand.com) Everything you need to know about Ko Pha-Ngan, from booking accommodation to finding out the Full Moon Party schedule. Doubles as a vast resource for the whole country as well.

Getting There & Away

As always, the cost and departure times are subject to change. Rough waves are known to cancel ferries between October and December.

AIR

Ko Pha-Ngan's new airport is scheduled to open in September 2014 with two daily flights to/from Bangkok on **Kan Air** (www.kanairlines.com). The flight will take 80 minutes. It's expected that services will increase over the next few years to include more Bangkok flights and other destinations as well.

BOAT

To/From Bangkok, Hua Hin & Chumphon

The **Lomprayah** (☎077 4277 656; www.lomprayah.com) and **Seatran Discovery** (☎0 2240 2582; www.seatrandiscovery.com) services have bus-boat combination packages (from around 1500B) that depart from the Th Khao San area in Bangkok and pass through Hua Hin and Chumphon. The whole voyage takes about 17 hours.

It is also quite hassle-free (unless your train breaks down, which happens a lot) to take the train from Bangkok or Hua Hin to Chumphon and switch to a ferry service. In this case expect to pay 300B for a train from Bangkok to Chumphon (about 8½ hours); the boat from Chumphon to Ko Pha-Ngan takes around 2½ hours and costs 800B to 1000B depending on the boat.

To/From Ko Samui

There are around a dozen daily departures between Thong Sala on Ko Pha-Ngan and Ko Samui. These boats leave throughout the day from 7am to 6pm, take from 20 minutes to an hour and cost 200B to 300B depending on the boat.

The **Haad Rin Queen** (☎0 7748 4668) goes back and forth between Hat Rin and Big Buddha Beach on Ko Samui four times a day. The voyage takes 50 minutes and costs 200B.

The *Thong Nai Pan Express* is a wobbly old fishing boat (not for the faint-hearted) that runs once a day from Mae Hat on Ko Samui to Hat Rin on Ko Pha-Ngan and then up the east coast, stopping at all the beaches as far as Thong Nai Pan Noi. Prices range from 200B to 400B depending on the destination. The boat won't run in bad weather.

To/From Ko Tao

Ko Tao-bound **Lomprayah** ferries (500B) depart from Thong Sala on Ko Pha-Ngan at 8.30am and 1pm and arrive at 9.45am and 2.15pm. The **Seatran** service (430B) departs from Thong Sala at 8.30am and 2pm daily. Taxis depart Hat Rin for Thong Sala one hour before the boat departure. The cheaper-but-slower **Songserm** (350B) leaves Ko Pha-Ngan at 12.30pm and alights at 2.30pm.

To/From Surat Thani & the Andaman Coast

There are about eight daily departures between Ko Pha-Ngan and Surat Thani on the **Songserm** (☎0 7737 7704; www.songserm-expressboat.com; 350B, 4½ hours) or **Lomprayah** (550B, 2¾ hours) services, both travelling via Ko Samui. These boats leave from Thong Sala throughout the day from 7am to 8pm. Every night, depending on the weather, a boat runs from Surat (350B, seven hours), departing at 11pm. Boats in the opposite direction leave Ko Pha-Ngan at 10pm.

Combination boat-bus tickets are available at any travel agency. Simply tell them your desired destination and they will sell you the necessary links in the transport chain. Most travellers will pass through Surat Thani as they swap coasts.

Getting Around

You can rent motorcycles all over the island for 150B to 250B per day. Always wear a helmet – it's the law on Ko Pha-Ngan, and local policemen are starting to enforce it. If you plan on riding over dirt tracks it is imperative that you rent a bike comparable to a Honda MTX125 – gearless scooters cannot make the journey. Bicycle rentals are discouraged unless you're fit enough to take on Lance Armstrong.

Pick-up trucks and *sŏrng·tăa·ou* chug along the island's major roads and the riding rates double after sunset. Ask your accommodation about free or discount transfers when you leave the island. The trip from Thong Sala to Hat Rin is 100B; further beaches will set you back around 150B to 200B.

Long-tail boats depart from Thong Sala, Chalok Lam and Hat Rin, heading to a variety of far-flung destinations such as Hat Khuat (Bottle Beach) and Ao Thong Nai Pan. Expect to pay anywhere from 50B for a short trip, and up to 300B for a lengthier journey. You can charter a private boat ride from beach to beach for about 150B per 15 minutes of travel.

Ko Tao เกาะเต่า

POP 1500

Once the baby of the Samui, Pha-Ngan, Tao trio, Ko Tao may still be the smallest in size but in many other ways it's grown up. The island is consistently gaining popularity and going more upscale, but for now this jungle-topped cutie has the busy vibe of Samui mixed with the laid-back nature of Pha-Ngan. But Tao also has its wildcard, something the others don't: easy-to-get-to, diverse diving right off its shores. Cavort with sharks and rays in a playground of tangled neon coral, toast the day with sunset cocktails on a white beach then get up and do it all over again the next day. But even while the island may be synonymous with diving, there is much more to the place. Hikers and hermits can re-enact an episode from *Lost* in the dripping coastal jungles. And when you're Robinson Crusoe-ed out, hit the pumpin' bar scene that rages on until dawn.

Activities

Diving

If you've never been diving before, Ko Tao is *the* place to lose your scuba virginity. The shallow bays scalloping the island are perfect for newbie divers to take their first stab

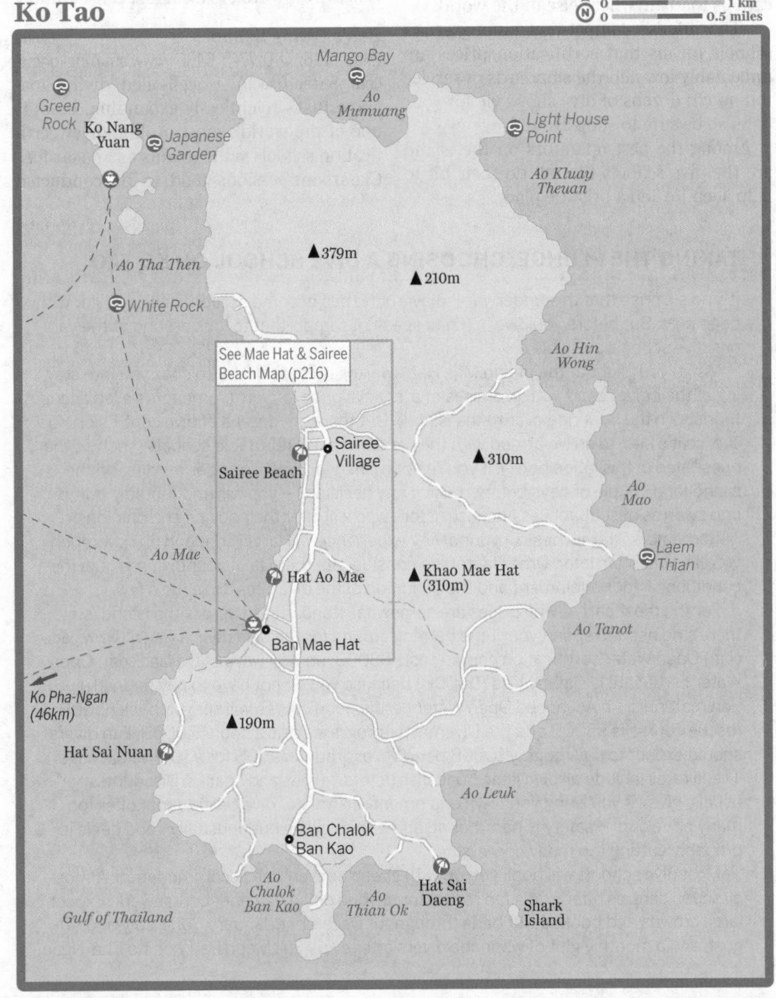

at scuba; the waters are crystal clear, there are loads of neon reefs and the temperatures feel like bathwater. The best dive sites are found at offshore pinnacles within a 20km radius of the island, but seasoned scubaholics almost always prefer the top-notch sites along the Andaman coast. The local marine wildlife includes groupers, moray eels, batfish, bannerfish, barracudas, titan triggerfish, angelfish, clownfish (Nemos), stingrays, reef sharks and frequent visits by mighty whale sharks.

Onshore, over 40 dive centres are ready to saddle you up with gear and teach you the ropes in a 3½-day Open Water certification course. The island issues more scuba certifications than anywhere else in the world.

The intense competition among scuba schools means that certification prices are unbeatably low and the standards of service top-notch; dozens of dive shops vie for your baht, so be sure to shop around.

Among the best operators on the island are the dive schools that all do their bit to help keep Ko Tao a pristine place:

ACE Marine Expeditions DIVING
(Map p216; www.divephotothai.com) The luxe choice. Go out on this James Bond-worthy speedboat and get to sites in a fraction of the time. The ingenious 'Whaleshark Watch' program keeps up-to-the-moment tabs on where sightings are taking place – they'll whisk you out to where the creatures are so you're chances of seeing them are greatly increased.

Roctopus DIVING
(Map p216; ☎0 7745 6611; www.roctopusdive.com; Sairee Beach) One of the newer places on the scene, Roctopus already has a near legendary reputation for its great staff and high standards. Groups are small and the centre is heavily involved in local reef conservation.

Ban's Diving School DIVING
(Map p216; ☎0 7745 6466; www.amazingkohtao.com; Sairee Beach) A well-oiled diving machine that's relentlessly expanding, Ban's is one of the world's most prolific diver certification schools yet it retains a five-star feel. Classroom sessions tend to be conducted

TAKING THE PLUNGE: CHOOSING A DIVE SCHOOL ON KO TAO

It's no surprise that this underwater playground has become exceptionally popular with beginners. But before you dive in (so to speak) it's important to look around at the various dive schools available.

When you alight at the pier in Mae Hat, swarms of touts will try to coax you into staying at their dive resort with promises of a 'special price for you' (some touts even accost tourists on the boat ride over to the island). But there are dozens of dive centres on Ko Tao, so it's best to arrive armed with the names of a few reputable schools (such as the ones listed in this guide book). If you're not rushed for time, consider relaxing on the island for a couple of days before making any decisions – you will undoubtedly bump into swarms of scubaphiles and instructors who will offer their advice and opinions.

Remember: the success of your diving experience will largely depend on how much you like your instructor. Other factors to consider are the size of your diving group, the condition of your equipment and the condition of the dive sites, to name a few.

For the most part, diving prices are somewhat standardised across the island, so there's no need to spend your time hunting around for the best deal. A **PADI** (www.padi.com) Open Water certification course costs 9800B; an **SSI** (www.ssithailand.com) Open Water certificate is slightly less (9000B) because you do not have to pay for instruction materials. An Advanced Open Water certification course will set you back 8500B, a rescue course is 9500B and the Divemaster program costs a cool 25,000B. Fun divers should expect to pay roughly 1000B per dive, or around 7000B for a 10-dive package. These rates include all dive gear, boat, instructors/guides and snacks. Discounts are usually given if you bring your own equipment. Be wary of dive centres that offer too many price cuts – safety is paramount, and a shop giving out unusually good deals is probably cutting too many corners.

Most dive schools will hook you up with cheap or even free accommodation. Almost all scuba centres offer gratis fan rooms for anyone doing beginner coursework. Expect large crowds and booked-out beds throughout December, January, June, July and August, and a monthly glut of wannabe divers after every Full Moon Party on Ko Pha-Ngan.

in large groups, but there's a reasonable amount of individual attention in the water. A breadth of international instructors means that students can learn to dive in their native tongue.

Big Blue Diving DIVING
(Map p216; ☎0 7745 6772, 0 7745 6415; www.bigbluediving.com; Sairee Beach) If Goldilocks were picking a dive school, she'd probably pick Big Blue – this midsize operation (not too big, not too small) gets props for fostering a sociable vibe while maintaining a high standard of service. Divers of every ilk can score dirt-cheap accommodation at their resort.

Buddha View DIVING
(☎0 7745 6074; www.buddhaview-diving.com; Chalok Ban Kao) Another big dive operation on Ko Tao, Buddha View offers the standard fare of certification and special programs for technical diving (venturing beyond the usual parameters of recreational underwater exploration). Discounted accommodation is available at its friendly resort.

Crystal Dive DIVING
(Map p216; ☎0 7745 6107; www.crystaldive.com; Mae Hat) Crystal is the Meryl Streep of diving operators, winning all the awards for best performance year after year. It's one of the largest schools on the island (and around the world), although high-quality instructors and intimate classes keep the school feeling quite personal. Multilingual staff members, air-conditioned classes and two on-site swimming pools sweeten the deal. Highly recommended.

New Heaven DIVING
(☎0 7745 6587; www.newheavendiveschool.com; Chalok Ban Kao) The owners of this small diving operation dedicate a lot of their time to preserving the natural beauty of Ko Tao's underwater sites by conducting regular reef checks and contributing to reef restoration efforts. A special CPAD research diver certification program is available in addition to the regular order of programs and fun dives.

Scuba Junction DIVING
(Scuba J; Map p216; ☎0 7745 6164; www.scubajunction.com; Sairee Beach) A groovy new storefront and a team of outgoing instructors lure travellers looking for a more intimate dive experience. Scuba Junction guarantees a maximum of four people per diving group.

ZERO TO HERO

It's the oldest story in the book: 'I came to Ko Tao on vacation and six months later I'm still here!' Seems like the island's magical magnetic energy catches hold of everyone, so don't be surprised if you too find yourself altering flight plans.

For those of you who anticipate embracing the castaway lifestyle, consider going from 'Zero to Hero' as they call it on Ko Tao. Over the last few years, several of the savvier diving operators started package deals where you can go from scuba newbie to pro over the course of a couple of months. You'll graduate through four levels of diving certifications, 'intern' as a divemaster at your dive school, then take a stab at the instructor program. Prices hover around 80,000B and include all the bells and whistles necessary to turn you into a fish. Accommodation is not included.

Snorkelling

Snorkelling is a popular alternative to diving, and orchestrating your own snorkelling adventure here is simple, since the bays on the east coast have small bungalow operations offering equipment rental for between 100B and 200B per day.

Most snorkel enthusiasts opt for the do-it-yourself approach on Ko Tao, which involves swimming out into the offshore bays or hiring a long-tail boat to putter around further out. Guided tours are also available and can be booked at any local travel agency. Tours range from 500B to 800B (usually including gear, lunch and a guide/boat captain) and stop at various snorkelling hotspots around the island. **Laem Thian** is popular for its small sharks, **Shark Island** has loads of fish (and ironically no sharks), **Ao Hin Wong** is known for its crystalline waters, and **Light House Point**, in the north, offers a dazzling array of colourful sea anemones. Dive schools will usually allow snorkellers on their vessels for a comparable price – but it's only worth snorkelling at the shallower sites such as Japanese Gardens. Note that dive boats visit the shallower sites in the afternoons.

Freediving

Over the last couple of years freediving (exploring the sea using breath-holding techniques rather than scuba gear) has grown rapidly in popularity. Several small schools have opened up across the island. We recommend the capable staff at **Apnea Total** (Map p216; ☎08 7183 2321; www.apnea-total.com; Sairee Beach) who have earned several awards in the freediving world and possess a special knack for easing newbies into this heart-pounding sport. The student-teacher ratio of three to one also ensures plenty of attention to safety. Also worth a special mention is **Blue Immersion** (Map p216; ☎08 7682 1886; www.blue-immersion.com; Sairee Beach) run by friendly Akim, a martial arts expert and a freediving pro – he was one of the first people in the world to freedive below 100m. Freediving prices are standardised across the island as well – a 2½-day SSI beginner course will set you back 5500B.

Technical Diving & Cave Diving

Well-seasoned divers and hardcore Jacques Cousteaus should contact **Tech Thailand** (www.techthailand.com) or one of a handful of other tech diving schools if they want to take their underwater exploration to the next level and try a technical dive. According to PADI, tec diving, as it's often known, is 'diving other than conventional commercial or recreational diving that takes divers beyond recreational diving limits'. Technical diving exceeds depths of 40m and requires stage decompressions, and a variety of gas mixtures are often used in a single dive.

Several years ago, Tech Thailand's old boat, MS *Trident,* made a name for itself in the diving community after successfully locating dozens of previously undiscovered wrecks in the Gulf of Thailand. Its most famous discovery was the USS *Lagarto,* an American naval vessel that sank during WWII. The gulf has long been an important trading route and new wrecks are being dis-

DIVE SITES AT A GLANCE

In general, divers don't have a choice as to which sites they explore. Each dive school chooses a smattering of sites for the day depending on weather and ocean conditions. Deeper dive sites such as Chumphon Pinnacle are usually visited in the morning. Afternoon boats tour the shallower sites such as Japanese Gardens. Recently, two large vessels have been sunk off the coast, providing scubaphiles with two new wreck dives. Divers hoping to spend some quality time searching for whale sharks at Sail Rock should join one of the dive trips departing daily from Ko Pha-Ngan.

➡ **Chumphon Pinnacle** (36m maximum depth), 13km west of Ko Tao, has a colourful assortment of sea anemones along the four interconnected pinnacles. The site plays host to schools of giant trevally, tuna and large grey reef sharks. Whale sharks are known to pop up once in a while.

➡ **Green Rock** (25m maximum depth) is an underwater jungle gym featuring caverns, caves and small swim-throughs. Rays, grouper and triggerfish are known to hang around. It's a great place for a night dive.

➡ **Japanese Gardens** (12m maximum depth), between Ko Tao and Ko Nang Yuan, is a low-stress dive site perfect for beginners. There's plenty of colourful coral, and turtles, stingray and pufferfish often pass by.

➡ **Mango Bay** (16m maximum depth) might be your first dive site if you are putting on a tank for the first time. Lazy reef fish swim around as newbies practise their skills on the sandy bottom.

➡ **Sail Rock** (34m maximum depth), best accessed from Ko Pha-Ngan, features a massive rock chimney with a vertical swim-through, and large pelagics like barracuda and kingfish. This is one of the top spots in Southeast Asia to see whale sharks.

➡ **Southwest Pinnacle** (33m maximum depth) offers divers a small collection of pinnacles that are home to giant groupers and barracudas. Whale sharks and leopard sharks are sometimes spotted (pun partially intended).

➡ **White Rock** (29m maximum depth) is home to colourful corals, angelfish, clown fish and territorial triggerfish. Another popular spot for night divers.

covered all the time, from old Chinese pottery wrecks to Japanese *marus* (merchant ships). In 2011 the *Trident* was purposefully sunk off the coast of Ko Tao to create an artificial reef. A miscalculation with the explosives has left the wreck a bit too deep for beginners.

Recently, cave diving has taken Ko Tao by storm, and the most intrepid scuba buffs are lining up to make the half-day trek over to Khao Sok National Park. Beneath the park's main lake lurks an astonishing submarine world filled with hidden grottos, limestone crags and skulking catfish. In certain areas divers can swim near submerged villages that were flooded in order to create a reservoir and dam. Most cave-diving trips depart from Ko Tao on the afternoon boat service and return to the island on the afternoon boat service of the following day. Overnight stays are arranged in or near the park.

Underwater Photography & Videography

If your wallet is already full of PADI certification cards, consider renting an underwater camera or enrolling in a marine videography course. Many scuba schools hire professional videographers to film Open Water certifications, and if this piques your interest, you could potentially earn some money after completing a video internship. Your dive operator can put you in touch with any of the half-dozen videography crews on the island. We recommend **ACE Marine Images** (Map p216; ☎0 7745 7054; www.acemarineimages.com; Sairee Beach), one of Thailand's leading underwater videography studios. An introductory course including camera, diving and instruction is 4500B and can also be used towards an Advanced PADI certification. **Deep Down Productions** (☎08 7133 4102; www.deepdown-productions.com) and **Oceans Below** (☎08 6060 1863; www.oceansbelow.net) offer videography courses and internships and each have their own special options.

Other Activities

★Flying Trapeze Adventures ACROBATICS
(FTA; Map p216; ☎08 0696 9269; www.flyingtrapezeadventures.com; Sairee Beach; ⏰4-8pm, lessons 4pm, 5pm & 6pm) Find out if you're a great catch during a one-hour group trapeze lesson (950B). Courses are taught by superfriendly Gemma and her posse of limber sidekicks, who take you from circus neophyte to soaring savant in four jumps or less. Book over the phone or show up at one of the nightly demos, which start at 7.30pm. Participants must be at least six years old.

Goodtime Adventures HIKING, ADVENTURE SPORTS
(Map p216; ☎08 7275 3604; www.gtadventures.com; Sairee Beach; ⏰noon-late) Hike through the island's jungly interior, swing from rock to rock during a climbing and abseiling session (from 2000B), or unleash your inner daredevil during an afternoon of cliff jumping (at your own risk). The Goodtime office, along the Sairee sands, doubles as a friendly cafe serving an assortment of international nibbles (including dip coffee!).

Shambhala YOGA
(Map p216; ☎08 4440 6755; Sairee Beach) Ko Tao's full-time yoga centre is housed in beautiful wooden *săh·lah* on the forested grounds of Blue Wind in Sairee Beach. The two-hour classes, led by Kester, the energetic yogi, cost 300B.

Ko Tao Bowling & Mini Golf BOWLING, MINIGOLF
(☎0 7745 6316; ⏰noon-midnight) Located on the main road between Mae Hat and Chalok Ban Kao, Ko Tao Bowling & Mini Golf has several homemade bowling lanes where the employees reset the pins after every frame (300B per hour). The 18-hole minigolf course has a landmark theme – putt your ball through Stonehenge or across the Golden Gate Bridge.

Sleeping

If you are planning to dive while visiting Ko Tao, your scuba operator will probably offer you free or discounted accommodation to sweeten the deal. Some schools have on-site lodging, while others have deals with nearby bungalows. It's important to note that you only receive your scuba-related discount on the days you dive. So, for example, if you buy a 10-dive package, and decide to take a day off in the middle, your room rate will not be discounted on that evening. Also, a restful sleep is important before diving, so scope out these 'great room deals' before saying yes – some of them are one cockroach away from being condemned.

There are also many sleeping options that have absolutely nothing to do with the island's diving culture. Ko Tao's secluded eastern coves are dotted with stunning retreats that still offer a true getaway experience, but these can be difficult to reach due to the island's dismal network of roads. You can often call ahead of time and arrange to be picked up from the pier in Mae Hat.

Note that many budget rooms are only available on a first come, first served basis and often aren't even advertised on hotel websites. Many midrange resorts offer budget rooms so take a look at all our listings to see each resort's (usually very big) price range. These rooms book fast so it can be prudent to call ahead and find out what may be available before you arrive.

Sairee Beach

Giant Sairee is the longest and most developed strip on the island, with a string of dive operations, bungalows, travel agencies, minimarkets and internet cafes. The northern end is the prettiest and quietest while there's more of a party scene and noise from the bars to the south. For most people, this is the choice beach to stay at since it has a great blend of scenery and action.

Blue Wind BUNGALOW $
(Map p216; 0 7745 6116; bluewind_wa@yahoo.com; bungalows 350-1400B;) Blue Wind offers a breath of fresh air from the high-intensity dive resorts strung along Sairee Beach. Sturdy bamboo huts are peppered along a dirt trail behind the beachside bakery. Large, tiled air-conditioned cabins are also available, boasting hot showers and TVs. It's rustic but relaxing.

LEARNING THE LOCAL LINGO

Due to the steady influx of international visitors, English is spoken just about everywhere; however, the locals on scuba-savvy Ko Tao regularly incorporate diving sign-language symbols into common parlance – especially at the bars.

Here are a few gestures to get you started:

I'm OK Make a fist and tap the top of your head twice.

Cool Bring together the tips of your index finger and thumb forming an 'O'.

I'm finished/I'm ready to go Hold your hand tight like a karate chop and quickly swing it back and forth perpendicular to your neck.

Spicytao Backpackers HOSTEL $
(Map p216; 08 1036 6683; www.spicyhostels.com; dm 200-250B;) Like your own supersocial country hang-out, Spicytao is hidden off the main drag in a rustic garden setting. Backpackers rave about the ambience and staff who are always organising activities. Book in advance!

Ban's Diving Resort RESORT $$
(Map p216; 0 7745 6466; www.amazingkohtao.com; r 600-29,700B;) This dive-centric party palace offers a wide range of quality accommodation from basic backpacker digs to sleek hillside villas, and it's getting bigger all the time. Post-scuba chill sessions happen on Ban's prime slice of beach or at one of the two swimming pools tucked within the strip of jungle between the two-storey, pillared and terraced white hotel blocks.

Sairee Cottage BUNGALOW $$
(Map p216; 0 7745 6126; www.saireecottagediving.com; bungalows 350-2800B;) Bungalows are connected by a sand path through a sun-splotched garden of palms and hibiscus. Even the smallest, most budget options here are of higher standard than most and very good value. The beach out front is slim and under the shade of a giant ironwood tree.

Big Blue Resort BUNGALOW $$
(Map p216; 0 7745 6050; www.bigbluediving.com; dm 400B, r 2000-7000B;) This scuba-centric resort has a summer camp vibe – diving classes dominate the daytime, while evenings are spent en masse, grabbing dinner or watching fire twirling. Both the basic fan bungalows and motel-style air-con rooms offer little when it comes to views, but who has the time to relax when there's an ocean out there to explore?

Palm Leaf & Bow Thong BUNGALOW $$
(Map p216; 0 7745 6266; www.bowthongresort.com; bungalows 700-4900B;) Palm Leaf is the swankier part of these conjoined resorts; Bow Thong has more popular lower-priced digs. Reception is a little awkward, the rooms are good though nothing spectacular, but the location, at the quieter northern section of silky Sairee Beach simply can't be beat. The lowest-priced bungalows are on a first come, first served basis.

In Touch Resort BUNGALOW $$
(Map p216; 0 7745 6514; www.intouchresort.com; bungalows 800-2500B;) Older bungalows

are a mishmash of bamboo and dark wood, while several rounded air-con rooms have a cave theme – it's all very *Flintstones*. This is as far south as you can get on Sairee, at the end of a skinny motorbike path, with a groovy bar and lush beach right out front and not too much of a racket.

Seashell Resort BUNGALOW **$$**
(Map p216; ☎0 7745 6271; www.seashell-kohtao.com; bungalows 1000-4800B;) Another place with a huge mix of lodging from simple wood bungalows to hotel-style rooms in a block. This is a busy resort with nicely tended grounds but we found the prices out of whack with what you can find elsewhere. It's a good backup that welcomes divers and non-divers.

★**Place** RESORT **$$$**
(www.theplacekohtao.com; villas 8000B;) Honeymooners will delight in this unique option – several private luxury villas nestled in the leaf-clad hills with sweeping ocean views down below. A private plunge pool is standard – naturally – and private chef services are available for those who choose to remain in their love nest instead of sliding down to Sairee for restaurant eats. It's about a 15-minute walk or five-minute taxi ride from this hilltop location to Sairee Beach.

Ko Tao Cabana BUNGALOW **$$$**
(Map p216; ☎0 7745 6250; www.kohtaocabana.com; bungalows 5300-14,000B; @) This prime piece of quiet beachside property offers timber-framed villas and crinkled white adobe huts with woven roofs dotted along the boulder-strewn beach and up the hill. Paths wind through the fern-laden, manicured jungle. The private villas are one of the more upscale options on the island although service isn't quite yet on par with what you'd hope for in this price bracket.

Koh Tao Coral Grand Resort BUNGALOW **$$$**
(Map p216; ☎0 7745 6431; www.kohtaocoral.com; bungalows 2600-9300B;) The plethora of pink facades at this family-friendly option feels a bit like Barbie's dream Thai beach house. Cottage interiors are coated in cheery primary colours framed by white truncated beams while pricier digs have a more distinctive Thai flavour, boasting dark lacquered mouldings and gold-foiled art. The setting is lovely, though the service is not all it could be.

Mae Hat

All ferry arrivals pull into the pier at the busy village of Mae Hat and nearly all the resorts on this beach will have a view and be in earshot of the constant ebb and flow of boat arrivals and departures. As such this isn't the best beach for a tranquil getaway although it's a good hub if your main goal is diving. Accommodation is spread throughout, but the more charming options extend in both directions along the sandy beach, both north and south of the pier.

Sai Thong Resort BUNGALOW **$**
(☎0 7745 6868; Hat Sai Nuan; bungalows 500-2000B;) As the rush of Mae Hat dwindles away along the island's southwest shore, Sai Thong emerges along quiet, sandy Hat Sai Nuan. Bungalows, in various, rustic incarnations of weaving and wood, have colourful porch hammocks and palm-filled vistas. Guests frequent the restaurant's relaxing sun deck – a favourite spot for locals too. The resort is accessed by a quick ride from the Mae Hat pier in a boat taxi.

Tao Thong Villa BUNGALOW **$**
(☎0 7745 6078; Ao Sai Nuan; bungalows 400-1800B; @) Very popular with long-termers seeking peace and quiet, these funky, no-frills bungalows have killer views. Tao Thong actually straddles two tiny beaches on a craggy cape about halfway between Mae Hat and Chalok Ban Kao. To reach it, grab a boat taxi for a short ride from the Mae Hat pier.

Crystal Dive Resort BUNGALOW **$$**
(Map p216; ☎0 7745 6107; www.crystaldive.com; bungalows 800-1500B;) The bungalow and motel-style accommodation at Crystal is reserved for its divers, and prices drop significantly for those taking courses. Guests can take a dip in the refreshing pool when it isn't overflowing with bubble-blowing newbie divers.

Ananda Villa HOTEL **$$**
(Map p216; ☎0 7745 6478; www.anandavilla.com; r 500-2000B;) This two-storey cream and white hotel has a colonial feel and is lined with decorative palms and plumeria. The cheapest rooms are fan only and are in another older block a bit further from the beach. Friendly reception.

Mae Hat & Sairee Beach

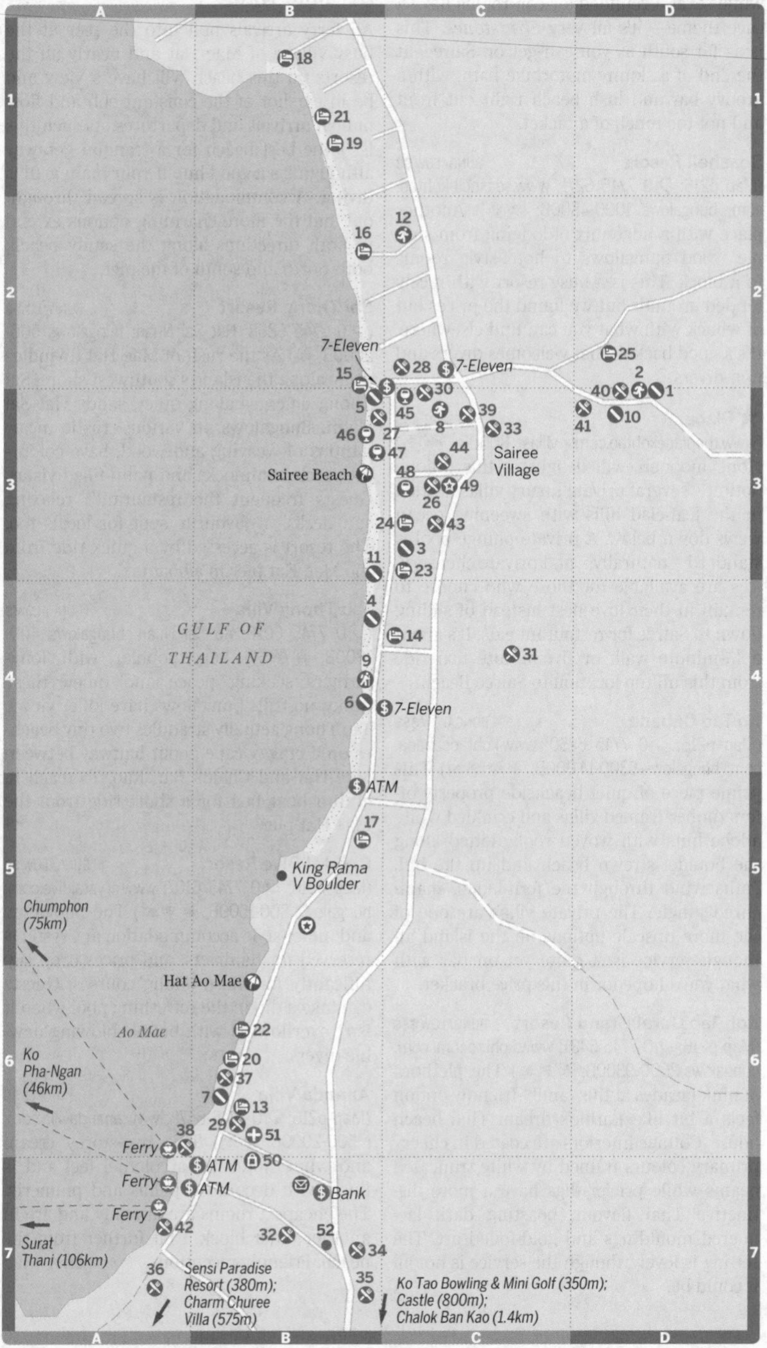

0 — 200 m
0 — 0.1 miles

A B C D
1 2 3 4 5 6 7

18
21
19
12
16
7-Eleven
15
28
7-Eleven
25
2
40
1
5
30
45
8
39
41
10
46
27
33
47
44
Sairee Village
Sairee Beach
48
49
26
24
43
3
11
23
4
14
GULF OF THAILAND
31
9
6
7-Eleven
ATM
17
King Rama V Boulder
Chumphon (75km)
Hat Ao Mae
Ao Mae
22
Ko Pha-Ngan (46km)
20
37
7
13
29
51
38
Ferry
ATM
50
Ferry
ATM
Bank
Ferry
Surat Thani (106km)
42
32
52
34
36
Sensi Paradise Resort (380m); Charm Churee Villa (575m)
35
Ko Tao Bowling & Mini Golf (350m); Castle (800m); Chalok Ban Kao (1.4km)

Mae Hat & Sairee Beach

Activities, Courses & Tours

1	ACE Marine Expeditions	D3
	ACE Marine Images	(see 1)
2	Apnea Total	C3
3	Ban's Diving School	B4
4	Big Blue Diving	B3
5	Blue Immersion	B4
	Crystal Dive	(see 15)
6	Flying Trapeze Adventures	C3
7	Goodtime Adventures	B4
8	Roctopus	D3
9	Scuba Junction	B3
10	Shambhala	C2

Sleeping

11	Ananda Villa	B6
12	Ban's Diving Resort	C4
13	Big Blue Resort	B2
14	Blue Wind	B2
15	Crystal Dive Resort	B6
16	In Touch Resort	B5
17	Ko Tao Cabana	B1
18	Koh Tao Coral Grand Resort	B1
19	Montra Resort & Spa	B6
20	Palm Leaf & Bow Thong	B1
21	Regal Resort	B6
22	Sairee Cottage	C3
23	Seashell Resort	C3
24	Spicytao Backpackers	D2

Eating

25	Barracuda Restaurant & Bar	C3
26	Big Blue East	B3
	Blue Wind Bakery	(see 14)
27	Café Corner	C2
28	Café del Sol	B6
29	Chopper's Bar & Grill	C3
30	Darawan	C4
31	Dolce Vita	B7
32	El Gringo	C3
33	Food Centre	B7
34	Greasy Spoon	B7
35	Pim's Guesthouse	A7
36	Pranee's Kitchen	B6
37	Safety Stop Pub	A6
38	Su Chili	C3
39	Taste of Home	D3
40	The Gallery	D3
41	Whitening	A7
42	ZanziBar	C3
43	Zest Coffee Lounge	C3

Drinking & Nightlife

44	Diza	C3
45	Fizz	B3
46	Lotus Bar	B3
47	Office Bar	C3

Entertainment

48	Queen's Cabaret	C3

Shopping

49	Avalon	B7

Regal Resort RESORT **$$**
(Map p216; ☎0 7745 6007; www.kohtaoregal.com; r 1900-3500B; ❄@📶🏊) This resort is just north of the pier so you get all the commotion along with your pretty stretch of white sand – the main pool is filled with divers most of the day. Rooms are large and some have beautiful sea views but it's all *Fawlty Towers*-esque with amenities breaking down etc. Decent value for the price though.

Montra Resort & Spa RESORT **$$$**
(Map p216; ☎0 7745 7057; www.kohtaomontra.com; r 4200-12,800B; ❄@📶🏊) The big, imposing Montra encircles an equally huge pool with a swim-up bar. This is a good location for Mae Hat, on the beach and steps away from all the action, although note that this is very close to the port.

Charm Churee Villa RESORT **$$$**
(☎0 7745 6393; www.charmchureevilla.com; bungalows 4300-18,700B; ❄📶🏊) Tucked under sky-scraping palms away from the bustle of the pier, the luxuriant villas of Charm Churee are dedicated to the flamboyant spoils of the Far East. Staircases, chiselled into the rock face, dribble down a palmed slope revealing teak huts strewn across smoky boulders. The villas' unobstructed views of the swishing waters are beguiling.

Sensi Paradise Resort RESORT **$$$**
(☎0 7745 6244; www.sensiparadise.com; bungalows 2100-7000B; ❄📶🏊) 'Natural chic' on the prettiest stretch of Mae Hat proper, right up against some boulder outcrops. You won't escape the noise of the pier, however. Rooms on the hillside are worn and not worth the price while newer models closer to the beach are quite lovely. Friendly caretakers and several airy teak *săh·lah* add an extra element of charm.

Chalok Ban Kao

Ao Chalok Ban Ko, about 1.7km south of Mae Hat by road, has the third-largest concentration of accommodation on Ko Tao. This is a slim stretch of sand in a scenic half-circle bay framed by boulders at either end. The milky blue water here is quite shallow and at low tide a sandbar is exposed that's fun to wade out to for prime sun bathing. This is the quietest of the main beaches but there's still a good selection of restaurants, diving and a more mellow but fun nightlife scene.

Tropicana GUESTHOUSE **$**
(0 7745 6167; www.koh-tao-tropicana-resort.com; r 500-1500B) Low-rise, basic hotel units peppered across a sandy, shady garden campus that provide fleeting glimpses of the ocean between fanned fronds and spiky palms.

JP Resort GUESTHOUSE **$**
(0 7745 6099; r from 600-1300B;) A colourful (some may say old-fashioned) menagerie of prim motel-style rooms stacked on a small scrap of jungle across the street from the sea.

★Viewpoint Resort RESORT **$$**
(0 7745 6666; www.kohtaoviewpoint.com; bungalows 1200-14,000B;) Lush grounds of ferns and palms meander across a boulder-studded hillside offering stunning views over the sea and the bay. All options, from the exquisite private suites that feel like Tarzan and Jane's love nest gone luxury to the huge, view-filled bungalows, use boulders, wood and concrete to create comfortable, naturalistic abodes. It's under new management and fantastic value.

Freedom Beach BUNGALOW **$$**
(0 7745 6596; bungalows 700-3500B;) On its own secluded beach shaded by tall, pretty bushes and connected to Ao Chalok Ban Kao by a boardwalk, Freedom feels like a classic backpacker haunt. Steep, concrete paths link the seaside bar to the accommodation (from wooden shacks to sturdier huts with air-con) that runs from the beach to high on the cliff. Reception is at Taahtoh Resort.

New Heaven Resort BUNGALOW **$$**
(0 7745 6422; www.newheavenkohtao.com; r & bungalows 700-3800B;) Just beyond the clutter of Chalok Ban Kao, New Heaven delivers colourful huts perched on a hill over impossibly clear waters. A steep path of chiselled stone tumbles down the shrubby rock face revealing views ripped straight from the pages of *National Geographic*.

Buddha View Dive Resort BUNGALOW **$$**
(0 7745 6074; www.buddhaview-diving.com; r 800-1500B;) Like the other large diving operations on the island, Buddha View offers its divers discounted on-site digs in a super-social atmosphere.

Ko Tao Resort RESORT **$$$**
(0 7745 6133; www.kotaoresort.com; r & bungalows 1850-9500B;) The entrance is a throwback to the days when taste and architecture weren't particularly synonymous, but inside the facilities fit the true definition of a resort. Rooms are split between 'pool side' and 'paradise zone' – all are well stocked, water sports equipment is on offer, and there are several bars primed to serve an assortment of fruity cocktails.

Chintakiri Resort RESORT **$$$**
(0 7745 6133; www.chintakiri.com; r & bungalows 2900-7000B;) Perched high over the gulf waters overlooking Chalok Ban Kao, Chintakiri is one of Ko Tao's more luxurious properties, helping the island furtively creep upmarket. Rooms are spread around the inland jungle, and sport crisp white walls with lacquered finishing.

Hin Wong

A sandy beach has been swapped for a boulder-strewn coast on the serene east side of the island, but the water is crystal clear. The road to Hin Wong is paved in parts, but sudden sand pits and steep hills can toss you off your motorbike.

Hin Wong Bungalows BUNGALOW **$**
(0 7745 6006; Hin Wong; bungalows 350-700B;) Pleasant wooden huts are scattered across vast expanses of untamed tropical terrain – it all feels a bit like *Gilligan's Island*. A rickety dock, jutting out just beyond the breezy restaurant, is the perfect place to dangle your legs and watch schools of black sardines slide through the cerulean water.

View Rock BUNGALOW **$**
(0 7745 6549, 0 7745 6548; viewrock@hotmail.com; Hin Wong; bungalows 500-2000B;) When coming down the dirt road into Hin Wong, follow the signs as they lead you north of Hin Wong Bungalows. View Rock is precisely that: views and rocks; the hodgepodge of wooden huts, which looks like a secluded fishing village, is built into the steep crags offering stunning views of the bay.

Ao Tanot (Tanote Bay)

Tanote Bay is more populated than some of the other eastern coves, but it's still rather quiet and picturesque. It is the only bay on the east coast that is accessible by a decent road. Discounted taxis (around 100B) bounce back and forth between Tanote Bay and Mae Hat; ask at your resort for a timetable.

Poseidon BUNGALOW $
(0 7745 6735; poseidonkohtao@hotmail.com; Ao Tanot; bungalows 400-1200B;) Poseidon keeps the tradition of the budget bamboo bungalow alive with a dozen basic-but-sleepable huts scattered near the sand.

Family Tanote BUNGALOW $$
(0 7745 6757; Ao Tanot; bungalows 800-3500B;) As the name suggests, this scatter of hillside bungalows is run by a local family who take pride in providing comfy digs to solitude seekers. Strap on a snorkel mask and swim around with the fish at your doorstep, or climb up to the restaurant for a tasty meal and pleasant views of the bay.

Ao Leuk & Ao Thian Ok

Jamahkiri Resort & Spa RESORT $$$
(0 7745 6400; www.jamahkiri.com; bungalows 6900-30,000B;) Wooden gargoyle masks and stone fertility goddesses abound amid swirling mosaics and multi-armed statues at this whitewashed estate. Feral hoots of distant monkeys confirm the jungle theme, as do the thatched roofs and tiki-torched soirees. The resort's seemingly infinite number of stone stairways can be a pain, so it's a good thing Ko Tao's most luxurious spa is on the premises.

Ko Nang Yuan

Photogenic Ko Nang Yuan, just off the northwest coast of Ko Tao, is easily accessible by the Lomprayah catamaran, and by water taxis that depart from Mae Hat and Sairee (100B each way). There's a 100B tax for all visitors to the island.

Ko Nangyuan Dive Resort BUNGALOW $$$
(0 7745 6088; www.nangyuan.com; bungalows 1500-9000B;) The rugged collection of wood and aluminium bungalows winds its way across three coolie-hatlike conical islands connected by an idyllic beige sandbar. Yes, this is a private island paradise but note it gets busy with day-trippers. The resort also boasts the best restaurant on the island, but then again, it's the only place to eat…

Eating

With super-sized Ko Samui lurking on the horizon, it's hard to believe that quaint little Ko Tao holds its own in the gastronomy category. Most resorts and dive operators offer on-site dining, and stand-alone establishments are multiplying at lightning speed in Sairee Beach and Mae Hat. The diverse population of divers has spawned a broad range of international cuisine dining options, including Mexican, French, Italian, Indian and Japanese. On our quest to find the tastiest Thai fare on the island, we discovered, not surprisingly, that our favourite local meals were being dished out at small, unnamed restaurants on the side of the road.

Sairee Beach

Su Chili THAI $
(Map p216; dishes 70-150B; lunch & dinner;) Fresh and tasty Thai food served by friendly waitstaff who always ask how spicy you want your food and somehow get it right. Try the delicious northern Thai specialities or Penang curries.

ZanziBar CAFE $
(Map p216; sandwiches 90-150B; breakfast, lunch & dinner) The island's outpost of sandwich yuppie-dom slathers an array of yummy ingredients between two slices of wholegrain bread.

Blue Wind Bakery INTERNATIONAL $
(Map p216; mains 50-180B; breakfast, lunch & dinner) This beachside shanty dishes out Thai favourites, Western confections and freshly blended fruit juices. Enjoy your thick fruit smoothie and flaky pastry while reclining on tattered triangular pillows and watching the waves roll in and out.

★**Barracuda Restaurant & Bar** ASIAN FUSION $$
(Map p216; 08 0146 3267; mains 180-400B; dinner) Chef Ed Jones caters for the Thai princess when she's in town but you can sample his exquisite cuisine for mere pennies in comparison to her budget. Locally sourced ingredients are used to make creative, fresh, fusion masterpieces. Try the seafood platter, basil stuffed fish or sashimi bruchetta – then wash it down with a lemon grass, ginger mojito.

The Gallery THAI FUSION $$

(Map p216; ☎0 7745 6547; mains 100-350B) One of the nicer settings in town, next to owner Chris Clark's gallery of beautiful island photography, the food here is equally special. The signature dish is *mok maprao* (chicken, shrimp and fish curry served in a young coconut) but the green curry red snapper is also phenomenal.

Taste of Home INTERNATIONAL $$

(Map p216; mains 180-250B; ⏲ lunch & dinner;) German-run and serving a bit of everything (Swedish meatballs, Turkish kofta, Greek salads and Weiner schnitzel to name a few), but everything is delicious and prepared with heart. It's a small, simple setting popular with expats. Don't forget to finish your meal with the owner's homemade Bailey's!

Darawan INTERNATIONAL $$

(Map p216; mains 120-450B; ⏲ lunch & dinner) Like a top-end dining venue plucked from the posh shores of Ko Samui, regal Darawan is the island's best place to take a date. Perched atop the trees at the back of Ban's sprawling resort, the outdoor balcony offers beautiful views of the setting sun (come around 6pm). Designer lighting, efficient waiters and two-for-one sunset gin and tonics seal the deal.

Chopper's Bar & Grill INTERNATIONAL $$

(Map p216; dishes 60-200B; ⏲ breakfast, lunch & dinner) So popular that it has become a local landmark, Chopper's is a two-storey hangout where divers and travellers can widen their beer belly. There's live music, sports on the TVs, billiards and a cinema room. On Friday nights the drinks are 'two for one', and dishes are half-priced as well. Cheers for scored goals are interspersed with chatter about the day's dive.

Café Corner CAFE $$

(Map p216; snacks & mains 30-180B; ⏲ breakfast & lunch) Prime real estate, mod furnishings and tasty iced coffees have made Café Corner a Sairee staple over the last few years. Swing by at 5pm to stock up for tomorrow morning's breakfast; the scrumptious baked breads are buy-one-get-one-free before being tossed at sunset.

Big Blue East THAI, INTERNATIONAL $$

(Map p216; dishes 70-250B; ⏲ breakfast, lunch & dinner) Big Blue Resort's busy chow house, located about 2m from the crashing tide, dispatches an assortment of Thai and international eats, including tasty individual pizzas. The joint fills up around sunset with divers chuckling at the daily dive bloopers shown on the big-screen TV.

El Gringo MEXICAN $$

(Map p216; dishes 80-200B; ⏲ breakfast, lunch & dinner) As if there aren't already enough nicknames in Thailand for *fa·ràng*. The self-proclaimed 'funky Mexican joint' slings burritos of questionable authenticity in both Sairee Beach and Mae Hat. Delivery is available.

Mae Hat

Bizzaro Tapas TAPAS $

(dishes 60-140B; ⏲ 4pm-1am, closed Tue) It's a bit out of the way, on the road between Mae Hat and Chalok Ban, but the setting in bamboo huts with cross-legged seating is great and the fun food – from ceviche and stuffed eggplant to barbecued pork ribs – is worth the drive.

Pim's Guesthouse THAI $

(Map p216; curry 70B; ⏲ lunch) Everyday Pim makes a curry (the massaman is everyone's favourite) at this humble spot, and everyday she sells out before the lunch hour is over. People from all over the island flock here. It's that good.

★Whitening INTERNATIONAL $$

(Map p216; dishes 150-400B; ⏲ dinner;) This starched, white, beachy spot falls somewhere between being a restaurant and a chic seaside bar – foodies will appreciate the tasty twists on indigenous and international dishes. Dine amid dangling white Christmas lights while keeping your bare feet tucked into the sand. And the best part? It's comparatively easy on the wallet.

Café del Sol INTERNATIONAL $$

(Map p216; dishes 70-320B; ⏲ breakfast, lunch & dinner;) Just steps away from the pier is our favourite breakfast spot on the island – go for the 'Del Sol breakfast' (delicious fruit salad, yoghurt and coffee) with a scrumptious spinach omelette on the side. Lunch and dinner dishes range from hearty pepper hamburgers to homemade pasta, though prices tend to be quite inflated.

Zest Coffee Lounge CAFE $

(Map p216; dishes 70-190B; ⏲ breakfast & lunch;) Indulge in the street-cafe lifestyle at Zest – home to the best cup of joe on the island. Idlers can nibble on ciabatta sandwiches or sticky confections while nursing their creamy caffe latte. There's a second branch in Sairee, although we prefer this location.

Dolce Vita ITALIAN $$
(Map p216; pizzas 170-270B; ⏲ noon-10pm) For the best Italian on Ko Tao, come and taste Dolce Vita's homemade pastas and fine pizzas.

Safety Stop Pub INTERNATIONAL $
(Map p216; mains 60-250B; ⏲ breakfast, lunch & dinner; 📶) A haven for homesick Brits, this pier-side restaurant and bar feels like a tropical beer garden. Stop by on Sundays to stuff your face with an endless supply of barbecued goodness; and the Thai dishes also aren't half bad.

Pranee's Kitchen THAI $
(Map p216; dishes 50-150B; ⏲ breakfast, lunch & dinner; 📶) An old Mae Hat fave, Pranee's serves scrumptious curries and other Thai treats in an open-air pavilion sprinkled with lounging pillows, wooden tables and TVs. English movies (with hilariously incorrect subtitles) are shown nightly at 6pm.

Food Centre THAI $
(Map p216; mains from 30B; ⏲ breakfast, lunch & dinner) An unceremonious gathering of hot-tin food stalls, Food Centre – as it's come to be known – lures lunching locals with veritable smoke signals rising up from the concrete parking lot abutting Mae Hat's petrol station. You'll find some of the island's best papaya salad here.

Greasy Spoon BREAKFAST $
(Map p216; English breakfast 140B; ⏲ breakfast & lunch) Although completely devoid of character, Greasy Spoon stays true to its name by offering a variety of heart-clogging breakfast treats: eggs, sausage, stewed vegies and chips (their speciality) that'll bring a tear to any Brit's eye.

Chalok Ban Kao

I ♥ Salad CAFE $$
(salads 160-200B; ⏲ breakfast & lunch; 📶) A healthy array of salads and wraps use fresh ingredients and are big and filling. There are also real fruit juices and healthy egg white-only breakfasts.

Viewpoint Restaurant INTERNATIONAL $$$
(☎ 0 7745 6444; 250-1250B; ⏲ breakfast, lunch & dinner) On a beautiful, wooden deck overlooking Ao Chalok Ban Kao, this is one of the most romantic settings on the island. The food is also the most upscale and holds its own against Samui's best – try the slow-roasted pork or the red snapper in green curry. Apart from the beef dishes, the prices are reasonable for the high standards.

Long Pae STEAKHOUSE $$$
(mains 100-430B; ⏲ dinner) Situated off the radar from most of the island's tourist traffic, 'Uncle Pae' sits on a scruffy patch of hilly jungle with distant views of the sea down below. The speciality here is steak, which goes oh-so-well with a generous smattering of pan-Asian appetisers.

Drinking & Nightlife

After diving, Ko Tao's favourite pastime is drinking, and there's definitely no shortage of places to get tanked. In fact, the island's three biggest dive centres each have bumpin' bars – **Fish Bowl**, **Crystal Bar** and **Buddha On The Beach** in Chalok Bak Kao – that attract swarms of travellers and expats alike. It's well worth stopping by even if you aren't a diver.

Flyers detailing upcoming parties are posted on various trees and walls along the island's west coast (check the two 7-Elevens in Sairee). Also keep an eye out for posters touting 'jungle parties' held on nondescript patches of scrubby jungle in the centre of the island. There's also a **Koh Tao Pub Crawl** (www.kohtaopubcrawl.com) that starts at Chopper's Bar & Grill (p220) on Hat Sairee every Monday, Wednesday and Friday at 7pm and bounces around to the most happening spots. The 380B cover includes a bucket, two shots and a T-shirt, so it's not a bad deal.

Several places, such as Chopper's and Safety Stop Pub, double as great hang-out joints for a well-deserved post-dive beer.

Just remember: don't drink and dive.

Clumped at the southern end of Sairee Beach, **AC Party Pub**, **In Touch** and **Maya Bar** take turns reeling in the partiers throughout the week.

Castle NIGHTCLUB
(www.thecastlekohtao.com; Mae Hat) Located along the main road between Mae Hat and Chalok Ban Kao, the Castle has quickly positioned itself as the most-loved party venue on the island, luring an array of local and

international DJs to its triad of parties each month.

Fizz BAR
(Map p216; Sairee Beach) Recline on mattress-sized pillows and enjoy designer cocktails while listening to Moby or Enya, mixed with hypnotic gushes of the rolling tide.

Lotus Bar BAR
(Map p216; Sairee Beach) Lotus is the de facto late-night hang-out spot along the northern end of Sairee. Muscular fire twirlers toss around flaming batons, and the drinks are so large there should be a lifeguard on duty.

Office Bar BAR
(Map p216; Sairee Beach) With graffiti proudly boasting 'No Gaga, and no Black Eyed F*^£*£ Peas', this hexagonal hut lures regulars with grunge beats and rickety wooden seats.

Diza BAR
(Map p216; Sairee Beach) Once a tatty shack that blasted music as it sold pirated DVDs, Diza has evolved into a casual hang-out at the crossroads of Sairee Village. Locals lounge on plastic chairs as they slurp their beer and people-watch.

☆ Entertainment

★ Queen's Cabaret CABARET
(Map p216; ⏲10.15pm nightly) FREE Wow! Every night is different at this intimate bar where acts range from your standard sparkling Abba and leg kicks extravaganza to steamy topless croons. If you're male, note you may get 'dragged' into the performance if you're sitting near the front. Drinks are pricey but worth it for the show.

Raw Art Moovment LIVE MUSIC
(⏲10am-late) FREE A place for art, music, socialising, drinking and, most importantly, the Sunday Art Jam when the island's talented musicians perform and the vibe is like a big, fun party at someone's house (in fact the venue is part of owner's Denny and Lisa's house). The first chords are strummed at 7.30pm, but come by any time.

Shopping

Although most items are cheap when compared to prices back home, diving equipment is a big exception to the rule. On Ko Tao you'll be paying Western prices plus shipping plus commission on each item (even with 'discounts') so it's better to do your scuba shopping at home or on your computer.

Avalon HAIR CARE
(Map p216; Mae Hat; ⏲10am-7pm Mon-Sat) If you're having trouble scrubbing the sea salt out of your hair, then stop by Avalon for some locally made (and eco-friendly) body and hair-care products.

ℹ Information

The ubiquitous *Koh Tao Info* booklet lists loads of businesses on the island and goes into some detail about the island's history, culture and social issues.

DANGERS & ANNOYANCES

There's nothing more annoying than enrolling in a diving course with your friends and then having to drop out because you scraped your knee in a motorcycle accident. The roads on Ko Tao are slowly being paved but are still horrendous. While hiring a moped is extremely convenient, this is not the place to learn how to drive. The island is rife with abrupt hills and sudden sand pits along gravel trails. Even if you escape unscathed from a riding experience, scamming bike shops may claim that you damaged your rental and will try to extort some serious cash from you.

Travellers should also be aware that mosquito-borne dengue fever (and a similar but less-severe cousin) is a real and serious threat. The virus can spread quickly due to tightly packed tourist areas and the small size of the island.

EMERGENCY

Police Station (Map p216; ☎0 7745 6631) Between Mae Hat and Sairee Beach along the rutted portion of the beachside road.

INTERNET ACCESS

Rates are generally 2B per minute, with a 20B minimum and discounts if you log on for one hour or longer. You may find, however, that certain useful tourism websites have been firewalled at internet cafes affiliated with travel agencies. The larger dive schools on the island usually have a wireless connection available for laptop-toting travellers.

MEDICAL SERVICES

All divers are required to sign a medical waiver before exploring the sea. If you have any medical condition that might hinder your ability to dive (including mild asthma), you will be asked to get medical clearance from a doctor on Ko Tao. If you're unsure about whether or not you are fit to dive, consider seeing a doctor before your trip as there are no official hospitals on the island, and the number of qualified medical professionals is limited. Also, make sure your traveller's insurance covers scuba diving. On-island medical 'consultations' (and we use that term very lightly) cost 300B. There are several walk-in clinics and mini-hospitals scattered around Mae Hat and Sairee. All serious medical needs should be dealt with on Ko Samui. If you are diving, ask your outfitter to point you in the proper direction of medical advice.

Diver Safety Support (Map p216; ☎08 1083 0533; kohtao@sssnetwork.com; Mae Hat; ⏲on call 24hr) Has a temporary hyperbaric chamber and offers emergency evacuation services.

MONEY

There are 24-hour ATMs at the island's 7-Elevens. There's also a cluster of ATMs orbiting the ferry docks at Mae Hat. There is a money exchange window at Mae Hat's pier and a second location near Chopper's in Sairee Beach. There are several banks near the post office in Mae Hat, at the far end of town along the island's main inland road. They are usually open 9am to 4pm on weekdays. Almost all dive schools accept credit cards, however there is usually a 3% or 4% handling fee.

POST

Post Office (Map p216; ☎0 7745 6170; ⏲9am-5pm Mon-Fri, 9am-noon Sat) A 10- to 15-minute walk from the pier; at the corner of Ko Tao's main inner-island road and Mae Hat's 'down road'.

TOURIST INFORMATION

There's no government-run TAT office on Ko Tao. Transportation and accommodation bookings can be made at most dive shops or at any of the numerous travel agencies, all of which take a small commission on services rendered.

Koh Tao Online (www.kohtaoonline.com) An online version of the handy *Koh Tao Info* booklet.

ℹ Getting There & Away

As always, costs and departure times are subject to change. Rough waves are known to cancel ferries between the months of October and December. When the waters are choppy we recommend taking the **Seatran** (☎0 2240 2582; www.seatrandiscovery.com) rather than the **Lomprayah** (☎077 4277 656; www.lomprayah.com) catamaran if you are prone to seasickness. The catamarans ride the swell, whereas the Seatran cuts through the currents as it crosses the sea. Note that we highly advise purchasing your boat tickets *several* days in advance if you are accessing Ko Tao from Ko Pha-Ngan after the Full Moon Party.

AIR

Nok Air (p234) jets passengers from Bangkok's Don Muang airport to Chumphon once daily in each direction from Monday to Saturday while **Happy Air** (www.happyair.co.th) has one to two flights per day from Bangkok's Suvarnabhumi International Airport and a flight five days a week to Ranong. Flights to/from Bangkok are usually around 3300B. Upon arriving in Chumphon, travellers can make a seamless transfer to the catamaran service bound for Ko Tao.

BOAT

To/From Ko Pha-Ngan

The **Lomprayah** catamaran offers a twice-daily service (500B), leaving Ko Tao at 9.30am and 3pm and arriving on Ko Pha-Ngan around 10.50am and 4.10pm. The **Seatran Discovery Ferry** (430B) offers an identical service. The **Songserm** express boat (350B) departs daily at 10am and arrives on Ko Pan-Ngan at 11.30am. Hotel pick-ups are included in the price.

To/From Ko Samui

The **Lomprayah** catamaran offers a twice-daily service (600B), leaving Ko Tao at 9.30am and 3pm and arriving on Ko Samui via Ko Pha-Ngan, around 11.30am and 4.40pm. The **Seatran Discovery Ferry** (600B) offers an identical service. The **Songserm** express boat (450B) departs daily at 10am and arrives on Samui (again via Ko Pha-Ngan) at 12.45pm. Hotel pick-ups are included in the price.

To/From Surat Thani & the Andaman Coast

The easiest option is to stop over on either Ko Pha-Ngan or Ko Samui to shorten the trip and lessen the number of connections. Otherwise, a combination bus-boat ticket from travel agents around the island shouldn't cost more than going it alone. But if you don't feel like being herded like a sheep onto a tourist bus, there are two routes you can take. The first, and more common, approach is to board a Surat-bound boat (you may have to transfer boats on Ko Pha-Ngan or Ko Samui), then transfer to a bus upon arrival.

The second option is to take a ferry to Chumphon on the mainland and then switch to a bus or train bound for the provinces further south.

BUS

Bus-boat package tickets to/from Bangkok are available from travel agencies all over Bangkok and the south; tickets cost about 1000B and the whole journey takes about 12 hours. Buses switch to boats in Chumphon and Bangkok-bound passengers can choose to disembark in Hua Hin (for the same price as the Ko Tao–Bangkok ticket).

TRAIN

Travellers can plan their own journey by taking a boat to Chumphon, then making their way to Chumphon's town centre to catch a train up to Bangkok (or any town along the upper southern gulf); likewise in the opposite direction. A

2nd-class ticket to Bangkok will cost around 300B and the trip takes around 8½ hours.

From Ko Tao, the high-speed catamaran departs for Chumphon at 10.15am and 2.45pm (600B, 1½ hours), and a Songserm express boat makes the same journey at 2.30pm (500B, three hours). There may be fewer departures if the swells are high.

Getting Around

MOTORCYCLE

Renting a motorcycle is a dangerous endeavour if you're not sticking to the main, well-paved roads. Daily rental rates begin at 150B for a scooter. Larger bikes start at 350B. Discounts are available for weekly and monthly rentals. Try **Lederhosenbikes** (Map p216; ☎ 08 1752 8994; www.lederhosenbikes.com; Mae Hat; ⏰ 8.30am-6pm Mon-Sat). Do not rent all-terrrain-vehicles (ATVs) or jet skis – they are unsafe.

SŎRNG·TĂA·OU

In Mae Hat *sŏrng·tăa·ou*, pick-up trucks and motorbikes crowd around the pier as passengers alight. If you're a solo traveller, you will pay 200B to get to Sairee Beach or Chalok Ban Kao. Groups of two or more will pay 100B each. Rides from Sairee to Chalok Ban Kao cost 150B per person, or 300B for solo tourists. These prices are rarely negotiable, and passengers will be expected to wait until their taxi is full unless they want to pay an additional 200B to 300B. Prices double for trips to the east coast, and the drivers will raise the prices when rain makes the roads harder to negotiate. If you know where you intend to stay, we highly recommend calling ahead to arrange a pick up. Many dive schools offer free pick-ups and transfers as well.

WATER TAXI

Boat taxis depart from Mae Hat, Chalok Ban Kao and the northern part of Sairee Beach (near Vibe Bar). Boat rides to Ko Nang Yuan will set you back at least 100B. Long-tail boats can be chartered for around 1500B per day, depending on the number of passengers carried.

Ang Thong Marine National Park

อุทยานแห่งชาติหมู่เกาะอ่างทอง

The 40-some jagged jungle islands of Ang Thong Marine National Park stretch across the cerulean sea like a shattered emerald necklace – each piece a virgin realm featuring sheer limestone cliffs, hidden lagoons and perfect peach-coloured sands. These dream-inducing islets inspired Alex Garland's cult classic *The Beach,* about dope-dabbling backpackers.

February, March and April are the best months to visit this ethereal preserve of greens and blues; crashing monsoon waves mean that the park is almost always closed during November and December.

Sights

Every tour stops at the park's head office on **Ko Wua Talap**, the largest island in the archipelago.

The naturally occurring stone arches on **Ko Samsao** and **Ko Tai Plao** are visible during seasonal tides and weather conditions. Because the sea is quite shallow around the island chain, reaching a maximum depth of 10m, extensive coral reefs have not developed, except in a few protected pockets on the southwest and northeast sides. There's a shallow coral reef near Ko Tai Plao and Ko Samsao that has decent but not excellent snorkelling. There are also several novice dives for exploring shallow caves and colourful coral gardens and spotting banded sea snakes and turtles. Soft powder beaches line **Ko Tai Plao**, **Ko Wuakantang** and **Ko Hintap**.

Viewpoint VIEWPOINT

The island's viewpoint might just be the most stunning vista in all of Thailand. From the top, visitors will have sweeping views of the jagged islands nearby as they burst through the placid turquoise water in easily anthropomorphised formations. The trek to the lookout is an arduous 450m trail that takes roughly an hour to complete. Hikers should wear sturdy shoes and walk slowly on the sharp outcrops of limestone. A second trail leads to **Tham Bua Bok**, a cavern with lotus-shaped stalagmites and stalactites.

Emerald Sea LAKE

The Emerald Sea (also called the Inner Sea) on **Ko Mae Ko** is another popular destination. This large lake in the middle of the island spans an impressive 250m by 350m and has an ethereal minty tint. You can look but you can't touch; the lagoon is strictly off limits to the unclean human body. A dramatic **viewpoint** can be found at the top of a series of staircases nearby.

Tours

The best way to experience Ang Thong is by taking one of the many guided tours departing Ko Samui and Ko Pha-Ngan. The tours usually include lunch, snorkelling equipment, hotel transfers and (with fingers crossed) a knowledgeable guide. If you're staying in luxury accommodation, there's a good chance that your resort has a private boat for providing group tours. Some mid-range and budget places also have their own boats, and if not, they can easily set you up with a general tour operator. Dive centres on Ko Samui and Ko Pha-Ngan offer **scuba trips** to the park, although Ang Thong doesn't offer the world-class diving that can be found around Ko Tao and Ko Pha-Ngan.

Due to tumultuous petrol prices, tour companies tend to come and go like the wind. Ask at your accommodation for a list of current operators.

Sleeping

Ang Thong does not have any resorts; however, on Ko Wua Talap the national park has set up five bungalows, each housing between two and eight guests. Campers are also allowed to pitch a tent in certain designated zones. Online bookings are possible, although customers must forward a bank deposit within two days of making the reservation. For advance reservations contact the **National Parks Services** (0 7728 6025; www.dnp.go.th; bungalows 500-1400B).

Getting There & Around

The best way to reach the park is to take a private day tour from Ko Samui or Ko Pha-Ngan (28km and 32km away, respectively). The islands sit between Samui and the main pier at Don Sak; however, there are no ferries that stop off along the way.

The park officially has an admission fee (adult/child 400/200B), although it should be included in the price of every tour (ask your operator if you are unsure). Private boat charters are also another possibility, although high petrol prices will make the trip quite expensive.

SURAT THANI PROVINCE

Surat Thani อำเภอเมืองสุราษฎร์ธานี

POP 128,990

Known in Thai as 'City of Good People', Surat Thani was once the seat of the ancient Srivijaya empire. Today, this unglamorous, busy junction has become a transport hub that indiscriminately moves cargo and people around the country. Travellers rarely linger here as they make their way to the popular islands of Ko Samui, Ko Pha-Ngan and Ko Tao, but it's a great stop if you enjoy real Thai working cities and good southern-style street food.

Sleeping

Staying in central Surat puts you in a bustling Thai city that can be refreshing after days in the primped-for-tourists gulf islands. Between the late-running markets, karaoke bars and frequent festivals, nights up to around midnight can be noisy and it's hard to escape the sounds of revelry even in high-rise hotels. Prices, however, are very low and you get a lot for relatively few baht.

For a quieter night and more modern amenities, escape the city centre and hop on a *sŏrng·tăa·ou* heading towards the Phang-Nga district. When you climb aboard, tell the driver 'Tesco-Lotus', and you'll be taken about 2km to 3km out of town to a large, boxlike shopping centre. A handful of hotel options orbit the mall.

If you're on a very tight budget, consider zipping straight through town and taking the night ferry to reach your island destination.

My Place @ Surat Hotel HOTEL $
(0 7727 2288; www.myplacesurat.com; 247/5 Na Meuang Rd; fan r with/without bathroom 260/199B, air-con r with bathroom 490B;) This spiffed-up Chinese hotel has surprising touches like bright paint, colourful throw cushions and modern art on the walls. It's clean, very central and the best bargain in town.

100 Islands Resort & Spa RESORT $
(0 7720 1150; www.roikoh.com; 19/6 Moo 3, Bypass Rd; r 900-1800B;) Across the street from the suburban Tesco-Lotus, 100 Islands is as good as it gets around here for a reasonable price. This teak palace looks out of place along the highway, but inside the immaculate rooms surround an overgrown garden and lagoonlike swimming pool.

Eating

Surat Thani is packed with delicious street food at lunch and then even more at dinner. Aside from the central night market listed below, stalls near the departure docks open for the daily night boats to the islands, and there's an afternoon **Sunday market** (4-9pm) near the TAT office. During the day many food stalls near the downtown bus terminal sell *kôw gài òp* (marinated baked chicken on rice).

Surat Thani

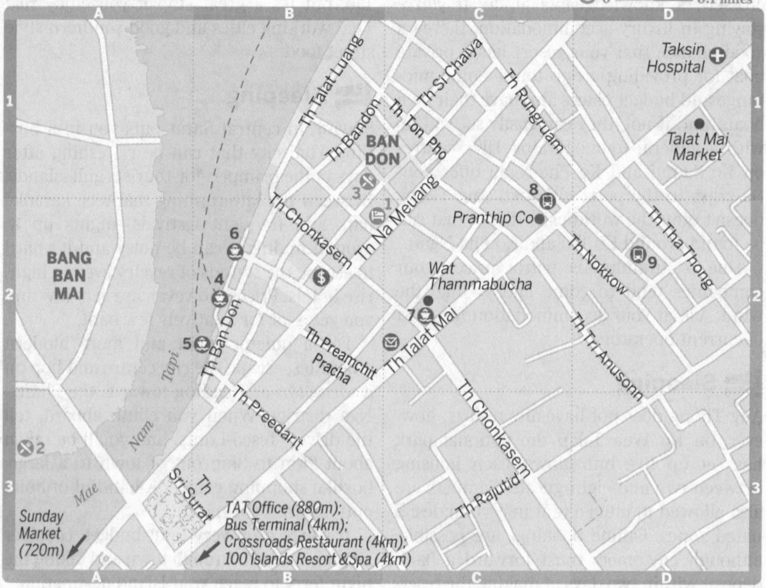

Surat Thani

Sleeping

1 My Place @ Surat Hotel B2

Eating

2 Crossroads Restaurant A3
3 Night Market B1

Transport

4 Ko Tao Night Ferry Pier B2
Lomprayah .... (see 6)
5 Night Boat to Ko Pha-Ngan B2
6 Seatran Discovery B2
7 Seatran Office C2
Songserm .... (see 6)
8 Talat Kaset 1 Bus Terminal C2
9 Talat Kaset 2 Bus Terminal D2

★ **Night Market** MARKET $
(Sarn Chao Ma; Th Ton Pho; dishes from 35B; ⏲6-11pm) A truly fantastic smorgasborg of food including lots of melt-in-your-mouth marinated meats on sticks, fresh fruit juices, noodle dishes and desserts. It's not that big so it's easy to browse the stalls before choosing what to eat.

Crossroads Restaurant INTERNATIONAL $$
(Bypass Rd; dishes 50-200B; ⏲lunch & dinner) Located southwest of Surat across from the Tesco-Lotus mall, Crossroads has a quaint bluesy vibe enhanced by dim lighting and live music. Try the oysters – Surat Thani is famous for its giant molluscs, and the prices are unbeatable.

Information

Th Na Meuang has a bank on virtually every corner in the heart of downtown. If you're staying near the 'suburbs', the Tesco-Lotus has ATMs as well.

Post Office (☎0 7728 1966, 0 7727 2013; ⏲8.30am-4.30pm Mon-Fri, 8.30am-12.30pm Sat) Across from Wat Thammabucha. The local One Tambon One People (OTOP) craft house is inside.

Taksin Hospital (☎0 7727 3239; Th Talat Mai) The most professional of Surat's three hospitals. Just beyond the Talat Mai Market in the northeast part of downtown.

Tourism Authority of Thailand (TAT; ☎0 7728 8817; tatsurat@samart.co.th; 5 Th Talat Mai; ⏲8.30am-4.30pm) Friendly office southwest of town. Distributes plenty of useful brochures and maps, and staff speak English very well.

Getting There & Away

In general, if you are departing Bangkok or Hua Hin for Ko Pha-Ngan or Ko Tao, consider taking the train or a bus-boat package that goes through Chumphon rather than Surat. You'll save time, and the journey will be more comfortable. Travellers heading to/from Ko Samui will most likely pass through. If you require any travel services, try **Pranthip Co** (Th Talat Mai) – both are reliable and English is spoken.

AIR

Although flights from Bangkok to Surat Thani are cheaper than the flights to Samui, it takes quite a bit of time to reach the gulf islands from the airport. Air Asia offers a convenient bus and boat shuttle with their flights that can alleviate some of the stress. There are daily shuttles to Bangkok on **Thai Airways International** (THAI; ☎0 7727 2610; 3/27-28 Th Karunarat), Air Asia (p234) and Nok Air (p234).

BOAT

Various ferry companies offer services to the islands. Try **Lomprayah** (☎077 4277 656; www.lomprayah.com), **Seatran Discovery** (☎0 2240 2582; www.seatrandiscovery.com) or **Songserm** (☎0 7737 7704; www.songsermexpressboat.com).

Bus-boat Combination Tickets

In the high season travellers can usually find bus-boat services to Ko Samui and Ko Pha-Ngan directly from the Phun Phin train station (which is 14km west of Surat). These services don't cost any more than those booked in Surat Thani and can save you some serious waiting time.

There are also several ferry and speedboat operators that connect Surat Thani to Ko Tao, Ko Pha-Ngan and Ko Samui. Most boats – such as the Raja and Seatran services – leave from Don Sak (about one hour from Surat; bus transfers are included in the ferry ticket) although the Songserm leaves from the heart of Surat town. Be warned that the Raja service can be a very frustrating experience, especially for travellers who are tight on time. The boat trip usually takes around 1½ hours to Ko Samui and 2½ hours to Ko Pha-Ngan, although often the captain will cut the engines to half propulsion, which means the journey can take up to five hours.

Night Ferry

From the centre of Surat there are nightly ferries to Ko Tao (eight hours, departs at 10pm), Ko Pha-Ngan (seven hours, departs at 10pm) and Ko Samui (six hours, departs at 11pm). These are cargo ships, not luxury boats, so bring food and water and watch your bags.

BUS & MINIVAN

The most convenient way to travel around the south, frequent buses and minivans depart from two main locations in town known as Talat Kaset 1 and Talat Kaset 2. Talat Kaset 1, on the north side of Th Talat Mai (the city's main drag) offers speedy service to Nakhon (120B, 1½ hours). This is also the location of Pranthip Co, one of the more trustworthy agencies in town. Buses to Phun Phin also leave from Talat Kaset 1.

At Talat Kaset 2, on the south side of Th Talat Mai, you'll find frequent transportation.

The 'new' bus terminal (which is actually a few years old now, but still referred to as new by the locals) is 7km south of town on the way to Phun Phin. This hub services traffic to and from Bangkok (380B to 800B, 11 to 14 hours).

BUSES & MINIVANS FROM SURAT THANI

DESTINATION	FARE	DURATION
Bangkok	421-856B	10hr
Hat Yai	160-240B	5hr
Khanom	100B	1hr
Krabi	150B	2½hr
Phuket	200B	6hr
Trang	190B	2hr 10min

TRAIN

When arriving by train you'll actually pull into Phun Phin, a nondescript town 14km west of Surat. From Phun Phin, there are buses to Phuket, Phang-Nga and Krabi – some via Takua Pa, a junction for Khao Sok National Park. Transport from Surat moves with greater frequency, but it's worth checking the schedule in Phun Phin first – you might be lucky and save yourself a slow ride between towns.

If you plan on travelling during the day, go for the express railcars. Night travellers should opt for the air-con couchettes. Trains passing through Surat stop in Chumphon and Hua Hin on their way up to the capital, and in the other direction you'll call at Trang, Hat Yai and Sungai Kolok before hopping across the border. The train station at Phun Phin has a 24-hour left-luggage room that charges around 20B a day. The advance ticket office is open from 6am to 6pm daily (with a nebulous one-hour lunch break somewhere between 11am and 1.30pm). The trip to Bangkok takes over 8½ hours and costs 107B to 1379B depending on class.

Getting Around

Air-conditioned vans to/from Surat Thani airport cost around 100B per person and they'll drop you off at your hotel.

To travel around town, *sŏrng·tăa·ou* cost 10B to 30B (it's 15B to reach Tesco-Lotus from the city centre).

Fan-cooled Orange buses run from Phun Phin train station to Surat Thani every 10 minutes (15B, 25 minutes). For this ride, taxis charge a cool 200B for a maximum of four people, while share taxis charge 100B per person. Other taxi rates are posted just north of the train station (at the metal pedestrian bridge).

WORTH A TRIP

WÁT SUAN MOKKHAPHALARAM

Surrounded by lush forest, **Wát Suan Mokkhaphalaram** (www.suanmokkh.org; Wat Suanmokkh), whose name means 'Garden of Liberation', charges 2000B for a 10-day program that includes food, lodging and instruction (although technically the 'teaching' is free). English retreats, run by the International Dhamma Hermitage, begin on the first day of every month and registration takes place the afternoon before. Founded by Ajan Buddhadasa Bhikkhu, arguably Thailand's most famous monk, the temple's philosophical teachings are ecumenical in nature, comprising Zen, Taoist and Christian elements, as well as the traditional Theravada schemata.

For details on reaching the temple, located 7km outside of Chaiya, check out www.suanmokkh-idh.org/idh-travel.html.

NAKHON SI THAMMARAT PROVINCE

Ao Khanom อ่าวขนอม

Lovely Ao Khanom, halfway between Surat Thani and Nakhon Si Thammarat, quietly sits along the blue gulf waters. Overlooked by tourists who flock to the jungle islands nearby, this pristine region, simply called Khanom, is a worthy choice for those seeking a serene beach setting unmarred by enterprising corporations.

The beach area is actually quite long and is comprised of two beaches: the main, long Hat Nadan and the smaller and more out of the way Hat Naiplau.

Sights

This area is home to a variety of pristine geological features including **waterfalls** and **caves** but the highlight for many are the pink dolphins.

Caves CAVE

There are two beautiful caves along the main road (Hwy 4014) between Khanom and Don Sak. **Khao Wang Thong** has a string of lights guiding visitors through the network of caverns and narrow passages. A metal gate covers the entrance; stop at the house at the base of the hill to retrieve the key (and leave a small donation). Turn right off the main highway at Rd 4142 to find **Khao Krot**, which has two large caverns, but you'll have to bring a torch (flashlight).

Samet Chun Waterfall WATERFALL

This is the largest waterfall in the area with tepid pools for cooling off, and great views of the coast. To reach the falls, head south from Ban Khanom and turn left at the blue Samet Chun sign. Follow the road for about 2km and, after crossing a small stream, take the next right and hike up into the mountain following the dirt road. After about a 15-minute walk, listen for the waterfall and look for a small trail on the right.

Hin Lat Falls WATERFALL

The scenic Hin Lat Falls is the smallest cascade, but it's also the easiest to reach. There are pools for swimming and several huts providing shade. It's south of Nai Phlao.

Dat Fa Mountain MOUNTAIN

For a postcard-worthy vista of the undulating coastline, head to Dat Fa Mountain, about 5km west of the coast along Hwy 4014. The hillside is usually deserted, making it easy to stop along the way to snap some photos.

Tours

Pink Dolphin Viewing Tours WILDLIFE

(day tours 1700B) The most special inhabitants of Khanom are the pink dolphins – a rare albino breed with a stunning pink hue. They are regularly seen from the old ferry pier and the electric plant pier around dawn and dusk but resorts are now offering full-day tours that include viewing the dolphins by boat and a car tour to the area's caves and waterfalls.

If you just want to see the dolphins you can hire a boat for a few hours (for up to six people) for 1000B. Enquire at your hotel.

Sleeping & Eating

In the last few years, there has been talk of further developing Khanom's beaches into a more laid-back alternative to the islands nearby. A recent surge in gulf oil rigging means developers are eyeing Khanom as a potential holiday destination for nearby workers, but for now it's still a very low-key retreat.

Many of the resorts see very few customers and the constant disuse (not regularly flushing the toilets etc) means that some rooms are dank as the relentless jungle reclaims them. It's best to stay away from the large hotels and stick to beachside bungalow operations. Note that all options are spaced very far apart so unless you have your own wheels don't expect to just show up and wander around looking for a place to stay.

For some cheap eats, head to **Hat Kho Khao** at the end of Rd 4232. You'll find a steamy jumble of barbecue stands offering some tasty favourites such as *mŏo nám đòk* (spicy pork salad) and *sôm·đam*. On Wednesday and Sunday there are markets further inland near the police station.

Suchada Villa BUNGALOW **$**
(☎0 7552 8459; www.suchadavilla.com; Hat Naiplau; bungalows 800B; ❄) Right off the main road and a short walk to the beach, Suchada is recognisable by its cache of brightly coloured bungalows. Rooms are cute and clean with quirky designer details such as strings of shells dangling in front of the bathroom doors. Friendly, English-speaking staff.

Khanom Hill Resort BUNGALOW **$$**
(☎0 7552 9403; www.khanom.info; Hat Naiplau; bungalows 2800-3800B; ❄📶≋) Travellers rave about this spot on a very small hill, that leads to a half-circle of dreamy white beach. Choose from modern, concrete villas with thatched roofs, cheaper models with Thai-style architecture or big family-sized apartments; all are clean and comfy.

Talkoo Beach Resort BUNGALOW **$$**
(☎0 7552 8397; yok_hana@yahoo.com; Hat Nadan; bungalows 1000-1500B; ❄📶≋) Probably the most efficiently run place on Hat Nadan. Talkoo has a range of bungalows in a garden on the beach and cheaper ones across the main road in a more dry, sparse area. All are in great shape, spacious, comfortable and have charming touches like naturalistic bathrooms. The owner is a character who engages with all her guests.

CC Beach Bar & Bungalows BUNGALOW **$$**
(www.ccbeachbarthai.wordpress.com; bungalows from 1500B; ❄📶≋) A social spot that's sprung from a friendly, fun beach bar on a stunning stretch of Hat Nadan. The clean and modern concrete bungalows are priced higher for what you can find elsewhere, with a foreigner-specific, chummy ambience.

Racha Kiri RESORT **$$$**
(☎0 7530 0245; www.rachakiri.com; bungalows 3550-18,500B; ❄📶≋) Khanom's upscale retreat is a beautiful campus of rambling villas. The big price tag means no crowds, which can be nice, although the resort feels like a white elephant when the property isn't being used as a corporate retreat.

Information

The police station and hospital are just south of Ban Khanom at the junction leading to Hat Kho Khao. There's a 7-Eleven (with an ATM) in the heart of Khanom town.

Getting There & Away

Minivans from both Surat Thani and Nakhon leave every hour on the hour from 5am to 5pm daily and drop passengers off in Khanom town, which is several kilometres from the beach. From Khanom town you can hire motorcycle taxis out to the beaches for about 20B to 80B depending on the distance you're going. If you've booked in advance your hosts may offer to pick you up in Khanom town for free.

A taxi to/from Don Sak pier for the gulf islands is 1000B and a motorcyle taxi is 300B.

Once at your lodging you'll be stranded unless you hire your own transport or take a tour with your hotel.

Nakhon Si Thammarat

อำเภอเมืองนครศรีธรรมราช

POP 120,836

The bustling city of Nakhon Si Thammarat (usually shortened to 'Nakhon') won't win any beauty pageants. However, travellers who stop in this historic town will enjoy a decidedly cultural experience amid some of the most important wát in the kingdom.

Hundreds of years ago, an overland route between the western port of Trang and the eastern port of Nakhon Si Thammarat functioned as a major trade link between Thailand and the rest of the world. This ancient influx of cosmopolitan conceits is still evident today in the local cuisine, and housed in the city's temples and museums.

Sights

Most of Nakhon's commercial activity (hotels, banks and restaurants) takes place in the northern part of the downtown. South of the clock tower, visitors will find the city's historic quarter with the oft-visited Wat Mahatat. Th Ratchadamnoen is the main thoroughfare and teems with cheap *sŏrng·tăa·ou* heading both north and south.

★Wat Phra Mahathat Woramahawihaan

TEMPLE

(Th Si Thamasok; ⌚8.30am-4.30pm) The most important wát in southern Thailand, stunning Wat Phra Mahathat Woramahawihaan (simply known as Mahathat) boasts 77 *chedi* (stupa) and an imposing 77m *chedi* crowned by a gold spire. According to legend, Queen Hem Chala and Prince Thanakuman brought relics to Nakhon over 1000 years ago, and built a small pagoda to house the precious icons.

The temple has since grown into a rambling site, and today crowds gather daily to purchase the popular Jatukham amulets. Don't miss the **museum** inside featuring antique statues from all eras and corners of Thailand.

Shadow Puppets

MUSEUM

(Th Si Thamasok Soi 3; ⌚8.30am-4pm) There are two styles of local shadow puppets: *năng đà·lung* and *năng yài*. At just under 1m tall, the former feature movable appendages and parts; the latter are nearly life-sized, and lack moving parts. Both are intricately carved from cow hide. Suchart Subsin's puppet house has a small museum where staff can demonstrate the cutting process and performances for visitors (50B).

National Museum

MUSEUM

(Th Ratchadamnoen; admission 30B; ⌚9am-4pm Wed-Sun) When the Tampaling (also known as Tambralinga) kingdom traded with merchants from Indian, Arabic, Dvaravati and Champa states, the region around Nakhon became a melting pot of crafts and art. Today, many of these relics are on display behind the run-down facade of the national museum.

Sleeping & Eating

Nakhon is a great place to sample cuisine with a distinctive southern twist. In the evening, Muslim food stands sell delicious *kôw mòk gài* (chicken *biryani*), *má·đà·bà* (*murdabag;* Indian pancake stuffed with chicken or vegetables) and roti. A good hunting ground is along Th Neramit, which turns into Th Pak Nakhon – the street bustles with food stalls every night.

Thai Hotel

HOTEL $

(0 7534 1509; fax 0 7534 4858; 1375 Th Ratchadamnoen; fan/air-con r 350/500B;) Thai Hotel is the most central sleeping spot in town. The lobby is musty, the walls are thin, but the rooms are clean, freshly painted and a good deal for the price. Each room has a TV

JATUKHAM RAMMATHEP

If you've spent more than 24 hours in Thailand, you've probably seen a Jatukham Rammathep dangling around someone's neck – these round amulets are everywhere.

The bearers of the Jatukham Rammathep are supposed to have good fortune and protection from any harm. The origin of the amulet's name remains a mystery, although a popular theory suggests that Jatukham and Rammathep were the aliases of two Srivajayan princes who buried relics under Nakhon's Wat Phra Mahathat some 1000 years ago.

A notorious Thai police detective first wore the precious icon, and firmly believed the guardian spirits helped him solve a particularly difficult murder case. He tried to popularise the amulet, but it wasn't a market success until his death in 2006. Thousands of people attended his funeral, including the crown prince, and the Jatukham Rammathep took off.

The talismans are commissioned at Wat Phra Mahathat, and in the last several years southern Thailand has seen a spike in economic activity. The first amulet was sold in 1987 for 39B, and today over 100 million baht are spent on the town's amulets every *week*. The desire for these round icons has become so frenzied that a woman was crushed to death on the temple grounds during a widely publicised discount sale (she was not wearing her talisman).

Every day, trucks drive along Nakhon's main roads blaring loud music to promote new shipments. These thumping beats have started to shake the ground beneath the temple, and the repeated hammering has, in an ironic metaphor, bent the main spire of Wat Phra Mahathat.

and the higher floors have good views of the urban bustle.

Nakorn Garden Inn HOTEL $
(☎0 7532 3777; 1/4 Th Pak Nakhon; r 450B; ❄📶) With all the foliage, this place feels more like a shady jungle than its location in the centre of town. All rooms have air-con, TV, hot water, fridge, tiled floors and bamboo-plaited walls, although most are quite dark and a little musty. It's a nice change from a cement block, though, a good deal and friendly.

Twin Lotus Hotel HOTEL $$
(☎0 7532 3777; www.twinlotushotel.net; 97/8 Th Phattanakan Khukhwang; r 1200-8200B; ❄📶🏊) Its age is showing, but Twin Lotus is still the place to go a little more upscale when in Nakhon. This 16-storey behemoth sits 2km southeast of the city centre.

Khrua Nakhon THAI $$
(Bovorn Bazaar; dishes 60-200B; ⏰breakfast & lunch) This joint has a great selection of traditional Nakhon cuisine. Order a sharing platter, which comes with five types of curry (including an unpalatable spicy fish sauce), or try the *kôw yam* (southern-style rice salad). There's one at a second location in Robinson Ocean shopping mall.

Rock 99 INTERNATIONAL $
(1180/807 Bovorn Bazaar; dishes 60-150B; ⏰4pm-midnight) The choice *fa·ràng* hang-out in Nakhon, Rock 99 has a good selection of international fare, from taco salads to pizzas (avoid the Thai fare though). There's live music on Wednesday, Friday and Saturday nights, but expect to bump into friendly expats almost all the time.

Information

Several banks and ATMs hug Th Ratchadamnoen in the northern end of downtown. There is an English-language bookstore on the 3rd floor of Robinson Ocean shopping mall.

Most hotels have free, useful city maps to give to guests.

Bovorn Bazaar (Th Ratchadamnoen) A mall housing a few internet cafes.

Police Station (☎1155; Th Ratchadamnoen) Opposite the post office.

Post Office (Th Ratchadamnoen; ⏰8.30am-4.30pm)

Tourism Authority of Thailand (TAT; ☎0 7534 6515; ⏰8.30am-4.30pm) Housed in a 1926-vintage building in the northern end of the Sanam Na Meuang (City Park). Has some useful brochures in English.

Getting There & Away

AIR

Several carriers such as Nok Air, Air Asia and Orient Thai Airlines (plus Thai Airways) fly from Bangkok to Nakhon daily. There are about six daily one-hour flights. One-way fares are around 1500B.

BUS

Ordinary buses to Bangkok leave from the bus terminal (mostly in the afternoon or evening), but a couple of private buses leave from booking offices on Th Jamroenwithi, where you can also buy tickets. The journey takes 12 hours and costs 454B to 1142B depending on the class of bus.

When looking for minivan stops to leave Nakhon, keep an eye out for small desks along the side of the downtown roads (minivans and waiting passengers may or may not be present nearby). It's best to ask around as each destination has a different departure point. Krabi and Don Sak minivans are grouped together – just make sure you don't get on the wrong one. Stops are scattered around Th Jamroenwithi, Th Wakhit and Th Yommarat.

TRAIN

There are two daily train departures to/from Bangkok to Nakhon (133B to 652B; stopping at Hua Hin, Chumphon and Surat Thani along the way). All are 12-hour night trains. These trains continue on to Hat Yai and Sungai Kolok.

Getting Around

Sŏrng·tăa·ou run north–south along Th Ratchadamnoen and Th Si Thammasok for 10B (a bit more at night). Motorcycle-taxi rides start at 30B and cost up to 50B for longer distances.

SONGKHLA PROVINCE

Songkhla's postal code is 90210, but this ain't no Beverly Hills! The province's two main commercial centres, Hat Yai and Songkhla, are less affected by the political turmoil plaguing the cities further south. Intrepid travellers will be able to count the number of other tourists on one hand as they wander through local markets, savour Muslim-Thai fusion cuisine and relax on breezy beaches.

Songkhla & Around สงขลา

POP 90,780

'The great city on two seas' lends itself perfectly to the click of a visitor's camera; however, slow-paced Songkhla doesn't see much

DON'T MISS

KHAO LUANG NATIONAL PARK

Known for its beautiful mountain and forest walks, cool streams, waterfalls and orchards, **Khao Luang National Park** (อุทยานแห่งชาติเขาหลวง; ☎0 7530 0494; www.dnp.go.th; adult/child 400/200B) surrounds the 1835m peak of Khao Luang. This soaring mountain range is covered in virgin forest. An ideal source for streams and rivers, the mountains show off impressive waterfalls and provide a habitat for a plethora of bird species – this place is a good spot for any budding ornithologist. Fans of flora will also get their kicks here; there are over 300 species of orchid in the park, some of which are found nowhere else on earth.

It's possible to rent **park bungalows** (per night 600-2000B), sleeping six to 12 people. There's a **restaurant** at park headquarters. **Camping** is permitted along the trail to the summit. To reach the park, take a *sŏrng·tăa·ou* (around 35B) from Nakhon Si Thammarat to Lan Saka; drivers will usually take you the extra way to park headquarters. The entrance to the park and the offices of the Royal Forest Department are 33km from the centre of Nakhon on Rte 4015, an asphalt road that climbs almost 400m in 2.5km to the office and a further 450m to the car park. Plenty of up-to-date details are available on the park's website.

in the way of foreign tourist traffic. Although the town hasn't experienced any of the Muslim separatist violence plaguing the provinces further south, it's still catching the same bad press. This is a shame, since it's the last safe city where travellers can experience the unique flavour of Thailand's predominately Muslim Deep South.

The population is a mix of Thais, Chinese and Malays, and the local architecture and cuisine reflect this fusion at every turn.

Sights

There's a **zoo** (สวนสัตว์สงขลา; www.songkhlazoo.com; Khao Rup Chang; admission adult/child 100/50B; ⏲9am-6pm) and **aquarium** (สงขลาอะควาเรียม; www.songkhlaaquarium.com; admission adult/child 300/200B; ⏲9.30am-4pm Tue-Fri, 9.30am-5pm Sat & Sun), both good outings if you have kids in tow.

★National Museum MUSEUM
(พิพิธภัณฑสถานแห่งชาติสงขลา; Th Wichianchom; admission 150B; ⏲9am-4pm Wed-Sun, closed public holidays) This 1878 building was originally built in a Chinese architectural style as the residence of a luminary. The museum is easily the most picturesque national museum in Thailand and contains exhibits from all Thai art-style periods, particularly the Srivijaya. Walk barefoot on the wood floors to view elaborate wood carvings, historical photos and pottery salvaged from a shipwreck.

Hat Samila BEACH
(หาดสมิหลา) Stroll this beautiful strip of white sand with the giggling local couples and enjoy the kite flying (a local obsession). A bronze **Mermaid sculpture**, in tribute to Mae Thorani (the Hindu-Buddhist earth goddess), sits atop some rocks at the northern end of the beach. Locals treat the figure like a shrine, tying the waist with coloured cloth and rubbing the breasts for good luck.

Don't expect to sunbathe here – the local dress code is too modest – but it's a wholesome spot to meet locals and enjoy a distinctly Thai beach scene.

Ko Yo ISLAND
(เกาะยอ) A popular day trip from Songkhla, this island in the middle of Thale Sap is actually connected to the mainland by bridges and is famous for its cotton-weaving industry. There's a roadside market selling cloth and ready-made clothes at excellent prices.

If you visit Ko Yo, don't miss **Wat Phrahorn Laemphor**, with its giant reclining Buddha, and check out the **Thaksin Folklore Museum** (☎0 7459 1618; admission 100B; ⏲8.30am-4.30pm), which actively aims to promote and preserve the culture of the region, and is a must-see. The pavilions here are reproductions of southern Thai-style houses and contain folk art, handicrafts and traditional household implements.

Tours

Singora Tram Tour TRAM TOUR
(⏲6 tours daily btwn 9am & 3pm) FREE These 40-minute tours in an open-air tram leave from next to the National Museum. You'll be lucky if you get any English narration but you will get a drive through the old part

of town past the Songkhla mosque, a Thai temple, Chinese shrine and then out to Hat Samila.

Sleeping & Eating

Songkhla's hotels tend to be lower priced than other areas in the gulf, which makes going up a budget level a relatively cheap splurge.

For quality seafood, head to the street in front of the BP Samila Beach Hotel – the best spot is the restaurant directly in the roundabout. If market munching is your game, you'll find a place to sample street food every day of the week. On Sundays try the bustling market that encircles the Pavilion Hotel. Monday, Tuesday and Wednesday feature a night market (which closes around 9pm) near the local fish plant and bus station, and the Friday morning market sits diagonally opposite the City Hall.

Queen Hotel GUESTHOUSE $
(☎0 7431 1138; 20 Th Traiburi; s/d/ste 330/380/550B; ❄) Central with basic, ageing but clean rooms with air-con, private hot-water bathrooms and friendly staff who speak minimal English. You can't beat the price.

BP Samila Beach Hotel HOTEL $$
(☎0 7444 0222; www.bphotelsgroup.com; 8 Th Ratchadamnoen; r 1600-2500B; ❄@≋) A landmark in quaint Songkhla, the city's poshest address is actually a great deal – you'd pay nearly double for the same amenities on the islands. The beachfront establishment offers large rooms with fridges, satellite TVs and a choice of sea or mountain views (both are pretty darn good).

Khao Noy THAI $
(☎0 7431 1805; 14/22 Th Wichianchom; dishes 30-50B; ⏲breakfast & lunch Thu-Tue) Songkhla's most lauded *ráhn kôw gaang* (curry shop) serves up an amazing variety of authentic southern-style curries, soups, stir-fries and salads. Look for the glass case holding several stainless-steel trays of food just south of the sky-blue Chokdee Inn.

Information

Banks can be found all over town.

Indonesian Consulate (☎0 7431 1544; Th Sadao)

Malaysian Consulate (☎0 7431 1062; 4 Th Sukhum)

Police Station (☎0 7432 1868; Th Laeng Phra Ram) North of the town centre.

Post Office (Th Wichianchom) Opposite the market; international calls can be made upstairs.

Getting There & Around

BUS

The bus and minibus station is a few hundred metres south of the Viva Hotel. Three 2nd-class buses go daily to Bangkok (1126B), stopping in Nakhon Si Thammarat and Surat Thani, among other places. For Hat Yai, buses (19B to 21B) and minivans (30B) take around 40 minutes, and leave from Th Ramwithi. *Sŏrng·tăa·ou* also leave from here for Ko Yo.

TRAIN

From Songkhla you'll have to go to Hat Yai to reach most long-distance destinations in the south (trains no longer pass through town).

Hat Yai หาดใหญ่

POP 191,696

Welcome to the urban hub of southern Thailand where Western-style shopping malls mingle with wafts of curry from the incredible range of busy street food stalls. Teenagers text each other between shopping and coffee shops and old Chinese men sit and watch the world go by on rickety chairs outside their junk shops – it's a lively mix of busy city and laid-back tropics. The town has long been a favourite stop for Malaysian men on their weekend hooker tours and you'll notice that the town's tourism scene is still predominantly Malaysian mixed with a few Western expats. An evening bar scene includes cosy pubs and bouncing discos.

The town is often said to be safe from the violent hullabaloo of the far south, however it hasn't been ignored. On March 31, 2012 the Lee Gardens Plaza Hotel was bombed, killing three people and injuring 400. In the past banks, malls and the airport have been targeted in more minor incidents. It's up to you if you want to stop here, but changing transport shouldn't be too risky. Those who get out and explore will be rewarded with some of the best food in the region and the dynamic flavour of the big smoke of southern Thailand.

Sleeping & Eating

Hat Yai has dozens of business-style hotels in the town centre, within walking distance of the train station. The city is the unofficial capital of southern Thailand's cuisine, offering Muslim roti and curries, Chinese noodles, duck rice and dim sum, and fresh Thai-style seafood from both the gulf and Andaman coasts. You'll find hawker stalls everywhere but a particularly good hunting ground is along Th Supasarnrangsan. Meals here cost between 25B to 80B.

Tune Hotel HOTEL $
(☎0 2613 5888; www.tunehotels.com; 152-156 Th Niphat Utit 2; r from 800B; ❄📶) In a great, central location, Air Asia's cookie cutter hotel chain works well in Hat Yai, with its affordable, extremely clean and slick rooms. Hopefully you like red and white. Prices change a lot depending on how far in advance you book and/or promotions and you save if you book a room with an Air Asia flight.

Night Market MARKET $
(Th Montri 1) The night market boasts heaps of local eats including several stalls selling the famous Hat Yai-style deep-fried chicken and *kà·nŏm jeen* (fresh rice noodles served with curry), as well as a couple of stalls peddling grilled seafood.

Information

Immigration Office (Th Phetkasem) Near the railway bridge, it handles visa extensions.

Tourism Authority of Thailand (TAT; tatsgkhla@tat.or.th; 1/1 Soi 2, Th Niphat Uthit 3; ⊙8.30am-4.30pm) The very helpful staff here speak excellent English and have loads of info on the entire region.

Tourist Police (Th Niphat Uthit 3; ⊙24hr) Near the TAT office.

Getting There & Away

AIR

Air Asia (www.airasia.com) Daily flights from Hat Yai to Bangkok and Kuala Lumpur.

Nok Air (www.nokair.com) Daily flights between Hat Yai and Bangkok's Don Muang Airport.

Thai Airways International (THAI; 182 Th Niphat Uthit 1) Operates several flights daily between Hat Yai and Bangkok.

Nearly all of the low-cost airlines now operate flights to and from Bangkok:

BUS

Most interprovincial buses and southbound minivans leave from the bus terminal 2km southeast of the town centre, while most northbound minivans now leave from a minivan terminal 5km west of town at Talat Kaset, a 60B túk-túk ride from the centre of town. Buses link Hat Yai to almost any location in southern Thailand.

Prasert Tour (Th Niphat Uthit 1) runs quicker minibuses to Surat Thani (4½ hours, 8am to 5pm), and **Cathay Tour** (93/1 Th Niphat Uthit 2) can also arrange minivans to many destinations in the south.

BUSES FROM HAT YAI

DESTINATION	PRICE	DURATION
Bangkok	688-1126B	15hr
Krabi	82-535B	5hr
Phuket	344-535B	8hr
Songkhla	19-21B	1½hr
Sungai Kolok	200B	4hr
Surat Thani	160-240B	6hr

TRAIN

There are four overnight trains to/from Bangkok each day (146B to 825B), and the trip takes at least 16 hours. There are also seven trains daily that run along the east coast to Sungai Kolok and two daily trains running west to Butterworth and Padang Besar, both in Malaysia.

There is an advance booking office and left-luggage office at the train station; both are open 7am to 5pm daily.

Getting Around

An **Airport Taxi Service** (☎0 7423 8452; 182 Th Niphat Uthit 1) makes the run to the airport four times daily (80B per person, 6.45am, 9.30am, 1.45pm and 6pm). A private taxi for this run costs 320B.

Sŏrng·tăa·ou run along Th Phetkasem (10B per person). Túk-túk and motorcycle taxis around town cost 20B to 40B per person.

DEEP SOUTH

Yala ยะลา

POP 76,853

Landlocked Yala wiggles its way south to the Malaysian border, making it Thailand's southernmost province. Its eponymous capital appears very different from other Thai metropolises. The city's big boulevards and well-organised street grid are set around a huge circular park and feel distinctly Western. Around three-quarters of the population are Muslim and it is a university town; the educational centre of the Deep South.

Sights

Yala's biggest attraction is **Wat Kuha Pi Muk** (also called Wat Na Tham or Cave-front Temple), one of the most important pilgrimage points in southern Thailand. Located 8km west of town on the road connecting Yala to Hat Yai (Rte 409), the Srivijaya-period cave temple features a reclining Buddha that dates back to AD 757. A statue of a giant guards the temple's entrance, and inside small natural openings in the cave's roof let in the sun's rays to illuminate a variety of ancient Buddhist cave drawings.

Further south, Betong is home to the largest **mail box** in Thailand, first built in 1924. Betong also functions as a legal, but inconvenient, border crossing to Malaysia; contact Yala's **immigration office** (0 7323 1292).

Sleeping & Eating

Many of Yala's cheapest lodgings double as unofficial brothels. There are excellent restaurants scattered around the park's perimeter.

Yala Rama HOTEL $

(0 7321 2815; 21 Th Sri Bumrung; r 500-600B;) Like most hotels in the region, this central and reputable place would be more expensive if it wasn't in the tourist-free Deep South. Clean, comfortable rooms and an OK attached restaurant.

Getting There & Around

There are five daily buses to and from Bangkok's southern bus terminal (689B to 1218B, 14 hours). The 2.30pm bus from Bangkok carries onto Betong.

Yala's bus station is south of the city centre. Four trains a day run between Bangkok and Yala (22 hours). Six trains travel daily from Yala to Sungai Kolok (three to four hours). The train station is just north of the city centre.

Buses to Hat Yai (160B, 2½ hours) stop several time a day on Th Sirirot, outside the Prudential TS Life office.

Minivans to Betong and Sungai Kolok (120B, two hours) depart hourly from opposite the train station.

Four trains a day run between Bangkok and Yala (22 hours). Six trains travel daily from Yala to Sungai Kolok (three to four hours).

Pattani ปัตตานี

POP 43,631

Once the heart of a large Muslim principality that included the neighbouring provinces of Yala and Narathiwat, Pattani Province has never adjusted to Thai rule. Although today's political situation has stunted the area's development, Pattani Town has a 500-year history of trading with the world's most notorious imperial powerhouses. The Portuguese established a trading post here in 1516, the Japanese passed through in 1605, the Dutch in 1609 and the British flexed their colonial muscle in 1612.

Yet despite the city's fascinating past, there's little of interest in Pattani except its access to some decent nearby beaches. The ongoing insurgency has made all but a handful of these sandy destinations unsafe for the independent traveller.

Sights

The Mae Nam Pattani (Pattani River) divides the older town to the east and the newer town to the west. Along Th Ruedi you can see what is left of old Pattani **architecture** – the Sino-Portuguese style that was once so prevalent in this part of southern Thailand. On Th Arnoaru there are several ancient but still quite intact Chinese-style homes.

Pattani could be one of the better beach destinations in the region. The coastline between Pattani Town and Narathiwat Province is stunning: untouched and deserted apart from fishing villages. But exploring much of this area independently is not a safe option at this time (see the boxed text on p238), nor is there any tourist infrastructure once you get to the beaches.

Locals frequent **Laem Tachi**, a sandy cape that juts out over the northern end of Ao Pattani. It can be reached by boat taxi from Pattani pier. **Hat Talo Kapo**, 14km east of Pattani near Yaring Amphoe, is another hotspot. Although it's technically in Songkhla Province, **Thepha district**, 35km northwest of Pattani, is the most developed beach destination in the area. There you'll find a few slightly aged resorts that cater mostly to middle-class Thais. At **Hat Soi Sawan**, near the Songkhla–Pattani border, several families have set up informal beachfront restaurants that are popular with weekend visitors. To reach Thepha, hop on any Songkhla-bound bus from Pattani (or vice versa); mention the name of your resort and you'll be deposited at the side of the road for the brief walk to the beach.

Matsayit Klang MOSQUE
(Th Naklua Yarang) Thailand's second-largest mosque is the Matsayit Klang, a traditional structure with a green hue that is probably still the south's most important mosque. It was built in the 1960s.

Sleeping & Eating

Palace Hotel HOTEL $
(☎0 7334 9171; 10-12 Pipit Soi Talattewiwat 2; r 200-350B; ❄) There's nothing palatial about this place. But it is the only budget option in town for foreigners and close to the night market. Go for the air-con rooms with hot water.

CS Pattani Hotel HOTEL $$
(☎0 7333 5093; www.cspattanihotel.com; 299 Moo 4, Th Nong Jik; r from 1100B; ❄@🛜🏊) The safest hotel, with soldiers outside and a metal detector in the lobby, this is where Thai politicians stay on their rare visits to the Deep South. The paucity of tourists means you get great rooms and facilities for a bargain price. It's about 2km west of the centre of town. The area around the hotel has a number of restaurants and bars.

Sakom Cabana RESORT $$
(☎0 7431 8065; 136 Moo 4, Tambon Sakom; r 600-1000B; ❄) Located about 40km from Pattani town in the Thepha district, this basic resort features a clean compound with several attractive wooden duplex bungalows a short walk from the beach.

> **MOBILE PHONES**
>
> When you arrive in the Deep South, you'll notice that your mobile (cell) phone won't work, whether or not you have a Thai SIM card. Mobile phone signals are routinely jammed to prevent insurgents using them to set off bombs. If you have a Thai SIM, you can reactivate it by visiting a local phone shop and handing over your passport and 50B. They'll make a note of your details, so that the authorities know whose phone it is should it be used for anything illegal, and an hour later your phone will work again.

Night Market SOUTHERN THAI $
(Soi Talattewiwat; ⏲4-9pm) Pattani shuts down far earlier than most Thai towns, but the night market offers solid seafood, as well as southern Thai-style curries and the usual noodle and fried rice options.

Information

There are several banks along the southeastern end of Th Pipit, near the Th Naklua Yarang intersection.

Pattani Hospital (☎0 7332 3414, 0 7332 3411; Th Nong Jik)

Police Station (☎0 7334 9018; Th Pattani Phirom) In a central location.

Getting There & Around

Minivans are the region's most popular mode of transport and there are frequent daytime departures to Hat Yai (100B, 1½ hours), Narathiwat (100B, two hours) and Sungai Kolok (130B, 2½ hours). Ask at your hotel for the departure points.

There is one daily bus to and from Bangkok's southern bus terminal (763B, 15 hours).

Motorbike taxis charge 10B to 30B for hops around town, but they become very scarce after dark.

Narathiwat นราธิวาส

POP 40,521

Sitting on the banks of the Bang Nara River, Narathiwat is probably the most Muslim city in Thailand, with many mosques scattered around town. There are still a few old Sino-Portuguese buildings lining the riverfront (although blink and you'll miss them), and there are some excellent beaches just outside town. But few tourists pass through, due to the security situation.

Sights

Matsayit Klang MOSQUE
Towards the southern end of Th Pichitbumrung stands Matsayit Klang, a wooden mosque built in the Sumatran style and known locally as the 'central mosque'. It was reputedly built by a prince of the former kingdom of Pattani over a hundred years ago.

Ao Manao BEACH
Five kilometres south of town, Ao Manao is a superb strip of palm tree-fringed sand. You'll likely have it all to yourself.

TRAVEL IN THE DEEP SOUTH: SHOULD YOU GO?

Despite the conflict, almost everyone in the Deep South – whether ethnic Malay Muslim or a Thai soldier – is happy to see a *fa·ràng*. So few foreigners make it here that you're guaranteed a lot of attention from the locals. Nor have tourists, or any Westerners, ever been targeted by the insurgents; this is a very insular war.

Yet by nature insurgencies are unpredictable, and bombs kill indiscriminately. Explosive devices planted on parked motorbikes outside shops are a common tactic of the separatists and have been used in the city centres of Yala, Pattani and Narathiwat on a number of occasions.

It's best not to linger on the streets for too long; you could be in the wrong place at the wrong time. Nor is travel in the countryside in the early morning or after dark advisable. This isn't an area to be riding a motorbike in if you can't be identified as a foreigner.

But perhaps the biggest drawback to travel in the region is that the insurgency has stifled tourism to such an extent that there is very little infrastructure for visitors. Apart from travelling between the major centres, you'll need private transport to get around. There are few hotels and restaurants and precious little nightlife, and hardly anyone speaks English. And those beautiful beaches have absolutely no facilities.

If you do want to travel here, research the current situation carefully and take advice from your embassy.

Hat Narathat BEACH
Just north of town is Hat Narathat, a 5km-long sandy beach fronted by towering pines, which serves as a public park for locals. The beach is only 2km from the town centre – you can easily walk there or take a *sǎhm·lór*.

Wat Khao Kong BUDDHIST TEMPLE
(⌚9am-5pm) FREE The tallest seated-Buddha image in southern Thailand is at Wat Khao Kong, 6km southwest on the way to the train station in Tanyongmat. Located in a park, the image is 17m long and 24m high, and made of reinforced concrete covered with tiny gold-coloured mosaic tiles that glint magically in the sun.

Sleeping & Eating

Most of the town's accommodation is located on and around Th Puphapugdee along the Bang Nara river. There are a few riverfront Thai restaurants which serve alcohol; the Muslim ones in town are booze-free.

Ocean Blue Mansion HOTEL $
(☎0 7351 1109; 297 Th Puphapugdee; r 400-500B; ❄📶) Sound budget choice with a riverfront location. Rooms are decent-sized and come with fridges and cable TV.

Imperial HOTEL $$
(☎0 7351 5041; narathiwat@imperialhotels.com; 260 Th Pichitbumrung; r 1000B; ❄@📶) Not the most exclusive hotel in town, but still a snip at the price and centrally located and secure. Rooms are large and comfortable. There are a few Thai restaurants/bars close by.

Jay Sani MUSLIM-THAI $
(50/1 Th Sophaphisai; dishes 40-80B; ⌚10am-9pm) This is where locals go for excellent Thai-Muslim food. Point to whatever curry or stir-fry looks good, but be sure not to miss the sublime beef soup.

Ang Mo CHINESE-THAI $
(cnr Th Puphapugdee & Th Chamroonnara; dishes 50-150B; ⌚10am-10pm) This exceedingly popular Chinese restaurant is both cheap and tasty, and has even fed members of the Thai royal family.

Information

The **Tourism Authority of Thailand** (TAT; ☎Narathiwat 0 7352 2411, nationwide call centre 1672) is inconveniently located a few kilometres south of town, just across the bridge on the road to Tak Bai.

Getting There & Around

Air Asia (☎nationwide call centre 0 2515 9999; www.airasia.com; Narathiwat Airport) flies daily to and from Bangkok (from 2390B, 1½ hours).

Two buses daily travel to and from Bangkok's southern bus terminal (685B to 1369B, 15 to 17 hours). Narathiwat's **bus terminal** (☎0 7351 1552) is 2km south of town on Th Rangae Munka.

THAILAND'S FORGOTTEN WAR

It may seem fantastic as you laze on the beach, or meditate at a peaceful hilltop temple, but the Deep South of Thailand is home to one of Southeast Asia's longest-running and bloodiest conflicts.

Just 300km or so south of the party islands of Ko Samui and Ko Pha-Ngan, a guerrilla war between ethnic Malay Muslims and the overwhelmingly Buddhist Thai state has claimed almost 5500 lives since 2004 and left close on 10,000 people injured.

The Deep South, which borders Malaysia, is a different world to the rest of the country. Foreign visitors are nonexistent and the pristine beaches deserted. Military convoys rumble through the villages and towns, checkpoints dominate the roads and mobile phone signals are jammed to prevent the insurgents from using them to set off bombs.

Around 80% of the 1.8 million people who live in Thailand's three southernmost provinces of Pattani, Narathiwat and Yala are ethnic Malay Muslims. They speak a Malay dialect and many want their own independent state, as the region once was hundreds of years ago.

For the estimated 12,500 to 15,000 separatist fighters here, the Deep South is 'Patani'; this is the name given to the Qatar-sized sultanate during its glory days in the 14th and 15th centuries. The separatists view the Thai government as a colonial power and Thai Buddhists as interlopers in their land.

Ranged against the insurgents are around 150,000 soldiers, police and militias. Targeted in ambushes along the coconut tree-lined roads of the region, or by increasingly sophisticated IEDs (improvised explosive devices), barely a day goes by without a member of the Thai security forces being killed or wounded.

At the same time, the insurgency has set neighbours against each other. Gruesome tit-for-tat killings occur, with both Buddhist and Muslim civilians being gunned down as they ride home on their motorbikes, or beheaded in the rubber plantations that are the mainstay of the local economy. Bombs are planted outside shops and in the markets of the towns, claiming random victims. The few remaining Buddhist monks in the region have to be escorted by the army when they collect alms every morning for fear they will be assassinated, while mosques are riddled with bullet holes.

Yet despite the appalling violence – one 2012 Australian study revealed that 5% of all global terrorist attacks between 2002 and 2009 occurred in the Deep South – the insurgency remains little-known both at home and overseas. With 24 million visitors a year, Thailand is fiercely proud and protective of its reputation as the 'Land of Smiles'. The media downplays the security situation, while Thai politicians act as if they are in denial about the sheer scale of the conflict.

The insurgents, too, have resisted attacking targets outside the Deep South, a tactic that would do huge damage to the Thai psyche and would garner them far more attention

Minivans heading to Hat Yai (160B, three hours), Pattani (100B, two hours), Songkhla (150B, two hours), Sungai Kolok (80B, one hour) and Yala (100B, 1½ hours) leave on an hourly basis from 5am to 5pm from the bus terminal.

Narathiwat is small enough to navigate by foot, although motorcycle taxis only charge 20B to 30B to get around.

Sungai Kolok สุไหงโกลก

POP 42,776

It's not the most prepossessing place to enter or exit the 'Land of Smiles', but Sungai Kolok is the main gateway between Thailand and Malaysia. As such, it's a scuzzy border town best known for smuggling and prostitution. Far less of a target than the other major towns in the region, the unstable situation in the Deep South has nevertheless severely diminished its 'sin city' reputation in recent years, with the Malaysian men who once came here for wild weekends now favouring safer Hat Yai. But there's still a small strip of booming bars on Th Charoenkhet, Soi 3 and behind the Marina Hotel. Fewer travellers, too, leave Thailand here now; more come in the opposite direction and immediately hop a train north.

around the world. Nor do they appear to be connected to the more radical Islamic militants of Indonesia and the Philippines.

Instead, they stay in the shadows, rarely issuing statements or talking to the press. Operating in independent cells, they belong to three different organisations all likely linked to each other. But there seems to be no common leader of the groups. That renders the sporadic peace talks that take place between the separatists and the Thai government meaningless, as no one is really sure if the representatives of the insurgents have any true control over them.

While the insurgency kicked into life in earnest in 2004, after 32 suspected Muslim rebels were cornered in an ancient mosque in Pattani Town and brutally killed by the Thai army, its roots go back hundreds of years. From the 16th century on, the sultanate of Patani was unwillingly under Thai rule for brief periods. But it wasn't until the Anglo-Siamese Treaty of 1909 that the Deep South was absorbed into Thailand proper. Britain recognised Thai sovereignty over the region, in return for Bangkok abandoning its claims to other parts of what were then the British-ruled Malay States.

Since then, Thailand, the most populous Buddhist country in the world, has set about attempting to remake the Deep South in its own image. Muslim schools have been shut down and all children made to study in Thai, even though most of them speak it only as a second language. They are also forced to learn about Buddhism, a part of the Thai national curriculum, despite following Islam. Officials from other parts of the country are imported to run the region.

By turns heavy-handed and paternalistic, the Thai government's policies began to fuel a separatist movement. Even now, there are no media outlets in the Malay dialect spoken by the majority of people in the Deep South. Having their children subject to the Thai school system remains a huge source of resentment for many Muslims. Regarded as symbols of the hated Thai state by the insurgents, over 300 schools have been burned down in recent years, while more than 150 Buddhist teachers have been assassinated.

But with the insurgency entirely confined to just three provinces, and a small part of neighbouring Songkhla Province, few Thais are even aware of why the fighting is taking place. Nor are they willing to contemplate giving into the separatists' demands. Imbued with the nationalism taught in their schools, the idea that the Deep South should want to secede from Thailand is unthinkable, both to ordinary Thais and the authorities.

Yet some form of autonomy for the region is likely the only way to end the violence. Until that happens, Thailand's forgotten war will carry on and the grim list of casualties will continue to grow.

Sleeping & Eating

Most hotels here are uniform in quality and price. Many of the real cheapies won't accept foreigners.

Stand-out restaurants are in short supply, although there is some tasty Malaysian and Chinese food around.

Tara Regent HOTEL **$**

(0 7361 1401; 45 Th Charoenkhet; r 600B;) Functional but clean and reasonably sized rooms are at this Malay-Chinese-owned place 400m walk from the train station. Little English spoken.

Genting Hotel HOTEL **$$**

(0 7361 3231; 250 Th Asia 18; r 700-800B;) More respectable than most hotels in town and, if you're the nervous type, the security is efficient. But the midrange rooms are rather scuffed for the price. It's a few hundred metres west of the train station on the other side of the road.

Kakyah Restaurant MALAYSIAN **$**

(43/11 Th Charoenkhet; dishes from 30B; 10am-10pm) Decent Malaysian food is on offer at this reliable, alcohol-free, Muslim-run place.

GETTING TO MALAYSIA: SUNGAI KOLOK TO RANTAU PANJANG

Getting to the Border The Thai border (open 5am to 9pm) is about 1.5km from the centre of Sungai Kolok or the train station. Motorbike taxis charge 30B.

At the Border This is a hassle-free, straightforward border crossing. After completing formalities, walk across the Harmony Bridge to the Malaysian border post.

Moving On Shared taxis and buses to Kota Bharu, the capital of Malaysia's Kelantan State, can be caught 200m beyond the Malaysian border post. Shared taxis cost RM$8 per person (80B) or RM$40 (400B) to charter the whole car yourself. The ride takes around 40 minutes. Buses make the hour-long journey for RM$5.10 (50B).

It's possible to continue south by the so-called 'jungle train', but the closest station is at Pasir Mas, located along taxi/bus routes to Kota Bharu.

Tak Bai, also in Narathiwat Province, and Betong, further south in Yala, are also legal crossing points for foreigners, but Sungai Kolok is by far the most convenient place to cross the border.

Night Market MARKET $

It's a small night market, but exceptionally good and cheap eats can be found at the stall in the centre that only has Chinese characters.

Information

In addition to the one at the border, there is an **immigration office** (0 7361 4114; Th Charoenkhet; 8am-5pm Mon-Fri) opposite the night market with helpful, English-speaking staff. A tourist police office sits at the border. There are plenty of ATMs in town as well as foreign-exchange booths, which are open during border-crossing hours.

Getting There & Away

The long-distance **bus station** (0 7361 2045) is an office on the corner of Th Wongwiwat and Th Worakamin in the east of town.

There are four buses daily to and from Bangkok's southern bus terminal (741B to 1481B, 17 to 20 hours).

Minivans heading north to Narathiwat (80B, one hour), Pattani (130B, 2½ hours), Yala (120B, two hours) and Hat Yai (200B, four hours) depart frequently during the day across the road from the Genting Hotel.

Two daily trains connect Sungai Kolok with Bangkok (607B to 1753B, 24 hours, departures at 11.20am and 2.20pm). Very slow local trains run to other points north. Trains in the Deep South are often delayed and subject to army and police searches.

Getting Around

Motorcycle taxis zoom around town for a flat rate of 30B.

Phuket & the Northern Andaman Coast

Includes ➡

Best Places to Eat

- Siam Indigo (p253)
- Suay (p252)
- Rum Jungle (p258)
- Ban Ra Tree (p276)
- Pad Thai Shop (p264)
- Kopitiam by Wilai (p251)

Best Places to Stay

- Six Senses Hideaway (p299)
- Elephant Hills (p289)
- Sabai Corner (p260)
- Pullman (p275)
- Dewa (p276)

Why Go?

Whether you've got designer-villa wishes, bamboo-hut desires or something in between, the northern Andaman coast serves it up hot with a shot of turquoise ocean to wash it down. Phuket, on the southern extremity, is the audacious starlet of the region, flaunting glitzy five-star hotels that grace ultrawhite beaches. Here, sleep is an afterthought to parties, water sports and spa pampering. Ranong, to the far north, is a mix of Burmese and Thais who eke out a living in an up-and-coming frontier that's opening more and more to tourism. Travel the 300km between, and you'll see it all: Muslim and Moken stilt villages and vertical limestone karsts, jaw-dropping resorts, and bays abuzz with jet skis, tangled mangrove swamps and skittish clouds of swallows.

When to Go

- May to October is the rainy season. That's when the surf kicks up, many resorts close and others slash their prices.
- The Vegetarian Festival is held in late September or October and involves parades of pierced, penitent worshippers, endless firecrackers and great meatless food.
- December to January is peak season for tourism. Prices soar, and accommodation and transport need to be booked well in advance.

Phuket & the Northern Andaman Coast Highlights

1. Staying at an over-the-top luxury spa resort on **Phuket** (p243)
2. Enjoying unmentionably wild nights in **Patong** (p264)
3. Searching for monkeys in the Jurassic Park of **Khao Sok** (p288)
4. Kayaking the surreal green waters of **Ao Phang-Nga** (p295) to empty coves
5. Catching up on your reading on a quiet **Ko Phayam beach** (p281)
6. Exploring the enchanting Sino-Portuguese architecture of the newly restored cafes, shops and galleries around **Phuket Town** (p249)
7. Snorkelling, diving or simply exploring the psychedelically green and blue **Surin** and **Similan Islands** (p285)
8. Beach-bumming, cycling and relaxing to the max on **Ko Yao Noi** (p298)

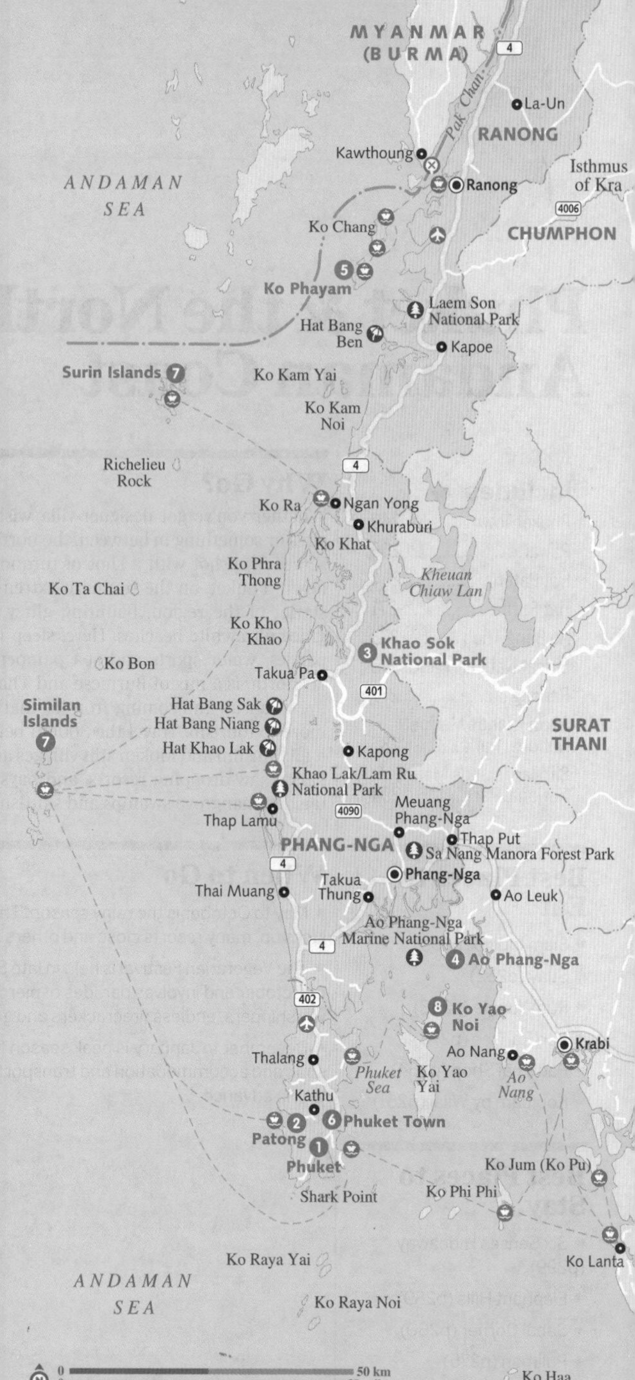

PHUKET PROVINCE

The island of Phuket has long been misunderstood. Firstly, the 'h' is silent. Ahem. And secondly, Phuket doesn't feel like an island at all. It's so huge (the biggest in Thailand) that you rarely get the sense that you're surrounded by water, which is probably the reason why Ko (meaning 'island') was dropped from its name. Dubbed the 'pearl of the Andaman' by marketing execs, this is Thailand's original flavour of tailor-made fun in the sun.

The island's sin city of Patong is the biggest town and busiest beach. It's the ultimate gong show where beachaholics sizzle off their hangovers and go-go girls play ping pong...without paddles. But ultimately the island's affinity for luxury far outshines its other stereotypes. Jet-setters come through in droves, getting pummelled during swanky spa sessions and swigging sundowners at one of the many fashion-forward nightspots or on their rented yacht. And you don't have to be an heiress to tap into Phuket's trendy to-do list. With deep-sea diving, high-end dining, and white beaches all within reach, it really is hard to say farewell.

Activities

Diving & Snorkelling

Phuket enjoys an enviable central location relative to the Andaman's top diving destinations. The much-talked-about Similan Islands sit to the north, while dozens of dive sites orbit Ko Phi-Phi and Ko Lanta to the south. Of course, this means that trips from Phuket to these awesome destinations cost slightly more than from places closer to the sites since you'll be forking over extra dough for your boat's petrol. Most operators on Phuket take divers to the nine decent sites orbiting the island, like Ko Raya Noi and Ko Raya Yai (also called Ko Racha Noi and Ko Racha Yai), but these spots rank lower on the wow-o-meter. The reef off the southern tip of Raya Noi is the best spot, particularly good for experienced divers, with soft corals and pelagic fish species aplenty. Manta and marble rays are also frequently glimpsed here and, if you're (very) lucky, you might even see a whale shark.

Typical one-day dive trips to nearby sites cost about 3500B to 4000B, including two dives and equipment. Nondivers (and snorkellers) are permitted to join these trips for a significant discount. PADI Open Water certification courses cost around 15,000B to 17,000B for three days of instruction equipment hire.

Snorkelling isn't wonderful off Phuket proper, though mask, snorkel and fins can be rented for around 250B a day in most resort areas. As with scuba diving, you'll find better snorkelling (with greater visibility and variety of marine life) along the shores of small outlying islands such as Ko Raya Yai and Ko Raya Noi.

As is the case elsewhere in the Andaman Sea, the best diving months are December to May when the weather is good and the sea is smooth and clear.

Sea Fun Divers DIVING
(Map p261; ☎0 7634 0480; www.seafundivers.com; 29 Soi Karon Nui, Patong; 2/3 dives per day 4100/4500B, open-water course 18,400B) An outstanding and very professional diving operation. Standards are extremely high and service is impeccable. There's an office at Le Meridien resort in Patong, and a second location at Katathani Resort in Kata Noi.

Rumblefish Adventure DIVING
(Map p261; ☎0 7633 0315; Scubatuna.com; 98/79 Th Kata; day trips 3200-3700B, open-water course 12,900B) A terrific boutique dive shop offering all the standard courses and overnight trips out of their Beach Center location. They have a hostel upstairs, too.

Dive Asia DIVING
(Map p261; ☎0 7633 0598; www.diveasia.com; 24 Th Karon, Kata; day trips 3400-3900B, open-water course 14,860B) There is a **second location** (Map p261; 623 Th Karon) near Hat Karon.

Offspray Leisure DIVING
(☎08 1894 1274; www.offsprayleisure.com; 43/87 Chalong Plaza, Chalong; day trips 3500-4500B, open-water course 15,900B) A dive and snorkelling excursion company specialising in small-load, intimate trips to the reefs around Ko Phi-Phi.

Adrenalin Sports

Cable Jungle Adventure Phuket ADVENTURE SPORTS
(☎08 9874 0066; www.ziplinephuket.com; 232/17 Moo 8, Th Bansuanneramit; per person 2150B; 9am-6pm) Tucked into the hills behind a quilt of pineapple fields, rubber plantations and mango groves is this maze of eight zip lines linking cliffs to ancient ficus trees. The zips range from 6m to 23m above the ground and the longest run is 100m long. Closed-toe shoes are a must.

ngy Jump ADVENTURE SPORTS
351; www.phuketbungy.com; 61/3 Th n, Kathu; jump 2100B) In opera- 92, this 20-storey bungy jump Patong is built and operated to Kiwi standards. Jumpers have the option to dunk in the water, leap in pairs or experience the Rocket Man, where you'll be shot 50m into the air, then do the bungy thing on the way down.

Phuket Wake Park WATER SPORTS
(☎0 7620 2527; www.phuketwakepark.com; 86/3 Moo 6, Th Wichitsongkram, Kathu; 2 hrs 500-650B, day pass 1200B; ⌚7:30am-11pm) Phuket's newest extreme addiction: buzz Kathu's lake backed by steep green hills on a wake board. They offer rides in two-hour blocks or by the day, and you can even book a week's worth of fun in advance. Best prices are offered in the early morning and evening.

Horse Riding

Phuket Riding Club HORSE RIDING
(☎0 7628 8213; www.phuketridingclub.com; 95 Th Viset, Rawai; 1hr/1½hr 1000B/1500B) Phuket Riding Club offers rides in the jungle around Rawai and along nearby beaches.

Sea Kayaking

Several companies based on Phuket offer canoe tours of scenic Ao Phang-Nga. Kayaks can enter semi-submerged caves inaccessible to long-tail boats. A day paddle costs from 3950B per person including meals, equipment and transfer. Many outfits also run all-inclusive, three-day (from 13,700B) or six-day (from 23,400B) kayaking and camping trips.

★ **John Gray's Seacanoe** BOATING
(☎0 7625 4505; www.johngray-seacanoe.com; 124 Soi 1, Th Yaowarat; adult/child from 3950/1975B) The original, the most reputable and by far the most ecologically sensitive company on the island. Like any good brand in Thailand, John Gray's 'Seacanoe' name and itineraries have been frequently copied. Located north of Phuket Town.

Paddle Asia BOATING
(Map p250; ☎0 7621 6145; www.paddleasia.com; 9/71 Moo 3, Th Rasdanusorn, Ban Kuku; day trips from 4300B) Another popular company that caters to small groups, Paddle Asia offers several day and multi-day trips to Ao Phang-Nga and Khao Sok National Park on classic kayaks rather than sit-on-tops or inflatables.

Surfing

Phuket is an undercover surf destination. Once the monsoons bring their midyear swell, glassy seas fold into barrels. The best waves arrive between June and September, when annual competitions are held in Kata and Kalim. **Phuket Surf** (Map p261; ☎08 1611 0791, 08 7889 7308; www.phuketsurf.com; Th Koktanod, Kata; lessons 1500B, board rental per hr/day 150/500B; ⌚Apr–late-Oct) is based in Kata, at the south end of the bay near the best break, which typically tops out at 2m. Hat Nai Han can get bigger waves (up to 3m) near the yacht club. Be warned: Kata and Nai Han have vicious undertows that can claim lives.

Hat Kalim, just north of Patong, is sheltered and has a consistent break that also gets up to 3m. This is a hollow wave, and is considered the best break on the island. Kamala's northernmost beach has a nice 3m beach break, and Laem Singh, just up the coast in front of the Amanpuri, gets very big and fast, plus it's sheltered from wind by the massive headland.

Hat Nai Yang has a consistent if soft wave that breaks more than 200m offshore. Hat Nai Thong gets better shape. Swells get up to 3m high a few times per year.

Kiteboarding

One of the world's fastest-growing sports is also one of Phuket's latest fads. The three best spots are Hat Nai Yang, Karon (in the low season) and Rawai (ideal conditions for beginners in the high season). Phuket's three kiteboarding outfitters are all affiliated with the International Kiteboarding Organization (PADI for kites).

Kiteboarding Asia WATER SPORTS
(☎08 1591 4594; www.kiteboardingasia.com; lessons from 4000B) Its main office is on Hat Nai Yang, but it has a kiosk on the south end of Hat Karon that's open in the low season. It also offers lessons off Rawai's Friendship Beach.

Kite Zone WATER SPORTS
(Map p257; ☎08 3395 2005; www.kitesurfing-phuket.com; 1hr beginner lessons from 1100B; half-day lesson 4400B; ⌚May–late-Oct) With locations in Nai Yang and Rawai, this is the younger, hipper school, with a tremendous perch on Friendship Beach. Courses range in length from an hour to five days.

Bob's Kite School Phuket WATER SPORTS
(www.kiteschoolphuket.com; Nai Yang; 1hr discovery lesson 1000B, 3hr course 3300B) Phuket's very

Ko Phuket

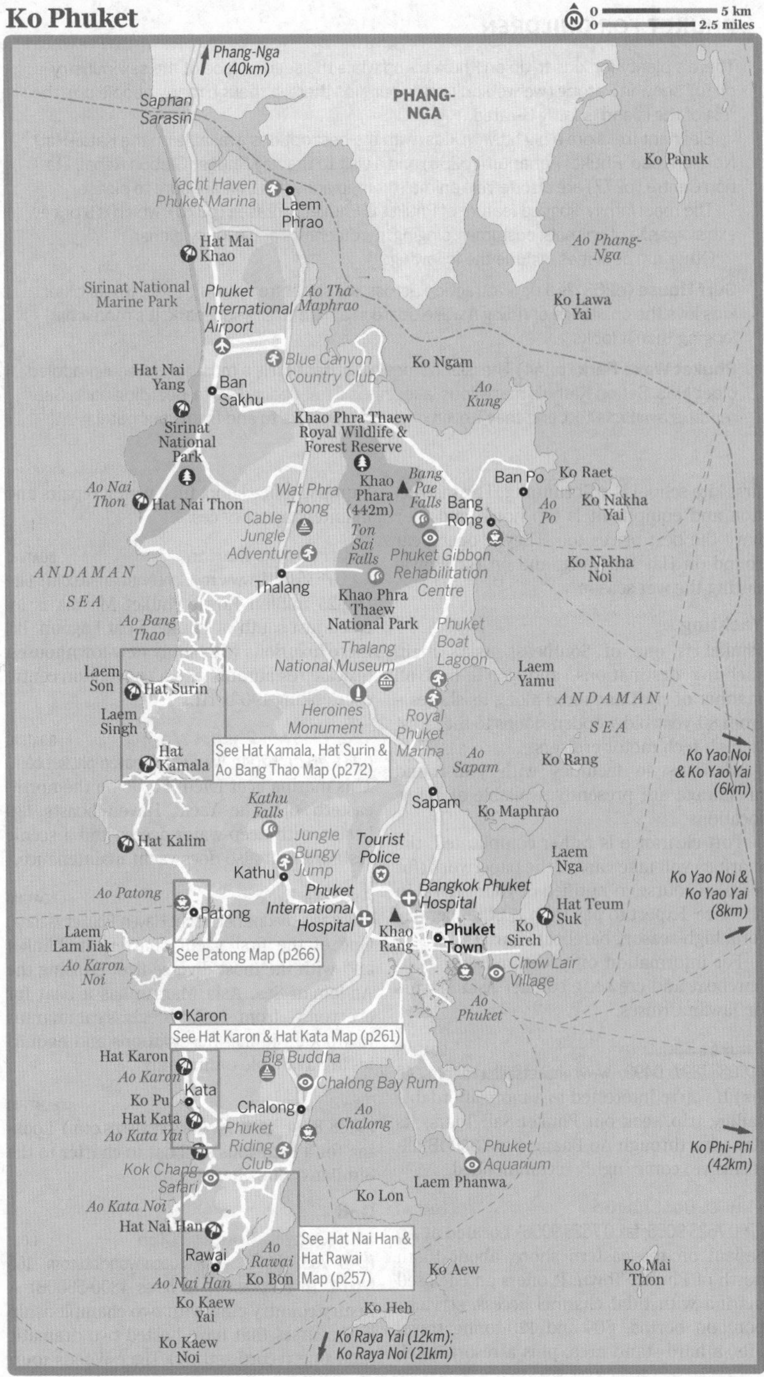
0 5 km
0 2.5 miles
Phang-Nga (40km)
PHANG-NGA
Saphan Sarasin
Ko Panuk
Yacht Haven Phuket Marina
Laem Phrao
Hat Mai Khao
Ao Phang-Nga
Sirinat National Marine Park
Phuket International Airport
Ao Tha Maphrao
Ko Lawa Yai
Blue Canyon Country Club
Ko Ngam
Hat Nai Yang
Ban Sakhu
Ao Kung
Sirinat National Park
Khao Phra Thaew Royal Wildlife & Forest Reserve
Ban Po
Ko Raet
Khao Phara (442m)
Bang Pae Falls
Bang Rong
Ao Po
Ko Nakha Yai
Ao Nai Thon
Hat Nai Thon
Wat Phra Thong
Cable Jungle Adventure
Ton Sai Falls
Phuket Gibbon Rehabilitation Centre
Ko Nakha Noi
ANDAMAN SEA
Thalang
Khao Phra Thaew National Park
Ao Bang Thao
Phuket Boat Lagoon
Thalang National Museum
Laem Son
Hat Surin
Laem Yamu
Heroines Monument
ANDAMAN SEA
Laem Singh
Royal Phuket Marina
Hat Kamala
See Hat Kamala, Hat Surin & Ao Bang Thao Map (p272)
Ao Sapam
Ko Rang
Ko Yao Noi & Ko Yao Yai (6km)
Sapam
Ko Maphrao
Kathu Falls
Hat Kalim
Jungle Bungy Jump
Tourist Police
Laem Nga
Kathu
Ko Yao Noi & Ko Yao Yai (8km)
Ao Patong
Phuket International Hospital
Bangkok Phuket Hospital
Patong
Hat Teum Suk
Laem Lam Jiak
Khao Rang
Phuket Town
Ko Sireh
See Patong Map (p266)
Ao Karon Noi
Chow Lair Village
Ao Phuket
Karon
See Hat Karon & Hat Kata Map (p261)
Hat Karon
Big Buddha
Ao Karon
Chalong Bay Rum
Kata
Ko Pu
Chalong
Ao Chalong
Hat Kata
Ao Kata Yai
Phuket Riding Club
Ko Phi-Phi (42km)
Phuket Aquarium
Kok Chang Safari
Laem Phanwa
Ko Lon
Ao Kata Noi
Hat Nai Han
See Hat Nai Han & Hat Rawai Map (p257)
Rawai
Ao Rawai
Ko Aew
Ko Mai Thon
Ao Nai Han
Ko Bon
Ko Kaew Yai
Ko Heh
Ko Kaew Noi
Ko Raya Yai (12km); Ko Raya Noi (21km)

PHUKET FOR CHILDREN

There's plenty for kids to do on Phuket. And while the seedier face of the sex industry is on full show in Patong (we wouldn't bring our kids there, although many people do), the rest of the island is fairly G-rated.

Elephant treks are a big hit with kids, with the best options available on the Kata–Hat Nai Han road. Phuket Aquarium (p256) and a visit to the tiny Phuket Gibbon Rehabilitation Centre (p277) are also terrific animal-themed activities that are sure to please.

The main family-flogged feature of Phuket is Phuket Fantasea (p270), which is a pricey extravaganza of animals, costumes, singing, pyrotechnics and a lousy dinner.

Other fun activities include the following:

Surf House (p263) is a new attraction across the street from Kata beach, where older kids love the challenge of riding a wake board in a man-made surf park. It's more challenging than it looks.

Phuket Wake Park (p244) The island's newest attraction is a must for adrenalin-addled older kids. Set on Kathu's marvelous lake, this is a full-fledged wake-boarding park. Gear rental is available too, and they'll even organise transfers to and from your hotel.

first kite school is still running. The instruction and equipment is top notch and they have the best prices too. They're open year round on Hat Nai Yang, and on Hat Rawai during the wet season.

Yachting

Phuket is one of Southeast Asia's main yachting destinations, and you'll find all manner of craft anchored along its shores – from 80-year-old wooden sloops to the latest in high-tech motor cruisers.

Marina-style facilities with year-round anchorage are presently available at a few locations.

Port clearance is rather complicated; the marinas will take care of the paperwork (for a fee, of course) if notified of your arrival in advance. Expect to pay from 17,000B per day for a high-season, bareboat charter.

For information on yacht charters (both bareboat and crewed), contact Asia Marine or Tawan Cruises.

Phuket Sail Tours BOATING
(☎08 7897 0492; www.phuketsailtours.com; Ao Por) If you're interested in a more affordable sailing trip, seek out Phuket Sail Tours. Its day trips through Ao Phang-Nga (3500B all-inclusive) come highly recommended.

Phuket Boat Lagoon BOATING
(☎0 7623 9055; fax 0 7623 9056) Located at Ao Sapam on the eastern shore, about 10km north of Phuket Town. It offers an enclosed marina with tidal channel access, serviced pontoon berths, 60- and 120-tonne travel lifts, a hard-stand area, plus a resort hotel, laundry, coffee shop, fuel, water, repairs and maintenance services.

Royal Phuket Marina BOATING
(☎0 7636 0811; www.royalphuketmarina.com) The US$25 million Royal Phuket Marina is located just south of Phuket Boat Lagoon. It's more luxurious with shiny new townhouses, upscale restaurants and a convention centre overlooking 190 berths.

Yacht Haven Phuket Marina BOATING
(☎0 7620 6704; www.yacht-haven-phuket.com) This marina is at Laem Phrao on the northeastern tip. The Yacht Haven boasts 130 berths with deep-water access and a scenic restaurant. It also does yacht maintenance.

Asia Marine BOATING
(www.asia-marine.net; Yacht Haven Phuket Marina) One of the first yacht charters in Phuket and with the most diverse fleet cruising the Andaman Sea, Asia Marine has a boat for everyone – from sleek fibreglass catamarans to wooden junks. Reservations and enquiries are available online only.

Tawan Cruises BOATING
(☎08 8194 3234; www.tawancruises.com) Looking for a luxurious sailboat to charter to the Similans? Start here.

Golf

Blue Canyon Country Club GOLF
(☎0 7632 8088; www.bluecanyonclub.com; 165 Moo 1, Th Thepkasatri; 18 holes 4800-5600B) A luxury country club with two championship golf courses that have hosted two dramatic (and one record-setting) Tiger Woods tour-

nament wins. There is also a full-service spa, two restaurants and luxury apartments on the property. The facilities are showing their age, but you'll come for the golf course.

Red Mountain GOLF
(☎0 7632 2000; www.redmountainphuket.com; 119 Moo 4, Th Vichitsongkram; 18 holes 5700B) The most popular course at research time was cut into the red soil of Kathu's steep mountains back in 2007.

Courses

★Suay Cooking School COOKING
(Map p250; ☎08 1797 4135; www.suayrestaurant.com; 50/2 Th Takuapa; per person 1800B) Learn from one of the best chefs on the island. Noy Tammasak will lead you through the local market and teach you how to make three dishes, before opening a bottle of wine for you to enjoy with your culinary creations. Highly recommended.

Mom Tri's Boathouse COOKING
(Map p261; ☎0 7633 0015; www.boathousephuket.com; 2/2 Th Kata, Patak West, Hat Kata) Offers a fantastic weekend Thai cooking class (per person one/two days 2200/3500B) with its renowned chef.

Blue Elephant Restaurant & Cookery School COOKING
(Map p250; ☎0 7635 4355; www.blueelephant.com; 96 Th Krabi, Phuket Town; half-day class 2800B) Phuket's newest culinary school is in the stunningly restored 1903 Sino-Portuguese–style Phra Phitak Chyn Pracha Mansion. There are a variety of options from short group lessons to five-day private training (78,000B). Morning classes include a market visit.

Phuket Thai Cookery School COOKING
(☎0 7625 2354; www.phuketthaicookeryschool.com; Ko Sireh; courses per day from 2900B; ⏱8.30am-5pm) Get intimate with aromatic Thai spices at this popular cooking school set on a quiet seafront plot on Ko Sireh's east coast. Courses can last up to six hours. It provides hotel pick-ups, market tours and a cookbook.

Pum Thai Cooking School COOKING
(Map p266; ☎0 7634 6269; www.pumthaifoodchain.com; 204/32 Th Rat Uthit, Patong; classes 500-7500B) This restaurant chain (with three locations in Thailand, two in France and one in the UK) holds several daily one-dish (30 minutes) to six-hour classes. Longer classes begin with a kitchen and pantry tour and end with a meal and three take-home cookbooks.

Tours

It's not hard to find elephant rides and 4WD tours of the island's interior, though none of these will win their way into the hearts of animal-rights activists or environmentalists. So why not take a bike ride?

Amazing Bike Tours CYCLING
(☎0 7628 3436; www.amazingbiketoursthailand.asia; 32/4 Moo 9, Th Chaofa, Chalong; day trips adult/child from 1600/1400B) Phuket's best adventure outfitter, Amazing Bike Tours leads small groups on half-day bicycle tours through the Khao Phra Thaew Royal Wildlife & Forest Reserve, and offers terrific day trips around Ko Yao Noi and the gorgeous beaches and waterfalls of Thai Muang in nearby Phang-Nga province. It also has unforgettable three-day packages to Krabi and luscious Khao Sok.

Information

DANGERS & ANNOYANCES

During the May to October monsoon, large waves and fierce undertows sometimes make it too dangerous to swim. Dozens of drownings occur every year on Phuket's beaches, especially on Laem Singh, Kamala and Karon. Red flags are posted to warn bathers of serious riptides.

Keep an eye out for jet skis when you are in the water. Although the Phuket governor declared jet skis illegal in 1997, enforcement of the ban is another issue. Long-tails can be hazardous too. Do not expect the boat to see you!

Renting a motorcycle or motorbike can be a high-risk proposition. Thousands of people are injured or killed every year on Phuket's highways. If you must rent one, make sure you at least know the basics and wear a helmet.

There have been late-night motorbike muggings and stabbings on the road leading from Patong to Hat Karon, and on the road between Kata and the Rawai–Hat Nai Han area. Random sexual assaults on women can happen as well. Women should think twice before sunbathing topless (a big no-no in Thailand anyway) or alone, especially on an isolated beach. It can also be dangerous to run alone at night or early in the morning.

MEDICAL SERVICES

Local hospitals are equipped with modern facilities, emergency rooms and outpatient-care clinics. Both Bangkok Phuket Hospital and Phuket International Hospital have hyperbaric chambers.

Bangkok Phuket Hospital (☎0 7625 4425; www.phukethospital.com; Th Yongyok Uthit) Reputedly the favourite with locals.

Phuket International Hospital (☎0 7624 9400; www.phuketinternationalhospital.com; Th Chalermprakiat) International doctors rate this hospital as the best on the island.

TOURIST INFORMATION

The weekly English-language *Phuket Gazette* (www.phuketgazette.net) publishes information on activities, events, dining and entertainment around the island, as well as the latest scandals. *Phuket Wan* (www.phuketwan.com) is frequently juicier – and more newsworthy.

WEBSITES

Jamie's Phuket (www.jamie-monk.com) A fun insider's blog written by a long-time Phuket expat resident with excellent photos and travel tips.

One Stop Phuket (www.1stopphuket.com) A user-friendly travel guide and internet booking referral service.

Phuket Dot Com (www.phuket.com) Offers a sophisticated compendium of many kinds of information, including accommodation on the island.

ℹ Getting There & Away

AIR

Phuket International Airport (p420) is 30km northwest of Phuket Town; it takes around 45 minutes to an hour to reach the southern beaches from here. Several international airlines fly to Phuket and have offices in Phuket Town, including **Malaysia Airlines** (☎0 7621 6675; www.malaysiaairlines.com; 1/8-9 Th Thungkha, Phuket Town) and **Silk Air** (Map p250; ☎0 7621 3891; www.silkair.com; 183/103 Th Phang-Nga, Phuket Town).

For domestic flights, **Bangkok Airways** (☎0 7622 5033; www.bangkokair.com; 58/2-3 Th Yaowarat, Phuket Town) and **THAI** (Map p250; ☎0 7621 1195; www.thaiairways.com; 78/1 Th Ranong, Phuket Town) have offices in Phuket Town.

FERRY & SPEEDBOAT

Phuket's Tha Rasada, southeast of Phuket Town, is the main pier for boats to Ko Phi-Phi, connecting onward to Krabi, Ko Lanta, the Trang Islands, Ko Lipe and even as far as Langkawi Island in Malaysia (where there are further ferry connections to Penang). For additional services to Krabi and Ao Nang via the Ko Yao Islands, boats leave from Tha Bang Rong north of Tha Rasada.

MINIVAN

Phuket travel agencies all around the island sell tickets (including ferry fare) for air-con minivans down to Ko Samui and Ko Pha-Ngan. Air-con minivan services to Krabi, Ranong, Trang, Surat Thani and several other locations are also available. Prices are slightly more than the buses, which all stop in Phuket Town.

ℹ Getting Around

Local Phuket transport is terrible. The systems in place make tourists either stay on their chosen beach, rent a car or motorbike (which can be hazardous) or take overpriced private car 'taxis' or túk-túk (pronounced *đúk đúk*). There are *sŏrng·tăa·ou* (passenger pick-up trucks) which run to the beaches from Phuket Town, but often you'll have to go via Phuket Town to get from one beach to another (say Hat Surin to Hat Patong), which can take hours.

That said, when it comes to transport to and from the airport, the stranglehold local drivers have enjoyed may be coming to an end. At research time, Phuket authorities had evicted the legions of drivers who used to gather at the

FLIGHTS TO/FROM PHUKET

DESTINATION	AIRLINE	FREQUENCY	PRICE
Bangkok	Air Asia	several daily	around 1480B
Bangkok	Bangkok Airways	daily	1725B
Bangkok	Nok Air	3-4 daily	1488B
Bangkok	THAI	7 daily	3000B
Chiang Mai	Air Asia	2 daily	1600B
Hong Kong	Air Asia	daily	5000-10,740B
Jakarta	Air Asia	Sun, Wed, Fri	from 2730B
Ko Samui	Bangkok Airways	daily	2380B
Kuala Lumpur	Air Asia	4 daily	1712B
Seoul	Korean Air	daily	roundtrip US$660
Singapore	Air Asia	daily	1400B

doors to baggage claim and haggle and tug for passengers. Now, just seven drivers, of metered taxis only, will be allowed in at any one time, making for a far more soothing first step on the island.

BUS

You'll find the bus terminal (Map p250; ☎ 0 7621 1977; Th Thepkrasattri) just to the east of central Phuket Town, within walking distance of the many hotels. Services from here are listed in the following table.

DESTINATION	BUS TYPE	FARE (B)	DURATION (HR)
Bangkok	2nd class	543	15
Bangkok	air-con	680	13-14
Bangkok	VIP	1058	13
Hat Yai	air-con	556	6-7
Ko Samui	air-con	430	8 (bus/boat)
Krabi	air-con	150	3½
Phang-Nga	ordinary	90	2½
Ranong	ordinary	209	6
Ranong	air-con	270	5
Surat Thani	ordinary	195	6
Surat Thani	air-con	220	5
Trang	air-con	240	5

Phuket Town เมืองภูเก็ต

POP 94,325

Long before tourist T-shirts or flip-flops, Phuket was an island of rubber trees, tin mines and cash-hungry merchants. Attracting entrepreneurs from as far away as the Arabian Peninsula, China, India and Portugal, Phuket Town was a colourful blend of cultural influences, cobbled together by tentative compromise and cooperation. Today the city is proof of the island's historical soul. Wander down streets clogged with Sino-Portuguese architecture housing arty coffee shops, galleries, wonderful inexpensive restaurants and hip little guesthouses; peek down alleyways to find Chinese Taoist shrines shrouded in incense smoke.

But it's not just some lost-in-time cultural archive. Bubbling up throughout the emerging Old Town is an infusion of current art, music and food that attracts a very hip crowd, most of it Thai. Investors have finally caught on that culture, not just slinky beaches and girly bars, is a commodity. Old shophouses and homes, once left to rot, are being bought up and restored, resulting in flash-forward gentrification.

Despite inflated real estate prices, if you're on a budget, Phuket Town has the best lodging bargains on the island. From here you can hop on regular *sŏrng·tăa·ou* to any of Phuket's beaches (which will take between 30 minutes and 1½ hours).

Sights & Activities

Sino-Portuguese Architecture ARCHITECTURE

Stroll along Thanons Thalang, Dibuk, Yaowarat, Ranong, Phang-Nga, Rasada and Krabi for a glimpse of some of the best architecture on offer. Soi Romanee off of Th Thalang is the most ambient area of town. The most magnificent examples of buildings are the **Standard Chartered Bank** (Map p250; Th Phang-Nga), Thailand's oldest foreign bank; the **THAI office** (Map p250; Th Ranong); and the **old post office building** (Map p250), which now houses the **Phuket Philatelic Museum** (Map p250; Th Montri; 9.30am-5.30pm) FREE, a first stop for stamp boffins.

The best-restored residential properties are found along Th Dibuk and Th Thalang. The fabulous Phra Phitak Chyn Pracha Mansion has been restored and turned into a branch of the upscale Blue Elephant restaurant chain and culinary school.

Khao Rang VIEWPOINT

(เขารัง; Phuket Hill) For a bird's-eye view of the city, climb (or drive) up Khao Rang, northwest of the town centre. It's at its best during the week, when the summit is relatively peaceful, but keep an eye out for the mobs of snarling dogs. If Phuket is indeed a corruption of the Malay word *bukit* (hill), then this is probably its namesake.

Phuket Thaihua Museum MUSEUM

(พิพิธภัณฑ์ภูเก็ตไทยหัว; Map p250; 28 Th Krabi; admission 200B; 9am-5pm) This museum, formerly a Chinese language school, is filled with photos and exhibits of Phuket's history. There's also an overview of the building's history, which is a stunning combination of Chinese and European architectural styles, including Art Deco, Palladianism and a Chinese gable roof and stucco.

Festivals & Events

Vegetarian Festival FESTIVAL

The Vegetarian Festival is Phuket's most important event and usually takes place during late September or October. If you plan to attend the street processions, consider bringing

Phuket Town

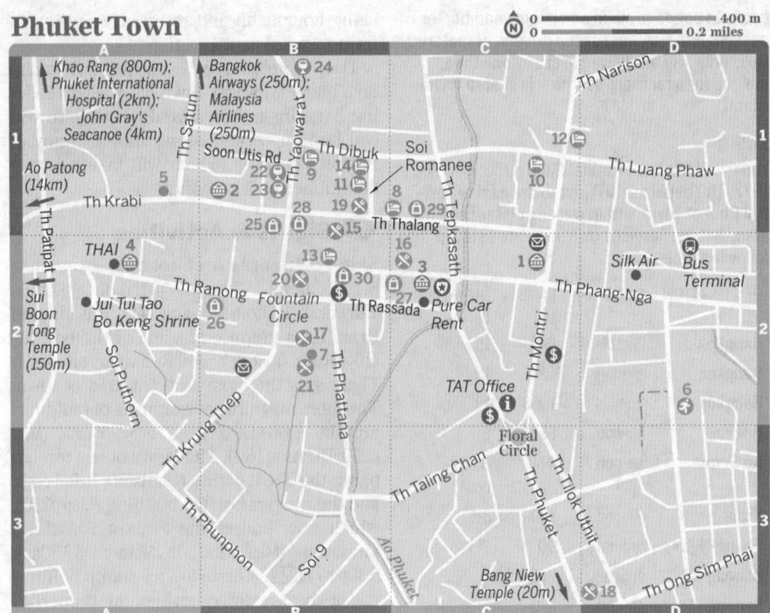

earplugs to shield your eardrums from the never-ending firecracker explosions.

Sleeping

The cheapest place on the island to get some zzz's, Phuket Town is a treasure trove of budget lodging. Head out to the beaches for more midrange and top-end options.

Al Phuket Hostel HOSTEL $

(Map p250; ☎0 7621 2881; www.aiphukethostel.com; 88 Th Yaowarat; dm 299B, d 699B; ❄@📶) Double rooms are spacious with wood floors, greenhouse windows and funky papered ceilings. Dorms are bright and clean and sleep eight. All share polished concrete baths and a cramped downstairs lounge for movies and hang time.

Phuket 346 GUESTHOUSE $

(Map p250; ☎08 0146 2800; www.phuket346.com; 15 Soi Romanee; r with fan/air-con from 400/800B; ❄📶) On charming Soi Romanee, this romantic old shophouse has been exquisitely restored to look like a cosy art gallery. Rooms have white patterned wallpaper, brightly coloured walls and modern art. Downstairs are fish ponds and a street-side cafe playing sultry jazz tunes.

★ **The Romanee** GUESTHOUSE $$

(Map p250; ☎08 9728 9871; Th Romanee; r standard/deluxe 890/1090B; ❄📶) They call themselves a boutique guesthouse, and it certainly has style with its polished concrete floors and wood block reception bar. Rooms likewise have an airy modern feel with wood floors, flat screens, pastel accent walls, fine linens and tasteful lighting. Deluxe rooms are huge and worth the extra coin.

The Memory at On On Hotel HOTEL $$

(Map p250; ☎0 7621 6161; www.thememoryhotel.com; 19 Th Phang-Nga; dm 400B, r 1600B; P❄📶) This longtime bare-bones classic snapped up a cameo in *The Beach* (2000), playing a shitty backpacker dive. And that's what it was until a recent refurbish put the antiquated shine on Phuket's first hotel. Private rooms have concrete floors, rain showers, flat screens and gorgeous shutters. Though some smell musty.

Dorms are even better, thanks to wood floors, old-school office desks, draped bunks and a fantastic lounge area, kitchen and laundry facilities.

99 Old Town Boutique Guesthouse GUESTHOUSE $$

(Map p250; ☎08 1693 2423, 0 7622 3800; 99oldtown@hotmail.co.th; 99 Th Thalang; s/d from

Phuket Town

650/790B;) Another shophouse-turned-B&B that's unpretentious at first glance but has surprisingly sumptuous rooms with four-poster beds and large attached polished cement bathrooms. It's run by a lovely family, and a fountain gurgles in the communal back courtyard.

Baan Suwantawe HOTEL $$
(Map p250; 0 7621 2879; www.baansuwantawe.co.th; 1/10 Th Dibuk; r from 1200B;) With Zen art, hardwood floors, good-sized bathrooms and comfy lounge areas, these studio-style rooms are a steal. Higher-priced rooms have terraces overlooking the blue-tiled pool and lily pond, and the whole place smells like lemongrass.

Sino House HOTEL $$$
(Map p250; 0 7623 2494; www.sinohousephuket.com; 1 Th Montri; r from 1600B;) Shanghai style meets *Mad Men* chic at this impressive Old Town offering. Rooms are massive with mod furnishings, fantastic handmade ceramic basins and quarter-moon shower tubs in the bathrooms. There's an on-site **Raintree Spa** (Map p250; 08 1892 1001; www.theraintreespa.com; Th Yaowarat; massages 500-1000B; 10am-9.30pm) and long-term rates are available.

Eating

There's good food in Phuket Town, and meals here cost a lot less than those at the beach.

Kopitiam by Wilai THAI $
(Map p250; 08 3606 9776; www.facebook.com/kopitiambywilai; 18 Th Thalang; mains 70-120B; 11am-10pm Mon-Sat;) Phuket soul food. It does Phuketian *pàt tai* with some kick to it, and a fantastic *mee sua:* think noodles sautéed with egg, greens, prawns, chunks of sea bass, and squid. Wash it down with fresh chrysanthemum juice.

Noodle Soup THAI $
(Map p250; cnr Th Romanee & Th Thalang; dishes 20-50B; 10am-6pm) A funky little street stall set up under a shade structure on a vacant street corner lot. It does simple Thai dishes and a range of noodle soups for locals. Super cheap.

Cook INTERNATIONAL-THAI $
(Map p250; 0 7625 8375; 101 Th Phang-Nga; pasta dishes 90-160B, pizzas 160-240B) The Thai owner-chef used to cook Italian at a mega-resort, so when he opened this ludicrously inexpensive Old Town cafe he fused the two cultures. Order the sensational green curry pizza with chicken or the pork curry coconut milk pizza, and fall in love.

DON'T MISS

VEGETARIAN FESTIVAL

Loud popping sounds similar to machine-gun fire fill the streets, the air is nearly opaque with grey-brown smoke and men and women traipse along blocked-off city roads, their cheeks pierced with skewers and knives or, more surprisingly, lamps and tree branches. Some of the flock have blood streaming down their fronts or open lashes across their backs. No this isn't a war zone, this is the Vegetarian Festival (p249), one of Phuket's most important festivals, centred in Phuket Town.

The festival, which takes place during the first nine days of the ninth lunar month of the Chinese calendar – usually late September or October – celebrates the beginning of 'Taoist Lent', when devout Chinese abstain from eating meat. But more obvious to outsiders are the daily processions winding their way through town with floats of ornately dressed children and ladyboys, near armies of flag-bearing colour-coordinated young people and, most noticeably, men and women engaged in outrageous acts of self-mortification. Shop owners along Phuket's central streets set up altars in front of their shopfronts offering nine tiny cups of tea, incense, fruit, firecrackers, candles and flowers to the nine emperor gods invoked by the festival.

Those participating as mediums bring the nine deities to earth by entering into a trance state, piercing their cheeks with an impressive variety of objects, sawing their tongues or flagellating themselves with spiky metal balls. Whatever form the self-flagellation takes, the mediums (primarily men) walk in procession, stopping at shopfront altars where they pick up the offered fruit. They also drink one of the nine cups of tea, grab flowers to stick in their waistbands or set strings of firecrackers alight. The shop owners and their families stand by with their palms together in a *wâi* gesture out of respect for these mediums who are temporarily possessed by deities. Surreal hardly describes it.

In Phuket Town, the festival activities are centred around five Chinese temples, with the **Jui Tui** temple on Th Ranong the most important, followed by **Bang Niew** and **Sui Boon Tong** temples. There are also events at temples in the nearby towns of Kathu (where the festival originated) and Ban Tha Reua. If you stop by the procession's starting point early enough in the morning, you may see a surprisingly professional, latex-glove-clad crew piercing the devotees' cheeks – not for the faint-hearted. Other ceremonies occur throughout the festival at the temples and can include firewalking and knife-ladder climbing. Beyond the headlining gore, fabulous vegetarian food stalls line the side streets offering a perfect opportunity to sample cheap local treats and strike up interesting conversations with the locals.

The TAT office in Phuket prints a helpful schedule of events for the Vegetarian Festival each year. The festival also takes place in Trang, Krabi and other southern Thai towns.

Oddly enough, there is no record of these sorts of acts of devotion associated with Taoist Lent in China. The local Chinese claim the festival was started by a theatre troupe from China that stopped off in nearby Kathu around 150 years ago. The story goes that the troupe was struck seriously ill because the members had failed to propitiate the nine emperor gods of Taoism. The nine-day penance they performed included self-piercing, meditation and a strict vegetarian diet.

For more info, visit www.phuketvegetarian.com.

★Suay INTERNATIONAL-THAI **$$**

(Map p250; ☎08 1797 4135; www.suayrestaurant.com; 50/2 Th Takuapa; dishes 90-350B; ⊙5-11pm) Fusion at this converted house just south of old town proper means salmon carpaccio piled with tart pomelo salad, an innovative take on *sôm·đam* featuring mangosteen that pops with flavour, yellowfin tuna *lâhp*, smoked eggplant served with roast chili paste and crab meat, and massaman curry with lamb chops.

But do not sleep on the mango with sticky rice. The rice is wrapped in a spring roll dough, fried and stuffed with mango. Plated with more mango, it's paired with black sesame ice cream that may have you hugging the chef with gratitude. We sure did. Tables are sprinkled inside the house and on the wrap-around porch. The wine list is proper, and the chef/owner also offers cooking classes.

China Inn INTERNATIONAL-THAI $$
(Map p250; ☎0 7635 6239; 20 Th Thalang; dishes 150-250B; ⊙11am-6pm Mon-Wed, to 10pm Thu-Sat; 🌿) The organic movement meets Phuket cuisine at this turn-of-the-20th-century shop-house. There's red curry with crab, grilled duck breast salad, a host of veggie options, homemade yoghurt and fruit smoothies flavoured with organic honey.

★**Siam Indigo** INTERNATIONAL-THAI $$
(Map p250; ☎0 7625 6697; www.siamindigo.com; 8 Th Phang-Nga; dishes 120-280B; ⊙2-11pm) One of Phuket's most stylish gems is set in an 80-year-old Sino-Portuguese relic and specialises in Thai cuisine – including classic recipes rarely seen these days, with a French-international twist. Meals are plated on gorgeous china, the room itself is glorious and the food is exceptional.

La Gaetana INTERNATIONAL $$$
(Map p250; ☎0 7625 0523; 352 Th Phuket; dishes 200-450B; ⊙noon-2pm Mon-Fri & 6-10pm Tue-Sun) An irresistibly intimate five-table restaurant, La Gaetana has black concrete floors, colourful walls and stemware, an open kitchen in the courtyard, and a superb Italian menu. Think duck breast carpaccio followed by osso bucco.

Ka Jok See THAI, INTERNATIONAL $$$
(Map p250; ☎0 7621 7903; kajoksee@hotmail.com; 26 Th Takua Pa; dishes 180-480B; ⊙6.30pm-late Tue-Sat) Dining here is reason enough to come to town. Dripping Old Phuket charm and creaking under the weight of the owner's fabulous trinket collection, this atmospheric little eatery offers great food, top-notch music and – if you're lucky – some sensationally camp cabaret.

Drinking & Nightlife

This is where you can party like a local. Bars buzz until late, patronised almost exclusively by Thais and local expats. If you're tired of the sleazy, resort party scene, the vibe here will feel like a fresh ocean breeze, even if it is another sweaty, windless night in Old Town.

★**Sanaeha** BAR
(Map p250; ☎08 1519 8937; 83, 85 Th Yaowarat, Phuket Town; ⊙6pm-late) Sanaeha is an upscale bohemian joint lit by seashell chandeliers, with plenty of dark corners where you can sip, snuggle, snack and dig that soulful crooner on stage.

Juice Raw JUICE
(Map p250; 91 Th Yaowarat; ⊙10am-9pm) A new and ambitious cafe serving fresh-pressed hangover tonics, tomato-, cucumber- or pomelo-based detox drinks and some outrageous smoothies. The J Passion is a blend of passion fruit, dates, orange, ginger and banana. Carrot Lava blends carrot, pineapple, ginger and almond milk. You can also customise your juice. As if you could do better.

Chino Cafe CAFE
(Map p250; ☎08 1979 6190; www.facebook.com/chinocafegallery; 4 Th Thalang; ⊙8:30am-8:30pm) A fun new cafe with a green ethos. In addition to the teas and good coffee, there's an art and gift gallery, small boxes of Phuket Town's famous cookies and nice offering of breakfast plates and Thai dishes (70-170B).

WORTH A TRIP

PHUKET'S CULINARY SPY

With the improvisational soul of a skater, Phuket's next great chef, Noy Tammasak, was born in Hat Yai but moved to Germany when he was 15, and that's where he came of age. After graduating from culinary school in Stuttgart, where he was trained in the classic European style, he was hired at the JW Marriott in Phuket and he returned to his homeland. At the time, he couldn't make a *pàt tai* to save his, yours or anyone else's life.

So off he went to Chiang Mai, Isan, as well as points south and west. He spied on village kitchens, was taught regional recipes and when he returned to the resort, he created an unforgettable Thai fusion menu, with an emphasis on seasonal and local ingredients, which you can enjoy at Suay, his own Phuket Town restaurant which he opened in 2010. His spaghetti carbonara comes with Isan spiced pork meatballs, lâhp is wrapped in spring-roll wrappers and flash fried, *sôm·đam* is made with mangosteen instead of green papaya, and braised rack of lamb is used in massaman curry. The dining experience is an absolute must, and he also offers one of the most laid-back, soulful and fun cooking school experiences in Thailand.

PHUKET'S MOO·AY TAI EXPLOSION

Over the past few years, spurred in no small part by the increasing global presence and popularity of mixed martial arts, several *moo·ay tai* (Thai boxing; also spelled *muay thai*) gyms catering to international male and female athletes have sprouted off the beach in Phuket. Based on the original *moo·ay tai* camp concept, fighters live and train on site with seasoned *moo·ay tai* professionals.

The whole thing started with Pricha 'Tuk' Chokkuea and his gym, Rawai Muay Thai, where he decided to train tourists as a fundraising mechanism so he could also train impoverished, up-and-coming Thai fighters, without dipping deeply into their fight purse (the traditional *moo·ay tai* business model, and something Tuk always resented). For years his was the only gym around. He's recently moved his operation to Khao Lak, but his gym still thrives as **Rawai Supa Muay Thai** (Map p257; ☎0 7668 1116; www.supamuaythai.com; 43/42 Moo 7, Th Sai Yuan; per session 300B, per week 3000B), one of a half dozen gyms in Rawai alone. The most popular gym in the area these days seems to be **Sinbi Muay Thai** (Map p257; ☎08 3391 5535; www.sinbi-muaythai.com; 100/15 Moo 7, Th Sai Yuan; per session 400B, per week 3000B). Wherever you enter the ring, be warned: this is no watered-down-for-Westerners theme-park ride. Prepare to sweat, cringe, grapple and bleed. And maybe, if you're the real deal, you'll win a fight under the Bang-la Stadium lights.

Timber Hut CLUB

(Map p250; ☎0 7621 1839; 118/1 Th Yaowarat, Phuket Town; ⊙6pm-2am) Thai and expat locals have been filling this old clubhouse every night for nearly 20 years. They gather at long wooden tables on two floors, converge around thick timber columns, swill whiskey, and sway to live bands that swing from hard rock to funk to hip-hop with aplomb. No cover charge.

Shopping

There are some fabulous bohemian-chic boutiques scattered throughout Old Town selling jewellery, women's fashions, fabrics and souvenirs, as well as a few whimsical art galleries.

★Drawing Room GALLERY

(Map p250; ☎08 6899 4888; isara380@gmail.com; 56 Th Phang Nga; ⊙9am-11pm) With a vibe reminiscent of pre-boom Brooklyn or East London, this wide open, almost reclaimed, co-operative is by far the most interesting gallery in a town full of them. Canvasses can be colourful abstract squiggles or dreamy pen and ink meanderings. A street art aesthetic pervades and house music thumps at low levels. Find it.

Ranida GALLERY

(Map p250; 119 Th Thalang; ⊙10am-6pm) An exquisite antique gallery featuring antiquated Buddha statues and sculpture, organic textiles and interesting fashions inspired by vintage Thai garments and fabrics. The clothing is striking and ambitious, and on the right woman it can be a tasteful high-fashion statement.

Ban Boran Textiles TEXTILES

(Map p250; ☎0 7621 1563; 51 Th Yaowarat; ⊙10.30am-6.30pm Mon-Fri) Simply put, this dusty hole-in-the-wall is the best shop on the island for silk, raw silk, cotton textiles and sarongs.

Oldest Herbs Shop HERBS

(Map p250; Th Thalang; ⊙7am-8pm) This concrete-floored dusty cubby hole has traded Chinese herbs since forever, and pulls you in with its aromas wafting from twigs, seeds, and earthy potions that promise health, wellness and, ahem, potency.

Day Market MARKET

(Map p250; Th Ranong; ⊙7am-3pm) This market near the town centre traces its history back to the days when pirates, Indians, Chinese, Malays and Europeans traded in Phuket. You might still find some fabrics from Southeast Asia, though it mostly sells food now.

Southwind Books BOOKSTORE

(Map p250; ☎08 9724 2136; 1/2/5 Th Phang-Nga; ⊙9am-7pm Mon-Sat, 10am-3pm Sun) Peruse the dusty secondhand stacks for titles in 18 languages, including Polish.

Information

There are numerous internet cafes and ATMs around Th Phuket, Th Ranong, Th Montri and Th Phang-Nga.

Main Post Office (Map p250; Th Montri; ⌚8.30am-4pm Mon-Fri, 9am-noon Sat)

Police (Map p250; ☎0 7622 3555, 191; cnr Th Phang-Nga & Th Phuket)

TAT Office (Map p250; ☎0 7621 23213; www.tourismthailand.org/Phuket; 191 Th Thalang; ⌚8.30am-4.30pm) Has maps, loads of brochures and info on boat trips to Ko Phi-Phi and the islands.

Getting There & Around

TO/FROM THE AIRPORT

Despite what airport taxi touts would like you to believe, a bright orange **government airport bus** (☎0 7623 2371; www.airportbusphuket.com; tickets 90B) runs between the airport and Phuket Town (45 minutes) via the Heroines Monument about every hour between 6am and 7pm. There's also a minibus service at the airport that will take you into Phuket Town for 150B per person; Patong, Kata and Karon beaches cost 180B if there are enough passengers. Chartered cars between the airport and Phuket Town cost 500B; between the airport and beaches is 700B to 1000B. Metered taxis should cost no more than 550B (including airport tax) to anywhere around the island.

BUS

The bus terminal (p249) is east of the town centre. For bus routes, see p249.

CAR

There are cheap car-rental agencies on Th Rasada near **Pure Car Rent** (Map p250; ☎0 7621 1002; www.purecarrent.com; 75 Th Rasada), a good choice in the centre of town. Suzuki jeeps go for about 1200B per day (including insurance), though in the low season the rates can go down to 750B. And if you rent for a week or more, you should get a discount.

The rates are always better at local places than at the better-known internationals, though you may be able to get deals with the familiar companies if you reserve in advance.

MOTORCYCLE

You can rent motorcycles on Th Rasada near Pure Car Rent, or from various places at the beaches. Costs are anywhere from 200B to 300B per day, and can vary depending on the season. Bigger bikes (over 125cc) can be rented at shops in Patong, Kata, Rawai and Karon.

SŎRNG·TĂA·OU & TÚK-TÚK

Large bus-sized *sŏrng·tăa·ou* run regularly from Th Ranong near the market to the various Phuket beaches (25B to 40B per person). These run from around 7am to 5pm; outside these times you have to charter a túk-túk to the beaches, which will set you back 500B (to Patong, Kata and Rawai) or 600B (to Karon and Kamala). You'll have to bargain. Beware of tales about the tourist office being 5km away, or that the only way to reach the beaches is by taxi, or even that you'll need a taxi to get from the bus terminal to the town centre (it is more or less in the town centre). For a ride around town, túk-túk drivers should charge 100B to 200B.

Motorcycle taxis around town cost 30B.

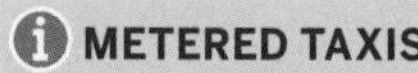

METERED TAXIS

To escape Phuket's 'taxi mafia' (an organisation of overpriced chartered cars that are often the only means of transport in the beach areas), get the phone number of a metered taxi and use the same driver throughout your stay in Phuket. The easiest way to do this is to take a metered taxi from the airport (one of the only places where you'll find them) when you arrive, then take down your driver's phone number. Metered taxis are found about 50m to the right as you exit the arrivals hall.

Ko Sireh เกาะสิเหร่

This tiny island, 4km east of the district capital and connected to the main island by a bridge, is known for its *chow lair* (sea gypsies; also spelled *chao leh*) village and a hilltop reclining Buddha at **Wat Sireh**.

The largest settlement of *chow lair* in Thailand is little more than a poverty-stricken cluster of tin shacks on stilts, plus one seafood restaurant. The Urak Lawoi, the most sedentary of the three *chow lair* groups, are found only between the Mergui archipelago and the Tarutao-Langkawi archipelago, and speak a mixture of Malay and Mon-Khmer.

A single road loops the island, passing a few residences, prawn farms, lots of rubber plantations and a bit of untouched forest. On the east coast there's a public beach called **Hat Teum Suk**, as well as a terrific cooking school on a quiet seafront plot, the Phuket Thai Cookery School (p247).

Laem Phanwa แหลมพันวา

Laem Phanwa is a wooded, elongated cape, jutting into the sea south of Phuket. Some say this is the last vestige of Phuket as it once was. It's an all-natural throwback and just 15 minutes from wonderful Phuket Town.

The biggest bloom of development can be found near the harbour at the cape's tip. That's where you'll find **Phuket Aquarium** (☎0 7639 1126; www.phuketaquarium.org; adult/child 100/50B; ⏰8.30am-4.30pm), which displays a varied collection of tropical fish and other marine life. The **seafood restaurants** along the Laem Phanwa waterfront are a great place to hang and watch the pleasure skiffs and painted fishing boats passing by.

On either side of the harbour, the beaches and coves remain rustic and protected by rocky headlands and mangroves. The sinuous coastal road is magic. If you just can't leave, check into the family-friendly **Panwha Beach Hotel** (☎0 7639 3300; www.marcopolohotels.com; 5/3 Moo 8, Ao Yon; r from 4000B; P❄📶🏊👪) on the east cape, for four-star setting and service at a three-star price tag. Or go with the adults-only boutique hotel **Cloud 19** (☎0 7620 0920; www.cloud19phuket.com; 30/10 Moo 8, Th Bor Rae-Ao Yon; r from 4150B; ❄📶🏊). For a splash of serious luxury above the main strip, find **Sri Panwha** (☎0 7637 1000; www.sripanwa.com; 88 Moo 8, Th Sakdidej; d from 14,280B; ❄📶🏊). This is as decadent as the cape gets.

To get to the cape, take Rte 4021 south and then turn down Rte 4023 just outside Phuket Town.

Rawai ราไวย์

Now this is a place to live, which is exactly why Phuket's rapidly developing south coast is teeming with retirees, Thai and expat entrepreneurs, and a service sector that, for the most part, moved here from somewhere else.

The region is not just defined by its beaches but also by the lush coastal hills that rise steeply and tumble into the Andaman Sea, forming **Laem Promthep**, Phuket's southernmost point. These hills are home to pocket neighbourhoods and cul-de-sacs that are knitted together by just a few roads – although more are being carved into the hills each year. Still, even with the growth you can feel nature, especially when you hit the beach.

Hat Nai Han, with its crescent of white sand backed by casuarinas, bobbing yachts, the seafront **Wat Nai Han** and a monsoon-season surf break, is the best beach in the area, but there are smaller, hidden beaches that are just as beautiful. **Hat Rawai** lacks Nai Han's good looks. It's just a rocky longtail and speedboat harbour, which makes it the perfect place to open up a seafood grill – and there is a string of them here. All are locally owned and serve equally delicious fare. This is where most of the luxury condo development seems to be proliferating. Sadly, you can almost envision the day when real-estate money will chase away all the seafood grills and tiki bars. Let's hope that's several decades off. Or at least one.

Sights

Chalong Bay Rum DISTILLERY
(☎09 3575 1119; www.chalongbayrum.com; 14/2 Moo 2, Soi Palai 2; ⏰tours 4-6pm Mon-Sat) FREE Nearby Chalong is home to Phuket's only working distillery, open for tours six days a week. You have to reserve ahead, mostly because you'll need directions as it can be hard to find. But upon arrival you'll be awarded a mojito, made with their delicious product and escorted on a delightful 30-minute tour. Then you'll get a refill.

Sleeping

Ao Sane Bungalows HOTEL $
(Map p257; ☎0 7628 8306; 11/2 Moo 1, Th Viset, Hat Nai Han; bungalows 600-1200B) Rickety cold-water, fan-cooled wooden bungalows sit on a secluded beach, with million-dollar views of Ao Sane and Ao Nai Han. There's a beachside restaurant, a dive centre and an old-hippy vibe.

Pineapple Apartments LODGE $$
(Map p257; ☎0 7661 3372; www.pineappleapartments.com; Th Viset; apt from 1500B; P❄📶) Freshly painted and serviced apartments in the rolling Rawai hills. It's one of several similar options in town, which tend to cater to visiting middle-aged men of a certain mindset. But the digs are comfortable, clean and a good value.

Vijitt HOTEL $$$
(Map p257; ☎0 7636 3600; www.vijittresort.com; 16 Moo 2, Th Viset; villas from 6700B; ❄) Arguably the area's most elegant property, Vijitt is sprinkled with deluxe villas that boast limestone floors, large bathtubs, outdoor showers and gorgeous sea views from private terraces. Its stunning, black-bottom infinity pool overlooks Friendship Beach. Their Sunday brunch is popular with local expats.

Royal Phuket Yacht Club HOTEL $$$
(Map p257; ☎0 7638 0200; www.royalphuketyachtclub.com; 23/3 Moo 1, Th Viset, Hat Nai Han;

Hat Nai Han & Hat Rawai

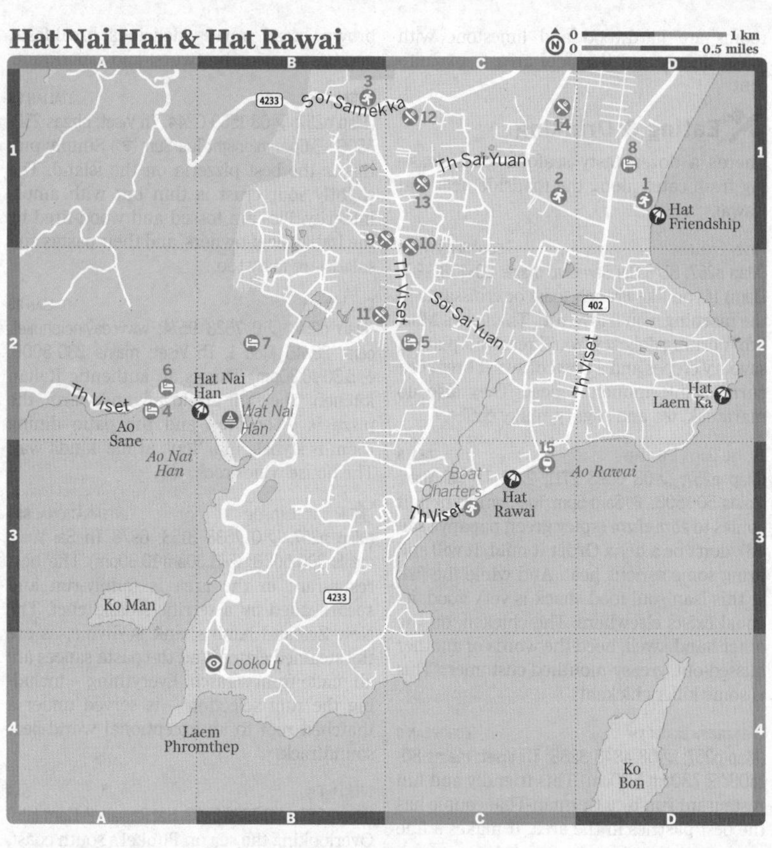

Hat Nai Han & Hat Rawai

Activities, Courses & Tours
1 Kite Zone D1
2 Rawai Supa Muay Thai C1
3 Sinbi Muay Thai B1

Sleeping
4 Ao Sane Bungalows A2
5 Pineapple Apartments C2
6 Royal Phuket Yacht Club A2
7 U Sunsuri B2
8 Vijitt D1

Eating
9 Da Vinci C1
10 German Bakery C1
11 MM's Pizzeria B2
12 Roti House C1
13 Rum Jungle C1
14 Som Tum Lanna C1

Drinking & Nightlife
15 Nikita's C3
Orange .... (see 10)

r from 6400B; ❄@🏊) Still a destination for many a transcontinental yachty, Royal Phuket Yacht Club has an air of old-world elegance, especially in its fabulous lobby-bar spinning with ceiling fans. Rooms feature large terraces – and stunning bay views – and there's every creature comfort you could imagine somewhere on site.

U Sunsuri RESORT **$$$**
(Map p257; ☎0 7633 6400; www.uhotelsresorts.com/usunsuriphuket; 11/5 Moo 1; d from 5500B; P❄@📶🏊👪) Rawai's newest luxe compound is made up of three vaguely modernist cubes swathed in earth tones and set on a ridge behind Nai Harn beach, which means ocean views from nearly every room. The

rooms are hardwood and limestone with plush linens, and the pool area is magnificent.

Eating & Drinking

There's a dozen tasty seafood grills roasting fresh catch along the roadside near Hat Rawai.

Roti House SOUTHERN THAI $

(Map p257; 81/6 Soi Sameka; mains 20-40B; 7-11am) If you like French toast or croissants in the morning, you'll love roti, Thailand's Muslim morning delicacy. You'll receive a plate of savoury crepes and a bowl of sweet breakfast curry. Dunk, munch, repeat. They also do martabak, tea and sugary, milky coffee.

Som Tum Lanna THAI $

(Map p257; 08 6593 2711; 2/16 Th Sai Yuan; mains 50-150B; 8am-5pm Tue-Sun) When it comes to *sôm·đam* (spicy green papapya salad), don't be a hero. Order it mild. It will still bring some serious heat. And while the fish at this Isan soul food shack is very good, its equal exists elsewhere. The chicken, on the other hand...well, heed the words of another blissed-out, greasy-mouthed customer: 'This is some killer chicken!'

German Bakery EUROPEAN $

(Map p257; 08 4843 3288; Th Viset; mains 80-180B; 7.30am-5.30pm) This friendly and fun restaurant run by a German-Thai couple has the best pastries in the area. It makes a fine brown bread, serves delicious breakfasts, and has amazing bratwurst and sauerkraut.

MM's Pizzeria ITALIAN $$

(Map p257; 08 1569 0244; Th Viset; pizzas 250-350B; 6pm-midnight Tue-Sun;) Simply put, this is the best pizzeria on the island. The slightly sour crust is thin but with ample integrity. Pies are tossed and wood-fired by the Italian chef-owners, and their pastas and salads are tasty too.

Da Vinci ITALIAN $$

(Map p257; 0 7628 9574; www.davinciphuket.com; 28/46 Moo 1, Th Viset; mains 230-800B; 5.30-10.30pm) This is an authentic Italian kitchen. The staff are lovely and warm, the pizza is wood-fired and the patio dining room is stylish, in a 'look at me' kinda way. The house wines rock, too.

★ **Rum Jungle** INTERNATIONAL $$$

(Map p257; 0 7638 8153; 69/8 Th Sai Yuan; meals 300-500B; 11.30am-10.30pm) The best restaurant in the area is family-run and spearheaded by a terrific Aussie chef. The New Zealand lamb shank is divine, as are the steamed clams, and the pasta sauces are all made from scratch. Everything – including the rum selection – is served under a thatched roof to an exceptional world-beat soundtrack.

Nikita's BAR

(Map p257; 0 7628 8703; Hat Rawai; 11am-late) Overlooking the sea on Phuket's south coast,

DON'T MISS

CHALONG BAY RUM: THE SPIRIT OF PHUKET

When a young couple, each born into a prestigious French wine family, met and fell in love, they bonded over booze. It wasn't the kind of booze coupling that involved indiscreet public nudity in spring break climes. Or maybe it was, we didn't ask. The point is, they both like to drink fine rum. Which is why they became master distillers and decided to launch their own distillery. But where?

They knew they wanted to make natural rum, rum in the French style, the kind they make in Martinique. Which meant they would be distilling sugarcane juice, rather than molasses. This is a departure from the norm as most rum is made from molasses, the industrial byproduct of sugar. As it happens, Thailand is the world's fourth-largest sugarcane producer with over 300 varieties currently in cultivation. They also noticed that nobody was distilling anything at all on Phuket. They saw an opportunity to incorporate one of the world's great islands into their brand. So they imported 40-year-old copper Armagnac stills to their land in Chalong, where they will soon be producing cane, and started bottling Chalong Bay Rum (p256). It's a new company and their rum is white, as they haven't begun ageing it just yet, but it has great flavour, took a silver medal at the Hong Kong International Wine & Spirits Competition, and it makes for a mean mojito. Which you'll be sipping as you tour their facility and learn way more about rum than you could ever imagine.

WORTH A TRIP

BIG BUDDHA

Set on a hilltop just northwest of Chalong circle and visible from almost half of land, the Big Buddha sits at the best viewpoint on Phuket. To get here you'll follow red signs from the main highway (Hwy 402) and wind up a country road, passing terraced banana groves and tangles of jungle. Once you're on top, pay your respects at the tented golden shrine, then step up to Big Buddha's glorious plateau where you can peer into Kata's perfect bay, glimpse the shimmering Karon strand and, on the other side, survey the serene Chalong harbour where the channel islands look like pebbles.

Construction began on Big Buddha in 2007, and he's dressed in Burmese alabaster, which isn't cheap. All in all, the price tag is north of 60 million baht, not that anybody minds. Over the last 20 years construction on Phuket hasn't stopped, so it means something when locals refer to the Big Buddha project as Phuket's most important development in the last 100 years.

Nikita's is a pleasant open-air hangout, with coffee, green tea and a nice selection of shakes and cocktails. If you're hungry you can order from the attached restaurant, Baan Rimlay (wood-fired pizzas from 200B).

Orange PUB
(Map p257; 41/7-8 Th Viset; ⏲5pm-2am; 📶) Billed as an Irish pub, though it doesn't look the part, this polished concrete block of a building offers a happening night scene thanks to its incredible house band imported from the Philippines. Fronted by a soulful diva, as beautiful as she is talented, they are a serious group and play anything and everything from Deep Purple to Beyoncé.

Getting There & Away

Rawai is about 18km from Phuket Town. *Sŏrng·tăa·ou* (30B) run from Phuket's fountain circle at Th Ranong – some continue to Hat Nai Han, but not all of them, so ask first. The túk-túk trip from Rawai to Nai Han is a hefty 200B.

You can hire taxis (which are actually just chartered cars) from Rawai and Hat Nai Han to the airport (800B), Patong (700B) and Phuket Town (500B).

Long-tail and speedboat charters are available from Hat Rawai. Destinations include Ko Bon (long-tail/speedboat 1000/2000B), Coral Island (long-tail/speedboat 1500/4000B) and Ko Kai (long-tail/speedboat 4000/9000B). Maximum six passengers.

Hat Kata หาดกะตะ

Kata attracts travellers of all ages with its shopping, surfing and lively beach, and without the seedy hustle endemic to Patong. While you might not find a secluded strip of sand, you will find lots to do and plenty of easy-going folks to clink beers with.

There's surfing in the shoulder and wet seasons, terrific day spas, fantastic food, and a top-notch yoga studio. The beach is divided in two by a rocky headland, and the road between them is home to Phuket's original millionaire's row. Hat Kata Yai is on the north end, while the more secluded Hat Kata Noi unfurls to the south. Both offer soft golden sand and attract a bohemian crowd.

The main commercial street of Th Thai Na is perpendicular to the shore and has most of its restaurants and shops, along with some cheaper places to stay.

Sights & Activities

The small island of **Ko Pu** is just offshore, but be careful of rip tides, heed the red flags and don't go past the breakers in the wet season unless you are a strong ocean swimmer with experience. Both Hat Kata Yai and Hat Kata Noi offer decent surfing from April to November. Board rental costs 100B to 150B for one hour or 300B to 600B for the whole day. Surf House (p263), a bar across the street from Hat Kata, has a manmade surf park (per hour 800B) that kids love.

Kata Hot Yoga YOGA
(Map p261; ☎0 7660 5950; www.katahotyoga.com; 217 Th Khoktanod; per class 500B; ⏲classes 9am, 5:15pm & 7:15pm) Crave more heat? Consider a class at Kata Hot Yoga, where Bikram's famed asana series is taught in a sweltering room with expertise by the owner and an international roster of visiting instructors. Beware: it is habit forming. So are the post-class coconuts.

Sleeping

These are average prices for the high season (May to October). Like Patong, it's getting harder and harder to find anything under 1000B during the high season, but prices drop radically when tourism is down.

Just before the turn toward Karon, hang a right into the **Beach Centre** (Map p261; Hat Kata), a complex of new build townhouses packed with way too many guesthouses to list. If you're stuck without shelter, you should find a room here.

Rumblefish Adventure HOSTEL $
(Map p261; ☎0 7633 0315; http://scubatuna.com; 98/79 Th Kata, Hat Kata; dm/s/d 250/600/700B; P ❄ ᯤ) A water sports flop house offering reasonably clean doubles with private baths, hot water and air con. Dorms sleep six and are airy with turquoise accent walls. There's a mini living area upstairs too. Why not get certified by day and crash here by night? It's in the Beach Center complex.

Fantasy Hill Bungalow HOTEL $
(Map p261; ☎0 7633 0106; fantasyhill@hotmail.com; 8/1 Th Patak West, Hat Kata; r with fan 600B, air-con 1000-1200B; P ❄ ᯤ) Sitting in a lush garden on a hill, the older but well-maintained bungalows here are great value. It's peaceful but central and the staff are super sweet. Angle for a corner air-con room with a view.

Chanisara Guesthouse GUESTHOUSE $
(Map p261; ☎08 5789 5701; 48/5 Soi Casa del Sol, Hat Kata; r from 1000B; ❄ ᯤ) One of several townhouse-style guesthouses on the Casa Del Sol cul de sac. Rooms are super bright, tiled affairs with air-con flat-screen TVs, recessed lighting and a little balcony. Beds are dressed in Thai linens and bottled water is delivered daily. Low season rates drop to 600B per night.

Kata Beach Center Hotel HOTEL $$
(Map p261; ☎0 7633 0868; http://katabeachcenterhotel.com; 98/47 Th Kata; r from 1300B; ❄ ᯤ) Cosy and clean little rooms with wood furnishings, crown mouldings and tiled floors in a three-floor walk up. One of many townhouse hotels in this part of town.

★ **Sabai Corner** BUNGALOWS $$
(☎0 9875 5525; www.sabaicorner.com; Th Karon Lookout; r 1950B) No room on this sweet island offers the view available from the two chalets set on the hillside above Sabai Corner. Each is an independent studio with granite tile in the baths, canopied bed, wall-mounted flat screen with satellite TV, sofa, wardrobe and security boxes. They also have wide outdoor patios that function as an outdoor living room.

And about that 270-degree ocean view. Yeah, you may want to look into that.

Kata Country House HOTEL $$
(Map p261; ☎0 7633 3210; www.katacountryhouse.com; 82 Th Kata; r 1600-2600B; ❄ ≋) Whether or not the retro '60s kitsch is intentional or just a lovely accident, the leafy setting, wagon-wheel railings, waterlily ponds and a Tiki-style (Polynesian) lounge are inviting and full of character. Their in-house country restaurant offers a cheap and authentic steam table pick-and-mix option at lunch.

The Color Kata HOTEL $$
(Map p261; ☎0 7633 0870; www.thecolorkata.com; 65-67 Th Ket Kwan; r from 2000B; ❄ @ ᯤ) Self-billed as a 'hip hotel', and splashed with loud colours and louder electronic music, it will definitely appeal to some. The 23 rooms are cluttered yet ambitious with beds suspended by cables and desks anchored dead centre. They are definitely going for…something. Worth a look if you are the clubbing kind.

Sugar Palm Resort HOTEL $$$
(Map p261; ☎0 7628 4404; www.sugarpalmphuket.com; 20/10 Th Kata; r incl breakfast from 3644B; ❄ @ ᯤ ≋) It's a 'chic chill-out world' at the Sugar Palm, as this Miami-meets-Thailand resort proclaims. Rooms, decorated in urban whites, blacks and lavender, are exceptional value and sparkling with recently updated electronics and retro tile. All surround a black-bottomed, U-shaped pool. The beach isn't far and you're in the heart of Kata's lively shopping and restaurant strip.

Kata Palm Resort HOTEL $$$
(Map p261; ☎0 7628 4334; www.katapalmresort.com; 60 Th Kata; r from 3750B; ❄ ᯤ ≋) Given the abundance of ever-creeping modernism, it's nice to see some classic Thai kitsch at this old standby. Expect Thai art on the walls, silks on the beds, fine wood furnishings, and handpainted columns in the lobby. Great deals are frequently available through the website.

Sawasdee Village HOTEL $$$
(Map p261; ☎0 7633 0979; www.phuketsawasdee.com; 38 Th Ked Kwan; bungalows from 5940B; ❄ @ ᯤ ≋) A boutique resort with an opulent but compact footprint built in classic

Thai style. Ornate, peaked-roof bungalows have wooden floors, beamed ceilings and open on to a thick tropical landscape laced with *koi* (carp) canals and gushing with waterfalls and Buddhist art installations. It will cost you in the high season, however.

Mom Tri's Boathouse BOUTIQUE HOTEL **$$$**
(Map p261; ☎0 7633 0015; www.boathouse-phuket.com; 2/2 Th Kata (Patak West); r from 6000B;) For Thai politicos, pop stars, artists and celebrity authors, the intimate and recently renovated Boathouse is still the only place to stay on Phuket. Rooms are spacious and gorgeous, some sporting large breezy verandas. The on-site restaurant, Boathouse Wine & Grill, is among the best on the island.

Katathani Resort & Spa HOTEL **$$$**
(Map p261; ☎0 7633 0124; www.katathani.com; 14 Th Kata Noi; r from 7800B;) Taking over a huge portion of lush, relatively quiet Hat Kata Noi, this glitzy spa resort offers all the usual trimmings in stylish surrounds. It features a spa, a handful of pools, a beauty salon and heaps of space. Excellent low-season deals are often available.

Mom Tri's Villa Royale HOTEL **$$$**
(Map p261; ☎0 7633 3568; www.villaroyalephuket.com; 12 Th Kata Noi; ste incl breakfast from 13,400B;) Tucked away in a secluded Kata Noi location with the grandest of views, Villa Royale offers romantic rooms, delicious food, an attached spa and a saltwater pool – if you

Hat Karon & Hat Kata

Hat Karon & Hat Kata

Activities, Courses & Tours
1 Dive Asia ... A3
2 Dive Asia ... A1
3 Kata Hot Yoga ... B4
Mom Tri's Boathouse ... (see 14)
4 Phuket Surf ... B4
Rumblefish Adventure ... (see 7)
Sea Fun Divers ... (see 13)

Sleeping
5 Andaman Seaview Hotel ... A2
6 Bazoom Haus ... A2
7 Beach Centre Complex ... B3
8 Chanisara Guesthouse ... B3
9 Fantasy Hill Bungalow ... A2
10 Kangaroo Guesthouse ... A2
Kata Beach Center Hotel ... (see 7)
11 Kata Country House ... B3
12 Kata Palm Resort ... B3
13 Katathani Resort & Spa ... B4
14 Mom Tri's Boathouse ... B4
15 Mom Tri's Villa Royale ... B4
16 Mövenpick ... A1
17 Rumblefish Adventure ... B3
18 Sawasdee Village ... B3
19 Sugar Palm Resort ... B3
20 The Color Kata ... B3

Eating
21 Bai Toey ... A1
Boathouse Wine & Grill ... (see 14)
22 Capannina ... B3
23 Kata Mama ... A3
24 Mama Noi's ... A2
25 Pad Thai Shop ... B2
26 Re Ka Ta Beach Club ... B4

Drinking & Nightlife
Chanisara Juice Stand ... (see 8)
27 Ska Bar ... A4
28 Surf House ... B4

prefer a tamer version of the real thing, which is just steps away.

Eating

There's some surprisingly classy cuisine in Kata, though you'll be paying for it. For cheaper eats, head to Th Thai Na and to the cluster of affordable, casual seafood restaurants on Th Kata (Patak West) near the shore.

Kata Mama THAI $
(Map p261; Th Hat Kata; mains 80-200B; ⊙11am-10pm) One of several cheapie seafood huts at the southern end of Hat Kata, this is our favourite for the charming management and their affordable and reliably tasty Thai standards.

★ **Sabai Corner** INTERNATIONAL-THAI $$
(☎0 9875 5525; www.sabaicorner.com; Th Karon Lookout; mains 200-499B; ⊙10am-10pm; 📶📱) There is no better view on the island than the one you'll glimpse from the deck at this superlative pub. From here you can see all the way to Patong in one direction, and an endless horizon of wide rippling blue ocean as it unfurls west and wraps around Phuket in the other. Sunsets just don't get any better.

Yet it's rare that a location like this gets the restaurant it deserves. That's why this Thai-Swiss-American owned indoor-outdoor patio restaurant is such a stellar find. Here is a soaring thatched roof, an island bar, and wide deck to take in the sun and stars. There's also a pool table, a flat screen for the ball games of the moment and the best service staff in town. The menu isn't innovative – wandering from grilled and fried fish to searing Thai curries to salads, pastas and some damn good pizza – but it satisfies. It's no wonder they lure such a consistent local expat scene. You'll find it downhill and around a bend from the Karon Lookout, a little over halfway between Rawai and Kata.

Capannina ITALIAN $$
(Map p261; ☎0 7628 4318; www.capannina-phuket.com; 30/9 Moo 2, Th Kata (Patak West); mains 200-700B) Everything here – from the pastas to the sauces – is made fresh. The ravioli and

TOP FIVE SPAS IN THE NORTHERN ANDAMAN

There seems to be a massage shop on every corner on Phuket. Most are low-key family affairs where a traditional Thai massage goes for about 300B per hour and a basic mani-pedi costs around 250B – a real steal. The quality of service at these places varies and changes rapidly as staff turnover is high. Go with your gut instinct or ask fellow travellers or your hotel staff for recommendations. No matter where you choose, it's still a massage and likely to be extremely pleasant and relaxing – especially if it's sporting a wood-fired herbal sauna on the premises.

If you're looking for a more Western spa experience, head to one of Phuket's plentiful spa resorts. These places are often affiliated with a ritzy hotel (but nearly all are open to nonguests). They are high-class affairs with sumptuous Zen designs and huge treatment menus. Prices vary depending on location, but sessions generally start at 1000B.

Here are our top five spa picks:

Siam Hot Spa (p277) Combining local flavour and price point with sumptuous treatments and an atmospheric location (right on a steaming river), this is the best bang for the buck in the entire region.

Six Senses Spa (p299) No luxury brand presents back to nature elegance like the Six Senses stilted 'spa village' on Ko Yao Noi. Their therapists are skilled in massage traditions from China, India and, of course, Thailand. Treatments from 3400B.

Hideaway Day Spa (p273) One of Phuket's first spas, the Hideaway still enjoys an excellent reputation. More reasonably priced than many hotel counterparts, it offers treatments in a tranquil setting by a lagoon.

Raintree Spa (p251) Another reasonably good, refreshing choice is located at Sino House in Phuket Town. When locals crave spa therapy, they come here.

Sarojin (p290) Their treatment rooms wander to the edge of the mangroves, open to the ocean breeze and the sound of the sea. One of the best massage settings of your life awaits.

gnocchi are memorable, the risotto comes highly recommended, and there are great pizzas, calzones and veal Milanese too. It gets crowded during the high season, so reserve ahead.

Re Ka Ta Beach Club INTERNATIONAL $$$
(Map p261; ☎0 7633 0421; www.rekataphuket.com; 184 Th Kotanod; meals 370-950B) Part of the Boathouse family, this gleaming white and modern beachside cafe does burgers and baguettes, a range of pastas and a fresh seafood grill at dinner. The ambience and view make up for the price tag.

★**Boathouse Wine & Grill** INTERNATIONAL $$$
(Map p261; ☎0 7633 0015; www.boathousephuket.com; 2/2 Th Kata (Patak West); mains 450-950B; ⊙11am-11pm) The perfect place to wow a fussy date, the Wine & Grill is the pick of the bunch for most local foodies. The atmosphere can be a little stuffy – this is the closest Phuket gets to old-school dining – but the Mediterranean fusion food is fabulous, the wine list expansive and the sea views sublime.

Drinking

Kata's nightlife veers toward mellow.

★**Ska Bar** BAR
(Map p261; 186/12 Th Koktanod, Kata; ⊙noon-late) At Kata's southernmost cove, tucked into the rocks and seemingly intertwined with the trunk of a grand old banyan tree, Ska is our choice for oceanside sundowners. The Thai bartenders add to the funky Rasta vibe, and the canopy dangles with buoys, paper lanterns and flags. Friday nights brings fire spinners to the beach.

Surf House BAR
(Map p261; ☎08 1979 7737; www.surfhousephuket.com; 4 Moo 2, Th Kata; ⊙10am-midnight) Perched across the street from Kata Beach, this bar serves both beer and waves. Well, man made ones, anyway. The bar pours icy Chang and serves decent pub grub. The attached surf attraction is a sloped slide that riders navigate on wake boards for as long as they can stay upright. Kids love it.

Chanisara Juice Stand JUICE
(Map p261; 48/5 Soi Casa Del Sol; ⊙8am-6pm) A terrific little stand, set in front of the guesthouse of the same name and run by the owner of both. There aren't many places you can blend more obscure fruits like mangosteen, rambutan, dragon and snake fruit with old reliables like banana, mango, papaya and pineapple.

Information

There are plenty of ATMs along Kata's main drag.

Post Office (Map p261; ⊙9am-4.30pm Mon-Fri, to noon Sat) On Rte 4028, at the end of Th Thai Na.

Getting There & Around

Sŏrng·tăa·ou to both Kata and Karon (per person 25B) leave frequently from the day market on Th Ranong in Phuket Town from 7am to 5pm. The main *sŏrng·tăa·ou* stop is in front of Kata Beach Resort.

Taxis from Kata go to Phuket Town (600B), Patong (600B) and Karon (200B).

Motorbike rentals (per day 300B) are widely available.

Hat Karon หาดกะรน

Hat Karon is like Hat Patong and Hat Kata's love child: it's chilled-out, a touch glamorous and a tad sleazy. There are two mega-resorts and package tourists aplenty here, but there's still more sand space per capita than at either Patong or Kata. The further north you go the more beautiful the beach gets, culminating at the northernmost edge, accessible from a rutted road that extends past the vendors and food stalls, where the water is like turquoise glass. Within the inland network of streets and plazas you'll find a blend of good local food, more Russian signage than seems reasonable, low-key girly bars, T-shirt vendors and lovely Karon Park, with its artificial lake and mountain backdrop. Fronting the whole mess is a fine stretch of sand.

Sleeping

★**Bazoom Haus** GUESTHOUSE $
(Map p261; ☎08 9533 0241; www.bazoomhostel.com; 269/5 Karon Plaza, Hat Karon; dm 300B, r 2700B; ❄@☜) The fabulous private rooms offer wood floors and furnishings, recessed lighting, flat screens and mosaic showers. There's a Jacuzzi and barbecue on the roof top deck, DJ decks in the in-house Korean restaurant (the owners are from Korea), and a dive shop too. Dorms have six beds to a room. Discounts of up to 65% in low season.

Kangaroo Guesthouse GUESTHOUSE $$
(Map p261; ☎0 7639 6517; www.kangarooguesthouse.com; 269/6-9 Karon Plaza, Hat Karon;

r 1200B; ❄📶) Basic, but very clean, sunny tiled rooms with hot water, air-con, a cute breakfast nook, and balconies overlooking a narrow, slightly seedy soi.

In On The Beach HOTEL $$$
(☎0 7639 8220; www.karon-inonthebeach.com; 695-697 Moo 1, Th Patak; r from 3500B; ❄@📶🏊) A sweet, tasteful inn on Karon Park. The location is sublime, and the rooms – think marble floors, wi-fi, air-con and ceiling fans – horseshoe the pool and come with sea views, though they are ageing fast. With substantial low-season discounts, it's still an ideal surf lair.

Sugar Palm Karon Beach HOTEL $$$
(☎0 7639 6611; www.sugarpalmkaron.com; 542/1 Th Patak; r from 3240B; P❄📶🏊) With louvres and exposed steel girders lofted from the roof, it's striking, gaudy and a little cheesy maybe, but it cannot be ignored. All 144 rooms are super clean and modern with wall-mounted flat screens, high ceilings, built-in wardrobes, rain showers and soaker tubs, and stylish wallpapered accents.

Andaman Seaview Hotel HOTEL $$$
(Map p261; ☎0 7639 8111; www.andamanphuket.com; 1 Soi Karon, Th Kata (Patak West); r from 4600B; ❄@📶🏊👪) The design here is Cape Cod meets the colonial South Pacific with its sky-blue-and-white exterior and chequerboard marble floors in the lobby. Rooms have a turn-of-the-20th-century Americana theme with marble tables, antiquated ceiling fans, art deco–ish bathroom tiles and white-shutter cabinet doors. There's a bubbling kid's pool and an adult pool.

Mövenpick HOTEL $$$
(Map p261; ☎0 7639 6139; www.moevenpick-hotels.com; 509 Th Patak West; r from 6525B; ❄📶🏊) Grab a secluded villa and choose from a private plunge pool or outdoor rainforest shower. Alternatively, chill in the cubelike rooms with huge floor-to-ceiling glass windows. There's a prime location across the street from a pretty stretch of the beach, a pool with swim-up bar, a spa, and an alfresco restaurant with a giant selection of wood-fired pizzas.

Eating

There are a few cheap Thai and seafood places off the roundabout (including a number of beachside seafood houses under one louvred roof 100m north) and a similar group on the main road near the southern end of Hat Karon.

★ Pad Thai Shop THAI $
(Map p261; Th Patak East; dishes 50-60B; ⌚9am-8pm) This glorified food stand offers rich and savoury chicken stew, a terrific stir-fried chicken and rice, absurdly good *kôw pàt Ƃoo* (crab fried rice) and the best *pàt tai* on planet earth. Spicy and sweet, packed with prawns, tofu, egg and peanuts, and wrapped in a fresh banana leaf, it will make you grateful. Don't miss the house-made chilli sauces.

Mama Noi's THAI, ITALIAN $
(Map p261; Karon Plaza; mains 60-185B; ⌚8am-10pm; 📶) A simple tiled cafe with a handful of plants out front that has been feeding the expat masses for nearly a generation. They do all the Thai dishes and some popular pasta dishes, too. Cheap and tasty, all of it arrives in ample portions.

Bai Toey THAI $$
(Map p261; ☎08 1691 6202; www.baitoeyrestaurant.com; 192/36 Th Patak West; meals 200-300B; ⌚11am-10pm; 📶) A charming Thai bistro with shaded outdoor patio and indoor seating. It has the traditional curry, stir-fry and noodle dishes, but you'd do well to sample its Thai-style grilled beef. It's a sliced fillet brushed in oyster sauce and served with sticky rice.

Hat Patong หาดป่าตอง

Sun-seared Russians in bad knock-off T-shirts, beach-buzzing wave runners, a complete disregard for managed development and a knack for turning the midlife crisis into a full-scale industry (sorry, Cialis, Patong was here first) make Patong rampant with unintentional comedy. But for all the concrete and silicon, and moral and gender bending, there's something honest about this place.

Patong is a free-for-all. Anything, from a Starbucks 'venti latte' to an, ahem, companion for the evening is available for the right price. And while that's true of dozens of other, phonier destinations, Patong doesn't try to hide it. Patong is what it is. And that's refreshing.

Of course, that doesn't mean you're going to like it. But when you arrive you'll take one look at the wide, white-sand beach and its magnificent crescent bay, and you'll understand how it all started.

TSUNAMI EARLY WARNING SYSTEM

On the morning of 26 December 2004, an earthquake off the coast of the Indonesian island of Sumatra sent enormous waves crashing against much of Thailand's Andaman coast, claiming around 8000 lives and causing millions of dollars of damage to homes and businesses. Over 10 years have passed; life and business on this stretch of the Andaman coast has bounced back and in many ways it is better than ever. Yet, the incident hasn't been forgotten. In fact, it's inspired action to prevent a repeat disaster.

Most significantly, in 2005 Thailand officially inaugurated a national disaster warning system, which was created in response to the country's lack of preparedness in 2004. The Bangkok-based centre anticipates that a tsunami warning can be issued within 30 minutes of the event being detected by existing international systems.

The public will be warned via the nationwide radio network, Channel 5 army TV network, the state-operated TV pool and SMS messages. For non-Thai speakers, the centre has installed warning towers along the high-risk beachfront areas that will broadcast announcements in various languages accompanied by flashing lights. The call centre also handles questions and tips from the public regarding potential or unfolding disasters.

As far as collective memory goes, the moving **Tsunami Memorial Park** in Baan Nam Kem, a squid fishing village that was nearly wiped off the map, was built to memorialise locals and tourists alike who lost their lives. The wave-shaped memorial is just north of Khao Lak, where a police boat is still moored inland where it was deposited by the wave. The more official entrance way and memorial displays augment what for years was an unofficial pilgrimage site for those who came to pay their respects and grasp nature's fury.

Diving and spa options abound, as well as upscale dining, street-side fish grills, campy cabaret, Thai boxing, dusty antique shops and one of Thailand's coolest shopping malls.

Sleeping

It's getting pretty difficult to find anything in Patong under 1000B between approximately November and April (the period that corresponds to the prices listed here), but outside this time rates drop by 40% to 60%.

Patong Backpacker Hostel HOSTEL $
(Map p266; ☎0 7625 6680; www.phuketbackpacker.com; 140 Th Thawiwong; dm 250-450B; ❄☜) This has a great location near the beach and the owner offers info on all the best, cheapest places to eat in town. Dorm prices vary depending on the number of beds in the room (four to 10). The top floor is the brightest, but dorm rooms on the lower floors each have their own attached bathrooms.

Casa Jip GUESTHOUSE $
(Map p266; ☎0 7634 3019; www.casajip.com; 207/10 Th Rat Uthit; r from 700B; ❄☜) Italian-run and great value, this place offers bright, spacious rooms with floating beds, brick accents on the walls, flat screens and rain showers along with stylish concrete wash basins. Deluxe rooms are enormous. This is the best three-star deal in Patong.

Merrison Inn HOTEL $$
(Map p266; ☎0 7634 0383; www.merrisoninn.com; 5/35 Th Hat Patong; r 1300B; ❄☜) Polished concrete floors, terrazzo bathrooms, wall-mounted flat-screens, queen-sized beds and more than a little Asian kitsch make this place a real bargain.

Tune Hotel HOTEL $$
(Map p266; ☎0 7634 1936; www.tunehotels.com; 56 Th Rat Uthit ; 1500B; P❄) Brand-new at research time, the Tune is a budding new Southeast Asian brand. They offer small but comfy rooms with wood floors, satellite TV, and plush linens. It's no frills, tidy three-star living. And it works.

Patong Station House GUESTHOUSE $$
(Map p266; ☎0 7629 2022; 205/3-4 Th Rat Uthit; r 1500B; ❄☜) A simple four-floor walk up, with wood furnishings, wall-mounted flat screens and nice mosaic baths. Some rooms smell mustier than others, but it's a good value.

Sino House GUESTHOUSE $$
(Map p266; ☎0 7629 3272; 205/10-11 Th Rat Uthit; r from 1500B; ❄☜) A cute guesthouse with Chinese art hanging on the flagstone hallway

Patong

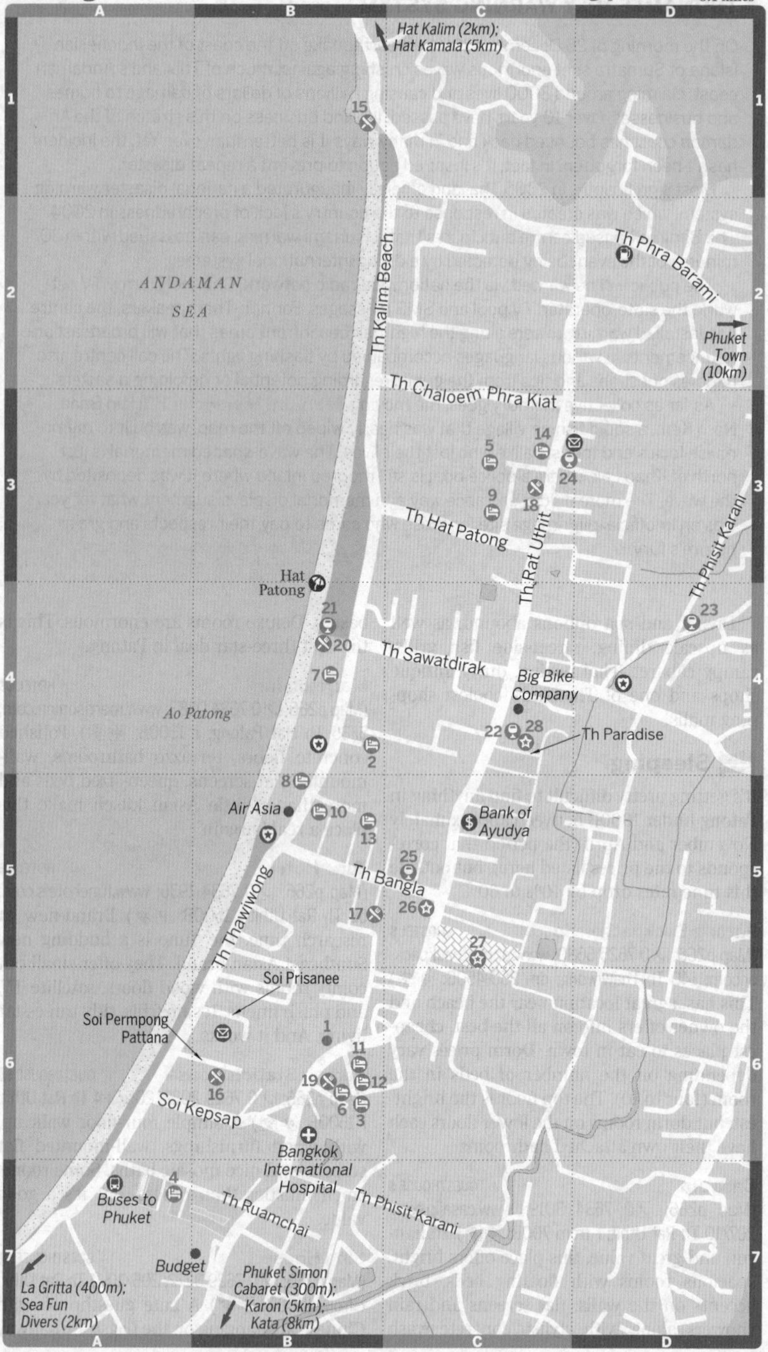

0 200 m
0 0.1 miles
A
B
C
D
1
2
3
4
5
6
7
Hat Kalim (2km);
Hat Kamala (5km)
15
Th Phra Barami
ANDAMAN
SEA
Th Kalim Beach
Phuket
Town
(10km)
Th Chaloem Phra Kiat
14
5
24
9
18
Th Hat Patong
Th Rat Uthit
Th Phisit Karani
Hat
Patong
21
23
20
Th Sawatdirak
7
Big Bike
Company
Ao Patong
22
28
Th Paradise
2
8
Air Asia
10
Bank of
Ayudya
13
25
Th Bangla
Th Thawiwong
17
26
27
Soi Prisanee
Soi Permpong
Pattana
1
11
16
19
12
6
Soi Kepsap
3
Bangkok
International
Hospital
4
Buses to
Phuket
Th Ruamchai
Th Phisit Karani
Budget
La Gritta (400m);
Sea Fun
Divers (2km)
Phuket Simon
Cabaret (300m);
Karon (5km);
Kata (8km)

walls, and clean and spacious, if basic, rooms with wood furnishings, burgundy drapes, safety boxes and floor-to-ceiling headboards.

Baan Pronphateep HOTEL $$
(Map p266; ☎0 7634 3037; http://baanpronphateep.com; 168/1 Th Thawiwong; r 1400-2800B; P❄📶) Banyan tree–shaded and nestled down a secluded soi, this is a quiet and simple three-star choice. Rooms are spacious and come with a full-sized fridge and a private patio. You may get propositioned by veteran hookers and/or bold lady boys on your way in and out. Just saying.

Baipho, Baithong & Sala Dee GUESTHOUSE $$
(Map p266; ☎0 7629 2738, 0 7629 2074; www.baipho.com; 205/12-13 & 205/14-15 Th Rat Uthit 200 Pee; r 1800-3300B; ❄📶) Three arty guesthouses are on the same soi and under the same management. Rooms and common areas are filled with Buddha imagery, and the dimly lit, nest-like rooms are all unique, so ask to see a few, if possible. The Lounge downstairs at Baithong serves cocktails and very good Italian and Thai food.

The Kee RESORT $$$
(Map p266; ☎0 7633 5888; www.thekeeresort.com; 152/1 Th Thawiwong; d from 3600B; P❄📶🏊) A splashy, sprawling chic spread for the masses. It's not uber exclusive or swanky, but it does feel that way compared to most Patong nests. There's a rooftop lounge and restaurant, and four-star quality rooms horseshoe a shallow blue pool. Promotional rates are terrific, but they'll probably climb soon.

Burasari HOTEL $$$
(Map p266; ☎0 7629 2929; www.burasari.com; 18/110 Th Ruamchai; r 3700-9300B; ❄📶🏊) A labyrinth of swimming pools and waterfalls, etched columns, cushion-strewn lounges and bars. Rooms are simple but chic with flat-screen TVs, queen-sized beds and bamboo accents. Their **Naughty Radish** cafe serves outrageous customizable salads (from 180B) and the streetside **It's Just For You** juice bar does terrific smoothies (120B).

Impiana Phuket Cabana HOTEL $$$
(Map p266; ☎0 7634 0138; www.impiana.com; 41 Th Thawiwong; r from 4500-7000B; ❄📶🏊) Cabana-style and plumb on the best part of the beach, the rooms here are laden with chic creature comforts and are close to all the action. Deep discounts when booked online.

La Flora HOTEL $$$
(Map p266; ☎0 7634 4241; www.laflorapatong.com; 39 Th Thawiwong; r from 7980B; ❄📶🏊) Here's where clean lines and minimalist decor spill onto the beach. Rooms are large with wooden furnishings (check out that floating desk), flat-screen TV and DVD player, bathtub and shower. The minibar is stocked with complimentary soft drinks, and there's a huge lap pool.

BYD Lofts HOTEL $$$
(Map p266; ☎0 7634 3024; www.bydlofts.com; 5/28 Th Rat Uthit; apt 4900-19,500B; ❄@📶🏊) If style and comfort are more important to you than beachfront location (although

Patong

Activities, Courses & Tours
1 Pum Thai Cooking School B6

Sleeping
2 Baan Pronphateep B4
3 Baipho, Baithong & Sala Dee B6
4 Burasari A7
5 BYD Lofts C3
6 Casa Jip B6
7 Impiana Phuket Cabana B4
8 La Flora B5
9 Merrison Inn C3
10 Patong Backpacker Hostel B5
11 Patong Station House B6
12 Sino House B6
13 The Kee B5
14 Tune Hotel C3

Eating
15 Baan Rim Pa B1
Chicken Rice Briley .... (see 18)
16 Ella B6
17 Mengrai Seafood B5
18 Patong Food Park C3
19 Shalimar B6
20 The Beach B4

Drinking & Nightlife
21 Barefoot Beach Shack B4
22 Boat Bar C4
23 Monte's D4
24 Nicky's Handlebar C3
25 Seduction C5

Entertainment
26 Bangla Boxing Stadium C5
27 Jung Ceylon C5
28 My Way C4

it's only a minute's walk), look no further. Urban-style apartments with lots of white (floors, walls, blinds) and sharp lines feel angelic compared to the seedy world on the streets below. There's a day spa, rooftop pool and excellent restaurant on the premises.

Eating

Patong has stacks of restaurants and the trick is to steer around the abundant watered-down Thai and poorly executed Western kitchens. The most glamorous restaurants are in a little huddle above the cliffs on the northern edge of town.

Bargain seafood and noodle stalls pop up across town at night – try the lanes on and around Th Bangla, or venture over to the **Patong Food Park** (Map p266; Th Rat Uthit; meals 100-200B; 4pm-midnight) once the sun drops.

Chicken Rice Briley THAI $

(Map p266; 0 7634 4079; Patong Food Park, Th Rat Uthit; meals 35-45B; 9am-3pm) The only diner in the Patong Food Park to offer sustenance when the sun shines. Steamed chicken breast is served on a bed of rice with a bowl of chicken broth with crumbled bits of meat and bone, and roast pork. Dip in the fantastic chilli sauce. There's a reason it's forever packed with locals.

Mengrai Seafood SEAFOOD $$

(Map p266; 08 7263 7070; Soi Tun; meals 120-300B) Located down a sweaty, dark soi off Th Bangla, Mengrai is nestled in a wonderful food court serving fresh, local food. The stalls towards the end serve daily curries that local expats swear by. This restaurant specialises in (very) fresh fish, prawns and mussels.

Ella INTERNATIONAL $$

(Map p266; 08 1540 1267; www.theellagroup.org; 100/19-20 Th Permpong Pattana (Soi Post Office); mains 150-250B;) A funky, mod, moulded concrete bar and bistro with creative all-day breakfasts featuring Rajistani scrambled eggs, omelettes stuffed with chicken and peas, and baguette french toast. At lunch and dinner they fire up the grill to barbecue everything from pork ribs to blackened slabs of tuna. They have guest rooms of a similar style and decor upstairs.

Shalimar INDIAN $$

(Map p266; 207/7, 8 Soi Patong Lodge, 200 Pee; dishes 120-600B, buffet 300B; 11am-11:30pm) This Indian kitchen offers a daily veggie lunch buffet as well as a menu with half a dozen dhal dishes, samosas, butter chicken, tandoori mixed grill and biryani. In a town with more than its share of Indian joints, these wood tables and leather seats are consistently packed.

The Beach THAI $$

(Map p266; 0 7634 5944; 49 Th Thawiwong; mains 180-350B; 8am-midnight) If you want decent Thai food and an array of seafood choices on the beach, come to this long-running shack. There are a string of choices here that are all slightly overpriced, but the setting is terrific.

Baan Rim Pa THAI $$$

(Map p266; 0 7634 4079; Th Kalim Beach; dishes 215-475B) Stunning Thai food is served with a side order of spectacular views at this institution. Standards are high, with prices to match, but romance is in the air, with candlelight and piano music aplenty. Book ahead, button up and tuck it in.

Drinking & Nightlife

Some visitors may find that Patong's bar scene is enough to put them off their *pàt tai,* but if you're in the mood for plenty of beer, winking neon and short skirts, it is certainly worth sampling.

Th Bangla is Patong's beer and bar-girl mecca and features a number of spectacular go-go extravaganzas, where you can expect the usual mix of gyrating Thai girls and often red-faced Western men. The music is loud (expect techno), the clothes are all but nonexistent and the decor is typically slapstick with plenty of phallic imagery. That said, the atmosphere is more carnival than carnage and you'll find plenty of peers pushing their way through the throng to the bar.

★ **Seduction** NIGHTCLUB

(Map p266; www.facebook.com/seductiondisco; 39/1 Th Bangla; 10pm-4am) International DJs, professional-grade sound system and the best dance party on Phuket, without question. Winner and still champion.

La Gritta BAR

(0 7634 0106; www.amari.com; 2 Th Meun-ngern; 10.30am-11.30pm) A spectacular, modern restaurant that doesn't fit in with the ageing bones of this once-great property, but who cares? With tiered booths, massive yet muted light boxes and a deck that is just centimetres above the boulder-strewn shore,

there are few better settings for a sunset cocktail in Patong.

Barefoot Beach Shack BAR

(Map p266; ☎08 9697 2337; www.facebook.com/BarefootBeachShack; Th Thawiwong; ⊙10am-10pm; 📶) A whimsically decorated retro bar with a Caribbean feel, crafted from reused corrugated tin and reclaimed wood. It's right on the beach, pulses with palatable pop tunes and is irrigated with middling cocktails and Chang draught. There are worse ways to spend an afternoon.

Monte's BAR

(Map p266; Th Phisit Karani; ⊙11am-midnight) Now this, my friends, is a tropical pub. There's a thatched roof, a natural-wood bar, dozens of orchids and a flat-screen TV for sport. The barflies swarm on Fridays for Monte's famous Belgian-style mussels, and on the weekends he fires up the grill.

Nicky's Handlebar BAR

(Map p266; ☎08 9866 9302, 0 7634 3211-3; www.nickyhandlebars.com; 41 Th Rat Uthit) Though it is a full restaurant and there are guestrooms too, we like coming here for drinks and to admire the vintage hogs in the rafters. Once a bit of a dive, Nicky's has never looked better, and they still offer motorcycle rentals and tours.

☆ Entertainment

Once you've done the go-go, there's plenty more to see. Cabaret and Thai boxing, in particular, are something of a speciality here.

Phuket Simon Cabaret CABARET

(☎0 7634 2011; www.phuket-simoncabaret.com; Th Sirirach; admission 700-800B; ⊙performances 6pm, 7.45pm & 9.30pm nightly) About 300m south of town, this cabaret offers entertaining transvestite shows. The 600-seat theatre is grand, the costumes are gorgeous and the ladyboys are convincing. Though the show is brief, the house is often full – book ahead.

Bangla Boxing Stadium THAI BOXING

(Map p266; ☎0 7282 2348; 198/4 Th Rat Uthit; admission 1000-1500B; ⊙9-11.30pm Tue, Wed, Fri & Sun) Old name, new stadium, same game: a packed line-up of competitive *moo·ay tai* (Thai boxing) bouts.

Jung Ceylon CINEMA

(Map p266; Th Rat Uthit) Catch new Hollywood releases in pristine, amphitheatre-style cinemas at the shopping mall.

Music NIGHTCLUB

(Th Bangla; ⊙9pm-2am) The newest dance club on Patong's sluttiest street takes up the top two floors of a long-running tin-roof beer and bar girl garden. The crowds descend and the energy picks up after 11pm.

ℹ Information

There are internet cafes and banks with ATM and currency-exchange facilities across town.

Post Office (Map p266; Th Thawiwong; ⊙9am-4.30pm Mon-Fri, to noon Sat)

GAY PRIDE IN PHUKET

Although there are big gay pride celebrations in Bangkok and Pattaya, the **Phuket Gay Pride Festival** is considered by many to be the best in Thailand, maybe even Southeast Asia. The date has changed several times, but it usually lands between February and April. Whenever it blooms, the whole island – but the town of Patong specifically – is packed with (mostly male) revellers from all over the world.

The main events of the four-day weekend party are a huge beach volleyball tournament and, of course, the Grand Parade, featuring floats, cheering crowds and beautiful costumes in the streets of Patong. In recent years, the festival has also included social-responsibility campaigns to increase awareness of child prostitution, substance abuse and HIV.

Any other time of year, the network of streets that link the Royal Paradise Hotel with Th Rat Uthit in Patong is where you'll find Phuket's gay pulse. The **Boat Bar** (Map p266; ☎0 7634 2206; www.boatbar.com; 125/20 Th Rat Uthit; ⊙9pm-late), Phuket's original gay nightspot and still its only disco, is usually jumping with a lively, mostly gay crowd. Make sure to arrive before the midnight cabaret! There's another good cabaret, some might say the original, at nearby **My Way** (Map p266; 125/15-17 Th Rat Uthit; ⊙9pm-late). For updates on future festivals or for more information about the scene in general, go to **Gay Patong** (www.gaypatong.com).

Tourist Police (Map p266; ☎1699; cnr Th Thawiwong & Th Bangla, Patong)

Getting There & Around

Air Asia (Map p266; ☎0 7634 1792; www.airasia.com; 39 Th Thawiwong; ⏰9am-9pm) has an office in town.

Túk-túks circulate around Patong for 50B to 100B per ride. There are numerous places to rent 125cc motorbikes and jeeps. **Big Bike Company** (Map p266; ☎0 7634 5100; 106 Th Rat Uthit) rents proper motorcycles (500B to 1000B per day) and Nicky's Handlebar rents Harleys. Keep in mind that the mandatory helmet law is strictly enforced in Patong, where roadblocks/checkpoints can spring up at a moment's notice. **Budget** (Map p266; ☎0 7629 2389; 44 Th Thawiwong; ⏰9am-4pm) has an office in the Patong Merlin Hotel.

Sŏrng·tăa·ou to Patong from Phuket Town leave from Th Ranong, near the day market and fountain circle; the fare is 25B. The after-hours charter fare is 500B. *Sŏrng·tăa·ou* then drop off and pick up passengers at the southern end of Patong beach. From here you can hop on a motorbike taxi (20B to 40B per ride), flag down a túk-túk (prices vary widely) or walk till your feet hurt.

Hat Kamala หาดกมลา

A chilled-out hybrid of Hat Karon and Hat Surin, calm but fun Kamala tends to lure a mixture of longer-term, lower-key partying guests, a regular crop of European families, and young couples. The bay is magnificent, turquoise and serene with shore breakers that lull you to sleep. Palms and pines mingle on the leafy and rocky northern end where the water is a rich emerald green and the snorkelling around the rock reef is halfway decent, while new resorts are ploughed into the southern bluffs above the gathering long-tails. The entire beach is backed with lush rolling hills, which one can only hope are left alone…forever. And it's the only beach with a walking path lined with this many restaurants, resorts and shops. Ditch the motorbike and step into Kamala bliss.

Sights & Activities

Local beach boffins will tell you that **Laem Singh**, just north of Kamala, is one of the best capes on the island. Walled in by cliffs, there is no road access so you have to park your car (40B) or motorbike (20B) on the headland and clamber down a narrow path, or you could charter a long-tail (1000B) from Hat Kamala. It gets crowded.

Phuket Fantasea THEATRE
(☎0 7638 5000; www.phuket-fantasea.com; admission with/without dinner 1900/1500B; ⏰shows 7pm & 9pm Wed & Fri, 9pm only Sat-Tue) This US$60 million cultural theme park is located just east of Hat Kamala. It's where the colour and pageantry Thai dance is combined with a state-of-the-art light-and-sound system of Vegas quality. Now add a herd of elephants. All of this takes place on a stage dominated by a full-scale replica of a Khmer temple.

Kids will be especially captivated by the spectacle, but it is over-the-top cheesy and cameras are forbidden. They recommend you arrive an hour before showtime.

Sleeping & Eating

Clear House HOTEL $$
(☎0 7638 5401; www.clearhousephuket.com; 121/2, 121/10 Th Rimhaad, Hat Kamala; r 1300B; ❄📶) Shabby chic with a mod twist, whitewashed rooms have pink accent walls, plush duvets, flat-screen TVs, wi-fi and huge pebbled baths. This place just feels good.

Layalina Hotel HOTEL $$$
(☎0 7638 5942; www.layalinahotel.com; r incl breakfast 5500-7700B; ❄@📶🏊) Nab one of the split-level suites with very private rooftop terraces at this small boutique hotel for romantic sunset views over white sand and blue sea. The decor is simple, Thai and chic, with fluffy white duvets and honey-toned wooden furniture.

Cape Sienna Hotel HOTEL $$$
(☎0 7633 7300; www.capesienna.com; 18/40 Moo 6, Th Nakalay; r 5400-13,050B; ❄@📶🏊) This flashy, romantic hotel dominates the southern headland and offers magnificent azure bay views from the lobby, the pool and every room. Rooms are modern, with all the amenities. The recently added cliffside residences make sense for groups who plan to stay awhile.

Beach Restaurants THAI, INTERNATIONAL $
(Hat Kamala; dishes 50-250B; ⏰11am-9pm) One of Kamala's highlights is its long stretch of eateries where you can dine in a swimsuit with your feet in the sand. There's everything from Thai to pizza, and plenty of cold beer. **Ma Ma Fati Ma**, at the far northern part of the beach, is our favourite.

Rockfish FUSION $$$
(☎0 7627 9732; www.rockfishrestaurant.com; 33/6 Th Kamala Beach; dishes 170-1000B; ⏲noon-late; 📶✎) Perched above the river mouth, with beach, bay and mountain views, Rockfish not only boasts prime real estate, but also Kamala's best international menu. Smoked salmon eggs benedict on English muffins for breakfast, garlic and pepper-infused fish and chips for lunch, and five-spice pork loin with crackling and roast potatoes for dinner – it's all hard to resist.

ℹ Getting There & Away

To catch a public *sŏrng·tăa·ou* from Kamala to Patong costs 50B per person, while a *sŏrng·tăa·ou* charter (starting in the evenings) costs 250B. Public *sŏrng·tăa·ou* to Surin and Phuket Town cost 20B and 40B respectively.

Hat Surin หาดสุรินทร์

Like that hot boy or girl in school who also happens to have style, soul, a fun personality and wealthy parents, Surin beach is the kind of place that can inspire (travel) lust in anyone who meets him or her. With a wide, blonde beach, water that blends from pale turquoise in the shallows to a deep blue on the horizon, and two lush, boulder-strewn headlands, Surin could easily attract tourists on looks alone. Ah, but there are stunning galleries, five-star spa resorts and wonderful beachfront dining options, too. So by the time you're done swimming, sunbathing, snacking at local fish grills and sipping cocktails at barefoot-chic beach clubs, don't be surprised if you've fallen in love.

Sleeping

Hat Surin is home to some of Phuket's classiest resorts, but there's little available for budgeteers.

Benyada Lodge HOTEL $$
(☎0 7627 1261; www.benyadalodge-phuket.com; 106/52 Moo 3, Th Chengtalay; r from 2800B; ❄📶🏊) Chic, modern rooms – with black louvred closets, terracotta-tiled bathrooms and silk, pastel-coloured throw pillows scattered in the lounging corner – are a great bargain for this area. Service is stellar. Admire the sunset at the rooftop bar or take the short walk to the beach.

★**Twin Palms** RESORT $$$
(☎0 7631 6500; www.twinpalms-phuket.com; 106/46 Moo 3, Th Surin Beach; r 8100-25,850B; ❄@📶🏊) Even the simplest rooms are extra spacious and have oversized bathrooms, sublimely comfortable beds and a supreme sense of calm. The minimalist, artsy swimming pools are fringed by delicate white frangipani, and it's a few minutes' walk to the beach.

Chava RESORT $$$
(☎0 7637 2600; www.thechavaresort.com; 113 Moo 3, Tambon Cherng Talay; apt 11,200-20,000B; ❄@🏊) Draped in flowering vines and blessed with gurgling fountains and shimmering reflection pools, this place is part hotel, part condo development and completely stylish. The massive two-, three- and four-bedroom apartments have fully stocked stainless-steel fridges, entertainment systems in the living room and another flat-screen TV in the master bedroom.

★**Surin Phuket** HOTEL $$$
(☎0 7662 1579; www.thesurinphuket.com; 118 Moo 3, Hat Pansea; r 17,000-58,000B; ❄📶🏊) Almost any place located on a private beach this quiet and stunning would have be a top pick. But the bungalows at the Surin (previously 'The Chedi'), hidden beneath the hillside foliage, offer earthy, luxurious interiors that make the site that much better. The restaurant has a dreamy *Robinson Crusoe* feel, yet the six-sided pool is rather abstract.

You'll have to be in decent shape for walking around the resort, since it can be quite a hoof up hills and over wooden walkways to get to many of the bungalows.

Amanpuri Resort RESORT $$$
(☎0 7632 4333; www.amanresorts.com; Hat Pansea; villas from US$1050; ❄@📶🏊) Over the top and luxurious, the Amanpuri is one of Phuket's most exclusive hotels and a celebrity magnet.

Eating & Drinking

There are plenty of excellent restaurants in and around Surin. For cheap seafood, your first stop should be the numerous, fun and delicious seafront dining rooms. For cheapest eats head to the huddle of food stalls in the parking lot in front of Wat Surin at the Surin beach crossroads. They grill chicken, burgers and corn, and fry up martabak and crepes.

Hat Kamala, Hat Surin & Ao Bang Thao

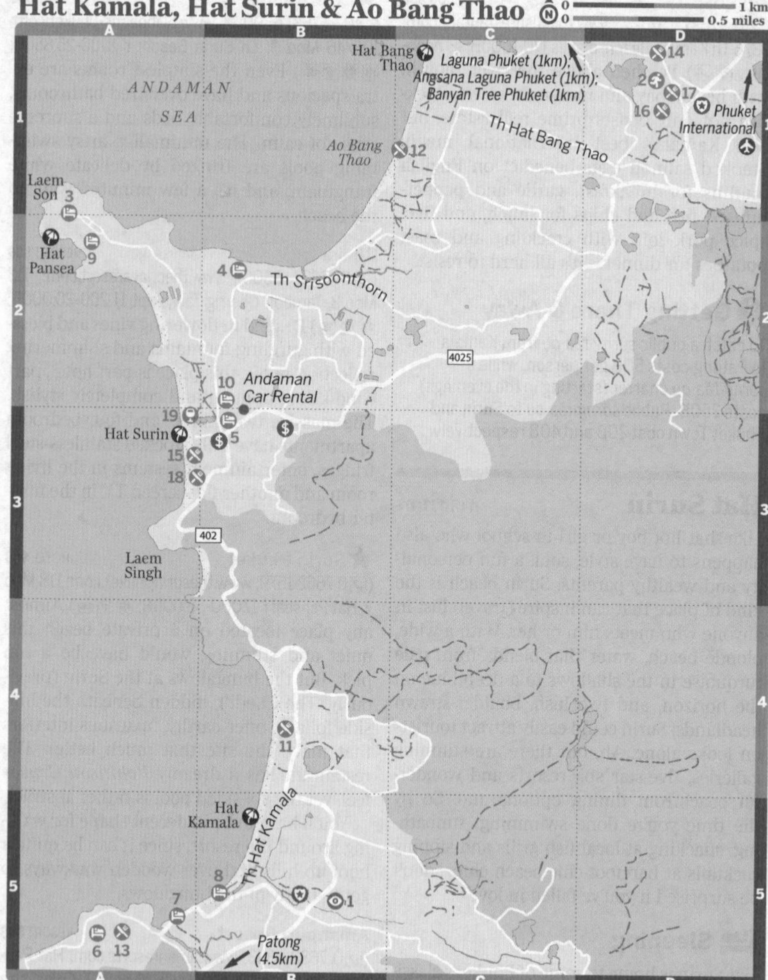

Twin Brothers THAI $$
(Hat Surin; mains 150-350B; ⏲10.30am-10.30pm) By day, one brother mans the wok, stirring up decent Thai food at local prices. At night, the other fires up a fresh seafood grill for beachside diners. It's a bit more down to earth than other Surin choices.

Taste FUSION $$
(☎08 7886 6401; www.tastesurinbeach.com; tapas 225-485B; 📶) The best of the urban-meets-surf eateries along the beach. Dine indoors or alfresco on meal-sized salads, perfectly cooked fillet mignon or a variety of Thai-Mediterranean starters and mains. Service is outstanding and there's an enticing attached gallery selling Tibetan, Nepali and local jewellery and art.

The Catch BEACH CLUB
(☎0 7631 6567; www.catchbeachclub.com; Hat Surin; beach club access per day 1500B; ⏲10:30am-10:30pm; 📶👪) Slip on your breeziest linen to dine and lounge at this draped cabana-style club right on the beach. It's part of Twin Palms, even though it's not attached, and has all the same classy attributes as the hotel in both ambience and cuisine.

Hat Kamala, Hat Surin & Ao Bang Thao

Sights
1 Phuket Fantasea B5

Activities, Courses & Tours
2 Hideaway Day Spa D1

Sleeping
3 Amanpuri Resort A1
4 Andaman Bangtao Bay Resort B2
5 Benyada Lodge B3
6 Cape Sienna Hotel A5
Chava .... (see 10)
7 Clear House A5
8 Layalina Hotel B5
9 Surin Phuket A2
10 Twin Palms B2

Eating
11 Beach Restaurants B4
12 Bliss Beach Club C1
Chaba .... (see 17)
13 Rockfish A5
14 Siam Supper Club D1
15 Taste A3
16 Tatonka D1
17 Tawai Restaurant D1
18 Twin Brothers A3

Drinking & Nightlife
BB's Pub .... (see 17)
19 The Catch A3

Entertainment
Diamond Beach Club .... (see 19)

Admission includes access to beach lounges and toys, as well as up to 1500B of food and drink. Or you could simply grab a table and order a la carte off the menu. The buffets are offered on Monday, Tuesday and Friday.

Diamond Beach Club BEACH CLUB
(☎0 7638 6550; www.diamondbeachclub.com; ⏰10am-2am; 📶) They too have DJs, beachside dining and more. It's slightly less expensive and a smidge less elegant than its chief competition, but with beach clubs, like night clubs, it all depends upon the scene of the moment.

Information

There is an ATM at Surin Plaza, just east of the beach on Rte 4025. Internet access is available at most hotels for 1B per minute and wi-fi is free at most restaurants.

Getting There & Away

A regular *sŏrng·tăa·ou* from Phuket Town's Th Ranong to Hat Surin costs 40B per person, and túk-túk or *sŏrng·tăa·ou* charters cost 600B.

Rent cars from **Andaman Car Rental** (☎0 7662 1600; www.andamancarrent.com; ⏰9am-9pm), opposite the entrance to Twin Palms. Vehicles can be rented from 1400B per day.

Ao Bang Thao อ่าวบางเทา

Almost as large and even more beautiful than Ao Patong, the stunning 8km-long white-sand sweep of Ao Bang Thao is the glue that binds the region's disparate elements. The southern half is home to a sprinkling of three-star bungalow resorts. Further inland you'll find an old fishing village laced with canals, along with a number of upstart villa subdivisions. Don't be alarmed if you see a herd of water buffalo grazing just 100m from a gigantic construction site. That's how fast Bang Thao has changed.

Smack in the centre of it all is the somewhat absurd Laguna Phuket complex – a network of five four- and five-star resort properties and an ageing shopping mall knitted together by an artificial lake (patrolled by tourist shuttle boats) and a paved nature trail. But in the north, Mother Nature asserts herself once more, and a lonely stretch of powder-white sand and tropical blue sea extends past all the bustle and change, and delivers the kind of peace you imagined when you booked your trip.

The **Hideaway Day Spa** (☎08 1750 0026; www.phuket-hideaway.com; 382/33 Th Srisoontorn, Chergtalay; treatments from 1500B) has an excellent reputation. It offers traditional Thai massage, sauna and mud body wraps in a tranquil wooded setting at the edge of a lagoon. The Hideaway also has its own line of spa products.

Sleeping

Laguna Phuket is home to five luxury resorts, an 18-hole golf course and 30 restaurants (the gargantuan Sheraton Grande alone has eight restaurants). Guests at any one of the resorts can use the dining and recreation facilities at all of them. Frequent shuttle buses make the rounds of all the hotels, as do pontoon boats (via the linked lagoons).

Andaman Bangtao Bay Resort HOTEL $$$
(☎0 7627 0246; www.andamanbangtaobayresort.com; bungalows 2900-5900B;) Every bungalow has a sea view and there's a summer-camp vibe at this pleasant little resort. The design is very Thai, with woodcarvings on the walls and coconuts hanging from the eaves of the roofs, but for this price we expect a little more luxury.

Angsana Laguna Phuket HOTEL $$$
(☎0 7632 4101; www.angsana.com; 10 Moo 4, Th Srisoonthorn; r from 5800B;) Gated away in Laguna Phuket, the Angsana Laguna Phuket is a remodel of the older Sheraton Grande Laguna. The gigantic hotel reopened in late 2011 and appeals to a lively, active crowd. It features a gigantic 323m-long pool, water-sports facilities galore and well over 400 rooms. Best rates are secured online.

Banyan Tree Phuket RESORT $$$
(☎0 7632 4374; www.banyantree.com; villas from 16,200B;) One of Phuket's finest hotels, and the first to introduce bungalows with their own private pool, the Banyan Tree Phuket (in Laguna Phuket) is an oasis of sedate, understated luxury. Accommodation is in villas – and, as long as you're here, the on-site spa should not be missed.

Eating & Drinking

Many of Phuket's finest eateries are found just outside Laguna's main gate, and there are even more at the seafood-oriented beach cafes south of the Banyan Tree Phuket.

Cafe de Bangtao INTERNATIONAL $$
(69/19 Moo 3, Hat Bang Tao; mains 130-450B; 8am-1am;) A cute terra-cotta tiled cafe with wood tables and a tiki bar, this is the most appealing eatery on the north end of Bang Tao. Dishes range from Western breakfasts and tasty and reasonably priced Thai dishes to pork tenderloin and tamarind-glazed spare ribs.

Tawai Restaurant THAI $$
(☎0 7632 5381; Moo 1, Laguna Resort Entrance; mains 180-300B; noon-10pm) Set in a lovely old house decorated with traditional art is this gem of a Thai kitchen, serving classics like roast duck curry and pork *lâhp*. Free shuttle service is available to and from the Laguna hotels.

Chaba THAI $$
(☎0 7627 1580; Moo 1, Laguna Resort Entrance; meals 400-800B; 11am-10pm) Upscale Thai served with flair on the lagoon just outside the Laguna gates. Just point and the restaurant will steam, grill or fry it.

Bliss Beach Club INTERNATIONAL $$
(☎0 7651 0150; www.blissbeachclub.com; 202/88 Moo 2; mains 290-480B; 11am-late) Even if you don't commit to a day indulging in its plush surrounds, try to stop in here for lunch. Bliss Beach Club's menu includes garlic prawn Neapolitan-style pizza, an assortment of fresh, crunchy baguettes, and a yummy chocolate mousse, all served with gorgeous sea views.

Tatonka INTERNATIONAL $$$
(☎0 7632 4349; Th Srisoonthorn; dishes 180-790B; 6pm-late Thu-Tue) This is the home of 'globetrotter cuisine', which owner-chef Harold Schwarz developed by taking fresh local products and combining them with cooking and presentation techniques learned in Europe, Colorado and Hawaii. The eclectic, tapas-style selection includes creative vegetarian and seafood dishes and such delights as Peking duck pizza (220B). Book ahead during the high season.

Siam Supper Club INTERNATIONAL $$$
(☎0 7627 0936; Hat Bang Thao; dishes 290-1290B; 6pm-1am) One of the hippest spots on Phuket where the 'infamous' come to sip cocktails, listen to breezy jazz and eat an excellent meal. Siam Supper Club's menu is predominantly Western with gourmet pizzas, seafood *cioppino* (Italian-style seafood stew) and hearty mains such as truffle-honey roast chicken and Australian grass-fed rib eye.

BB's Pub PUB
(☎08 1787 5354; Moo 1, Laguna Phuket entrance; noon-1am) The rickety 'ye olde codger's thinking bar' is reason enough for a round or two at this ageing Laguna standby. The pub grub is decent. It has a pool table and a dartboard, and live music on Friday nights.

Getting There & Away

A *sŏrng·tăa·ou* between Ao Bang Thao and Phuket Town's Th Ranong costs 40B per person. Túk-túk charters are 700B.

Sirinat National Park อุทยานแห่งชาติสิรินาถ

Comprising the exceptional beaches of Nai Thon, Nai Yang and Mai Khao, as well as the former Nai Yang National Park and Mai Khao wildlife reserve, **Sirinat National Park** (☎0 7632 8226; www.dnp.go.th; adult/child 200/100B; ⏲8am-5pm) encompasses 22 sq km of coastal land, plus 68 sq km of sea.

The whole area is 15 minutes or less from Phuket International Airport, which makes it particularly convenient for a first stop after a long trip. This is one of the sweetest slices of the island.

Sleeping & Eating

Hat Nai Thon หาดในทอน

If you're after a lovely arc of fine golden sand, away from the buzz of Phuket busyness, **Hat Nai Thon** is it. One of the best beaches on the island, swimming is exceptional here except at the height of the monsoon, and there is some coral near the headlands at either end of the bay. The closest ATM is in Nai Yang, so stock up on baht before you come. There are a handful of beach restaurants strung along the sand.

Phuket Naithon Resort HOTEL $$
(☎0 7620 5233; www.phuketnaithonresort.com; 24 Moo 4; r 2500B; ❄📶) A great midrange choice set across from the beach and smack in the middle of the strip. Rooms are spacious tiled affairs with floating queen beds, built-in day beds, mini fridge, desk, tub and shower. Check-in at the **Wiwan Restaurant**.

★**Pullman** RESORT $$$
(☎0 7630 3299; www.pullmanphuketarcadia.com; 22/2 Moo 4, Hat Nai Thon; r from 3100B; P❄@📶🏊) The area's newest resort is a stunner. Set high on the cliff above Hat Nai Thon, the lobby alone will make you weak in the knees, with its soothing grey and lavender colour scheme, hardwood floors, and exposed rough-cut limestone walls, plus the dreamy network of reflection pools extending out above the sea, which extends for 180 degrees to the horizon. Thankfully there are rocking chairs and day beds aplenty to catch you when you fall.

Rooms, set in two- and three-storey wood chalets, are spacious with wide terraces that function as outdoor living areas. It's big (277 rooms), but it sure is pretty and service is divine.

Naithonburi HOTEL $$$
(☎0 7620 5500; www.naithonburi.com; Moo 4, Th Hat Nai Thon; r from 3500B; ❄@📶🏊👪) A mellow megaresort if ever there was one. Yes, it has 222 rooms, but it rarely feels too crowded. Rooms are spacious with terracotta tile floors, Thai silks on the bed and private balconies, and the enormous pool is lined with lounges and daybeds.

Hat Nai Yang & Hat Mai Khao หาดในยาง/หาดไม้ขาว

Hat Nai Yang's bay is sheltered by a reef that slopes 20m below the surface – which makes for both good snorkelling in the dry season and decent surfing in the monsoon season. Along the dirt road is a seemingly endless strip of seafood restaurants, beach bars and, oddly enough, tailor shops. It's all refreshingly rough around the edges.

About 5km north of Hat Nai Yang is **Hat Mai Khao**, Phuket's longest beach. Sea turtles lay their eggs here between November and February. Take care when swimming, as there's a strong year-round undertow. Except on weekends and holidays, you'll have this place almost to yourself.

Sirinat National Park CAMPING, BUNGALOWS $
(☎0 7632 7152; www.dnp.go.th/parkreserve; campsites 30B, bungalows 700-1000B) There are campsites (bring your own tent) and large, concrete bungalows at the park headquarters on a gorgeous, shady, white-sand bluff. Check in at the visitors centre or book online.

Discovery Beach Resort GUESTHOUSE $
(65/17 Moo 5, Hat Nai Yang; r with fan/air-con 800/1500B; ❄📶) With wooden Thai accents on the facade and lacquered timber handrails and furnishings, this spotless, budget three-star spot has enough motel kitsch to make it interesting, and its location – right on the beach – makes it a terrific value.

Nai Yang Beach Resort HOTEL $$$
(☎0 7632 8300; www.naiyangbeachresort.com; 65/23-24 Th Hat Nai Yang; r from 3600B; ❄@📶🏊👪) This midrange workhorse is as clean as it is busy and rambles from the road into the casuarinas only steps from Hat Nai Yang. The lowest-end rooms are fan-cooled, while higher-end ones are decorated in modern Thai style and are quite chic.

Dang Sea Beach GUESTHOUSE $$
(☎08 1477 2879; www.dangseabeach.com; 90/4 Moo 5, Th Saku; r 2500B; ❄📶) Rooms are set in

duplex and triplex pods set across from one another and bisected by a paved path to the sand. They're super clean, with high ceilings, recessed lighting, air-con and hot water. It's a superb low season value.

Sala Resort & Spa HOTEL **$$$**
(☎0 7633 8888; www.salaphuket.com; 333 Moo 3, Tambon Maikhao; r from 4800B, villas from 9040B; ❄@📶🏊) This uberstylish boutique property is a blend of Sino-Portuguese and art deco influences with mod flair. Even 2nd-floor rooms have outdoor bathrooms. The gem of the property is the beachfront black-granite infinity pool where the bar area includes cushy, circular sofa lounges.

★**Dewa** RESORT **$$$**
(☎0 7637 2300; www.dewaphuketresort.com; 65 Tambon Sakoo; condos & villas from 7000B; P❄📶🏊) An independently owned boutique resort that offers one- and two-bedroom condos and luscious pool villas, just steps from the virgin national park beach. You'll have more space and a full kitchen in the condos, but the villas are secluded pods with reclaimed wood accents, vintage wrought-iron motifs, and a wall-mounted flat screen.

Huge outdoor baths with a soaker tub and rain shower spill into a garden with a sizable plunge pool. The restaurant is sensational and borders the sexy common pool area, blessed with magnificent sunset views. Service could not be better.

Indigo Pearl HOTEL **$$$**
(☎0 7632 7006; www.indigo-pearl.com; r 8250-16,500B; ❄@📶🏊) One of the most unique and hip of Phuket's high-end resorts takes its design cues from the island's tin-mining history. Hardware, such as vices, scales and other mining tools, are used in the decor – even the toilet-paper rolls are big bolts – and the common lounge areas are infused with indigo light.

The gardens are modern and lush, and surround a pool area oasis.

Anantara Phuket HOTEL **$$$**
(☎0 7633 6100; www.phuket.anantara.com; 888 Moo 3, Tumbon Mai Khao; villas from 13,125B; ❄@📶🏊) This all-villa property opens onto a serene lotus-filled lagoon that extends to the beach. Luxurious, classic Thai pool villas are connected to the lobby, bars and restaurants, and to the beach by old timber board-walks that wind beneath swaying palms. It also offers the Bua Luang Spa; the Sea Fire Salt Restaurant is worth a romantic splurge.

★**Ban Ra Tree** THAI **$$**
(Hat Nai Yang; mains 90-350B; ⏰11am-10:30pm) The best choice on the Hat Nai Yang beach strip; its plastic tables are elegantly dressed in turquoise and white linen and sunk in the sand beneath parasols. The seafood is dynamite: think green curry fried rice topped with coconut milk. Ask for yours with crab, and it won't just include hints of crab meat. It will be topped with a whole, meaty cracked crab for just 220B!

They also do fresh fish in myriad ways. Try it fried in yellow or red curry. They steam and sauce Phuket lobster, slather prawns in tamarind sauce, and make wonderful smoothies. Service is superb.

Fiesta INTERNATIONAL-THAI **$$**
(Hat Nai Yang; mains 150-350B; ⏰noon-10pm) Hidden in the jumble of bamboo seafood joints is this unique kitchen owned by a former resort chef who presents Thai classics with a twist. He does *pá·naang* fish curry and a mixed seafood *lâhp*, and everything is spiced for the *fa·ràng* palate and presented with flair on powder-blue wooden tables sunk in the sand.

ℹ Getting There & Away

If you're coming from the airport, a taxi costs about 200B. There is no regular *sŏrng·tăa·ou*, but a túk-túk charter from Phuket Town costs about 800B.

Khao Phra Thaew Royal Wildlife & Forest Reserve

อุทยานสัตว์ป่าเขาพระแทว

It's not all sand and sea. In the north of the island, this park protects 23 sq km of virgin island rainforest (evergreen monsoon forest). There are some pleasant hikes over the hills and a couple of photogenic waterfalls, including **Nam Tok Ton Sai** and **Nam Tok Bang Pae**. The falls are best seen in the rainy season between June and November; in the dry months they are less impressive. The highest point in the park is **Khao Phara** (442m). Because of its royal status, the reserve is better protected than the average national park in Thailand.

A German botanist discovered a rare and unique species of palm in Khao Phra Thaew about 50 years ago. Called the white-backed palm – or *langkow* palm – the fan-shaped plant stands 3m to 5m tall and is found only here and in Khao Sok National Park.

Tigers, Malayan sun bears, rhinos and elephants once roamed the forest here, but nowadays resident mammals are limited to humans, pigs, monkeys, slow loris, langurs, civets, flying foxes, squirrels, mousedeer and other smaller animals. Watch out for cobras and wild pigs.

The tiny **Phuket Gibbon Rehabilitation Centre** (☎0 7626 0492; www.gibbonproject.org; admission 10B; ⏲9am-4pm), in the park near Nam Tok Bang Pae, is open to the public. Financed by donations (1500B will care for a gibbon for one year), the centre adopts gibbons that have been kept in captivity in the hopes they can be reintroduced to the wild.

Park rangers may act as guides for hikes in the park on request; payment for services is negotiable.

To get to Khao Phra Thaew from Phuket Town, take Th Thepkasatri north about 20km to Thalang District and turn right at the intersection for Nam Tok Ton Sai, which is 3km down the road.

Thalang District อำเภอถลาง

A few hundred metres northeast of the famous **Heroines Monument** in Thalang District on Rte 4027, and about 11km northwest of Phuket Town, is **Thalang National Museum** (☎0 7631 1426; admission 30B; ⏲9am-4pm). The museum contains five exhibition halls chronicling southern themes such as the history of Thalang-Phuket and the colonisation of the Andaman coast. The legend of the 'two heroines' (memorialised on the nearby monument), who supposedly drove off an 18th-century Burmese invasion force by convincing the island's women to dress as men, is also recounted in detail.

Also in Thalang District, just north of the crossroads near Thalang town, is **Wat Phra Thong** (admission by donation; ⏲dawn-dusk), Phuket's 'Temple of the Gold Buddha'. The image is half buried so that only the head and shoulders are visible. According to local legend, those who have tried to excavate the image have become very ill or encountered serious accidents. The temple is particularly revered by Thai-Chinese, many of whom believe the image hails from China. During Chinese New Year pilgrims descend from Phang-Nga, Takua Pa and Krabi.

RANONG PROVINCE

Ranong ระนอง

POP 29,096

On the eastern bank of the Sompaen River's turbid, tea-brown estuary, the frontier town of Ranong is a short boat ride – or a filthy swim – from Myanmar. This border town par excellence (shabby, frenetic, slightly seedy) has a thriving Burmese population (keep an eye out for men wearing traditional *longyi,* Burmese sarongs), a clutch of hot springs and some tremendous street food.

Once a gritty, grotty backwater, today the town is basking in transit tourism to Ko Phayam and Ko Chang, and clearly benefiting from a stabilised political situation in Myanmar. Suddenly there are boutique hotels and a style-conscious local scene, relatively speaking. Meanwhile, more and more dive operators specialising in live-aboard trips to the Surin Islands and Burma Banks are establishing themselves here too, adding a pinch of an expat feel. Ranong is absolutely worthy of a night or two.

Activities

Rakswarin Hot Springs HOT SPRINGS
(Th Petchkasem; ⏲8am-5pm) FREE Ranong healing waters bubble from a sacred spring hot enough to boil eggs (65°C). The riverside pools have received a recent update and are now blessed with chequered mosaic tile, and that hot concrete floor – essentially one giant heating pad – is where you lay that bad back and let the heat penetrate your gnarliest knots.

★ **Siam Hot Spa** SPA
(☎0 7781 3551; www.siamhotsparanong.com; 73/3 Th Petchkasem; treatments from 300B) Opposite the public springs, this place offers a more sterilised mineral bath experience. You can dip into a private Jacuzzi or standard tubs, and pair it with a salt scrub or a massage, which is divine. Highly recommended.

Diving

Live-aboard diving trips to world-class bubble-blowing destinations, including the Burma Banks and the Surin and Similan Islands, are deservedly popular. Try **A-One-Diving** (☎0 7783 2984; www.a-one-diving.com; 256 Th Ruangrat; 3-night packages from 16,900B; ⏲Oct-Apr) or **Aladdin Dive Safari** (☎08 7288 6908; www.aladdindivesafari.com; Ko Phayam Pier;

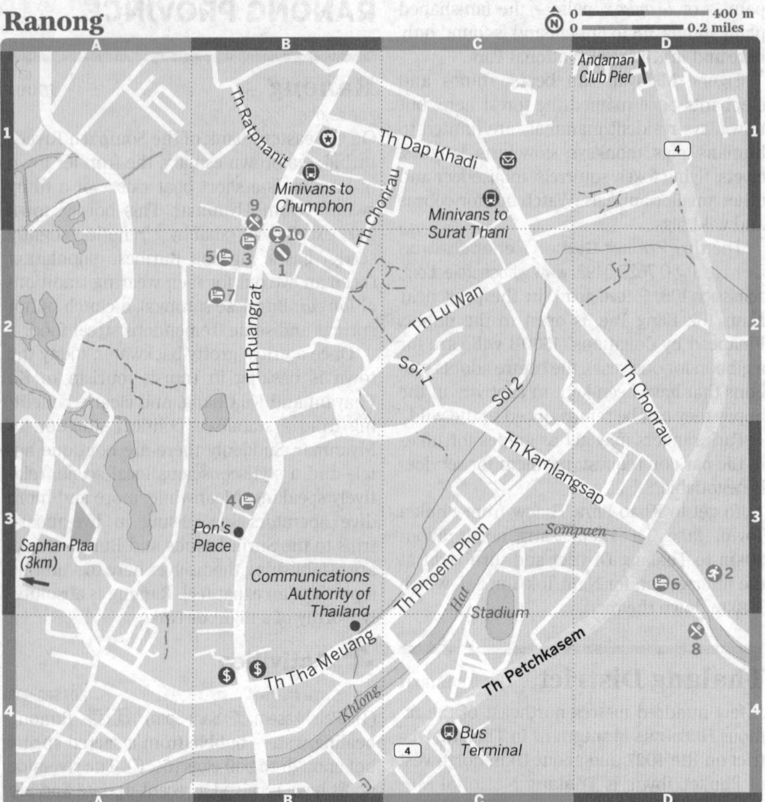

Ranong

Activities, Courses & Tours

Sleeping

Eating

Drinking & Nightlife

live-aboard trips from 14,900B; ⏲ Oct-Apr) located at the Ko Phayam pier.

Sleeping

Accommodation in town can help you arrange a visa run and transport to the islands.

The places on or near Th Petchkasem (Hwy 4) can be reached from town by *sŏrng·tăa·ou* 2.

Suta House Bungalows GUESTHOUSE $
(☎0 7783 2707; Th Ruangrat; r with fan/air-con 380/420B; ❄📶) Right in the town centre, this off-the-road, very popular place has a cluster of simple ageing bungalows – and plenty of flowers. Beds are hard but their sheets are crisp and showers are hot.

Dahla House GUEST HOUSE $
(☎0 7781 2959; http://dahla.siam2web.com; 323/5 Th Ruangrat; r with fan/air-con 400/500B; ❄📶) Funky little concrete bungalows with tiled floors and pebbled tile baths line a garden;

it's set off the main drag. It's got the friendliest vibe in town and management will happily arrange a late check-out if you're on a visa run.

Luang Poj GUESTHOUSE $
(☎08 7266 6333, 0 7783 3377; www.facebook.com/luangpojhostel; 225 Th Ruangrat; r 500B; ❄📶) This new and expanding place is a gorgeous remodel of a 1920s-era building that was Ranong's first hotel. Rooms are windowless and share warm-water bathrooms, but each is spotless, very comfy and decorated in a signature colour, with mod-meets-vintage flair: think Indian art, birdcages, one-of-a-kind light fixtures and retro photography.

★**Thansila Hot Spring Resort** HOTEL $$
(☎08 1797 4674; www.thansila-hotspring-resort.com; 129/2 Th Petchkasem; r 700-900B) A groovy new spot downriver from the hot springs, the best digs are stone-wall lodge rooms with fantastic river views, grotto-like baths with hot water, and flat screens with satellite TV. The hotel rooms offer high ceilings and an artsy flair.

The hotel is owned by a Thai architect who renovated over two years. She recently added a hip and homey cafe, serving Western breakfasts and simple Thai meals.

The B HOTEL $$
(☎0 7782 3111; www.thebranong.com; 295/1-2 Th Ruangrat; superior/deluxe 1100/1300B) This chunk of polished concrete modernism is proof of a new era in Ranong. Rooms have floating beds, flat-screen TVs, rain showers, high ceilings and excellent service. There's also a billiards and snooker bar, an open-air restaurant, and a rooftop infinity pool overlooking town and the surrounding green hills.

Eating & Drinking

Ranong has a lively, young and very local drinking scene involving lots of karaoke.

On Th Kamlangsap, not far from Hwy 4, there is a night market that sells great Thai dishes at low prices. The day market on Th Ruangrat offers inexpensive Thai and Burmese meals.

Appreski Resort SCANDINAVIAN $
(☎08 7817 7033; 129/6 Moo 1, Th Petchkasem; sandwiches from 45B; ⏲8am-8pm) Built into Ranong Canyon across the river from the hot springs, this eatery has cultivated a reputation for Danish-style open sandwiches piled with imported cheese, pork liver pâté or gravlax cured in-house.

Sophon's Hideaway THAI, INTERNATIONAL $$
(☎0 7783 2730; www.sophonshideaway.asia; 323/7 Th Ruangrat; mains 45-350B; ⏲10am-11pm; 📶) An attractive if weathered steak house unfurls beneath this stilted bamboo roof that has been serving expats and border businessmen for years. They do decent Thai dishes and have a pizza oven, but their speciality is steak – all kinds of steak, from venison, ostrich, and salmon to T-bones and ribeyes.

Some Time BAR
(☎0 7782 4333; Th Ruangrat; ⏲5pm-1am) The thinking person's border-run bar, this super hip spot has been crafted from upcycled wood panelling to accentuate its old teak bones. There is an attractive patio and a bandstand offering frequent live music which lures a local crowd for drinks and cheap Thai eats.

PON'S PLACE: RANONG'S TOURISM EXPERT

Pon's Place (☎08 1597 4549; www.pon-place-ranong.com; Th Ruangrat; ⏲7.30am-midnight) is the go-to spot in Ranong for everything from Western breakfasts (from 40B) to Ranong Air bookings and information about bus schedules. Pon himself is a high-energy, friendly guy. If you need help with anything, consider Pon your fixer.

Information

Internet can be found along Th Ruangrat for 20B per hour. A cluster of ATMs are at the intersection of Th Tha Meuang and Th Ruangrat. Most restaurants have wi-fi.

IMMIGRATION OFFICES

The main Thai immigration office is on the road to Saphan Plaa, about halfway between town and the main piers, across from a branch of Kasikorn Bank. If entering Thailand from Myanmar via Kawthoung, you'll have to visit this office to get your passport stamped with a visa on arrival, but you'll still only get 15 days.

There is also a smaller immigration post in the vicinity of Tha Saphan Plaa. If you're just going in and out of Myanmar's Kawthoung for the day, a visit to the small post will suffice.

POST

Main Post Office (Th Chonrau; ⏲9am-4pm Mon-Fri, to noon Sat)

TELEPHONE

Communications Authority of Thailand (CAT; Th Tha Meuang; ⏲24hr) For phone services.

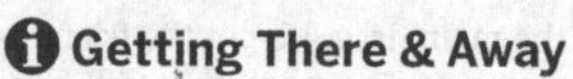

Getting There & Away

AIR

Ranong Air (☎0 7783 2222; www.ranongair.com) runs five flights per week between Ranong and Bangkok. **Happy Air** (☎08 1891 5800; www.happyair.co.th) and **Nok Air** (☎0 2900 9955; www.nokair.com), the only one to operate out of Don Muang Airport, also make the run.

GETTING TO MYANMAR: RANONG TOWN TO VICTORIA POINT (KAWTHOUNG)

The dusty, tumbledown port at the southernmost tip of mainland Myanmar was named Victoria Point by the British, but is known as Ko Song (Second Island) by the Thais. The Burmese appellation, Kawthoung, is most likely a corruption of the Thai name. Most travellers come here to renew their visas, but the place also makes an interesting day trip.

Fishing and trade with Thailand keep things ticking over, but Kawthoung also churns out some of Myanmar's best kickboxers. Nearby islands are inhabited by bands of nomadic *chow lair* (sea gypsies; also spelled *chao leh*).

The easiest way to renew your visa is to opt for one of the 'visa trips' (from 1000B per person including visa fees) offered by travel agencies in Ranong such as Pon's Place, but it's relatively easy to do the legwork yourself, and you'll save around 200B.

Getting to the border When the Thailand–Myanmar border is open, boats to Kawthoung leave from the pier at **Saphan Plaa** (Pla Bridge) about 5km from the centre of Ranong. Take *sŏrng·tăa·ou* (passenger pick-up truck) 3 from Ranong (20B) to the pier, where long-tail captains will lead you to the immigration window then to their boat (per person one-way/return 150/300B). When negotiating your price, confirm whether it is per person or per ride, and one-way or return.

At the border At the checkpoint, you must inform the authorities that you're a day visitor if you don't plan on staying overnight – in which case you will pay a fee of US$10 (it must be a crisp bill; you can get one from harbour touts for 500B). The only big hassles come from 'helpers' on the Myanmar side who offer to do everything from carrying your day pack to collecting forms, then ask for tips, but they're generally more friendly than aggravating.

If you're just coming to renew your Thai visa, the whole process will take a minimum of two hours. Bear in mind when you are returning to Thailand that Myanmar's time is 30 minutes behind Thailand's. This has caused problems in the past for returning visitors who got through Burmese immigration before its closing time only to find the **Thai Immigration office** (⏲8.30am-4.30pm) closed. It's a good idea to double-check Thai immigration closing hours when leaving the country – if you don't get stamped in you'll have to return to Myanmar again the next day.

A quicker, easier (especially for self-drivers) and much more polished alternative – albeit sterilised and less interesting – is to find the **Andaman Club** (www.andamanclub.com; Hwy 4; 850B; ⏲8.30am-3.30pm) pier, just north of town, off Hwy 4. At the terminal, you'll get your passport stamped in minutes, and a Myanmar bound ferry (25 minutes each way) leaves hourly from 8.30am to 3.30pm, docking at a flash casino resort. The whole trip costs 850B, and for an additional 490B you can take a half-day tour along the Myanmar coast from the casino.

Moving on It's possible to stay overnight in one of Victoria Point's dingy, overpriced hotels, but you'd probably rather not. If you have a valid Myanmar visa in your passport, which you'll have to apply for at the Myanmar Embassy in Bangkok (or a third country), you'll be permitted to stay for up to 28 days and exit anywhere you like, taking your passport with you. If not, you'll have to leave your passport at the border and grab it on your way back to Ranong.

Book flights at Pon's Place. The airport is 22km south of town.

BUS

The bus terminal is on Th Petchkasem 1km from town, though some Bangkok-bound buses stop at the main market. *Sŏrng·tăa·ou* 2 (blue) passes the terminal.

DESTINATION	FARE (B)	DURATION (HR)
Bangkok	360-725	10
Chumphon	130	3
Hat Yai	420	5
Khao Lak	180	3½
Krabi	210	6
Phang-Nga	190	5
Phuket	260	5-6
Surat Thani	190	4-5

Minivans head to Surat Thani (190B, 3½ hours, four times daily) and Chumphon (120B, three hours, hourly from 6am to 5pm).

Getting Around

Motorcycle taxis will take you almost anywhere in town for 50B, and to the pier for boats to Ko Chang, Ko Phayam and Myanmar for 70B. Pon's Place can assist with motorcycle and car rentals and offers shuttle vans from its office to the ferry docks for 70B. Minivan shuttles (per person 350B) meet flights and run from the airport to the Ko Phayam pier.

Ko Phayam

เกาะพยาม

Technically part of Laem Son National Park, little Ko Phayam is fringed with beautiful beaches and – for now – is managing to go mainstream while still holding onto its soul. The spectacular northwest and southwest coasts are dotted with beach bungalows, breezy restaurants and bars, and its wooded interior is laced with narrow concrete streets, so you can certainly understand the appeal. Fauna in the area includes wild pigs, monkeys and snakes, and there is tremendous bird life. Look for sea eagles, toucans and hornbills. The one 'village' on the island, where you will also find the main pier and a majestic golden Buddha at **Wat Phayam**, caters mostly to tourists. But hit it during a festival (such as the Cashew Festival in April) and you'll see that islanders still have a firm grip on their homeland. Motorcycle pathways run down the middle of the island, feeding smaller concrete roadways and dirt trails, some of which can be rutted to the point of hazardous – drive slowly.

The main drawback of Ko Phayam is that the snorkelling isn't great, as high sea temperatures have killed off all the coral. But the Surin Islands are closer to here than anywhere else and you can hop on live-aboard dive expeditions or speedboat transfers. For dive trips and PADI courses contact **Phayam Divers** (08 6995 2598; www.phayamlodge.com; Ao Yai).

Sleeping & Eating

Room capacity has doubled in the past four years, and most resorts are now open year round with attached eateries serving middling Thai fare. Most places have wi-fi or internet for 2B per minute. The cheapest, and some of the best, Thai eats are found in town near the pier. Electricity is often only available from sunset to 10pm or 11pm.

Ao Khao Kwai & Ao Hin Khow

★ **June Horizon** BUNGALOWS $
(08 0145 9771; Ao Khao Kwai; bungalows 450-600B; Nov-May) A joyful addition tucked into a mangrove inlet at the south end of the beach. Bunk in one of the creatively styled circular concrete bungalows brushed with fanciful murals, or grab a beach hut nailed together with reclaimed and distressed wood panels and crowned with a grass ceiling. All have outdoor baths. The wonderful 'gypsy bar' is worth a tipple.

Jansom Bungalows HOTEL $
(08 1968 5720; Ao Khao Kwai; bungalows 500-600B) The wooden bungalows here are basic but the view from the terraces over white sand, grey boulders and aqua sea is stunning. The landscaped gardens and stone pathways also make this place feel more upscale. It's right off the beach and the restaurant is reliably good.

PP Land HOTEL $
(08 1678 4310; www.payampplandbeach.com; Ao Hin Khow; bungalows 650B; wi-fi) This eco-lodge, north of the pier on the little-visited eastside of the island, offers stylish concrete bungalows powered by the wind and sun with terraces that overlook the sea. The Belgian-Thai owners also preserved a vast tract of jungle south of the resort, and good birdwatching is available from the top floor of their restaurant.

They have an organic garden, make their own all-natural laundry detergent and treat their sewage. Some talk green; these folks live it.

Mr Gao BUNGALOWS $
(☎0 7787 0222; www.mr-gao-phayam.com; Ao Khao Kwai; bungalows from 350B;) The varnished wood-and-brick or bamboo bungalows are popular with activity-oriented couples and families. It has 24-hour electricity and kayak rental, and arranges transport and multi-day trips to the Surin Islands.

Chomjan Resort HOTEL $$
(☎08 5678 4166; www.chomjanresort.com; Ao Khao Kwai; bungalows 900-1500B) Tidy concrete bungalows are perched on a beach-side slope and have sea views through mature trees just before the bay's jade curl. All have terraces with lounging cushions and open-to-sky bathrooms, but otherwise the decor is fairly bland and slightly frayed. The restaurant here serves excellent Thai fare.

Heaven Beach GUESTHOUSE $$
(☎08 2806 0413; www.ppland-heavenbeach.com; Ao Khao Kwai; r 2000B;) A two-year old resort with an idyllic slice of real estate on luscious Ao Khao Kwai. Their tiled bungalows are spacious with outdoor baths, hot showers, all-day electricity and wide decks with rattan lounges. Enjoy a coconut shake at the cute beachfront restaurant with turquoise benches, hand-painted menu boards, and tables sunk in the sand.

Buffalo Bay Vacation Club HOTEL $$
(☎08 5107 9473; www.buffalobayclub.com; Ao Khao Kwai; bungalows 1300-2500B;) Buffalo's spotless, airtight, concrete bungalows with sliding glass doors, hot water and TVs are posh by Phayam standards and a decent value. Their restaurant serves everything from fajitas to authentic Thai curries.

Ao Yai

Aow Yai Bungalows GUESTHOUSE $
(☎08 9819 8782, 0 7787 0216; Ao Yai; bungalows 200-400B) The thatched bamboo bungalow pioneer that started it all 24 years ago. This French-Thai operation was Phayam's first. Choose between small wooden-and-bamboo bungalows in the palm grove and a larger beachfront model on the southern end of Ao Yai. It rents snorkelling gear, kayaks and bodyboards, too.

Friends Bungalow BUNGALOWS $
(☎08 5679 9568; www.payamfriends.jimdo.com; Ao Yai; tents from 400B, bungalows from 800B) This property has potential. They offer spacious tents on wood platforms with their own private tiled baths, and some interesting wood-and-concrete bungalows with simple but nice touches like hand-painted designs on concrete porches, sliding doors, built-in platform beds and outdoor baths. They have electricity all night.

Bamboo Bungalows GUESTHOUSE $$
(☎0 7782 0012; www.bamboo-bungalows.com; Ao Yai; bungalows 750-1500B;) A very popular and social beachfront property. There's a lush garden and an attractive lounge-restaurant with hammocks and log swings out front. Bungalows range from sagging bamboo jobs to fairly luxurious peaked-

KO PHAYAM'S BEACHES

Ko Phayam is dotted with small beaches, but these two long stretches of sandy bliss are where most folks end up.

Ao Khao Kwai (Buffalo Bay) A luscious cove with golden sand, jungled bluffs and a rock reef offshore – it's the most stunning location on the island. Lovers of peace and quiet head here along with some hippies and the occasional German package tourist. It's a terrific swimming beach as well, except at low tide when the sea recedes leaving mud flats at the southern end. Of course, that's where the sand is at its finest and whitest, streaked with great brush strokes of tiny pink shells. Hundreds – no, thousands – are piled evocatively in thick drifts by the sea.

Ao Yai Long, wide and chilled out yet social, this beach attracts everyone from gap-year backpackers and glam-packing couples to young families and retirees. Surf kicks up in the fringe and low seasons, with a consistent right-hand break. The best beginner's break is directly in front of Bamboo Bungalows. You can rent boogie boards and surfboards at guesthouses along the beach. The swimming is great here and the island's best snorkelling (still, don't expect much) is found off Laem Rung, Ao Yai's northernmost point.

roof cottages that have tiled floors, ceiling fans and outdoor rain showers. There's 24-hour electricity and kayaks, surf- and bodyboards available for guests.

Frog Beach House HOTEL $$
(☎08 3542 7559; www.frogbeachhouse.com; Ao Yai; bungalows 1000B; 📶) Traditional Thai-style hardwood chalets with wooden floors, outdoor bathrooms, glass-bowl sinks and mosquito nets are all lined up just off the beach next to a small stream, with a nice slab of beach out front.

Phayam Lodge BUNGALOWS $$$
(☎08 6995 2598; www.phayamlodge.com; Ao Yai; bungalows 2500-3900B; ❄📶) The flashiest compound on this beach is set up for divers who have the Similan and Surin Islands in their sights. Bungalows are set up around a fledgling garden and offer wooden beds, ceiling fans and air-con, recessed lighting, hot water and plush linens. They have an in-house dive centre, and their Bubble Bar is right on the beach.

Drinking

Hippy Bar BAR
(Ao Khao Kwai; ⏱11am-2am Nov-Apr) An amazing beach bar cobbled out of foraged driftwood, bottles, seashells and anything else that happened to wash up on shore. The lounge resembles the bow of a pirate ship. There are orchids, waterfall fountains and dub tunes on the sound system.

Getting There & Away

From Ranong, take *sŏrng·tăa·ou* 3 from Th Ruangrat Market (25B) or one of the many shuttles that service most guesthouses (50B) to the Phayam Pier near Saphan Plaa. If you have three or more people in your group it makes better sense to hire a driver (100B).

There is a daily ferry from here to Ko Phayam's main pier (150B, 1½ to two hours) at 9.30am, and speedboats (350B, 45 minutes) at 10am, noon, 2.30pm & 4pm. From Ko Phayam back to Ranong the boats run at 9am, noon and 3.30pm. Long-tail boat charters to Ko Chang are 1500B.

Getting Around

Motorcycle taxis provide transport around Ko Phayam; there are no cars. A motorcycle taxi from the pier to the main beaches costs 50B to 80B per person each way, depending on the beach. Walking is possible but distances are long – it's about 45 minutes from the pier to Ao Khao Kwai, the nearest bay. Motorbike rentals (200B) are available in the village and from most of the larger resorts, and you'll need one to properly explore the island. It's best to rent yours immediately after getting off the boat in the village. Bicycles are widely available as well.

Ko Chang เกาะช้าง

This little-visited rustic isle is a long way – in every respect – from its much more popular Trat Province namesake. Its speciality is no-frills living, and, yes, electricity is a frill here, but its absence gives as much as it denies. The whole island is saturated in an all-pervading quiet, where the blip and buzz of modern life are replaced with the slosh of the sea, the intoxicating murmur of the cicadas and the far off rumbling of a long-tail.

Pass the time exploring the island's tiny village capital (where the boats dock during the wet season) or wend your way around the island on one of the dirt trails. Sea eagles, Andaman kites and hornbills all nest here and, if you're lucky, you'll catch sight of them floating above the mangroves and the jungled east coast. The wide, west-coast beach of **Ao Yai** has gorgeous marbled white and black sand in the south, which obscures the otherwise clear water. A short trail leads over the bluff to **Ao Tadeng**, another marbled beach strewn with boulders and the island's best sunset spot. White-sand snobs will be happiest on Ao Yai's north end. In the dry season you'll be dropped off directly in front of your bungalow.

There are no banks or cars on Ko Chang, but internet has arrived at **Cashew Resort** (Ao Yai; per min 2B) and Crocodile Rock (p284) (1B per minute). Yoga and tai chi classes are held at **Om Tao** (☎08 5470 9312; www.omtao.net; Ao Yai), next door.

Trails lead south from the village in the island's interior to the national park station on the east coast. That's where you'll find the island's best stretch of intact jungle. Elsewhere it's all been tamed into cashew orchards and rubber plantations.

Sleeping & Eating

Basic bamboo huts reign supreme on Ko Chang and, for the most part, they're only open from November to mid-April. Electricity is limited and a few places have solar and wind power.

Ao Yai is where you'll find most lodging options and a few more places are tucked away on Ao Tadeng, to the south, which is linked to Ao Yai via a short walking track. More isolated options can be found on the beaches to the north and far south of the island.

Sunset Bungalows GUESTHOUSE $
(☎08 0693 8577, 08 4339 5224; Ao Yai; bungalows 250-500B) Sweet wooden bungalows with bamboo decks and attached Thai-style bathrooms sit back in the trees lining Ao Yai's northern end and its slender yet clean stretch of sand. The restaurant is charming and offers a tasty menu, and the staff is as friendly as they come.

Lae Ta Wan BUNGALOWS $
(☎08 0698 6227; Ao Tadeng; bungalows 300-500B) Here are some of Ko Chang's best, though rustic, wooden bungalows, brushed with bright purple trim and scattered on a scrubby hillside that tumbles down to the beach around a ramshackle restaurant in a shady grove.

★**Crocodile Rock** GUESTHOUSE $
(☎08 0533 4138; tonn1970@yahoo.com; Ao Yai; bungalows 400-500B; @) Outstanding bamboo bungalows perched on Ao Yai's serene southern headland. Although it's not 'on' the beach, it has superb bay views. Its classy kitchen turns out homemade yoghurt, breads, cookies, good espresso, and a variety of veggie and seafood dishes. This place has its own pier, so ask to be dropped here by long-tail. Three-night minimum.

Full Moon Bungalow BUNGALOWS $
(Ao Yai; seafront/garden bungalows 450/250B) A handful of quaint A-frame cottages, some brushed sky blue, some cream coloured. One is pink. Frills are few (or none), but the location under the trees and steps from the sea is superb.

Sawasdee GUESTHOUSE $
(☎08 1803 0946, 08 6906 0900; www.sawadeekohchang.com; Ao Yai; bungalows 350-600B) A-frame wooden bungalows have vented walls to keep things cool, sunken bathrooms painted bright colours and hammocks on the terraces. Its alfresco restaurant (dishes 80-160B) – think driftwood furniture spread beneath a massive tree dangling with lanterns – is as classy as it is delicious.

Mama's GUESTHOUSE $
(☎08 0530 7066, 0 7782 0180; mamasbungalows@yahoo.com; Ao Tadeng; huts 250-500B) One of three good choices on Ao Tadeng, Mama's is tucked into a pretty corner on a rocky, hibiscus-laden hillside. The good-sized wooden huts here all have private bathrooms. Mama serves some of the best Thai food on the island.

ℹ Getting There & Away

From Ranong take a *sŏrng·tăa·ou* (25B) from the day market on Th Ruangrat to Tha Ko Phayam near Saphan Plaa. Alternatively, most Ranong guesthouses will arrange for a taxi to shuttle you to the pier for 50B to 100B.

Two speedboats to Ao Yai (per person 350B, 45 minutes, 9.30am and 2pm) leave daily from late October to April. They return to Ranong at 9am and 1pm. It's cheaper and just as convenient to travel on one of two daily long-tail taxi boats (per person 150B, two hours, 8.30am and 2pm). In the dry season, they stop at all the west-coast beaches. Taxi boats return at 7.30am and 1.30pm. During the monsoon months only morning boats make the crossing three days a week, docking at the main pier on the northeast coast.

You can also charter a long-tail boat to Ko Phayam through Koh Chang Resort (1500B). In high season inquire about a once-daily taxi boat to the island.

Laem Son National Park

อุทยานแห่งชาติแหลมสน

This **national park** (☎0 7786 1431; www.dnp.go.th; adult/child 200/100B) covers 315 sq km and includes about 100km of Andaman Sea coastline – the longest protected shore in the country – and over 20 islands. Much of the coast here is edged with mangroves and laced with tidal channels, home to various species of birds, fish, deer and monkeys. Sea turtles nest on Hat Praphat.

The most accessible beach is the gorgeous 3km white sweep of **Hat Bang Ben**, where the park headquarters are located. Look south and peninsulas jut out into the ocean like so many fingers hiding isolated coves accessible only by long-tail boat. All of the beaches are said to be safe for swimming year-round. From here you can also see several islands, including the nearby Ko Kam Yai, Ko Kam Noi, Mu Ko Yipun, Ko Khang Khao and, to the north, Ko Phayam. If there is a prettier sunset picnic spot on the north Andaman coast, we missed it.

Sleeping & Eating

Most accommodation options are at Hat Bang Ben. At research time, the national park bungalows were closed and camping was no longer available on the beach.

Wasana Resort GUESTHOUSE $

(☎0 7786 1434; bungalows 400-600B; ❄📶) A family-run ring of cosy bungalows wrap around the colourful on-site restaurant. The owners, a Dutch-Thai couple, have plenty of great ideas for exploring Laem Son (ask about the stunning 10km trek around the headland) and can take you on a day trip to Ko Kum (per person 550B), and on a boat trip through the mangroves (per person 200B).

Getting There & Away

The turn-off for Laem Son National Park is about 58km from Ranong down Hwy 4 (Petchkasem Hwy), between the Km 657 and Km 658 markers. Buses heading south from Ranong can drop you off here (ask for Hat Bang Ben). Once you're off the highway, however, you'll have to flag down a pickup truck going towards the park. If you can't get a ride all the way, it's a 10km walk from Hwy 4 to the park entrance. The road is paved, so if you're driving it's a breeze.

PHANG-NGA PROVINCE

Khuraburi คุระบุรี

Blink and you'll miss it. But if you keep your eyes wide open you'll enjoy this soulful, dusty gateway to the Surin Islands and some of the south's best community-based tourism opportunities. For locals it's a market town relied on by hundreds of squid fishermen who live in ramshackle stilted bamboo villages or new royally-sponsored subdivisions tucked away in the rolling jade hills.

For tourist information try **Tom & Am Tour** (☎08 6272 0588) across from the bus station.

Sleeping & Eating

Don't miss the **morning market** (⊙6-10am daily) across from Boon Piya Resort, where you'll sniff stalls frying up chickens and grilling coconut waffles (7B), and kettles bubbling with Thai donuts (per bag 20B) to be dipped in thick sugary green curry. Choose your flavour, then sit at one of the long wooden tables under the shelter in the middle of the market and ask for a cup of tea (10B). It will come caramel coloured and floating on a raft of condensed milk. Stir it. Sip it. Dunk your donuts in it. Then sip the herbal tea afterwards. You'll be among the few *fa·ràng* here. This is travelling.

★ **Boon Piya Resort** GUESTHOUSE $

(☎08 1752 5457, 0 7649 1969; 175/1 Th Pekasem; bungalows 600B; ❄📶) These spacious, sparkling and modern concrete bungalows with tiled floors and hot-water bathrooms are set in a garden compound off the main road and the best in town. The owner books transport to the Surin Islands.

Greenview Resort HOTEL $$

(☎0 7640 1400; www.kuraburigreenviewresort.com; 129 Moo 5 Bangwan; r incl breakfast 1500-3500B; ❄📶🏊) Five kilometres south of town is this lovely landscaped jungle property with unique rooms and bungalows made from stone, wood or bamboo, with high-end touches such as waterfall-style showers in outdoor bathrooms and Thai art on the walls. There's a new adobe-style addition with floating beds and polished concrete floors, a shaded pool and a lake for canoeing.

Getting There & Away

Any Ranong- or Phuket-bound bus will stop in Khuraburi. Take a Phuket-bound bus to Takua Pa, about 50km south of Khuraburi, to transfer to destinations such as Surat Thani (ordinary/air-con 100/160B, three hours), Krabi (ordinary 180B, four hours) and Khao Sok National Park (60B to 100B, one hour).

The pier for the Surin Islands is about 9km north of town. Whoever books your boat to the islands will arrange free transfer.

Surin Islands Marine National Park อุทยานแห่งชาติหมู่เกาะสุรินทร์

The five gorgeous islands that make up the **Surin Islands Marine National Park** (www.dnp.go.th; adult/child 500/300B; ⊙mid-Nov–mid-May) sit 60km offshore, just 5km from the Thailand–Myanmar marine border. Healthy rainforest, pockets of white-sand beach in sheltered bays and rocky headlands that jut into the ocean characterise these granite-outcrop islands. The clearest of water makes for great marine life, with underwater visibility often up to 35m. The islands' sheltered waters also attract *chow lair* – sea gypsies – who live in a village onshore during the monsoon season from May to November. Around here they are known as Moken, from the local word *oken* meaning 'salt water'.

Ko Surin Neua (north) and Ko Surin Tai (south) are the two largest islands. Park headquarters and all visitor facilities are at Ao Chong Khad and Ao Mai Ngam on Ko Surin Neua, near the jetty. The shapes and colours are what you'll remember most. The flaxen sand and sparkling blue-green bays, the purpling depths, and the sheer granite peninsulas that tumble down in a permanent geological avalanche forming arrow-like points and natural breakwaters are spectacular.

Khuraburi is the jumping-off point for the park. The pier is about 9km north of town, as is the mainland **national park office** (☎0 7649 1378; ⊙8am-5pm), with good information, maps and helpful staff.

Sights & Activities

Ban Moken VILLAGE

(Moken Village Tour per person 300B) Moken have long settled in this one sheltered bay on Ao Bon where a major ancestral worship ceremony (Loi Reua) takes place in April. They experienced no casualties during the tsunami that wiped the entire village away, because they read the signs and evacuated to the hilltop.

The national park offers a Moken Village Tour. You'll stroll through the village where you should ask locals for permission to hike the 800m Chok Madah trail over the jungled hills to an empty beach. Tours depart at 9.15am and must be reserved the day before. You can also organise a ride from the park's headquarters (per person 100B). Handicrafts are for sale to help support the local economy and there's a clothing donation box at park headquarters for the Moken – this is the best place to lighten your load.

Diving & Snorkelling

Dive sites in the park include **Ko Surin Tai** and **HQ Channel** between the two main islands. **Richelieu Rock** (a seamount 14km southeast) is also technically in the park and happens to be one of the best, if not the best, dive sites on the Andaman coast. Whale sharks are sometimes spotted here during March and April. There's presently no dive facility in the park itself, so dive trips (four-day live-aboards from around 20,000B) must be booked from the mainland.

Snorkelling isn't as good as it used to be due to recent bleaching of the hard corals, but you'll still see fish and soft corals. Two-hour snorkelling trips (per person 100B, gear per day 40B) leave the park headquarters at 9am and 2pm daily. Expect to be mostly in the company of Thais, who generally splash around fully clothed and in life jackets. If you'd like a more serene snorkelling experience, charter your own long-tail from the national park (half day 1500B) or, better yet, directly from the Moken themselves in Ban Moken. The best section of reef is between the white buoys along the northern peninsula. There are more fish off tiny **Ko Pajumba**, but the coral isn't in great shape. **Ao Suthep** is also a good snorkel spot though there seems to be some bombing damage here, as well as bleaching. Still, there are hundreds of colourful fish, big and small.

Wildlife & Hiking

Around park headquarters you can explore the forest fringes and spot crab-eating macaques and some of the 57 resident bird species, which include the fabulous Nicobar pigeon, endemic to the Andaman islands. Along the coast you're likely to see the Brahminy kite soaring and reef herons on the rocks. Twelve species of bat live here, most noticeably the tree-dwelling fruit bats (also known as flying foxes).

A rough-and-ready **walking trail** winds 2km along the coast, through forest and back down to the beach at **Ao Mai Ngam**, which has camping facilities and its own canteen. At low tide it's easy to walk along the coast between the two campsites.

Sleeping & Eating

Park accommodation is decent, but because of the island's short, narrow beaches it can feel seriously crowded when full (around 300 people). Book online at www.dnp.go.th or with the mainland national park office (p286) in Khuraburi. The clientele is mostly Thai, giving the place a lively holiday-camp feel. You can camp on both Ao Chong Khad and Ao Mai Ngam. The former has the more spectacular beach; the latter fills up last, is more secluded and, with its narrow white-sand shallow bay, feels a bit wilder.

Bungalows (weekday/weekend 1400/2000B) on Ao Chong Khad have wooden floors and private terraces, as well as private terracotta bathrooms and fans that run all night. There are no bungalows on Ao Mai Ngam. **Tents** (2-/4-person 300/450B, bedding per person 60B) are available for rent at both beaches or you can pitch your own tent (per night 80B). There's generator power until 10pm.

A park **restaurant** (dishes from 80B, set menus 170-200B) serves decent Thai food. Change your cash for camp coupons at the activities desk, then head to the canteen to place your order.

Getting There & Away

Tour operators now use speedboats (return 1700-1900B, 60-75 minutes) exclusively. They leave around 9am and honour open tickets. Return whenever you please, but ask the park office to confirm your ticket the night before.

Several tour operators also run day tours (2900B including food and park lodging) to the park. The best in safety, service and value is **Greenview** (0 7640 1400; Khuraburi Pier). Agencies in Hat Khao Lak, Phuket and Ranong are the most convenient booking options for live-aboard dive trips. Transfers from the place of purchase are always included.

Ko Phra Thong & Ko Ra เกาะพระทอง/เกาะระ

Legend has it that many centuries ago, pirates docked at Ko Phra Thong and buried a golden Buddha beneath the sands. The legendary statue was never found but the modern-day treasures at Ko Phra Thong (Golden Buddha Island) are its endless sandy beaches, mangroves, vast bird life and rare orchids.

The long, slender, wooded island is as quiet as a night on the open ocean and as flat as Kansas, and fishing (squid, prawns and jellyfish) remains its key industry. The local delicacy is pungent *gà·Ъì* (fermented prawn paste). On one side, the wide tidal inlet laps a brown sand beach that rolls into mud flats; on the other is 11km of virgin golden sand beach kissed by a blue sea.

Nearby and even quieter is Ko Ra, encircled by golden beaches and mangroves. This small isle is a mountainous jungled slab with an impressive array of wildlife (including leopard cats, flying lemurs, scaly anteaters and slow loris) and has a welcoming local population of fisherfolk.

Sleeping

Mr Chuoi's GUESTHOUSE $

(08 7898 4636, 08 4855 9886; www.mrchuoibarandhut.com; Ko Phra Thong; bungalows 500-700B) Nice, simple, artsy bungalows close to the village on north end of the island. There's a fun bar-restaurant here as well, enlivened by Mr. Chuoi himself. Call and he'll arrange transport between Ko Phra Thong and Khuraburi.

Ko Ra Eco-Resort BUNGALOWS $$

(08 9867 5288; www.kohraecolodge.com; bungalows 1400-2800B) Nestled in the trees off its own small private beach, this older place offers everything from meditation retreats to spectacular wildlife hikes and diving and snorkelling tours to the most pristine and secret coves as well as the relatively nearby Surin Islands. Bungalows are basic, but the restaurant serves excellent local specialities.

★ **Golden Buddha Beach Resort** BUNGALOWS $$$

(08 1892 2208; www.goldenbuddharesort.com; bungalows 3200-14,000B) The area's most posh resort attracts yoga aficionados and families keen for a secluded getaway. Accommodation is in naturalistic-chic privately owned wooden houses rented out short- or long-term. All have open-air bathrooms with

COMMUNITY-BASED TOURISM IN PHANG-NGA PROVINCE

Post-tsunami, Phang-Nga looks pretty much back to normal if you stay in tourist areas. What the majority of visitors don't know is that many fishing communities have had their way of life changed forever, either by the loss of key family members, the destruction of fishing equipment or relocation inland out of necessity or fear. Recovery nowadays is taking the form of community development and visitors can help by enjoying a glimpse of 'real life' on the Andaman coast via community tourism.

Andaman Discoveries (08 7917 7165; www.andamandiscoveries.com; Khuraburi) runs highly recommended community-based tours featuring cultural and handicraft activities, fishing and snorkelling trips to uninhabited islands, and village homestays.

They also manage three community-service projects: a learning centre for children of Burmese migrant workers, an orphanage outside of Khao Lak, and a school for special-needs children in Ranong. Volunteer placement is available.

views of the sea and the surrounding forest. There's also a dive centre.

Future plans include an updated and renovated club house, and a group retreat centre featuring smaller, cheaper guest rooms. At research time, renovations were scheduled to be completed in January 2014.

Getting There & Away

There are no regular boats to Ko Phra Thong, but you could theoretically charter a long-tail from the Khuraburi pier for around 1500B each way – boatmen are hard to find. It's better and probably cheaper to contact your resort in advance to arrange transport.

Locals of Tung Dap village on the southern tip of Ko Phra Thong have requested that tourists not visit their area, so please be respectful and avoid this corner.

Khao Sok National Park

อุทยานแห่งชาติเขาสก

If your leg muscles have atrophied after one too many days of beach-bumming, consider venturing inland to the wondrous Khao Sok National Park (0 7739 5025; www.khaosok.com; park admission adult/child 200/100B). Many believe this lowland jungle – the wettest spot in Thailand – to be over 160 million years old, making it one of the oldest rainforests on the globe. It features dramatic limestone formations and waterfalls that cascade through juicy thickets drenched with rains and morning dew. A network of dirt trails snakes through the quiet park, allowing visitors to spy on an exciting array of indigenous creatures.

The best time of year to visit is between December and April – the dry season. During the June to October wet season, trails can be extremely slippery, flash flooding is common and leeches come out in force. However, animals leave their hidden reservoirs throughout the wet months, so you're more likely to stumble across big fauna.

Sights & Activities

Khao Sok's vast terrain makes it one of the last viable habitats for large mammals. During the wetter months you may happen upon bears, boars, gaur, tapirs, gibbons, deer, wild elephants and perhaps even a tiger. There are more than 300 bird species, 38 bat varieties and one of the world's largest flowers, the rare *Rafflesia kerrii,* which, in Thailand, is found only in Khao Sok. These giant flowers can reach 80cm in diameter.

The stunning **Chiaw Lan** sits about an hour's drive (65km) east of the visitors centre. The lake was created in 1982 by an enormous shale-clay dam called Ratchaprapha (Kheuan Ratchaprapha or Chiaw Lan). The limestone outcrops protruding from the lake reach a height of 960m, over three times higher than the formations in the Phang-Nga area. Technical divers can drop into the emerald waters and glimpse ghostly stalagmites with a number of the Khao Lak–based dive operations. Trips always start and finish at Khao Lak, but you can also arrange to be dropped in Khao Sok afterward.

Tham Nam Thalu cave contains striking limestone formations and subterranean streams, while **Tham Si Ru** features four converging passageways used as a hideout by communist insurgents between 1975 and 1982. The caves can be reached on foot from the southwestern shore of the lake. You can rent boats from local fishermen to explore the coves, canals, caves and cul-de-sacs along the lakeshore.

Elephant trekking, kayaking and rafting are popular park activities. The hiking is also excellent, and you can arrange park tours from any guest house – just be sure you get a certified guide (they wear an official badge). Various trails you can hike independently from the visitors centre lead to the waterfalls of **Sip-Et Chan** (4km), **Than Sawan** (9km) and **Than Kloy** (9km), among other destinations. The park office hands out free trail maps.

Outside the park proper, **Wat Tham Phan Turat** is worth a visit; it's known locally as the Monkey Temple because of the monkey mob that hangs out in the trees here, which is great fun to feed. The cave and temple itself are rather sacred. You'll see massive candles flickering and the rumbling of chanting monks if you time it right.

Sleeping

The road leading into the park is lined with simple, charming guesthouses, all of which offer a variety of park tours and guide services. We recommend going on a two-day, one-night trip (2500B per person) to Chiaw Lan where you sleep in floating huts on the lake and go on a variety of canoe and hiking excursions.

Morning Mist Resort HOTEL $
(☎08 9971 8794; www.khaosokmorningmistresort.com; r 450-1000B; P 🛜 👪) Clean, tiled, fan-cooled bungalows all have balconies or patios, and are set in split-level duplex style blocks. The most expensive overlook the river.

Art's Riverview Jungle Lodge GUESTHOUSE $$
(☎09 0167 6818; http://krabidir.com/artsriverviewlodge; 54/3 Moo 6; bungalows 650-1500B) In a monkey-filled jungle bordering a clear river with a natural limestone cliff-framed swimming hole, this is the prettiest guesthouse property in Khao Sok. Stilted brick, shingled and all-wooden bungalows are spacious and creative; all have river views and the charming restaurant overlooks the sublime swimming hole.

Tree House GUESTHOUSE $$
(☎0 7739 5169; www.khaosok-treehouse.com; 233 Moo 6; r with fan/air-con 1000/2000B; ❄ 🛜 🏊) Don't be dissuaded by the Disney-esque facade: here is a complex of excellent and spacious bungalows connected by raised paths and bridges. The best nests have flat screens, air-con and two terraces. Fan rooms are simpler and smaller but very clean.

Khao Sok Hotel & Spa HOTEL $$
(☎08 1537 7555; www.khaosoknationalparkhotel.com; 265 Moo 6; r from 1900B; P ❄ 🛜 🏊) More organised and official than much of what you'll find in Khao Sok proper, these brick cottages come with private patios, air-con, high-end tile floors, safety boxes, exposed brick walls and wood panelled ceilings; they also include breakfast. The family house sleeps four. They have a spa (treatments from 200B), pool and tennis courts.

Cliff & River Jungle Resort HOTEL $$
(☎08 7271 8787; www.thecliffandriver.com; bungalows incl breakfast from 2000B; ❄ 🏊) This beautiful property with stilted bamboo bungalows is set below the jagged cliffs and is removed from Khao Sok's budget huddle. If you need air-con, come here.

★ **Elephant Hills** RESORT $$$
(☎0 7638 1703; www.elephant-hills.com; 170 Moo 7 Tambon Klong Sok; d all-inclusive from 12,500B; P 🛜 👪) 🍃 Whether you are a family of five, honeymooning backpackers or a soloist, this is one of those resorts that makes everyone smile. Set above the Sok River, at the base of stunning limestone mountains draped in misty jungle, the area's only tented camp offers rootsy luxury you'd most associate with the Serengeti. Airy tents have wood floors, stone baths, skylights, wood furnishings and hammocks on the porch.

It's all inclusive and the price includes average meals, guided hikes through the jungle and a canoe trip downriver to their elephant camp where 15 lovely ladies – rescues from other camps where they were forced to carry tourists around – are treated kindly. You can't ride them. But you do get to feed, bathe, and spend some quality time with them. The kids love it. The inner-kid loves it. It really is a special experience. And after a few days in the hills consider adding a night at their **Rainforest Camp** (www.rainforestcamp.com; Chiaw Lan Lake): a floating tented camp on Chiaw Lan Lake. Reservations only.

> **ℹ KHAO SOK TOURS**
>
> Tours in and around Khao Sok can be up to 50% cheaper when booked at guesthouses or from travel agents around the park itself. Tours booked from further-afield destinations such as Phuket or Khao Lak will include higher-priced transport and tour agent commissions.

ℹ Information

The **park headquarters** (☎0 7739 5025; www.khaosok.com; park admission adult/child 200/100B) and visitors centre are 1.8km off Rte 401, close to the Km 109 marker.

There's an ATM outside the Morning Mist Mini-Mart. Internet is available near the park entrance for 2B per minute, but most guest houses offer free wi-fi.

ℹ Getting There & Around

Minivans to Surat Thani (300B, one hour), Krabi (350B, two hours) and a handful of other destinations leave daily. Otherwise, from Surat catch a bus going towards Takua Pa and, on the Andaman coast, take a Surat Thani–bound bus. Buses drop you off along the highway (Rte 401), 1.8km from the visitors centre. If guesthouse touts don't meet you, you'll have to walk to your chosen nest (from 50m to 2km).

To explore Chiaw Lan on your own, charter a long-tail (2000B per day) at the dam's entrance.

Hat Pakarang & Hat Bang Sak หาดปะการัง/หาดบางสัก

This long, sleepy, unbroken stretch of sand took a fierce hit from the 2004 Tsunami, but each year since the tourists have been returning in greater numbers. And it's no wonder folks love it: with thick mangroves, ample rolling pasture and rubber-tree plantations forming a wide buffer between the coast and highway, you really do feel like you've escaped from it all when you land here.

Sleeping & Eating

There are just a few hotels along these pretty beaches, making them ideal romantic hideaways.

★Sarojin HOTEL $$$
(0 7642 7900-4; www.sarojin.com; Hat Pakarang; r US$450-700;) A quiet retreat with stellar service and an elegant and intimate setting. The very private spa (treatments from 2300B), which takes in views of coconut groves and mangroves, is one of the best on the Andaman coast. Cooking classes take place on the banks of the Takuapa River, where you can watch water buffalo amble by. No kids allowed.

There are two restaurants here: a Thai seafood kitchen on the beach and a gorgeous Mediterranean restaurant tucked into the trees. Both are exceptional.

VILLAGE OF THE DEAD

Ban Sok, the village on the banks of the Sok River, near the entrance to the Khao Sok National Park, has a past so dark it had to change its name. In the 1940s a smallpox epidemic swept through Takuapa and Phuket in a vicious wave of death. Populations were decimated and some chose to escape, hiking high into these limestone mountains and hoping for the plague to pass. That was not to be, and death followed in such numbers that the village they settled in 1944 became known as Ban Sop, or Village of the Dead. By 1961, when the road was built to connect the Gulf Coast at Surat Thani with Phang Nga, the villagers had re-branded, naming their village Ban Sok, which technically means nothing at all.

Le Méridien HOTEL $$$
(0 7642 7500; www.lemeridienkhaolak.com; Hat Bang Sak; r from 5550B, villas from 14,705B;) A four-star megaresort, its 243 rooms and 20 villas are the only nests on Hat Bang Sak. It lacks a boutique touch and five-star service, but it is relatively affordable for an international resort and certainly majestic, sprawling nearly all the way from the highway to the sea.

White Sand Beach SEAFOOD $$
(0 7648 7580; Hat Pakarang; mains 90-300B) Next door to the Sarojin is this rambling compound of bamboo lounges, private dining pagodas, showers, massage areas and a good seafood restaurant. Come for lunch and stay for the day.

Hat Khao Lak หาดเขาหลัก

Hat Khao Lak is a beach for folks who shun the glitz and cheesiness of Phuket's bigger resort towns, but still crave comfort, shopping and plenty of facilities. With long stretches of white sand backed by forested hills, warm waves to frolic in and easy day trips to the Similan and Surin Islands, Khao Sok and Khao Lak/Lam Ru National Parks, or even Phuket, the area is a central and kick-back base for exploring the northern Andaman. About 2.5km north of Hat Khao Lak, **Hat Bang Niang** is an even quieter version of sandy bliss with skinnier beaches and fewer people. Khao Lak proper (also called Khao Lak Town by locals) – a hodgepodge of restaurants, tourist markets and low-rise hotels along a grey highway – isn't exactly eye-catching, but it is convenient and you'll probably spend your days at the beach or further afield.

Internet is widely available and banks and ATMs are everywhere.

Sights

Khao Lak/Lam Ru National Park NATIONAL PARK
(อุทยานแห่งชาติเขาหลัก-ลำรู่; 0 7642 0243; www.dnp.go.th; adult/child 200/100B; 8am-4.30pm) Immediately south of Hat Khao Lak, the vast 125-sq-km Khao Lak/Lam Ru National Park is a collage of sea cliffs, 1000m-high hills, beaches, estuaries, forested valleys and mangroves. Wildlife includes hornbills, drongos, tapirs, gibbons, monkeys and Asiatic black bears.

The visitors centre, just off Hwy 4 between the Km 56 and Km 57 markers, has little in the way of maps or printed information, but there's a very nice open-air restaurant perched on a shady slope overlooking the sea. From the restaurant you can take a fairly easy 3km round-trip nature trail that heads along the cape and ends at often-deserted Hat Lek beach.

Khlong Thap Liang NATURE RESERVE

Guided hikes along the coast or inland can be arranged through many tour agencies in town, as can long-tail boat trips up the scenic Khlong Thap Liang estuary. The latter affords opportunities to view mangrove communities of crab-eating macaques.

Between Khao Lak and Bang Sak is a network of sandy beach trails – some of which lead to deserted beaches – which are fun to explore on foot or by rented motorcycle. Most of the hotels in town rent out motorbikes for 250B per day.

Boat 813 MONUMENT

Perched in an open field nearly 1km from shore, this boat was hurled to its current location by the powerful 2004 Boxing Day tsunami. A decade later, it remains the region's most prominent reminder of the disaster.

There's a regal monument-worthy entryway, an information booth nearby with a tsunami timeline in both Thai and English, as well as some compelling photo books for sale. It's just a 50B *sŏrng·tăa·ou* ride between here and Khao Lak.

Activities

Diving or snorkelling day excursions to the Similan and Surin Islands are immensely popular but, if you can, opt for a live-aboard. Since the islands are around 60km from the mainland (about three hours by boat), you'll have a more relaxing trip and experience the islands sans day trippers. All dive shops offer live-aboard trips from around 17,000/29,000B for three-/five-day packages and day trips for 4900B to 6500B.

On these two-, three-, four- or five-day trips, you'll wake up with the dawn and slink below the ocean's surface up to four times per day in what's commonly considered to be one of the top 10 diving realms in the world. While both the Similan and Surin Islands have experienced vast coral bleaching recently, **Richelieu Rock** is still the crème de la crème of the region's sites and **Ko Bon** and **Ko Ta Chai** are two other

Khao Lak

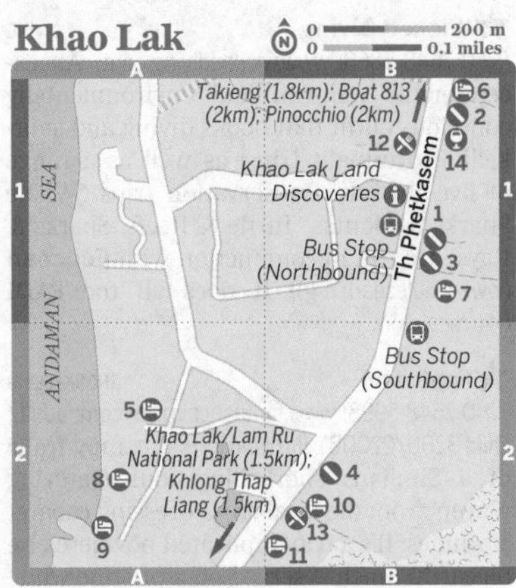

Khao Lak

Activities, Courses & Tours
1 IQ Dive ... B1
2 Sea Dragon Diver Centre ... B1
3 Similan Seven Sea Club ... B1
4 Wicked Diving ... B2

Sleeping
5 Greenbeach ... A2
6 Khao Lak Youth Club ... B1
7 Khaolak Banana Bungalows ... B1
8 Nangthong Bay Resort ... A2
9 Nangthong Beach Resort ... A2
10 PhuKhaoLak ... B2
11 Walker's Inn ... B2

Eating
12 Go Pong ... B1
13 Phu Khao Lak ... B2

Drinking & Nightlife
14 Happy Snapper ... B1

good sites due to the traffic of giant manta rays.

Although geared towards divers, all dive shops welcome snorkellers who can hop on selected dive excursions or live-aboards for a discount of around 40%; otherwise, tour agencies all around town offer even cheaper snorkelling trips to the Similan Islands for around 3200B. PADI Open Water certification courses cost anywhere from 10,000B to 18,000B depending on where you dive. You can go on a 'discover scuba' day trip to the Similans for around 6000B to 6500B.

★**Wicked Diving** DIVING
(☎0 7648 5868; www.wickeddiving.com) An exceptionally well-run and environmentally conscious outfit that books diving and snorkelling overnight trips, as well as a range of live-aboards. Conservation trips (Whale Sharks & Mantas, Turtle & Reefs, Sharks & Rays) are run in conjunction with **Ecocean** (www.whaleshark.org). It does all the PADI courses, too.

★**Fantastic** SNORKELLING
(☎0 7648 5998; www.fantasticsimilan.com; adult/child 3200/2200B) Fantastic is a campy frolic of a Similans snorkelling tour featuring players from the local cross-dressing cabaret as guides. It's a trip duplicated nowhere else on earth: lunch is served on a pristine white sand beach and they get you to the prime snorkel sites, too. No booking office; meet at the pier or Fantastic can arrange pick-ups from your hotel.

Sea Dragon Diver Centre DIVING
(☎0 7648 5420; www.seadragondivecenter.com; Th Phetkasem) One of the older operations in Khao Lak, Sea Dragon has maintained high standards throughout the years.

Similan Seven Sea Club DIVING
(☎0 7648 5237; www.similansevenseaclub.com; Th Phetkasem) A new, highly recommended dive outfitter for day trips and live-aboards to the Similans.

IQ Dive DIVING
(☎0 7648 5614; www.iq-dive.com; Th Phetkasem; diving day trips from 5100B) A quality operation that focuses on diving and snorkelling day trips. The website has good information about the gamut of live-aboards operating in the region.

Sleeping

Cheaper accommodation predominates in the congested centre of town, while three- and four-star resorts dominate the coast.

Walker's Inn GUESTHOUSE $
(☎08 6281 7668, 08 4840 2689; www.walkersinn.com; Th Phetkasem; dm/r 200/600B; ❄📶) A long-running backpacker fave and classic old-school guest house that offers bright and spacious air-con rooms, decent dorms, and a fine downstairs pub serving full English breakfasts. It offers a laundry service and motorbike rental too.

Khaolak Banana Bungalows BUNGALOWS $
(☎0 7648 5889; www.khaolakbanana.com; 4/147 Moo 7; r 500-1200B; ❄🏊) These adorable little bungalows have swirls painted on the cement floors and sun-filled indoor-outdoor bathrooms. A cute pool with deckchairs sweetens the deal.

Khao Lak Youth Club GUESTHOUSE $
(☎0 7648 5900; www.khaolakyouthclub.com; Th Phetkasem; r 700-1200B, bungalows 1600B; P❄📶🏊) You have several choices at this incongruent spot in the Book Tree mall. Standard rooms are enormous with high ceilings and decked out with dangling lanterns, but we liked the newly refurbished, more traditional bungalows still under renovation at research time. Cheapest rooms are fan cooled and share baths.

PhuKhaoLak BUNGALOWS $
(☎08 9874 1018, 0 7648 5141; www.phukhaolak.com; r with fan 700, with air-con 500-1800B) Air-con rooms are decent stand-alone casitas with high ceilings, dark wood furnishings, recessed lighting, ceramic tiled floors and huge baths. Fan rooms are basic but super clean. All have front porches and face a palm grove blanketed with a rolling lawn, set back from the main highway and against the jungled hills.

Khao Lak/Lam Ru National Park Bungalows BUNGALOWS $
(☎0 2562 0760; www.dnp.go.th; bungalows 800-2000B) There is a handful of four- and six-bed bungalows in the national park. The standards are basic, but the setting will suit those after an eco-experience.

Greenbeach HOTEL $$
(☎0 7648 5845; www.khaolakgreenbeachresort.com; bungalows 1400-2300B; ❄👪) On an excellent stretch of beach and extending back into a garden, this place has a warm, family-style soul. The wooden bungalows have glass doors, air-con and fan, shady terraces and views of a towering, ancient banyan tree. Even the cheapest rooms have sea views.

Nangthong Bay Resort HOTEL $$
(☎0 7648 5088; www.nangthong.com; r 1800B, bungalows 2500-3000B; ❄@📶🏊👪) Until its sister property opened, this was the best midranger on the beach. Rooms are designed with a sparse black-and-white chic decor. The cheapest rooms are set back from the beach, but are fantastic value. Grounds are lush and service is excellent.

Nangthong Beach Resort HOTEL $$
(☎0 7648 5911; www.nangthong2.com; r 2000-2200B, bungalows 2500-3000B;) Still one of our favourites in Khao Lak proper. The large, well-appointed rooms and even larger bungalows are ageing, but they do offer ceramic-tile floors, dark-wood furnishings, a burgeoning garden, solid service and the best stretch of sand in town.

Monochrome BOUTIQUE HOTEL $$$
(☎0 7642 7700; www.monochromeresort.com; 67/238 Moo 5, Ban Niang; r/ste from 3900/7900B;) Just four months old at research time, the newest and splashiest address in Khao Lak is set on the road to Bang Niang, about 200m from the beach. It's modern, with a vertical louvred facade, a beer garden off the entry way and pool in the courtyard, and with lots of charcoal grey and natural cherry wood to soothe the eye.

Pricier suites include a full living room and soaker tub in the bedroom. Yes, the bedroom. It's unique, yet strangely alluring.

Eating & Drinking

This is no culinary capital, but there are a few local haunts where tourists congregate to rehash the day's diving yarns. Early-morning divers will be hard pressed to find a place to grab a bite before 8.30am.

★Takieng THAI $$
(☎08 6952 7693; 26/43 Moo 5, Bang Niang; dishes 80-350B; ⏲11am-10pm) On the east side of the highway just before the Bang Niang turn are two open-air Thai restaurants beneath stilted tin roofs. This is the more visually appealing of the two, and the dishes are also stylish. They steam fresh fish in green curry, do a scintillating chicken or pork *lâhp*, and fry squid in chilli paste. Service is impeccable.

Go Pong THAI $
(Th Phetkasem; dishes 30-100B; ⏲noon-10pm) Get off the tourist taste-bud tour at this terrific little streetside diner where they stir fry noodles and spicy rice dishes and simmer an aromatic noodle soup which attracts a local lunch following. If you dig the pig, try the stewed pork leg with rice or maybe the Chinese broccoli with crispy pork. Both look worthy.

Jumbo Steak & Pasta ITALIAN $$
(☎08 7269 3928; Th Phetkasem, Ban Khukkhuk; mains 70-220B; ⏲10:30am-10pm Thu-Tue) A hole-in-the-wall joint in Ban Khukkhuk, just past the police boat, launched by a former line chef at Le Méridien who does beautiful pasta dishes of all flavours. Here are penne arrabiata, spaghetti alla carbonara, a host of pizzas and some terrific steaks. Dishes are an incredible value (hence the local expat scene), though portions aren't huge.

Pinocchio ITALIAN $$
(☎0 7644 3079; 67/61 Soi Bang Muang, Hat Bang Niang; mains 200-380B) This beautiful candle-lit garden restaurant features a huge stone pizza oven, imported wine and cheese, tremendous sourdough bread, even better pizza, homemade pasta and gelato.

Phu Khao Lak INTERNATIONAL, THAI $$
(☎0 7648 5141; Th Phetkasem; dishes 80-300B; ⏲8am-10pm) With its clothed tables spilling to the edges of a lawn at the south end of the Khao Lak strip, it's hard to miss. And you shouldn't because there's a huge menu of Western and Thai dishes with ample descriptions, all well prepared.

Happy Snapper BAR
(☎0 7648 5500; www.happysnapperbar.com; Th Phetkasem) The bar is stocked with good liquor, there's an atlas on the ceiling, the tree of life on the wall and a rockin' house band on stage six nights a week in the high season, led by the owner, Pitak, a Bangkok-born bass legend.

Information

For diving-related emergencies, call the **SSS Ambulance** (☎08 1081 9444), which rushes injured persons down to Phuket for treatment. The ambulance can also be used for car or motorcycle accidents. There is also one nurse in Bang Niang who caters to diving-related injuries.

There are numerous travel agencies scattered about that rent motorbikes for around 250B per day. The best is **Khao Lak Land Discovery** (☎0 7648 5411; www.khaolakland discovery.com; Th Petchkasem).

Getting There & Away

Any bus running along Hwy 4 between Takua Pa (60B, 45 minutes) and Phuket (100B, two hours) will stop at Hat Khao Lak if you ask the driver.

Khao Lak Land Discovery runs hourly minibuses to Phuket International Airport (600B, 75 minutes). Alternately you can take **Cheaper Than Hotel** (☎08 6276 6479, 08 5786 1378), which admittedly is an odd name for a taxi and transport service. They make the run to the Phuket airport (1000B) and points south. Or tell a Phuket-bound bus-driver to drop you at the 'airport' – you'll be let off at an intersection from which motorcycle taxis will take you to the airport (10 minutes, 100B). It sounds sketchy, but works every time.

Similan Islands Marine National Park อุทยานแห่งชาติหมู่เกาะสิมิลัน

Known to divers the world over, the beautiful **Similan Islands Marine National Park** (www.dnp.go.th; adult/child 400/200B; ⏲Nov-May) is 70km offshore. Its smooth granite islands are as impressive above water as below, topped with rainforest, edged with white-sand beaches and fringed with coral reefs. Unfortunately recent coral bleaching has killed off many of the hard corals, but soft corals are still intact, the fauna is there and it's still a lovely place to dive.

Two of the nine islands, Island 4 (Ko Miang) and Island 8 (Ko Similan), have ranger stations and accommodation; park headquarters and most visitor activity centres are on Island 4. 'Similan' comes from the Malay word *sembilan,* meaning 'nine', and while each island is named, they're more commonly known by their numbers. Relatively recently, the park was expanded to included Ko Bon and Ko Tachai; both have remained unscathed by coral bleaching making them some of the better diving and snorkelling areas.

Hat Khao Lak is the jumping-off point for the park. The pier is at Thap Lamu, about 10km south of town.

Sights & Activities

Diving & Snorkelling

The Similans offer diving for all levels of experience, at depths from 2m to 30m. There are rock reefs at **Ko Payu** (Island 7) and dive-throughs at **Hin Pousar** (Elephant Head), with marine life ranging from tiny plume worms and soft corals to schooling fish and whale sharks. There are dive sites at each

Similan Islands

of the six islands north of Ko Miang (Island 4); the southern part of the park (Islands 1, 2 and 3) is a turtle nesting ground and off-limits to divers. No facilities for divers exist in the national park itself, so you'll need to take a dive tour. Agencies in Hat Khao Lak and Phuket book dive trips (three-day live-aboards from around 15,000B).

You can hire snorkelling gear (per day 150B) from the park headquarters. Day-tour operators usually visit three or four different snorkelling sites. Plenty of tour agencies in Hat Khao Lak offer snorkelling-only day/overnight trips (from around 3000/5000B), and the beach can become positively packed. It's clear that nobody is really monitoring the numbers of day trip visitors, to the park's detriment. Some snorkelling outfits go so far as to feed the fish, which is a big ecological no-no. That would never happen if this place were a national park! Oh, wait...

Wildlife & Hiking

The forest around the park headquarters on Ko Miang (Island 4) has a couple of walking trails and some great wildlife. The fabulous Nicobar pigeon, with its wild mane of grey-green feathers, is common here. Endemic to the islands of the Andaman Sea, it's one of some 39 bird species in the park. Hairy-legged land crabs and fruit bats (flying foxes) are relatively easy to spot in the forest, as are flying squirrels.

A small **beach track**, with information panels, leads 400m to a tiny snorkelling bay. Detouring from the track, the **Viewpoint Trail** – 500m or so of steep scrambling – has panoramic vistas from the top. A 500m walk to **Sunset Point** takes you through forest to a smooth granite platform facing west.

On Ko Similan (Island 8) there's a 2.5km forest hike to a **viewpoint**, and a shorter, steep scramble off the main beach to the top of **Sail Rock** (aka Balance Rock).

Sleeping & Eating

Accommodation in the park is available for all budgets. Book online at www.dnp.go.th or with the mainland **national park office** (☎ 0 7645 3272) at Hat Khao Lak. Tour agents in Hat Khao Lak also arrange overnight and multi-day trips that include transport, food and lodging at the park – these cost little more than it would to go solo.

On Ko Miang (Island 4) there are sea-view **bungalows** (2000B; ❄ 📶) with balconies, two dark five-room wood-and-bamboo **longhouses** (r 1000B; ❄) with fans, and **tents** (2-/4-person 300/450B). There's electricity from 6pm to 6am.

Tents are also available on Ko Similan (Island 8). You can pitch your own **tent** (per night 80B) on either island.

A **restaurant** (dishes 100-150B) near the park headquarters serves simple Thai food.

Getting There & Away

There's no official public transport to the park, but theoretically independent travellers can book a speedboat transfer (return 1700B, 1½ hours one way) with a Hat Khao Lak snorkelling operator, though they much prefer that you join the snorkelling tour and generally discourage independent travel to the Similans. Most will collect you from Phuket or Hat Khao Lak, but if you book through the national park (which uses the same tour operators' boats anyway), be aware that you'll have to find your own way to their office and then wait for a transfer to the pier.

Agencies in Hat Khao Lak and Phuket book day/overnight tours (from around 3000/5000B) and dive trips (three-day live-aboards from around 15,000B). Generally these cost little more than what you'd pay trying to get to the islands independently when you factor in meals, bus tickets and so on.

Ao Phang-Nga & Phang-Nga อ่าวพังงา

With turquoise bays peppered with craggy limestone rock towers, brilliant-white beaches and tumbledown fishing villages, Ao Phang-Nga is one of the region's most spectacular landscapes. Little wonder then that it was here, among the towering cliffs and swifts' nests, that James Bond's nemesis, Scaramanga *(The Man with the Golden Gun)*, chose to build his lair. Wanted assassins with goals of world domination would not be recommended to hide out here nowadays, since the area is swarming with tourists in motorboats and sea kayaks nearly year-round. Much of the bay, and some of the coastline, has now been incorporated into the Ao Phang-Nga National Marine Park.

Sights & Activities

Phang-Nga is a scruffy, luckless town backed up against sublime limestone cliffs. There isn't a whole lot to see or do unless you happen to be here during the annual **Vegetarian Festival** in late September or October.

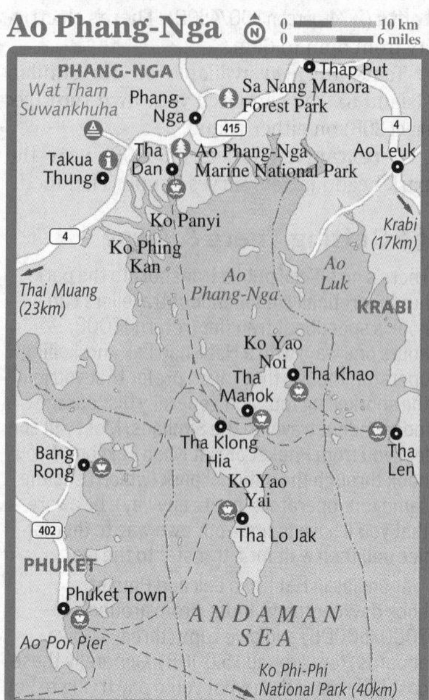

About 8.5km south of the town centre is Tha Dan. From here, you can charter boats to see half-submerged **caves**, oddly shaped islands and **Ko Panyi**, a Muslim village on stilts. There are tours to the well-trodden **Ko Phing Kan** (James Bond Island) and **Ao Phang-Nga National Marine Park** (500B per person for a two- to three-hour tour). Takua Thung, another pier area about 10km further west of Tha Dan, also has private boats for hire at similar prices to tours. The park office, inside Ao Phang-Nga National Marine Park, also offers boat tours.

Although it can be a pain to haggle with boatmen, it's nice to create your own itinerary. Of course, it's easier (and cheaper) to go with an organised tour through an agency in town. Several are clustered around the bus station. **Sayan Tours** (08 1397 4717, 08 3692 0537; www.sayantour.com) has been doing tours of Ao Phang-Nga for many years, and continues to receive good reviews from travellers. **Mr Kean Tour** (08 9871 6092, 0 7643 0619), owned by the man himself, is another great choice. He's been running tours in the area for over 20 years. Half- and full-day tours cost from 700B to 1600B per person and include **Tham Lawt** (a large water cave), Ko Phing Kan and Ko Panyi, among other destinations. You can even add a bit of kayaking.

Sleeping & Eating

Phang-Nga won't entice too many folks into sleepovers. Most choose to swing through on a day trip, though there are three decent sleeps. Several food stalls on the main street of Phang-Nga sell delicious *kà·nŏm jeen* (thin wheat noodles) with chicken curry, *nâm yah* (spicy ground-fish curry) or *nâm prík* (spicy sauce). There's a morning market open from 5am to 10am daily and a small night market on Tuesday, Wednesday and Thursday evenings, located just south of Soi Lohakit.

Phang-Nga Guest House GUESTHOUSE $
(0 7641 1358; 99/1 Th Petchkasem; r with fan/air-con 350/480B;) A simple yet super tidy inn with tiled rooms brushed in cheery pastels, halls dressed in Thai tapestries, and wall-mounted flat screens. A touch of colour in the otherwise drab centre of town.

Baan Phang Nga GUESTHOUSE $$
(0 7641 3276; 100/2 Th Petchkasem; r 650-850B;) It's a mom-and-pop kind of place with spacious, spotless rooms in an old relic. Ceilings are high, the concrete floors are painted and they even have rain showers and hot water in the bathrooms. Good coffee and Western breakfasts are served in the downstairs bakery.

Phang-Nga Inn HOTEL $$
(0 7641 1963; 2/2 Soi Lohakit; r 700-1500B;) This converted residential villa is an absolute gem and features heavy wooden staircases, louvred cabinets and peaceful gardens. It's well furnished, there's a little eatery and the staff are gracious.

★ **Kror Son Thong** THAI $
(08 4182 4684; 29/1 Th Rongua; mains 70-200B; 11am-10pm) Overlooking the river south of the commercial strip is this kitchen, which verges on gourmet. Try the *Ɓlah tôrt kà·mîn* (turmeric-fried fish), crab omelette or roast duck with kale.

Around Phang-Nga

Ao Phang-Nga National Marine Park อุทยานแห่งชาติอ่าวพังงา

Established in 1981 and covering an area of 400 sq km, **Ao Phang-Nga National**

Marine Park (☎0 7641 1136; www.dnp.go.th; adult/child 200/100B; ⌚8am-4pm) is noted for its classic karst scenery. There are over 40 islands with huge vertical cliffs, some with caves that are accessible at low tide and lead into hidden *hôrng* (lagoons surrounded by solid rock walls). The bay itself is composed of large and small tidal channels including Khlong Ko Panyi, Khlong Phang-Nga, Khlong Bang Toi and Khlong Bo Saen. These channels run through vast mangroves in a north–south direction and today are used by fisher folk and island inhabitants as aquatic highways. They are the largest remaining primary mangrove forests in Thailand.

In the peak season the bay can become a package-tourist superhighway. But if you explore in the early morning (best done from Ko Yao Noi or Ko Yao Yai) or stay out a bit late, you'll find a slice of beach, sea and a limestone karst to call your own. The best way to experience the park is by kayak.

Sights & Activities

Ko Phing Kan (James Bond Island) ISLAND

The biggest tourist drawcard in the park is the so-called James Bond Island, known to Thais as Ko Phing Kan (literally 'Leaning on Itself Island'). Once used as a location setting for *The Man with the Golden Gun*, the island is now full of vendors hawking coral and shells that should have stayed in the sea. It's much wiser to venture further afield.

★John Gray's Seacanoe BOATING

(☎0 7622 6077; www.johngray-seacanoe.com) John Gray was the first kayak outfitter in the bay and remains the most ecologically minded. He's constantly clamouring for more protection for his beloved *hôrng* among local park rangers and their supervisors in Bangkok. His **Hong by Starlight trip** (per person 3950B) dodges the crowds, involves plenty of sunset paddling and will introduce you to Ao Phang-Nga's famed bioluminescence once night falls.

Getting There & Around

From the centre of Phang-Nga, drive about 6km south on Hwy 4, turn left onto Rte 4144 (the road to Tha Dan) and travel 2.6km to the park headquarters. Without your own transport you'll need to take a *sŏrng·tăa·ou* to Tha Dan (30B).

From the park office, you can hire a boat (1500B, maximum four passengers) for a three-hour tour of the surrounding islands.

Suan Somdet Phra Sinakharin Park สวนสมเด็จพระศรีนครินทร์

This public **park** (⌚dawn-dusk) FREE has two entrances. The most dramatic is through a huge hole in a limestone cliff near the Phang-Nga Bay Resort Hotel in Tha Dan. The main (and less scenic) entrance is at the southern end of Phang-Nga. Surrounded by limestone cliffs and bluffs, the park is cut through with caves and tunnels. Wooden walkways link the water-filled caverns so visitors can admire the ponds and amazing limestone formations. One of the larger caves, **Tham Reusi Sawan**, is marked by a gilded statue of a *reu·sĕe* (Hindu sage). The other main cavern is known locally as **Tham Luk Seua** (Tiger Cub Cave).

Wat Tham Suwankhuha วัดถ้ำสุวรรณคูหา

Wat Tham Suwankhuha (Heaven Grotto Temple; admission 20B; ⌚dawn-dusk) is a cave temple full of Buddha images. The shrine consists of two main caverns, the larger one containing a 15m-high reclining Buddha and tiled with *lai·krahm* and *benjarong* (two coloured patterns more common in pottery). The smaller cavern displays spirit

ROCK ART IN AO PHANG-NGA

Many of the limestone islands in Ao Phang-Nga feature prehistoric rock art painted on or carved into the walls and ceilings of caves, rock shelters, cliffs and rock massifs. In particular you can see rock art on Khao Khian, Ko Panyi, Ko Raya, Tham Nak and Ko Phra At Thao. Khao Khian (Inscription Mountain) is probably the most visited of the sites. The images contain scenes of human figures, fish, crabs, prawns, bats, birds and elephants, as well as boats and fishing equipment, and seem to reference some sort of communal effort tied to the all-important sea harvest. The rock paintings don't fall on any one plane of reference; they may be placed right-side up, upside-down or sideways. Most of the paintings are monochrome, while some have been traced in orange-yellow, blue, grey and black.

flags and a *reu·sěe* statue. It's swarming with monkeys.

The wát is 10km southwest of Phang-Nga. To get here without your own transport, hop on any *sŏrng·tăa·ou* running between Phang-Nga and Takua Thung (90B). The wát is down a side road.

Ko Yao เกาะยาว

With mountainous backbones, unspoilt shorelines, a large variety of birdlife and a population of friendly Muslim fishermen and their families, **Ko Yao Yai** and **Ko Yao Noi** are laid-back vantage points for soaking up Ao Phang-Nga's beautiful scenery. The islands are part of the Ao Phang-Nga National Marine Park but are most easily accessed from Phuket.

Please remember to respect the beliefs of the local Muslim population and wear modest clothing when away from the beaches.

Sights & Activities

Despite being the relative pipsqueak of the Ko Yao Islands, Ko Yao Noi is the main population centre, with fishing, coconut farming and tourism sustaining its small, year-round population. Bays on the east coast recede to mud flats at low tides, and don't expect postcard-perfect white-sand beaches and turquoise lagoons even when the tide is high. That said, **Hat Pa Sai** and **Hat Paradise** are both gorgeous.

Ko Yao Yai is far less developed than Ko Yao Noi; it offers an even more remote and wild getaway. It's twice the size of Yao Noi with a fraction of the development, which is why villagers are still pleasantly surprised to see tourists pedalling their bicycles or buzzing the concrete streets on rented motorbikes. If you explore some of the island's dirt trails that wind into the hills you may glimpse wild boar, monkeys, flying squirrels or small barking deer.

Hat Lo Pa Red and **Hat Tiikut** are two of the island's best beaches – the former lined with coconut palms, the latter with casuarina trees. But **Hat Chonglard**, best accessed from Thwison Beach Resort, trumps them both. The powder-white sand extends into a jutting palm-shaded peninsula to the north, and it's perfectly oriented to the limestone islands that layer the eastern horizon.

Ko Bele, a small island east of the twin Ko Yao islands, features a large tidal lagoon, three white-sand beaches, and easily accessible caves and coral reefs.

If you enjoy self-propulsion, rent a mountain bike (200B per day from most guest houses) and explore either island's numerous dirt trails (though bikes are far more readily available on Ko Yao Noi), or join up with Phuket's **Amazing Bike Tours** (☎08 7263 2031; www.amazingbiketoursthailand.com; day trip 2900B). Their Ko Yao Noi tour from Phuket is extremely popular, and they'll leave you and your bags on the island upon request.

Kayak rental is widely available on Ko Yao Noi, which enables paddlers to ply the island's glassy bays. Sabai Corner (p298) rents them out for 500B per day.

Diving & Snorkelling

Koh Yao Diver DIVING
(☎08 9868 8642, 08 7895 7515; www.kohyaodiver.com) Koh Yao Diver services both islands and leads dive trips around the bay and beyond. Half-day three-island snorkelling tours (1700B, maximum six passengers) through Ao Phang-Nga are easily organised from any guest house or with long-tail captains on the beach.

Elixir Divers DIVING
(☎08 7897 0076; www.elixirdivers.com; 99 Moo 3) Based in Ko Yao Yai, they lead two-tank dive trips in and around Ao Phang Nga.

Rock Climbing

Mountain Shop Adventures ROCK CLIMBING
(☎08 3969 2023; www.themountainshop.org; Tha Khao) The Mountain Shop Adventures offers half-day and full-day rock-climbing trips for 2500B and 4000B respectively. There are over 150 climbs on Ko Yao Noi and owner Mark has routed most of them himself – many trips involve boat travel to get to remote limestone cliff faces. Most climbs are equipped with titanium bolts and beginner to advanced trips are available.

Sleeping & Eating

Ko Yao Noi

Sabai Corner Bungalows GUESTHOUSE $$
(☎0 7659 7497; www.sabaicornerbungalows.com; Ko Yao Noi; bungalows 1000-1600B) Tucked into a rocky headland, the wooden and bamboo bungalows here are full of character and blessed with gorgeous views. The restaurant (p262) is also good and a great place to hang out.

Ulmur's Nature Lodge BUNGALOWS $$
(☎0 7658 2728, 08 9290 0233; ulmar_nature_lodge@hotmail.com; Hat Tha Khao; bungalows with fan/air-con 1000/1600B; ❄📶) This place is set on the semi-private beach, Hat Tha Khao – a fringe of sand on the mangrove-shrouded toe of the bay. This lodge is a collection of nice wooden, octagonal bungalows with sliding glass doors that peel back onto marvellous views. All are super clean, with hot water and hardwood floors. There's an on-site yoga studio (classes 7.30am & 4.30pm) here, too.

Ko Yao Beach Bungalows GUESTHOUSE $$
(☎0 7645 4213, 08 1693 8935; www.kohyaobeach.com; Hat Tha Khao; bungalows 1500B; ❄📶) Attractive, spacious, tiled bungalows with hot water and air-con, as well as smaller, older thatched wooden huts. The whole compound is set across the road from a fantastic swimming beach, and either choice is a great value.

★ **Six Senses Hideaway** HOTEL $$$
(☎0 7641 8500; www.sixsenses.com/hideaway-yaonoi; Ko Yao Noi; villas from 20,377B; ❄@≋) This swanky five-star property – where hillside pool villas (and their tremendous spa) have been built to resemble an old *chow lair* village – doesn't disappoint. Views of distant limestone are jaw-dropping, its loungy bar and white-sand beach are both worthy of the fashionistas that frequently parachute in, and its commitment to sustainability is unparalleled among global five-star chains.

Lom Lae BUNGALOWS $$$
(☎0 7659 7486; www.lomlae.com; Ko Yao Noi; bungalows 2500-6000B; 👪) Stylish wooden bungalows are fronted by a stunning and secluded beach with views of Phang-Nga's signature karst islands. There's a dive centre, a good restaurant and plenty of activities on offer. We found the bungalows a bit rustic for the price, but the setting and service do merit extra baht. They close during the wet season.

Koyao Island Resort RESORT $$$
(☎0 1606 1517; www.koyao.com; Ko Yao Noi; villas 7000-14,500B; ❄@≋) Open-concept thatched bungalows offer serene views across a palm-shaded garden and infinity pool to a skinny white beach. We love the elegant, nearly safari-esque feel of the villas, with their fan-cooled patios and indoor/outdoor bathrooms. There's a posh restaurant bar and service is stellar.

Rice Paddy THAI, INTERNATIONAL $$
(☎08 2331 6581, 0 7645 4255; Hat Pasai; mains 150-250B; ⏰6-10pm Tue-Sun; 🖉) Just around the corner from Pasai Beach, this cute, all-wood Thai and international kitchen is German owned, and all the dishes are special. They fry barracuda filets and smother them in curry, flash fry *sôm dam*, and the felafel and hummus get high marks too. They do a number of veggie dishes featuring chicken, lamb and seafood substitutes.

Ko Yao Yai

Fa Sai Beach Bungalows GUESTHOUSE $
(☎08 1691 3616; bungalows 500B) Basic but clean cold-water bungalows are stilted in the mangroves south of Tha Lo Jak, and just back from a gorgeous strip of white sand.

Thiwson Beach Resort GUESTHOUSE $$$
(☎08 1737 4420; www.thiwsonbeach.com; Ko Yao Yai; bungalows 3200B; ❄👪) Easily the sweetest of the island's humbler bungalow properties. Here are proper wooden bungalows with polished floors, outdoor baths and wide patios facing the best beach on the island. Beachfront bungalows are the largest, but fan rooms are tremendous value in the low season, when prices drop significantly.

Elixir HOTEL $$$
(☎08 7808 3838; www.elixirresort.com; Ko Yao Yai; bungalows 3331-9000B; ❄@≋) The eldest of Yao Yai's three four-star resorts offers tasteful beachfront and hillside peaked-roof villas steeped in classic Thai style. It's set on a private beach, where you'll also find a common pool, a dive centre, massage pagodas and spectacular sunsets over Phuket.

Santhiya RESORT $$$
(☎0 7659 2888; www.santhiya.com; villas from 13,600B; ❄@📶≋) Seventy-nine rooms and antiquated teak wood villas – inspired by the ancient kingdom of Lanna in Northern Thailand – are set amid 15 hectares of tropical forest and virgin beach scenery at Ko Yao Yai's newest luxury resort. There's a luscious spa, marvellous views from basically everywhere, and terrific service. Villas have private pools.

ℹ Information

In Ta Khai, the largest settlement on Ko Yao Noi, there's a 7-Eleven with an attached ATM, one of five on the island. You won't be cash poor here.

On Ko Yao Yai, there were three ATMs operating at research time, but it would still be wise

BUSES FROM PHANG-NGA

Phang-Nga's bus terminal is located just off the main street on Soi Bamrung Rat. Bangkok buses to/from Phang-Nga include VIP (960B, 12 hours, one daily), 1st class (600B, 12 to 13 hours, two daily) and 2nd class (480B, 12 hours, three to four daily).

Other bus connections include the following:

DESTINATION	FARE (B)	DURATION (HR)	FREQUENCY
Hat Yai	237-306	6	hourly
Krabi	80	1½	every 2-3hr
Phuket	90	1½	every 2-3hr
Ranong	170	5	4 daily
Surat Thani	150	3	every 2-3hr
Trang	200	3½	every 2-3hr

to carry plenty of cash in the low season, when re-supply can be an issue.

Getting There & Away

FROM PHUKET

To get to Ko Yao Noi from Phuket, take a taxi (600B to 800B) to Tha Bang Rong. From here, there are hourly long-tails (120B, 20 minutes) or three daily speedboats (200B, 20 minutes) between 7.15am and 5.40pm. They dock at Tha Klong Hia on Ko Yao Yai upon request before crossing to Ko Yao Noi. Boats begin returning to Phuket at 6.30am. Returning to Phuket from Ko Yao Noi, taxis run from Tha Bang Rong to the resort areas for 600B to 800B, or there's one *sŏrng·tăa·ou* (80B) to Phuket Town at 2.30pm daily.

The best way to reach Ko Yao Yai from Phuket is to catch a speedboat or ferry from Tha Rasada near Phuket Town. Ferries depart at 8.30am, 10.30am and 2pm (one hour, 100B). Speedboats (30 minutes, 150B) make the run at 4pm and 5pm. On Fridays the schedule shifts to accommodate prayer times.

FROM KRABI

There are four 'express' boats (470B, 1½ hours) and two speedboats (600B, 45 minutes) per day from Krabi's Tha Len pier to Ko Yao Noi piers at Tha Manok and Tha Khao.

FROM PHANG-NGA

From Tha Sapan Yao in Phang-Nga there's a 9am ferry to Ko Yao Noi continuing to Ko Yao Yai (200B, 1½ hours) that makes an excellent budget cruise of Ao Phang-Nga. It leaves Ko Yao Noi for the return trip at 7.30am the next morning.

Getting Around

To get from Ko Yao Noi to Ko Yao Yai, catch a shuttle boat from Tha Manok (100B to 150B, 15 minutes) to Tha Klong Hia. On the islands, you can travel by túk-túk for about 150B per ride or rent a motorbike from most guest houses for around 200B to 300B per day. It's 100B for túk-túk transport to the resorts.

Ko Phi-Phi & the Southern Andaman Coast

Includes ➡

Best Places to Eat

- Kruthara (p312)
- Nee Papaya (p357)
- Trang Night Market (p339)
- Lanta Seafood (p334)
- Libong Beach Resort (p345)

Best Places to Stay

- Rayavadee (p317)
- Railei Beach Club (p315)
- Castaway (p356)
- Pak-Up Hostel (p303)
- Islanda Hotel (p305)

Why Go?

Island hoppers, this is your dreamland. The south is the quieter half of the Andaman coast; even the regional star, Ko Phi-Phi, can't rival the glam and crowds of Phuket. Just slowly putter from white-sand isle to white-sand isle – and prepare for serious relaxation, outdoor fun and chummy nights at beachside bars.

Social seekers will love the developed beauties, such as Ko Phi-Phi and Ko Lanta, where you can party into the wee hours and meet plenty of fellow ramblers on the beach yet still find a peaceful strip of sand. And roads less travelled are just next door: head down through the lightly developed Trang Islands to the even-less-visited Satun Province to find powder-white beaches, outrageous snorkelling and plenty of spicy southern Thai culture.

When to Go

- The weather can be a big concern for travellers in this region. The Andaman coast receives more rain than the southern gulf provinces, with May to October being the months of heaviest rainfall. During this time passenger boats to some islands, such as Ko Tarutao, are suspended. If you find the weather on the Andaman coast unpleasant, you can easily travel to the southwestern gulf coast, where you're more likely to find the sun shining.
- Top daytime temperatures average 32°C year-round with high humidity during the wet season.

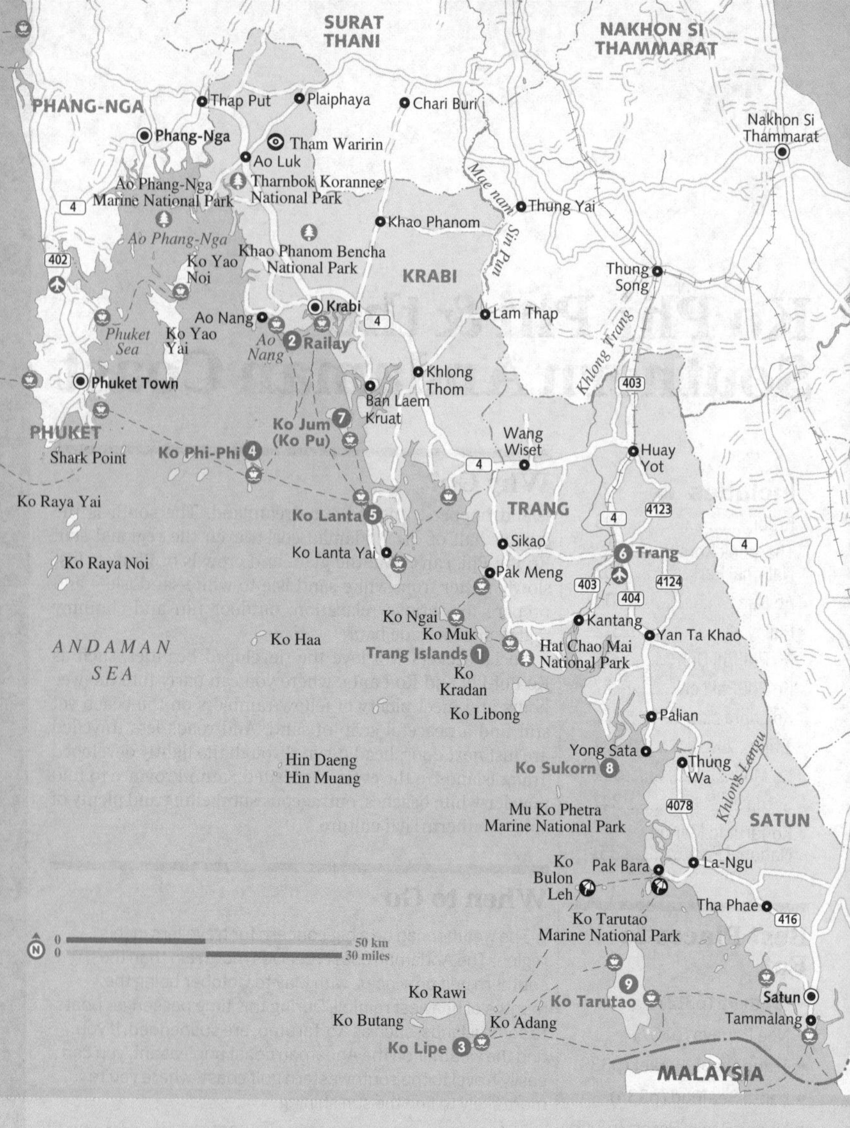

Ko Phi-Phi & the Southern Andaman Coast Highlights

1. Island hopping the serene **Trang Islands** by local longtail (p340)
2. Climbing karst formations over seas of emerald glass in **Railay** (p312)
3. Sipping cold ones on the soft, star-lit sands of **Ko Lipe** (p354)
4. Trying to decide if **Ko Phi-Phi** is more beautiful above or below water (p318)
5. Motorbiking along the wild jungle east coast of **Ko Lanta** (p327)
6. Trying everything from spicy seafood salads to fried grubs at the **Trang Night Market** (p339)
7. Having a stretch of sand almost to yourself on jungle island **Ko Jum** (p336)
8. Listening to the mosque as you pedal past water buffalo on **Ko Sukorn** (p346)
9. Jungle trekking, exploring caves and cycling the forgotten roads on **Ko Tarutao** (p351)

KRABI PROVINCE

When travellers talk about the amazing Andaman, they are probably talking about Krabi, with its trademark karst formations curving along the coast like a giant limestone fortress. Rock climbers will find their nirvana in Railay, while castaway wannabes should head to Ko Lanta, Ko Phi-Phi or any of the other 150 islands swimming off the bleach-blonde shores.

Krabi กระบี่

POP 30,882

Krabi Town is majestically situated among impossibly angular limestone karsts jutting from the mangroves, but mid-city you're more likely to be awe-struck by the sheer volume of guest houses and travel agencies packed into this compact, quirky little town. Western restaurants are ubiquitous, as are gift shops that all sell the same old trinkets. Yet if you hang out awhile, you'll also see that there's a very real provincial scene going on between the cracks. Though lately, it is the increasingly moneyed side of Krabi Town that seems to be blooming and growing.

Sights & Activities

Khao Khanap Nam CLIFFS, CAVES

(ถ้ำเขาขนาบน้ำ) It's possible to climb one of these two limestone massifs, just north of the town centre. A number of human skeletons were found in the caves here, thought to be the remains of people trapped during an ancient flood. To get here, charter a long-tail boat from Khong Kha pier for about 400B.

Sea Kayak Krabi BOATING

(0 7563 0270; www.seakayak-krabi.com; 40 Th Ruen Rudee) Offers a wide variety of sea-kayaking tours, including to Ao Thalane (half/full day 900/1500B), which has looming sea cliffs; Ko Hong (full day 1800B), famed for its emerald lagoon; and Ban Bho Tho (full day 1700B), which has sea caves with 2000- to 3000-year-old cave paintings. All rates include guides, lunch, fruit and drinking water.

Tours

Various companies offer day trips to Khlong Thom, about 45km southeast of Krabi on Hwy 4, taking in some nearby hot springs and freshwater pools. Expect to pay around 1000B to 1200B, including transport, lunch and beverages; bring a swimsuit and good walking shoes. Various other 'jungle tour' itineraries are available.

Pak-up Hostel offers mangrove and cave tours in Bho Tho for 800B.

Sleeping

It's never hard to find a cheap sleep in Krabi, but midrange and top-end options leave much to be desired (go to Ao Nang if you crave luxury).

★ **Pak-up Hostel** HOSTEL $

(0 7561 1955; www.pakuphostel.com; 87 Th Utarakit; dm 220-270B, d 500-600B;) The grooviest hostel on the Andaman coast and ranked as one of Asia's three best, this converted school house (Krabi's first) features several uber-hip polished-cement 8- and 10-bed dorms, all co-ed and named for school subjects. The big wooden bunks are built into the wall; each is equipped with a personal locker.

There's only two double rooms, constructed in the same style. All rooms share massive, modern bathrooms with hot water. There are two on-site bars (one with nightly live music) and a young, fun-loving vibe. Consider it your Real World Spring Break waking dream. You may never leave.

Blue Juice GUESTHOUSE $

(0 7563 0679; www.bluejuice.com; Th Chao Fah; r with/without bathroom 350/180B;) They don't dive anymore, but this is still a great value guest house. Rooms are simple and fan cooled, with high ceilings and old wood floors. Their kitchen is best known for tasty burgers (mains 60B-120B).

NAVIGATING KRABI

Th Utarakit is the main road into and out of Krabi and most places of interest are on the soi (lanes) that branch off it. Ferries to Ko Phi-Phi, Ko Lanta and other islands leave from Khlong Chilat (Krabi passenger pier) about 4km southwest of town, while long-tail boats to Railay depart from Khong Kha (Chao Fa) pier on Th Khong Kha. The Krabi bus terminal is north of the town centre at Talat Kao, near the junction of Th Utarakit, while the airport is nearly 17km northeast on Hwy 4.

Krabi

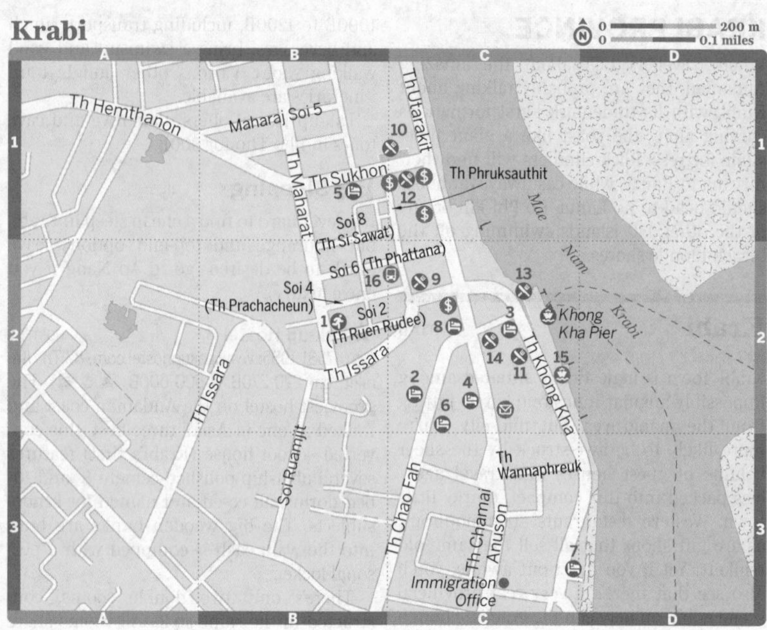

Krabi

Activities, Courses & Tours

1 Sea Kayak Krabi B2

Sleeping

2 A Mansion Hotel C2
3 Blue Juice C2
4 Chan Cha Lay C2
5 Hometel B1
6 K Guesthouse C2
7 Krabi River Hotel C3
8 Pak-up Hostel C2

Eating

9 Cucina Italiana Viva C2
10 Day Market C1
11 Kotung Restaurant C2
12 Krabi Station C1
13 Night Market C2
14 Relax Coffee C2

Drinking & Nightlife

Playground .... (see 8)

Transport

15 PP Family Co C2
16 Sŏrng•tăa•ou to Ao Nang C2

Chan Cha Lay GUESTHOUSE $
(☎0 7562 0952; www.chanchalay.com; 55 Th Utarakit; r with/without bathroom 400/200B; ❄📶) The en-suite rooms here, all decorated in tasteful Mediterranean blues and whites with white-pebble and polished-concrete semi-outdoor bathrooms, are among Krabi's most comfortable. Shared-bathroom, fan-only rooms are plain but spotless with firm beds.

K Guesthouse GUESTHOUSE $
(☎0 7562 3166; kguesthouse@yahoo.com; 15-25 Th Chao Fah; r 200-600B; ❄@📶) An old teak lodge with Wild West accents and varnished wooden rooms that line a second-storey verandah overlooking the street.

A Mansion Hotel HOTEL $
(☎0 7563 0511; www.a-mansionkrabi.com; 12/6 Th Chao Fah; d fan/air-con 350/500B; P❄📶) This hotel right in the centre of town is not as snazzy as the lobby first appears, but rooms are brushed in pastel tones and are clean and spacious with high ceilings.

Hometel HOTEL $
(☎0 7562 2301; 7 Soi 2, Th Maharat ; r 750B; ❄📶) A modern and funky boutique sleep with 10

rooms on three floors crafted entirely from polished concrete. Abstract art brings the colour, there are rain showers, some rooms have two terraces and all have high ceilings. There's a tour desk which can arrange any and all transport wishes as well as a sunny cafe serving Western breakfasts.

Krabi River Hotel HOTEL **$$**
(☎0 7561 2321; krabiriver@hotmail.com; 73/1 Th Khong Kha; r from 1000B; ❄) Sure, it feels like a flashback from the early 1980s, but rooms have newly tiled bathrooms and queen-sized beds, and offer terrific views of the dark river and misty mangroves. Quiet, yet in town, it's a simple place in a five-star location.

Krabi Maritime Park & Spa HOTEL **$$**
(☎0 7562 0028; www.maritimeparkandspa.com; r from 2040B; ❄@📶🏊) On lovely riverside grounds and framed by those signature limestone karsts, this dated, once-glorious hotel is 2km from Krabi town proper. It sports a nightclub, pool, fitness centre, spa and even a lake on which you can pedal swan-shaped boats. There are free shuttle buses to Krabi town and Ao Nang, and shuttle boats to Railay.

Eating & Drinking

★Night Market THAI **$**
(Th Khong Kha; meals 20-50B) The most popular spot for an evening meal is this market near the Khong Kha pier. The menus are in English but the food is authentic and excellent. Stalls here sell *sôm·đam* (spicy green papaya salad), fried noodles, *đôm yam gûng* (prawn and lemon grass soup), grilled snapper, huge skillets of egg-battered and fried oysters, all things satay, plus sweet, creamy Thai desserts.

Day Market THAI **$**
(Th Sukhon; meals 20-60B) This market is even more authentic than the night market. Among the bouquets of flowers and weighty tropical-fruit stands are simmering curry pots and banquet trays of steaming noodles with fried squid, sautéed beef, devilled eggs, fried fish and boiled corn. Eat daringly. Though called the day market, it's open most nights too.

Krabi Station THAI **$**
(☎0 7561 2501; www.krabistation.com; 3/1 Th Sukhon; 59-139B; ⏲8am-10pm) A tour agent, a hit-and-miss boutique and a Thai diner all in one. They do a range of authentic stir fries and curries, and forgettable Western fare on the cheap.

Kotung Restaurant THAI **$**
(☎0 7561 1522; 36 Th Khong Kha; dishes 80-150B; ⏲11am-10pm Mon-Sat) The tables are dressed in red linen and packed with upwardly mobile locals who descend for crab omelettes, baked prawns with glass noodles and pork *pá·naang* curry among other flavours. All of it affordable.

Relax Coffee CAFE **$**
(Th Chao Fah; mains 45-220B; ⏲7:30am-6pm; 📶) Krabi's best coffee shop offers both Thai and Western breakfasts and ample salads, sandwiches and curries at lunch, and it does pizza too. It's all served in a charming, restored wooden storefront near the river.

Cucina Italiana Viva ITALIAN **$$**
(☎0 7563 0517; 29 Th Phruksauthit; mains 120-560B) This is the place to sample tasty, thin-crust pizza, with a variety of cheeses and toppings to choose from. It has calzones, Italian wine, steaks and chops, ice cream and coffee, and it delivers.

OFF THE BEATEN TRACK

KO KLANG

One of the most fun and least visited sights in the Krabi town area is the island of **Ko Klang**. Set just across the channel and accessible by long-tail ferry (per person/motorbike 10/20B), this traditional Muslim farming island cultivates rice, fish and shrimp and is laced with narrow concrete streets with no cars at all. The thing to do is to rent a bike and go over for the day, pedalling around the flat streets and along brackish canals. Head to the far side to get to the broad sandy beach with incredible sunset views over Railay. Although ferries run into the night, you may wish to sleep over at the **Islanda Hotel** (☎08 9616 2333; www.islandakrabi.com; Ko Klang; d from 3000B; P❄@📶🏊), a special four-star boutique hotel made up of stylish polished concrete bungalows blessed with sumptuous outdoor baths and private sun porches set around a stunning infinity pool. The restaurant is top notch, so is the service. It's not for budgeteers, but is an exceptional value at this price.

Playground BAR
(87 Th Utarakit; 📶) Pak-up Hostel's rollicking downstairs courtyard bar is where the fun and games gather and bloom. From beer pong and open-mic nights to live music and game nights, there is always something on and new friends to enjoy.

Information

Many of Krabi's guest houses and restaurants offer free wi-fi. There are numerous banks and ATMs.

Immigration Office (☎0 7561 1350; Th Chamai Anuson; ⏰8.30am-4pm Mon-Fri) Handles visa extensions.

Krabi Hospital (☎0 7561 1210; Th Utarakit) Located 1km north of town.

Post Office (Th Utarakit) Just south of the turn-off to Khong Kha pier.

Getting There & Away

AIR

Most domestic carriers offer service between Bangkok and Krabi International Airport. **Bangkok Air** (www.bangkokair.com) has daily service to Ko Samui.

BOAT

Boats to Ko Phi-Phi and Ko Lanta leave from the passenger pier at Khlong Chilat, about 4km southwest of Krabi. Travel agencies will arrange free transfers when you buy a boat ticket with them.

The largest boat operator is **PP Family Co** (☎0 7561 2463; www.phiphifamily.com; Th Khong Kha), which has a ticket office right beside the pier in town. In the high season there are boats to Ko Phi-Phi (300B, 1½ hours) at 9am, 10.30am, 1.30pm and 3pm, while in low season the schedule is reduced to two boats per day.

From November to May, there is only one daily boat to Ko Lanta (400B to 450B, two hours), leaving Krabi at 11.30am. These can also stop at Ko Jum (one hour), where long-tails shuttle you to shore (though you'll pay the full fare). During the wet season, you can only get to Ko Lanta by frequent air-con vans (300B, 2½ hours), which also run throughout the high season.

If you want to get to Railay, long-tail boats leave from Krabi's Khong Kha pier to Hat Railay East (150B, 45 minutes) from 7.45am to 6pm. The boatmen will wait until they can fill a boat with 10 people before they leave; if you're antsy to go before then, you can charter the whole boat for 1500B.

To get to Phuket or the Ko Yao Islands, the quickest route is with direct boats from the pier at Ao Nang. *Sŏrng·tăa·ou* run between the two piers for 50B, or a taxi costs 400B to 500B.

MINIVAN

Dozens of travel agencies in Krabi run air-con minivans and VIP buses to popular tourist centres throughout southern Thailand, but you may end up crammed cheek-to-jowl with other backpackers. Most travel agencies also offer combined minivan and boat tickets direct to Ko Samui (550B, 5½ hours) and Ko Pha-Ngan (700B, 7½ hours). Destinations from Krabi include the following:

DESTINATION	FARE (B)	DURATION (HR)
Ao Luk	80	1
Hat Yai	350	3
Ko Lanta	300	1½
Phuket	300-350	2-3
Satun	600-650	5
Trang	350	2

SŎRNG·TĂA·OU

Sŏrng·tăa·ou (passenger pick-up trucks) run from the bus station to central Krabi and on to Hat Noppharat Thara (50B), Ao Nang (50B) and the Shell Cemetery at Ao Nam Mao (50B). There are services from 6am to 6.30pm. In the high season there are less frequent services until

BUSES TO/FROM KRABI

Taking a government bus from the **Krabi bus terminal** (☎0 7561 1804; cnr Th Utarakit & Hwy 4) in nearby Talat Kao, about 4km from Krabi, is an altogether more relaxing option than taking a cramped minivan.

DESTINATION	FARE (B)	DURATION (HR)	FREQUENCY
Bangkok	794-1000	12	4 per day
Hat Yai	169	5	hourly
Phuket	150	3½	hourly
Ranong	205	6	2 per day
Surat Thani	140	1½	every 2-3 hr
Trang	90-115	2	every 2-3hr

10pm for a 10B surcharge. For Ao Luk (80B, one hour) there are frequent *sŏrng·tăa·ou* from the corner of Th Phattana and Th Phruksauthit; the last service leaves at around 3pm.

Getting Around

Central Krabi is easy to explore on foot, but the bus terminal and airport are both a long way from the town centre. A taxi from the airport to town will cost 400B. In the reverse direction, taxis cost 350B, while motorcycle taxis cost 300B. Agencies in town can arrange seats on the airport bus for 100B. *Sŏrng·tăa·ou* between the bus terminal and central Krabi cost 50B.

Hiring a vehicle is an excellent way to explore the countryside around Krabi. Most of the travel agencies and guest houses in town can rent you a Yamaha motorbike for 150B to 200B per day. Pak-up Hostel (p303) has a gleaming fleet and provides helmets. They also rent push bikes for 120B per day. A few of the travel agencies along Th Utarakit rent out small 4WDs for 1200B to 1800B per day.

Wat Tham Seua วัดถ้ำเสือ

A sprawling hill and cave temple complex 8km northwest of Krabi, **Wat Tham Seua** (Tiger Cave Temple) is an easy and very worthwhile daytrip from Krabi Town. Although the main *wí·hăhn* (hall) is built into a long, shallow limestone cave at the wát's entrance, where there's also a shiny new pagoda to explore, the best part of the temple grounds can be found by following a loop trail through a little forest valley behind the ridge where the *bòht* (central sanctuary) is located. You'll find several limestone caves hiding Buddha images, statues and altars as well as some of the monks' rustic jungle huts, behind which they hang out their saffron robes to dry. Troops of monkeys cackle from the trees.

> **WHAT NOT TO WEAR AT THE WAT**
>
> Wat Tham Seua sees a large amount of Western visitors, many of whom unfortunately arrive in shorts, swimsuits and even shirtless as if they just stepped off the beach. Signs are posted around the wát asking visitors to dress respectfully but the monks themselves, as well as most Thais, are too polite to say anything to those disregarding their kind request. This is a sacred area of worship, so please be respectful and dress modestly: trousers or skirts past the knees, shirts covering the shoulders and nothing too tight.

Back near the park entrance again, you'll come to a gruellingly steep 1237 steps (you'll have the number memorised if you climb them) leading to a 600m karst peak. The fit and fearless are rewarded with a Buddha statue, a gilded stupa and spectacular views; on a clear day you can see well out to sea.

Getting There & Away

A motorcycle taxi or túk-túk from Krabi to Wat Tham Seua costs 100B. By *sŏrng·tăa·ou*, get on at Krabi's Th Utarakit for 50B, and tell the driver 'Wat Tham Seua'. If no one else is going to the wát, the driver may ask an extra fee to drive you down the 300m lane from the main road to the wát's entrance. It's just as easy to get off at the road and walk. Motorcycle taxis and túk-túks hang out in the wát parking lot, or you could flag one down on the main road.

Tharnbok Korannee National Park อุทยานแห่งชาติธารโบกขรณี

Close to the small town of Ao Luk, a stunning 46km drive northwest of Krabi, **Tharnbok Korannee National Park** (Than Bok; adult/child under 14yr 200/100B) protects a large area of islands, mangroves and limestone caves. The most important cave here is **Tham Pee Hua Toe** (Big-Headed Ghost Cave), reached by long-tail boat or sea kayak from the pier at Ban Bho Tho, 7km south of Ao Luk. Legend has it that a huge human skull was found in the cave, but the ghost story probably has more to do with the 2000- to 3000-year-old cave paintings that adorn the cave walls. Nearby **Tham Lot** (Tube Cave) can also be navigated by boat. Both caves are popular destinations for kayaking tours from Krabi or Ao Nang, but you can also hire sea kayaks from local guides who grew up in the shadow of the Bho Tho pier. Long-tails are available for 500B to 600B.

There are at least seven other caves in the park, including **Tham Sa Yuan Thong** – a few kilometres southeast of Ao Luk – which has a natural spring bubbling into a pool. The national park also includes the uninhabited island of **Ko Hong**, which has fine beaches, jungle-cloaked cliffs and a scenic hidden lagoon.

Just to the south of Ao Luk, the park headquarters is a popular picnic spot. You'll find an 1800m nature trail that links a series of babbling brooks and shady emerald pools connected by little waterfalls. The usual vendors sell noodles, fried chicken and *sôm·đam*. There's also a brand-new **visitors centre** (8am-4pm) that has photo mural displays in Thai and English.

Nearby **Ao Them Lem** is another stunning panorama of limestone and mangroves laced with concrete streets and sandy lanes. Day-trippers buzz in for long-tail trips to nearby *hôrng* (semisubmerged island caves) and lagoons, but otherwise this is a mellow, very local village with a few modest resorts.

Discovery Resort (08 1298 9533; 500 Moo 1 Kao Tong; bungalows from 1100B;) is the tightest operation. The owner-operator speaks English and her attractive peaked-roof bungalows have cable TV and there's a pool.

Getting There & Away

The park headquarters is about 1.5km south of Ao Luk town along Rte 4039. Buses and *sŏrng·tăa·ou* from Krabi stop on Hwy 4. Catch a government bus to Pha-Ngan or Phuket and ask to be let off at Ao Luk (80B, one hour), from where you can walk down to the park headquarters or take a motorcycle taxi for 20B. The easiest way to get to Tham Pee Hua Toe and Tham Lot is on a sea-kayaking tour from Krabi or Ao Nang.

To get to Ban Bho Tho from Ao Luk under your own steam, take a motorcycle taxi (70B) or a Laem Sak *sŏrng·tăa·ou* (30B) to the Tham Pee Hua Toe turn-off on Rte 4039. From the junction it's about 2km to Ban Bho Tho along the first signposted road on the left.

Sŏrng·tăa·ou from Krabi also travel directly to Ao Them Lem (60B).

Ao Nang อ่าวนาง

POP 12,400

First, the hard truths. Thanks to its unchecked and rather unsightly development huddled in the shadows of stunning karst scenery, Ao Nang is ugly pretty, and there's a touch of the Twilight Zone in the air here too, with the countless Indian-owned 'Italian' restaurants and naughty bar-girl sois.

So, yes, it's a little trashy, but if you forgive all that and focus on the beaches, framed by limestone headlands tied together by narrow strips of golden sand, there's an awful lot to like here. In the dry season the sea glows a turquoise hue; in the wet season, rip-tides stir up the mocha shallows. If you're hankering for a swim in crystalline climes at any time of year, you can easily book a trip to the local islands that dot the horizon.

Ao Nang is compact and easy to navigate, and with the onrush of attractive, midrange development, accommodation standards are high, with substantial discounts possible. It's not nearly as cheap (or as authentic) as Krabi town, but it's cleaner and sunnier. There's plenty to do (mangrove tours, snorkelling trips) and it's only 40 minutes away from the Krabi airport and a smooth 20-minute long-tail boat ride from stunning Railay.

Activities

Loads of activities are possible at Ao Nang, and children under 12 typically get a 50% discount.

Kayaking

Several companies offer kayaking tours to mangroves and islands around Ao Nang. Popular destinations include the scenic sea lagoon at Ko Hong (1500B to 1800B) to view collection points for sea swallow nests (spurred by the ecologically dubious demand for bird's-nest soup). There are also trips to the lofty sea cliffs and wildlife-filled mangroves at Ao Thalane (half/full day 500/800B) and to the sea caves and 2000- to 3000-year-old paintings at Ban Bho Tho (half/full day 700/900B). Rates will vary slightly, but always include lunch, fruit, drinking water, sea kayaks and guides.

Diving & Snorkelling

Ao Nang has numerous dive schools offering trips to 15 local islands, including Ko Si, Ko Ha, Yava Bon and Yava Son. It costs about 2500B to 3300B for two local dives. Ko Mae Urai is one of the more unique local dives, with two submarine tunnels lined with soft and hard corals. Other trips run further afield to King Cruiser (three dives from 4200B) and Ko Phi-Phi (two dives 3400B to 3900B). A PADI Open Water course will set you back 14,900B to 16,000B. Reliable dive schools include **Kon-Tiki Diving & Snorkelling** (0 7563 7826; www.kontiki-thailand.com; 161/1 Moo 2 Tambon Ao Nang; dive trips from 3900B; 9am-1pm & 4-9pm), **The Dive** (08 2282 2537; www.thediveaonang.com; 249/2 Moo 2; dive trips 2500-4200B), and **Aqua Vision** (0 7563 7415; www.aqua-vision.net; Ao Nang; around 3000B for two dives). Most dive companies can also arrange snorkelling trips in the area.

WORTH A TRIP

KHAO PHANOM BENCHA NATIONAL PARK

This 50-sq-km **park** (อุทยานแห่งชาติเขาพนมเบญจา; ☎0 7566 0716; adult/child under 14yr 200/100B) protects a dramatic area of virgin rainforest along the spine of 1350m-high Khao Phanom Bencha, 20km north of Krabi. The park is full of well-signed trails to scenic waterfalls, including the 11-tiered **Huay To Falls**, 500m from the park headquarters. Nearby and almost as dramatic are Huay Sadeh Falls and Khlong Haeng Falls. On the way into the park you can visit **Tham Pheung**, a dramatic cave with shimmering mineral stalactites and stalagmites. The numerous trails that wend through the area are excellent for hiking.

The park is home to abundant wildlife – but only monkeys are commonly seen. Many bird-spotters come here to see white-crowned and helmeted hornbills, argus pheasants and the extremely rare Gurney's pitta. Local guides aren't absolutely necessary here, considering the well-marked trails, but visitors who hire guides tend to spot more wildlife, and have a deeper experience in general.

There is no public transport to the park, but it's easy to get here from Krabi by hired motorcycle; follow the sign-posted turn-off from Hwy 4. Park your motorcycle by the park headquarters and remember to apply the steering lock. Alternatively, you can hire a túk-túk (pronounced *đúk đuk*; motorised three-wheeled pedicab) for around 800B round-trip.

Tours

Any agency worth its salt can book you on one of the popular four- or five-island tours for around 2500B. The **Ao Nang Long-tail Boat Service** (☎0 7569 5313) offers private charters for up to six people to Hong Island (2500B) and Bamboo Island (3800B), and the standard five-island tour, of course. You can also book half-day trips to Poda and Chicken Islands (2000B, four hours) for up to four people.

Several tour agencies offer tours to **Khlong Thom**, including visits to freshwater pools, hot springs and the **Wat Khlong Thom Museum**; the price per adult/child is 1500/1000B.

You can also arrange day tours to Ko Phi-Phi on the **Ao Nang Princess** (adult/child 1400/1000B). The boat leaves from the Hat Noppharat Thara National Park headquarters at 9am and visits Bamboo Island, Phi-Phi Don and Phi-Phi Leh. Free transfers from Ao Nang to Hat Noppharat Thara are included in the price.

Sleeping

Prices at all these places drop by 50% during the low season.

★Glur HOSTEL $

(☎08 9001 3343, 0 7569 5297; www.krabiglurhostel.com; 22/2 Moo 2, Soi Ao Nang; dm 600B, d 1300-1500B; P❄@🛜🏊) Another sneaky, great Krabi-area hostel. Designed, built, owned and operated by a talented Thai architect and his wife, the gleaming white lodge complex incorporates shipping containers, glass and moulded, polished concrete to create sumptuous dorms – with curtained-off turquoise beds and airy private rooms. The pool was under construction at research time.

J Hotel HOTEL $$

(☎0 7563 7878; www.jhotelaonang.com; Th Ao Nang; r 1500B; ❄@) J Hotel is an old standby that caters well to backpackers. Large, bright rooms have new tiled floors, built-in desks, wardrobes and satellite TV, but some smell a bit musty. Sniff before you commit.

Amorn Mansion HOTEL $$

(☎0 7563 7695; 310 Moo 2, Soi Ao Nang; r 1600B incl breakfast; P❄🛜) Four floors of decent-value tiled rooms with air-con and private terraces. Expect fresh bath tile, satellite TV and wi-fi throughout. One of the better no-frills joints in town.

The Nine @ Ao Nang HOTEL $$

(☎0 7569 5668; www.thenineaonang.com; 348 Moo 2, Soi Ao Nang; d 1700-2200B; ❄🛜) Dig the dancing Ganesh statues framed in the lobby and the floating beds and slightly sunken baths in the stylish guest rooms. Rooms also have private terraces (some with cliff views), mini-fridges, wall-mounted flat screens and their own little Ganesh standing sentry on the desk. It all adds up to one of Ao Nang's most stylish three-star sleeps.

Somkiet Buri Resort HOTEL $$
(0 7563 7320; www.somkietburi.com; 236 Moo 2, Ao Nang; r from 1800-3000B;) This place just might inspire you to slip into a yoga pose. The lush jungle grounds are filled with ferns and orchids, while lagoons, streams and meandering wooden walkways guide you to the 26 large and creatively designed rooms. A great swimming pool is set amid it all – balconies face either this pool or a peaceful pond.

Ban Sainai RESORT $$$
(0 7581 9333; 11/1 Soi Ao Nang; bungalows from 3000B;) One of the newest properties in town sports cushy, thatched faux-adobe bungalows sprinkled amid the palms and set so close to the cliffs you can almost kiss them. Expect high-end tiled floors, polished concrete baths, timber wash basins and pebbled showers. Low season deals (1750B) are fabulous.

Red Ginger Chic Resort HOTEL $$$
(0 7563 7777; www.redgingerkrabi.com; 88 Moo 3, Th Ao Nang; r from 3000B;) Fashionable and colourful with detailed tiles, large paper lanterns, and a frosted glass bar in the lobby. Large rooms feature elegant wallpaper, modern furnishings and large balconies overlooking an expansive pool.

Pakasai RESORT $$$
(0 7563 7777; www.pakasai.com; 88 Moo 3, Th Ao Nang; r from 3400B;) This sprawling family-owned resort has been around a while – though you wouldn't know it from the handsome, well-maintained rooms graced with stylish blonde wood furnishings, tasteful light fixtures, rain showers and soaker tubs on the terrace. Low season rates plummet to 1500B.

Golden Beach Resort HOTEL $$$
(0 7563 7871, 0 7563 7870; www.goldenbeach-resort.com; 254 Moo 2, Th Ao-Nang; r 3500-6100B, bungalows 5100-8500B;) This sprawling, unpretentious resort dominates the southernmost 400m of Ao Nang's beachfront – the best part of the beach. It's made up of large hotel blocks and stylish white-cement, wood-trimmed bungalows arranged in garden foliage around a big pool. It's only verging on hip but it definitely feels good to be here. Check the website for specials.

Phra Nang Inn HOTEL $$$
(0 7563 7130; www.phrananghotels.com; Th Ao Nang; r incl breakfast from 3600B;) A sprawling thatched explosion of rustic coconut wood, bright orange and purple paint and plenty of elaborate Thai tiles. There are two pools, and a similarly designed branch is across the road from the original. It could use a refresh, but it has a sweet perch and plenty of life.

Ananta Burin HOTEL $$$
(0 7566 1551; www.anantaburinresort.com; 166 Moo 3; r from 6000B;) A boutique resort with an impressive vaulted-roof lobby and hotel blocks that horseshoe around a pool. Rooms feature nice design elements, including built-in dark-wood furnishings. First-floor rooms spill directly into the pool. Rooms are half price in low season.

Eating

Ao Nang is full of mediocre roadside restaurants serving Italian, Scandinavian, Indian, Thai and fast food. Prices are a bit inflated but you won't go hungry. For budget meals, a few stalls pop up at night on the road to Krabi (near McDonald's). You'll find *roti* (pancakes), *gài tôrt* (fried chicken), hamburgers and the like, and around lunch time streets stalls also set up just north of Krabi Resort. Glur (p309), the grooviest hostel in town, also has a seasonal sandwich shop that makes some of the best sandwiches and burgers in all of Krabi. Of course, the best meal in the Ao Nang area (and beyond) can be found at Kruthara (p312) in nearby Nopparat Thara. It's well worth the trip.

Bamboo Food Huts THAI $
(meals 35-90B) If you're in the mood for a ramshackle local food joint, walk a few minutes up the main road to Krabi from the beach to find a row of thatched beach-style eateries. Ignore the Western dishes and dig into something tasty, spicy and authentic, like fried squid with hot basil, seafood *đôm yam* or massaman curry. There are plenty of vegie options too. **Lucky Yim Restaurant** is particularly good.

Ao Nang Cuisine THAI
(mains 50-300B; 9:30am-10pm;) This place claims to be the first proper restaurant in town, and it does feel delightfully dated, with its brick columns and breezy patio perch across the road from the beach. They do a mix of Chinese and Thai dishes, including more obscure delicacies like steamed crab with glass noodles and fried tofu with crab meat.

WORTH A TRIP

SHELL CEMETERY สุสานหอย

About 9km east of Ao Nang at the western end of Ao Nam Mao is the Shell Cemetery, also known as Gastropod Fossil or Su-San Hoi. Here you can see giant slabs formed from millions of tiny 75-million-year-old fossil shells. There's a small **visitors centre** (admission 50B; ⏲8am-4pm), with geological displays and various stalls selling snacks. *Sŏrng·tăa·ou* from Ao Nang cost 40B.

Soi Sunset SEAFOOD **$$**
(☎0 7569 5260; Soi Sunset; dishes 60-400B; ⏲noon-10pm) At the western end of the beach is this narrow pedestrian-only alley with several romantic seafood restaurants with gorgeous views. They all have model ice boats at the entrance showing off the day's catch and smiling staff to beckon you to take a seat.

Jeanette's Restaurant SWEDISH, THAI **$$**
(☎08 9474 6178; www.jeanettekrabi.com; dishes 120-350B; ⏲8am-10pm) The most popular place in town thanks to its signature bench seating, inkblot art on the walls and traditional Thai menu augmented with Swedish hits.

Drinking & Nightlife

Last Café CAFE, BAR
(⏲11am-7pm) At the far southern end of Hat Ao Nang is this barefoot beach cafe, with cold beer and cool breezes. Come here for a welcome blast of Ao Nang natural.

Entertainment

Aonang Krabi Muay Thai Stadium THAI BOXING
(☎0 7562 1042; admission 800B, ringside 1200B) If you get tired of the beach bars and video movies on the strip, this place has boisterous *moo·ay tai* (Thai boxing; often spelled *muay thai*) bouts two days a week (check current schedules at any travel agent in town) from 8.45pm. A free *sŏrng·tăa·ou* runs along the strip at Ao Nang, collecting punters before the bell.

Information

All the information offices on the strip are private tour agencies, and most offer international calls and internet access for around 1B per minute. Most cafes and hotels have free wi-fi. Several banks have ATMs and foreign-exchange windows (open from 10am to 8pm) on the main drag.

Getting There & Around

BOAT

Boats to Railay's Hat Railay West are run by **Ao Nang Long-tail Boat Service** (☎0 7569 5313; www.aonangboatco-op.com) and rates are fixed at 100B per person from 7.30am to 6pm or 150B per person from 6pm to 6am. It's a 15-minute journey – boats leave when there are a minimum of eight passengers or you can charter the whole boat by paying for the equivalent of eight people. During rough seas, boats leave from a sheltered cove about 200m west of Ao Nang – you can get here from Ao Nang by motorcycle taxi (30B), *sŏrng·tăa·ou* (10B) or on foot.

Ferries and speedboats leave for Ko Phi-Phi, Ko Lanta, Phuket and the Ko Yao Islands from the nearby pier at Hat Noppharat Thara.

CAR, BUS & MINIVAN

Ao Nang is served by regular *sŏrng·tăa·ou* from Krabi (50B, 20 minutes). These start at the Krabi bus terminal (add 10B to the fare) and then pass by the 7-Eleven on Th Maharat and the Khong Kha pier in Krabi, continuing on to Hat Noppharat Thara, Ao Nang and finally the Shell Cemetery. From Ao Nang to Hat Noppharat Thara or the Shell Cemetery it's 40B. Airport buses to and from Ao Nang cost 80B to 100B and leave throughout the day. Private taxis from the airport cost about 800B. Minibuses go to destinations all over the south including Phuket (350B to 400B, three to four hours), Pak Bara (300B, 3½ hours) and Koh Lanta (400B, two hours).

Dozens of places along the strip rent out small motorcycles for 150B to 200B. Budget Car Hire has desks at most of the big resort hotels and charges around 1600B per day for a dinky Suzuki micro-4WD.

Around Ao Nang

Hat Noppharat Thara หาดนพรัตน์ธารา

North of Ao Nang, the golden beach goes a bit more *au naturel* as it curves around a headland for 4km with limited development, until the sea eventually spills into a natural lagoon at the Ko Phi-Phi Marine National Park headquarters. Here, scores of long-tails mingle with fishing boats and speedboats against a stunning limestone backdrop. The small visitors centre has displays on coral reefs and mangrove ecology, labelled in Thai and English.

Several resorts here advertise a 'central Ao Nang' location – so if you don't like reading fine print, you might end up sleeping out here (though you might prefer it anyway).

Sleeping & Eating

Around the national park headquarters there are several restaurants serving the usual Thai snacks, such as fried chicken and papaya salad, and there's a handful of dining stalls and seafood restaurants along the frontage road.

Government Bungalows BUNGALOWS $$
(0 7563 7200; bungalows 1000B) These wooden, fan-cooled bungalows across the street from the beach are rustic yet well maintained and a terrific budget choice. Prices don't go up in the high season, but you'd better book ahead. Check in at national park headquarters near the harbour. Meals are no longer served on-site.

Sabai Resort HOTEL $$
(0 7563 7791; www.sabairesort.com; bungalows 1300-1600B) The most professionally run of the area's bungalow properties. The tiled-roof bungalows are fan cooled and have pebbled concrete patios overlooking a palm-shaded swimming pool and a flower garden. It offers massage and accepts credit cards.

★ **Kruthara** SEAFOOD $$
(0 7563 7361; Hat Nopparat Thara; meals from 300B; 11am-10pm; P) This cavernous, tin-roof delight is the best restaurant in the south Andaman, and one of the best seafood kitchens in Thailand, which places it high in the running for best worldwide. There is no pretension here, just the freshest fish, crab, clams, oysters, lobster and prawns done dozens of ways, some of which are very special.

The crab fried in yellow curry is spectacular, with meaty legs half cracked and waiting, and the guts and roe scrambled in eggs which are drenched in curry and piled on top of the crab itself. The fried rice is fluffy and light, and the snapper fried in red curry is scintillating and moist and one of the best fish dishes we've ever eaten in Thailand (and we've had hundreds). Simply put, this is a meal that can turn enemies into friends, friends into lovers and lovers into life partners.

Getting There & Away

Sŏrng·tăa·ou between Krabi and Ao Nang stop in Hat Noppharat Thara; the fare is 50B from Krabi or 20B from Ao Nang.

From November to May the *Ao Nang Princess* runs between Ko Phi-Phi Marine National Park headquarters and Ko Phi-Phi (400B, two hours). The boat leaves from the national park jetty at 9am, returning from Ko Phi-Phi at 1.30pm. It also stops at Railay's Hat Railay West. This boat can also be used for day trips to Ko Phi-Phi. During the same high-season months, there's also a 3pm boat to Phuket (700B, four hours), leaving from the same pier, and a 10.30am boat to Koh Lanta (470B, 1½ hours).

A faster alternative to Phuket is to take the *Green Planet* speedboat (950B, 75 minutes), which goes from Hat Noppharat Thara to Bang Rong Pier, north of Phuket Town via Ko Yao Noi and Ko Yao Yai (both 470B, 45 minutes). The boat leaves Hat Noppharat Thara at 10.30am and 4pm, and transport to your Phuket accommodation is included in the fare.

Railay ไร่เล

Krabi's fairytale limestone crags come to a dramatic climax at Railay (also spelled Rai Leh), the ultimate jungle gym for rock-climbing fanatics. This quiet slice of paradise fills in the sandy gaps between each craggy flourish, and although it's just around the bend from chaotic tourist hustle in Ao Nang, the atmosphere here is nothing short of laid-back, Thai-Rasta heaven.

Sights

At the eastern end of Hat Phra Nang is **Tham Phra Nang** (Princess Cave), an important shrine for local fishers. Legend has it that a royal barge carrying an Indian princess foundered in a storm here during the 3rd century. The spirit of the drowned princess came to inhabit the cave, granting favours to all who paid their respects. Local fishermen – both Muslim and Buddhist – still place carved wooden phalluses in the cave as offerings in the hope that the spirit will provide plenty of fish.

About halfway along the path from Hat Railay East to Hat Phra Nang, a crude path, with somewhat dodgy footing (especially after rain), leads up the jungle-cloaked cliff wall to a murky hidden lagoon known as **Sa Phra Nang** (Princess Pool). There's a dramatic viewpoint over the peninsula from the nearby cliff top. This is a strenuous, if brief, hike.

Railay

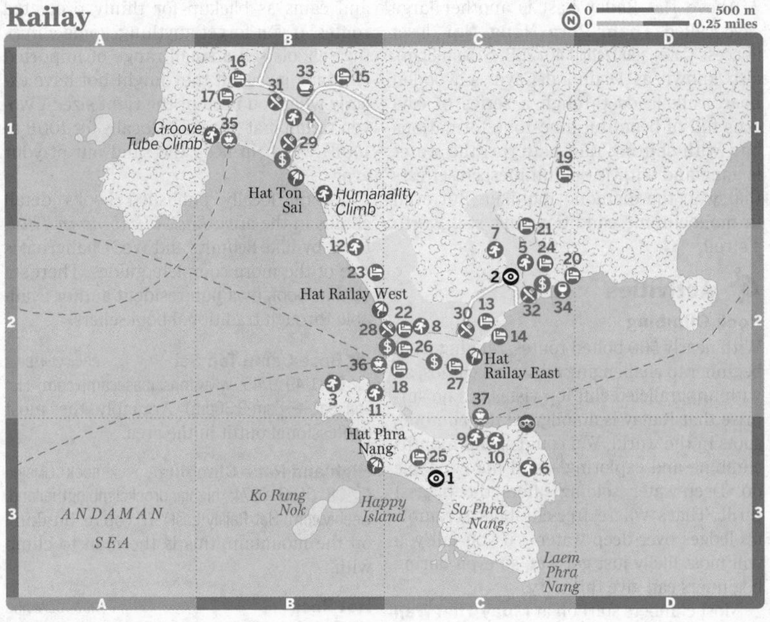

Railay

Sights
1 Tham Phra Nang ... C3
2 Tham Phra Nang Nai ... C2

Activities, Courses & Tours
3 Ao Nang Tower ... B2
4 Base Camp Ton Sai ... B1
5 Diamond Cave ... C2
6 Hidden World ... C3
7 Highland Rock Climbing ... C2
8 Hot Rock ... C2
King Climbers ... (see 14)
9 Muay Thai Wall ... C3
10 One, Two, Three Wall ... C3
11 Thaiwand Wall ... B2
12 Wee's Present Wall ... B2

Sleeping
13 Anyavee ... C2
14 Bhu Nga Thani ... C2
15 Forest Resort ... B1
16 Mountain View Resort ... B1
17 Paasook ... B1
18 Railay Bay Resort & Spa ... C2
19 Railay Cabana ... C1
20 Railay Garden View ... C2
21 Railay Phutawan Resort ... C2
22 Railay Village Resort & Spa ... C2
23 Railei Beach Club ... B2
24 Rapala Rockwood Resort ... C2
25 Rayavadee ... C3
26 Sand Sea Resort ... C2
27 Sunrise Tropical Resort ... C2

Eating
28 Flame Tree ... C2
29 Mama's Chicken ... B1
30 Mangrove Restaurant ... C2
31 Pyramid Bar & Restaurant ... B1
32 Seaview ... C2

Drinking & Nightlife
33 Backyard Bar & Cafe ... B1
Highland Rock Climbing ... (see 7)
34 Lucky Last Bar ... C2
Small World Bar ... (see 31)

Information
Clinic ... (see 18)

Transport
35 Long-Tail Boats to Ao Nang ... B1
36 Long-Tail Boats to Ao Nang ... B2
37 Long-Tail Boats to Krabi ... C2

Above Hat Railay East is another large cave called **Tham Phra Nang Nai** (Inner Princess Cave; adult/child 40/20B; ⏲5am-8pm), also known as Diamond Cave. A wooden boardwalk leads through a series of caverns full of beautiful limestone formations but, with shifting rain patterns, the water is gone and with it the luminescent effects that won the diamond moniker. But even in monochrome conditions, it's still worth a stroll.

Activities

Rock Climbing

With nearly 500 bolted routes, ranging from beginner to challenging advanced climbs, all with unparalleled cliff-top vistas, it's no surprise that Railay is among the top climbing spots in the world. You could spend months climbing and exploring – and many people do. Deep-water soloing offers the biggest thrill. That's where free-climbers scramble up ledges over deep water – if you fall you will most likely just get wet, so even daring beginners can give this a try.

Most climbers start off at **Muay Thai Wall** and **One, Two, Three Wall**, at the southern end of Hat Railay East, which have at least 40 routes graded from 4b to 8b on the French system. The mighty **Thaiwand Wall** sits at the southern end of Hat Railay West and offers a sheer limestone cliff with some of the most challenging climbing routes.

Other top climbs include **Hidden World** (some classic routes for intermediate climbers), **Wee's Present Wall** (an overlooked 7c+ gem), **Diamond Cave** (another beginner-to-intermediate favourite) and **Ao Nang Tower** (a three-pitch climbing wall reached only by long-tail).

The going rate for climbing courses is 800B to 1000B for a half-day and 1500B to 2000B for a full day. Private instruction runs 3000B for a half-day and 5000B for a full-day. Three-day courses (6000B) will involve lead climbing, where you clip into bolts on the rock face as you ascend. Experienced climbers can rent gear sets for two people from any of the climbing schools for 800/1300B for a half/full day – the standard set consists of a 60m rope, two climbing harnesses and climbing shoes. If you're planning to climb independently, you're best off bringing your own gear from home; be sure to bring plenty of slings and quickdraws, chalk (sweaty palms are inevitable in the tropics) and a small selection of nuts and cams as backup for thinly protected routes. If you forget anything, some climbing schools sell a small range of imported climbing gear, but they might not have exactly what you need or the right size. A woven rattan mat (available locally for 100B to 150B) will help keep the sand out of your gear.

Several locally published books detail climbs in the area; *Rock Climbing in Thailand*, by Elke Schmitz and Wee Changrua, is one of the more complete guides. There's a similar book by a non-resident author available through traditional booksellers.

★**Base Camp Ton Sai** ROCK CLIMBING
(☎08 1149 9745; www.tonsaibasecamp.com; Hat Ton Sai; ⏲8am-9:30pm) Arguably the most professional outfit in the area.

Highland Rock Climbing ROCK CLIMBING
(☎08 0693 0374; highlandrockclimbingthailand.weebly.com; Hat Railay East) If you're bunking on the mountain, this is the man to climb with.

Hot Rock ROCK CLIMBING
(☎0 7562 1771; www.railayadventure.com; Hat Railay West) Has a very good reputation and is owned by one of the granddaddies of Railay climbing.

King Climbers ROCK CLIMBING
(☎0 7563 7125; www.railay.com; Hat Railay East) One of the biggest, oldest, most reputable and commercial schools.

Water Sports

Several **dive** operations in Railay run trips out to Ko Poda and other dive sites. Two local dives at outlying islands cost about 2000B while a three- or four-day PADI Open Water dive course is 12,000B to 15,000B.

Full-day, multi-island **snorkelling** trips to Ko Poda, Chicken Island and beyond can be arranged through any of the resorts for about 2000B (maximum six people) or you can charter a long-tail (half/full-day 1800/2500B) from Hat Railay West beach. If you just want to snorkel off Railay, most resorts can rent you a mask set and fins for 100B to 150B each.

Flame Tree Restaurant (p315) rents out **sea kayaks** for 200B per hour or 800B per day. Overnight trips to deserted islands can be arranged with local boat owners, but you'll need to bring your own camping gear and food.

Sleeping & Eating

Hat Railay West

It's all midrange and top-end options on this beach (where sunsets are fabulous), but rates often drop by 30% in the low season.

Sand Sea Resort HOTEL $$
(0 7562 2608; www.krabisandsea.com; Hat Railay West; bungalows 1950-5950B;) The lowest-priced resort on this beach offers everything from ageing fan-only bungalows to newly remodelled cottages with every amenity. The grounds aren't as swank as the neighbours, but rooms are comfy enough and there's a peaceful karst-view, foliage-enclosed pool – if you're able to tear yourself away from that sublime beach out the front.

★**Railei Beach Club** VILLAS $$$
(08 6685 9359; www.raileibeachclub.com; houses from 3000B;) At the northern end of the beach, hidden in forested grounds that stretch all the way back to luscious limestone cliffs, is this collection of Thai-style homes, each unique in size and design, rented out on behalf of absentee owners. They come with patios, kitchens and amenities, and some have pools to make extended stays very comfortable.

Houses sleep between two and eight people. It's a superb deal and a romantic location, so book well in advance for the high season. The in-house massage therapist is a cheerful former Muay Thai boxer, and she'll happily pummel you deep into wellness.

Railay Bay Resort & Spa HOTEL $$$
(0 7562 2571, 0 7562 2570; www.railaybayresort.com; bungalows 3500-18,500B;) The amoeba-shaped blue pool here faces onto the best bit of the beach, so you can switch between salt and fresh water. Elegant bungalows with big windows, white walls and rustic-chic timber terraces run right across the peninsula to Hat Railay East via gorgeously planted grounds and a second pool.

Bungalows on the east side are older, with dark-tinted windows, and are the least expensive. The spa, which also overlooks the sea, offers a host of treatments at reasonable prices.

Railay Village Resort & Spa HOTEL $$$
(0 7563 7990; www.railayvillagekrabi.com; bungalows 5250-10,500B;) Posh bungalows with private hot tubs are spread throughout gardens of lily ponds, tall palms and gurgling fountains. The cheapest digs are set in two-storey modern hotel blocks, with bottom-floor rooms spilling directly into one of two pools. The open-air restaurant serves convincing Western-style pastas that are a boon if you're travelling with children.

Flame Tree THAI $$
(dishes 150-395B; 7.30am-10pm) Flame Tree is well situated on the walking street and has a bit of a monopoly on nightlife in Hat Railay West, and though the Thai food is middling and the prices inflated, it's still a chilled place to relax with a beer and watch the sun fall.

Hat Railay East

Hat Railay East, also called Sunrise Beach, recedes to mud flats during low tide and can get steamy hot if the breezes aren't blowing your way. That said, this is where the cheaper restaurants and bars are concentrated, and it's only a five-minute walk to better beaches.

Rates usually drop by half during the low season.

Rapala Rockwood Resort HOTEL $
(0 7562 2586; bungalows 500-750B) Ramshackle bamboo bungalows have verandahs, bathrooms, mosquito nets and fans, and beds plopped on the floor. The delightful location atop a hill means breezes and views of the sea (and your neighbours), but you're here for the price point.

Anyavee HOTEL $$
(0 7581 9437; www.anyavee.com; tents 300B, bungalows from 1700B;) A quirky resort, bungalows here have lots of windows making them bright but not private. Interiors are country chic, with duvets and plenty of hardwoods. Their recently added and cheaply tarped backpacker tents are the cheapest digs on the beach and they heat up, but they also have electricity and will do for some for a night or two.

Railay Garden View BUNGALOWS $$
(08 5888 5143; www.railaygardenview.com; Hat Railay East; bungalows 1300B) A collection of tin-roof, woven-bamboo bungalows, stilted high above the mangroves on the east beach. They look weather-beaten from the outside, but are spacious and super clean, and are graced with Thai linens and creative

concrete baths. There's a cushioned seating area on the floor, too. Bring mosquito repellent and all will be peachy.

Sunrise Tropical Resort HOTEL $$$
(0 7562 2599; www.sunrisetropical.com; bungalows incl breakfast 2500-6750B;) Bungalows here rival the better ones on Hat Railay West but are priced for Hat Railay East – so we think this is one of the best deals in Railay. Expect hardwood floors, Thai-style furniture, lush bathrooms with bright aqua tiles and private balconies or patios.

Bhu Nga Thani HOTEL $$$
(0 7581 9451; www.bhungathani.com; r from 5100B, villas from 12,200B;) The splashiest and easily the priciest spot on Railay East. The entry is elegant with louvred bridges over reflection pools. Rooms are exceptionally well built with high ceilings, limestone floors and all the amenities of a 4½-star property, including wide terraces with magnificent karst views. They have a full spa.

Mangrove Restaurant THAI $
(dishes 70-120B; 8am-10pm) This humble, local-style place, set beneath a stilted thatched roof on the recently detoured trail between the east and west beaches, turns out all your spicy Thai faves cheaply, from beef salad and noodles to curries and *sôm đam*. Praise goes to the kitchen's matriarch. She means business, and her husband can turn a spoon just fine, too.

Seaview THAI $$
(mains 99-359B; 5pm-10pm) The most intriguing new dinner choice is all about the setting. It's part of the Railay Viewpoint Resort complex, but it's set apart on a reclaimed barge, docked in the mangroves. The deck is sprinkled with candlelit wooden tables, there's a kitschy cute bar, they grill snapper, yellowtail and tiger prawns, and offer European fare too.

Railay Highlands

The resorts in the highlands above the beach are among the best-value lodging in the area.

WHERE TO STAY IN RAILAY

There are four beaches around Railay, or you can choose to stay up on the headland. It's only about a five-minute walk between Hat Railay East, Hat Railay West, Hat Phra Nang and the headlands. Hat Ton Sai is more isolated, and to get to the other beaches you'll need to take a long-tail (50B) or hike – it takes about 20 minutes to scramble over the rocks from Hat Railay West.

Hat Railay East The most developed beach. The shallow, muddy bay lined with mangroves is not appetising for swimming, but the beach is lined with hotels and guest houses, and those headlands and limestone cliffs are miraculous.

Hat Railay West A near flawless white wonder and the best place to swim, join an afternoon pick-up football game or just watch the sun go down. Tastefully designed midrange resorts are sprinkled throughout, and long-tail boats pick up and drop off here to/from nearby Ao Nang.

Hat Phra Nang Quite possibly one of the world's most beautiful beaches, with a crescent of pale, golden sand, framed by karst cliffs carved with caves. Those distant limestone islets peeking out of the cerulean sea are Chicken (Ko Hua Khwan) and Poda islands. Rayavadee (p317), the peninsula's most exclusive resort, is the only one on this beach, but anyone can drop a beach towel.

Hat Ton Sai The grittier climbers' retreat. The beach here isn't spectacular, but with so many good climbs all around, most people don't mind. Bars and bungalows are nestled in the jungle behind the beach and it's a lively, fun scene.

Railay Highlands Where sea breezes cool the jungle canopy, and the quiet, charming community will welcome you warmly. To get here, you'll have to walk about 500m from either Hat Railay West or East. From Hat Railay West follow 'Walking Street', veer left onto a dirt path then follow the signs to Ya-Ya Bar. From Hat Railay East turn right on the cement road accessible via the beachside Diamond Cave Restaurant.

Railay Cabana GUESTHOUSE $

(☎08 4534 1928, 0 7562 1733; Railay Highlands; bungalows 350-600B) Superbly located in a bowl of karst cliffs, this is your hippy tropical mountain hideaway. Rustic yet clean thatched-bamboo bungalows are surrounded by mango, mangosteen, banana and guava groves. The only sounds are birds chirping and children laughing. Plans for concrete, air-conditioned bungalows were being hatched at research time, and will be worth exploring.

Railay Phutawan Resort HOTEL $$

(☎0 7581 9479, 08 4060 0550; www.railayphutawan.com; r from 1850B, bungalows from 2150B; ❄@) The super-spacious polished-cement bungalows highlighted with creamy yellow walls and big rain-shower bathrooms offer all the trimmings of a high-end resort. Tiled rooms in an apartment-style block are a step down in luxury, but very comfortable.

Hat Tham Phra Nang หาดถ้ำพระนาง

There's only one place to stay on this magnificent beach and it's a doozy.

★**Rayavadee** HOTEL $$$

(☎0 7562 0741, 0 7562 0740; www.rayavadee.com; pavilions from 14,500B, villas from 75,000B; ❄🛜🏊) This exclusive resort has sprawling grounds that are filled with banyan trees and flowers, dotted with meandering ponds, and navigated by golf buggies. It's arguably one of the best hunks of beachfront property in Thailand. The two-storey, mushroom-domed pavilions are filled with antique furniture and every mod con – including butler service.

There are yoga classes for guests, tours offered in luxury speedboats and a first-rate spa. Two restaurants grace Hat Tham Phra Nang (one is half inside an illuminated cave) and nonguests can stop in for pricey but divine Thai or Mediterranean meals.

Hat Ton Sai หาดต้นไทร

This is the beach to go to if you're serious about climbing; there are plenty of backpacker options here. For the best cheap eats find the row of food shacks leading inland from the beach.

Paasook HOTEL $

(☎08 9648 7459; Hat Ton Sai; bungalows 200-900B) The cheaper, pink cinder-block cells are clean and do-able, but the wooden cottages are huge, have floor-to-ceiling windows and concrete floors and are far more appealing. This place is at the far western end of the beach, right beneath Groove Tube. The gardens are lush, management is friendly and there's a rustic-chic outdoor restaurant, perfect for steamy evenings.

Forest Resort HOTEL $$

(☎08 0143 8261; Hat Ton Sai; bungalows 400-1000B) The concrete floor cells are mouldy and uninhabitable, while the bamboo bungalows are slightly less scruffy. The best bet are the wood-and-brick-tiled bungalows with tiled floors and tin roofs. All are fan cooled when the electricity is running (5pm to 6am daily)

Mountain View Resort HOTEL $$

(☎08 9783 4008, 0 7581 9819; www.citykrabi.com; bungalows 1300-1900B; ❄) Bright, cheery and immaculate with mint-green walls, tiled floors and crisp sheets in lodge-like environs. Some rooms are slightly musty, so sniff around. They offer yoga classes in the high season.

Mama's Chicken THAI $

(Hat Ton Sai; 50-90B; ⊙7.30am-10pm) One of the more popular of the Ton Sai beach stalls offers Western breakfasts, fruit smoothies and a range of cheap Thai dishes, including a massaman tofu, which is a rarity. Grab a table and watch management engage in their daily battle with a thieving mob of macaques, who do love their mangoes.

Pyramid Bar & Restaurant INTERNATIONAL $

(dishes from 60B, drinks from 30B) The most popular hangout in Ton Sai. It does fresh fruit lassis, shakes, ciabatta and baguette sandwiches with home-baked loaves, and tasty espresso drinks in thatched treehouse environs. Hit one of the hammocks or lounge on the floor cushions and stay a while. Often closed in the wet season.

Drinking & Nightlife

There's a bunch of cool places on the beaches where you can unwind and get nicely inebriated.

★**Lucky Last Bar** BAR

(⊙11am-late) A multi-level tiki bar that rambles to the edge of the mangroves on Hat Railay East, Lucky Last has cushioned seating on one deck, candlelit tables on another and a bandstand closer to the walking street. It's no wonder the crowds gather here.

Backyard Bar & Cafe CAFE
(8am-9pm) Good coffee, organic teas, a tasty chai, and a range of cakes and cookies, including 'Happy Cookies'. Which are, well, quite happy. Or so we hear. Brunch is served between 8am and 2pm.

Small World Bar BAR
(11am-11pm) A slack line, a fire show, 'shroom lanterns, 'peace cake', live music, ramshackle charm. You get the idea.

Highland Rock Climbing CAFE
(08 0693 0374; Railay Highlands) Part climbing school, part cafe, this place has been cobbled together from driftwood and is dangling with orchids. The owner, Chaow, sources his beans from sustainable farms in Chiang Rai and serves the best coffee on the peninsula.

Information

The website www.railay.com has lots of information about Railay. There are two ATMs along Hat Railay East. On Hat Ton Sai there is one ATM near the Ton Sai Bay Resort. Several of the bigger resorts can change cash and travellers cheques. For minor climbing injuries there's a small clinic at Railay Bay Resort & Spa.

Wi-fi is widely available in hotels and cafes.

Getting There & Around

Long-tail boats to Railay run from Khong Kha pier in Krabi and from the seafronts of Ao Nang and Ao Nam Mao. Boats between Krabi and Hat Railay East leave every 1½ hours from 7.45am to 6pm when they have six to 10 people (150B, 45 minutes). Chartering a special trip will set you back 1500B.

Boats to Hat Railay West or Hat Ton Sai leave from the eastern end of the promenade at Ao Nang and cost 100B (15 minutes) from 7.30am to 6pm or 150B at other times; boats don't leave until six to eight people show up. Private charters cost 800B. If seas are rough, boats leave from a sheltered cove just west of Krabi Resort in Ao Nang. You can be dropped at Hat Phra Nang or Hat Ton Sai for the same fare.

During exceptionally high seas the boats from Ao Nang and Krabi stop running, but you may still be able to get from Hat Railay East to Ao Nam Mao (100B, 15 minutes), where you can pick up a *sŏrng·tăa·ou* to Krabi or Ao Nang.

From October to May the *Ao Nang Princess* runs from Hat Noppharat Thara National Park headquarters to Ko Phi-Phi with a stop at Hat Railay West. Long-tails run out to meet the boat at around 9.15am from in front of the Sand Sea Resort. The fare to Ko Phi-Phi from Railay is 350B.

Ko Phi-Phi Don เกาะพีพีดอน

Oh, how beauty can be a burden. Like Marilyn Monroe, Phi-Phi Don's stunning looks have become its own demise. Everyone wants a piece of her. Though not exactly Hollywood, this is Thailand's Shangri-La: a hedonistic paradise where tourists cavort in azure seas and snap pictures of longtails puttering between craggy cliffs. With its flashy, curvy, blonde beaches and bodacious jungles, it's no wonder that Phi-Phi has become the darling of the Andaman coast. And, like any good starlet, this island can party hard all night and still look like a million bucks the next morning. Unfortunately, nothing can withstand this glamorous pace forever, and unless limits are set, Phi-Phi is in for an ecological crash.

Activities

The strenuous climb to the **Phi-Phi viewpoint** (Map p320) is a rewarding short hike. Follow the signs from the road heading east towards Ao Lo Dalam from the Tourist Village (central Tonsai). The viewpoint is reached via a 300m vertical climb that includes hundreds of steep steps and narrow twisting paths. The views from the top are amazing – this is where you can see Phi-Phi's lush mountain butterfly brilliance in full bloom. From here you can head over the hill through the jungle to the peaceful eastern beaches for a DIY snorkelling tour.

Ao Lo Dalam is ripe for exploration. Stop at the **kayak rental stall** (Map p322; per hr 200B, full day 600B) on the sand in front of Slinky Bar, paddle out to the headland and dive in.

Diving

Crystal Andaman water and abundant marine life make the perfect recipe for top-notch scuba. Popular sights include the **King Cruiser Wreck**, sitting a mere 12m below the surface; **Anemone Reef**, teeming with hard corals and clownfish; **Hin Bida**, a submerged pinnacle attracting turtles and large pelagic fish; and **Ko Bida Nok**, with its signature karst massif luring leopard sharks. **Hin Daeng** and **Hin Muang**, to the south, are expensive ventures from Ko Phi-Phi – it's cheaper to link up with a dive crew in Ko Lanta.

An Open Water certification course costs around 12,900B to 13,800B, while the standard two-dive trips cost from 2500B to 3200B.

Trips out to Hin Daeng or Hin Muang will set you back about 5500B.

Adventure Club DIVING
(Map p322; ☎08 1970 0314; www.phi-phi-adventures.com) Our favourite diving operation on the island runs an excellent assortment of educational, eco-focused diving, hiking and snorkelling tours. You won't mind getting up at 6am for the much-loved shark-watching snorkel trips on which you're guaranteed to cavort with at least one reef shark.

Blue View Divers DIVING
(Map p320; ☎0 7581 9395; www.blueviewdivers.com) Focuses on community involvement and beach clean-ups (its latest cleared up 700 tonnes of rubbish) and is the only shop to offer dives from a long-tail.

Sea Frog Diving DIVING
(Map p322; ☎0 7560 1073; www.ppseafrog.com) This long-running dive shop has a solid reputation.

Snorkelling

A popular snorkelling destination is **Ko Mai Phai** (Bamboo Island), north of Phi-Phi Don. There's a shallow area here where you may see small sharks. Snorkelling trips cost between 600B and 2400B, depending on whether you travel by long-tail or motorboat. On Ko Phi-Phi there is good snorkelling along the eastern coast of **Ko Nok**, near Ao Ton Sai, and along the eastern coast of **Ko Nai**. If you're going on your own, most bungalows and resorts rent out a snorkel, mask and fins for 150B to 200B per day.

Rock Climbing

Yes, there are good limestone cliffs to climb on Ko Phi-Phi, and the views are spectacular. The main climbing areas are **Ton Sai Tower** (Map p320), at the western edge of Ao Ton Sai, and **Hin Taak** (Map p320), a short long-tail boat ride around the bay. Climbing shops on the island charge around 1200B for a half-day of climbing or 2000B for a full day, including instruction and gear. **Spider Monkey** (Map p322; ☎0 7581 9384; www.spidermonkeyphiphi.com) is run by Soley, one of the most impressive climbers on Phi-Phi. **Ibex Climbing & Tours** (Map p322; ☎08 4309 0445, 0 7560 1423; www.ibexclimbingandtours.com) is one of the newest and best outfitters in the village.

Courses

Pum Restaurant & Cooking School COOKING
(Map p322; ☎08 1521 8904; www.pumthaifoodchain.com; classes 399-1200B; ⏲classes 1pm & 4pm) Thai-food fans can take cooking courses here in the Tourist Village. You'll learn to make some of the excellent dishes that are served in the restaurant and go home with a great cookbook.

Tours

Ever since Leonardo DiCaprio smoked a spliff in Alex Garland's *The Beach*, Phi-Phi Leh has become somewhat of a pilgrimage site. Aside from long-tail boat tours to Phi-Phi Leh and Ko Mai Phai, tour agencies can arrange sunset tours to Monkey Bay and the beach at Wang Long, both on Phi-Phi Leh, for 600B. Adventure Club (p319) is a

KO PHI-PHI DIVE SITES

Leopard sharks and hawksbill turtles are very common on the dive sites around Ko Phi-Phi. Whale sharks sometimes make cameo appearances around Hin Daeng, Hin Muang, Hin Bida and Ko Bida Nok in February and March. The top five dives at Ko Phi-Phi are the following:

DIVE SITE	DEPTH (M)	FEATURES
Anemone Reef	17-26	Hard coral reef with plentiful anemones and clownfish
Hin Bida Phi-Phi	5-30	Submerged pinnacle with hard coral, turtles, leopard sharks and occasional mantas and whale sharks
Hin Muang	19-24	Submerged pinnacle with a few leopard sharks, grouper, barracuda, moray eels and occasional whale sharks
Ko Bida Nok	18-22	Karst massif with gorgonians, leopard sharks, barracuda and occasional whale sharks
Phi-Phi Leh	5-18	Island rim is covered in coral and oysters, with moray eels, octopus, seahorses and swim-throughs

Ko Phi-Phi Don

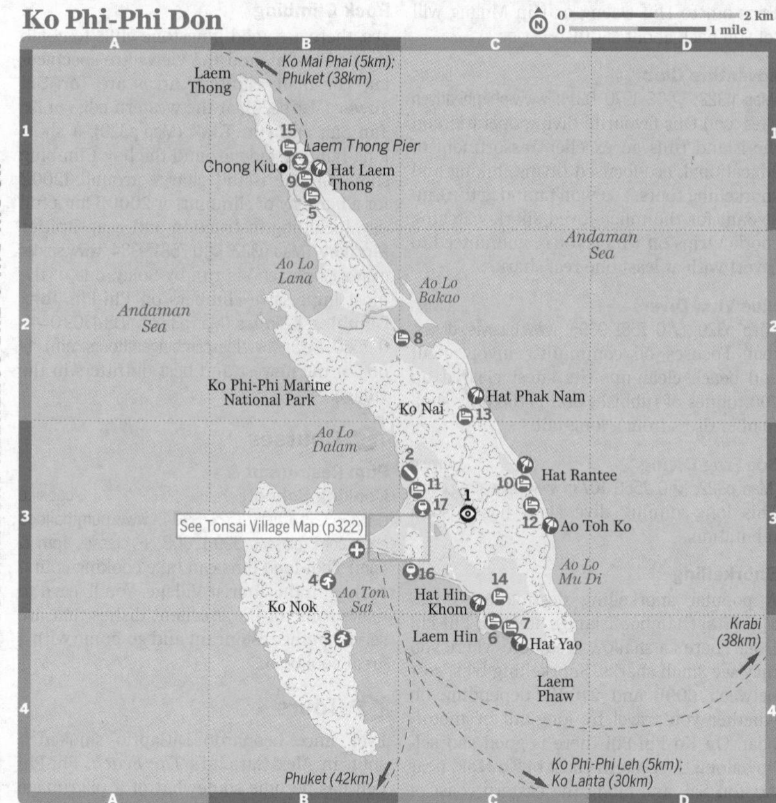

good choice. **U-Rip** (☎0 7560 1075; per person 600B) offers the same trip and is also highly recommended.

You can no longer camp on Maya Beach, but you can join the **Plankton Sunset Cruise** (www.mayabaytours.com; per person 1200B), and sleep aboard the boat just off shore. They only take on-line bookings.

Captain Bob's Booze Cruise (☎08 4848 6970; www.phiphiboozecruise.com; men/women 3000/2500B; ⏲departs at 1pm, returns at 7pm) is the latest buzz-worthy excursion and is exactly what it sounds like. You're cruising the waters around Phi Phi Don and Phi Phi Leh, on a sail boat, adult beverage in hand.

Another unique choice is the **Watersports Experience** (www.facebook.com/watersportsexperience; per person with/without sports 1500/2500B), where guests can stand-up paddle (SUP), wake board, water ski and snorkel the waters around Phi Phi Don and Phi Phi Leh. You'll lunch on Ao Rantee. You'll be zipping around in the Ali Baba speedboat, and guests who don't wish to get sporty are welcome at a discount. Best booked at any of the tour offices in the village.

Sleeping

Finding accommodation on this ever-popular island has never been easy and you can expect serious room shortages at peak holiday times. Masses of touts meet incoming boats and, while often annoying, can make your life easier.

Be sure you lock the door while you sleep and close all the windows when you go out. Break-ins can be a problem.

Ao Ton Sai & Ao Lo Dalam
อ่าวต้นไทร/อ่าวโละดาลัม

During high season the pedestrian-only streets in this area get so packed it's like moving through crowds at a rock concert.

Euphemistically, central Tonsai is called the 'Tourist Village'.

The beach at Ao Dalam is the island's prettiest – a screensaver-worthy crescent of white sand backed by stunning karst cliffs. But it's clogged with people and long-tail boats, and locals complain the water is polluted from the beach-bar clientele's cigarette butts and day-visitors' sunscreen, urine and boat fuel.

The Ao Ton Sai coastline is even busier with the main ferry pier and a concrete ocean-front promenade, but peace can be found at the far western end, which has been roped off for swimming.

Blanco HOSTEL $

(Map p322; ☎0 7562 8900; Tonsai Village; dm 300B; wi-fi) This bare bones (better bring your own top sheet) yet stylish hostel offers eight-bed dorms in bamboo chalets with concrete floors. Digs are cramped and mattresses are gym-mat hard, but this is where the cool kids stay, thanks to a fun-loving Thai owner and his super groovy beach bar.

The bar itself is arced concrete, and there are cushioned lounges and a handful of candlelit white tables sunk in the sand with Dalam views. The food is good too. Of course, with this location you'll be keeping vampire hours. But how sexy is that?

Rock Backpacker HOSTEL $

(Map p322; ☎08 1607 3897; Tonsai Village; dm 300B, r from 400-600B) A proper hostel on the village hill, with clean dorms lined with bunk beds, tiny private rooms, an inviting restaurant-bar and a rugged, graffiti-scrawled exterior.

Marine House GUESTHOUSE $

(Map p322; r from 700B) Good-value rooms with wood-tiled floors, tasteful paint jobs and baths with porcelain sinks, floral touches and a vibe that falls somewhere in the ramshackle elegant category, which works. It's steps from the dock and far from the night noise. Walk-ins only. No reservations are accepted.

Oasis Guesthouse GUESTHOUSE $

(Map p322; ☎0 7560 1207; Tonsai Village; r 800-900B; air-con) It's worth the walk up the side road east of the village centre to find this cute guest house with wooden shutters surrounded by trees. The innkeeper can be surly, but freshly painted rooms have sparkling bathrooms. He won't take reservations. It's first-come, first-serve only.

Tee Guesthouse GUESTHOUSE $

(Map p322; ☎08 4851 5721; Tonsai Village; r with fan/air-con 800/1200B; air-con) A fun and funky choice tucked down a side road. Rooms are simple with graceful touches like exposed brick and lavender walls, queen beds, mosaic tiled baths, and a welcome blast of graffiti on the exterior. They have a darling little cafe (p326) here, too.

★ **JJ Residence** INN $$

(Map p322; ☎0 7560 1098; d 1900-2500B; air-con wi-fi pool) Expect spacious tiled rooms with funky wood panelling, beamed ceilings, duvees, mini fridge, flat screens, built-in desks and wardrobes and private terraces. Those on the first floor spill right onto the pool. One of the nicer choices in Ton Sai.

Tropical Garden Bungalows BUNGALOWS $$

(☎08 9729 1436; www.thailandphiphitravel.com; r 1000-200B; air-con) If you don't mind walking 10 minutes to eat, drink or sunbathe, then you'll love Tropical Garden. At the far end of the main path heading north from the eastern end of Ao Ton Sai, it feels pretty isolated in its fragment of flourishing hillside jungle. The great cabins are frontier-style log affairs and there's even a lofty pool, surrounded by flora, halfway up the hill.

Tonsai Village

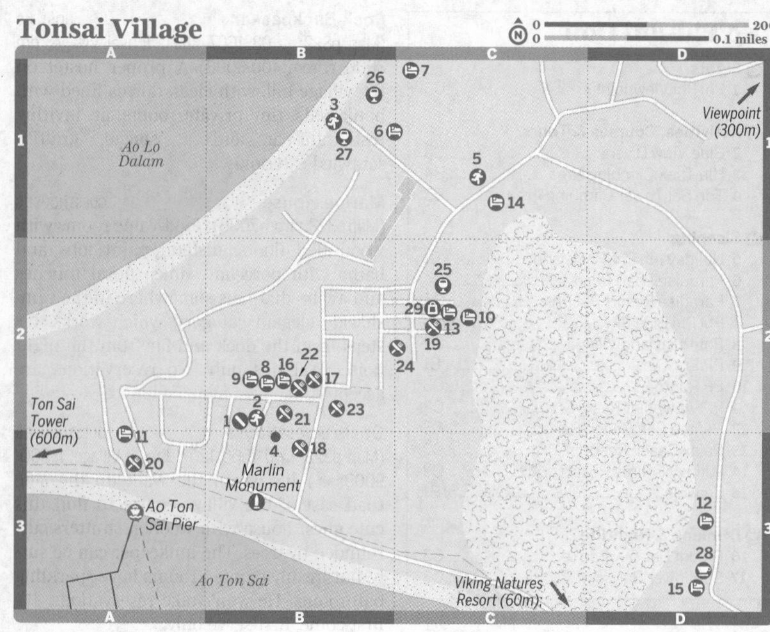

Tonsai Village

Activities, Courses & Tours

1 Adventure Club ... B2
2 Ibex Climbing & Tours ... B2
3 Kayak Rental Stall ... B1
4 Pum Restaurant & Cooking School ... B3
Sea Frog Diving ... (see 21)
5 Spider Monkey ... C1

Sleeping

6 Anita Resort ... B1
7 Blanco ... C1
8 Ivory ... B2
9 JJ Residence ... B2
10 Kinnaree House ... C2
11 Marine House ... A3
12 Oasis Guesthouse ... D3
13 Orange Tree ... C2
14 Rock Backpacker ... C1
15 Tee Guesthouse ... D3
16 White ... B2

Eating

17 Cosmic ... B2
18 Cosmic 2 ... B3
19 La Mamita ... C2
20 Le Grand Bleu ... A3
21 Local Food Market ... B2
22 Matt's Joint ... B2
23 Papaya 2 ... B2
24 Papaya Restaurant ... C2
Unni's ... (see 21)

Drinking & Nightlife

25 Banana Sombrero ... C2
Breakers ... (see 19)
26 Ibiza ... B1
27 Slinky Bar ... B1
28 Tee Cafe ... D3

Shopping

29 D's Bookshop ... C2

Information

Internet ... (see 29)

Orange Tree GUESTHOUSE $$
(Map p322; ☎08 1439 3924; www.orangetree-phiphi.com; r 1300-1500B; ❄☜) A chic four-room guesthouse tucked down a narrow soi, with windowless dark pods for rooms that still feel really good thanks to high-end tiled floors, exposed concrete and brick walls, flat screens and tastefully tiled baths. From a design point of view, it's by far the best option in the village. But it's not for light sleepers.

Kinnaree House GUESTHOUSE $$
(Map p322; ☎0 7560 1139; www.kinnareehouse.com; r 1300B; ❄) Tiled rooms are brushed in pastels, cooled with air-con and outfitted with desks, safety boxes and queen beds. Factor in the cute decorative touches – dig those ceramic flowers embedded in the hallway floors – and you've got a nice value. It can get loud at night, however.

White INN $$
(Map p322; ☎0 7560 1300; www.whitephiphi.com; r 1500-1800B; ❄@📶) White has two decent and surprisingly quiet locations in Tonsai Village – the better being the White 2, which has a few rooftop suites with patios. Rooms are decked out with TVs, safes and huge beds, and are very white (of course), with hip touches like tiny black-and-white-tiled hot-water bathrooms. They aren't as clean as they could be.

Ivory INN $$
(Map p322; ☎0 7560 1149; www.ivoryphiphi.com; r from 1650B; ❄📶) A collection of simple but not soulless tiled rooms in a three-star inn behind the market. There's a pink accent wall, flat screens, hot water bubblers and wi-fi throughout.

Anita Resort RESORT $$
(Map p322; ☎0 7560 1282; www.phiphianita-resort.com; r from 2200B, bungalows from 2600B; ❄📶🏊) For something sweet on Ao Dalam, seek out this three-star resort where rooms are tastefully done up with blue and black accents, with flat screens on the wall, the rare floor-to-ceiling headboard, a sliding glass door that opens onto a grassy courtyard and hammocks swinging on private decks. Breakfast is included.

PP Viewpoint Resort HOTEL $$
(Map p320; ☎0 7561 8111, 0 7560 1200; www.phiphiviewpoint.com; bungalows 1700-3500B; ❄🏊) At the far northeastern end of Ao Lo Dalam, wooden bungalows sit high on stilts and enjoy awesome views. It has a small swimming pool that practically drops into the ocean below and a glass-walled tower with 360-degree views where you can pamper yourself with a Thai massage. The Ao Dalam party can be heard up here, so bring earplugs.

Hat Hin Khom หาดหินคม

This area actually has a few small white-sand beaches in rocky coves, some of which are relatively quiet. It's about a 15-minute jungle walk from both Hat Yao and the Ao Ton Sai bustle, which unfortunately means you will hear whatever the DJs are spinning.

Viking Natures Resort HOTEL $$
(Map p320; ☎0 7581 9399; www.vikingnaturesresort.com; bungalows 1500-12,000B; 📶) OK, it's funky (in all senses of the word) and not the place to stay if you're afraid of jungle insects and critters, but the wood, thatch and bamboo bungalows here are creative and stylish with lots of driftwood, shell mobiles and hammock-decked lounging spaces with outrageous views of Ko Phi-Phi Leh.

We say splurge for one of several wooden lodge rooms. They open onto inviting verandahs, are well lit with groovy lanterns and have huge bathrooms and high ceilings.

Hat Yao หาดยาว

You can either walk here in about 30 minutes from Tonsai via Hat Hin Khom or take a long-tail (100B to 150B) from Tonsai pier. This long stretch of pure-white beach is perfect for swimming and well worth the walk but don't expect to have it to yourself – it's popular with families and sporty types playing volleyball. A trail leads from here over to beautiful and secluded Ao Lo Mu Di.

Paradise Pearl Resort RESORT $$
(Map p320; ☎0 7560 1246; www.phiphiparadisepearl.com; d from 2000-3000B; ❄📶) A collection of dark wood Thai chalets, decked out with art and updated electronics, tucked into the rocky headland on the southern curl of Hat Yao. There's tasteful lounges on the beach and a restaurant that rambles on timber tables to the edge of the sand. It's typically packed with young couples. Free wi-fi is available in the lobby only.

★**Paradise Resort Phi Phi** HOTEL $$$
(Map p320; ☎08 1968 3982; www.paradiseresort.co.th; bungalows from 3000B; ❄📶) Rooms in the uber-white lodge have South Beach echoes and are plush with granite tiled floors, wood panelled walls, floating beds, flat screens and desks. There are also standalone beach cottages with similar furnishings in older bones. Low-season deals are superb.

Phi Phi Blue Sky BUNGALOWS $$$
(Map p320; ☎08 9881 7929; www.phiphibluesky.com; bungalows from 3500B; ❄📶) Slightly overpriced during the high season, these

simple, spacious, tiled bungalows, sprinkled along the beach and in a sweet garden behind it, are a good low-season value when prices plummet.

Hat Rantee & Ao Toh Ko หาดรันตี

Still fairly low-key, this series of small, remote eastern bays is home to a few modest family-run bungalows (some starting at 600B). The pretty beaches here are grey-gold and have rocky outcroppings and excellent snorkelling. You can either get here by long-tail from Ao Ton Sai pier (300B – although most resorts provide free pick up if you reserve; the return trip is 150B) or by making the strenuous 45-minute hike over the viewpoint.

PP Rantee BUNGALOWS $$
(Map p320; ☎08 1597 7708; Hat Rantee; bungalow with fan 1200-1600B, air-con 2000B; ⏰restaurant 7am-10pm; ❄📶) Here are basic yet acceptable woven bamboo bungalows and newer, super clean tiled bungalows with wide porches overlooking a trim garden path that leads to the sand. There is also the best restaurant (mains 80B to 100B) on this beach, and a big wooden swing on the tree out front.

Rantee Cliff Beach Resort BUNGALOWS $$
(Map p320; ☎08 9725 4411; www.ranteecliffbeach.com; bungalows 2000-5800B; ❄📶) The newest offering on Phi Phi was nearing completion at research time. Expect stylish bamboo bungalows with soaring thatched roofs, french doors opening onto private patios, gauzy mosquito netting and sunken baths. It's tucked into the headland at the southern end of Hat Rantee.

Hat Phak Nam หาดผักน้ำ

The beach is pretty rocky and somewhat gritty at low tide, but given that it's nestled on the same bay as a small fishing hamlet, there is a certain romance to it. To get here, you can either charter a long-tail from Ao Ton Sai for around 500B (150B by shared taxi boat upon your return) or make the very sweaty one-hour hike over the viewpoint.

★ **Relax Beach Resort** HOTEL $$
(Map p320; ☎08 9475 6536, 08 1083 0194; www.phiphirelaxresort.com; bungalows 1800-4900B; @🏊) There are 47 unpretentious lacquered Thai-style bungalows with wood floors, two-tiered terraces with lounging cushions and mosaic baths in the sweetest nests. Some suffer from a tinge of must and scuffed-up walls. All are rimmed by lush jungle.

The resort has a good restaurant and breezy bar, and it's worked by incredibly charming staff who greet and treat you like family. You can walk to Hat Rantee at low tide.

Ao Lo Bakao อ่าวโละบาเกา

This fine stretch of palm-backed sand ringed by dramatic hills is one of Phi-Phi's most lovely, with offshore views over aqua bliss to the Bamboo and Mosquito Islands. Phi-Phi Island Village arranges transfers for guests, but on your own a charter from Ao Ton Sai will cost 800B.

SLEEPING (OR TRYING TO) ON KO PHI-PHI

Noise pollution on Phi-Phi is bad and centred around central Ao Ton Sai and Ao Dalam – although you shouldn't expect an early night on Hat Hin Khom either. At the time of writing, bars had a 2am curfew in Ao Dalam and 1.30am in Ton Sai – which are more or less observed – but that doesn't stop inebriated revellers from making plenty of other noises (like door slamming and dry heaving).

The most peaceful accommodation can be found on:

- Phi-Phi's east coast
- the back road that connects the southeast end of Ao Ton Sai with Ao Lo Dalam
- the hill near the road up to the viewpoint
- the far western section of Ao Ton Sai
- Hat Yao

Of course, the best option may be to simply grab a bucket and join the scrum.

Phi-Phi Island Village HOTEL $$$
(Map p320; ☎0 7636 3700; www.ppisland.com; bungalows 7200-21,500B; ❄📶🏊) This place really is a village unto itself: its whopping 100 bungalows take up much of the beachfront with palms swaying between them. Facilities vary from the family friendly and casual to romantic dining experiences and pampering spa treatments. It offers dozens of activities and excursions.

The infinity pool blends seamlessly into the ocean, and fresh flowers are artfully arranged throughout the resort. Good living with a whiff of old-school luxury if you have the means.

Hat Laem Thong หาดแหลมทอง

The beach here is long, white and sandy with a small, rubbish-strewn *chow lair* (sea gypsy) settlement of corrugated metal shacks at the north end. Despite the upmarket offerings, the beach is really busy and all the hotels are packed together. There are a few local-style seafood restaurants within the bustle that are worth a try. A long-tail charter from Ao Ton Sai costs 800B. Operators can also arrange transfers.

PP Erawan HOTEL $$$
(Map p320; ☎08 1968 5690; www.pperawanpalms.com; r 3000-4000B; ❄@📶🏊) Step onto the grounds and let the stress fall away, as you follow a meandering path through the garden to bright modern rooms decorated with Thai art and handicrafts. There's an inviting pool bar and excellent service here too. Breakfast is included.

Holiday Inn Phi-Phi Island HOTEL $$$
(Map p320; ☎0 7562 7300; www.phiphi.holidayinn.com; bungalows 8297-10,400B; ❄📶🏊) This is your standard Thailand-issue Holiday Inn – which means it's comfortable, white-concrete-with-dark-trim chic and filled with active types milling around the pool. You'll find tennis courts, beckoning hammocks, a spa and a dive centre. The restaurant has a gorgeous alfresco deck with sea views.

Zeavola HOTEL $$$
(Map p320; ☎0 7562 7000; www.zeavola.com; bungalows 9900-26,900B; ❄@📶🏊) Hibiscus-lined pathways lead to teak bungalows with sleek, distinctly Asian indoor-outdoor floorplans. Each comes with glass walls on three sides, beautiful 1940s fixtures and antique furniture, a patio and impeccable service. Some villas come with a private pool and there's a fabulous couples-oriented spa. If you were nitpicky, you might say that the electronics could use an update.

Eating

Most of the resorts, hotels and bungalows around the island have their own restaurants. Ao Ton Sai is home to some reasonably priced restaurants, but don't expect haute cuisine.

Local Food Market THAI $
(Map p322; Ao Ton Sai; meals 30-60B; ⏰8am-8pm) The cheapest and most authentic eats are at the market. A handful of local stalls huddle on the narrowest sliver of the isthmus and serve up scrumptious *pàt tai,* fried rice, *sôm·đam* and smoked catfish. Walls are scrawled with the blessings of a thousand travellers.

La Mamita ITALIAN, MEXICAN $
(Map p322; mains 80-250B; ⏰11am-11pm) The latest offering from the Cosmic family, this atmospheric room, tucked down a narrow soi, feels like a grotto, and is known for pasta, pizza, fajitas and burritos. They reportedly do a nice moussaka here too.

Papaya Restaurant THAI $
(Map p322; ☎08 7280 1719; dishes 80-300B; ⏰11am-11pm) Cheap, tasty and spicy. Here's some real-deal Thai food served in heaping portions. It has your basil and chilli, all the curries and *đôm yam,* too. They're so popular they decided to open a second **cafe** (Map p322; ☎08 7280 1719; Ton Sai Village; dishes 80-300B) a block away.

Cosmic INTERNATIONAL, THAI $$
(Map p322; mains 90-200B, pizzas from 150B; ⏰8am-11pm) This long-standing favourite still cranks out some of Phi-Phi's best pizzas as well as Western and Thai fare. It's packed so frequently that they recently opened a **second branch** (Map p322) closer to the dock in Ton Sai village.

Le Grand Bleu INTERNATIONAL-THAI $$
(Map p322; ☎08 1979 9739; mains 140-265B; ⏰11am-2pm, 6.30-10pm) Thai–Euro fusion set in a charming wooden house just off the main pier. It serves French and Aussie wines, and you can get your duck wok-fried with basil or oven-roasted and caramelised with mango.

Matt's Joint BARBECUE **$$**
(Map p322; mains 159-250B, buffet 299B; ⏲10.30am-10.30pm) Continental comfort food is served in heaping steam-table portions at this nightly all-you-can-eat BBQ buffet. The menu is stocked with favourites from salmon steaks and fish and chips to ham and eggs and Caesar salad. But the buffet is the best-value play here.

Unni's INTERNATIONAL **$$**
(Map p322; mains 200-320B; ⏲8am-10pm) Local expats rave about the Western fare here, which is good – not great – and ranges from homemade bagels topped with everything from smoked salmon to meatballs. There are also massive salads, Mexican food, tapas, cocktails and more. It's a chic cafe lounge-style place with cooling overhead fans and jazzy mood music.

Drinking

A rowdy nightlife saturates Phi-Phi. Buckets of cheap whiskey and Red Bull and sticky-sweet cocktails make this the domain for spring-break wannabes and really bad hangovers. This is also the only place in Thailand where you're beckoned into bars by scantily clad *fa·ràng* (Western) girls, who are workin' it for free booze – yup, Phi-Phi is that kind of place. The truth is that if you're nesting within earshot of the wilds, you may as well enjoy the chaos.

★ **Sunflower Bar** BAR
(Map p320; Ao Lo Dalam) Poetically ramshackle, this driftwood gem is still the chillest bar in Phi-Phi. Destroyed in the 2004 tsunami, it was rebuilt with reclaimed wood by the Captain (as he is known). The long-tail booths are named for the four loved ones he lost in the flood.

Slinky Bar NIGHTCLUB
(Map p322; Ao Lo Dalam) Forever the beach dancefloor of the moment. One of several nightspots with the standard fire show, buckets of souped-up candy juice and throngs of Thais, local expats and tourists mingling, flirting and flailing to throbbing bass on the sand.

Ibiza NIGHTCLUB
(Map p322; Ao Lo Dalam) Another of Dalam's beach dens of inebriation and iniquity (but, you know, in a good way). Relax on beachside cushions, toke a shisha pipe, and marvel at expert fire twirlers and drunken daredevils as they jump through fiery hoops, limbo beneath a fiery cane and jump a fiery rope to bone rattling bass.

Breakers BAR
(Map p322; Ton Sai Village; ⏲11am-2am; 📶) A sportsbar as good for TV football as it is for people-watching and Western comfort food. The burgers and steaks work, and the appetisers, from yummy buffalo wings to potato skins, will satisfy most pint swillers.

Chukit Bar & Karaoke BAR
(Map p320; ⏲11am-2am) Part of the otherwise forgettable Chukit Resort complex, this fine bar extends over a long-tail harbour on the lip of Ao Ton Sai. In addition to bar stools with a supreme view, they have a pool table, live bands and a happy hour crowd.

Tee Cafe CAFE
(Map p322; ⏲8am-4pm) They do crepes and salads, but we love this intimate Moroccan-themed cafe for its coffee, tea and fresh-pressed juices.

Banana Sombrero BAR
(Map p322; ☎08 7330 6540; www.facebook.com/BananaBarPhiPhi/info; ⏲11-2am; 📶) The Mexican food with its appealing aroma and professional presentation is definitely tempting, but the 2nd-floor bar, festooned with flat screens and blessed with a ping pong table for late night beer pong battles, is what makes this new village spot a winner.

Information

ATMs are spread thickly throughout the Tourist Village but aren't available on the more remote eastern beaches. Wi-fi is widely available, so Instagram your hearts out.

D's Bookshop (Map p322; ⏲7am-10pm), in the heart of the Tourist Village, sells new and used fiction and brews a decent espresso.

Phi Phi Island Hospital (Map p320) offers some emergency care, but for anything truly serious, you'll be on the first boat back to Krabi. It's set beyond the beach bars from town on Ao Ton Sai.

Getting There & Away

Ko Phi-Phi can be reached from Krabi, Phuket, Ao Nang, Railay and Ko Lanta. Most boats moor at Ao Ton Sai, though a few from Phuket use the isolated northern pier at Laem Thong. The Phuket and Krabi boats operate year-round, while the Ko Lanta and Ao Nang boats only run in the October-to-April high season.

Krabi and Ao Nang Boats depart from Krabi for Ko Phi-Phi (300B, 1½ hours) at 9am,

10.30am, 1.30pm and 3.30pm, returning at 7.30am, 10.30am, 1.30pm and 3.30pm. From Ao Nang (350B, 1½ hours) there's one boat per day at 3.30pm.

Phuket From Phuket, boats leave at 9am, 2pm, and 2.30pm, and return from Ko Phi-Phi at 10am, 3.30pm and 4pm (250B to 350B, 1¾ to two hours).

Ko Lanta To Ko Lanta, boats leave Phi-Phi at 11.30am, 2pm and 3pm and return from Ko Lanta at 1pm, 3.30pm and 4.30pm (350B, 1½ hours).

Railay For Railay (350B, 1¼ hours), take the Ao Nang–bound ferry.

Getting Around

There are no roads on Phi-Phi Don, so transport on the island is mostly by foot, although long-tails can be chartered at Ao Ton Sai for short hops around Ko Phi-Phi Don and Ko Phi-Phi Leh.

Long-tails leave from the Ao Ton Sai pier to Hat Yao (100B to 150B), Laem Thong (800B), Hat Rantee (500B) and Viking Cave (500B). Chartering speedboats for six hours costs around 6500B, while chartering a long-tail boat costs 1500B for three hours or 3000B for the whole day.

Ko Phi-Phi Leh เกาะพีพีเล

Rugged Phi-Phi Leh is the smaller of the two islands and is protected on all sides by soaring cliffs. Coral reefs crawling with marine life lie beneath the crystal-clear waters and are hugely popular with day-tripping snorkellers. Two gorgeous lagoons await in the island's interior – **Pilah** on the eastern coast and **Ao Maya** on the western coast. In 1999 Ao Maya was controversially used as the setting for the filming of *The Beach,* based on the popular novel by Alex Garland. Visitor numbers soared in its wake.

At the northeastern tip of the island, **Viking Cave** (Tham Phaya Naak) is a big collection point for swifts' nests. Nimble collectors scamper up bamboo scaffolding to gather the nests. Before ascending, they pray and make offerings of tobacco, incense and liquor to the cavern spirits. This cave gets its misleading moniker from 400-year-old graffiti left by Chinese fishermen.

There are no places to stay on Phi-Phi Leh and most people come here on one of the ludicrously popular day trips out of Phi-Phi Don. Tours last about half a day and include snorkelling stops at various points around the island, with detours to Viking Cave and Ao Maya. Long-tail trips cost 800B; by motorboat you'll pay around 2400B. Expect to pay a 400B national park day-use fee upon landing.

It is no longer possible to camp on Phi-Phi Leh, but you can still visit Maya Beach at dusk and sleep on board a boat bobbing just offshore with Plankton Sunset Cruise (p320).

Ko Lanta เกาะลันตา

POP 20,000

Once the domain of backpackers and sea gypsies, Lanta hasn't just gentrified, it's morphed almost completely from a luscious southern Thai backwater into a midrange getaway for French, German and Swedish package tourists who come for divine beaches (though the northern coast is alarmingly eroded) and nearby dive spots, Hin Daeng, Hin Muang and Ko Ha. Within eyeshot of Phi-Phi, Lanta remains far more calm and real, however, and effortlessly caters to all budget types. It's also relatively flat compared to the karst formations of its neighbours, and laced with good roads, so is easily explored by motorbike. A quick loop reveals a colourful crucible of cultures – fried-chicken stalls sit below slender minarets, stilted *chow lair* villages cling to the island's east side, and small Thai wát hide within green-brown tangles of curling mangroves.

Ko Lanta is technically called Ko Lanta Yai, the largest of 52 islands in an archipelago protected by the Mu Ko Lanta Marine National Park. Almost all boats pull into Ban Sala Dan, a dusty two-street town at the northern tip of the island.

Sights

Ban Ko Lanta TOWN

Halfway down the eastern coast, Ban Ko Lanta (Lanta Old Town) was the original port and commercial centre for the island, and provided a safe harbour for Arabic and Chinese trading vessels sailing between Phuket, Penang and Singapore. Some of the gracious and well-kept wooden stilt houses and shopfronts here are over 100 years old.

Pier restaurants offer a fresh catch and have views over the sea. There's a small afternoon market on Sundays, and if you're looking for hip, handmade goods, stop by **Malee Malee** (☎08 4443 8581; 55/3 Moo 2, Ban Ko Lanta; ⏰9am-9pm), a bohemian wonderland trading in silk-screened and hand-painted T-shirts, silk scarves, journals, toys,

Ko Lanta

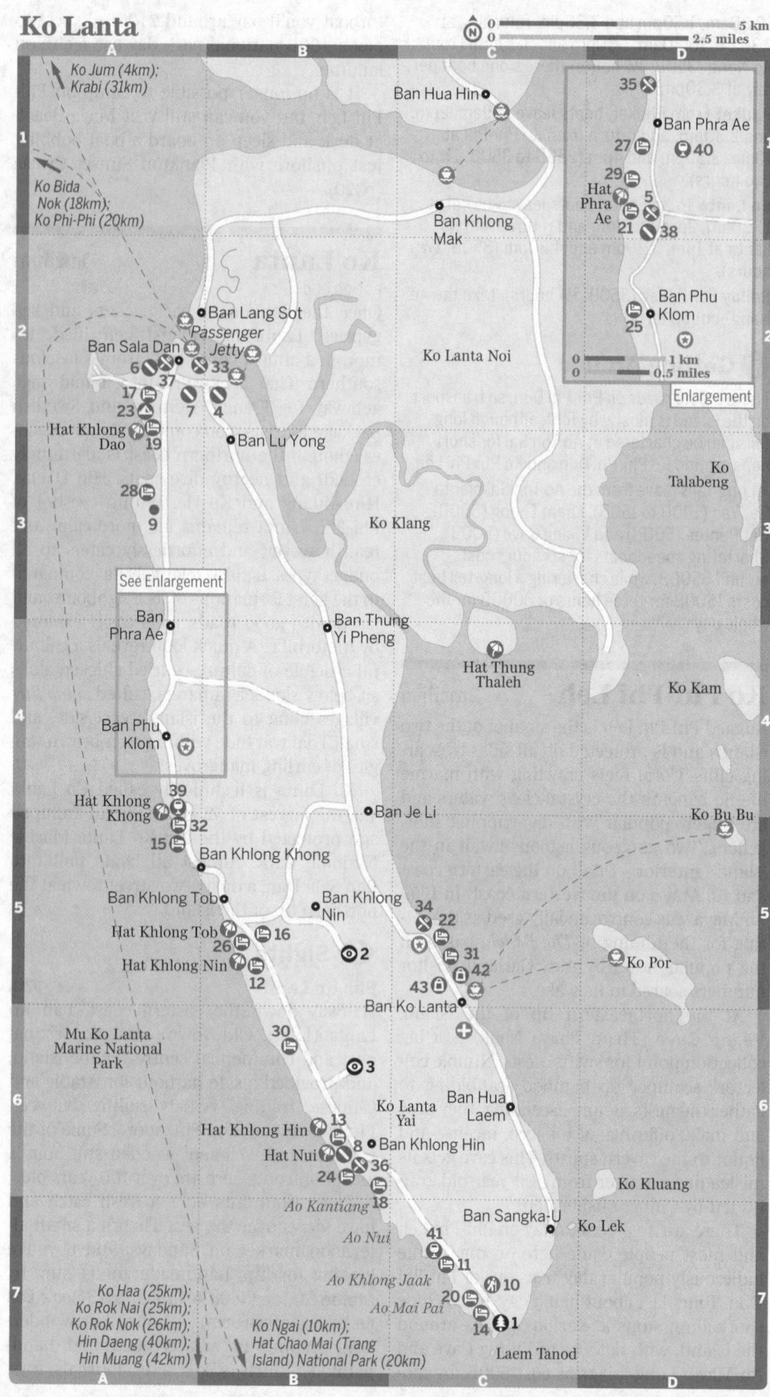

0 5 km
0 2.5 miles
Ko Jum (4km); Krabi (31km)
Ko Bida Nok (18km); Ko Phi-Phi (20km)
Ban Hua Hin
Ban Khlong Mak
Ban Lang Sot
Passenger Jetty
Ban Sala Dan
Hat Khlong Dao
Ban Lu Yong
Ko Lanta Noi
Ko Klang
See Enlargement
Ban Phra Ae
Ban Phu Klom
Ban Thung Yi Pheng
Hat Thung Thaleh
Ko Talabeng
Ko Kam
Hat Khlong Khong
Ban Je Li
Ko Bu Bu
Ban Khlong Khong
Ban Khlong Tob
Ban Khlong Nin
Hat Khlong Tob
Hat Khlong Nin
Ko Por
Ban Ko Lanta
Mu Ko Lanta Marine National Park
Ko Lanta Yai
Ban Hua Laem
Hat Khlong Hin
Ban Khlong Hin
Hat Nui
Ko Kluang
Ao Kantiang
Ban Sangka-U
Ko Lek
Ao Nui
Ao Khlong Jaak
Ao Mai Pai
Laem Tanod
Ko Haa (25km); Ko Rok Nai (25km); Ko Rok Nok (26km); Hin Daeng (40km); Hin Muang (42km)
Ko Ngai (10km); Hat Chao Mai (Trang Island) National Park (20km)
Hat Phra Ae
0 1 km
0 0.5 miles
Enlargement

Ko Lanta

Sights
- 1 Ko Lanta Marine National Park C7
- 2 Tham Khao Maikaeo B5
- 3 Tham Seua B6

Activities, Courses & Tours
- 4 Blue Planet Divers B2
- 5 Dive & Relax D1
- 6 Go Dive A2
- 7 Lanta Diver A2
- Lanta Paddlesports .... (see 28)
- Liquid Lense .... (see 8)
- Palm Beach Divers .... (see 29)
- 8 Scubafish B6
- 9 Time for Lime A3
- 10 Waterfall Trail C7

Sleeping
- 11 Andalanta Resort C7
- 12 Andalay Resort B5
- Andaman Sunflower .... (see 21)
- 13 Baan Laanta Resort & Spa B6
- 14 Baan Phu Lae C7
- 15 Bee Bee Bungalows A5
- 16 Clean Beach Resort B5
- 17 Costa Lanta A2
- Hutyee Boat .... (see 21)
- 18 Kantiang Bay View Resort B6
- La Laanta .... (see 14)
- 19 Lanta Bee Garden A2
- 20 Lanta Darawadee C7
- 21 Layana Resort D1
- Mango House .... (see 42)
- 22 Maya Beach Resort C5
- 23 Mu Ko Lanta Marine National Park Headquarters A2
- 24 Phra Nang Lanta B6
- 25 Relax Bay D2
- 26 Round House B5
- 27 Sanctuary D1
- 28 Slow Down Villas A3
- 29 Somewhere Else D1
- 30 Sri Lanta B6
- 31 Sriraya C5
- 32 Where Else? A5

Eating
- Apsara .... (see 42)
- 33 Bai Fern A2
- 34 Beautiful Restaurant C5
- 35 Country Lao D1
- 36 Drunken Sailors B6
- 37 Lanta Seafood A2
- Lym's Rice Bowl .... (see 21)
- 38 Red Snapper D1

Drinking & Nightlife
- 39 Moonwalk A4
- 40 Opium Bar D1
- Pirate's Bar .... (see 29)
- 41 Same Same But Different C7

Shopping
- 42 Hammock House C5
- 43 Malee Malee C5

baby clothes, paintings and handbags. Prices are low and it's a super fun browse. For quality hammocks don't miss **Hammock House** (www.jumbohammock.com; 10am-5pm).

Tham Khao Maikaeo CAVE

(ถ้ำเขาไม้แก้ว) Reached via a guided trek through the jungle, this complex of forest caverns and tunnels was created by monsoon rains pounding away at the limestone cracks and crevices for millions of years. There are chambers as large as cathedrals, thick with stalactites and stalagmites, and tiny passages that you have to squeeze through on hands and knees.

There's even a subterranean pool you can take a chilly swim in. Sensible shoes are essential, and total coverage in mud is almost guaranteed. A local family runs treks to the caves (with torches) for around 200B. The best way to get here is by rented motorcycle; alternatively, most resorts can arrange transport.

Close by, but reached by a separate track from the dirt road leading to the marine national park headquarters, **Tham Seua** (Tiger Cave) also has interesting tunnels to explore; elephant treks run up here from Hat Nui.

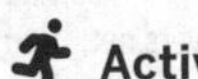

Activities

Vacationers on Ko Lanta will be delighted to find that some of Thailand's top diving spots are within arm's reach. The best diving can be found at the undersea pinnacles called **Hin Muang** and **Hin Daeng**, about 45 minutes away. These lone coral outcrops in the middle of the sea act as important feeding stations for large pelagic fish such as sharks, tuna and occasionally whale sharks and manta rays. Hin Daeng is commonly considered to be Thailand's second-best dive site after Richelieu Rock, near the Burmese border. The sites around **Ko Haa** have consistently good visibility, with depths of 18m to 34m, plenty of marine life and a cave known as 'the Cathedral'. Lanta dive outfitters also

WORTH A TRIP

KO LANTA MARINE NATIONAL PARK

Established in 1990, the **Ko Lanta Marine National Park** (อุทยานแห่งชาติเกาะลันตา; www.dnp.go.th; adult/child 200/100B) protects 15 islands in the Ko Lanta group, including the southern tip of Ko Lanta Yai. The park is increasingly threatened by the runaway development on the western coast of Ko Lanta Yai. The other islands in the group have fared slightly better.

Ko Rok Nai is still very beautiful, with a crescent-shaped bay backed by cliffs, fine coral reefs and a sparkling white-sand beach. Camping is permitted on **Ko Rok Nok** and nearby **Ko Haa**, with permission from the national park headquarters. On the eastern side of Ko Lanta Yai, **Ko Talabeng** has some dramatic limestone caves that you can visit on sea-kayaking tours. The national park fee applies if you visit any of these islands.

The national park headquarters is at Laem Tanod, on the southern tip of Ko Lanta Yai, reached by a steep and corrugated 7km dirt track from Hat Nui. There are some basic hiking trails and a scenic lighthouse, and you can hire long-tails here for island tours during the low season. They also offer camping facilities and bungalows for rent.

run trips up to the King Cruiser Wreck, Anemone Reef and Ko Phi-Phi.

Trips out to Hin Daeng and Hin Muang cost around 4500B to 5500B, while trips to Ko Haa tend to be around 3300B to 4000B. PADI Open Water courses will set you back around 14,000B to 17,000B.

Numerous tour agencies along the strip can organise snorkelling trips out to Ko Rok Nok, Ko Phi-Phi and other nearby islands.

Scubafish DIVING
(☎0 7566 5095; www.scuba-fish.com; Ban Sala Dan) A long-running operator with a good reputation, Scubafish runs personal and personable programs tailored to your needs, including the **Liquid Lense** (www.liquidlense.co.uk) underwater photography program. The three-day dive packages (9975B) are quite popular.

Blue Planet Divers DIVING
(☎0 7566 2724; www.blueplanetdivers.net; Ban Sala Dan) The first Lanta school to specialise in free-diving instruction.

Lanta Diver DIVING
(☎0 7568 4208; www.lantadiver.com; Ban Sala Dan) Their main shop is near the pier, but they have smaller concessions at a few of the island's nicer resorts, as well.

Dive & Relax DIVING
(☎08 4842 2191; www.diveandrelax.com; Hat Phra Ae) In the Lanta Castaway Beach Resort.

Palm Beach Divers DIVING
(☎0 7568 4603, 08 7806 4314; www.palmbeach-divers.com; Hat Phrae Ae) Based on Hat Phrae Ae and a convenient choice for those staying in the area.

Go Dive DIVING
(☎0 7566 8321; www.godive-lanta.com; Ban Sala Dan) One of the island's newest outfitters.

Lanta Paddlesports BOATING
(☎0 9113 8117; per hour 400B; ⏲11am-4pm) Set just south of Slow Down Villas, this new concession rents kayaks and SUP boards by the hour.

Lanta Garden Hill SNORKELLING
(www.lantaislandtours.com; long-tail/big boat/speedboat 850/900/1500B) One of a few comers who offer four-island snorkel tours linking Lanta and the Trang islands. If you bring your gear, you can hop off anywhere you like along the way.

Courses

Time for Lime COOKING
(☎0 7568 4590; www.timeforlime.net; per class 1800B) On Hat Khlong Dao, this place has a huge, hip and professional moulded-concrete kitchen with plenty of room to run amok. It offers excellent cooking courses with a slightly more exciting selection of dishes than most cookery schools in Thailand; five-hour courses cost 1800B with substantial discounts if you take more than one class. Profits from the school finance Lanta Animal Welfare.

Sleeping

Ko Lanta is home to many long stretches of good-looking beach packed with accommodation. Some resorts close for the May-to-October low season; others drop their rates by 50% or more. Resorts usually have their own restaurants and tour-booking facilities, which can arrange island snorkelling, massages, tours and motorcycle rental.

The building boom means that in addition to the waterfront resorts suggested here, there are now dozens of good-value roadside spots available, though views will probably leave you wanting. Reservations are a must in high season.

Hat Khlong Dao หาดคลองดาว

Once an outstanding 2km stretch of white sand with no rocks and perfect for swimming, erosion has gotten so bad that at high tide there is no beach here at all, just a sea wall. That's a big issue throughout northern Lanta.

Lanta Bee Garden GUESTHOUSE $$
(08 1606 6344; www.lantabeegarden.com; Hat Khlong Dao; bungalows with fan/air-con 800/1500B;) A mix of concrete rooms with fans and tinted windows, just off the main road, and nicer, newer air-con rooms in the two-storey annex, with burgundy accent walls and hot water. There is no beach here, though.

★**Costa Lanta** HOTEL $$$
(0 7566 8168; www.costalanta.com; Hat Khlong Dao; r from 6800B;) Zen-like standalone abodes nestled in a garden shaded by coconut palms and laced with tidal canals at the north end of Hat Khlong Dao. Everything from the floors to the walls to the washbasins is polished concrete, and the barn doors of each small cabana open on two sides to maximise space and air flow.

The restaurant is stunning, as is the black spill-over pool on the edge of the sand. Discounts are available if booked through the website. Low-season rates are a steal.

Maya Beach Resort HOTEL $$$
(0 7568 4267; mayalanta.com; Hat Khlong Dao; r from 3000B;) It's a bit weathered these days, but this place still offers attractive, large, Ikea-chic rooms on two floors. There are (flaking) louvred railings on the terrace, Buddhist shrines on the sand and a pool that blends with the nearby sea. And there's actually a sliver of beach here too.

Slow Down Villas VILLAS $$$
(08 4999 6780; www.slowdownlanta.se; villas per week 25,000B;) These modern two- and three-bedroom wood-and-shingle villas are all about clean lines, open spaces, comfy beach living and family-style holidays. The website is only in Swedish but everyone's welcome. The nine villas are privately owned by expats but can be rented by the week and month.

Hat Phra Ae หาดพระแอ

A large travellers' village has grown up along the extensive, sandy Hat Phra Ae (also called 'Long Beach'), with *fa·ràng*-oriented restaurants, beach bars, internet cafes and tour offices. The beach has suffered erosion in recent years and is getting extremely thin on the southern end, but there is a nice stretch on its northern flank near Somewhere Else.

Hutyee Boat GUESTHOUSE $
(08 9645 1083, 08 3633 9723; Hat Phra Ae; bungalows 350-400B) A hidden, hippy paradise of big, solid bungalows with tiled bathrooms and mini fridges in a forest of palms and bamboo. It's just back from the beach behind Nautilus. It's run by a Muslim family, who are as sweet and kind as can be.

Sanctuary GUESTHOUSE $
(08 1891 3055; sanctuary_93@yahoo.com; Hat Phra Ae; bungalows 600-1200B) The original Phra Ae resort is still a delightful place to stay. There are artistically designed wood-and-thatch bungalows with lots of grass and a hippy-ish atmosphere that's low-key and friendly. The restaurant offers Indian and vegetarian eats and the Thai usuals. The guesthouse also holds yoga classes.

Andaman Sunflower BUNGALOWS $
(0 7568 4668; Hat Phra Ae; bungalows 850B; Oct-Apr;) A terrific collection of wood and bamboo bungalows with built-in platform beds, high palm-leaf ceilings, polished wood floors, and glass bowl sinks in the bath. Set back from the beach, these are some of the best budget bungalows around.

Somewhere Else GUESTHOUSE $
(08 1536 0858; Hat Phra Ae; bungalows 600-1200B;) Choose among small, basic and clean thatched bamboo bungalows with terracotta tiled baths and newish wood floors, larger versions of the same, or snag a much bigger polished-concrete job with high ceilings. All are fan-cooled and steps from the best stretch of Long Beach.

Relax Bay HOTEL $$
(0 7568 4194; www.relaxbay.com; bungalows with fan 1550-2100B, air-con 2450-4050B, luxury tents 2750B;) This gorgeous French-run place sprawls over a tree-covered headland

by a small beach. Its wooden bungalows sit on stilts with large decks overlooking the bay and stunning sunsets. For a more unique experience, sleep in a seaview luxury tent perched over the rocks on a wooden platform. And there's a stylish open-air bar and restaurant.

Layana Resort RESORT **$$$**
(0 7560 7100; www.layanaresort.com; r from 15,000B, bungalows from 18,000B;) Yes, it's crowded with package tourists, but the location and the fabulous palm-lined pool make them lucky to be here. Comfy and big hardwood rooms with soothing neutral decor make it that much nicer. Rack rates are steep but internet deals can make it a bargain. Expect 50% discounts in the low season.

Hat Khlong Khong หาดคลองโขง

This is thatched-roof, Rasta-bar bliss with plenty of beach volleyball games, moon parties and the occasional well-advertised mushroom shake. Still, it's all pretty low-key and all ages are present. The beach, a thinning yet ample stretch of sand, goes on forever in either direction lapped by turquoise shallows.

Where Else? BUNGALOWS **$**
(0 7566 7173, 08 1536 4870; www.lanta-whereelse.com; Hat Khlong Khong; bungalows 300-800B) One of Ko Lanta's little slices of bohemia. The bungalows may be a bit shaky but there is great mojo here and the place buzzes with backpackers. The restaurant is a growing piece of art in itself. The pricier bungalows are all unique multilevel abodes sleeping up to four people.

★**Bee Bee Bungalows** BUNGALOWS **$**
(08 1537 9932; www.beebeebungalows; Hat Khlong Khong; bungalows 900B;) One of the best budget spots on the island, Bee Bee's super-friendly staff care for a dozen creative bamboo cabins – every one is unique and a few are stilted in the trees. The on-site restaurant has a library of tattered paperbacks to keep you busy while you wait for your delicious Thai staples.

Lanta Darawadee HOTEL **$$**
(0 7566 7094; www.lantadarawadee.com; bungalows 1000-1600B;) If you dig the Hat Khlong Khong scene but can't live without air-con, here's a great-value option right on the beach. It's bland, but the new rooms are clean and have good beds, terraces, mini fridges and TVs. Water is solar heated and rates include breakfast.

Hat Khlong Nin หาดคลองนิน

After Hat Khlong Tob, the main road heading south forks. Veer left for the inland road, which runs to the east coast, and head right for the country road, which hugs the coastline for 14km to the tip of Ko Lanta. On the right fork the first beach is picturesque Hat Khlong Nin. There are lots of small, inexpensive guest houses at the north end of this white sand beach that are usually attached to restaurants. It's easy to get dropped off here, then shop around for a budget place to stay.

Round House GUESTHOUSE **$**
(08 1606 0550; www.lantaroundhouse.com; Hat Khlong Nin; r/bungalow/house 800/1000/2400B;) A cute little find on the north end of this beach with three options. The wooden and bamboo bungalows are closest to the beach, just behind the breezy restaurant, but they also have a cool adobe round house (hence the name) off the road and a nearby beach house perfect for families.

Clean Beach Resort RESORT **$$**
(0 7566 2652, 08 9645 6068; www.cleanbeachresort.com; Hat Khlong Nin; superior 2300B, deluxe 2600-3800B; P) A rather swish collection of new tiled bungalows with wide private decks, set across the road from the beach in a lush garden. Deluxe pool-view rooms are the priciest, but all are reduced by 50% or more during the wet season.

Sri Lanta HOTEL **$$**
(0 7566 2688; www.srilanta.com; Hat Khlong Nin; cottages 1800-6200B; @) At the southern end of the beach, this sophisticated resort consists of minimalist wooden villas in wild gardens stretching from the beach to a landscaped hillside. There's a stylish beach-side area with a restaurant, infinity pool and private massage pavilions. The resort strives for low environmental impact by using biodegradable products and minimising energy use and waste.

Andalay Resort HOTEL **$$$**
(0 7566 2699; www.andalaylanta.com; Hat Khlong Nin; bungalows 5400B;) Rooms at this stylish boutique resort open onto porches perched above a lotus pond, which blends into the pool and sea. Inside find

rose-coloured concrete floors, ceiling fan and air-con, built-in wood furnishings, and satellite TV. Low-season rates can plummet to 1600B, which is a steal.

Ao Kantiang อ่าวกันเตียง

This superb sweep of sand backed by mountains is also its own self-contained village complete with mini-marts, internet cafes, motorbike rental and restaurants. Much of the beach here is undeveloped, although there are lots of sailboats and motorboats anchored in the bay. It's far from everything. If you land here, don't expect to move much.

Kantiang Bay View Resort HOTEL $

(0 7566 5049; www.kantiangbay.net; Ao Kantiang; r from 800B, bungalows from 1200B;) Choose between the cheap, rickety, not-exactly-spotless wooden-and-bamboo bungalows or the more expensive, candy-coloured tiled rooms with minifridge. The bamboo-clad restaurant serves decent, *fa·ràng*-friendly Thai dishes.

Baan Laanta Resort & Spa HOTEL $$

(0 7566 5091; www.baanlaanta.com; Ao Kantiang; bungalow pool/seaview from 2000/3000B;) Landscaped grounds wind around stylish wooden bungalows and a pool that drops off to a stretch of white sandy beach. The bungalows' centrepiece is a futon-style bed on a raised wooden platform under a gauzy veil of mosquito netting.

★Phra Nang Lanta INN $$$

(0 7566 5025; Ao Kantiang; studios 2500-8500B;) These gorgeous Mexican-style adobe-looking concrete studios are huge. Interiors are decorated with clean lines, hardwoods and whites accented with bright colours. Outside, flowers and foliage climb over bamboo lattice sunshades, and the pool and lush restaurant-bar look over the beautiful beach.

Ao Khlong Jaak อ่าวคลองจาก

There's a splendid beach here. The namesake waterfall is further inland.

Andalanta Resort HOTEL $$$

(0 7566 5018; www.andalanta.com; bungalows 2600-6900B;) You'll find beach-style, modern air-con bungalows (some with loft) and simple fan-cooled ones, and they all face the sea. The garden is a delight, there's an ambient restaurant and the waterfall is just a 30- to 40-minute walk away.

Ao Mai Pai อ่าวไม้ไผ่

A luscious, nearly forgotten cove at the southwestern curve just before the cape, this is our favourite beach on the island. Backed by elegant palm groves, with a rock reef jutting north, a jungle-swathed headland to the south and jade waters in between. Nature magic gleams here.

Baan Phu Lae BUNGALOWS $

(08 5474 0265, 0 7566 5100; www.baanphulae.com; Ao Mai Pai; bungalows 800-1000B) Set on the rocks at the end of this tiny beach, the last before the cape, are a collection of romantic, canary-yellow concrete bungalows with thatched roofs, bamboo beds and private porches. The restaurant's rickety deck juts over the sea. Baan Phu Lae can arrange diving with Go Dive (p330), offers cooking classes and massage, and books transport.

★La Laanta BOUTIQUE HOTEL $$$

(0 7566 5066; www.lalaanta.com; Ao Mai Pai; bungalows 2800-6200B;) Owned and operated by a young, hip, English-speaking Thai–Vietnamese couple, this is the grooviest spot on the island. Thatched bungalows have polished-concrete floors, platform beds, floral-design motifs and decks overlooking a pitch of sand, which blends into a rocky fishing beach. Set down a rutted dirt road, it's the last turn before the national park. Steep low-season discounts are available.

Laem Tanod แหลมโตนด

The road to the marine national park headquarters fords the *klorng* (canal), which can get quite deep in the wet season. This jungled mountainous corner of the island is the best, offering sheer drops and massive views to intrepid motorbikers.

Directly opposite the large, seasonal Andalanta Resort a private 2km **trail** leads to a waterfall. Elephant treks in the area are run by the landowners who also present a possibly upsetting baby elephant show, but hikers can walk it for free.

Mu Ko Lanta Marine National Park Headquarters CAMPING GROUND $

(in Bangkok 0 2561 4292; www.dnp.go.th; with own tent per person 30B, with tent hire 225B, 2-/4-room bungalows 1500/3000B) The secluded grounds of the national park headquarters are a wonderfully serene place to camp. The flat camping areas are covered in shade and sit in the wilds of the tropical jungle. Out front lie craggy outcroppings and the sounds of the ocean lapping up against the rocks.

There are toilets and running water, but you should bring your own food. You can rent basic but decent bungalows or get permission for camping on Ko Rok or Ko Ha. National park entry fees apply.

Ban Ko Lanta บ้านเกาะลันตา

There are a handful of inns open for business in Lanta's oft-ignored, wonderfully dated and incredibly rich Old Town.

Sriraya GUESTHOUSE $
(0 7569 7045; Ban Ko Lanta; r with shared bathrooms 500B) Sleep in a simple but beautifully restored, thick-beamed Chinese shophouse, that's possibly the very best value on the island. Walls are brushed in earth tones and bathrooms are shared. Angle for the street-front balcony room that overlooks the old town's ambient centre.

★**Mango House** GUESTHOUSE $$
(0 7569 7181; www.mangohouses.com; Ban Ko Lanta; suites 1500-3000B; Oct-April) These 100-year-old Chinese teak pole houses and former opium dens are stilted over the harbour. The original time-worn wood floors are still intact, ceilings soar and the four, house-sized rooms are decked out with satellite TVs, DVD players and ceiling fans. One has a full kitchen.

There are plans for an additional suite and two smaller studios in the coming year. Maid service is just twice weekly here and 50% discounts are offered in the low season.

Eating

The best places to grab a bite are at the seafood restaurants along the northern edge of Ban Sala Dan. With tables on verandahs over the water, they offer fresh seafood sold by weight (which includes cooking costs).

Bai Fern THAI $
(0 7566 8173; Ban Sala Dan; mains 40-100B; 8am-9pm) Cheap, tasty and authentic Thai salads, noodles and curry served over the water in a stilted dining room.

★**Lanta Seafood** SEAFOOD $$
(0 7566 8411; Ban Sala Dan; mains 80-300B) The best of the seafood-by-weight options. Order the *Ƀlah tôrt kà-mîn*: deep-fried white snapper rubbed with fresh, hand-ground turmeric and garlic. It's not oily, but it is smoky, spicy and juicy. The steamed mussels are also divine. There's even a wine list.

Beautiful Restaurant SEAFOOD $$
(0 7569 7062; www.beautifulrestaurantkolanta.com; Ban Ko Lanta; mains 100-200B;) The best of Old Town's seafood houses. Tables are scattered on four piers that extend into the sea. Fish is fresh and exquisitely prepared.

Drunken Sailors INTERNATIONAL-THAI $$
(0 7566 5076; Hat Nui; dishes 100-200B; 11am-late) This hip, ultra-relaxed octagonal pod is smothered with beanbags. The coffee drinks are top-notch and go well with interesting bites like the chicken green curry sandwich.

Lym's Rice Bowl THAI $$
(Hat Phra Ae; mains 80-180B, seafood dinners 450B; 8am-10pm Oct-Apr;) Authentic curries, noodles, soups and stir fries are served under the casuarinas and right on the beach. At dinner time they also do fresh fish – steamed, grilled and fried. If you eat and drink here, you are welcome to their beach lounges all day long.

Apsara THAI $$
(Ban Ko Lanta; dishes 100-160B; 10am-9pm) A new and lovely Old Town restaurant with a handful of weathered tables and chairs on a pier overlooking the east coast. It's romantic, relaxing and serves all the Thai faves, from steamed fish and shrimp with black pepper sauce to chicken with basil or cashew nuts.

Country Lao THAI $$
(08 5796 3024; Ban Phra Ae; mains 80-400B) A huddle of bamboo umbrellas and thatched pagodas on the main road notable for its house speciality: crispy papaya salad (150B). Green papaya shreds are battered and crispy fried. They're served in a heap alongside a bowl of lime dressing swimming with peanuts, green beans and juicy cherry tomatoes, and three tiger prawns. Your job: combine, devour.

Red Snapper INTERNATIONAL $$$
(0 7885 6965; www.redsnapper.lanta.com; Hat Phra Ae; tapas 35-295B, mains 295-525B; 5-11pm Thu-Tue) When local expats want a splurge, they find this Dutch-run roadside tapas restaurant with a romantic garden setting, serving everything from Indian lamb curry

and house marinated olives to roasted pork tenderloin and a popular grilled duck breast. There are decent vegetarian choices here too.

Drinking & Nightlife

During the high season Ko Lanta has some nightlife, but there are so many driftwood-style reggae bars along the west coast that it can become diluted. Low season is beyond mellow.

Same Same But Different BAR
(08 1787 8670; Ao Kantiang; 8am-11pm) In a sweet seaside setting, you can sample middling Thai cuisine and sip cocktails beneath massive trees, thatched pagodas or in a bamboo chair sunk into the sand. The location is the thing.

Moonwalk BAR
(0 7566 7214; www.moonwalkresort.com; Hat Khlong Khong; 7am-11pm;) A sprawling, thatched bar and restaurant that brings a little Thai funk back to what is becoming an increasingly plotted, planned and international island. Expect tasty cocktails, Jack Johnson in stereo and seafood barbecue in the high season. There's also a number of well-kept rooms (fan/air-con 1000/2800B) available.

Pirate's Bar BAR
(Hat Phrae Ae; 11am-late) A fun, well-managed tiki bar with tables and chairs scattered under private thatched shelters on the beach and a larger stilted roof which hosts the main semi-circular bar, complete with tree stump bar stools and sound system. The beer's cold, too.

Opium Bar NIGHTCLUB
(www.opiumbarkohlanta.com; Hat Phra Ae; from 6pm) This chic club has live music some nights, guest DJs and a big dance floor. It's still the top party spot on Lanta.

Information

Ban Sala Dan has plenty of restaurants, minimarts, internet cafes (1B per minute), travel agencies, dive shops and motorcycle rentals. There are several 7-Elevens spread along the island's west coast – each one has an ATM.

Ko Lanta Hospital (0 7569 7085) The hospital is 1km south of Ban Ko Lanta (Old Town).

Police Station (0 7569 7017) North of Ban Ko Lanta.

Getting There & Away

Most people come to Ko Lanta by boat or air-con minivan. If you're coming on your own steam, you'll need to use the frequent vehicle ferries (motorcycle 10B, pedestrian 23B, car 170B; 7am-8pm) between Ban Hua Hin and Ban Khlong Mak (Ko Lanta Noi) and on to Ko Lanta Yai.

Several information desks in Ban Sala Dan can fix you up with minivan and boat tickets and so can your guest house. Prices are standard and shouldn't vary.

BOAT

There are two piers at Ban Sala Dan. The passenger jetty is about 300m from the main strip of shops; vehicle ferries leave from a second jetty that's several kilometres further east.

There is one passenger ferry connecting Krabi's Khlong Chilat pier with Ko Lanta. It departs from Ko Lanta at 8.30am (400B, two hours) and returns from Krabi at 11am. It also stops at Ko Jum (for the full 400B fare).

Boats between Ko Lanta and Ko Phi-Phi technically run year-round, although service can peter out in the low season if there are too few passengers. Ferries usually leave Ko Lanta at 8am and 1pm (300B, 1½ hours); in the opposite direction boats leave Ko Phi-Phi at 11.30am and 2pm. From Ko Phi-Phi you can transfer to ferries to Phuket.

From around 21 October through May, you can join a four-island snorkelling tour to the Trang Islands and hop off with your bags at any destination you choose (350B). Boats stop on Ko Ngai (two hours), Ko Muk (three hours) and Ko Kradan (four hours).

There are also several speedboats that buzz from Ko Lanta to the Trang Islands on the so-called four-island tours, the fastest being the **Satun-Pak Bara Speedboat Club** (08 2433 0114, 0 7475 0389; www.tarutaolipeisland.com), which stops in Ko Ngai (650B, 30 minutes), Ko Muk (900B, one hour) and Ko Bulone Leh (1600B, two hours) then continues to Ko Lipe (1900B, three hours). Lanta Garden Hill (p330) offers the same trip.

Tigerline (08 1092 8800; www.tigerlinetravel.com), a high-speed ferry, runs between Ban Sala Dan on Ko Lanta and Ko Lipe (1500B, four hours), stopping at Ko Ngai (500B, 30 minutes), Ko Kradan (750B, 1½ hours) and Ko Muk (750B, two hours). The service leaves at 1pm. The next day the same boat makes the return trip from Ko Lipe, departing at 9am and arriving in Ban Sala Dan at noon.

MINIVAN

Minivans run year-round and are your best option from the mainland. Daily minivans to Krabi airport (300B, 1½ hours) and Krabi Town (250B,

1½ hours) leave hourly between 8am and 4pm in both directions. Minivans to Phuket (500B, four hours) leave every two hours or so, but are more frequent in the high season. There are also several daily air-con minivans to Trang (300B, three hours) and less frequent services to Khao Lak (500B, six hours), Ko Samui (800B including boat ticket) and other popular destinations.

Getting Around

Most resorts send vehicles to meet the ferries – a free ride to your resort. In the opposite direction expect to pay 80B to 350B. Alternatively, you can take a motorcycle taxi from opposite the 7-Eleven in Ban Sala Dan; fares vary from 50B to 350B, depending on distance.

Motorbikes (250B per day) can be rented all over. Unfortunately, very few places provide helmets and none provide insurance, so take extra care on the bumpy roads.

Several places rent out small 4WDs for around 1600B per day, including insurance.

Ko Jum & Ko Si Boya

เกาะจำ/เกาะศรีบอยา

Just north of Ko Lanta, Ko Jum and its neighbour Ko Si Boya have surprisingly little development; what's there is tucked away in the trees, making the islands look and feel nearly deserted. Although technically one island, the locals consider only the flatter southern part of Ko Jum to be Ko Jum; the northern hilly bit is called Ko Pu.

Ko Jum was once the exclusive domain of Lanta's *chow lair* people, but ethnic Chinese began arriving after Chairman Mao came to power in the 1950s. At the time there were no Thai people living here at all, but eventually the three cultures merged into one, which is best sampled in the warm early morning, amid the ramshackle poetry of **Ban Ko Jum**, the island's fishing village. It has a few restaurants, an **internet cafe** (Ban Ko Jum; per min 3B) and one dive shop, **Ko Jum Divers** (☎08 2273 7603; www.kohjum-divers.com; Ko Jum Beach Villas).

Sleeping & Eating

Ko Jum

Upwards of 30 properties are spread out along Ko Jum's west coast. Some places rent out sea kayaks and most have a restaurant. Public transport to Ko Jum and Ko Si Boya is limited in the low season, so some resorts close between May and October.

Bodaeng BUNGALOWS $
(☎08 1494 8760; Hat Yao; bungalow with/without bathroom 200/150B) A good old-fashioned hippie vortex with dirt-cheap lean-to wood and bamboo bungalows sprinkled in the trees. It ain't fancy. Expect squat toilets in the corrugated tin baths. It is open year-round and there's a restaurant, too.

★ **Woodland Lodge** GUESTHOUSE $$
(☎08 1893 5330; www.woodland-koh-jum.com; Hat Yao; standard/family bungalows 1000/1500B) Tasteful, clean bamboo huts with proper thatched roofs, polished wood floors and verandahs. Family bungalows sleep three people, and the exceptionally friendly British-Thai owners can organise boat and fishing trips and have an excellent, sociable restaurant. Great value and ambience.

Oon Lee Bungalows GUESTHOUSE $$
(☎08 7200 8053; http://kohjumoonleebungalows.com; Ko Pu; bungalows 600-4000B) This Crusoe-chic, Thai-French family-run resort is on a deserted white beach on the Ko Pu part of Ko Jum. Wooden stilted bungalows are in a shady garden and plenty of activities, including some of the island's best hiking, are on offer. The fantastic fusion restaurant here is reason enough for a visit.

Joy Bungalow GUEST HOUSE $$
(☎08 9875 2221, 0 7561 8199; www.kohjum-joy-bungalow.com; Hat Yao; bungalows 650-3050B) On the southwestern coast of Ko Jum, Joy has some very attractive stilted, polished-wood cottages on a tremendous stretch of beach. The best are raised 2m high in the trees. This was the first resort on Ko Jum and it's still very popular.

Ting Rai Bay Resort HOTEL $$
(☎08 7263 3881, 08 4944 6141; www.tingrai.com; Ko Pu; bungalows 900-3200B; ⊙May-Mar; ❄≋) The bungalows here, which vary in size and comfort, are built in a horseshoe on a sloping landscaped hill and all have sea views.

Koh Jum Resort HOTEL $$
(☎08 0221 4040; www.kohjumresort.com; Ko Pu; bungalows 1500-6000B; ≋) Three stunning two-storey, ranch-style teak chalets are built with crooked, polished wood and designed with cylindrical turrets. The seven bamboo huts, attached to wide sun terraces stilted high above the sea, are rustic for the price but the excellent landscaping makes that easy to overlook.

★**Koh Jum Beach Villas** VILLAS $$$
(☎08 6184 0505; www.kohjumbeachvillas.com; Hat Yao; villas 6000-16,000B; 📶) Spacious wooden homes with plenty of living spaces, lush decks with cushioned seating and views of the sea are spread along a luscious white nub of Hat Yao. Houses are privately owned and rented out by the night.

The community is devoted to keeping the place as environmentally and socially responsible as possible (note there's no air-con but the houses have been constructed to catch ocean breezes). The staff are delightful, the restaurant and bar scrumptious.

Koh Jum Lodge HOTEL $$$
(☎0 7561 8275; www.kohjumlodge.com; Hat Yao; bungalows 4500-5500B; 📶) An eco-lodge with style: imagine lots of hardwoods and bamboo, gauzy mosquito netting, potted orchids, Thai carvings, manicured grounds and a hammock-strewn curve of white sand out front. It strikes that hard-to-get balance of authenticity and comfort. Bliss.

Kung Nang Seafood SEAFOOD $
(☎08 7264 9185; Ban Ko Jum; meals 150-200B; ⏲8am-7pm) A terrific local seafood house in main village. Order your fish early in the day and it will be ready for you at dinner time. Southern Thai delicacies like *Ƀlah tôrt kà·mîn* (fried fish with turmeric) and *Ƀlah đôm kà·mîn* (fish soup) are excellent.

Mama Cooking THAI $
(Ban Ko Jum; dishes 20-50B) If you love your Thai breakfasts, join the fishermen for milky tea, flavoured sticky rice and freshly made Thai donuts in the village.

Ko Si Boya

Low-lying, rural Ko Si Boya has yet to garner more than a trickle of the annual tourism stream, and that's just fine with repeat visitors – almost all of whom land at a single, exceptional bungalow compound.

Siboya Resort HOTEL $
(☎08 1979 3344, 0 7561 8026; www.siboyabungalows.com; bungalows 350B, houses 600-1200B; @📶) OK, the beach itself isn't spectacular. But the mangrove setting is wild and full of life, and the bungalows and private homes are large, tasteful and affordable. The restaurant rocks and is wired with high-speed internet. No wonder ever-smiling, secretive 50-somethings flock here like it's a retiree's version of Alex Garland's *The Beach*.

Getting There & Around

From November to May, boats between Krabi and Ko Lanta can drop you at Ko Jum, but you'll pay full fare (400B, one hour). In the fringe months of November and May only the early boat will drop you. In the high season there's a long-tail ferry to Ko Phi-Phi (600B, 1½ hours) that leaves between 8am and 9am and picks guests up from the Hat Yao resorts.

There are also small boats to Ko Jum from Ban Laem Kruat, a village about 30km southeast of Krabi, at the end of Rte 4036, off Hwy 4. The boat (100B) leaves at 9am, 10am, 11.30am, 1pm, 2pm, 4pm, 5.30pm and 6.15pm, and returns the following day at 6.30am, 7.15am, 7.35am, 7.55am, 8.15am, 1.30pm, 2.30pm and 4pm. Private charters cost from 1200B to 1500B.

If you plan to arrive in Ko Jum via Laem Kruat, make sure to call your guesthouse in advance so they can arrange your transfer from the pier. Otherwise, you may be relying on the kindness of strangers. A handful of places on the main road in Ban Ko Jum rent out bicycles (100B), mountain bikes (130B to 150B) and motorbikes (250B) at standard rates.

Boats to Ko Si Boya (50B) make the 10-minute hop from Laem Hin, just north of Ban Laem Kruat, every hour between 8am and 5pm. Call Siboya Resort to arrange transfer from the pier.

TRANG PROVINCE

Lining the Andaman Sea south of Krabi, Trang Province has an impressive limestone-covered coast with several sublime islands. For the adventurous, there's also plenty of big nature to explore in the lush interior, including dozens of scenic waterfalls and limestone caves. And it's nowhere near as popular as Krabi, which means you're more likely to see working rubber plantations here than rows of vendors selling 'same same but different' T-shirts. Transport links are improving every year, and during the high season it's now possible to island-hop all the way to Malaysia.

Trang ตรัง

POP 67,080

Most visitors to Trang are in transit to nearby islands, but if you're an aficionado of culture, Thai food or markets, plan to stay a day or more. Here is an easy-to-manage, old-school Thai town where you can get lost in wet markets by day and hawker markets and late-night Chinese coffee shops by night.

Trang Province

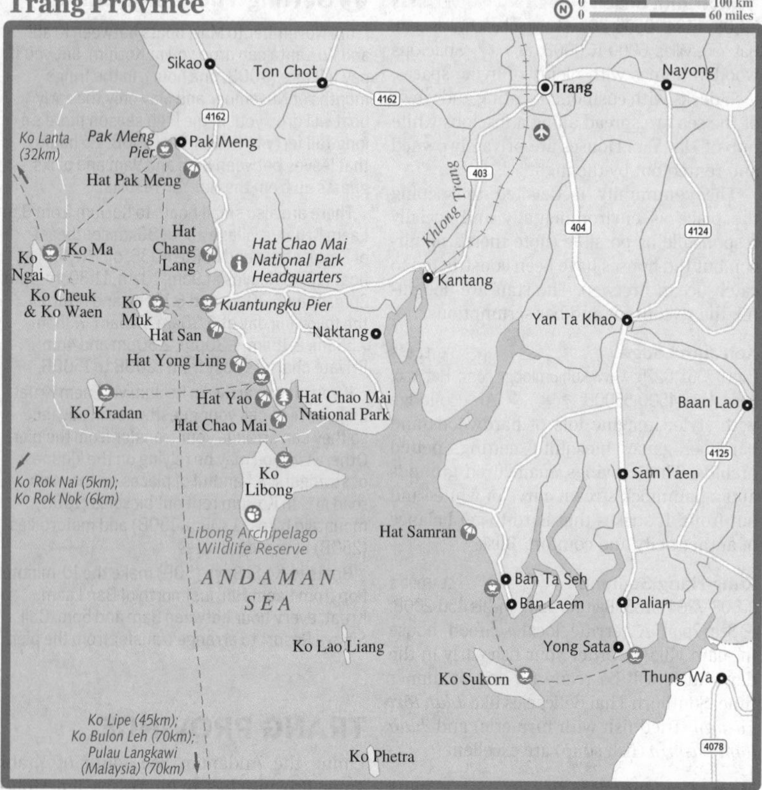

At nearly any time of the year, there's likely to be some minor festival that oozes local colour.

Most of the tourist facilities lie along the main drag, Th Praram VI, between the clock tower and the train station.

Sights

Trang is more of a business centre than a tourist town. **Wat Tantayaphirom** (Th Tha Klang) has a huge white *chedi* (stupa) enshrining a footprint of the Buddha that's mildly interesting. The Chinese **Meunram Temple**, between Soi 1 and Soi 3, sometimes sponsors performances of southern Thai shadow theatre. It's also worth strolling around the large **wet & dry markets** on Th Tha Klang and Th Sathani.

Activities

Tour agencies around the train station and along Th Praram VI offer various tours around Trang. **Boat trips** to Hat Chao Mai National Park and the Trang Islands start at 750B plus national park fees. **Snorkelling** trips on private long-tails to Ko Rok (per person 1300B) and trips to local **caves and waterfalls** (1800B, maximum three people) by private car can also be arranged by most agencies.

Festivals & Events

Trang's Chinese population celebrates the wonderful **Vegetarian Festival** every October, coinciding with the similar festival in Phuket.

Sleeping & Eating

Trang is famous for its *mŏo yâhng* (crispy barbecued pork) and *ráhn goh·Ђée* (coffee shops) that serve real filtered coffee. You can find *mŏo yâhng* in the mornings at some coffee shops or by weight at the wet market on Th Ratchadamnoen. To really get into the local scene, get to a dim sum depot early in the morning and stay out late at the coffee shops along Th Ratsada.

Koh Teng Hotel HOTEL $
(☎0 7521 8622; 77-79 Th Praram VI; r with fan 200-260, air-con 320B; ❄) The undisputed king of backpacker digs in Trang. If you're feeling optimistic, the huge, window-lit rooms here have an adventuresome kind of shabby charm to them; if not, the grunge factor might get you down.

Sri Trang Hotel HOTEL $$
(☎0 7521 8122; www.sritrang.com; 22-26 Th Praram VI; r 640-840B; ❄📶) There is a range of fan-cooled and air-con rooms in this renovated 60-year-old building (it opened for business in 1952) with high ceilings, a winding wooden staircase, groovy paint jobs, and wi-fi throughout. There's also a pleasant cafe-bar downstairs.

Rua Rasada Hotel HOTEL $$$
(☎0 7521 4230; www.ruarasadahotel.com; 188 Th Trang-Phattalung; r incl breakfast from 2600B; ❄📶🏊) Trang's slickest choice is a 10-minute (25B) túk-túk ride from the train station. Chic rooms have comfortable beds and a dusky blue, dark mauve and grey colour scheme. It's a five-minute walk to Robinson's Shopping Mall and Cinema City.

★**Night Market** MARKET $
(btwn Th Praram VI & Th Ratchadamnoen; meals around 30B) The best night market on the Andaman coast will have you salivating over bubbling curries, fried chicken and fish, *pàt tai* and an array of Thai desserts. Go with an empty stomach and a sense of adventure. On Friday and Saturday nights there's a second, even more glorious night market right in front of the train station.

Asia Ocha THAI $
(Th Kantang; meals from 35-40B; ⏰7am-10pm) In business for 65 years, Asia Ocha serves filtered coffee to an all-Thai clientele who sit at vintage marble tables in an antiquated building. Don't miss the food either – the roast duck and crispy pork are delectable, as are the Thai breakfasts.

ℹ Information

You'll find several internet cafes and various banks with ATMs and foreign-exchange booths on Th Praram VI.

My Friend (☎0 7522 5984; 25/17-20 Th Sathani; per hr 30B) Has the best 24-hour internet cafe in town.

Post Office (cnr Th Praram VI & Th Kantang)

ℹ Getting There & Away

AIR

Nok Air (www.nokair.com) operates daily flights from Bangkok (Don Muang) to Trang, but note that flights may be cancelled if there is heavy rain. The airport is 4km south of Trang; minivans meet flights and charge 80B to town. In the reverse direction a taxi or túk-túk will cost 100B to 120B.

MINIVAN & SHARE TAXI

Hourly vans heading to Surat Thani (180B, 2½ hours), with connections to Ko Samui and Ko Pha-Ngan, leave from a depot just before Th Tha Klang crosses the railway tracks. Several daily air-con minivans between Trang and Ko Lanta (250B, 2½ hours) leave from the travel agents across from the train station. There are share taxis to Krabi (150B, two hours) and air-con minivans to Hat Yai (150B, two hours) from offices just west of the Trang bus terminal.

Local transport is mainly by air-con minivan rather than *sŏrng·tăa·ou*. Minivans leave regularly from the depot on Th Tha Klang for Pak Meng

BUSES TO/FROM TRANG

Buses leave from the Trang **bus terminal** (Th Huay Yot). Air-con buses from Trang to Bangkok cost 600B to 680B (12 hours, morning and afternoon). More comfortable are the VIP 24-seater buses at 5pm and 5.30pm (1050B). From Bangkok, VIP/air-con buses leave between 6.30pm and 7pm.

Other services include the following:

DESTINATION	FARE (B)	DURATION (HR)	FREQUENCY
Hat Yai	110	3	every 2-3hr
Krabi	90-115	2	every 2-3hr
Phang-Nga	200	3½	hourly
Phuket	240	5	hourly
Satun	110	3	every 2-3hr

Trang

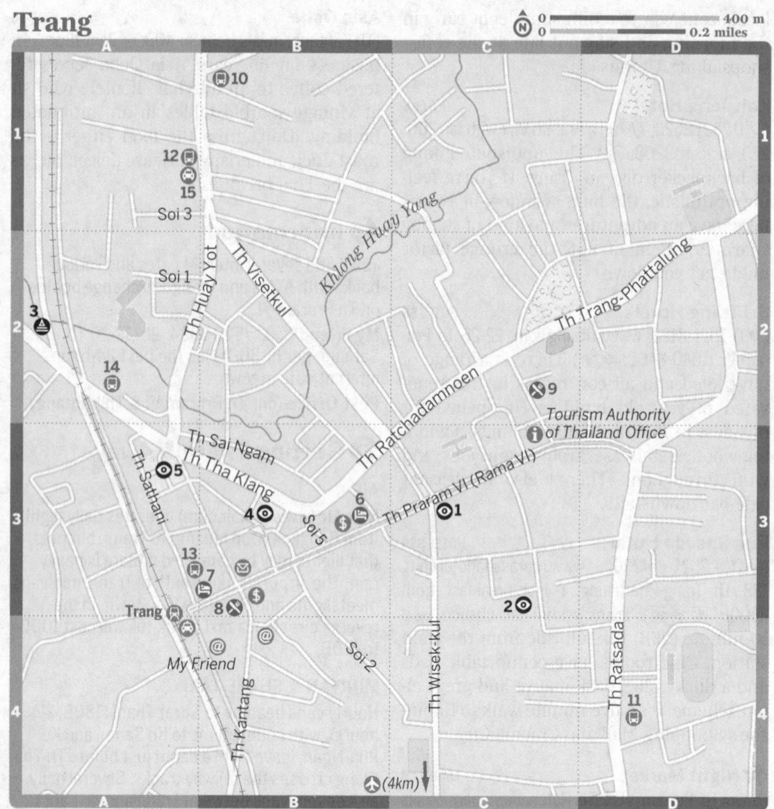

(100B, 45 minutes), Hat Chao Mai (150B, one hour) and Kuantungku pier (150B, one hour).

TRAIN

Only two trains go all the way from Bangkok to Trang: the express 83 and the rapid 167, which both leave from Bangkok's Hualamphong station in the afternoon and arrive in Trang the next morning. From Trang, trains leave in the early and late afternoon. Fares are around 1480B/831B for a 1st-/2nd-class air-con sleeper and 285B for 3rd class.

Getting Around

Túk-túk mill around near the train station and should charge 30B for local trips and 250B per hour. Motorbike taxis charge the same price. Motorcycles can be rented at travel agencies for about 200B per day. Most agencies can also help you arrange car rental for around 1500B per day.

Trang Beaches & Islands

Think: limestone karsts rising from steamy palm-studded valleys and swirling seas. Trang's beaches are mostly just jumping-off points to the islands, but if you have the time, stop and enjoy the scenery.

The mythical Trang Islands feel like the lost fragments of the Andaman's iconic limestone that have tumbled into the sea, and most have pure white sand beaches, home to roving sea gypsies.

Hat Pak Meng & Hat Chang Lang
หาดปากเมง/หาดฉางลาง

Thirty-nine kilometres from Trang in Amphoe Sikao (Sikao District), Hat Pak Meng is the main jumping-off point for Ko Ngai. There's a wild-looking stretch of coastline here, and though the beach is scruffy, the backdrop – jutting limestone karsts on all

Trang

Sights

1 Clock Tower....C3
2 Meunram Temple....C3
3 Wat Tantayaphirom....A2
4 Wet & Dry Market (Th Ratchadamnoen)....B3
5 Wet & Dry Market (Th Sathani)....A3

Sleeping

6 Koh Teng Hotel....B3
7 Sri Trang Hotel....B3

Eating

8 Asia Ocha....B3
9 Night Market....C2

Transport

10 Bus Terminal....B1
11 Buses to Satun & La-Ngu....D4
12 Minivans to Hat Yai....A1
13 Minivans to Ko Lanta....A3
14 Minivans to Pak Meng, Hat Chao Mai, Kuantungku & Surat Thani....A2
15 Share Taxis to Krabi....A1

sides that rival the best of Railay and Phi-Phi – is spectacular. The main pier is at the northern end of the beach and there are several seafood restaurants with deck chairs under casuarinas where Rte 4162 meets the coast, which attract Thai day trippers and weekend warriors.

Tour agencies at the jetty organise one-day boat tours to Ko Muk, Ko Cheuk, Ko Ma and Ko Kradan for 750B per person (minimum three people), including lunch and beverages. There are also snorkelling day tours to Ko Ngai (450B) and Ko Rok (1200B to 1400B, plus national park fees). Mask and snorkel sets and fins can be rented by the pier for 50B each.

Hat Chang Lang is the next beach south from Hat Pak Meng and it continues the casuarina-backed-beach motif. At the southern end of Hat Chang Lang, where the beachfront road turns inland, is the headquarters of **Hat Chao Mai National Park** (อุทยานแห่งชาติหาดเจ้าไหม; ☎0 7521 3260; adult/child 200/100B; ⏲6am-6pm).

The 231-sq-km park covers the shoreline from Hat Pak Meng to Laem Chao Mai and encompasses the islands of Ko Muk, Ko Kradan and Ko Cheuk plus a host of small islets. In various parts of the park you may see endangered dugong and rare black-necked storks, as well as more common species such as sea otters, macaques, lang[...] pangolins, little herons, Pacific [...] white-bellied sea eagles and monit[...]

Sleeping

National Park Headquarters CAMPING GROUND, CABINS $
(☎0 7521 3260; www.dnp.go.th; camping with own tent 30B, with tent hire 200B, cabins 800B) Simple cabins sleep up to six people and have fans, or you can camp under the casuarinas. There's also a restaurant and a small shop.

Anantara Sikao HOTEL $$$
(☎0 7520 5888; www.sikao.anantara.com; Hat Cheng Leng; r from 5100B; P ❄ 📶 🏊) Set on the northern edge of Hat Chang Leng, Anantara's glamorous yet hip vibe has refreshed these old bones. Deluxe oceanfront rooms have wood floors, floating desks, flat-screen TVs and amazing views of Pak Meng's signature karsts. There are impressive timber columns and Balinese wood furnishings in the lobby, and the view from its Acqua restaurant is jaw dropping.

Take the free shuttle to its guests-only beach club on seductive Ko Kradan.

Getting There & Away

There are several daily boats between Pak Meng and Ko Ngai. Boats leave Ko Ngai for Pak Meng (450B) at 8.30am and return to Ko Ngai at noon. A long-tail charter is 1500B.

Regular air-con minivans from Th Kha Klang in Trang run to Hat Pak Meng (60B, 45 minutes) and Chao Mai (80B, one hour). Or you can charter a taxi from Trang for around 800B.

The Chao Mai National Park headquarters is about 1km off the main road, down a clearly signposted track.

Ko Ngai เกาะไหง (ไห)

The long blonde wind-swept beach along the developed eastern coast of Ko Ngai (Ko Hai) extends into blue water with a sandy bottom (perfect for children) that ends at a reef drop-off with excellent snorkelling. Coral and clear waters actually encircle the entire densely forested island – it's a stunning place. With no indigenous population living here, several spiffy resorts have the whole island to themselves. There is one dive centre (dives from 1500B). Snorkel sets and fins can be rented from resorts for 100B each, sea kayaks for around 150B to 180B per hour, or you can take a boat tour around the island (550B) or a half-day snorkelling tour

…0B per person). Inter… is slow and costs 100B …i is iffy. … technically a part of …land's mainland link is

Eating

…cidedly midrange and come with restaurants and 24-hour electricity. The boat pier is at Koh Ngai Resort, but if you book ahead resorts on the other beaches will arrange transfers.

Ko Hai Camping CAMPING GROUND $
(☎08 1970 9804; seamoth2004@yahoo.com; tent 500-600B) Big fan-cooled tent-bungalows on the beach have shared bathrooms and are run by friendly Tu, who also manages the adjacent Sea Moth Dive Center.

Thanya Beach Resort HOTEL $$
(☎0 7520 6967; www.kohngaithanyaresort.com; bungalows 1890-5775B; ❄@) Ko Ngai's Bali-chic choice has dark but spacious teak bungalows with indoor hot showers and outdoor country-style bucket showers (don't knock it till you've tried it). Stroll to your seafront terrace and gaze at the palm-dappled lawn, which rolls towards the sea.

Mayalay Resort HOTEL $$
(☎08 3530 7523; www.mayalaybeachresort.com; r 2500-5000B; ❄@≋) This charming resort has huge bungalows, all with double beds plus day beds by the window, draped in mosquito nets. The Thai-Western beachside terrace restaurant is a little pricey but the view is sublime and portions are big and tasty.

★**Coco Cottages** HOTEL $$$
(☎08 9724 9225; www.coco-cottage.com; bungalows 3600-4800B; ❄wi-fi) As the name suggests, cottages are coconut extravaganzas with thatched roofs, coconut-wood walls and coconut-shell lanterns. Decks and interiors catch plenty of breezes, so air-con isn't always necessary. Grab a sea-view fan bungalow if you can. There are bamboo lounges on the beach, massage pavilions and a terrific restaurant and beachfront bar.

Thapwarin Resort RESORT $$$
(☎08 1894 3585; www.Thapwarin.com; garden/ocean view bungalows 3500/6500B; ❄wi-fi) Expect attractive and spacious bamboo cottages, each with private deck nestled in the trees on its own dock above the sea. Comfy and cosy with attractive mosquito netting, throw pillows and paper lanterns, they are a touch overpriced. Still, **Laytrang Diving**, their in-house shop, is the only dive centre on the island and the bar and restaurant have style.

Ko Ngai Seafood THAI $$
(☎08 1367 8497; mains 100-300B; ⏲Nov-Apr; ❄) One of the best kitchens on the island. The coconut-milk crab curry with big chunks of de-shelled fresh crab is a dream come true. They have a collection of bungalows too.

Getting There & Away

Ko Ngai Villa runs the daily boats from Ko Ngai to Hat Pak Meng (450B, 1½ hours) at 10.30am, returning to Ko Ngai at noon. You can also privately charter a long-tail to and from Pak Meng for 1500B, as well as Ko Muk (1500B) and Ko Kradan (1800B). Ko Ngai Seafood and Ko Ngai Villa are the best sources for long-tail charters.

In the high season, the **Tigerline** (☎08 1092 8800; www.tigerlinetravel.com) high-speed ferry runs between Ban Sala Dan (750B, 30 minutes) on Ko Lanta and Ko Lipe (1600B, four hours), stopping at the pier on Ko Muk, where you can connect to Ko Ngai. **Satun Pakbara Speedboat Club** (☎08 2433 0114, 0 7475 0389; www.tarutaolipeisland.com) is the more direct and comfortable choice from Ko Lanta (650B, 30 minutes). You can charter a long-tail to Lanta for 2000B to 2500B.

Ko Muk เกาะมุก

Motoring into Ko Muk is unforgettable whether you land on the sugary white sand bar of **Hat Sivalai** or spectacular **Hat Farang** (aka Hat Sai Yao, aka Charlie's Beach) where jade water kisses a perfect beach. Unfortunately, the lodging options aren't tremendous, and there's a steady stream of Speedo-clad package tourists tramping the beach and even more in the speedboats that buzz to Tham Morakot (Emerald Cave) from Ko Lanta. Still, the west coast sunsets are glorious, it's easy to hop from here to any and every island in the province and you may be shocked to feel Ko Muk's topography stir something deep and wild in your primordial soul.

Sights & Activities

Tham Morakot (Emerald Cave) is a beautiful limestone tunnel that leads 80m into a *hôrng* (semisubmerged island cave). No wonder long-gone pirates buried treasure here. You have to swim or paddle through the tunnel, part of the way in pitch blackness, to a small white-sand beach surrounded by lofty limestone walls; a piercing shaft of light illuminates the beach around midday. The cave features prominently on most tour itineraries, so it can get ridiculously crowded in the high season. Better to arrange a long-tail boat (600B to 800B) or rent a kayak (per hour/day 150/500B) to zip over to the cave at daybreak or late afternoon when you'll have it to yourself – but note you can't get inside the cave at high tide.

Between Ko Muk and Ko Ngai are the small karst islets of **Ko Cheuk** and **Ko Waen**, both of which have good snorkelling and small sandy beaches.

Ko Mook Garden Resort rents out bikes (per day 100B) with maps for self-guided island tours, and you can also spend hours walking through rubber plantations and the island's devout Muslim sea shanty villages (please cover up).

Sleeping & Eating

Hat Sivalai & Hat Lodung หาดสิวลัย

Most places in Hat Sivalai and Hat Lodung are a short walk from either side of the pier. If you're facing the sea, humble, local-flavoured Hat Lodung is to your left after a stilt village and some mangroves; stunning Hat Sivalai wraps around the peninsula to the right. Though beautiful, that murky backwash from the mangrove villages on mainland does lap these shores. You can even see the oily sheen sometimes. The sea is cleaner on Hat Farang.

Ko Mook Garden Resort GUESTHOUSE $
(☎09 0703 3570; Hat Lodung; r 400-800B) Wooden rooms are large while bamboo bungalows are small and basic. Staying here means you're in with a local family who take guests snorkelling, rent bikes (100B), and give out detailed maps of all the island's secret spots.

Pawapi Resort BUNGALOWS $$
(☎08 6444 7543; www.pawapi.com; Hat Sivalai; bungalows incl breakfast from 1600B; ❄) The upscale bamboo bungalows here are perched on stilts about 1.5m off the ground so that breezes ventilate the room; the 180-degree view of islands and turquoise sea is insane. A collection of newer concrete jobs were nearing completion at the time of writing.

Sivalai HOTEL $$$
(☎08 9723 3355; www.komooksivalai.com; Hat Sivalai; bungalows incl breakfast 4000-8000B; ❄🛜🏊) Straddling an arrow-shaped peninsula of white sand and surrounded by views of karst islands and the mainland, this location is sublime. Elegant thatched-roof cottages are almost encircled with glass doors, to maximise that view. The vibe is a little stiff, the pool is disappointing and the electronics could use an update, but the beach is special.

Hat Farang หาดฝรั่ง

You'll be part of a blend of travellers and package tourists more liable to relish the calm than to party. More and more places are opening inland from the beach, so shopping around is worthwhile. Most boats will pick up and drop you off here, but if not you'll have to take a 10-minute motorbike taxi to or from the main pier (50B).

Hadfarang GUESTHOUSE $
(☎08 7884 4785, 08 1584 4648; www.kohmookhadfarang.com; Hat Farang; r with fan/air-con 500/1200B; ❄🛜) A short walk inland, these tiled air-con rooms are set in wood-panelled duplexes. The fan rooms are tiny white-washed plywood constructs with tin roofs. Nothing special, but well priced.

Sawasdee Resort GUESTHOUSE $
(☎08 0127 4717; www.kohmook-sawadeeresort.com; Hat Farang; bungalows 800B) Unremarkable, somewhat scruffy wooden bungalows with terraces right on the quiet, shady north end of Hat Farang. You're paying for the location – which is beautiful.

Charlie Beach Resort HOTEL $$
(☎0 7520 3283, 0 7520 3281; www.kohmook.com; Hat Farang; bungalows 1300-3850B; ❄@) Bungalow options range from basic beach shacks to three-star, air-con cottages at this sprawling resort, which dominates the beach and is laced with sandy footpaths. Staff, although not always helpful, can organise snorkelling tours to Tham Morakot and other islands for around 1000B. Skip the restaurant. It's open year-round.

★**Ko Yao Viewpoint** SEAFOOD $
(Hat Farang; meals 100-200B; ⏲8am-9pm) This family-owned patio restaurant is perched on the cliffs, with wooden tables scattered beneath a string of lights – views are astounding. The beer is cold, and the fish is fresh

and steamed in a smouldering broth of chilli and lime.

Getting There & Away

Boats to Ko Muk leave from the pier at Kuantungku. There are daily departures at 8am, 9am, and 2pm (200B to 300B, 30 minutes), which make the return trip to the mainland an hour later; the early morning ferry is the cheapest. Minibuses to/from Trang (350B to 450B, one hour) meet the 9am and 3pm boats. Minivans to the Trang airport (550B) meet the 2pm boat only. A chartered long-tail from Kuantungku to Ko Muk (800B, 30 minutes) and to either Pak Meng or Hat Yao is around 1200B (45 minutes to one hour).

Long-tail charters to Ko Kradan (600B, 30 minutes) and Ko Ngai (1000B, one hour) are easily arranged on the pier or at Rubber Tree Bungalow or Ko Yao Restaurant on Hat Farang.

From November to May, Ko Muk is one of the stops on the speedboats connecting Ko Lanta and Ko Lipe.

Lanta Garden Hill's (p330) speed boat makes the Lanta–Nga–Muk connection leaving Ko Muk daily at 10.30am.

Ko Kradan เกาะกระดาน

Kradan is dotted with slender, silky white-sand beaches, bathtub-warm shallows and limestone karst views. There's a small but lush tangle of remnant jungle inland, where a short track leads past Paradise Lost over the ridge to **Sunset Beach**, a mostly wet and rocky beach with open seas in the offing, and a fun place to get a little beachside privacy.

Sadly, although the water is clean, clear, warm and inviting on Kradan, the coral structure has been decimated and the snorkelling is a major disappointment. Nevertheless, it is nice to swim here.

For internet access and boat tickets go to Kradan Beach Resort, the biggest spread of mediocre bungalows on the main beach.

Sleeping & Eating

Paradise Lost GUESTHOUSE $$
(☎08 9587 2409; www.kokradan.wordpress.com; bungalows with/without bathroom 1200/600B) One of the first places built on Kradan and still one of the best, this groovy, inland Thai-American-owned bungalow property has easy access to the island's more remote beaches. Small bamboo nests have solid wood floors and shared baths. Larger bungalows are all wood and have private facilities. Its kitchen (dishes 120B to 180B) is the best on the island.

Kalumé Village BUNGALOWS $$
(☎08 0522 8220; www.kalumekradan.com; bungalows 1300-1900B) A basic place with attractive but simple wooden and bamboo bungalows and plans for new ones at research time. The location at the far end of Kradan – with a shady garden and just steps from blue water – is spectacular.

Coral Garden BUNGALOWS $$$
(www.coralgardenresort.com; bungalows from 3000B) A rather stunning collection of spacious, multi-hued natural wood bungalows decked out with floating queen beds, rattan wardrobes, recessed lighting, and private patios, and set at the wooded northwestern end of the island. Online reservations only.

Seven Seas Resort HOTEL $$$
(☎08 2490 2442; www.sevenseasresorts.com; r 6600-7600B, bungalows 11,750-15,600B;) This boutique resort's ultra-slick rooms have terrazzo floors and enormous beds that could sleep four. Beach bums will adore this stretch of sand. The breezy restaurant, hugging the jet-black infinity pool, is attractive, but serves an overpriced mix of middling Western and Thai dishes. Pricey? Sure. But the amazing staff more than make up for it.

NICE DAY FOR A WET WEDDING

Every Valentine's Day, Ko Kradan is the setting for a rather unusual wedding ceremony. Around 35 brides and grooms don scuba gear and descend to an underwater altar amid the coral reefs, exchanging their vows in front of the Trang District Officer. How the couples manage to say 'I do' underwater has never been fully explained, but the ceremony has made it into the *Guinness World Records* for the world's largest underwater wedding. Before and after the scuba ceremony, the couples are paraded along the coast in a flotilla of motorboats. If you think this might be right for your special day, visit the website www.underwaterwedding.com.

Getting There & Away

Daily boats to Kuantungku leave at 9am and noon; tickets include the connecting minibus all the way to Trang (450B). A chartered long-tail from Kuantungku will cost around 800B to 1000B one-way (45 minutes to one hour); you can also charter boats from Kradan to other islands within the archipelago.

Tigerline (08 1092 8800; www.tigerlinetravel.com) connects Kradan with Ko Lanta (850B, 1½ hours) and Hat Yao (1050B, one hour).

Hat Yao หาดยาว

A scruffy fishing hamlet just south of Hat Yong Ling, Hat Yao is sandwiched between the sea and imposing limestone cliffs, and sits at the mouth of a thick mangrove estuary. A rocky headland at the southern end of Hat Yao is pocked with caves and there's good snorkelling around the island immediately offshore. The best beach in the area is tiny **Hat Apo**, hidden away among the cliffs. **Tham Chao Mai** is a vast cave full of crystal cascades and impressive stalactites and stalagmites that can be explored on a kayak tour (650B).

Just south of the headland is the Yao pier, the main departure point for Ko Libong and the midpoint in the Tigerline ferry route that connects Lipe to Lanta.

Sleeping

Haad Yao Nature Resort GUEST HOUSE $

(08 1894 6936; www.natureresortsgroup.com; r with fan/air-con 800/1200B;) Set in the harbour, this place offers a variety of environmentally focused tours in the Hat Yao area. It has large cottages with wide terraces, TV and DVD, simpler motel-style rooms and a few overwater bungalows.

Getting There & Around

From here, you can catch one of the regular long-tail boats to Ko Libong (50B, 20 minutes). You can also charter long-tail boats to Ko Libong (800B, 20 minutes) or to Ko Muk (1500B, one hour) each way. *Sŏrng·tăa·ou* to Trang (70B, one hour) leave when full from the pier and meet arriving boats. **Tigerline** (08 1092 8800; www.tigerlinetravel.com) is the area's high-speed ferry service, which docks in Hat Yao for lunch on its way between Lanta (850B, two hours) and Lipe (850B, two hours).

Ko Libong เกาะลิบง

Trang's largest island is just 20 minutes by long-tail from Hat Yao. Less visited than neighbouring isles, it's a gorgeous, lush mountainous pearl, wrapped in rubber trees, thick with mangroves and known for its captivating flora and fauna (especially the resident dugong) more than its thin reddish-brown beaches. The island is home to a small Muslim fishing community and has a few resorts on the west coast. Libong's scruffy sweetness and backwater charm has a way of making you feel humble, grateful and open, if you let it.

Sights

Libong Archipelago Wildlife Reserve NATURE RESERVE

(0 7525 1932) This reserve on the eastern coast of Ko Libong at **Laem Ju Hoi** is a large area of mangroves protected by the Botanical Department. The sea channels are one of the dugong's last habitats, and around 40 of them graze on the lush sea grass that flourishes in the bay.

The Haad Yao Nature Resort in Hat Yao and the resorts here on Ko Libong (the reserve is not far from the Libong Beach Resort) offer dugong-spotting tours by sea kayak, led by trained naturalists, for around 1500B. Sea kayaks can also be rented at most resorts for 200B per hour.

Sleeping

Le Dugong Resort HOTEL $

(08 7475 8310, 08 7475 8310; www.libongresort.com; Ko Libong; bungalows 900B) The best digs are rustic yet stylish wood-and-bamboo bungalows with terracotta sinks, woven walls and shuttered doors that open the whole room to the sea and setting sun.

Libong Beach Resort BUNGALOWS $$

(08 4849 0899, 08 9647 7030; www.libongbeachresort.com; Ko Libong; bungalows with fan 800-1000B, air-con 2000B;) There are several options here, from bland slap-up shacks behind a murky stream to comfortable varnished wood-and-thatch chalets on the beachfront. It offers a slew of trips, motorbike rental (300B) and internet access (per hour 100B), and the **Jolly Roger Dive Center** is based here, too. The kitchen rocks. Order the *đôm yam kà·mîn* (turmeric fish soup).

Libong Sunset Resort HOTEL $$
(☎08 0522 2421; www.libongsunsetresort.com; bungalows 800-1000B, r 1800B; ❄📶) Set on its own rocky, sandy beach tucked up against a headland, this family-owned resort is a good choice. Bungalows are simple, fan-cooled and spotless. The bigger air-con rooms have sitting area and TV. All have private porches with seaviews.

Getting There & Away

Long-tail boats to Ban Ma Phrao on the eastern coast of Ko Libong leave regularly from Hat Yao (20 minutes) during daylight hours for 50B per person; the long-tail jetty at Hat Yao is just west of the newer Yao pier. On Ko Libong, motorcycle taxis run across to the resorts on the western coast for 100B. A chartered long-tail directly to the resorts will cost 800B each way.

Tigerline (p335) links Ko Libong with Lanta (1050B, 2½ hours) and Lipe (1050B, 2½ hours).

Ko Lao Liang เกาะเหลาเลียง

Ko Lao Liang is actually two islands right next to each other: Ko Lao Liang Nong is the smaller of the two and is where you'll find the only resort. Ko Lao Liang Pi is the larger island; there's a small fishing settlement here. The islands are stunning vertical karst formations with small white-sand beaches, clear water and plenty of coral close to shore.

The only place to stay is the rock climbing-oriented **Laoliang Island Resort** (☎08 4304 4077; www.laoliangresort.com; per person 1000-1700B). Lodging is in comfy tents equipped with mattresses and fans, right on the beach, and there are plenty of activities on offer, including snorkelling, climbing the islands' karst cliffs and sea kayaking. At night there's a small bar and the restaurant fires up its seafood barbecue regularly – it's like summer camp for grown-ups (although the kids are happy, too). Rates include all meals, snorkel gear and sea kayaks.

If organised in advance, **Tigerline** (☎08 1092 8800; www.tigerlinetravel.com) stops just off Ko Lao Liang between Lanta (1050B, 2½ hours) and Lipe (1050B, 2½ hours).

Ko Sukorn เกาะสุกร

Sukorn is a cultural paradise of tawny beaches, light-green sea, black-rock headlands shrouded in jungle, and stilted shack neighbourhoods home to about 2800 Muslim inhabitants, whose rice fields, watermelon plots and rubber plantations unfurl along narrow concrete roads. Bike past fields occupied only by water buffalo, through pastel villages where folks are genuinely happy to see you and sleep soundly through deep, black nights. Sukorn's simple stillness is breathtaking, its authenticity a tonic to the jaded, road-weary soul.

With few hills, stunning panoramas, lots of shade and plenty of opportunities to meet locals, renting a bike (150B) is the best way to see the island. Please be respectful of local culture and cover up when you leave the beach.

Sleeping

Sukorn Cabana BUNGALOWS $$
(☎08 9724 2326; www.sukorncabana.com; Ko Sukorn; bungalows 800-1500B; ❄@) Sloping landscaped grounds dotted with papaya, frangipani and bougainvillea hold large,

REMARKABLE RUBBER TREES

If you ever wondered where the bounce in your rubber comes from, wonder no further: unlike money, it grows on trees. All over the Trang region, particularly on the islands floating off its coast, you are likely to come across rubber-tree plantations.

Rubber trees produce the milky liquid known as latex in vessels that grow within the bark of the tree. The trees are 'tapped' by making a thin incision into the bark at an angle parallel with the latex vessels (note that latex isn't the tree's sap). A small cup collects the latex as it drips down the tree. New scores are made every day – you can see these notched trees and collection cups throughout the region.

Latex from multiple trees is collected, poured into flat pans and mixed with formic acid, which serves as a coagulant. After a few hours, the very wet sheets of rubber are wrung out by squishing them through a press. They're then hung out to dry. You'll see these large, yellowish pancakes drying on bamboo poles wherever rubber trees are grown. The gooey ovals are then shipped to processing plants where they are turned into rubber as we know it.

clean bungalows with thatched roofs, varnished wood interiors and plush verandahs. The gorgeous beach has stunning views over Ko Phetra.

★**Sukorn Beach Bungalows** HOTEL $$
(☎08 1647 5550, 0 7520 7707; www.sukorn-island-trang.com; Ko Sukorn; bungalows 1000-2200B; ❄📶) Easily the most professionally run place on this island. The concrete-and-wood bungalows all have comfy verandahs and a long swimming beach out the front, from which you can watch the sun set over outlying islands. The friendly Dutch and Thai owners are chock-full of information, arrange excellent island-hopping tours and offer guided tours of Sukorn (per person 400B).

Oh, and the food (mains 85B to 300B) is the best in the Trang Islands. If you land here during the monsoon season, look for the break close to the beach – you just may see a dolphin show.

Getting There & Away

The easiest way to get to Sukorn is by private transfers from Trang, arranged through your resort (1850B per person). The cheapest way is to take a *sŏrng·tăa·ou* from Trang to Yan Ta Khao (80B, 40 minutes), then transfer to Ban Ta Seh (50B, 45 minutes), where long-tails (50B) leave the pier when full.

Otherwise, book a private taxi or *sŏrng·tăa·ou* from Trang to Ban Ta Seh (800B), where you can charter a long-tail to Ban Saimai (300B), the main village on Ko Sukorn. The resorts are a 20-minute walk or 50B motorcycle-taxi ride from Ban Saimai. You can also charter long-tails directly to the beach resorts (750B).

From Ko Sukorn you can charter long-tails to meet the high-speed **Tigerline** (☎08 1092 8800; www.tigerlinetravel.com) ferry that connects Lanta with Lipe.

SATUN PROVINCE

Until recently, Satun was mostly overlooked, but that's all changed thanks to the dynamic white sands of Ko Lipe – a one-time backpacker secret turned mainstream beach getaway. Beyond Ko Lipe, the rest of the province passes by in the blink of an eye as visitors rush north to Ko Lanta or south to Pulau Langkawi in Malaysia. Which means, of course, that they miss the untrammelled beaches and sea caves on Ko Tarutao, the rugged trails and ribbon waterfalls of Ko Adang and the rustic beauty of Ko Bulon Leh.

Largely Muslim in make-up, Satun has seen little of the political turmoil that plagues the neighbouring regions of Yala, Pattani and Narathiwat. Around 60% of people here speak Yawi or Malay as a first language, and the few wát in the region are quite humble and vastly outnumbered by mosques.

Satun สตูล

POP 33,720

Lying in a steamy jungle valley surrounded by limestone cliffs and framed by a murky river, isolated Satun is a surprisingly bustling little city – the focal point of a province home to a quarter million people. Malaysia-based yachties, passing through for cheap repairs in Satun's acclaimed boat yard, are the only travellers who seem to hang around, but if you wander a bit before you leave, you'll see some interesting religious architecture, lots of friendly smiles and plenty of gritty charm.

Sights & Activities

Ku Den Museum MUSEUM
(Satun National Museum; Soi 5, Th Satun Thanee; admission 20B; ⏲8.30am-4.30pm Wed-Sun) Housed in an old Sino-Portuguese mansion, this excellent museum was constructed to house King Rama V during a royal visit, but the governor snagged the roost when the king failed to show up. The building has been restored and the exhibits feature dioramas with soundtracks covering every aspect of southern Muslim life.

Monkey Mountain WALK
This jungled mound of limestone, teeming with primates, winds around **Spirit Rock**, a kitschy but locally beloved Buddhist shrine. You can also walk over a bridge here to stroll through a stilted fishing village just a kilometre west of town.

Mangrove Walk WALK
A self-guided walk along a boardwalk with a river viewpoint behind the football stadium. It's especially popular at sunset.

Sleeping

On's Guesthouse GUESTHOUSE $$
(☎0 7472 4133; 36 Th Burivanich; r with/without bathroom 750/650B) Satun's dynamic tourism matriarch, On, has redone an old downtown

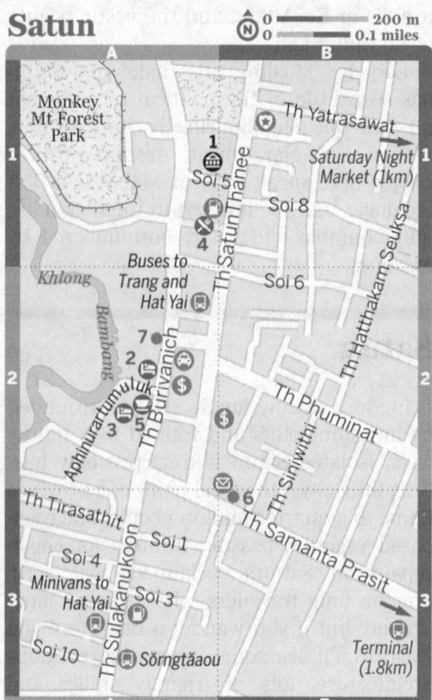

Satun

Sights
1 Ku Den Museum A1

Sleeping
2 On's Guesthouse A2
3 Sinkiat Buri Hotel A2

Eating
4 Night Markets A1
The Kitchen .... (see 2)

Drinking & Nightlife
5 On's, The Living Room A2

Information
6 CAT Office B3
7 Immigration Office A2

shophouse and turned it into a sparkling and affordable guest house with spacious rooms featuring wood furnishings, cute end tables and desks and other homey touches. The 2nd-floor room has a private bath and good wi-fi connectivity. Cheaper rooms on the 3rd floor share a bath.

Sinkiat Buri Hotel HOTEL $$
(☎0 7472 1055; www.sinkiathotel.com; 20 Th Aphinurartumuluk; r with/without breakfast 1200/1400B; ❄📶🏊) Just five months old at research time, rooms are fresh and bright with granite desktops and wood floors, air-con and wooden wardrobes, rain-shower heads and flat screens. It's new, modern and a welcome addition.

Eating & Drinking

Quick and cheap Chinese and Muslim restaurants can be found on Th Burivanich and Th Samanta Prasit. The Chinese food stalls specialise in *kôw mŏo daang* (red pork with rice), while the Muslim restaurants offer roti with southern-style chicken curry (around 50B each). Satun also has a fun **wet market** (6am-noon) in a warehouse-like shelter by the riverside with great Thai breakfast stalls and an array of seafood and meat for sale along with chilli, spices, fruits and Thai sweets. It's a wonderful neighbourhood scene.

Night Markets MARKET $
(Th Satun Thanee) There are some excellent night markets in Satun. The daily market begins just north of Satun Tanee Hotel, comes to life around 5pm, and serves delectable fried fish, squid skewers and spicy, southern-style curries. There's also a much larger Saturday night market on Th Burivanich and a Monday night market 1km from town on Th Yatrasawat.

The Kitchen THAI, INTERNATIONAL $$
(☎0 7472 4133; 36 Th Burivanich; mains 100-300B; ⌚8am-10pm; 📶) The ground-floor cafe in On's Guesthouse (p347) produces tasty pizzas and standard Thai mains, as well as popular steak dinners and a Thursday night poker game, frequented by visiting yachties and young expat English teachers. Don't tell them we told you.

On's, The Living Room CAFE, BAR
(☎0 7472 4133; 48 Th Burivanich; ⌚8am-late; 📶) With its bamboo tables, sarong-draped tables and leafy front porch, the original On's remains the place to hang out in Satun (which explains the yachtie bar flies). It also has the best travel information in town.

Information

Bangkok Bank (Th Burivanich) Has a foreign-exchange desk and an ATM.

CAT Office (Th Satun Thanee) The Communications Authority of Thailand (Telecom) office; same location as the post office.

Immigration Office (☎0 7471 1080; Th Burivanich; ⌚8.30am-4.30pm Mon-Fri) Handles visa issues and extensions for long termers. It's easier and cheaper for tourists to exit Thailand via the border checkpost at Tammalang pier and immediately re-enter to obtain a new 15-day tourist visa. You will need to catch the boat and enter Malaysia before you come back, however.

If you have wheels, hop the border in driveable Malaysia via Thale Ban National Park.

Post Office (cnr Th Satun Thanee & Th Samanta Prasit)

Siam Commercial Bank (Th Satun Thanee) Also has foreign exchange and an ATM.

Getting There & Away

BOAT

Boats to Malaysia leave from Tammalang pier, 7km south of Satun along Th Sulakanukoon. Large long-tail boats run daily at 9.30am and 4.30pm to Kuala Perlis in Malaysia (300B one-way, one hour). From Malaysia the fare is M$30.

For Pulau Langkawi in Malaysia, boats leave from Tammalang pier daily at 9.30am, 1.30pm and 4pm (300B, 1½ hours). In the reverse direction, boats leave from Pulau Langkawi at 8.30am, 12.30pm and 3pm and cost M$27. Keep in mind that there is a one-hour time difference between Thailand and Malaysia. You can buy boat tickets for these trips in Satun at the pier.

BUS

Buses leave from the **bus terminal** (Th Samanta Prasit), 2km east of the town centre. Air-con services to Bangkok (800B to 1200B, 14 hours) leave at 7am, 7.30am, 3pm and 4pm. Air-con buses to Trang (110B, 1½ hours) leave hourly. There are also a few daily buses to Krabi (220B, four hours) and Phuket (360B, seven hours). Buses to Hat Yai (70B, two hours) and local (no air-con) buses to Trang (90B, two hours) will stop and pick up passengers on Th Satun Thanee as they slowly make their way north.

MINIVAN & SHARE TAXI

There are regular minivans to the train station in Hat Yai (80B, one hour) from a depot south of Wat Chanathipchaloem on Th Sulakanukoon. Occasional minivans run to Trang, but buses are much more frequent. If you're arriving by boat at Tammalang pier, there are direct air-con minivans to Hat Yai and Hat Yai airport (90B).

Getting Around

Small orange *sŏrng·tăa·ou* to Tammalang pier (for boats to Malaysia) cost 40B and leave from the 7-Eleven on Th Sulakanukoon 40 minutes before ferry departure. A motorcycle taxi from the same area costs 60B.

Around Satun

Pak Bara ปากบารา

The small fishing community of Pak Bara is the main jumping-off point for the islands in the Mu Ko Phetra and Ko Tarutao Marine National Parks. Tourist facilities are slowly improving as Pak Bara becomes increasingly busy with tourists discovering these dazzling isles. The peaceful town has forgettable sleeping options, and, aside from the great seafood, there's no pressing reason to stick around.

The main road from La-Ngu terminates at the pier where there are several travel agencies, internet cafes, cheap restaurants and shops selling beach gear. There's a brand-new, huge **visitors centre** (☎0 7478 3485) for Ko Tarutao Marine National Park just back from the pier, which is really more of a massive passenger waiting terminal for Lipe- and Tarutao- bound speedboats. You can book Tarutao accommodation and obtain permission for camping here as well. Local travel agencies can also arrange tours to the islands in the national parks.

Tours

There are several travel agencies near the pier that will vie for your attention. **Adang Seatours** (☎0 7478 3338; www.adangseatour.com) is one of the more reliable agencies and also has an ATM. **My Friend Travel** (☎08 9974 7267, 08 1766 8640) is another reliable source for speedboat bookings. Shop around for kayaking day trips through the impressive caves at **Tham Chet Khok** (per person incl lunch 1800B).

During the high season, the **Satun Pakbara Speedboat Club** (☎0 7478 3643; www.tarutaolipeisland.com) runs speedboat tours to Ko Tarutao, Ko Bulon Leh and Ko Lipe – visit the website for the latest details.

Sleeping & Eating

There are several elementary restaurants and vendors near the Pak Bara pier that serve good Malay Muslim food for 40B to 80B. There's also a series of tasty seafood stalls along the coast south of town that get smoking just before sunset. They're a popular local hang-out on Sundays.

Best House Resort BUNGALOWS **$$**
(☎08 1189 6906; www.besthouseresort.com; bungalows 590-690B; P ❄ 🛜) This place is 100m

inland from the pier and has tidy concrete bungalows around a murky pond. Management is pleased to offer travel tips.

Red Boat THAI, INTERNATIONAL $
(☎0 7478 3498; dishes 70-150B; ⏰7am-11pm; 📶) Stop here while waiting for your ferry. Red Boat does Western breakfasts, espresso drinks, cocktails and tasty fried prawns in tamarind sauce.

Getting There & Away

BUSES

There are hourly buses between 7am and 4pm from Hat Yai to the pier at Pak Bara (100B, 2½ hours). Coming from Satun, you can take an ordinary bus towards Trang and get off at La-Ngu (70B, 30 minutes), continuing by *sŏrng·tăa·ou* to Pak Bara (20B, 15 minutes).

MINIVANS

Air-con minivans leave hourly for Hat Yai (150B, two hours) from travel agencies near Pak Bara pier. There are also minivans to Trang (200B, 1½ hours), which connect to numerous destinations such as Krabi (450B, four hours) and Phuket (650B, six hours).

BOATS

From 21 October to the end of May there are several speedboats to Ao Pante Malacca on Ko Tarutao and on to Ko Lipe. Boats depart from Pak Bara at 11.30am, 2.30pm, 3pm and sometimes 5pm (return 1300B, one hour); in the reverse direction boats leave from Ko Lipe at 9.30am and 1.30pm only. From 16 November these boats also stop at Ko Adang for the same price. For Ko Bulon Leh, boats depart at 12.30pm, arriving in Ko Bulon Leh one hour later (return 800B), before buzzing on to Ko Lipe. If you miss the Bulon boat, you can easily charter a long-tail from local fishermen (2000B, 1½ hours). During the wet season, services to Ko Lipe are weather and demand dependent, but generally operate daily. All boats depart from the new national park office.

Ko Bulon Leh เกาะบุโหลนเล

This pretty island, 23km west of Pak Bara, is surrounded by the Andaman's signature clear waters and has its share of faultless beaches with swaying casuarinas. Gracious Ko Bulon Leh is in that perfect phase of being developed enough to offer comfortable facilities, yet not so popular that you have to book beach time days in advance.

The exceptional white-sand **beach** extends along the east coast from Bulone resort, on the northeast cape, to Pansand. In places the beach narrows a bit, especially where buffered by gnarled mangroves and strewn with thick sun-bleached logs. But those nooks and crannies make it easy to find your own secret shady spot with dreamy views.

Bulon's lush interior is interlaced with a few tracks and trails that are fun to explore, though the dense, jungled rock that makes up the western half remains inaccessible on foot. Bulon's wild beauty is accessible on the southern coast at **Ao Panka Yai**, which is blue and laden with coral gravel. There's good snorkelling around the western headland, and if you follow the trails through remnant jungle and rubber plantations – with eyes open wide lest you miss one of Bulon's enormous monitor lizards – you'll wind your way to **Ao Muang**, where you'll find an authentic *chow lair* squid-fishing camp. **Ao Panka Noi** is another fishing village with long-tails docking on a fine gravel beach. Here you'll find beautiful karst views and a clutch of simple but very good restaurants.

Resorts can arrange snorkelling trips (2000B, four hours) to other islands in the Ko Bulon group for a maximum of six people, and fishing trips for 400B per hour. Trips usually take in the glassy emerald waters of **Ko Gai** and **Ko Ma**, whose gnarled rocks have been ravaged by wind and time. But the most stunning sight has to be **White Rock** – bird-blessed spires rising out of the open sea. Beneath the surface is a rock reef crusted with mussels and teeming with colourful fish. Snorkelling is best at low tide. The area's best coral reef is off Laem Son near Bulone Resort, where you can rent masks, snorkels (100B), fins (70B) and kayaks (200B).

Bulone Resort also offers internet (per minute 3B), and battery-charging services for laptops (50B) and digital cameras (10B).

Sleeping & Eating

Most places here shut down in the low season. Those that persevere rent out bungalows at discount rates. For eating, it's worth hiking over to Ao Panka Noi.

There are a few local restaurants and a small shop in the Muslim village next to Bulon Viewpoint.

Marina Resort HOTEL $
(☎08 5078 1552, 08 1598 2420; bungalows 1000B) Log-built and shaggy with stilted decks, louvred floors and high ceilings, thatched

huts never looked or felt so good. There's a tasty kitchen attached to an inviting patio restaurant with cushioned floor seating. The ever-gracious Max will be your wise-guy host. The resort arranges speedboat tickets and snorkelling tours. It's located just inland from Pansand resort.

Bulon Hill Resort BUNGALOWS **$$**
(☎08 6960 3890, 08 0709 8453; www.bulonhill.com; bungalows 1000-1500B) A collection of decent, spacious wooden bungalows and smaller bamboo ones stilted on the hill just inland from Bulone Resort. They are only open in high season.

Pansand Resort RESORT **$$**
(☎0 7521 1010; www.pansand-resort.com; cottages from 1800B; @) Pansand sits on the south end of the island's gorgeous white-sand beach. Brick-and-bamboo bungalows are fan cooled and come with sea views. The actual lodging isn't any better than elsewhere on the island – you're paying for a sublime location and a larger, organised resort setting. Cheaper wooden bungalows are set back in the trees.

Bulone Resort HOTEL **$$**
(☎08 6960 0468; www.bulone-resort.com; bungalows 2500-3500B) Perched on the northeast cape with access to two exquisite stretches of white sand, these cute wooden and bamboo bungalows have the best beachside location on Bulon. Queen-sized beds come with iron frames and ocean breezes. It has electricity all night and serves up a tremendous mango smoothie with honey, lime and fresh yoghurt.

Getting There & Away

The boat to Ko Bulon Leh (450B) leaves from Pak Bara at 12.30pm daily if there are enough takers. Ship-to-shore transfers to the beach by long-tail cost 50B – save yourself some sweat and ask to be dropped off on the beach closest to your resort. In the reverse direction, the boat moors in the bay in front of Pansand Resort at 9.30am. You can charter a long-tail from Pak Bara for 1500B to 2000B.

From November to May there is a daily speedboat (600B, one hour) from Ko Bulon Leh to Ko Lipe in Ko Tarutao Marine National Park. Boats, which originate in Ko Lanta and make stops in the Trang Islands, depart from in front of the Pansand Resort at 3pm. It returns from Lipe at 9am.

Ko Tarutao Marine National Park

อุทยานแห่งชาติหมู่เกาะตะรุเตา

One of the most exquisite and unspoilt regions in all of Thailand, **Ko Tarutao Marine National Park** (☎0 7478 1285; adult/child 400/200B; ⏲Nov–mid-May) encompasses 51 islands covered with well-preserved virgin rainforest teeming with fauna and surrounded by healthy coral reefs and radiant beaches.

One of the first marine national parks in Thailand, the main accommodations in the park are small, ecofriendly government-run cabins and longhouses. Pressure from big developers to build resorts on the islands has so far (mostly) been ignored, though concessions were made for the filming of the American reality-TV series *Survivor* in 2001. And there is the minor issue of a private fishing resort on Ko Adang, which is supposed to be off-limits to developers. It was originally slated to open in 2010, but local environmentalists have appealed to the Thai courts to keep it shuttered.

Rubbish on the islands can be a problem – removal of beach and visitor rubbish only happens sporadically. Do your part and tread lightly. Within the park, you can spot dusky langurs, crab-eating macaques, mouse deer, wild pigs, sea otters, fishing cats, tree pythons, water monitors, Brahminy kites, sea eagles, hornbills and kingfishers.

Ko Tarutao is the biggest and second-most visited island in the group. It's home to the park headquarters and government accommodation. Note that there are no foreign-exchange facilities at Ko Tarutao – you can change cash and travellers cheques at travel agencies in Pak Bara and there's an ATM at La-Ngu.

Many travellers choose to stay on Ko Lipe which, despite being part of the park, is fast becoming a popular and increasingly paved resort island with tourist facilities and bungalows aplenty. Curiously, the island has managed to evade the park's protection because it is home to communities of *chow lair* (sea gypsy) people, making it exempt from zero development laws.

Long-tail tours to outlying islands can be arranged through travel agencies in Satun or Pak Bara, through the national park headquarters on Ko Tarutao, or through resorts and long-tail boat operators on Ko Lipe.

Ko Tarutao เกาะตะรุเตา

Most of Ko Tarutao's whopping 152 sq km is covered in old-growth jungle, which rises sharply up to the park's 713m peak. Mangrove swamps and typically impressive limestone cliffs circle much of the island, and the western coast is pocked with caves and lined with quiet white-sand beaches. This is one of Thailand's wildest islands. The park entrance fee, payable on arrival, is 200B.

Tarutao's sordid history partly explains its preservation. Between 1938 and 1948, more than 3000 Thai criminals and political prisoners were incarcerated here, including interesting inmates such as So Setabutra, who compiled the first Thai–English dictionary while imprisoned on Tarutao, and Sittiporn Gridagon, son of Rama VII. During WWII, food and medical supplies from the mainland were severely depleted and hundreds of prisoners died from malaria. The prisoners and guards mutinied, taking to piracy in the nearby Strait of Malacca until they were suppressed by British troops in 1944.

Sights & Activities

The overgrown ruins of the camp for political prisoners can be seen at **Ao Taloh Udang**, in the southeast of the island, reached via a long overgrown track. The prison camp for civilian prisoners was over on the eastern coast at **Ao Taloh Waw**, where the big boats from Satun's Tammalang pier now dock.

Next to the park headquarters at Ao Pante Malacca, a steep trail leads through the jungle below a limestone karst dripping with precipitation, and up a series of steps that have been chiselled from the stone to the top of **Toe-Boo Cliff**, a dramatic rocky outcrop with fabulous views towards Ko Adang and the surrounding islands.

Ao Pante Malacca has a lovely alabaster beach shaded by pandanus and casuarinas. If you follow the large stream flowing inland, you'll reach **Tham Jara-Khe** (Crocodile Cave), once home to deadly saltwater crocodiles. The cave is navigable for about 1km at low tide and can be visited on longtail tours from the jetty at Ao Pante Malacca.

Immediately south of Ao Pante Malacca is **Ao Jak**, which has another fine sandy beach, and **Ao Molae**, which also has fine white sand and a ranger station with bungalows and a camp site. A 30-minute boat ride or 8km walk south of Ao Pante is **Ao Son**, an isolated bay where turtles nest between September and April. You can camp here but there are no facilities. Ao Son has decent snorkelling, as does **Ao Makham** further south. From the small ranger station at Ao Son you can walk inland to **Lu Du Falls** (about 1½ hours) and **Lo Po Falls** (about 2½ hours).

Sleeping & Eating

There's accommodation both at Ao Pante Malacca and Ao Molae, open mid-November to mid-May. Water is rationed, rubbish is (sporadically) transported back to the mainland, lighting is provided by power-saving lightbulbs and electricity is available between 6pm and 7am only.

The biggest spread of options is at Ao Pante Malacca, conveniently near all the facilities, where there are **bungalows** (800-1000B), simple **longhouse rooms** (550B) sleeping up to four people with shared bathrooms, and **camp sites** (with/without tent rental 375/150B).

Ao Molae is quieter, much more isolated and arguably prettier. But that's splitting hairs. Basic and reasonably clean (but not spotless) one- and two-room **duplexes** (r 600-1000B) are right on the beach. Accommodation can be booked at the **park office** (☎0 7478 3485) in Pak Bara. National park entry fees can be paid at Ao Pante Malacca or Ao Taloh Waw.

Camping is also permitted under casuarinas at Ao Molae and Ao Taloh Waw, where there are toilet and shower blocks, and on the wild beaches of Ao Son, Ao Makham and Ao Taloh Udang, where you will need to be self-sufficient. The cost is 30B per person with your own tent, or you can hire tents for 225B. Camping is also permitted on Ko Adang and other islands in the park. Note that local monkeys have a habit of going into tents and destroying or eating everything they find inside – so shut everything tight.

The park authorities run **canteens** (dishes 40-120B; ⏰7am-2pm & 5-9pm) at Ao Pante Malacca and Ao Molae. The food is satisfying, but you can find beer only at Ao Molae.

Getting There & Around

Boats connecting Pak Bara and Ko Lipe stop at Ko Tarutao (450B each way, at least four times daily). Oddly, though, only the 9.30am boat directly from Lipe drops passengers at Tarutao. The island officially closes from the end of May to 15 September. Regular boats run from 21 October to the end of May. During the high season,

Ko Tarutao National Park & Around

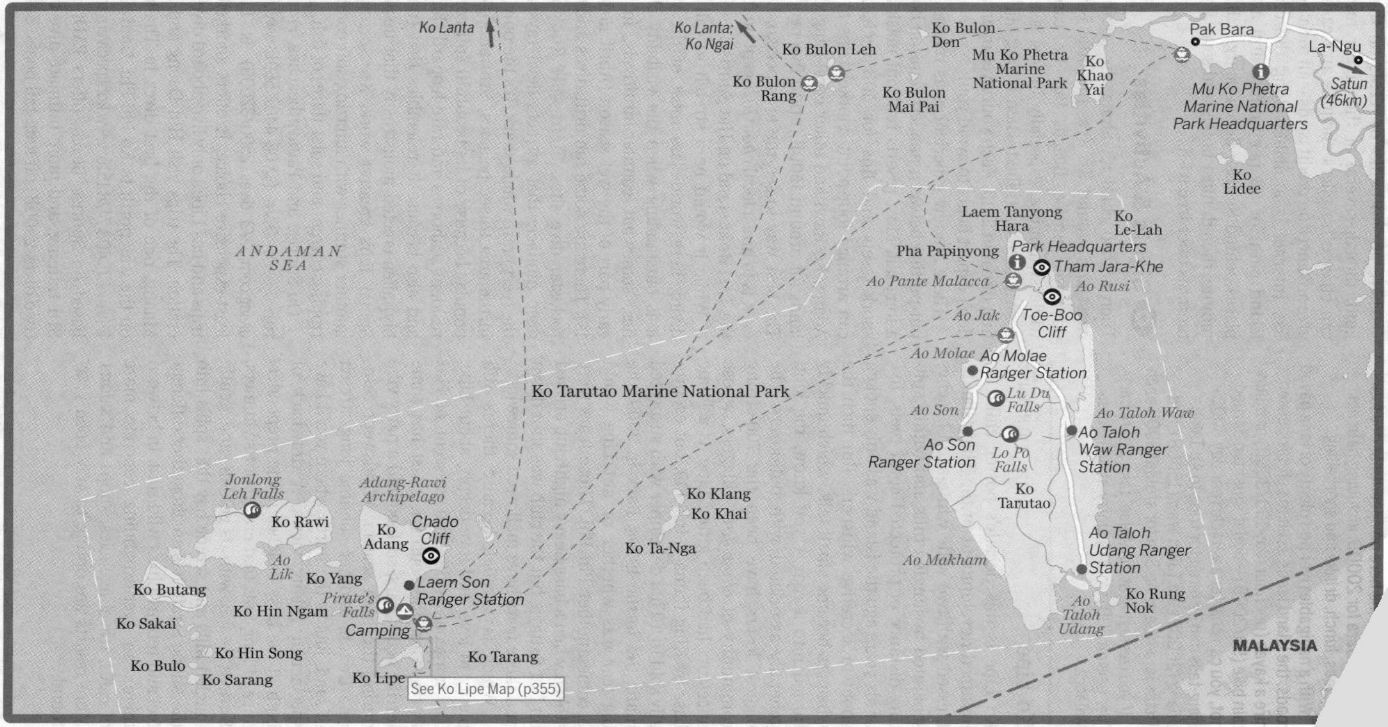

0 — 10 km
0 — 5 miles

Ko Lanta
Ko Lanta; Ko Ngai
Ko Bulon Leh
Ko Bulon Rang
Ko Bulon Don
Ko Bulon Mai Pai
Mu Ko Phetra Marine National Park
Ko Khao Yai
Pak Bara
La-Ngu
Satun (46km)
Mu Ko Phetra Marine National Park Headquarters
Ko Lidee
ANDAMAN SEA
Laem Tanyong Hara
Ko Le-Lah
Pha Papinyong
Park Headquarters
Tham Jara-Khe
Ao Pante Malacca
Ao Rusi
Ao Jak
Toe-Boo Cliff
Ao Molae
Ao Molae Ranger Station
Ko Tarutao Marine National Park
Lu Du Falls
Ao Son
Ao Taloh Waw
Ao Son Ranger Station
Lo Po Falls
Ao Taloh Waw Ranger Station
Ko Tarutao
Jonlong Leh Falls
Adang-Rawi Archipelago
Ko Klang
Ko Khai
Ko Rawi
Ko Adang
Chado Cliff
Ko Ta-Nga
Ao Taloh Udang Ranger Station
Ao Makham
Ao Lik
Ko Yang
Laem Son Ranger Station
Ko Rung Nok
Ko Butang
Pirate's Falls
Ko Hin Ngam
Ao Taloh Udang
Ko Sakai
Camping
Ko Hin Song
Ko Tarang
MALAYSIA
Ko Bulo
Ko Lipe
Ko Sarang

See Ko Lipe Map (p355)

…on speedboat day tours …0B, including national …ks and snorkelling.

…river and plenty of long paved …lends itself to self-propulsion: …per hour/day 100/300B) or moun-…0/200B) – or if it's just too darned …an charter a vehicle (per day 600B). Lon…ils can be hired for trips to Ao Taloh Udang (2000B), Ao Taloh Waw (1500B), and Tham Jara-Khe or Ao Son for around 800B each.

If you're staying at Ao Molae, take a park car (per person 60B) from the jetty at Ao Pante Malacca.

Ko Lipe เกาะหลีเป๊ะ

Ko Lipe is this decade's poster child for untamed development in the Thai Islands. Blessed with two wide white-sand beaches separated by jungled hills and within spitting distance of protected coral reefs, five or six years ago the island was only spoken about in secretive whispers. But then the whispers became small talk, which quickly turned into a roar – you know, the kind generally associated with bulldozers. The biggest losers have been the 700-strong community of *chow lair* villagers, whose ancestors had been gifted Lipe as a home base by King Rama V in 1909, but eventually sold to a Thai developer with suspected mafia ties in the 1970s. Back in 2009, the big fear was whether or not Lipe would become another Phi Phi. Those fears were stoked when a bass heavy nightclub arrived on Hat Pattaya, but the club was shut down and those fears have mellowed somewhat.

Which is a relief, because there's still plenty to love, and love deeply, about Lipe. The gorgeous white-sand crescent of **Hat Pattaya** on the southern coast has some terrific beach bars, seafood and a party vibe during the high season. Windswept **Sunrise Beach**, another sublime long stretch of sand, juts to the north where you'll have spectacular Adang views. A drawback of both of the busy beaches is the preponderance of long-tails that crowd out swimmers. **Sunset Beach**, with its golden sand, gentle jungled hills and serene bay that spills into the Adang Strait, has an altogether different feel and retains Lipe's wild soul. In between there's an ever-expanding concrete maze of cafes, travel agencies, shops and salons. More resorts are opting to stay open year-round.

There are no banks or ATMs on the island, though several of the bigger resorts can change travellers cheques and cash or give advances on credit cards – all for a hefty fee. Internet is available along the cross-island path for 3B per minute and a few places behind Sunrise Beach charge 2B per minute, though most hotels and several restaurants offer free wi-fi.

Sights & Activities

There's good coral all along the southern coast and around **Ko Kra**, the little island opposite Sunrise Beach. But be careful while swimming, especially in low season. A swimmer was killed when a long-tail ran him down in 2013. Keep your eyes open and don't expect boats to avoid you!

There are few experiences as relaxing as put-putting between jungled gems on board a long-tail. Most resorts rent out mask and snorkel sets and fins for 50B each, and can arrange four-point snorkel trips to Ko Adang, Ko Rawi and other coral-fringed islands for around 1500B (up to five people). The best way to see the archipelago, however, is to hire a local *chow lair* captain from the **Taxi Boat** stand on Hat Sunrise.

While it would be a stretch to call the diving here world-class most of the year, it is outstanding when the visibility clarifies, somewhat counter-intuitively, in the early part of the wet season (April 15-June 15). There are some fun drift dives and two rock-star dive sites. **Eight Mile Rock** is a deep pinnacle that attracts devil rays and the (very) rare whale shark. It's the only site in the area to see pelagics. **Stonehenge** is popular because of its beautiful soft corals, resident seahorses and rare leopard sharks, and also because it resembles that (possibly) alien-erected monstrosity that inspired Spinal Tap's greatest work. **Ko Sorong** is another stunner with amazing soft corals, a ripping current and solar flares of fish.

On Sunrise and Pattaya beaches, French-run **Forra Dive** (☎08 4407 5691; www.forradiving.com; 2/3 dives 2500/3200B) is Lipe's least-expensive choice. It offers snorkelling trips and has Lipe's only live-aboard dive operation. The trips visit Hin Daeng and Hin Muang, one of the best dives in Thailand on the way north to Ko Phi-Phi. **Castaway Divers** (☎08 7478 1516; www.kohlipedivers.com), based on Sunrise Beach, offers PADI and SDI training, and more intimate dive trips (two dives 2800B) off long-tail boats. **Sabye**

Ko Lipe

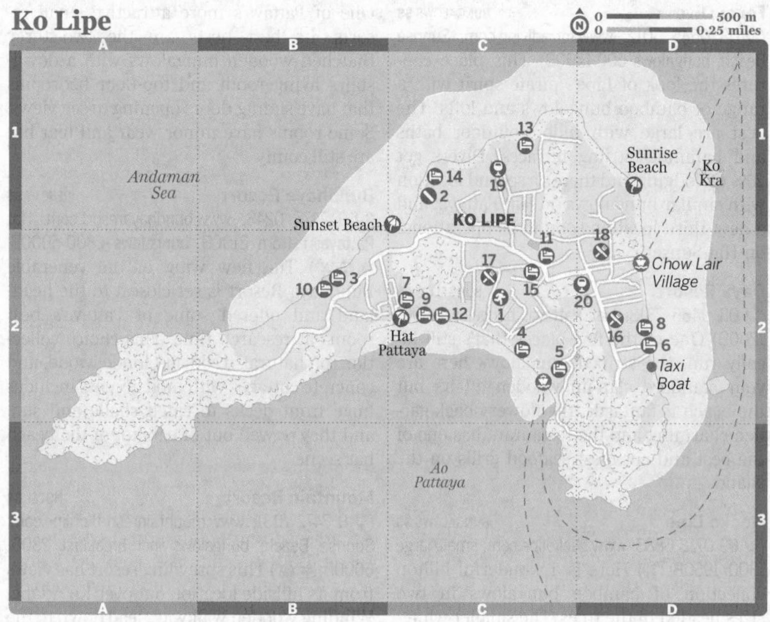

Divers (☎08 9464 5884; www.sabye-sports.com) is the small Greenfins-certified shop on Sunset Beach owned by a long-time expat.

While it may look inviting, do not try to swim the narrow strait between Lipe and Adang at any time of year. Currents are swift and can be deadly.

After all that activity, you may need a little recovery time. That's when you should find Khun Rund at **Chao Shop Thai Massage** (300B). She may be small but she's powerful and an unassuming master of the traditional Thai massage art form.

Or if you'd rather stretch and twist under your own power, head to Gecko Lipe (p356) for their twice-daily yoga classes under the trees (classes at 6.45am & 7.30pm; non-guests 300-400B)

Sleeping

More and more resorts on Ko Lipe are staying open year round. Book well ahead during high season and around Thai holidays. On Lipe, progress means big charmless package-tour type resorts are colonising Hat Pattaya in a big way. There are still a few collections of humble bamboo bungalows on that beach, but they are disappearing rapidly.

Ko Lipe

Activities, Courses & Tours

- Castaway Divers ....(see 6)
- 1 Chao Shop Thai Massage C2
- Forra Dive ....(see 8)
- 2 Sabye Divers C1

Sleeping

- 3 Bila Beach B2
- 4 Blue Tribes C2
- 5 Bundhaya Resort C2
- 6 Castaway Resort D2
- 7 Daya Resort C2
- 8 Forra Dive D2
- 9 Forra Dive 2 ....C2
- 10 Forra Dive 3 ....B2
- 11 Gecko Lipe C2
- 12 Mali Resort C2
- 13 Mountain Resort C1
- 14 Sunset Beach C1
- 15 The Box C2

Eating

- 16 Nee Papaya D2
- 17 Papaya Mom C2
- 18 Som Tam D2
- Zanom Sunrise ....(see 6)

Drinking & Nightlife

- 19 Home Bar C1
- 20 Pooh's Bar D2

Forra Dive BUNGALOWS $$
(☎08 0545 5012; www.forradiving.com; Sunrise Beach; bungalows 600-1400B) This place captures the look of Lipe's pirate spirit with a range of bamboo bungalows and lofts. The best are large with indoor-outdoor baths and hammock-strung terraces. Divers get 25% off lodging and there's a second location with similar bungalows on Hat Pattaya, and a new, third location soon to be operational on Hat Sunset.

Daya Resort BUNGALOWS $
(☎08 9466 7318; Hat Pattaya; bungalows 800-1200B) One of the few places that's still locally run, the striped bungalows here are your standard slap-up wooden affairs but the beach is fantastic, the flowery back garden charming and the restaurant has one of the best and cheapest seafood grills on the island.

Gecko Lipe BUNGALOWS $$
(☎09 0716 6883; www.geckolipe.com; small/large 1300/1950B; [wi-fi]) Here is a wonderful hilltop collection of bamboo bungalows in two sizes nestled in the trees. The smaller whitewashed varietal offers blonde floors and cold-water baths. The larger, shaggy-haired, golden-bamboo edition offers stylish hot-water baths and thicker mattresses. Expect deep discounts in the low season. They offer yoga classes here too.

Bila Beach BUNGALOWS $$
(☎08 7570 3684; www.bilabeach.com; Sunset Beach; bungalow 1500B) A killer bamboo reggae bar and beachfront restaurant lurk below stylish cliffside, shaggy-haired bungalows set above a tiny, private white-sand cove, which is strewn with boulders and adjacent to Sunset Beach. It's the perfect setting for your hippy honeymoon and a short jog over the hill from Pattaya.

Sunset Beach BUNGALOWS $$
(☎08 7479 5326; www.lipesunsetbeach.com; bungalows 1800B; [wi-fi]) Here's a refreshing collection of damn fine braided-bamboo bungalows with king beds, moulded concrete baths and shady front porches perched above the rocky far end of Hat Sunset, just before the curve to Mountain Resort. Book ahead and management will scoop you up in their deluxe off-road golf cart.

Blue Tribes HOTEL $$
(☎08 6285 2153; www.bluetribeslipe.com; Hat Pattaya; r/bungalows from 1700/2400B; [air-con][internet][wi-fi]) One of Pattaya's more attractive small resorts, its best nests are the two-storey thatched wooden bungalows with a downstairs living room and top-floor bedrooms that have sliding doors opening to sea views. Some rooms have minor wear and tear but are still comfy.

Bundhaya Resort RESORT $$
(☎0 7475 0248; www.bundhayaresort.com; Hat Pattaya; r from 2100B, bungalows 2800-5000B; [air-con][wi-fi][pool]) The new wing of the venerable Bundhaya Resort is set closest to the headland and offered some of Pattaya's best rooms at research time. This choice collection of natural, reddish-blonde wood and concrete cottages with mod accents includes huge front decks to catch shade and sun, and they're well out of earshot of the beach bar scene.

Mountain Resort HOTEL $$
(☎0 7472 8131; www.mountainresortkohlipe.com; Sunrise Beach; bungalows incl breakfast 2300-6000B; [air-con][internet]) This sprawling resort has views from its hillside location out over Ko Adang. Winding wooden walkways lead down to the sublime beach on Sunrise Beach's northern sand bar and there is a flashy new array of wooden bungalows and condo-like flats that are called villas, all with the expected mod cons and private lanai.

Their footprint is impressively compact and it's a rather stunning sight from the sea. Yes, they do cater to package tourists, but before you roll your eyes, check out their stretch of beach. Wow! Like, wow!

The Box HOTEL $$
(d 1200-2900B, family units 4600-5200B; [air-con][wi-fi]) An alluring boutique hotel crafted from shipping containers, dressed up in natural wood panelling and connected by wooden paths through the garden. Interiors are spare, simple and stylish with bamboo beds, accent walls and wooden wash basins.

Castaway Resort HOTEL $$$
(☎08 3138 7472; www.castaway-resorts.com; Sunrise Beach; bungalows 3500-5000B; [internet][wi-fi]) The Castaway's roomy wood bungalows with hammock-laden terraces, cushions everywhere, overhead fans and fabulous, modern-meets-natural bathrooms are among the most chic on Lipe. The resort is also one of the most environmentally friendly, with solar water heaters and lights. Cool room sleepers beware: it can get hot upstairs and that ceil-

ing fan isn't always strong enough to keep things comfortable.

Mali Resort RESORT $$$

(www.maliresortkohlipe.com; bungalows from 3800B) Chic and laid back, the gorgeous new bungalows at this rebranded, American-owned resort on Pattaya offer dark wood floors, thatched beamed ceilings, built-in day beds and huge outdoor baths with dual shower heads. There are also have older and more affordable garden cottages with plush linens and flat screens.

All offer access to the stunning beach bar – the best on the island bar none – and an ideal slab of Pattaya beachfront.

Eating & Drinking

Hat Pattaya's resorts put on fresh seafood barbecues nightly; Daya's is arguably the best. Cheap eats are best found at the roti stands and small Thai cafes along Walking Street, the main paved path.

Good coffee is the new thing on Lipe and there is an abundance of coffee shops sprinkled all over the island, most prominently on the walking street that links Pattaya and Sunrise. Almost all have free wi-fi.

Thankfully, driftwood-clad Rasta bars are still found on all beaches. At least some things never change.

★ **Nee Papaya** THAI $

(08 7714 5519; mains 80-200B; 8am-10pm;) Delightful Nee offers an affordable fish grill nightly, all the standard curries (including a dynamite *pá·naang* vegetable), noodles and stir fries with beef, chicken, seafood or veggie, as well as tremendous array of fiery Isan dishes. Ask for a *lâhp Ɓla*, one of her new off-the-menu specialities.

She will tone down the chilli quotient upon request, but her food is best when spiced for the local palate, which is why she attracts droves of Thai tourists, who know what good food is.

Papaya Mom THAI $

(mains 80-160B; 10am-10pm) Another cute Isan food stall between two beaches, notable for authentic eats popular with local Thais (grilled spicy pork neck, *lâhp*). Meat dishes are so varied and succulent they may make an omnivore out of even the least-conflicted vegan. Okay, maybe not. Vegans can raid the luscious fruit stand.

Som Tam CAFE $

(Sunrise Beach; dishes 20-50B) There was no name when we passed by, but this tiny cafe on the corner of Walking Street and the Sunrise Beach road serves fantastic *sôm·đam* with lip-smacking fried chicken – a perfect lunch.

Zanom Sunrise SEAFOOD $$

(08 7381 3494; www.facebook.com/zanomsunrise; dishes 80-150B, seafood 250-350B) While service is not always swift, it does come with a warm smile, and they have a tasty seafood grill, with local tuna, king prawns, snapper and more all lined up for the weighing and choosing. They also have decent-value wood and bamboo thatched bungalows (1200B) set back from the beach.

Home Bar BAR

(11am-10pm) An alluring ramshackle driftwood assemblage of a reggae bar that seems to have washed up and been pieced together by some supernatural jah love force in the banana tree hills above Hat Sunrise (translation: a lot of really high people burned the blueprint and devoted countless man hours here). It's more than a bar, it's a work of art.

Pooh's Bar BAR

(0 7472 8019; www.poohlipe.com; 7am-10pm;) This expansive complex was built by a Lipe pioneer and includes bungalows, a dive shop and several restaurants. It's a very popular local expat hang-out, especially in the low season. Each night it projects films onto its big screen, and there is live music on weekends.

Getting There & Away

From 21 October through to the end of May, several speedboats run from Pak Bara to Ko Lipe via Ko Tarutao or Ko Bulon Leh at 9.30am, 11am, 12.30pm and 2pm (550B to 650B, 1½ hours); in the reverse direction boats leave at 9.30am, 10am and 1.30pm. Low-season transport depends on the weather, but there are usually three direct boats per week. A boat charter to Ko Lipe from Pak Bara is a hefty 4000B each way.

Tigerline (08 1092 8800; www.tigerline-travel.com) offers the cheapest high-speed ferry service to Ko Lanta (1700B, five hours), stopping at Ko Muk (1600B, 3½ hours), Ko Kradan (1800B, 3½ hours) and Ko Ngai (1600B, four hours). It departs from Ko Lipe at 9.30am. You'll net up to 20% discounts when booked online.

The daily and more comfortable **Satun-Pak Bara Speedboat Club** (08 2433 0114, 0 7475 0389; www.tarutaolipeisland.com) speedboat departs from Ko Lipe for Ko Lanta (1900B, three hours) at 9am, stopping at Ko Bulon Leh (600B, one hour), Ko Muk (1400B, two hours) and Ko Ngai (1600B, 2½ hours). The same boat makes the return trip from Ko Lanta at 1pm.

Both of these speedboats also offer daily trips to Pulau Langkawi (1400B, one hour) in Malaysia; departure is at 7.30am, 10.30am and 4pm. Be at the immigration office at the Bundhaya Resort early to get stamped out. In reverse, boats leave from Pulau Langkawi for Ko Lipe at 7.30am, 9.30am and 2.30pm Malay time.

No matter which boat you end up deciding to use, you will have to take a long-tail shuttle (per person 50B) to and from the floating pier at the edge of the bay. Yes, it's a minor inconvenience, but it's also part of a local agreement to share the flow. Though it's really more of a trickle.

Ko Adang & Ko Rawi

เกาะอาดัง/เกาะราวี

The island immediately north of Ko Lipe, Ko Adang has brooding, densely forested hills, white-sand beaches and healthy coral reefs. Snorkelling tours generally stop on a cordoned-off slice of Adang that's about 100m long with decent snorkelling. Inland are a few short jungle trails and tumbling waterfalls, including the ramble up to **Pirate's Falls**, which is rumoured to have been a freshwater source for pirates (and is more of a cascading river than a waterfall). There are great views from **Chado Cliff** above the main beach, where green turtles lay their eggs between September and December.

Ko Rawi, a long, rocky, jungled ellipse 11km west of Ko Adang, has first-rate beaches and large coral reefs offshore. Camping at Ao Lik is allowed, with permission from the national park authorities. Excellent snorkelling spots include the northern side of **Ko Yang** and tiny **Ko Hin Ngam**, which has underwater fields of giant clams, vibrant anemones and striped pebble beaches. Legend has it that the stones are cursed and anyone who takes one away will experience bad luck until the stone is returned to its source. There is a small restaurant here, but bring your lunch from Lipe, where it's cheaper and (much) tastier. Even a short stop on the island will cost you the park's entrance fee (adult/child 200/100B).

Park accommodation on Ko Adang is located near the ranger station at Laem Son. There are new and attractive **bungalows** (3-9 people 600-1800B), scruffier **longhouses** (3-bed dm 300B) with attached bathrooms, and facilities for **camping** (sites per person 30B, with tent hire 250B). A small restaurant provides good Thai meals.

Long-tails from Ko Lipe will take you to Ko Adang and Ko Rawi for 50B to 100B per person, although you might have to do a bit of bargaining.

Understand Thailand's Islands & Beaches

Thailand's Islands & Beaches Today

Thailand continues to ride the wave of prosperity from increased business, tourism and development. The standard and cost of living have increased, the coming ASEAN Economic Community (AEC) promises increased business opportunities and tourism has discovered a new influx of visitors from China. Thailand's relations with its neighbours, especially once cloistered Myanmar, have never been better. And the cities continue to modernise, with fashionable shopping centres filled with cafes and boutiques replacing soot-stained shophouses.

Top Books

Very Thai (Philip Cornwell-Smith) Colourful photos and essays on Thailand's quirks.

Chronicle of Thailand (William Warren) History of the last 50 years.

King Bhumibol Adulyadej: A Life's Work (Nicholas Grossman et al.) Official biography of the king.

Top Films

Uncle Boonmee Who Can Recall His Past Lives (Apichatpong Weerasethakul; 2010) Winner of Cannes 2010 Palm d'Or.

Paradoxocracy (Pen-ek Ratanaruang; 2013) Traces the country's political history from the 1932 revolution to today.

OK Baytong (2007) Touches on the violence between the Thais and Muslims.

Top News Analysis Sites

The Diplomat (thediplomat.com) Current affairs magazine covering Asia Pacific.

New Mandala (asiapacific.anu.edu.au/newmandala) Commentary on news, society and culture in Southeast Asia.

Asia Times Online (atimes.com) Respected Southeast Asia reporting.

The Post Coup Years

Though Thaksin Shinawatra was removed from the prime minister's position by a military coup in 2006 and later fled the country to avoid a gaol term, he still exerts a strong gravitational pull on Thailand's political process. Thaksin's politically allied party, Puea Thai, won a majority of parliamentary seats in 2011, when his sister Yingluck Shinawatra was elected as Thailand's first female prime minister. This is the fifth straight electoral win for a Thaksin-backed political party. She is often viewed as a proxy for her brother, and Thais rarely distinguish between the two. Despite the unusual balance of power, Yingluck's administration has brought about a degree of political unity with the military.

The Shinawatra dynasty still polarises Thai society. The legislature has spent two years debating the details of the so-called amnesty bill, which would allow Thaksin to return to the country by absolving him of criminal charges, which he is evading through self-imposed exile. The bill also provides amnesty for those found guilty of wrongdoing in the 2010 military crackdown on Red Shirt activists; these include members of the military and even then–prime minister Abhisit Vejjajiva. The unpopularity of the extension of amnesty to the 'other' side shows a potential rift between Thaksin's political party (Puea Thai) and his grassroots supporters (Red Shirts; also known as the United Front of Democracy Against Dictatorship). As such it is unpopular with both ends of the political spectrum, although popular with Thaksin sympathisers. Thais in the political middle are fatigued from the political discord, which undermines a deep-seated sense of a unified 'Thai-ness' and a cultural aversion to displays of violence and anger.

Tensions mounted in protests against Yingluck at the end of 2013, which culminated in protesters shutting down Bangkok with their sheer numbers. Their goal: make the prime minister step down and begin an overhaul of the political system. Rice farmers became involved when the government's multi-billion-baht rice pledging scheme failed amid rumours of large-scale corruption, leaving thousands of farmers with critical levels of debt. At the time of writing it remained to be seen how peaceful the protests would remain and when or if this great rift in the views of the Thais could be mended.

Southern Separatism

Thailand's south is mostly synonymous with golden beaches and sky-scraping palms, but in the Deep South, abutting the Malaysian border, life is far from peaceful. Several of Thailand's southernmost provinces, including Yala, Pattani and Narathiwat, were once part of the sultanate of Pattani, which ruled the region from the 15th century until the turn of the 20th century when Buddhist Siam claimed the land. These areas have retained their culture and Muslim religion, and speak their own language (Yawi), and here a deep-seeded separatist sentiment has prevailed.

Government forces continue their attempts to contain the conflict (via force, surveillance, patrols) until political solutions are negotiated. Peace talks (arranged by exiled ex-Prime Minister Thaksin and Malaysian leader Najib Razak) that began in Kuala Lumpur in March 2013 were abandoned during the October anniversary of the 2004 Tak Bai killings (when Thai security forces opened fire on 1500 protestors and around 85 people were killed).

There were plans to restart negotiations in November 2013. Insurgents are demanding the release of prisoners and the inclusion of outside groups including ASEAN and the Organization of Islamic Cooperation (OIC) in the peace talks. Political observers are pessimistic about whether negotiations will succeed. While Thailand fears losing sovereignty in the region many analysts believe the only way to bring resolution is for the government to loosen its grip on the region, perhaps by serving as an administrator only.

While politics were heating up in Bangkok and all eyes were on the capital at the end of 2013 and into early 2014, a bomb shattered 20 shops, wounding 27 people in southern Songkla Province, the first time there have been attacks in that region. On that same day a bomb was discovered in Phuket that had been scheduled to go off in August 2013; it was big enough to destroy a 10-storey building.

POPULATION: **67.4 MILLION**

GDP: **US$662.6 BILLION**

GDP PER CAPITA: **US$10,300**

UNEMPLOYMENT: **0.7%**

POPULATION BELOW THE POVERTY LINE: **7.8%**

if Thailand were 100 people

75 would be Thai
14 would be Chinese
11 would be Other

belief systems

(% of population)

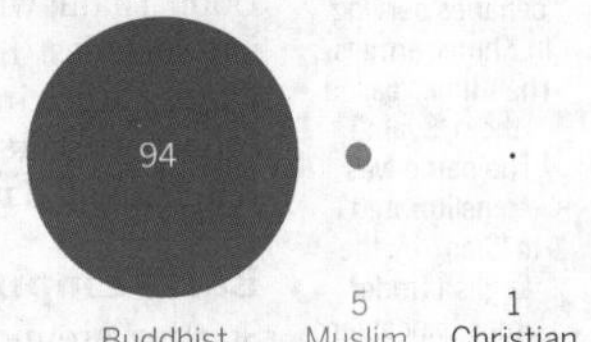

population per sq km

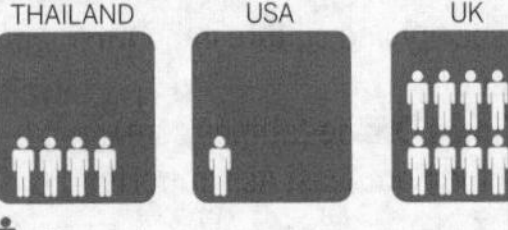

History & Politics

Thailand's history begins in Neolithic times, moves through the dawn of Hindu and Buddhist civilizations and morphs into a time of great immigrations, wars and kingdoms. From 1932 the country has been a democracy but the road has been bumpy as it has led to today's escalating ideological clashes.

History

Thai history began with immigrants from all directions exchanging dominance over the land. Eventually the country fused a national identity around language, religion and monarchy. While the kings resisted colonisation from the expansionist West, they ceded their absolute grip on the country when challenged by forces within. Since the transition to a constitutional monarchy in 1932, the military has predominantly ruled the country with a few democratic hiccups in between. Thailand's history is still unfolding in the political dramas of today.

Ancient History

Little evidence remains of the cultures that existed in Thailand before the middle of the 1st millennium AD. *Homo erectus* fossils in Thailand's northern province of Lampang date back at least 500,000 years, and the country's most important archaeological site is Ban Chiang, outside Udon Thani, which provides evidence of one of the world's oldest agrarian societies. It is believed that the Mekong River Valley and Khorat Plateau were inhabited as far back as 10,000 years ago by farmers and bronze-workers. Cave paintings in Pha Taem National Park near Ubon Ratchathani date back some 3000 years.

Relief carvings at Angkor Wat depict Tai mercenaries serving in Khmer armies. The Khmer called them 'Syam'. The name was transliterated to 'Siam' by the English trader James Lancaster in 1592.

Early Empires

Starting around the 10th century, the 'Tai' people, who are considered the ancestors of the contemporary Thais, began emigrating from south-

TIMELINE

4000–2500 BC

Prehistoric Neolithic people develop pottery, rice and cereal cultivation, cattle and pig farming and bronze metallurgy in northern Thailand.

6th–11th centuries AD

The Buddhist and Hindu Indian-influenced Dvaravati, thought to be predominantly of the Mon ethnicity, establish city-states in central Thailand.

9–13th centuries

Angkor extends control across parts of Thailand. The region is still influenced by the extravagant architectural and sculpture style of this once dominant Southeast Asia culture.

ern China into present-day Southeast Asia. These immigrants came in consecutive waves and spoke Tai-Kadai, a family of monosyllabic and tonal languages said to be the most significant ethno-linguistic group in Southeast Asia. Some settled in the river valleys of modern-day Thailand while others chose parts of modern-day Laos and the Shan state of Myanmar.

They settled in villages as farmers, hunters and traders and organised themselves into administrative units known as *meu·ang,* under the rule of a lord, which became the building block of the Tai state. Over time, the Tai expanded from the northern mountain valleys into the central plains and northeastern plateau, where there existed several important trading centres ruled by various indigenous and 'foreign' empires, including the Mon-Dvaravati, Khmer (Cambodia) and Srivijaya (Malay).

Top History Reads

Thailand: A Short History (2003) by David K Wyatt

A History of Thailand (2009) by Chris Baker and Pasuk Phongpaichit

Chronicle of Thailand: Headlines Since 1946 (2010) by William Warren

Dvaravati

The Mon dominated parts of Burma (present-day Myanmar), western Thailand and the central plains. In the 6th to 9th centuries, the Dvaravati culture emerged as a distinct Buddhist culture associated with the Mon people. Little is known about this period but it is believed that Nakhon Pathom might have been the centre and that overland trade routes and trading outposts extended west to Burma, east to Cambodia, north to Chiang Mai and Laos, and towards the northeast, as evidenced by findings of distinctive Dvaravati Buddha images, temples and stone inscriptions in Mon language.

The Dvaravati was one of many Indian-influenced cultures that established themselves in Southeast Asia at the time, but scholars single out the Dvaravati because of its artistic legacy and the trade routes that might have provided an early framework for what would become the core of the modern-day Thai state.

Khmer

While the Dvaravati are a historical mystery, the Khmers were Southeast Asia's equivalent of the Roman Empire. This kingdom became famous for its extravagant sculpture and architecture and had a profound effect on the art and religion of the region. Established in the 9th century, the Khmer kingdom built its capital in Angkor (modern-day Cambodia) and expanded westward across present-day central and northeastern Thailand. Administrative centres anchored by Angkor-style temples were built in Lopburi (then known as Lavo), Sukhothai and Phimai (near Nakhon Ratchasima) and linked by road to the capital.

The Khmer's large-scale construction projects were a symbol of imperial power in its frontier regions and examples of the day's most

10th century
Arrival of Tai peoples in Thailand from Southern China in several waves. Settlements expand from the northern mountain valleys to the central plains and northeast plateau.

1240–1438
Approximate dates of Sukhothai kingdom which the Thais consider the first real Thai kingdom. The period is marked by flourishing arts and culture.

1283
Early Thai script invented by King Ramkhamhaeng of Sukhothai. The script is based on Indian, Mon and Khmer scripts. Buddhism is established as the official religion.

1292
Chiang Mai becomes the capital of Lanna. King Mengrai, a skilled diplomat, creates ties that dispel outside threats and allow the culture to grow.

advanced technologies. Khmer elements – Hinduism, Brahmanism, Theravada Buddhism and Mahayana Buddhism – mark the cultural products of this period in Thailand.

Srivijaya

While mainland Thailand was influenced by forces from the north and west, the Malay peninsula was economically and culturally fused to cultures further south. Between the 8th and 13th centuries, the Malay peninsula was under the sway of the confederation of the Srivijaya, which controlled maritime trade between the South China Sea and Indian Ocean. The Srivijaya capital is believed to have been in Palembang on Sumatra.

Of the series of Srivijaya city-states that grew to prominence along the Malay peninsula, Tambralinga established its capital near present-day Nakhon Si Thammarat and adopted Buddhism in the 13th century, while the states further south fell under the influence of Islam, creating a religious boundary that persists to this day. Remains of Srivijaya culture can be seen around Chaiya and Nakhon Si Thammarat. Many art forms of the Srivijaya kingdom, such as *năng đà·lung* (shadow theatre) and *lá·kon* (classical dance-drama), persist today.

Emerging Tai Kingdoms

In the 13th century, the regional empires started to decline and prosperous Tai city-states emerged with localised power and military might. The competing city-states were ultimately united into various kingdoms that began to establish a Thai identity. Scholars recognise Lanna, Sukhothai and Ayuthaya as the unifying kingdoms of the period.

Lanna

The Lanna kingdom, based in northern Thailand, dates its formation to the upper Mekong River town of Chiang Saen in the middle of the 12th century by King Mengrai, who settled the bickering between neighbouring towns by conquering them. He then migrated south to Chiang Mai (meaning 'new city') in 1292 to establish his capital. The king was a skilled diplomat and forged important alliances with potential rivals, notably King Ngam Muang of Phayao and King Ramkhamhaeng of Sukhothai; a bronze statue commemorating this confederation stands in Chiang Mai today. King Mengrai is also credited for successfully repulsing Mongol invasions in the early 14th century and building diplomatic ties in lieu of future attacks.

The Lanna kingdom is also recognised for its royal patronage of the Sinhalese tradition of Theravada Buddhism, now widely practised in Thailand, and of the distinctive northern Thai culture that persists in

1351–1767

Reign of Ayuthaya which at its height in the 1600s controls parts of Burma, Laos and Cambodia, making it the predominant power of Southeast Asia at the time.

1511

Portuguese Duarte Fernandes becomes the first European to establish diplomatic relations with Thailand when he founds a foreign mission in Ayuthaya; other European nations follow.

1688

Pro-foreign King Narai dies and is followed by the Palace Revolution and the expulsion of the French. As a result, Thailand's ties with the West are near-severed until the 1800s.

1767

The capital city of Ayuthaya is sacked by the Burmese which ultimately, after 14 months of siege, brings an end to the kingdom.

the region. The Lanna kingdom never went through an extensive expansion period as it was plagued by dynastic intrigues and wars, especially against Sukhothai and Ayuthaya.

Sukhothai

During the 13th century, several principalities in the central plains united and wrested control from the dying Khmer empire, making their new capital at Sukhothai (meaning 'Rising of Happiness'). Thais consider Sukhothai the first true Thai kingdom and the period is recognised as an artistic and cultural awakening.

The most revered of the Sukhothai kings was Ramkhamhaeng, who is credited for developing the modern Thai writing system, which is based on Indian, Mon and Khmer scripts. He also established Theravada Buddhism as the official religion.

In its prime, the Sukhothai kingdom extended as far as Nakhon Si Thammarat in the south, to the upper Mekong River Valley in Laos and to Bago (Pegu) in southern Myanmar. For a short time (1448–86) the Sukhothai capital was moved to Phitsanulok, but by that time another star was rising in Thailand, the kingdom of Ayuthaya.

Ayuthaya

In the mid-14th century, the Ayuthaya kingdom began to dominate the Chao Phraya River basin during the twilight of the Khmer period. It survived for 416 years, defining itself as Siam's most important early kingdom. It had an expansive sphere of influence (including much of the former Khmer empire) and played a fundamental role in organising the modern Thai state and social structure.

With a strategic island location formed by encircling rivers, Ayuthaya grew wealthy through international trade during the 17th century's age of commerce and fortified itself with superior Portuguese-supplied firearms and mercenaries. The river system connected to the Gulf of Thailand and to the hinterlands as well.

During this period Western traders 'discovered' Southeast Asia, and Ayuthaya hosted many foreign settlements. Accounts by foreign visitors mention Ayuthaya's cosmopolitan markets and court. In 1690 Londoner Engelbert Campfer proclaimed, 'Among the Asian nations, the kingdom of Siam is the greatest'.

Ayuthaya adopted Khmer court customs, honorific language and ideas of kingship. The monarch styled himself as a Khmer *devaraja* (divine king) rather than Sukhothai's *dhammaraja* (righteous king); Ayuthaya continued to pay tribute to the Chinese emperor, who rewarded this ritualistic submission with generous gifts and commercial privileges.

KING NARESUAN

King Naresuan is portrayed as a national hero and became a cult figure, especially worshipped by the Thai army. His story inspired a high-budget, blockbuster film trilogy, *King Naresuan*, by filmmaker Chatrichalerm Yukol, funded in part by the Thai government.

1768

Thai Chinese King Taksin establishes a new capital in Thonburi which brings the Thais back into power and begins the brief Thonburi Period.

1782

Founding of the Chakri dynasty with Bangkok as the new capital. King Rama I is ruler and his lineage continues to hold the throne to this day.

1851–68

Reign of King Mongkut (Rama IV) and a period of Western influence. The king moves the country to modernise and integrates it into the world market of the day.

➡ Rama IV statue, Bangkok

FRIENDS OF THE KING

In the 1680s many foreign emissaries were invited to Ayuthaya by King Narai, who was keen to acquire and consume foreign material, culture and ideas. His court placed orders for spyglasses, hourglasses, paper, walnut trees, cheese, wine and marble fountains. He joined the French Jesuits to observe the eclipse at his palace in Lopburi and received a gift of a globe from France's King Louis XIV.

In the 1680s, Narai recruited the services of the Greek adventurer Constantine Phaulkon, who was later accused of conspiring to overthrow the ailing king. Instead, the accusers led a coup and executed Constantine.

The glories of Ayuthaya were interrupted by the expansionist Burmese. In 1569 the city had fallen to the great Burmese king, Bayinnaung, but regained independence under the leadership of King Naresuan. Then, in 1765, Burma's ambitious and newly established Kongbaung dynasty pushed eastward to eliminate Ayuthaya as a political and commercial rival. Burmese troops laid siege to the capital for a year before destroying it in 1767. The city was devastated, its buildings and people wiped out. The surrounding areas were deserted. So chilling was this historic sacking and razing of Ayuthaya that the perception of the Burmese as ruthless foes and aggressors still persists in the minds of many Thais to this day.

The Bangkok Era

With Ayuthaya in ruins, the line of succession of the kings was broken and chaos ensued. A former general, Taksin, claimed his right to rule, handily defeating potential rivals, and established his new capital in Thonburi, a settlement downriver from Ayuthaya with better access to trade. Consolidating his power, King Taksin, the son of a Chinese father and Thai mother, strongly promoted trade with China.

Landmarks of the Bangkok Era

- *Wat Arun*
- *Wat Phra Kaew and Grand Palace*
- *Dusit Palace Park*

The king was deposed in 1782 by the military. One of the coup organisers, Chao Phraya Chakri, assumed the throne as Phraphutthayotfa Chulalok (r 1782–1809; posthumously known as Rama I) and established the Chakri dynasty, which still rules today. The new monarch moved the capital across the Chao Phraya River to modern-day Bangkok.

The first century of Bangkok rule focused on rebuilding what had been lost when Ayuthaya was sacked. Surviving knowledge and practices were preserved or incorporated into new laws, manuals of government practice, religious and historical texts, and literature. At the same time, the new rulers transformed their defence activities into expansion by means of war, extending their influence in every direction. Destroying the capital cities of both Laos and Cambodia, Siam contained Burmese aggression and made a vassal of Chiang Mai. Defeated populations were

1855
Bowring Treaty between Siam and Britain stimulates the Thai economy by granting extraterritorial rights to British subjects in Siam and liberalising trade rules and regulations.

1868–1910
Reign of King Chulalongkorn (Rama V) who continues replacing the old political order with the model of the nation state. Increase of European imperialism in neighbouring countries.

1874
Slavery and the state labour system that had been in place since the Ayuthaya period is abolished. A salaried bureaucracy, police force and army are created.

1890
Siam's first railway, run by the Royal State Railway of Siam, connects Bangkok with Ayuthaya. This is the beginning of what will become the Northern Line.

resettled and played an important role in increasing the rice production of Siam, much of which was exported to China.

Unlike the Ayuthaya rulers, who identified with the Hindu god Vishnu, the Chakri kings positioned themselves as defenders of Buddhism. They undertook compilations and Thai translations of essential Buddhist texts and constructed many royal temples.

In the meantime, a new social order and market economy was taking shape in the mid-19th century. Siam turned to the West for modern scientific and technological ideas and reforms in education, infrastructure and legal systems. One of the great modernisers, King Mongkut (Rama IV) never expected to be king. Before his ascension he had spent 27 years in a monastery, founding the Thammayut sect based on the strict disciplines of the Mon monks he had followed. During his monastic career, he became proficient in Pali, Sanskrit, Latin and English and studied Western sciences.

During Mongkut's reign, Siam concluded treaties with Western powers that integrated the kingdom into the world market system, ceded royal monopolies and granted extraterritorial rights to British subjects.

Mongkut's son, King Chulalongkorn (Rama V) was to take much greater steps in replacing the old political order with the model of the nation-state. He abolished slavery and the corvée system (state labour), which had lingered on ineffectively since the Ayuthaya period. Chulalongkorn's reign oversaw the creation of a salaried bureaucracy, a police force and a standing army. His reforms brought uniformity to the legal code, law courts and revenue offices. Siam's agricultural output was improved by advances in irrigation techniques and increasing peasant populations. Schools were established along European lines. Universal conscription and poll taxes made all men the king's men.

In 'civilising' his country, Chulalongkorn relied greatly on foreign advisers, mostly British. Within the royal court, much of the centuries-old protocol was abandoned and replaced by Western forms. The architecture and visual art of state, like the new throne halls, were designed by Italian artists.

Like his father, Chulalongkorn was regarded as a skilful diplomat and is credited with successfully playing European powers off one another to avoid colonisation. In exchange for independence, Thailand ceded territory to French Indochina (Laos in 1893, Cambodia in 1907) and British Burma (three Malayan states in 1909). In 1902, the former Pattani kingdom was ceded to the British, who were then in control of Malaysia, but control reverted to Thailand five years later. (The Deep South continues to consider itself an occupied land by the Thai central government.)

Siam was becoming a geographically defined country in a modern sense. By 1902, the country no longer called itself Siam but Prathet Thai

In 1868 King Mongkut (Rama IV) abolished a husband's right to sell his wife or her children without her permission. The older provision, it was said, treated the woman 'as if she were a water buffalo'.

Chulalongkorn (Rama V) enjoys a cult-like devotion due in part to the endearing photographs of him in European dress, ordinary farmer garb or military pomp. He defied tradition by allowing himself to be seen in public by his subjects and to have his image widely disseminated.

1893

French blockade the Chao Phraya River over disputed Indochina territory. Bangkok is forced to cede the territory to France, strengthening French influence in the region.

1902

Siam annexes Yala, Pattani and Narathiwat from the former sultanate of Patani.

1909

Anglo–Siamese Treaty outlines Siam's southern boundary and gives it Yala, Pattani and Narathiwat from the former Malay sultanate, Pattani. Territories south later become part of the Unfederated Malay States.

1913

King Vajiravudh requires all citizens to adopt surnames. Before this time most Thais used only a first name. Each last name is required to be unique to the family.

(the country of the Thai) or Ratcha-anachak Thai (the kingdom of the Thai). By 1913, all those living within its borders were defined as 'Thai'.

Democracy vs Military

In 1932 a group of young military officers and bureaucrats calling themselves Khana Ratsadon (People's Party) mounted a successful, bloodless coup that marked the end of absolute monarchy and introduced a constitutional monarchy. The leaders of the group were inspired by the democratic ideology they had encountered during their studies in Europe.

In the years after the coup, rival factions (royalists, military, civilians) struggled for the upper hand in the new power regime. Even the People's Party was not unified in its vision of a democratic Thailand, and before general elections were held the military wing of the party seized control of the government. The leader of the civilian wing of the People's Party, Pridi Phanomyong, a French-educated lawyer, was forced into exile in 1933 after introducing a socialist-leaning economic plan that angered the military generals. King Prajadhipok (Rama VII) abdicated in 1935 and retired to Britain. Thailand's first general election was held in 1937 for half of the seats in the People's Assembly, the newly instated legislative body. General Phibul Songkhram, one of the leaders of the military faction of the People's Party, became prime minister, a position he held from 1938 to 1944 and again from 1948 to 1957.

Phibul's regime coincided with WWII and was characterised by strong nationalistic tendencies centring on 'nation' and 'Thai-ness'. He collaborated with the Japanese and allowed them to use Thailand as a staging ground for its invasion of other Southeast Asian nations. By siding with the Japanese, the Phibul government hoped to gain international leverage and reclaim historical territory lost during France's expansion of Indochina. Thailand intended to declare war on the US and Britain during WWII. But Seni Pramoj, the Thai ambassador in Washington and a member of Seri Thai (the Thai Liberation Movement), refused to deliver the formal declaration of war, and thus saved Thailand from bearing the consequences of defeated-nation status. Phibul was forced to resign in 1944 and was tried for war crimes.

In an effort to suppress royalist sentiments, Ananda Mahidol, the nephew of the abdicated king, was crowned Rama VIII in 1935, though he was only 10 years old and spent much of his childhood studying abroad. After returning to Thailand, he was shot dead under mysterious circumstances in his bedroom in 1946. In the same year, his brother, His Majesty Bhumibol Adulyadej (pronounced *poomípon adunyádèt*) was appointed as the ninth king of the Chakri dynasty, going on to become the longest-reigning king in Thai history, as well as the world's longest-reigning, living monarch.

NAME CHANGE

Prime Minister Phibul Songkhram changed the name of the country in 1939 from 'Siam' to 'Prathet Thai' (or 'Thailand' in English); it was considered an overt nationalistic gesture intended to unite all the Tai-speaking people.

1916

The first Thai university, Chulalongkorn University, is established by King Vajiravudh. Even today diplomas are handed out by members of the royal family.

1917

Siam sends troops to join the Allies in WWI in hopes of gaining popularity with the French and British, thus protecting the country's sovereignty.

1924

Don Muang International Airport (opened as a military base in 1914) welcomes its first commercial flight, opening up the country to nonmilitary air travel.

1932

Bloodless coup ends absolute monarchy and puts in place a constitutional monarchy. Leaders of the coup are inspired by democratic ideology learned from studies in Europe.

For a brief period after the war, democracy flourished: full elections for the National People Assembly were held, and the 1946 Constitution sought to reduce the role of the military and provide more democratic rights. It lasted until the death of King Ananda, the pretext the military used to return to power with Phibul at the helm.

Without the job of being absolute monarch, King Bhumibol had to find new work so he started the Royal Project Foundation in 1969 to help struggling farmers. The foundation's most lauded effort was eradication of opium cultivation among the northern hill tribes.

Military Dictatorships

In 1957 Phibul's successor, General Sarit Thanarat, subjected the country to a military dictatorship: abolishing the constitution, dissolving the parliament and banning political parties. In the 1950s, the US directly involved itself in Southeast Asia to contain communist expansion in the region. During the Cold War, the US government gave economic and military support to the Sarit government and continued that relationship with subsequent military dictators, Thanom Kittikachorn and Praphat Charusathien, who ruled from 1964 to 1973. They negotiated a package of economic deals with the USA in exchange for allowing the development of US military bases in Thailand to support the Vietnam War.

By 1973, an opposition group of left-wing activists, mainly intellectuals and students, along with peasants, workers and portions of the middle class, organised political rallies demanding a constitution from the military government. On 14 October that year the military suppressed a large demonstration in Bangkok, killing 77 people and wounding more than 800. The event is commemorated by a monument on Th Ratchadamnoen Klang in Bangkok, near the Democracy Monument. King Bhumibol

LIBERAL COUNTERWEIGHT

Pridi Phanomyong (1900–83) was a French-educated lawyer and a civilian leader in the 1932 revolution and People's Party. His work on democratic reforms in Thailand was based on constitutional measures and attempts to restrict by law military involvement in Thai politics. He supported nationalisation of land and labour, state-led industrialisation and labour protection. In 1934, he founded Thammasat University. He also served as the figurehead of Seri Thai (the resistance movement against WWII Japanese occupation of Thailand) and was Thailand's prime minister (1946).

Though acknowledged as a senior statesman, Pridi Phanomyong was a controversial figure and a major foe of Phibul and the military regimes. He was accused of being a communist by his critics and forced out of the country under suspicion of regicide following the mysterious death of King Ananda Mahidol. Since the thawing of the Cold War, his legacy has been re-examined and recognised for its democratic efforts and the counterbalancing effects it had on military interests. He was named one of Unesco's great personalities of the 20th-century world in 2000.

1939

The country's English name is officially changed from Siam to Thailand to align the name more closely with the majority ethnic group.

1941

Japanese forces enter Thailand during WWII, using the country for access to invade British Malaya and Burma. Japanese pressure leads to Thailand signing an alliance with Japan.

1945

WWII ends; Thailand cedes seized territory from Laos, Cambodia and Malaysia that it gained from the French and British during the war.

1946

King Bhumibol Adulyadej (Rama IX) ascends the throne and will become the longest reigning monarch in Thai history; Thailand joins the UN.

stepped in and refused to support further bloodshed, forcing Thanom and Praphat to leave Thailand.

In the following years, the left-oriented student movement grew more radical, creating fears among working-class and middle-class Thais of home-grown communism. In 1976 Thanom returned to Thailand (ostensibly to become a monk) and was received warmly by the royal family. In response, protestors organised demonstrations at Thammasat University against the perceived perpetrator of the 14 October massacre. Right-wing, anti-communist civilian groups clashed with students, resulting in bloody violence. In the aftermath, many students and intellectuals were forced underground, and joined armed communist insurgents – known as the People's Liberation Army of Thailand (PLAT) – based in the jungles of northern and southern Thailand.

Prem Tinsulanonda serves as lifelong head of the Privy Council of King Bhumibol and is widely believed to have been the architect of the 2006 coup.

Military control of the country continued through the 1980s. The government of the 'political soldier', General Prem Tinsulanonda, enjoyed a period of political and economic stability. Prem dismantled the communist insurgency through military action and amnesty programs. But the country's new economic success presented a challenging rival: prominent business leaders who criticised the military's role in government and their now-dated Cold War mentality. Communists, they maintained, should be business partners, not enemies.

It's Just Business

In 1988, Prem was replaced in fair elections by Chatichai Choonhavan, leader of the Chat Thai Party, who created a government dominated by well-connected provincial business people. His government shifted power away from the bureaucrats and set about transforming Thailand into an 'Asian Tiger' economy. But the business of politics was often bought and sold like a commodity and Chatichai was overthrown by the military on grounds of extreme corruption. This coup marked an emerging trend in Thai politics: the Bangkok business community and educated classes siding with the military against Chatichai, his provincial business-politicians and their money politics approach to governance.

In 1992, after reinstating elections, an unelected military leader inserted himself as prime minister. This was met with popular resistance and the ensuing civilian-military clash was dubbed 'Black May'. Led by former Bangkok governor and major general, Chamlong Srimuang, around 200,000 protestors (called the 'mobile phone mob', representing their rising urban affluence) launched a mass demonstration against the military rulers in Bangkok that resulted in three nights of violence with armed soldiers. On the night of 20 May, King Bhumibol called an end to the violence.

1957

Sarit Thanarat leads a coup that introduces military rule, which lasts until 1973. The constitution is abolished, parliament is dissolved and political parties are banned.

1959

Thailand's first tourism authority is created. The first overseas office opens in New York in 1965 and a regional office opens in Chiang Mai in 1968.

1965

Thailand hosts and commands US military bases during the Vietnam War under a 'gentlemen's agreement'. Around 80% of US airstrikes in Northern Vietnam will originate from Thailand.

1968

Thailand is a founding member of the Association of Southeast Asian Nations (ASEAN), to promote regional economic growth, social progress, peace and stability.

After Black May, a new wave of democracy activists advocated for constitutional reforms. For most of the 1990s, the parliament was dominated by the Democrat Party, which represented the urban middle class and business interests. Its major base of support came from the southern Thai population centres. Formerly port towns, these were now dominated by tourism and exports (rubber, tin and fishing). On the other side of the spectrum were the former pro-military politicians based in the central plains and the people of the agrarian northeast in new provincial towns who focused on state-budget distribution to their provinces. These political lines exist today.

In 1997, the boom years went bust and the Asian economic crisis unfolded. The country's economy was plagued by foreign-debt burdens, an overextension in the real-estate sector and a devalued currency. Within months of the crisis, the Thai currency plunged from 25B to 56B per US$1. The International Monetary Fund (IMF) stepped in to impose financial and legal reforms and economic liberalisation programs in exchange for more than US$17 billion to stabilise the Thai currency.

In the aftermath of the crisis, the Democrats returned to power uncontested, but were viewed as ineffective as the economy worsened.

Thaksinocracy

In 2000, the economic slump began to ease and business interests eclipsed the military as the dominant political force in Thai politics. The telecommunications billionaire and former police officer, Thaksin Shinawatra, through his Thai Rak Thai (TRT or 'Thai Loving Thai') party, capitalised on this rising nationalism and won a majority in the elections of 2001. Self-styled as a CEO-politician, Thaksin swiftly delivered on his campaign promises for rural development, including agrarian debt relief, village capital funds and cheap health care.

Thanks to the 1997 constitutional reforms designed to strengthen the prime minister's position, Thaksin's government was one of Thai history's most stable. The surging economy and his bold, if strong-arm, leadership won an outright majority in 2005, effectively introducing one-party rule. His popularity among the working class and rural voters was immense.

In 2006 Thaksin was accused of abusing his powers and of conflicts of interest, most notably in his family's sale of their Shin Corporation to the Singaporean government for 73 billion baht (US$1.88 billion), a tax-free gain thanks to telecommunications legislation that he had helped craft. Demonstrations in Bangkok called for him to be ousted, and on 19 September 2006 the military staged a bloodless coup that forced Thaksin into exile. The TRT party was dissolved by court order and party executives were barred from politics for five years. As promised, the interim

FOUR YEARS

Thaksin was the first prime minister in Thai history to complete a four-year term of office.

1973

Thai students, workers and farmers demonstrate for the reinstallation of a democratic government.

1976

Violent suppression of student movement by the military. King Bhumibol steps in to prevent further bloodshed and forces Thanom and Praphat to leave the country.

1979

After three years of military rule, elections and parliament restored. Thai authorities give safe haven to Khmer Rouge fleeing the North Vietnamese invasion of Cambodia.

1980

Prem Tinsulanonda's government works to undermine the communist insurgency movement with military action and amnesty programs and eventually ends it with a political solution.

government held general elections in December, returning the country to civilian rule, but the outcome was unsatisfactory to the military and the Bangkok upper and middle classes when Thaksin's political allies won a majority and formed a government led by Samak Sundaravej.

Demonstrations against the Thaksin-aligned government were led by Chamlong Srimuang (Black May activist and former Bangkok governor) and Sondhi Limthongkul (a long-time business and political rival of Thaksin). Their group, the People's Alliance for Democracy (PAD), earned the nickname 'Yellow Shirts' because they wore yellow (the king's birthday colour) to express their royalist allegiances; it was believed that Thaksin was so successfully consolidating power during his tenure that he had designs on the throne or at least planned to interrupt the royal succession.

In September 2008, Samak Sundaravej was unseated by the Constitutional Court on a technicality: while in office, he hosted a TV cooking show that the court found to be a conflict of interest. Still not politically satisfied, the Yellow Shirts seized control of Thailand's main airports, Suvarnabhumi and Don Muang, for a week in November 2008 until the military manoeuvred a silent coup and another favourable court ruling that further weakened Thaksin's political proxies. Through last-minute coalition building, Democrat Abhisit Vejjajiva was elected in a parliamentary vote, becoming Thailand's 27th prime minister.

Thaksin supporters organised their own counter-movement, the United Front For Democracy Against Dictatorship, better known as the 'Red Shirts'. Supporters hail mostly from the north and northeast, and include anti-coup, pro-democracy activists as well as die-hard Thaksin fans. There is a degree of class struggle, with some Red Shirts expressing bombastic animosity towards the aristocrats. The Red Shirts' most provocative demonstration came in 2010 when Thailand's Supreme Court ordered the seizure of US$46 billion of Thaksin's assets after finding him guilty of abusing his powers as prime minister. Red Shirts occupied Bangkok's central shopping district for two months and demanded the dissolution of the government and reinstatement of elections. Protest leaders and the government were unable to reach a compromise and in May 2010 the military used forced to evict the protestors, resulting in bloody clashes (91 people were killed) and a smouldering central city (crackdown-related arson, done by certain groups within the protest movement, caused damage estimated at US$15 billion).

In 2011, general elections were held and Thaksin's politically allied Puea Thai party won a parliamentary majority making his sister, Yingluck Shinawatra, prime minister.

Thailand has had 17 constitutions, all rewritten as a result of 18 (this number is debatable) coups. Each reincarnation seeks to allocate power within the branches of government with a bias for the ruling interest (military, royalist or civilian) and against their political foes.

1988

Chatichai Choonhavan becomes first elected PM since 1976 and creates a government dominated by well-connected provincial business people.

1991–92

General Suchinda attempts to seize power due to the extreme corruption of Chatichai's government; King Bhumibol intervenes to halt civil turmoil surrounding 'Black May' protests.

1997

Asian economic crisis; passage of historic 'people's constitution'. International Monetary Fund steps in to reform and stabilise the Thai currency.

2001

Self-styled CEO-politician Thaksin Shinawatra is elected prime minister. Campaign promises of rural development, agrarian debt and cheaper healthcare are quickly delivered.

Troubles in the Deep South

Starting in 2001, Muslim separatist insurgents have been waging a low-scale war against the central government in Thailand's southernmost provinces of Pattani, Narathiwat and Yala. These three provinces once comprised the area of the historic kingdom of Pattani until it was conquered by the Chakri kings. Under King Chulalongkorn, the traditional ruling elite were replaced with central government officials and bureaucrats from Bangkok. During WWII, a policy of nation-building set out to transform the multi-ethnic society into a unified and homogenous Thai Buddhist nation. This policy was resisted in the Deep South and gave birth to a strong separatist movement fighting for the independence of Pattani. In the 1980s and 1990s, the assimilation policy was abandoned and then-prime minister Prem promised support for Muslim cultural rights and religious freedoms. He also offered amnesty to the armed insurgents and implemented an economic development plan for the historically impoverished region.

The Thaksin regime took another approach to the region, which still ranks among the most economically and educationally depressed in the country. Greater central control was exerted; this was viewed as a thinly disguised policy to break up the traditional stronghold of the Democrat Party. The policy succeeded in weakening relations between the local elite, southern voters and the Democrats who had served as their representative in parliament. However, it did not take into consideration the sensitive and tenacious Muslim culture of the Deep South. In 2002, the government dissolved the long-standing inspectorate and the army-run joint civilian-police-military border security office – a unit often lauded for maintaining peace and stability and providing a communication link between the Thai government and the southern Muslims. In its place the Thai provincial police assumed control of security, though they lacked a perceived moral authority and the support of the local population. In 2004, the government responded harshly to demonstrations that resulted in the Krue Se Mosque and Tak Bai incidents, which together cost the lives of at least 180 Muslims, many of them unarmed civilians. In 2005, martial law was declared in the area.

After more than a decade of violence, Thailand's national government announced peace talks with Barisan Revolusion Nasional (BNR), a Malaysian-based insurgent group claiming a leading role in the southern war. But meetings have been suspended due to spikes in violence and concerns that BNR doesn't exert significant organisational control.

Sacred Landmarks of Note

Tham Phraya Nakhon, Khao Sam Roi Yot National Park

Sanctuary of Truth, Pattaya

Wat Phra Mahathat Woramahawihaan, Nakhon Si Thammarat

Khmer temples, Phetchaburi

Big Buddha, Phuket

2003

Government stages a huge, controversial crackdown on drugs during which some 2000 people are killed. Human rights groups blame the government; the government blames gangs.

2004

Indian Ocean tsunami kills 5000 people and damages tourism and fishing industries; Muslim insurgency reignites in the Deep South after brewing steadily since 2001.

2006

King Bhumibol celebrates 60th year on the throne; Thaksin government overthrown in a coup and prime minister forced into exile. Thaksin's allies win the following elections.

2008

Cambodia successfully petitions Unesco to list Phra Wihan (known as Phrea Vihear in Cambodia) as a World Heritage Site, reigniting border tensions with Thailand.

Politics

Government

Much of the political drama that has unfolded since the 2006 coup involves a long-standing debate about how to structure Thailand's legislative body and, ultimately, who gets greater control. The National Assembly (or parliament of Thailand) currently has 630 members divided into two chambers (House of Representatives and the Senate) with a mix of seats being popularly elected and elected by party vote. The ratio of seats being popularly elected changes with each replacement constitution. The 1997 constitution, dubbed the People's Constitution, called for both chambers to be fully elected by popular vote. This power to the people paved the way for Thaksin and his well-loved Thai Rak Thai party to gain nearly complete control. The military and the elites have since rescinded this structure, often arguing that full democratic representation doesn't work in Thailand.

The Democrat Party (Phak Prachathipat), founded in 1946, is now the longest-surviving political party in Thailand.

When Thai voters go to the polls they cast a ballot for the constituency MP (member of parliament) and for their preferred party, the results of which are used to determine individual winners and proportional representation outcomes for the positions assigned by party vote.

The prime minister is the head of the government and is elected via legislative vote by the majority party. Under the most recent constitution, the prime minister must be a sitting MP, though this has not always been the case.

Voting in Thailand is compulsory for all eligible citizens (over the age of 18) but members of the clergy are not allowed to vote. Voter turnout for national elections has steadily increased since the new millen-

SIGNS OF ELECTION

Preceding an election, Thai candidates paper the roadways and electricity poles with political billboards and signs. Traditional posters show the candidate posing seriously in an official uniform but recent trends include ad-like approaches with catchy slogans and evocative imagery.

Always a trendsetter, Chuvit Kamolvisit, former brothel owner turned political whistle-blower, won over voters with his 2011 'Angry Man' campaign ads, featuring him in grimacing and glaring poses expressing frustration and anger with the government. (Incidentally, one of his first acts in office was to expose an illegal Bangkok casino run by high-ranking police.)

Residents complain about the signs' obstruction of traffic but signmakers like the boost in business. All candidate posters are vulnerable to vandalism or theft, but the plastic ones are particularly desired as makeshift sunshades or roof patches.

2008

Yellow Shirt, anti-Thaksin, pro-royalist activists seize Bangkok's international airports, causing a weeklong shut-down.

2010

Red Shirt, pro-Thaksin activists occupy central Bangkok for two months demanding dissolution of the government and re-instatement of elections; military crackdown results in 91 deaths.

➡ Political protestor, Bangkok

nium with 78% of registered voters casting ballots in 2007. Charges of vote-buying typically accompany every election. Anecdotally, local party leaders make their rounds through the villages handing out money for the promise of a vote. In some cases, villagers will accept money from competing parties and report that they have no loyalty at the ballot box.

The ballots include a 'no' vote if the voter wishes to choose 'none of the above'. It is also common to 'spoil' the ballot, or disqualify it, by writing on it or defacing it. During the 2005 general election a large number of ineligible ballots contained anti-Thaksin messages.

Media

Southeast Asian governments are not usually fond of uncensored media, but Thailand often bucked this trend during the 1990s, even ensuring press freedoms in its 1997 constitution, albeit with fairly broad loopholes. This ended with the ascension of Thaksin Shinawatra, a telecommunications billionaire, at the beginning of the 21st century. With Thaksin as prime minister and his party holding a controlling majority, the press encountered the kind of censorship and legal intimidation not seen since the 1970s era of military dictatorships. The government filed a litany of defamation lawsuits against individuals, publications and media groups who printed embarrassing revelations about the Thaksin regime.

After the 2006 ousting of Thaksin, the media managed to retain its guarantees of press freedoms in the new constitution, but this was a 'paper promise' that did little to rescue the press from intimidation, lawsuits and physical attacks. Sweeping powers to ensure national security, often invoked against the press, were added to the emergency powers laws that went into effect after the coup.

Press intimidation in Thailand is made easier because of the country's lèse majesté laws (causing offence against the dignity of the monarchy) which carry a jail term of three to 15 years. Often the media exercises self-censorship with regard to the monarchy, mainly out of respect for the crown, but also out of fear that political enemies will file lèse majesté charges.

Filing of lèse majesté charges has increased since 2006, mainly against political rivals, but also against journalists and even average citizens. Charges have been filed against a Thai Facebook user who posted a negative comment about the king and an overseas Thai who posted translations of a banned book about the king on his blog.

Publications that the government views as presenting an unflattering view of the monarchy are often banned. Several critical issues of *The Economist* have been banned since 2006. Internet censorship is also on the rise and so-called Red Shirt (pro-Thaksin) radio stations based in the northeast have been shut down by the government.

Somsak Jiamteerasaku, a university professor long critical of the lèse majesté laws, was arrested after delivering a speech proposing reform measures to the institution of the monarchy. The Thai academic community was surprised that such a politically motivated tool would be applied to previously off-limits intellectuals.

2011

Puea Thai party wins general election; Yingluck Shinawatra (Thaksin's younger sister) becomes Thailand's first female prime minister on a platform of reconciliation.

2012

More Yellow Shirt protests, culminating with a 10,000-strong march against Prime Minister Yingluck, whom protestors see as a puppet of ousted Prime Minister Thaksin.

2013

The International Court Justice rules that Phra Wihan is part of Cambodia, although the area surrounding it and another 100km of border are still disputed.

2014

Anti-Yingluck protestors shut down Bangkok calling for the prime minister to step down. Demands include a proposed overhaul of the political system; tensions are high.

People & Culture

Thailand's cohesive national identity provides a unifying patina for ethnic and regional differences that evolved through historical migrations and geographic kinships with ethnically diverse neighbours.

Ethnic Makeup

Some 75% of the citizens of Thailand are ethnic Thais, providing a superficial appearance of sameness, but subtle regional differences do exist. In the central plains (Chao Phraya delta), Siamese Thais united the country through historic kingdoms and promulgated its culture and language. Today the central Thai dialect is the national standard and the capital, Bangkok, exports unified culture through media and standardised education.

Southern Thais (Ɓàk đâi) define the characteristics of the south. The dialect is a little faster than standard Thai, the curries are a lot spicier, and there is more mixing of Muslim folk beliefs into the regional culture thanks to the geographic proximity to Malaysia and the historic Muslim population.

People of Chinese ancestry – second- or third-generation Hakka, Teochew, Hainanese or Cantonese – make up 14% of the population. Bangkok and the nearby coastal areas have a large population of immigrants from China who came for economic opportunities in the early to mid-20th century. The mercantile centres of most Thai towns are run by

CHOW LAIR

Southern Thailand is home to one of Thailand's smallest ethnic groups, the *chow lair*, literally, 'people of the sea' (also spelt *chao leh*). Also known as Moken *(mor·gaan)*, or sea gypsies, the *chow lair* are an ethnic group of Malay origin who are found along coasts as far north as Myanmar and as far south as Borneo. The remaining traditional bands of *chow lair* are hunter-gatherers who are recognised as one of the few groups of humans that live primarily at sea, although in recent years many have turned to shanty-like settlements on various islands. Perhaps as a result of generations of this marine lifestyle, many *chow lair* can hold their breath for long periods of time and also have an uncanny ability to see underwater. Life at sea has also helped them in other ways: during the 2004 tsunami, virtually no *chow lair* were killed, as folk tales handed down from generation to generation alerted them to the dangers of the quickly receding tide, and they were able to escape to higher ground.

The *chow lair* were mostly ignored until recently when their islands became valuable for tourism. Entrepreneurs bought up large tracts of beachfront land and the *chow lair* moved on to smaller, less valuable islands. With these pressures, it was perhaps inevitable that the *chow lair* culture would slowly disappear. Many sea gypsies now make a living ferrying tourists around the islands or harvesting fish for seafood buffets at tourist resorts. One vestige of traditional *chow lair* life you may see is the biannual 'boat floating' ceremony in May and November, in which an elaborate model boat is set adrift, carrying away bad luck.

Thai-Chinese families and many places in the country celebrate Chinese festivals such as the annual Vegetarian Festival.

The second-largest ethnic minority are the Malays (4.6%), most of whom reside in the provinces of the Deep South. The remaining minority groups in the south include a smaller percentage of non-Thai-speaking Moken (*chow lair,* also spelt *chao leh;* people of the sea, or 'sea gypsies'). A small number of Europeans and other non-Asians reside in Bangkok and the provinces.

Regional Identity

Religion, royalty and tradition are the defining characteristics of Thai society. That Thailand is the only country in Southeast Asia never colonised by a foreign power has led to a profound sense of pride in these elements. However, the country is not homogenous, and in the south a strong cultural identity prevails that is more in tune with the Islamic culture of nearby Malaysia.

Before modern political boundaries divided the Malay peninsula into two countries, the city states, sultanates and villages were part of an Indonesian-based Srivijaya empire – with intermingled customs and language – all vying for local control over shipping routes. Many southern Thai towns and geographic names bear the hallmark of the Bahasa language, and some village traditions would be instantly recognised by a Sumatran but not by a northern Thai. Chinese culture is also prominent in southern Thailand, as seen in the numerous temples and clan houses, and it is this intermingling of domestic and 'foreign' culture that defines the south.

Lifestyle

The ordinary life of southern Thais can be divided into two categories: country and city.

Those in rural coastal areas are typically employed in rubber farming or fishing, though rice and livestock farming are also evident. Rubber farmers live in small, typically inland settlements identified by straight rows of trees and pale sheets of drying latex; many islands on the Andaman coast are dotted with these shady rubber forests. Traditional Muslim villages are built directly over the water in a series of connected stilt houses. Because the Andaman Sea had a history of tranquil behaviour, there was no fear of the ocean's wrath, a preconception painfully destroyed by the 2004 tsunami.

Within the cities, life looks a lot like the rest of the country (busy and modern), but the presence of Chinese and Indian merchants marks the uniqueness of southern Thai cities. The commercial centres are also the market towns, where the brightly coloured fishing boats ease into the harbour, unloading the catch and filling the marina with the aroma of fish.

Thailand Demographics

Population: 66.8 million

Fertility rate: 1.6

Percentage of people over 65: 9.2%

Urbanisation rate: 34%

Life expectancy: 73 years

Family Values

The importance of the family unit in Thai society is immediately apparent to a visitor in the many family-owned and -operated businesses. It is still common to see three generations employed in a family-run guesthouse, or sharing the same house. The elderly are involved in day-to-day life, selling sweets to neighbourhood kids or renting motorcycles to tourists, for example. Although tourism has significantly altered the islanders' traditional way of life, these jobs help to keep many ambitious children from seeking employment on the mainland.

THE INVISIBLE BURMESE

During the most oppressive years of the Myanmar state, an exodus of Burmese made their way to Thailand. Approximately 150,000 people have entered the kingdom as political and ethnic refugees, but the vast majority are economic migrants (estimated at two to three million, of which less than half are documented). They fill the low-level jobs – fish-processing, construction, and domestic and factory work – that used to employ unskilled northeastern Thai labourers. In the south, most of the hotel and restaurant staff you meet day to day will likely be from Myanmar. Many Thais believe Thailand needs this imported workforce as the population is ageing faster than it is reproducing.

However, the emerging immigration 'situation' has not been dealt with as swiftly by the government as the private sector. Because many of immigrants are residing and working in Thailand illegally, they are subjected to exploitative relationships with employers; many human rights activists describe their working conditions as modern-day slavery. These people can't return home due to possible persecution by the Myanmar regime and they can't turn to the Thai authorities in cases of workplace abuse because they would risk deportation.

Economy

Due to tourism, fishing, prawn farming and rubber, the south is Thailand's wealthiest region. Most rubber tappers are born into the industry, inheriting the profession of their fathers and mothers. Prawn and fish farming, on the other hand, are relatively new industries, introduced as an economic development program for rural communities losing ground to commercial fishing operations. The venture proved profitable and Thailand is one of the leading exporters of farm-raised prawns. However, fish farms have been largely unregulated until recently, leading to a host of environmental problems, such as water pollution and the destruction of mangrove forests.

Tourism has undoubtedly had the most tangible impact on the economy of the area, transforming many small villages into bilingual enterprises. Women who would otherwise sell products at markets have studied Thai traditional massage. Other do-it-yourself franchises, so prolific in Thai communities, have been tailored to tourists: shops along beach thoroughfares sell sunscreen and postcards instead of rice whisky and grilled fish, itinerant vendors hawk sarongs and henna tattoos instead of feather dusters and straw brooms, while fishermen sometimes abandon their nets for bigger catches – tourists on snorkelling trips.

Across Thailand, the size of the middle class is growing with successive decades, bridging the gap between rich and poor. Thailand doesn't suffer from poverty of sustenance; even the most destitute Thai citizens can have shelter and food. Rather, the lower rung of Thai society suffers from poverty of material: money isn't available for extensive education, material goods or health care. This is most obvious when you look at the numbers: the average Thai income stands at around US$2000 a year, but many people in rural provinces earn as little as US$570 a year.

Lifestyle Statistics

Average age of marriage for a Thai man/woman: 27/24 years

Minimum daily wage in Bangkok: 300B

Entry-level government salary: 10,000B per month

Religion

Buddhism

Approximately 95% of Thais follow Theravada Buddhism, also known as Hinayana or 'Lesser Vehicle' Buddhism to distinguish it from the Mahayana or 'Great Vehicle' school of Buddhism. The primary difference between the faiths is that Theravada Buddhists believe individuals are responsible for their own enlightenment, while Mahayana Buddhists believe in putting others' salvation over one's own.

The ultimate end of all forms of Buddhism is to reach *nibbana* (from Sanskrit, nirvana), which literally means the 'blowing out' or extinction of all desire and thus of all *dukkha* (suffering). Having achieved *nibbana*, an individual is freed from the cycle of rebirths and enters the spiritual plane. In reality, most Thai Buddhists aim for rebirth in a 'better' existence in the next life, rather than striving to attain *nibbana*. To work towards this goal, Buddhists carry out meritorious actions *(tam bun)* such as feeding monks, giving donations to temples and performing regular worship at the local wát (temple). The Buddhist theory of karma is well expressed in the Thai proverb *tam dee, dâi dee; tam chôo·a, dâi chôo·a* (do good and receive good; do evil and receive evil).

There is no specific day of worship in Thai Buddhism; instead the faithful go to temples on certain religious holidays, when it is convenient or to commemorate a special family event. Most temple visits occur on *wan prá* (excellent days), which occur four times a month, according to phases of the moon. Other activities include offering food to the temple *sangha* (community of monks and nuns), meditating, listening to monks chanting *suttas* (discourses of the Buddha) and attending talks on *dhamma* (right behaviour).

Monks & Nuns

There are about 32,000 monasteries in Thailand and 200,000 monks, many of whom are ordained for life. Traditionally, every Thai male is expected to spend time as a monk, usually between finishing school and marrying or starting a career. Even His Majesty King Bhumibol served as a novice at Wat Bowonniwet in Banglamphu, Bangkok. Traditionally boys would devote a year or more to monastic life, but these days most men enter the *sangha* for two weeks to three months during *pan·săh* (Buddhist Lent), which coincides with the rainy season.

Instead of a handshake, the traditional Thai greeting is the *wâi* – a prayerlike gesture with the palms placed together.

Women can become *mâa chee* (eight-precept nuns) but this is held in slightly lower regard than the status of male monks, as most Thais believe that a woman can only achieve *nibbana* if she is reincarnated as a man. Both monks and nuns shave their heads and wear robes (orange for men, white for women), give up most of their personal belongings and live on charity. Thais donate generously to the local wát, so monks often live quite comfortable lives.

An increasing number of foreigners are coming to Thailand to be ordained as Buddhist monks or nuns. If you want to find out more, visit the website **Buddha Net** (www.buddhanet.net).

As long as you dress appropriately and observe the correct etiquette you will be welcome at most monasteries. However, take care not to disturb monks while they are eating or meditating – nothing breaks the concentration quite like tourists snapping photographs!

Islam

Thailand is home to 1.6 million Muslims (just over 4% of Thailand's population), concentrated in the south of the country. Most Thai Muslims are of Malay origin and generally follow a moderate version of the Sunni sect mixed with pre-Islamic animism.

A decade-long revival movement has cultivated stricter Islamic practices and suspicions of outside influences. Under this interpretation of Islam, many folk practices have been squeezed out of daily devotions and local people see the mainly Buddhist government and education system as intolerant of their way of life. Schools and infrastructure in the Muslim-majority south are typically underfunded, and frustration with the Bangkok government is sometimes defined as a religious rather than political struggle.

There are mosques throughout southern Thailand but few are architecturally interesting and most are closed to women. If you do visit a mosque, remember to cover your head and remove your shoes.

Other Religions

Half a per cent of the population – primarily hill tribes converted by missionaries and Vietnamese immigrants – is Christian, while another half a per cent is made up of Confucians, Taoists, Mahayana Buddhists and Hindus. Chinese temples and joss houses are a common sight in the south and in Bangkok's Chinatown, and Bangkok is also home to the large, colourful Hindu Sri Mariamman Temple.

Arts

Much of Thailand's creative energy has traditionally gone into the production of religious and ceremonial art. Painting, sculpture, music and theatre still play a huge role in the ceremonial life of Thais, and religious art is very much a living art form.

Literature

The most pervasive and influential work of classical Thai literature is the *Ramakian,* based on the Hindu holy book, the *Ramayana,* which was brought to Southeast Asia by Indian traders and introduced to Thailand by the Khmer about 900 years ago. Although the main theme remains the same, the Thais embroidered the *Ramayana* by providing much more biographical detail on arch-villain Ravana (Thotsakan in the *Ramakian*) and his wife Montho. The monkey-god, Hanuman, is also transformed into something of a playboy.

The epic poem *Phra Aphaimani* was composed by poet Sunthorn Phu (1786–1855) and is set on the island of Ko Samet. *Phra Aphaimani* is Thailand's most famous classical literary work, and tells a typically epic story of an exiled prince.

The leading postmodern writer is Prabda Yoon, whose short-story collection *Probability* won the 2002 SEA Write award. Although his works have yet to be translated, he wrote the screenplay for *Last Life in the Universe* and other Pen-ek Ratanaruang–directed films, and in 2004 was commissioned by Thailand's Ministry of Culture to write a piece on the 2004 tsunami. The result, *Where We Feel: A Tsunami Memoir by an Outsider,* was distributed free along the Andaman coast.

Thai literature is usually written in Thai, however some modern works you may find translated include:

- *Pisat, Evil Spirits* by Seni Saowaphong deals with conflicts between the old and new generations.
- *Lai Chiwit (Many Lives)* by Kukrit Pramoj is a collection of short stories.
- *Monsoon Country* by Pira Sudham brilliantly captures the northeast's struggles against nature.
- *The Judgement by Chart Korbjitti* is a drama about a young village man wrongly accused of a crime.
- *Jasmine Nights* by SP Somtow is an upbeat coming-of-age novel that fuses traditional ideas with modern Thai pop culture.
- *Married to the Demon King* by Sri Doruang adapts the Ramayana into modern Bangkok.

Several Thai novels and short stories translated by Marcel Barang, including stories by Chart Korbjitti and two-time SEA Write winner Win Lyovarin, can be downloaded as e-books at www.thaifiction.com.

Recommended Fiction

- *The Lioness in Bloom: Modern Thai Fiction about Women (translated by Susan Fulop Kepner)*
- *Four Reigns (Kukrit Pramoj)*
- *Bangkok 8 (John Burdett)*
- *Fieldwork: A Novel (Mischa Berlinski)*

SAVING FACE

Thais believe strongly in the concept of saving face, ie avoiding confrontation and endeavouring not to embarrass themselves or other people (except when it's *sà·nùk* – or 'fun' – to do so). The ideal face-saver doesn't bring up negative topics in conversation, doesn't express firm convictions or opinions, and doesn't claim to have an expertise. Agreement and harmony are considered to be the most important social graces.

While Westerners might find a heated discussion to be good sport, Thais avoid such confrontations and regard any instance where voices are raised as rude and potentially volatile. Losing your temper causes a loss of face for everyone present, and Thais who have been crossed often react in extreme ways.

Minor embarrassments, such as tripping or falling, might elicit giggles from a crowd of Thais. In this case they aren't taking delight in your mishap, but helping you save face by laughing it off.

Cinema

Thailand has a lively homespun movie industry, producing some very competent films in various genres. The most expensive film ever made in the country, not to mention the highest grossing, was director Prince Chatrichalerm Yukol's epic *Legend of Suriyothai* (2003), which tells the story of a 16th-century warrior princess. But what has propelled Thai viewers to forsake Hollywood imports are generally action flicks such as *Ong Bak: Thai Warrior* and the follow-ups including *Tom Yum Goong*, directed by Prachya Pinkaew.

Thailand has cropped up in various foreign film festivals over the years, with several critically acclaimed art-house movies. Pen-Ek Ratanaruang's clever and haunting movies, such as *Last Life in the Universe* and *6ixty9ine*, have created a buzz on the film-festival circuit. Apichatpong Weerasethakul leads the avant-garde pack with his Cannes-awarded *Tropical Malady* and *Blissfully Yours*.

The Thai government is now actively touting Thailand as a location for foreign film-makers. The most famous film to be made here in recent years was *The Beach* (2000). Based on the Alex Garland novel, it was filmed at Maya Bay on Ko Phi-Phi, Phuket, and several jungle locations near Krabi and Khao Yai National Park. The film caused controversy for allegedly damaging the environment in Maya Bay, which was also a location for the 1995 pirate stinker *Cutthroat Island*. Other famous films made here include the James Bond romp *The Man with the Golden Gun* (1974), which was filmed in Ao Nang Bay, *Good Morning Vietnam* (1987), *The Killing Fields* (1984), *The Deer Hunter* (1978), *Bridget Jones: The Edge of Reason* (2004) and *The Hangover II* (2011).

Music

Traditional Thai music may sound a little strange to visitors, as the eight-note Thai octave is broken in different places to the European octave. Thai scales were first transcribed by Thai-German composer Phra Chen Duriyanga (Peter Feit), who also composed Thailand's national anthem in 1932.

The classical Thai orchestra is called the *Ɓèe·pâht* and can include anything from five to 20 musicians. The most popular stringed instrument is the *ja·kêh*, a slender guitarlike instrument played horizontally on the ground. Woodwind instruments include the *klòo·i*, a simple wooden flute, and the *Ɓèe*, a recorderlike instrument with a reed mouthpiece. You'll hear the *Ɓèe* being played if you go to a Thai boxing match. Perhaps the most familiar Thai instrument is the *kĭm* or hammer dulcimer,

There is no universally accepted method of transliterating from Thai to English, so some words and place names are spelled a variety of ways.

responsible for the plinking, plunking music you'll hear in Thai restaurants across the world.

The contemporary Thai music scene is strong and diverse. The most popular genre is undoubtedly *lôok tûng* (a style analogous to country and western in the USA), which tends to appeal most to working-class Thais. The 1970s ushered in a new style dubbed *pleng pêu·a chee·wít* (literally 'music for life'), inspired by the politically conscious folk rock of the USA and Europe. The three biggest modern Thai music icons are rock staple Carabao, pop star Thongchai 'Bird' MacIntyre, and *lôok tûng* queen Pumpuang Duangchan, who died tragically in 1995.

Today there are hundreds of youth-oriented Thai bands, from chirpy boy and girl bands to metal rockers, making music that is easy to sing along with and maddeningly hard to get out of your head.

In the 1990s an alternative pop scene – known as *pleng tâi din* (underground music) – grew in Bangkok. Modern Dog, a Britpop-inspired band, is generally credited with bringing independent Thai music into the mainstream, and their success paved the way for more mainstream alternative acts such as Apartmentkunpha, Futon, Chou Chou and Calories Blah Blah. Thai headbangers designed to fill stadiums include perennial favourite Loso, as well as Big Ass, Potato and Bodyslam.

Architecture

Most traditional Thai architecture is religious in nature. Thai temples, like Thai Buddhism, gladly mix and match different foreign influences, from the corn-shaped stupa inherited from the Khmer empire to the bell-shaped stupa of Sri Lanka. Despite the foreign flourishes, the roof lines of all Thai temples mimic the shape of the *naga* (mythical serpent) that protected the Buddha during meditation and is viewed as a symbol of life. Green and gold tiles represent scales while the soaring eaves are the head of the creature.

Bangkok's finest teak building is Vimanmek Teak Mansion, said to be the largest golden-teak building in the world. Teak houses are typically raised on stilts to minimise damage caused by flooding and provide a space for storage and livestock. In the south, houses have traditionally been simpler, relying heavily on bamboo poles and woven bamboo fibre. You might also see Malay-style houses, which use high masonry foundations rather than wooden stilts.

Architecture over the last 100 years has been influenced by cultures from all over the world. In the south, you can still see plenty of Sino-Portuguese *hôrng tăa·ou* (shophouses) – these are plastered Chinese-style masonry houses with shops below and living quarters above. Classic examples of this style can be found in Phuket Town. Since WWII the main trend in Thai architecture has been one of function over form, inspired by the European Bauhaus movement. As a result, there are lots of plain buildings that look like egg cartons turned on their sides.

Thai architects began experimenting during the building boom of the mid-1980s, resulting in creative designs such as Sumet Jumsai's famous

THE NICKNAME GAME

At birth Thai babies are given auspicious first names, often bestowed by the family patriarch or matriarch. These poetic names are then relegated to bureaucratic forms and name cards, while the child is introduced to everyone else by a one-syllable nickname. Thai nicknames are usually playful and can be inspired by the child's appearance (Moo, meaning 'pig', if he/she is chubby) or a favourite pastime (Toon, short for 'cartoon' for avid TV-watchers). Girls will typically be named Lek or Noi (both of which mean 'small').

robot-shaped Bank of Asia on Th Sathon Tai in Bangkok, or the Elephant Building off Th Phaholyothin in northern Bangkok.

Painting

Except for the prehistoric and historic cave paintings found in the south of the country, not much ancient formal painting exists in Thailand, partly due to the devastating Burmese invasion of 1767. The vast majority of what exists is religious in nature, and typically takes the form of temple paintings illustrating the various lives of the Buddha.

Since the 1980s boom years, Thai secular sculpture and painting have enjoyed increased international recognition, with a handful of Impressionism-inspired artists among the initial few to have reached this vaunted status. Succeeding this was the 'Fireball' school of artists, such as Manit Sriwanichpoom, who specialise in politically motivated, mixed-media art installations. In recent years Thai artists have again moved away from both traditional influences and political commentary and towards contemporary art, focusing on more personal themes, such as those seen in the gender-exploring works of Pinaree Sanpitak, or Maitree Siriboon's identity-driven work.

Theatre & Dance

Traditional Thai theatre consists of four main dramatic forms: *kŏhn* is a formal masked dance-drama, traditionally reserved for royalty, depicting scenes from the *Ramakian; lá·kon* is dance-drama performed for common people; *lí·gair* is a partly improvised, often bawdy, folk play featuring dancing, comedy, melodrama and music; and *hùn lŏo·ang (lá·kon lék)* is traditional puppet theatre enacting religious legends or folk tales.

Most of these forms can be enjoyed in Bangkok, both at dinner shows for tourists and at formal theatrical performances. There are also some distinctively southern theatrical styles, predating the arrival of Islam on the Malay peninsula. The most famous is *má·noh·rah,* the oldest surviving Thai dance-drama, which tells the story of Prince Suthon, who sets off to rescue the kidnapped Manohraa, a *gin·ná·ree* (woman-bird) princess. As in *lí·gair,* performers add extemporaneous, comic rhymed commentary. Trang also has a distinctive form of *lí·gair,* with a storyline depicting Indian merchants taking their Thai wives back to India for a visit.

Another ancient theatrical style in the south is shadow-puppet theatre (also found in Indonesia and Malaysia), in which two-dimensional figures carved from buffalo hide are manipulated against an illuminated cloth screen. The capital of shadow puppetry today is Nakhon Si Thammarat, which has regular performances at its festivals. While sadly a dying art, puppets are popular souvenirs for tourists.

Recommended Arts Reading

- *The Thai House: History and Evolution (2002; Ruethai Chaichongrak)*
- *The Arts of Thailand (1998; Steve Van Beek)*
- *Flavours: Thai Contemporary Art (2005; Steven Pettifor)*
- *Bangkok Design: Thai Ideas in Textiles & Furniture (2006; Brian Mertens)*
- *Buddhist Temples of Thailand: A Visual Journey Through Thailand's 40 Most Historic Wats (2010; Joe Cummings)*

The Sex Industry in Thailand

Prostitution has been widespread in Thailand since long before the country gained a reputation among international sex tourists. Throughout Thai history the practice was accepted and common, though it has not always been respected by society as a whole. Today prostitution is technically illegal but anti-prostitution laws are ambiguous and often unenforced.

Entertainment places fine a worker if she doesn't smile enough, arrives late or doesn't meet the drink quota. These deductions often exceed the worker's monthly base salary.

History & Cultural Attitudes

Prostitution was declared illegal in 1960 under pressure from the UN. But a separate law passed in 1966 allows for entertainment places (go-go bars, beer bars, massage parlours, karaoke bars and bathhouses) that can legally provide nonsexual services (such as dancing, massage, a drinking buddy); sexual services are brokered through these venues but they are not technically the businesses' primary purpose.

With the arrival of the US military forces in Southeast Asia during the Vietnam War era, enterprising forces adapted the existing framework to a new clientele. The industry targeted to foreigners is very visible with multiple red-light districts in Bangkok alone, but there is also a more clandestine domestic sex industry and myriad informal channels of sex-for-hire.

In 1998 the International Labour Organization, a UN agency, advised Southeast Asian countries, including Thailand, to recognise prostitution as an economic sector and income generator. It is estimated that one-third of the entertainment establishments are registered with the government and the majority pay an informal tax in the form of police bribes. In 2003, measures to legalise prostitution cited the Thai sex industry as being worth US$4.3 billion (about 3% of GDP), employing roughly 200,000 sex workers. A study conducted in 2003 by Thailand's Chulalongkorn University estimated 2.8 million sex workers, of which 1.98 million were adult women, 20,000 were adult men and 800,000 were children, defined as any person under the age of 18.

PROS & CONS

Women's rights groups take oppositional approaches to the question of prostitution. Abolitionists see prostitution as exploitation and an infraction of basic human rights. Meanwhile, mitigators recognise that there is demand and supply and try to reduce the risks associated with the activity, through HIV/AIDS prevention and education programs (especially for economic migrants). Sex-worker organisations argue that prostitution is a legitimate job and the best way to help women is to treat the issue from a workers' rights perspective, demanding fair pay and compensation, legal redress and mandatory sick and vacation time. According to pro-sex worker unions, the country's quasi-legal commercial sex establishments provide service industry jobs (dishwashers, cooks, cleaners) to non sex workers, who would otherwise qualify for employment protection if the employer were a restaurant or hotel.

HIV/AIDS

Thailand was lauded for its rapid and effective response to the AIDS epidemic through an aggressive condom-use campaign in the 1990s. But infection rates throughout the population have spiked as public education has declined. A 2007 study found that HIV prevalence among sex workers is highest in the freelance community (at a rate of 19%) compared to sex workers in commercial establishments (4.3%). Of the country's 490,000 people living with HIV/AIDS, intravenous drug users (22%) and gay men (between 20% to 31%) made up the largest portion of HIV prevalence.

Economic Motivations

Regardless of their background, most women in the sex industry are there for financial reasons: many find that sex work is one of the highest-paying jobs for their level of education, and they have financial obligations (be it dependents or debts). The most comprehensive data on the economics of sex workers comes from a 1993 survey by Kritaya Archavanitkul. The report found that sex workers made a mean income of 17,000B per month (US$18 per day), the equivalent of a mid-level civil servant job, a position acquired through advanced education and family connections. At the time of the study, most sex workers did not have a high-school degree.

These economic factors provide a strong incentive for rural, unskilled women (and to a lesser extent, men) to engage in sex work.

As with many in Thai society, a large percentage of sex workers' wages are remitted back to their home villages to support their families (parents, siblings and children). Kritaya's 1993 report found that between 1800B and 6100B per month was sent back home to rural communities. The remittance-receiving households typically bought durable goods (TVs and washing machines), bigger houses and motorcycles or automobiles. Their wealth displayed their daughters' success in the industry and acted as free advertisement for the next generation of sex workers.

NGOs

Ecpat (www.ecpat.net): anti-child prostitution and trafficking group.

Coalition Against Trafficking in Women (CATW; www.catwinternational.org): anti-trafficking NGO.

Empower Foundation (www.empowerfoundation.org): sex workers union.

Child Prostitution & Human Trafficking

According to Ecpat (End Child Prostitution & Trafficking), there are currently 30,000 to 40,000 children involved in prostitution in Thailand, though estimates are unreliable. According to Chulalongkorn University, the number of children is as high as 800,000, though this number includes anyone under the age of 18.

In 1996, Thailand passed a reform law to address the issue of child prostitution defined into two tiers: 15 to 18 years old and under 15. Fines and jail time are assigned to customers, establishment owners and even parents involved in child prostitution. Under the old law only prostitutes were culpable. Many countries also have extraterritorial legislation that allows nationals to be prosecuted in their own country for such crimes committed in Thailand.

Urban job centres such as Bangkok have large populations of displaced and marginalised people (migrant workers, ethnic hill-tribe members and impoverished rural Thais). Children of these fractured families often turn to street begging, which is an entryway into prostitution usually through low-level criminal gangs.

Suspicious behaviour involving child-sex tourism can be reported on a dedicated hotline (☎1300).

Thailand is also a conduit and destination for people trafficking from Myanmar, Laos, Cambodia and China. In 2007, the US State Department labelled Thailand as not meeting the minimum standards of prevention of human trafficking. Reliable data about trafficked people, including minors, does not exist.

Food & Drink

There's an entire universe of amazing dishes once you get beyond 'pàt tai' and green curry, and for many visitors food is one of the main reasons for choosing Thailand as a destination. Even more remarkable, however, is the love for Thai food among the locals: Thais become just as excited as tourists when faced with a bowl of well-prepared noodles or when seated at a renowned hawker stall. This unabashed enthusiasm for eating, not to mention an abundance of fascinating ingredients and influences, has generated one of the most fun and diverse food scenes of anywhere in the world.

Staples & Specialities

Rice & Noodles

Thailand is the world's third-largest exporter of rice and in 2012 exported 6.9 million tonnes of the grain.

Rice is so central to Thai food culture that the most common term for 'eat' is *gin kôw* (literally, 'eat rice') and one of the most common greetings is *Gin kôw rĕu yang?* (Have you eaten rice yet?). To eat is to eat rice, and for most of the country, a meal is not acceptable without this staple. The highest grade is *kôw hŏrm má·lí* (jasmine rice), a fragrant long grain that is so coveted by neighbouring countries that there is allegedly a steady underground business in smuggling out fresh supplies.

Rice is customarily served alongside main dishes like curries, stir-fries or soups, which are lumped together as *gàp kôw* 'with rice'. When you order plain rice in a restaurant you use the term *kôw Ƅlòw,* 'plain rice' or *kôw sŏoay,* 'beautiful rice'.

You'll find four basic kinds of noodle in Thailand. Hardly surprising, given the Thai fixation on rice, is the overwhelming popularity of *sên gŏo·ay đĕe·o,* noodles made from rice flour mixed with water to form a paste, which is then steamed to form wide, flat sheets. The sheets are folded and sliced into various widths.

Also made from rice, *kà·nŏm jeen* is produced by pushing rice-flour paste through a sieve into boiling water, much the way Italian-style pasta is made. *Kà·nŏm jeen* is a popular morning market meal that is eaten doused with various spicy curries and topped with a self-selection of fresh and pickled vegetables and herbs.

The third kind of noodle, *bà·mèe,* is made from wheat flour and egg. It's yellowish in colour and is sold only in fresh bundles.

Finally there's *wún·sên,* an almost clear noodle made from mung-bean starch and water. Often sold in dried bunches, *wún·sên* (literally 'jelly thread') is prepared by soaking it in hot water for a few minutes. The most common use of the noodle is in *yam wún sên,* a hot and tangy salad made with lime juice, fresh sliced *prík kêe nŏo* (tiny chillies), shrimp, ground pork and various seasonings.

Curries & Soups

In Thai, *gaang* (it sounds somewhat similar to the English 'gang') is often translated as 'curry', but it actually describes any dish with a lot of liquid and can thus refer to soups (such as *gaang jèut*) as well as the classic chilli paste–based curries for which Thai cuisine is famous. The preparation of the latter begins with a *krê·uang gaang*, created by mashing, pounding and grinding an array of fresh ingredients with a stone mortar and pestle to form an aromatic, extremely pungent-tasting and rather thick paste. Typical ingredients in a *krê·uang gaang* include dried chilli, galangal, lemon grass, kaffir lime zest, shallots, garlic, shrimp paste and salt.

Another food celebrity that falls into the soupy category is *đôm yam*, the famous Thai spicy and sour soup. Fuelling the fire beneath *đôm yam*'s often velvety surface are fresh *prík kêe nŏo* or, alternatively, half a teaspoonful of *nám prík pŏw* (a roasted chilli paste). Lemon grass, kaffir lime leaf and lime juice give *đôm yam* its characteristic tang.

Thai Food, by David Thompson, is widely considered the most authoritative English-language book on Thai cooking. Thompson's latest book, *Thai Street Food*, focuses on less formal street cuisine.

Stir-Fries & Deep-Fries

The simplest dishes in the Thai culinary repertoire are the various stir-fries *(pàt)*, introduced to Thailand by the Chinese, who are world famous for being able to stir-fry a whole banquet in a single wok.

The list of *pàt* dishes seems endless. Many cling to their Chinese roots, such as the ubiquitous *pàt pàk bûng fai daang* (morning glory flash-fried

FRUIT FOR THOUGHT

Thailand is home to an entire repertoire of fruit you probably never knew existed. Many are available year-round nowadays, but April and May is peak season for several of the most beloved varieties, including durian, mangoes and mangosteen.

Custard apple Known in Thai as *nóy nàh*, the knobbly green skin of this fruit conceals hard black seeds and sweet, gloopy flesh with a granular texture.

Durian Known in Thai as *tú·ree·an*, the king of fruit is also Thailand's most infamous, due to its intense flavour and odour, which can suggest everything from custard to onions.

Guava A native of South America, *fa·ràng* is a green, applelike ball containing a pink or white flesh that's sweet and crispy.

Jackfruit The gigantic green pod of *kà·nŭn* – it's generally considered the world's largest fruit – conceals dozens of waxy yellow sections that taste like a blend of pineapple and bananas (it reminds us of Juicy Fruit chewing gum).

Langsat Strip away the yellowish peel of this fruit, known in Thai as *long·gong*, to find a segmented, perfumed pearlescent flesh with a lychee-like flavour.

Longan *Lam yai* takes the form of a tiny hard ball; it's like a mini lychee with sweet, perfumed flesh. Peel it, eat the flesh and spit out the hard seed.

Lychee The pink skin of *lín·jèe* conceals an addictive translucent flesh similar in flavour to a grape; it's generally only available between April and June.

Mangosteen The hard purple shell of *mang·kút*, the queen of Thai fruit, conceals delightfully fragrant white segments, some containing a hard seed.

Pomelo Like a grapefruit on steroids, *sôm oh* takes the form of a thick pithy green skin hiding sweet, tangy segments; cut into the skin, peel off the pith and then break open the segments and munch on the flesh inside.

Rambutan People have different theories about what *ngó* look like, not all repeatable in polite company. Regardless, the hairy shell contains sweet translucent flesh that you scrape off the seed with your teeth.

Rose apple Known in Thai as *chom·pôo*, rose apple is an elongated pink or red fruit with a smooth, shiny skin and pale, watery flesh; a good thirst quencher on a hot day.

Salak Also known as snake fruit because of its scaly skin; the exterior of *sàlà* looks like a mutant strawberry and the soft flesh tastes like unripe bananas.

Starfruit The star-shaped cross-section of *má·feu·ang* is the giveaway; the yellow flesh is sweet and tangy and believed by many to lower blood pressure.

with garlic and chilli), while some are Thai-Chinese hybrids, such as *pàt pèt* (literally 'hot stir-fry'), in which the main ingredients, typically meat or fish, are quickly stir-fried with red curry paste.

Tôrt (deep-frying in oil) is mainly reserved for snacks such as *glôo·ay tôrt* (deep-fried bananas) or *Ƀò·Ƀée·a tôrt* (fried spring rolls). An exception is *Ƀlah tôrt* (deep-fried fish), which is a common way to prepare fish.

Bangkok's Top 50 Street Food Stalls, by Chawadee Nualkhair, also functions well as a general introduction and guide to Thai-style informal dining.

Hot & Tangy Salads

Standing right alongside curries in terms of Thai-ness is the ubiquitous *yam,* a hot and tangy 'salad' typically based around seafood, meat or vegetables. Lime juice provides the tang, while the abundant use of fresh chilli generates the heat. Most *yam* are served at room temperature or just slightly warmed by any cooked ingredients. The dish functions equally well as part of a meal, or on its own as *gàp glâam,* snack food to accompany a night of boozing.

Nám Prík

Although they're more home than restaurant food, *nám prík,* spicy chilli-based 'dips' are, for the locals at least, among the most emblematic of all Thai dishes. Typically eaten with rice and steamed or fresh vegetables and herbs, they're also among the most regional of Thai dishes, and you could probably pinpoint the province you're in by simply looking at the *nám prík* on offer.

Fruits

Being a tropical country, Thailand excels in the fruit department. *Má·môo·ang* (mangoes) alone come in a dozen varieties that are eaten at different stages of ripeness. Other common fruits include *sàp·Ƀà·rót* (pineapple), *má·lá·gor* (papaya) and *đaang moh* (watermelon), all of which are sold from the ubiquitous vendor carts and are accompanied by a dipping mix of salt, sugar and ground chilli.

ETHNIC SPECIALITIES

In addition to geography, the country's predominant minorities – Muslims and Chinese – have had different but profound influences on the local cuisine.

Thai-Muslim Cuisine

Muslims are thought to have first visited Thailand during the late 14th century. Common Thai-Muslim dishes include:

➡ *Gaang mát·sà·màn* – 'Muslim curry' is a rich coconut milk–based dish. As with many Thai-Muslim dishes, there is an emphasis on the sweet.

➡ *Kôw mòk* – biryani, a dish found across the Muslim world. In Thailand it is typically made with chicken and served with a dipping sauce and a bowl of chicken broth.

➡ *Sà·đé (satay)* – the savoury peanut-based dipping sauce served with these grilled skewers of meat is often mistakenly associated with Thai cooking.

Thai-Chinese Cuisine

Chinese labourers and vendors most likely introduced the wok and several noodle dishes to Thailand. Thai-Chinese dishes you're likely to run across include:

➡ *Bà·mèe* – Chinese-style wheat and egg noodles are typically served with slices of barbecued pork, a handful of greens and/or wontons.

➡ *Gŏo·ay đĕe·o kôo·a gài* – wide rice noodles fried with little more than egg, chicken, squid and garlic oil; a popular dish in Bangkok's Chinatown.

➡ *Kôw man gài* – chicken rice, originally from the Chinese island of Hainan, is now found in just about every corner of Thailand.

THE RIGHT TOOL FOR THE JOB

If you're not offered chopsticks, don't ask for them. Thai food is eaten with fork and spoon, not chopsticks. When *fa·ràng* (Westerners) ask for chopsticks to eat Thai food, it only puzzles the restaurant proprietors.

Chopsticks are reserved for eating Chinese-style food (such as noodles) from bowls, or for eating in all-Chinese restaurants. In either case you will be supplied with chopsticks without having to ask. Unlike their counterparts in many Western countries, restaurateurs in Thailand won't assume you don't know how to use them.

Sweets

English-language Thai menus often have a section called 'Desserts', but the concept takes two slightly different forms in Thailand. *Kŏrng wăhn,* which translates as 'sweet things', are small, rich sweets that often boast a slightly salty flavour. Prime ingredients for *kŏrng wăhn* include grated coconut, coconut milk, rice flour (from white rice or sticky rice), cooked sticky rice, tapioca, mung-bean starch, boiled taro and various fruits.

Thai sweets similar to the European concept of pastries are called *kà·nŏm.* Probably the most popular type of *kà·nŏm* in Thailand are the bite-sized items wrapped in banana leaves, especially *kôw đôm gà·tí* and *kôw đôm mát.* Both consist of sticky rice grains steamed with *gà·tí* (coconut milk) inside a banana-leaf wrapper to form a solid, almost taffylike, mass.

Although foreigners don't seem to immediately take to most Thai sweets, two dishes few visitors have trouble with are *rođee,* the backpacker staple 'banana pancakes' slathered with sugar and condensed milk, and *ai·đim gà·tí,* Thai-style coconut ice cream. At more traditional shops, the ice cream is garnished with toppings such as kidney beans or sticky rice, and is a brilliant snack on a sweltering Thai afternoon.

Pok Pok, by Andy Ricker with JJ Goode, features recipes of the rustic regional Thai dishes served at Ricker's eponymous Portland, Oregon, and New York City restaurants.

Regional Variations

One particularly unique aspect of Thai food is its regional diversity. Despite having evolved in a relatively small area, Thai cuisine is anything but a single entity, and takes a slightly different form every time it crosses a provincial border. The food of Thailand's southern provinces is no exception to this – see the boxed text on p185 for more information.

Drinks

Coffee, Tea & Fruit Drinks

Thais are big coffee drinkers, and good-quality arabica and robusta are cultivated in the hilly areas of northern and southern Thailand. The traditional filtering system is nothing more than a narrow cloth bag attached to a steel handle. This type of coffee is served in a glass, mixed with sugar and sweetened with condensed milk – if you don't want either, be sure to specify *gah·faa dam* (black coffee) followed with *mâi sài nám·đahn* (without sugar).

Black tea, both local and imported, is available at the same places that serve real coffee. *Chah tai,* Thai-style tea, derives its characteristic orange-red colour from ground tamarind seed added after curing.

Fruit drinks appear all over Thailand and are an excellent way to rehydrate after water becomes unpalatable. Most *nám pŏn·lá·mái* (fruit juices) are served with a touch of sugar and salt and a whole lot of ice. Many foreigners object to the salt, but it serves a metabolic role in helping the body to cope with tropical temperatures.

The authors of Eating Thai Food (www.eatingthaifood.com) have put together an 88-page illustrated PDF guide to identifying and ordering Thai dishes for foreign visitors.

Beer & Spirits

There are several brands of beer in Thailand, ranging from domestic brands (Singha, Chang, Leo) to foreign-licensed labels (Heineken, Asahi, San Miguel) – all largely indistinguishable in terms of taste and quality.

Domestic rice whisky and rum are favourites of the working class, struggling students and family gatherings, as they're more affordable than beer. Once spending money becomes a priority, Thais often upgrade to imported whiskies. These are usually drunk with lots of ice, soda water and a splash of coke. On a night out, buying a whole bottle is the norm in most of Thailand. If you don't finish it, it will simply be kept at the bar until your next visit.

Where to Eat & Drink

Appon's Thai Food (www.khiewchanta.com) features nearly 1000 authentic, well-organised Thai recipes – many with helpful audio recordings of their Thai names – written by a native Thai.

Prepared food is available just about everywhere in Thailand, and it shouldn't come as a surprise that the locals do much of their eating outside the home. In this regard, as a visitor, you'll fit right in.

Open-air markets and food stalls are among the most popular places for Thais to eat. In the mornings, stalls selling coffee and Chinese-style doughnuts spring up along busy commuter corridors. At lunchtime, eaters might grab a plastic chair at yet another stall for a simple stir-fry, or pick up a foam box of noodles to scoff down at the office. In most small towns, night markets often set up in the middle of town with a cluster of vendors, metal tables and chairs, and some shopping as an after-dinner mint.

There are, of course, restaurants *(ráhn ah·hăhn)* in Thailand that range from simple food stops to formal affairs. Lunchtime is the right time to point and eat at the *ráhn kôw gaang* (rice-and-curry shop), which sells a selection of premade dishes. The more generic *ráhn ah·hăhn đahm sàng* (food-to-order shop) can often be recognised by a display of raw ingredients – Chinese kale, tomatoes, chopped pork, fresh or dried fish, noodles, eggplant, spring onions – for a standard repertoire of Thai and Chinese dishes. As the name implies, the cooks attempt to prepare any dish you can name, a slightly more difficult operation if you can't speak Thai.

COFFEE, SOUTHERN STYLE

In virtually every town or city in southern Thailand, you'll find numerous old-world cafes known to locals as *ráhn goh·bée*. The shops are almost exclusively owned by Thais of Chinese origin, and often seem suspended in time, typically sporting the same decor and menu for decades. Characteristics of *ráhn goh·bée* include marble-topped tables, antique mugs and dishes, and an almost exclusively male clientele that also seems not to have budged since opening day. Some of the most atmospheric *ráhn goh·bée* in Thailand can be found in the town of Trang.

The beans used at *ráhn goh·bée* are sometimes grown abroad, but are roasted domestically. Atlhough the beans are as black as the night, the drink typically tends to lack body. This may be due to the brewing method, which involves pouring hot water through a wind-socklike piece of cloth that holds the loose grounds. Typically, *ráhn goh·bée* is served over a dollop of sweetened condensed milk and a tablespoon (or more) of sugar in small, handleless glasses. For those lacking a sweet tooth, try *goh·bée or* (black coffee), or just ask them to hold the sugar. All hot coffee drinks are served with a 'chaser' of weak green tea.

Ráhn goh·bée are also a great place for a quick bite. Upon arriving at the more traditional ones, you'll be greeted by a tray of steamed Chinese buns, sweet snacks such as sticky rice wrapped in banana leaf, or baked goods.

CAN I DRINK THE ICE?

Among the most common concerns we hear from first-time visitors to Thailand is about the safety of the country's ice. At the risk of sounding fatalistic, if it's your first time in Thailand, the ice is probably the least of your concerns – you're most likely going to get sick at some point. Considering that you're exposing yourself to a different cuisine and a new and unfamiliar family of bacteria and other bugs, it's virtually inevitable that your body will have a hard time adjusting.

In most cases this will mean little more than an upset tummy that might set you back a couple hours. You can avoid more serious setbacks, at least initially, by trying to frequent popular restaurants and vendors where dishes are prepared to order and only drinking bottled water.

And the ice? We've been lacing our drinks with it for years and have yet to trace it back to any specific discomfort, though we still recommend avoiding ice in remote areas.

Vegetarians & Vegans

Vegetarianism isn't a widespread trend in Thailand, but many of the tourist-oriented restaurants cater to vegetarians, and there are also a handful of *ráhn ah·hăhn mang·sà·wí·rát* (vegetarian restaurants) in Bangkok and several provincial capitals where the food is served buffet-style and is very inexpensive. Dishes are almost always 100% vegan (ie no meat, poultry, fish or fish sauce, dairy or egg products).

During the Vegetarian Festival, celebrated by Chinese Buddhists in October, many restaurants and street stalls in Bangkok, Phuket and in the Chinese business districts of most Thai towns go meatless for one month. See p252 for more information.

The phrase 'I'm vegetarian' in Thai is *pŏm gin jair* (for men) or *dì·chăn gin jair* (for women). Loosely translated this means 'I eat only vegetarian food', which includes no eggs and no dairy products – in other words, total vegan.

Maintained by a Thai woman living in the US, She Simmers (www.shesimmers.com) is a good resource for those making Thai food outside of Thailand.

Habits & Customs

Like most of Thai culture, eating conventions appear relaxed and informal but are orchestrated by many implied rules.

Whether at home or in a restaurant, Thai meals are always served 'family-style' – that is, from common serving platters – and the plates appear in whatever order the kitchen can prepare them. When serving yourself from a common platter, put no more than one spoonful onto your plate at a time. Heaping your plate with all 'your' portions at once will look greedy to Thais unfamiliar with Western conventions. Another important factor in a Thai meal is achieving a balance of flavours and textures. Traditionally, the party orders a curry, a steamed or fried fish, a stir-fried vegetable dish and a soup, taking great care to balance cool and hot, sour and sweet, salty and plain.

Originally Thai food was eaten with the fingers, and it still is in certain regions of the kingdom. In the early 1900s, Thais began setting their tables with fork and spoon to affect a 'royal' setting, and it wasn't long before fork-and-spoon dining became the norm in Bangkok and later spread throughout the kingdom. To use these tools the Thai way, use a serving spoon to take a single mouthful of food from a central dish, and ladle it over a portion of your rice. The fork is then used to push the now food-soaked portion of rice back onto the spoon before entering the mouth.

Written, photographed and maintained by the author of this section, www.austinbushphotography.com covers food and dining in both Bangkok and provincial Thailand.

Food Spotter's Guide

Spanning four distinct regions, influences ranging from China to the Middle East, a multitude of exotic ingredients, and a reputation for spice, Thai food can be a bit intimidating. To point you in the direction of the good stuff, we've put together a shortlist of must-eat dishes from Bangkok and Thailand's south.

1. Kôw yam
A popular breakfast in southern Thailand, this dish includes rice topped with sliced herbs, bean sprouts, dried prawns, toasted coconut and powdered red chilli, served with a sour/sweet fish-based sauce.

2. Pàt tai
This dish of thin rice noodles fried with egg, tofu and shrimp, and seasoned with fish sauce, tamarind and dried chilli, has emerged as the poster boy for Thai food – and justifiably so.

3. Gŏoay đĕeo reua
Known as boat noodles because they were previously served from canals in central Thailand, these intense pork- or beef-based bowls are among the most full-flavoured of all Thai noodle dishes.

4. Oh đow
This dish, a speciality of Phuket Town, takes the form of small chunks of taro fried with egg and tiny oysters, and topped with deep-fried pork rind.

5. Ngóp
Something of a grilled curry, this dish combines coconut cream, a herb paste and seafood, all wrapped in a banana leaf and grilled until firm.

6. Loh bà
A Phuket Town delicacy; deep-fried savoury snacks served with a slightly sweet dipping sauce.

7. Kôw mòk
The Thai version of biryani couples golden rice and tender chicken with a sweet-and-sour dip and a savoury broth.

8. Đôm yam
The 'sour Thai soup' moniker featured on many English-language menus is a feeble description of this mouth-puckeringly tart and intensely spicy herbal broth.

9. Gaang kĕe·o wăhn
Known outside of Thailand as green curry, this intersection of a piquant, herbal spice paste and rich coconut milk is single-handedly emblematic of Thai cuisine's unique flavours and ingredients.

10. Yam
This family of Thai 'salads' combines meat or seafood with a tart and spicy dressing and fresh herbs.

1

2

3

4
AUSTIN BUSH ©
8
AUSTIN BUSH ©
5
AUSTIN BUSH ©
9
AUSTIN BUSH ©
6
AUSTIN BUSH ©
10
AUSTIN BUSH ©
7
AUSTIN BUSH ©

Environment

Bound to the east by the Gulf of Thailand and to the west by the Andaman Sea, an extension of the Indian Ocean, Thailand possesses one of the most alluring coastlines in the world, with exquisitely carved limestone formations above water and tremendously rich coral reefs below. Hundreds of tropical islands of all shapes and sizes adorn the coast, from flat sand bars covered in mangroves to looming karst massifs licked by azure waters and ringed by white sand beaches.

The Land

Thailand's odd shape – bulky and wide up north, with a long pendulous arm draping to the south – has often been compared to the head of an elephant. Roughly the size of France, about 517,000 sq km, Thailand stretches an astounding 1650km along a north–south axis and experiences an extremely diverse climate, including two distinct monsoons from both the southwest and northwest. The north of the country rises into high forested mountains, while the south consists of a long ridge of limestone hills, covered in tropical rainforest.

Both the Andaman and the Gulf Coasts have extensive coral reefs, particularly around the granitic Surin Islands and Similan Islands in the Andaman Sea. More reefs and Thailand's most dramatic limestone islands sit in Ao Phang-Nga near Phuket. The west coast is of particular interest to divers because the waters are stunningly clear and extremely rich in marine life.

WHITE ELEPHANT

If anyone in Thailand comes across a white elephant, it must be reported to the Bureau of the Royal Household, and the King will decide whether it meets the criteria to be a royal white elephant.

Wildlife

With its diverse climate and topography, it should come as no surprise that Thailand is home to a remarkable diversity of flora and fauna. What is more surprising is that Thailand's environment is still in relatively good shape, particularly considering the relentless development going on all over the country. That said, there are certainly problems for some endangered species and marine environmental issues.

Animals & Birds

Animals that live on the coasts and islands of Thailand must adapt to shifting tides and the ever-changing mix of salt water and freshwater. Rather than elephants and tigers, keep your eyes open for smaller creatures, such as the odd little mudskipper, a fish that leaves the water and walks around on the mudflats when the tide goes out; or the giant water monitor, a fearsome 350cm-long lizard that climbs and swims effortlessly in its search for small animals.

Without a doubt you will see some of the region's fabulous birdlife – Thailand is home to 10% of the world's bird species – especially sandpipers and plovers on the mudflats, and herons and egrets in the swamps. Look overhead for the sharply attired, chocolate-brown and white Brahminy kite, or scan low-lying branches for one of the region's many colourful kingfishers. You are likely to spot a troop of gregarious and noisy crab-eating macaques, and don't be surprised to see these monkeys swimming from shore. With luck you may glimpse a palm civet, a complexly marbled catlike creature, or a serow, the reclusive 'goat-antelope' that bounds fearlessly among inaccessible limestone crags.

The oceans on either side of the Thai peninsula are home to hundreds of species of coral, and the reefs created by these tiny creatures provide the perfect living conditions for countless species of fish, crustaceans and tiny invertebrates. You can find one of the world's smallest fish (the 10mm-long goby) or the largest (a 10m-long whale shark), plus reef denizens such as clownfish, parrotfish, wrasse, angelfish, triggerfish and lionfish. Deeper waters are home to larger species such as groupers, barracudas, sharks, manta rays, marlin and tunas. You might also encounter turtles, whales and dolphins.

Endangered Species

Thailand is a signatory to the UN Convention on International Trade in Endangered Species of Wild Fauna and Flora (Cites) but the enforcement of these trade bans is notoriously lax – just walk around the animal section of Bangkok's Chatuchak Weekend Market to see how openly the rules are flouted. Due to habitat loss, pollution and poaching, a depressing number of Thailand's mammals, reptiles, fish and birds are endangered, and even populations of formerly common species are diminishing at an alarming rate. Rare mammals, birds, reptiles, insects, shells and tropical aquarium fish are routinely smuggled out to collectors around the world or killed to make souvenirs for tourists.

Many of Thailand's marine animals are under threat, including whale sharks, although they have been seen more frequently in Thai waters recently, and sea turtles, which are being wiped out by hunting for their eggs, meat and shells. Many other species of shark are being hunted to extinction for their fins, which are used to make shark-fin soup.

The rare dugong (similar to the manatee and sometimes called a sea cow), once thought extinct in Thailand, is now known to survive in a few small pockets, mostly around Trang in southern Thailand, but is increasingly threatened by habitat loss and the lethal propellers of tourist boats.

The Thai government is slowly recognising the importance of conservation, perhaps in part due to the efforts and leadership of Queen Sirikit, and many of the kingdom's zoos now have active breeding and conservation programs. Wildlife organisations such as the Phuket Gibbon Rehabilitation Centre are working to educate the public about native wildlife and have initiated a number of wildlife rescue and rehabilitation projects.

Plants

Southern Thailand is chock-full of luxuriant vegetation, thanks to its two monsoon seasons. The majority of forests away from the coast are evergreen rainforests, while trees at the ocean edge and on limestone formations are stunted due to lack of fresh water and exposure to harsh minerals.

The most beautiful shoreline trees are the many species of palm trees occurring in Thailand, including some found nowhere else in the world. All have small tough leaves with characteristic fanlike or featherlike shapes that help dissipate heat and conserve water. Look for the elegant cycad palm on limestone cliffs, where it grows in cracks despite the complete absence of soil. Collected for its beauty, this common ornamental plant is disappearing from its wild habitat.

Thailand is also home to nearly 75 species of salt-tolerant mangroves – small trees highly adapted to living at the edge of salt water. Standing tiptoe-like on clumps of tall roots, mangroves perform a vital ecological function by trapping sediments and nutrients, and by buffering the coast from the fierce, erosive power of monsoons. This habitat serves as a secure nursery for the eggs and young of countless marine organisms, yet Thailand has destroyed at least 50% of its mangrove swamps to make way for prawn farms and big hotels.

National Parks

National parks in Thailand are a huge draw for beach visitors. The popular island getaways of Ko Chang and Ko Samet sit just off the mainland along the eastern gulf coast. Ko Tarutao Marine National Park is remote and undeveloped for real back-to-nature vacations. Ao Phang-Nga, north of Phuket, is endlessly photogenic with its limestone cliffs jutting out of the aquamarine water while knotted mangrove roots cling to thick mudflats. Meanwhile the Similan Islands and Surin Islands Marine National Parks, in the waters of the Andaman Sea, have some of the world's best diving.

Approximately 13% of Thailand is covered by 112 national parks and 44 wildlife sanctuaries, which is a very respectable rate by international standards. Of Thailand's protected areas, 18 parks protect islands and mangrove environments. Thailand's parks and sanctuaries contain more than 850 resident and migratory species of birds and dwindling numbers of tigers, clouded leopards, koupreys, elephants, tapirs, gibbons and Asiatic black bears, among other species.

Despite promises, official designation as a national park or sanctuary does not always guarantee protection for habitats and wildlife. Local farmers, well-moneyed developers and other business interests will often prevail, either legally or illegally, over environmental protection in Thailand's national parks. Islands that are technically exempt from development often don't adhere to the law and there is little government muscle to enforce regulations. Ko Chang, Ko Samet and Ko Phi-Phi are all curious examples of national parks with development problems.

Students at Dulwich International College in Phuket collected 5000kg of garbage from the beach in a single day; help them out by picking up rubbish whenever you can.

For foreigners, parks charge entry fees of 100B to 400B per adult and 50B to 200B for children. In recent years these rates were doubled, then rescinded on a case-by-case basis, so what you pay may differ from park to park. In some cases the **Royal Forestry Department** (☎0 2561 4293, 0 2561 4292; 61 Th Phahonyothin, Chatuchak) rents out accommodation; make reservations in advance as this is a popular option for locals. All parks are best visited in the dry season, particularly marine national parks, which can have reduced visibility in the water during the monsoon.

Environmental Issues

Thailand is in a different developmental stage to most Western countries and this affects both the environmental problems and how people react to them. Thailand is wealthier, better developed and more educated than its regional neighbours, so there is an awareness of environmental issues that barely exists in countries such as Cambodia and Myanmar. But that awareness is often limited in scope and, while this is slowly changing, it rarely develops into the sort of high-profile, widespread movements seen in Europe, North America or Australia.

As such most issues have a very low profile, with only the most visible problems, such as pollution, overdevelopment and a lack of adequate planning, making it onto a visitor's radar. Look a little deeper and you'll see the environment has often been the victim in Thailand's rapid modernisation, with short-term considerations usually to the fore. Few Thais see any problem with cutting down mangroves to make prawn farms, or powering their development with energy from dams in Laos and dubious natural gas concerns in Myanmar.

So many well-meaning laws have been put on the books that it might seem Thailand is turning the corner towards greater ecological consciousness. But when the implementation of these laws is investigated it is often revealed that corruption and lack of political resolve have severely hampered efforts to enforce these environmental laws. With the deep split within Thai politics showing no signs of being healed and governments having to make all sorts of undesirable concessions just to stay in power, it seems the political will to enforce these laws remains some way off. Ironically, however, this same lack of political stability has also scared off investors.

The Land Environment

The main area in which Asia exceeds the West in terms of environmental damage is deforestation, though current estimates are that Thailand still has about 25% of its forests remaining, which stands up favourably against the UK's dismal 5%. The government's National Forest Policy, introduced in 1985, recommended that 40% of the country should be forested, and a complete logging ban in 1989 was a big step in the right direction. By law Thailand must maintain 25% of its land area as 'conservation forests'. But the logging ban has simply shifted the need for natural resources elsewhere. While illegal logging persists in Thailand on a relatively small scale, in neighbouring Cambodia, Laos and particularly Myanmar the scale has been huge since the 1989 ban. A great number of logs are illegally slipped over the border from these countries.

Despite Thailand being a signatory to Cites, all sorts of land species are still smuggled out of Thailand, either alive or as body parts for traditional Chinese medicines. Tigers may be protected by Thai law, but the kingdom remains the world's largest exporter of tiger parts to China (tiger penis and bone are believed to have medicinal effects and to increase libido). Other animal species are hunted (often illegally) to make souvenirs for tourists, including elephants, jungle spiders, giant insects and butterflies; and along the coast clams, shells and puffer fish.

The government has cracked down on restaurants serving *ah·hăhn Ъàh* (jungle food), which includes endangered wildlife species such as barking deer, bears, pangolins, gibbons, civets and gaurs. A big problem is that national park officials are underpaid and undertrained, yet are expected to confront armed poachers and mercenary armies funded by rich and powerful godfathers.

The widely touted idea that ecotourism can act as a positive force for change has been extensively put to the test in Thailand. In some instances tourism has definitely had positive effects. The expansion of Thailand's national parks has largely been driven by tourism. In Khao Yai National Park, all hotel and golf-course facilities were removed to reduce damage to the park environment. As a result of government and private-sector pressure on the fishing industry, coral dynamiting has been all but eliminated in the Similan and Surin Islands, to preserve the area for tourists.

However, tourism can be a poisoned chalice. Massive developments around and frequently in national parks have ridden roughshod over the local environment in their rush to provide bungalows, luxury hotels, beach bars and boat services for tourists. Ko Phi-Phi and Ko Samet are two national parks where business interests have definitely won out over the environment. In both cases, the development began in areas set aside for *chow lair* (also spelt *chao leh;* sea gypsies, the semi-nomadic people who migrate up and down the coast). Ko Lipe in Ko Tarutao Marine National Park and Ko Muk in Hat Chao Mai National Park now seem to be heading the same way.

Rubbish and sewage are growing problems in all populated areas, even more so in heavily visited areas where an influx of tourists overtaxes the local infrastructure. One encouraging development was the passing of the 1992 Environmental Act, which set environmental quality

FISHY BUSINESS

The famous white sands of Thailand's beaches are actually tiny bits of coral that have been defecated by coral-eating fish.

standards, designated conservation and pollution-control areas, and doled out government clean-up funds. Pattaya built its first public wastewater treatment plant in 2000 and conditions have improved ever since.

While Thais generally remain reluctant to engage in broader environmental campaigns, people are increasingly aware of the issues, particularly when they will be affected. Local people have campaigned for years against the building of dams, though usually without success. Damage to a favourite beach during the filming of *The Beach* in Ko Phi-Phi Marine National Park triggered demonstrations around the country and the filming of the US TV show *Survivor* in Ko Tarutao Marine National Park provoked a similar outcry. As a result, strict production and filming bans have been put in place to avoid similar issues in the future. The construction of a petroleum pipeline to Songkhla in 2002 created a remarkable level of grassroots opposition among ordinary village people.

A group of ecologically engaged Buddhist monks, popularly known as Thai Ecology Monks, uses peaceful activism to empower local communities in their fight against monolithic projects.

The Marine Environment

Thailand's coral reef system, including the Andaman coast from Ranong to northern Phuket and the Surin and Similan Islands, is one of the world's most diverse. Some 600 species of coral reef fish, endangered marine turtles and other rare creatures call this coastline home.

THAILAND'S NATIONAL PARKS

PARK	FEATURES	ACTIVITIES
Ang Thong Marine National Park	40 tropical islands with coral reefs, lagoons and limestone cliffs	sea kayaking, hiking, snorkelling
Ao Phang-Nga National Marine Park	coastal bay with limestone cliffs, islands and caves; coral reefs and mangroves	sea kayaking, snorkelling, diving
Hat Chao Mai National Park	coastal park with beaches, mangroves, lagoons and coral islands; dugong and mangrove birds	sea kayaking, snorkelling, diving
Kaeng Krachan National Park	mainland park with waterfalls and forests; plentiful birdlife and jungle mammals	bird-watching
Khao Laem Ya/Mu Ko Samet National Park	marine park with beaches, near-shore coral reefs	snorkelling, diving, boat trips, sailboarding
Khao Lak/Lam Ru National Park	coastal park with cliffs and beaches; hornbills, monkeys and bears	hiking, boat trips
Khao Luang National Park	mainland park with forested mountain peaks, streams and waterfalls; jungle mammals, birds and orchids	hiking
Khao Phanom Bencha National Park	mainland mountain jungle with tumbling waterfalls; monkeys	hiking
Khao Sam Roi Yot National Park	coastal park with caves, mountains, cliffs and beaches; serow, Irrawaddy dolphins and 300 bird species	cave tours, bird-watching, kayaking
Khao Sok National Park	mainland park with rainforest, waterfalls and rivers; tigers, monkeys, *rafflesia* and 180 bird species	hiking, elephant trekking, tubing

The 2004 tsunami caused high-impact damage to about 13% of the Andaman coral reefs. However, damage from the tsunami was much less than first thought and relatively minor compared to the ongoing environmental degradation that accompanies an industrialised society. It is estimated that about 25% of Thailand's coral reefs have died as a result of industrial pollution and that the annual loss of healthy reefs will continue at a rapid rate. Even around the dive centre of Phuket, dead coral reefs are visible on the northern coast. The biggest threat to corals is sedimentation from coastal development: new condos, hotels, roads and houses. High levels of sediment in the water stunts the growth of coral. Other common problems include pollution from anchored tour boats or other marine activities, rubbish and sewage dumped directly into the sea, and agricultural and industrial run-off. Even people urinating in the water as they swim creates by-products that can kill sensitive coral reefs.

The environmental wake-up call from the tsunami emphasised the importance of mangrove forests, which provide a buffer from storm surges. Previously mangroves were considered wastelands and were indiscriminately cut down. It is estimated that about 80% of the mangrove forests lining the gulf coast and 20% of those on the Andaman coast have been destroyed for conversion into fish and prawn farms, tourist development or to supply the charcoal industry. Prawn farms constitute the biggest threat because Thailand is the world's leading producer of black tiger prawns, and the short-lived, heavily polluting farms are built

PARK	FEATURES	ACTIVITIES
Ko Phi-Phi Marine National Park	archipelago marine park with beaches, lagoons and sea cliffs; coral reefs and whale sharks	sea kayaking, snorkelling, diving
Ko Tarutao Marine National Park	archipelago marine park with remote jungle islands and tropical beaches; monkeys, jungle mammals and birds	snorkelling, hiking, diving
Laem Son National Park	coastal and marine park with 100km of mangroves; jungle and migratory birds	bird-watching, boat trips
Mu Ko Chang National Marine Park	virgin rainforests, waterfalls, beaches and coral reefs	snorkelling, diving, elephant trekking, hiking
Mu Ko Lanta Marine National Park	archipelago marine park with scenic beaches; coral reefs and reef sharks	sea kayaking, elephant trekking, hiking, snorkelling, diving
Mu Ko Phetra Marine National Park	rarely visited archipelago marine park; dugongs, birds and coral reefs	sea kayaking, snorkelling
Similan Islands Marine National Park	marine park with granite islands; coral reefs and seabirds; underwater caves	snorkelling, diving
Sirinat National Park	coastal park with casuarina-backed beaches; turtles and coral reefs	walking, snorkelling, diving
Surin Islands Marine National Park	granite islands; coral reefs, whale sharks and manta rays	snorkelling, diving
Tharnbok Korannee National Park	coastal park with mangrove forests and limestone caves; monkeys, orchids and seabirds	sea kayaking

in pristine mangrove swamps at a terrific environmental and social cost. Prawn farms are big business (annual production in Thailand has soared from 900 tonnes to 277,000 tonnes in the past 10 years), and the large prawn-farming businesses are often able to operate in spite of environmental protection laws. Protesting voices rarely get heard in the media.

Contributing to the deterioration of the overall health of the ocean are Thailand and its neighbours' large-scale fishing industries, frequently called the 'strip-miners of the sea'. Fish catches have declined by up to 33% in the Asia-Pacific region in the past 25 years and the upper portion of the Gulf of Thailand has almost been fished to death. Most of the commercial catches are sent to overseas markets and rarely see a Thai dinner table. The seafood sold in Thailand is typically from fish farms, another large coastal industry for the country.

Making a Difference

It may seem that the range of environmental issues in Thailand is overwhelming, but there is actually much that travellers can do to minimise the impact of their visits, or to even make a positive impact. The way you spend your money has a profound influence on the kingdom's economy and on the profitability of individual businesses. Ask questions up front and take your money elsewhere if you don't like the answers. For instance, a number of large-scale resorts that lack road access transport clients across fragile mudflats on tractors (a wantonly destructive practice), so when booking a room inquire about transport to the hotel. Of the region's countless dive shops, some are diligent about minimising the impact their clients have on the reefs; however, if a dive shop trains and certifies inexperienced divers over living reefs, rather than in a swimming pool, then it is causing irreparable harm to the local ecosystem. As a rule, do not touch or walk on coral, monitor your movements so you avoid accidentally sweeping into coral, and do not harass marine life (any dead puffer fish you see on the beach probably died because a diver poked it until it inflated).

Make a positive impact on Thailand by checking out one of the many environmental and social groups working in the kingdom. If you do some research and make arrangements before arriving, you may connect with an organisation that matches your values.

GOING GREEN

A growing number of overseas tourism companies now insist that Thailand's tourism operators have environmental policies in place before doing business with them.

The **Wild Animal Rescue Foundation of Thailand** (WAR; Map p68; ☎0 2712 9715; www.warthai.org; 65/1 3rd fl, Soi 55, Th Sukhumvit, Bangkok) is one of the leading advocates for nature conservation in Thailand and currently runs four wildlife sanctuaries that use volunteers to rehabilitate and return former pets to the wild.

The **Bird Conservation Society of Thailand** (☎0 2691 4816; www.bcst.or.th) provides a plethora of information about the birds of Thailand, offering field trip reports, sightings of rare birds, bird festivals, bird surveys and a birding online forum.

The **Sanithirakoses-Nagapateepa Foundation** (www.sulak-sivaraksa.org), started by the 1995 Alternative Nobel Prize winner Sulak Sivaraksa, is an umbrella organisation associated with numerous environmental and social justice groups in Thailand including the Foundation for Children, Forum of the Poor, the Thai-Tibet Centre and Pun Pun, an organic farm and sustainable living centre. These groups offer countless opportunities to help empower local communities and get involved in issues important to the people of Thailand. They have also started an alternative college called Spirit in Education Movement (SEM) that offers a spiritually based, ecologically sound alternative to mainstream education.

Other groups promoting environmental issues in Thailand include:

Thailand Environment Institute (☎0 2503 3333; www.tei.or.th)
Wildlife Friends Foundation Thailand (☎0 3245 8135; www.wfft.org)
WWF Thailand (☎0 2524 6168; www.wwfthai.org)

Thai Massage

To many visitors Thai massage is just another way to relax and perhaps relieve back kinks earned from a long plane ride. However, this complex art is a major part of traditional Thai medicine and is the fruit of spiritual and medicinal roots that reach back to the time of the historical Buddha.

Spiritual & Philisophical Origins

The Thai form of massage can be traced to Tantric Buddhist Vajrayana teachings that originated in India and Tibet. Translated from the Sanskrit, Vajrayana means 'Diamond Vehicle' or 'Thunderbolt Vehicle', and marks a transition in Mahayana Buddhism when practices became more ritualised as opposed to primarily using abstract meditations to reach nirvana. Among other things, Vajrayana introduced the ideas of Mantra (a symbol, word or group of words that can help spiritual transformation) and Mandala (a symbol, often artistically depicted, that represents the universe). The school of thought flourished in India and Tibet between the 6th and 11th centuries, but its main influence on Thailand was its healing arts.

Like the Thai culture itself, influences on medicine came from many directions including China, India and other Southeast Asian regions. Both ayurvedic and traditional Chinese medicine are at the roots of Thai massage. Practitioners generally follow the ten Sen lines (see p402), or channels through the body with specific pressure points along them, which are similar to the Chinese meridians and Indian nadis. In Thai theory, these lines carry several types of 'wind' (depending on the Sen line), from air that is inhaled through the lungs. When a line is blocked or unbalanced, illness or symptoms will ensue. At the same time, yoga *asana* stretches are used to open joints, aided by the loosening power of rocking, thumb pressure and rhythmic compression.

Thai massage is often called the 'expression of loving kindness' because at the the heart of the practice is the compassionate intent of the healer. In its true form, the masseur will bond with the client in a meditative state and both parties will experience a deeper sense of awareness through humility and concentration.

History

Jivaka Komarabhacca, the physician to the historical Buddha himself, is said to be the father of Thai massage and Thai traditional medicine. Although he wasn't mentioned at length in Buddhist scriptures, Dr Jivaka holds extremely high status in Thai lore; there's a statue of him at the Grand Palace in Bangkok and you'll often see his likeness next to statues of the Buddha, like a protector. It's said that the doctor spread the practice of massage to monasteries to help ease the monks' pain after long hours of meditation. Today's massage practitioners still practise *wâi kroo* (the Thai tradition of giving prayers and offerings to a teacher) devoted to the revered physician with chants that include his name.

King Rama V commissioned a textbook, completed in 1900, of traditional Thai medicine that included massage

Massage techniques and knowledge were passed down through the generations by masters to their disciples within the monasteries. With the support of royalty and the devotion of the practitioners, techniques evolved for healing the sick and injured of the community. Everything was passed down orally until the 1830s when Wat Pho was built and included stone engravings and statues explaining and depicting Thai massage arts. It wasn't until the 1920s that Thai massage became a profession.

Getting a Massage

Where & How Much

Any tourist area in southern Thailand will have many massage options. Most places are in salon-looking air-conditioned shops with big reclining chairs for foot massages and manicures/pedicures and another area for a row or two of mattresses with curtained partitions for full body massages. Some shops also offer body scrubs and other spa services. Along busy beaches you'll find sheltered, elevated platforms with rows of mattresses where you can be pummelled in your swimsuit with a view of the sea. There may only be a masseuse or two in more remote areas, but these independent practitioners tend to be more skilled than those working in the big shops.

In general massages are most expensive near more posh resorts, but this isn't always the case. Sometimes just walking a minute or two off the main drag or further down the beach will yield lower prices. Expect to pay 200B to 500B for a one-hour Thai massage or foot massage. Prices

THE TEN SEN

Thai massage is based on these 10 energy pathways and the goal of a good practitioner will be to balance and/or unblock these channels.

SEN	LOCATION	MAIN INDICATIONS
Sen Sumana	Tip of the tongue to the solar plexus region	Digestive system, asthma, heart disease, bronchitis
Sen Ittha	Left nostril, over the head, down the back to the left knee	Headache, sinus problems, urinary tract, back pain
Sen Pingkhala	Same as Sen Ittha but on right side	Same as Sen Ittha plus gallbladder and liver disease
Sen Kalathari	Two lines make an X across body from tips of toes to shoulders and down to fingertips	Digestive system, hernia, arthritis, mental disorder
Sen Sahatsarangsi	Left eye, down left side around to back of left leg, under foot, up front of left leg to navel	Toothache, eye function, depression, gastrointestinal disease
Sen Thawari	Same as Sen Sahatsarangsi but on the right side	Same as Sen Sahatsarangsi plus appendicitis and jaundice
Sen Lawusang	Left ear to left nipple to mid solar plexus region	Ear disorders, cough, toothache, gastrointestinal disorders
Sen Ulangwa	Same as Sen Lawusang but on the right side	Same as Sen Lawusang plus itchy skin and insomnia
Sen Nanthakrawat	Two lines, each from the navel: one to urine passageway and other to the anus	Infertility, impotence, diarrhoea, irregular menstruation
Sen Kitchanna	Navel to penis in men, navel to uterus in women	Same as Sen Nanthakrawat plus balances libido

WAT PHO

Wat Pho next to the Royal Palace in Bangkok is the ground zero of Thai massage. Before the royal wát was built on this site by Rama I in the late 1800s, a centre for traditional Thai medicine was here. The future wát incorporated this history into its curriculum and eventually became home to the first official school of Thai massage; inscribed tablets of the Sen pathways grace the temple's interior walls. Today the school is still considered the best in the country and visitors can attend training programs or simply come in and have a massage. In 2008 Wat Pho was recognised by Unesco in its Memory of the World Program. The manager of the school, Khun Serat, is the founder's grandson and many of the instructors are descendents of the original faculty.

Check the website www.watphomassage.com for details on everything from 30-hour Thai massage or foot massage courses to several month-long training programs. Course prices start at 7500B or you can get a half hour or hour-long traditional massage at the wát for 260B to 420B.

go up for additions like oil, aloe for sunburn, aromatherapy or hot herbal compresses.

A more upscale option is to get a deluxe massage at an independent or resort spa. Practitioners here tend to have more credentials than the street shop or beach masseuses although that doesn't always mean that they're better. The real advantage here is the more luxurious surroundings that may include beautiful views, trickling water and teak furniture, a relaxing soundtrack, lots of pleasant smells and more privacy. At a spa you'll also have a bevy of other services on offer from body wraps to flower baths and foot scrubs. Massage prices at spas tend to start at around 1000B.

Check-in

On busier, sleazier beaches there may be a tout outside the salon hustling tourists by crooning 'meestaa, want massage?' and you'll be called mister even if you're female; in classier parts of town services are announced by a spa menu outside the door or perhaps a group of giggling masseuses hanging out on the front step. If the practitioners are dressed professionally, usually in matching uniforms, the place will probably be a straightforward massage parlour. If the women are very young, scantily dressed or heavily made up, this is a red flag that fuller services may be on offer. Private massage rooms at the back of the salon in lieu of the more common curtained-off massage areas can be another clue that the salon may be geared towards less savoury practices. A man asking for an 'oil massage' may also sometimes lead to techniques not on the advertised menu, even at what appear to be classy establishments.

Once you're inside, take off your shoes and follow your masseuse. Sometimes you'll be asked to leave your clothes on while at other places you'll be given a pair of Thai-style pajamas or a sarong. In the case of the latter, strip down to your underwear either behind your curtain or in a changing area, and put on the supplied garments. On the beach you'll usually be massaged in your swimsuit, and a sarong is sometimes offered to women who wish to take off their bikini tops.

DRINK WATER

Practitioners recommend drinking lots of water or green tea after a massage to flush out any dislodged toxins.

The Massage

Thai massage is not for wimps. The session usually begins with relaxing kneading of the back, arms and legs and the practitioner will often ask you if the pressure is light or strong enough. Then it gets gnarly. First there's the chiropractic-like popping of joints – mostly fingers and toes but sometimes whole legs and arms as well as the back and neck. Then,

TRADITIONAL THAI MEDICINE

Much like other schools of Asian medicine, traditional Thai medicine (TTM) takes a holistic approach to health to include the physical body, heart, mind, spirit and flow of energy through the Sen. Much is based on the four elements of fire, water, air and earth, with each element ruling body parts and functions – earth rules the organs, air rules the 'wind' (generally meaning respiration and digestion), water rules bodily fluid and fire rules four types of bodily heat (including circulation). Living in harmony with nature, eating well and being in tune with one's own natural cycles (from night and day to ageing) are the keys to health by TTM standards.

Tastes are important to Thais in a culinary sense and this extends into the realm of medicine. How a herbal remedy tastes determines how it balances the elements and what ailment it can treat. For example, sweet treats fatigue, salty is good for constipation and bitter helps fight infection. TTM treatments generally include herbal remedies, massage and lifestyle changes.

even the tiniest masseuses will muscle you into yoga contortions that arch the back, extend the legs and arms and so much more that it feels like you're being turned into a human pretzel. You'll start the session on your back, get moved to a prone position about midway and then end with your head in the practitioner's lap for a final head massage and a popping back stretch. Overall the treatment itself isn't very relaxing, but you'll feel incredible afterwards. Let your massage therapist know in advance if you have any injuries and don't be afraid to tell them to ease up on a stretch or joint pop. As with any good workout, know your limits.

All this said, Thai massage in many tourist areas has become very watered down and you may end up with just a light massage without being contorted or popped in the slightest. Older ladies tend to give the most violent yet rewarding massages, but even with younger ones, you won't know until your nose is hitting your knee what kind of torturous therapy they're capable of.

A foot massage begins with a foot bath and moisturising treatment before the practitioner strongly works pressure points.

If this sounds too scary, Swedish and other types of massage are also often available, but you'll be missing out on a big cultural and maybe even spiritual experience. A more simple reflexology foot massage (available at almost all salons) may be a good place to start if you've never had a professional massage or are wary of the practice in any way.

Survival Guide

Responsible Travel

CULTURAL ETIQUETTE

Monarchy and religion are treated with extreme deference in Thailand. Thais avoid criticising or disparaging the royal family for fear of offending someone or, worse, being charged for lèse majesté, which carries a jail sentence.

Buddha images are sacred objects. Thais consider it bad form to pose in front of one for a photo or to clamber upon them (in the case of temple ruins); instead they show respect by performing a *wâi* (a prayerlike gesture) to the figure no matter how humble it is. As part of their ascetic vows, monks are not supposed to touch or be touched by women. If a woman wants to hand something to a monk, the object is placed within reach of the monk or on the monk's 'receiving cloth'.

From a spiritual viewpoint, Thais regard the head as the highest and most sacred part of the body and the feet as the dirtiest and lowest. Shoes are not worn inside private homes and temple buildings, as a sign of respect and for sanitary reasons. Thais also step over the threshold, which is where the spirit of the house is believed to reside.

Thais don't touch each other's head or ruffle their hair as a sign of affection. Occasionally you'll see young people touching each other's head, which is a teasing gesture, maybe even a slight insult, between friends.

Social Conventions & Gestures

The traditional Thai greeting is made with a prayerlike palms-together gesture known as *wâi*. The depth of the bow and the placement of the fingers in relation to the face is dependent on the status of the person receiving the *wâi*. Adults don't *wâi* children and in most cases service people (when they are doing their jobs) aren't *wâi-ed*, though this is a matter of personal discretion.

In the more traditional parts of the country, it's not proper for members of the opposite sex to touch one another, either as lovers or as friends. But same-sex touching is quite common and is typically a sign of friendship, not sexual attraction. Older Thai men might grab a younger man's thigh in the same way that buddies slap each other on the back. Thai women are especially affectionate with female friends, often sitting close to one another or linking arms.

Thais hold modesty in personal dress in high regard, though this is changing among the younger generation. The importance of modesty extends to the beach as well. Except for urbanites, most provincial Thais swim fully clothed. For this reason, sunbathing nude or topless is not acceptable and in some cases is even illegal. Remember that swimsuits are not proper attire off the beach; wear a cover-up in between the sand and your hotel.

TOURISM

Most forms of tourism, despite the prevailing prejudices, have a positive economic effect on the local economy in Thailand by providing jobs for young workers and business opportunities for entrepreneurs. But in an effort to be more than just a consumer, many travellers look for opportunities to spend where their money might be needed, either on charitable causes or activities that preserve traditional ways of life.

Diving

The popularity of Thailand's diving industry places immense pressure on fragile coral sites. To help preserve the ecology, adhere to these simple rules.

- Avoid touching living marine organisms, standing on coral or dragging equipment (such as fins) across the reef. Coral polyps can be damaged by even the gentlest contact.

ESSENTIAL ETIQUETTE

Dos

Stand respectfully for the national anthem It is played on TV and radio stations as well as public and government places at 8am and 6pm. If you're inside a building you don't have to stand.

Rise for the royal anthem It is played in movie theatres before every screening.

Smile a lot It makes everything easier.

Bring a gift if you're invited to a Thai home Fruit, drinks or snacks would be acceptable; flowers are usually for merit-making purposes not home decor.

Take off your shoes When you enter a home, temple building or wherever there are sandals piled up at the door.

Lower your head slightly When passing between two people having a conversation or when passing near a monk; it is a sign of respect.

Dress modestly for temple visits Cover to the elbows and ankles and always remove your shoes when entering any building containing a Buddha image.

Give and receive politely Extend the right hand out while the left hand gently grips the right elbow when handing an object to another person or receiving something – truly polite behaviour.

Respect all Buddha images and pictures of the monarchy Signs of disrespect can have serious consequences.

Sit in the 'mermaid' position inside temples Tuck your feet beside and behind you so that your feet aren't pointing at the Buddha image.

Don'ts

Don't get a tattoo of the Buddha It is considered sacrilegious.

Don't criticise the monarchy The monarchy is revered and protected by defamation laws.

Don't prop your feet on tables or chairs Feet are considered dirty and people have to sit there.

Don't step on a dropped bill to prevent it from blowing away Thai money bears a picture of the king. Feet + monarchy = grave offence.

Never step over someone or their personal belongings Aaah, attack of the feet.

Avoid tying your shoes to the outside of your backpack They might accidentally brush against someone, gross.

Don't touch a Thai person on the head It is considered rude, not chummy.

Women cannot touch monks or their belongings Step out of the way when passing a monk on the footpath and do not sit next to them on public transport.

➡ When treading water in shallow reef areas, be careful not to kick up clouds of sand, which can easily smother the delicate reef organisms.

➡ Take great care in underwater caves where your air bubbles can be caught within the roof and leave previously submerged organisms high and dry.

➡ Join a coral clean-up campaign that's sponsored by dive shops.

➡ Don't feed the fish or allow your dive operator to dispose of excess food in the water. The fish become dependent on this food source and don't tend to the algae on the coral, causing harm to the reef.

For more information, see p43.

Elephant Encounters

Throughout Thai history, elephants have been revered for their strength, endurance and intelligence, working alongside their mahouts harvesting teak, transporting goods through mountainous terrain or fighting ancient wars.

But many of the elephants' traditional roles have either been outsourced to machines or outlawed (logging was banned in 1989), leaving the domesticated animals and their mahouts without work. Some mahouts turned to begging on the streets in Bangkok and other tourist centres, but most elephants found work in Thailand's tourism industry; their jobs vary from circus-like shows to elephant camps giving rides to tourists. Other elephant encounters include mahout-training schools, while sanctuaries and rescue centres provide modest retirement homes to animals that can no longer work and are no longer financially profitable to their owners.

It costs about 30,000B (US$1000) per month to provide a comfortable living standard for an elephant; this amount is equivalent to the salary of Thailand's upper middle class and the work life of an elephant is about 50 years. Welfare standards within the tourism industry are not standardised or subject to government regulations so it's up to the conscientious consumer to encourage the industry to ensure safe working conditions for elephants.

Here are some questions to ask the elephant camps to make sure you've chosen a well-run operation.

➡ Does the camp employ a veterinarian?

➡ What is its policy on procuring new elephants? Some camps buy illegally caught wild elephants whose registration has been forged so they appear to be born in captivity.

➡ How many hours per day do the elephants work? A brisk-paced walk for about four hours per day (with breaks for eating and drinking in between) is considered adequate exercise.

➡ How many adults do the elephants carry? An elephant can carry a maximum of 150kg (330lb) of weight on its back, plus a mahout on its neck. Tally up you own and your partner's combined weight and request a separate elephant if you tip the scales.

➡ Are the elephants kept in a shady spot near fresh water and a food source? What do they eat? A balanced diet includes a mixture of fruit, grasses, bamboo and pineapple shoots.

➡ Do the elephants have noticeable wounds? This is often a sign of mistreatment.

➡ What kind of seat is used for elephant riding? Wooden seats, custom-made to fit the elephant's back, cause less irritation and stress on the animal.

➡ What is the camp's birth/death rate? Happy elephants have babies.

VOLUNTEERING

Thailand is still technically a developing country, lacking a tight-knit social safety net, an executed environmental protection program and equal labour protections. There are a myriad volunteering organisations in Thailand but be aware that so-called 'voluntourism' has become a big business and that not every organisation fulfils its promise of meaningful experiences. Before committing, do your homework on the tour organiser and the volunteer facility.

Environmental & Animal Welfare Work

At centres and sanctuaries that rely on volunteer labour, your hard work is often rewarded with meaningful interactions with the animals. There are also smaller organisations listed in the On the Road chapters.

Starfish Ventures (www.starfishvolunteers.com) Places volunteers in conservation, teaching and animal welfare programs throughout Thailand.

Wild Animal Rescue Foundation (WARF; www.warthai.org) Operates the Phuket Gibbon Rehabilitation Centre and a conservation education centre in Ranong Province on the Andaman coast. Job placements include assisting with the daily care of gibbons that are being rehabilitated for life in the wild or counting and monitoring sea-turtle nests.

Wildlife Friends of Thailand Rescue Centre (www.wfft.org; Phetchaburi) Puts volunteers to work caring for sun bears, macaques and gibbons at its animal rescue centre.

Humanitarian & Educational Work

Organisations require varying time commitments but in order to be an effective volunteer, you should dedicate at least a month to the program.

The following grassroots organisations are worth investigating.

Andaman Discoveries (☎08 7917 7165; www.andamandiscoveries.com; Phang-Nga) Manages a learning centre for children of migrants from Myanmar, an orphanage and a school for disabled children in southern Thailand.

Isara (☎0 4246 0827; www.isara.org) Places teachers in underprivileged schools around Thailand; one of the few volunteer programs that is free and placements include housing and some meals.

Open Mind Projects (☎08 7233 5734; www.openmindprojects.org) Offers volunteer positions in IT, health care, education and community-based ecotourism throughout Thailand.

Volunthai (www.volunthai.com) A family-run operation that places volunteers in teaching positions at rural schools with homestay accommodation.

Directory A–Z

Accommodation

Thailand offers a wide variety of accommodation from cheap and basic to pricey and luxurious.

Guesthouses

Guesthouses are generally the cheapest accommodation in Thailand and can be found all along the backpacker trail. In more remote areas like the eastern seaboard, guesthouses (as well as tourists) are not as widespread.

Rates vary according to facilities and location. In provincial towns, the cheapest rooms range from 150B to 350B, and usually have shared bathrooms and rickety fans. Private facilities, air-con and sometimes a TV can be had for 600B to 800B. But prices are much higher in the beach resorts, where a basic fan room can start at 600B to 800B. Many guesthouses make their bread and butter from the on-site restaurants that serve classic backpacker fare (banana pancakes and fruit shakes). Although these restaurants are convenient and a good way to meet other travellers, don't judge Thai food based on these dishes.

Most guesthouses cultivate a travellers' ambience with friendly, knowledgeable staff and book exchanges. But there are also plenty of guesthouses with grumpy, disgruntled clerks.

SLEEPING PRICE RANGES

The following price ranges refer to a double room with bathroom in high season. Unless otherwise stated, tax is not included in the price which only applies to larger hotels and high-end options.

- $ less than 1000B
- $$ 1000–3000B
- $$$ more than 3000B

Increasingly, guesthouses can handle advance reservations, but due to inconsistent cleanliness and quality it is advisable to always look at a room in person before committing. In tourist centres, there are usually alternatives nearby if your preferred place is full. Guesthouses typically only accept cash payments.

COMMISSION HASSLES

In the popular tourist spots you'll be approached, sometimes surrounded, by touts or transport drivers who get a commission from the guesthouse for bringing in potential guests. While it's annoying for the traveller, this is an acceptable form of advertising among small-scale businesses in Thailand. As long as you know the drill, everything should work out in your favour. Touts get paid for delivering you to a guesthouse or hotel (whether you check in or not). Some places refuse to pay commissions, so in return the touts will steer customers away from those places (by saying they are closed or burned down). In less scrupulous instances, they'll tell you that the commission-paying hotel is the one you requested. If you meet with resistance, call the guesthouse for a pick-up, as they are often aware of these aggressive business tactics.

Hotels

In provincial capitals and small towns, the only options are often older Thai-Chinese hotels, once the standard in Thailand. Most cater to Thai guests and English is usually limited.

These hotels are multistorey buildings and might offer a range of rooms from mid-range options with private bathrooms, air-con and TVs to cheaper ones with shared

BOOK YOUR STAY ONLINE

For more accommodation reviews by Lonely Planet authors, check out http://lonelyplanet.com/hotels/. You'll find independent reviews, as well as recommendations on the best places to stay. Best of all, you can book online.

bath facilities and a fan. In some of the older hotels, the toilets are squats and the 'shower' is a *klong* (large terracotta basin from which you scoop out water for bathing). Although these Thai-Chinese hotels have tonnes of accidental retro charm, we've found that, unless they've been recently refurbished, they are too old and worn to represent good value compared to guesthouses.

In recent years, there has been a push to fill the budget gap for older backpackers and young affluent travellers who want the ambience of a guesthouse with the comforts of a hotel. 'Flashpacker' hotels in major tourist towns have dressed up the utilitarian options of the past with stylish decor and more creature comforts.

International chain hotels can be found in Bangkok, Phuket and other high-end beach resorts. Many of these upscale resorts combine traditional Thai architecture and modern minimalism.

Most top-end hotels and some midrange hotels add a 7% government tax (VAT) and an additional 10% service charge. The additional charges are often referred to as 'plus plus'. A buffet breakfast will often be included in the room rate. If the hotel offers Western breakfast, it is usually referred to as 'ABF', meaning 'American breakfast'.

Midrange and chain hotels, especially in major tourist destinations, can be booked in advance and some offer internet discounts through their websites or online agents. They also accept most credit cards, but fewer places accept American Express.

National Parks Accommodation

Most national parks have bungalows or campsites available for overnight stays. Bungalows typically sleep as many as 10 people and rates range from 800B to 2000B, depending on the park and the size of the bungalow. These are popular with extended Thai families who bring enough provisions to survive the Apocalypse. A few parks also have *reu·an tăa·ou* (longhouses).

Camping is available at many parks for 60B to 90B per night. Some parks rent tents and other sleeping gear, but the condition of the equipment can be poor.

Reservations for all park accommodation must be made in advance through the **central booking system** (☎reservations 0 2561 0777; www.dnp.go.th/parkreserve). Do note that reservations for campsites and bungalows are handled on different pages within the website.

Customs Regulations

The **customs department** (www.customsclinic.org) maintains a helpful website with specific information about customs regulations.

Climate

Bangkok

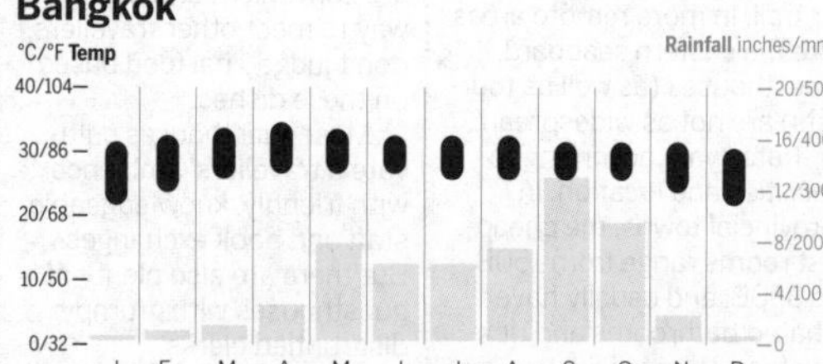

Phuket

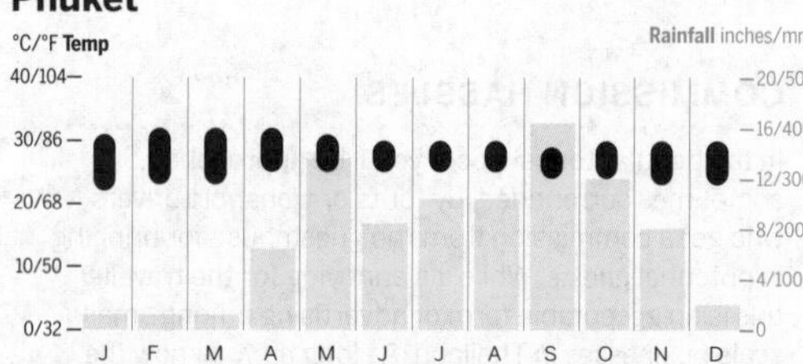

Surat Thani

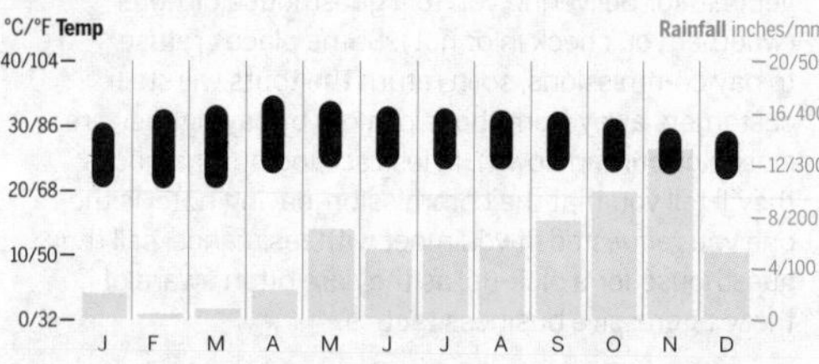

Thailand allows the following items to enter duty free:

- reasonable amount of personal effects (clothing and toiletries)
- professional instruments
- 200 cigarettes
- 1L of wine or spirits

Thailand prohibits the import of the following items:

- firearms and ammunition (unless registered in advance with the police department)
- illegal drugs
- pornographic media

When leaving Thailand, you must obtain an export licence for any antiques, reproductions or newly cast Buddha images (except personal amulets). Submit two front-view photos of the object(s) and a photocopy of your passport, along with the purchase receipt and the object(s) in question, to the **Department of Fine Arts** (☎0 2628 5032). Allow four days for the application and inspection process to be completed.

Electricity

Thailand uses 220V AC electricity; power outlets most commonly feature two-prong round or flat sockets.

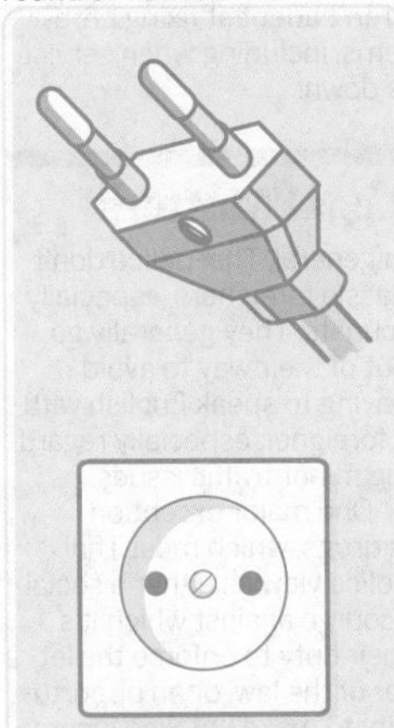

Embassies & Consulates

Foreign embassies are located in Bangkok.

Australian Embassy (☎0 2344 6300; www.thailand.embassy.gov.au; 37 Th Sathon Tai (South); ⌚8.30am-4.30pm Mon-Fri; Ⓜ Lumphini exit 2)

Burmese (Myanmar) Embassy (Map p66; ☎0 2233 7250; www.myanmarembassybkk.com; 132 Th Sathon Neua (North); ⌚9am-4.30pm (embassy), 9am-noon & 1-3pm Mon-Fri (visa section); Ⓢ Surasak exit 3)

Cambodian Embassy (☎0 2957 5851; 518/4 Th Pracha Uthit/Soi Ramkhamhaeng 39; ⌚9am-noon Mon-Fri; Ⓜ Phra Ram 9 exit 3 & taxi)

Canadian Embassy (☎0 2646 4300; www.canadainternational.gc.ca; 15th fl, Abdulrahim Pl, 990 Th Phra Ram IV; ⌚7.30am-12.15pm & 1-4.15pm Mon-Thu, to 1pm Fri; Ⓜ Si Lom exit 2, Ⓢ Sala Daeng exit 4)

Chinese Embassy (☎0 2245 7044; www.fmprc.gov.cn; 57 Th Ratchadaphisek)

Danish Embassy (☎0 2343 1100; thailand.um.dk; 10 Soi 1, Th Sathon Tai) Consulates in Phuket and Pattaya.

French Bangkok Visa & Culture Services (☎0 2627 2150; ambafrance-th.org; 29 Th Sathon Tai)

French Embassy (☎0 2657 5100; www.ambafrance-th.org; 35 Soi 36, Th Charoen Krung; ⌚8.30am-noon Mon-Fri; ⛴ Tha Oriental) Consulates in Phuket and Surat Thani.

German Embassy (☎0 2287 9000; www.bangkok.diplo.de; 9 Th Sathon Tai (South); ⌚8.30-11am Mon-Fri; Ⓜ Lumphini exit 2)

Indian Embassy (Map p68; ☎0 2258 0300-6; indianembassy.in.th; 46 Soi Prasanmit/Soi 23, Th Sukhumvit) Consulate only in Chiang Mai.

Indian Visa Centre (Map p68; ☎0 2664 1200; www.indiavisathai.com; Th Sukhumvit, 253 Soi 21/Asoke; ⌚IVS Global Services, 22nd fl)

Indonesian Embassy (Map p64; ☎0 2252 3135; www.kemlu.go.id/bangkok; 600-602 Th Phetchaburi)

Irish Honorary Consulate (Map p66; ☎0 2632 6720; www.irelandinthailand.com; 62 Th Silom, 4th fl, Thaniya Bldg) Consulate only; the nearest Irish embassy is in Kuala Lumpur.

Israeli Embassy (Map p68; ☎0 2204 9200; bangkok.mfa.gov.il; 25 Soi 19, Th Sukhumvit, Ocean Tower 2, 25th fl)

Japanese Embassy (☎0 2207 8500; www.th.emb-japan.go.jp; 177 Th Witthayu/Wireless Rd)

Laotian Embassy (☎0 2539 6678; www.laoembassybkk.com; Th Ramkamhaeng, 502/1-3 Soi Sahakarnpramoon, Pracha Uthit/Soi 39)

Malaysian Embassy (☎0 2629 6800; www.kln.gov.my/web/tha_bangkok/home; 35 Th Sathon Tai (South); ⌚8am-4pm; Ⓜ Lumphini exit 2) Consulate in Songkhla.

Nepalese Embassy (☎0 2391 7240; nepalembassybangkok.com; 189 Soi 71, Th Sukhumvit)

Netherlands Embassy (Map p64; ☎0 2309 5200; thailand.nlembassy.org; 15 Soi Tonson; ⌚8.30-11.30am Mon-Wed, 8.30-11.30am & 1.30-3pm Thu (consular office); ⓈChit Lom exit 4)

New Zealand Embassy (Map p64; ☎0 2254 2530; www.nzembassy.com/thailand; 14th fl, M Thai Tower, All Seasons Pl, 87 Th Witthayu (Wireless Rd); ⌚8am-noon & 1-2.30pm Mon-Fri; ⓈPhloen Chit exit 5)

Philippine Embassy (Map p68; ☎0 2259 0139; www.bangkokpe.com; 760 Th Sukhumvit)

Russian Embassy (Map p66; ☎0 2234 9824; www.thailand.mid.ru; 78 Soi Sap, Th Surawong) Consulates in Pattaya and Phuket.

Singaporean Embassy (Map p66; ☎0 2286 2111; www.mfa.gov.sg/bangkok; 129 Th Sathon Tai)

South African Embassy (Map p64; ☎0 2659 2900; www.dirco.gov.za; 87 Th Witthayu (Wireless Rd), 12th A fl, M Thai Tower, All Seasons Pl)

Spanish Embassy (Map p68; ☎0 2661 8284; es.embassyinformation.com; 193 Th Ratchadaphisek, 23 fl, Lake Ratchada Office Complex)

Swiss Embassy (Map p64; ☎0 2674 6900; www.eda.admin.ch/bangkok; 35 Th Witthayu/Wireless Rd)

UK Embassy (Map p64; ☎0 2305 8333; www.gov.uk/government/world/organisations/british-embassy-bangkok; 14 Th Witthayu (Wireless Rd); ⌚8am-4.30pm Mon-Thu, to 1pm Fri; ⓈPhloen Chit exit 5) Consulates in Chiang Mai and Pattaya.

US Embassy (Map p64; ☎0 2205 4049; http://bangkok.usembassy.gov; 95 Th Witthayu (Wireless Rd))

Vietnamese Embassy (Map p64; ☎0 2251 5838, 0 2251 5836; www.vietnamembassy-thailand.org; 83/1 Th Witthayu (Wireless Rd))

Food

For in-depth information on Thailand's glorious cuisine, see Food & Drink (p386).

Gay & Lesbian Travellers

Thai culture is relatively tolerant of both male and female homosexuality. There are fairly prominent gay and lesbian scenes in Bangkok, Pattaya and Phuket. With regard to dress or mannerism, lesbians and gays are generally accepted without comment. However, public displays of affection – whether heterosexual or homosexual – are frowned upon. **Utopia** (www.utopia-asia.com) posts lots of Thailand information for gay and lesbian visitors and publishes a guidebook to the kingdom for homosexuals.

Insurance

A travel-insurance policy to cover theft, loss and medical problems is a good idea. Policies offer differing medical-expense options and there is a wide variety of policies available, so check the small print. Be sure that the policy covers ambulances or an emergency flight home.

Some policies specifically exclude 'dangerous activities', which can include scuba diving, motorcycling or even trekking. A locally acquired motorcycle licence is not valid under some policies. Do not dive without diver's insurance.

You may prefer a policy that pays doctors or hospitals directly rather than you having to pay on the spot and claim later. If you have to claim later, make sure you keep all documentation.

Worldwide travel insurance is available at www.lonelyplanet.com/travel_services. You can buy, extend and claim online any time – even if you're already on the road.

Thailand has been considering a new regulation requiring foreign visitors to be covered by health insurance before arrival. This measure aims to curb Phuket's annual bill of 5 million baht in unpaid hospital bills from foreign patients. At the time of writing, it was unclear if this or a 500B arrival fee would go into effect.

EATING PRICE RANGES

The following price ranges refer to a standard main course meal.

- $ less than 100B
- $$ 100–250B
- $$$ more than 250B

Internet Access

You'll find plenty of internet cafes just about everywhere. The going rate is anywhere from 20B to 120B an hour. Connections tend to be pretty fast and the machines are usually well maintained. Wireless access (wi-fi) is available in most hotels and guesthouses, though staff aren't adept at fixing problems, including when service is down.

Legal Matters

In general, Thai police don't hassle foreigners, especially tourists. They generally go out of their way to avoid having to speak English with a foreigner, especially regarding minor traffic issues.

One major exception is drugs, which most Thai police view as either a social scourge against which it's their duty to enforce the letter of the law, or an opportunity to make untaxed income via bribes.

If you are arrested for any offence, the police will allow you the opportunity to make a phone call to your embassy or consulate in Thailand, if you have one, or to a friend or relative, if you don't. There's a whole set of legal codes governing the length of time and manner in which you can be detained before being charged or put on trial, but a lot of discretion is left to the police. In the case of foreigners the police are more likely to bend these codes in your favour. However, as with police worldwide, if you don't show respect, you will make matters worse.

Thai law does not presume an indicted detainee to be either 'guilty' or 'innocent' but rather a 'suspect', whose guilt or innocence will be decided in court. Trials are usually speedy.

The **tourist police** (☎1155) can be very helpful in cases of arrest. Although they typically have no jurisdiction over the kinds of cases handled by regular cops, they may be able to help with translations or with contacting your embassy. You can call the hotline number 24 hours a day to lodge complaints or request assistance with regard to personal safety.

Maps

ThinkNet (www.thinknet.co.th) produces high-quality, bilingual city and country maps, including interactive-map CDs. For GPS users in Thailand, most prefer the Garmin units and associated map products, which are accurate and fully routed.

Money

The basic unit of Thai currency is the baht. There are 100 satang in one baht; coins include 25-satang and 50-satang pieces and baht in 1B, 2B, 5B and 10B coins. Older coins have Thai numerals only, while newer coins have Thai and Arabic numerals. The 2B coin is similar in size to the 1B coin but it is gold in colour. The two satang coins are typically only issued at supermarkets where prices aren't rounded up to the nearest baht.

Paper currency is issued in the following denominations: 20B (green), 50B (blue), 100B (red), 500B (purple) and 1000B (beige).

ATMs & Credit/Debit Cards

Debit and ATM cards issued by a bank in your own country can be used at ATMs in Thailand to withdraw cash (in Thai baht only) directly from your account back home. ATMs are widespread throughout the country. You can also buy baht at foreign-exchange booths at some banks.

Thai ATMs charge a 150B foreign-transaction fee on top of whatever currency conversion and out-of-network fees your home bank charges. Before leaving home, shop around for a bank account that has free international ATM usage and reimburses fees incurred at other institutions' ATMs.

Aeon is the only Thai bank that we know of that doesn't charge the 150B usage fee on foreign accounts, but its ATM distribution is somewhat limited – many ATMs are located in Big C stores.

Credit cards, as well as debit cards, can be used for purchases at some shops, hotels and restaurants. The most commonly accepted cards are Visa and MasterCard. American Express is typically only accepted at high-end hotels and restaurants.

To report a lost or stolen credit/debit card, call your card's hotline in Bangkok.

American Express (☎0 2273 5544)

MasterCard (☎001 800 11887 0663)

Visa (☎001 800 11 535 0660)

Changing Money

Banks or the rarer private moneychangers offer the best foreign-exchange rates. When buying baht, US dollars are the most accepted currency, followed by British pounds and Euros. Most banks charge a commission and duty for each travellers cheque cashed.

Current exchange rates are printed in the *Bangkok Post* and the *Nation* every day, or you can walk into any Thai bank to see a daily rate chart.

Foreign Exchange

Visitors must declare cash over US$20,000 when arriving or departing. There are also certain monetary requirements for foreigners entering Thailand; demonstration of adequate funds varies per visa type but typically does not exceed a traveller's estimated trip budget. It's rare that you'll be asked to produce such financial evidence, but be aware that these laws do exist. The **Ministry of Foreign Affairs** (www.mfa.go.th) can provide more detailed information.

It's legal to open a foreign-currency account at any commercial bank in Thailand. As long as the funds originate from out of the country, there aren't any restrictions on maintenance or withdrawal.

Tipping

Tipping is not generally expected in Thailand. The exception is loose change from a large restaurant bill; if a meal costs 488B and you pay with a 500B note, some Thais will leave the 12B change. It's not so much a tip as a way of saying 'I'm not so money grubbing as to grab every last baht'.

At many hotel restaurants or other upmarket eateries, a 10% service charge will be added to your bill. When this is the case, tipping is not expected. Bangkok has adopted some standards of tipping, especially in restaurants frequented by foreigners.

Opening Hours

All government offices and banks are closed on public holidays.

Banks 9.30am to 3.30pm Monday to Friday; ATMs accessible 24 hours.

Bars 6pm to midnight (officially); closing times vary due to local enforcement of curfew laws; bars close during elections and certain religious public holidays.

Clubs (discos) 8pm to 2am; closing times vary due to local enforcement of curfew laws; clubs close during elections and certain religious public holidays.

Government offices 8.30am to 4.30pm Monday to Friday; some close for lunch (noon to 1pm), while others are open Saturday (9am to 3pm).

Live-music venues 6pm to 1am; closing times vary due to local enforcement of curfew laws; venues close during elections and certain religious public holidays.

Restaurants 10am to 10pm; some shops specialise in morning meals and close by 3pm.

Stores Local stores: 10am to 6pm daily; department stores: 10am to 10pm daily. In some small towns, local stores close on Sunday.

Photography

Thais are gadget fans and they readily snap pics with cameras or camera phones. Memory cards for most digital cameras are generally widely available in the electronic sections of most shopping malls. In the tourist areas, many internet shops have CD-burning software if you want to offload your pictures. Alternatively, most places have sophisticated enough connections that you can quickly upload digital photos to a remote storage site.

Be considerate when taking photographs of the locals. Learn how to ask politely in Thai and wait for an embarrassed nod.

Post

Thailand has a very efficient postal service and local postage is inexpensive. Typical provincial post offices are open between 8.30am and 4.30pm on weekdays and 9am and noon on Saturdays. Larger main post offices in provincial capitals may also be open for a half-day on Sundays.

Most provincial post offices will sell do-it-yourself packing boxes. Don't send cash or other valuables through the mail.

Thailand's poste restante service is generally very reliable. When you receive mail, you must show your passport and fill out some paperwork.

Public Holidays

1 January New Year's Day

February (date varies) Makha Bucha Day, Buddhist holy day

6 April Chakri Day, commemorating the founder of the Chakri dynasty, Rama I

13–15 April Songkran Festival, traditional Thai New Year and water festival

1 May Labour Day

5 May Coronation Day, commemorating the 1946 coronation of HM the King and HM the Queen

May/June (date varies) Visakha Bucha, Buddhist holy day

July (date varies) Asanha Bucha, Buddhist holy day

12 August Queen's Birthday

23 October Chulalongkorn Day

October/November (date varies) Ork Phansaa, the end of Buddhist Lent

5 December King's Birthday

10 December Constitution Day

31 December New Year's Eve

Safe Travel

Although Thailand is not a dangerous country to visit, it is smart to exercise caution, especially when it comes to dealing with strangers (both Thai and foreigners) and travelling alone. In reality, you are more likely to be ripped off or have a personal possession surreptitiously stolen than you are to be physically harmed.

Assault

Assault of travellers is rare in Thailand, but it does happen. Causing a Thai to 'lose face' (feel public embarrassment or humiliation) can sometimes elicit an inexplicably strong and violent reaction. Often alcohol is the number one contributor to bad choices and worse outcomes.

Women, especially solo travellers, need to be smart and somewhat sober when interacting with the opposite sex, be they Thai or *fa·ràng*. Opportunists pounce when too many whisky buckets are involved. Also be aware that an innocent flirtation might convey firmer intentions to a recipient who does not share your culture's sexual norms.

Border Issues & Hot Spots

Thailand enjoys generally amicable relations with its neighbours and most land borders are fully functional passages for goods and people. However, the ongoing violence in the Deep South has made the crossing at Sungai Kolok into Malaysia completely off limits and the entire Muslim-majority provinces (Yala, Pattani and Narathiwat) should be avoided by casual visitors.

Cross-border relations between Thailand and Myanmar have significantly normalised, though borders are subject to closing without warning. Borders are usually closed due to news-making events, like elections, so keeping abreast of current events prior to arriving at the border will prevent potential problems.

The long-contested area at Khao Phra Wihan (known as 'Preah Vihear' in Cambodia), along the Thai–Cambodian border, is still a source of military clashes and should be avoided until a lasting peace is found.

Check with your government's foreign ministry for current travel warnings.

Drug Possession

It is illegal to buy, sell or possess opium, heroin, amphetamines, hallucinogenic mushrooms and marijuana in Thailand. Belying Thailand's anything-goes atmosphere are strict punishments for possession and trafficking that are not relaxed for foreigners. Possession of drugs can result in at least one year or more of prison time. Drug smuggling – defined as attempting to cross a border with drugs in your possession – carries considerably higher penalties, including execution.

Scams

Thais can be so friendly and laid-back that some visitors are lulled into a false sense of security, making them vulnerable to scams of all kinds. Bangkok is especially good at long-involved frauds that dupe travellers into thinking that they've made a friend and are getting a bargain on highly valuable gem stones (which are actually pretty, sparkling glass).

Follow the Tourism Authority of Thailand's number-one suggestion: 'Disregard all offers of free shopping or sightseeing help from strangers.' These invariably take a commission from your purchases.

Theft & Fraud

Exercise diligence when it comes to your personal belongings. Ensure that your room is securely locked and carry your most important effects (passport, money, credit cards) on your person. Take care when leaving valuables in hotel safes.

Follow the same practice when you're travelling. A locked bag will not prevent theft on a long-haul bus.

When using a credit card, don't let vendors take your card out of your sight to run it through the machine. Unscrupulous merchants have been known to rub off three or four or more receipts with one purchase. Sometimes they wait several weeks – even months – between submitting each charge receipt to the bank so that you can't remember whether you've been billed by the same vendor more than once.

To avoid losing all of your travel money in an instant, use a credit card that is not directly linked to your bank account back home so that the operator doesn't have access to immediate funds.

Contact the **tourist police** (☎24hr hotline 1155) if you have any problems with consumer fraud.

Touts & Commissions

Touting is a longtime tradition in Asia, and while Thailand doesn't have as many touts as, say, India, it has its share. In Bangkok, túk-túk drivers, hotel employees and bar girls often take new arrivals on city tours; these almost always end up in high-pressure sales situations at silk, jewellery or handicraft shops.

Touts also steer customers to certain guesthouses that pay a commission. Travel agencies are notorious for talking newly arrived tourists into staying at badly located, overpriced hotels.

Some travel agencies often masquerade as TAT, the government-funded tourist information office. They might put up agents wearing fake TAT badges or have signs that read TAT in big letters to entice travellers into their offices where they can sell them bus and train tickets for a commission. Be aware that the official TAT offices do not make hotel or transport bookings. If such a place offers to do this for you, then it is a travel agency not a tourist information office.

When making transport arrangements, talk to several travel agencies to look for the best price, as the commission percentage varies greatly between agents. Also resist any high-sales tactics from an agent trying to sign you up for everything: plane tickets, hotel, tours etc. The most honest Thais are typically very low-key and often sub-par salespeople.

PRACTICALITIES

- *Bangkok Post* and the *Nation* are the daily English-language newspapers.
- There are more than 400 AM and FM radio stations; short-wave radios can pick up BBC, VOA, Radio Australia, Deutsche Welle and Radio France International.
- Six VHF TV networks carry Thai programming; TrueVision cable provides international programming.
- Thailand follows the international metric system. Gold and silver are weighed in *bàht* (15g).

BARGAINING

If there isn't a sign stating the price for an item, then the price is negotiable. Bargaining for nonfood items is common in street markets and some mum-and-dad shops. Prices in department stores, minimarts, 7-Elevens and so forth are fixed.

Thais respect a good haggler. Always let the vendor make the first offer, then ask 'Can you lower the price?'. This usually results in a discount. Now it's your turn to make a counter-offer; always start low but don't bargain at all unless you're serious about buying.

It helps immeasurably to keep the negotiations relaxed and friendly, and always remember to smile. Don't lose your temper or raise your voice as drama is not a good leveraging tool.

Shopping

Many bargains await you in Thailand but don't go shopping in the company of touts, tour guides or friendly strangers, as they will inevitably take a commission on anything you buy, thus driving prices up beyond an acceptable value and creating a nuisance for future visitors.

Antiques

Real Thai antiques are increasingly rare. Today most dealers sell antique reproductions or items from Myanmar. Bangkok is the centre of the antique and reproduction trade.

Real antiques cannot be taken out of Thailand without a permit. No Buddha image, new or old, may be exported without the permission of the Department of Fine Arts.

Clothing

Clothes tend to be inexpensive in Thailand but ready-made items are not usually cut to fit Westerners' body types. Increasingly, larger-sized clothing is available in metropolitan malls or tourist centres. Markets sell cheap everyday items and are handy for picking up something when everything else is dirty. For chic clothes, Bangkok and Ko Samui lead the country with design-minded fashions. The custom of returns is not widely accepted in Thailand, so be sure everything fits before you leave the store.

Thailand has a long sartorial tradition, practised mainly by Thai-Indian Sikh families, but this industry is filled with cut-rate operators and commission-paying scams. Be wary of the quickie 24-hour tailor shops; they often use inferior fabric and have poor workmanship. It's best to ask long-time foreign residents for a recommendation and then go for two or three fittings.

Fakes

In Bangkok and other tourist centres there's a thriving black-market street trade in fake designer goods. No one pretends they're the real deal, at least not the vendors. Technically it is illegal for these items to be produced and sold, and Thailand has often been pressured by intellectual-property enforcement agencies to close down the trade. Rarely does a crackdown by the police last and often the vendors develop more surreptitious means of distribution, further highlighting the contraband character of the goods. In Patpong market, for example, vendors might show you a picture of a knock-off watch, you pay for it and they go around the corner to fetch it. They usually come back, but you'll wait long enough to wonder.

Furniture

Rattan and hardwood furniture items are often good purchases and can be made to order. Due to the ban on teak harvesting and the subsequent exhaustion of recycled teak, 70% of export furniture produced in Thailand is made from parawood, a processed wood from rubber trees that can no longer be used for latex production.

Gems & Jewellery

Thailand is a leading exporter of gems and ornaments, rivalled only by India and Sri Lanka. However, rough-stone sources in Thailand have decreased dramatically, and stones are now imported from Myanmar, Sri Lanka and other countries to be cut, polished and traded.

Although there are a lot of gem and jewellery stores in Thailand, it has become so difficult to dodge the scammers that the country no longer represents a safe and enjoyable place to buy these goods. It is better just to window shop.

Lacquerware

Lacquerware furniture and decorative items were traditionally made from bamboo and teak but these days mango wood might be used as the base. From start to finish it can take five or six months to produce a high-quality piece of lacquerware, which may have as many as five colours. Flexibility is one characteristic of good lacquerware: a well-made bowl can have its rim squeezed together until the sides meet without suffering damage.

Textiles

At Bangkok's Chatuchak Weekend Market and at many of the popular tourist-friendly markets throughout the islands and beaches, you can find a slew of traditional textiles from all over the kingdom, including the culturally rich regions of the north.

Fairly nice *bah·dé* (batik) is available in the south in patterns that are more similar to the batik found in Malaysia than in Indonesia.

Telephone

The telephone country code for Thailand is ☎66 and is used when calling the country from abroad. All Thai telephone numbers are preceded by a '0' if you're dialling domestically (the '0' is omitted when calling from overseas). After the initial '0', the next three numbers represent the provincial area code, which is now integral to the telephone number. If the initial '0' is followed by an '8' or a '9' then you're dialling a mobile phone.

International Calls

If you want to call an international number from a telephone in Thailand, you must first dial an international access code plus the country code followed by the subscriber number.

The standard international direct-dial prefix is ☎001. It is operated by the Communications Authority of Thailand (CAT) and is considered to have the best sound quality; it connects to the largest number of countries but is also the most expensive. The next best is ☎007, a prefix operated by the telecommunications company TOT, with reliable quality and slightly cheaper rates.

Dial ☎100 for operator-assisted international calls or reverse-charges (or collect) calls. Alternatively, contact your long-distance carrier for its overseas operator number, a toll-free call, or try ☎001 9991 2001 from a CAT phone and ☎1 800 000 120 from a TOT phone.

Mobile Phones

The easiest phone option in Thailand is to acquire a mobile phone equipped with a local SIM card.

Thailand is on the GSM network and mobile phone providers include AIS, DTAC and True Move.

You have two phone options. You can buy a mobile phone in Thailand at one of the urban shopping malls or phone stores near the markets in provincial towns. Or you can use an imported phone that isn't SIM-locked (and supports the GSM network). To get started buy a SIM card from one of the carriers (AIS and DTAC are most popular), which includes an assigned telephone number. Once your phone is SIM-enabled you can buy minutes with prepaid phonecards. SIM cards and refill cards (usually sold in 300B to 500B denominations) can be bought from 7-Elevens throughout the country.

Thailand finally has a 3G network and True Move is offering 4G LTE coverage in Bangkok. Coverage and quality of the different carriers varies from year to year based on network upgrades and capacity. As of 2013, True was regarded as having the highest data connectivity though this could change. Carriers usually sell talk-data packages based on usage amounts.

There are various promotions but rates typically hover at around 1B to 2B per minute anywhere in Thailand and between 5B and 9B for international calls. SMS is usually 3B per message, making it the cheapest 'talk' option. The 299B 'Happy Internet' SIM card (through DTAC), that's usually offered to tourists, offers one week of free data and is probably the best deal for those staying for two weeks or less in Thailand who use data on their phones.

Calling overseas through phones in most hotel rooms usually incurs additional surcharges (sometimes as much as 50% over and above the CAT rate); however, sometimes local calls are free or at standard rates. Some guesthouses will have a mobile phone or landline that customers can use for a per-minute fee for overseas calls.

Time

Thailand's time zone is seven hours ahead of GMT/UTC (London). At government offices and local cinemas, times are often expressed according to the 24-hour clock, eg 11pm is written '23.00'.

Toilets

Increasingly, the Asian-style squat toilet is less of the norm in Thailand. There are still specimens in rural places, provincial bus stations, older homes and modest restaurants, but the Western-style toilet is becoming more prevalent and appears wherever foreign tourists can be found.

If you encounter a squat, here's what you should know. You should straddle the two footpads and face the door. To flush use the plastic bowl to scoop water out of the adjacent basin and pour into the toilet bowl. Some places supply a small pack of toilet paper at the entrance (5B); otherwise bring your own stash or wipe the old-fashioned way with water.

Even in places where sit-down toilets are installed, the septic system may not be designed to take toilet paper. In such cases there will be a waste basket where you're supposed to place used toilet paper and feminine hygiene products. Some modern toilets also come with a small spray hose – Thailand's version of the bidet.

Tourist Information

The government-operated tourist information and promotion service, **Tourism Authority of Thailand** (TAT; www.tourismthailand.org), produces excellent pamphlets on sightseeing, accommodation and transport. TAT's head office is in Bangkok and there are 22 regional offices throughout the country.

TAT also has a number of overseas information offices; check TAT's website for contact information.

Travellers with Disabilities

Thailand presents one large, ongoing obstacle course for the mobility impaired. With its high curbs, uneven footpaths and nonstop traffic, Bangkok can be particularly difficult. Many streets must be crossed via pedestrian bridges flanked with steep stairways, while buses and boats don't stop long enough even for the fully abled. Rarely are there any ramps or other access points for wheelchairs.

A number of more expensive top-end hotels make consistent design efforts to provide disabled access to their properties. Other deluxe hotels with high employee-to-guest ratios are usually good about accommodating the mobility-impaired by providing staff help where building design fails. For the rest, you're pretty much left to your own resources.

Counter to the prevailing trends, **Worldwide Dive & Sail** (www.sirenfleet.com) offers live-aboard diving programs for the deaf and hard of hearing.

Some organisations and publications that offer tips on international travel include the following.

Accessible Journeys (www.disabilitytravel.com)

Mobility International USA (www.miusa.org)

Society for Accessible Travel & Hospitality (SATH; www.sath.org)

Visas

The **Ministry of Foreign Affairs** (www.mfa.go.th) oversees immigration and visa issues. Check the website or the nearest Thai embassy or consulate for application procedures and costs.

Tourist Visas & Exemptions

The Thai government allows tourist-visa exemptions for 55 different nationalities, including those from Australia, New Zealand, the USA and most of Europe, to enter the country without a prearranged visa. Some Eastern Europeans, Indians and Chinese qualify for a visa on arrival valid for 15 days, though talks are under way to allow Chinese visa exemptions. Asean countries are moving towards visa-waiving programs.

For those arriving in the kingdom by air, a 30-day visa is issued without a fee. For those arriving via a land border, the arrival visa is 15 days. Some countries (including Brazil, South Korea, Argentina, Chile and Peru) receive a 90-day free visa at all borders.

Without proof of an onward ticket and sufficient funds for the projected stay any visitor can be denied entry, but in practice this is a formality that is rarely checked.

If you plan to stay in Thailand longer than 30 days (or 15 days for land arrivals), you should apply for the 60-day tourist visa from a Thai consulate or embassy before your trip. Contact the nearest Thai embassy or consulate to obtain application procedures and determine fees for tourist visas.

Non-Immigrant Visas

The Non-Immigrant Visa is good for 90 days and is intended for foreigners entering the country for business, study, retirement and extended family visits. There are multiple-entry visas available in this visa class; you're more likely to be granted multiple entries if you apply at a Thai consulate in Europe, the US or Australia than elsewhere. If you plan to apply for a Thai work permit, you'll need to possess a Non-Immigrant Visa first.

Visa Extensions & Renewals

If you decide you want to stay longer than the allotted time, you can extend your visa by applying at any immigration office in Thailand. The usual fee for a visa extension is 1900B. Those issued with a standard stay of 15 or 30 days can extend their stay for seven to 10 days (depending on the immigration office) if the extension is handled before the visa expires. The 60-day tourist visa can be extended by up to 30 days at the discretion of Thai immigration authorities.

Another visa-renewal option is to cross a land border. A new 15-day visa will be issued upon your return and some short-term visitors make a day trip out of the 'visa run'.

If you overstay your visa, the usual penalty is a fine of 500B per day, with a 20,000B limit. Fines can be paid at the airport or in advance at an immigration office. If you've overstayed only one day, you don't have to pay. Children under 14 travelling with a parent do not have to pay the penalty.

Foreign residents in Thailand should arrange visa extensions at the immigration office closest to their in-country address.

Volunteering

There are many wonderful volunteering organisations in Thailand that provide meaningful work and cultural engagement. **Volunteer Work Thailand** (www.volunteerworkthailand.org) maintains a database of opportunities.

Women Travellers

Women face relatively few problems in Thailand. With the great amount of respect afforded to women, an equal measure should be returned.

Thai women, especially the younger generation, are showing more skin than in the recent past. That means almost everyone is now dressing like a bar girl and you can wear spaghetti-strap tops and navel-bearing shirts (if only they were still trendy) without offending Thais' modesty streak. But to be on the safe side, cover up if you're going deep into rural communities or to temples.

Attacks and rapes are not common in Thailand, but incidents do occur, especially when an attacker observes a vulnerable target: a drunk or solo woman. If you return home from a bar alone, be sure to have your wits about you. Avoid accepting rides from strangers late at night or travelling around in isolated areas by yourself – common sense stuff that might escape your notice in a new environment filled with hospitable people.

While Bangkok might be a men's paradise to some, foreign women are finding their own Romeos on the Thai beaches. As more couples emerge, more Thai men will make themselves available. Women who aren't interested in such romantic encounters should not presume that Thai men have merely platonic motives. Frivolous flirting could unintentionally cause a Thai man to feel a loss of face if attention is then diverted to another person and, in some cases where alcohol is involved, the spurned man may become unpleasant or even violent.

Transport

GETTING THERE & AWAY

Flights, tours and rail tickets can be booked online at lonelyplanet.com/bookings.

Entering the Country

Entry procedures for Thailand, by air or by land, are straightforward: you'll have to show your passport and you'll need to present completed arrival and departure cards. Blank arrival and departure cards are usually distributed on the incoming flight or, if you're arriving by land, can be picked up at the immigration counter.

You do not have to fill in a customs form on arrival unless you have imported goods to declare. In that case, get the form from Thai customs officials at your point of entry. There can also be minimum funds requirements.

Air

Airports

Bangkok is Thailand's primary international and domestic gateway. Smaller airports throughout the country serve domestic and sometimes inter-regional routes.

Suvarnabhumi International Airport (BKK; ☎0 2132 1888; www.bangkokairportonline.com) Receives nearly all international flights and most domestic flights. It is located in Samut Prakan, 30km east of Bangkok and 110km from Pattaya. The airport name is pronounced *sù·wan·ná·poom.*

Don Muang International Airport (DMK; ☎0 2535 1111; www.donmuangairportonline.com) Bangkok's second airport is used for domestic flights operated by Nok Air, Air Asia and Orient Thai (formerly One-Two-Go).

Phuket International Airport (☎0 7632 7230; www.phuketairportonline.com) International destinations include Seoul, Hong Kong, Singapore, Australia, and several Chinese cities on Air Asia. Air Asia also flies to Abu Dhabi. Direct charter flights from Europe are also available.

Ko Samui Airport (USM; www.samuiairportonline.com) International Asian destinations include Hong Kong, Singapore and Kuala Lumpur.

Airlines

Bangkok is a major airline hub. Here are some of the main carriers:

Air Asia (☎0 2515 9999; www.airasia.com)

Air Canada (Map p66; ☎0 2718 1839; www.aircanada.com)

Air China (Map p66; ☎0 2108 1888; www.airchina.com)

Air France (☎001 800 441 0771; www.airfrance.fr)

Air New Zealand (Map p66; www.airnewzealand.com)

Bangkok Airways (☎1771; www.bangkokair.com)

British Airways (Map p66; ☎001 800 441 5906; www.britishairways.com)

CLIMATE CHANGE & TRAVEL

Every form of transport that relies on carbon-based fuel generates CO_2, the main cause of human-induced climate change. Modern travel is dependent on aeroplanes, which might use less fuel per kilometre per person than most cars but travel greater distances. The altitude at which aircraft emit gases (including CO_2) and particles also contributes to their climate change impact. Many websites offer 'carbon calculators' that allow people to estimate the carbon emissions generated by their journey and, for those who wish to do so, to offset the impact of the greenhouse gases emitted with contributions to climate-friendly initiatives. Lonely Planet offsets the carbon footprint of all staff and author travel.

Cathay Pacific Airways (Map p64; ☎0 2263 0606; www.cathaypacific.com)

China Airlines (Map p64; ☎0 2250 9898; www.china-airlines.com)

Delta Airlines (☎001 800 658 228; www.delta.com)

Emirates (Map p68; ☎0 2664 1040; www.emirates.com)

Eva Air (☎0 2269 62300; www.evaair.com)

Garuda Indonesia (Map p68; ☎0 2285 6470; www.garuda-indonesia.com)

Japan Airlines (Map p64; ☎001 800 811 0600; www.jal.co.jp)

Jetstar Airways (☎0 2267 5125; www.jetstar.com)

KLM Royal Dutch Airlines (☎001 800 441 5560; www.klm.com)

Korean Air (☎0 2620 6900; www.koreanair.com)

Lao Airlines (☎0 2236 9822; www.laoairlines.com)

Lufthansa Airlines (Map p68; ☎0 2264 6800; www.lufthansa.com)

Malaysia Airlines (Map p64; ☎0 2263 0565; www.mas.com.my)

Myanmar Airways International (Map p68; ☎0 2261 5060; www.maiair.com)

Qantas Airways (Map p66; ☎0 2632 6611; www.qantas.com.au)

Singapore Airlines (Map p66; ☎0 2353 6000; www.singaporeair.com)

Thai Airways International (Map p58; ☎0 2356 1111; 6 Th Lan Luang, Banglamphu; ⏲8am-5pm Mon-Sat, 9am-1pm Sun; ⛴Tha Phan Fah)

United Airlines (Map p64; ☎0 2353 3939; www.united.com)

Vietnam Airlines (Map p64; ☎0 2655 4137; www.vietnamair.com)

Tickets

In some cases, eg when travelling to neighbouring countries or to domestic destinations, it is still convenient to use a travel agent in Thailand. The amount of commission an agent will charge often varies so shop around. Paying by credit card generally offers protection, as most card issuers provide refunds if you can prove you didn't get what you paid for. Agents who accept only cash should hand over the tickets straightaway and not tell you to 'come back tomorrow'. After you've made a booking or paid a deposit, call the airline to confirm the booking was made.

Airfares during the high season (December to March) can be expensive.

Land

Thailand shares land borders with Laos, Malaysia, Cambodia and Myanmar. Travel between all of these countries can be done by land via sanctioned border crossings.

Bus, Car & Motorcycle

Road connections exist between all of Thailand's neighbours, and these routes can be travelled by bus, shared taxi and private car. In some cases, you'll take a bus to the border point, pass through immigration and then pick up another bus or shared taxi on the other side. In other cases, especially when crossing the Malaysian border, the bus will stop for immigration formalities and then continue to its destination across the border.

Train

Thailand's and Malaysia's state railways meet at Butterworth (93km south of the Thai–Malaysian border), which is a transfer point to Penang (by boat) or to Kuala Lumpur and Singapore (by Malaysian train).

There are several border crossings for which you can take a train to the border and then switch to automobile transport on the other side. The Thai–Cambodian border crossing of Aranya Prathet to Poipet and the Thai–Laos crossing of Nong Khai to Vientiane are two examples.

Another rail line travels to the Malaysian east-coast border town of Sungai Kolok, but because of ongoing violence in Thailand's Deep South we don't recommend this route for travellers.

Border Crossings

CAMBODIA

Cambodian tourist visas are available at the border for US$20, though some borders charge 1500B. Bring a passport photo and try to avoid the runner boys who want to issue a health certificate or other 'medical' paperwork for additional fees.

The most direct land route between Bangkok and Angkor Wat is Aranya Prathet to Poipet. Several more remote crossings include O Smach to Chong Chom (periodically closed due to fighting at Khao Phra Wihan) and Chong Sa to Ngam Choam, but they aren't as convenient as you'll have to hire private transport (instead of a share taxi) on the Cambodian side of the border.

Hat Lek to Krong Koh Kong The coastal crossing for those heading to/from Ko Chang/Sihanoukville.

Pong Nam Ron to Pailin A backdoor route from Ko Chang (via Chanthaburi) to Battambang and Angkor Wat.

LAOS

It is fairly hassle-free to cross into Laos from northern and northeastern Thailand. Lao visas (US$35 to US$50) can be obtained on arrival; bring a passport photo.

The main transport gateway to Laos is the first Thai–Lao Friendship Bridge at Nong Khai to Vientiane. Other crossings include Chiang Khong to Huay Xai, Mukdahan to Savannakhet, Nakhon Phanom to Tha Khaek and Chong Mek to Vangtao.

MALAYSIA

Malaysia, especially the west coast, is easy to reach via bus, train and even boat.

Hat Yai to Butterworth The western spur of the train line originating in Bangkok terminates at Butterworth, the mainland transfer point to Penang. Less popular these days due to unrest in the Deep South.

Ko Lipe to Pulau Langkawi Boats provide a convenient high-season link between these two Andaman islands.

Satun to Pulau Langkawi/ Kuala Perlis Boats shuttle from this mainland port to the island of Langkawi and the mainland town of Kuala Perlis.

Other crossings include Hat Yai to Padang Besar and Sungai Kolok to Kota Bharu, but we don't recommend these routes due to the violence in the Deep South.

MYANMAR

Myanmar has lifted travel restrictions at four of its borders with Thailand. Of these, Ban Phu Nam Ron to Htee-Khee is a new crossing requiring major infrastructure investment; the Thai government intends to develop this route as a link between Bangkok and Myanmar's Dawei port in the Andaman Sea.

The Mae Sai to Tachileik crossing is popular with travellers to renew their Thai visas as it is convenient to Chiang Mai and Chiang Rai.

Other crossings include Mae Sot to Myawadi which was open at the time of research.

Ranong to Kawthoung This is a popular visa-renewal point in the southern part of Thailand.

GETTING AROUND

Air

Hopping around the country by air continues to be affordable. Most routes originate from Bangkok, but Ko Samui and Phuket all have a few routes to other Thai towns.

Thai Airways International operates many domestic air routes from Bangkok to provincial capitals. Bangkok Air is another established domestic carrier. Orient Thai Airlines and Nok Air are the domestic budget carriers.

ISLAND TRANSFER TICKETS

You may see air tickets on low-cost carriers (mostly Air Asia) that go to islands that don't have airports, such as Ko Phi Phi, Ko Lanta and Ko Ngai. These tickets fly to the nearest airport then include bus and boat transport to the island. The cost is about the same as arranging the ground transport by yourself except you don't have the hassle that goes with it.

In other cases carriers may say they go to islands that have airports (like Ko Samui or Ko Pha-Ngan) but actually fly into a nearby airport and include ground and boat transportation in the cost. Make sure you check the details before booking. In these cases the ticket price is usually cheaper than flying to the island direct although the travel time will be much longer.

Boat

Long-tail boats are a staple of transport on rivers and canals in Bangkok and in the south.

Between the mainland and islands in the Gulf of Thailand or the Andaman Sea, you may also see 8m- to 10m-long wooden boats, with an inboard engine and a simple roof to shelter passengers and cargo. Faster, more expensive hovercraft or jetfoils are available in tourist areas.

Bus & Minivan

The bus network in Thailand is prolific and reliable. The Thai government subsidises the Transport Company *(bò·rí·sàt kŏn sòng)*, usually abbreviated to Baw Khaw Saw (BKS). Every city and town in Thailand linked by bus has a BKS station, even if it's just a patch of dirt by the side of the road.

By far the most reliable bus companies in Thailand are the ones that operate out of the government-run BKS stations. We do not recommend using bus companies that operate directly out of tourist centres, such as Bangkok's Th Khao San, because of repeated instances of theft and commission-seeking stops.

Increasingly, minivans are the middle-class option. Minivans are run by private companies and because their vehicles are smaller they can depart from the market (instead of the out-of-town bus stations) and will deliver guests directly to their hotel.

Bus Classes

The cheapest and slowest are the *rót tam·má·dah* (ordinary fan buses) that stop in every little town and for every waving hand along the highway. Only a few of these ordinary buses, in rural locations or for local destinations, still exist since most have been replaced by air-con buses.

The bulk of the bus service consists of faster, more comfortable air-con buses, called *rót aa* (air bus). Longer routes offer at least two classes of air-con buses: 2nd class and 1st class. The latter have toilets. 'VIP' and 'Super VIP' buses have fewer seats so that each seat reclines further; sometimes these are called *rót norn* (sleeper bus).

Bring a jacket, especially for long-distance trips, as the air-con can turn the cabin into a deep freeze.

On overnight journeys the buses usually stop en route

Air Fares & Train Routes Map

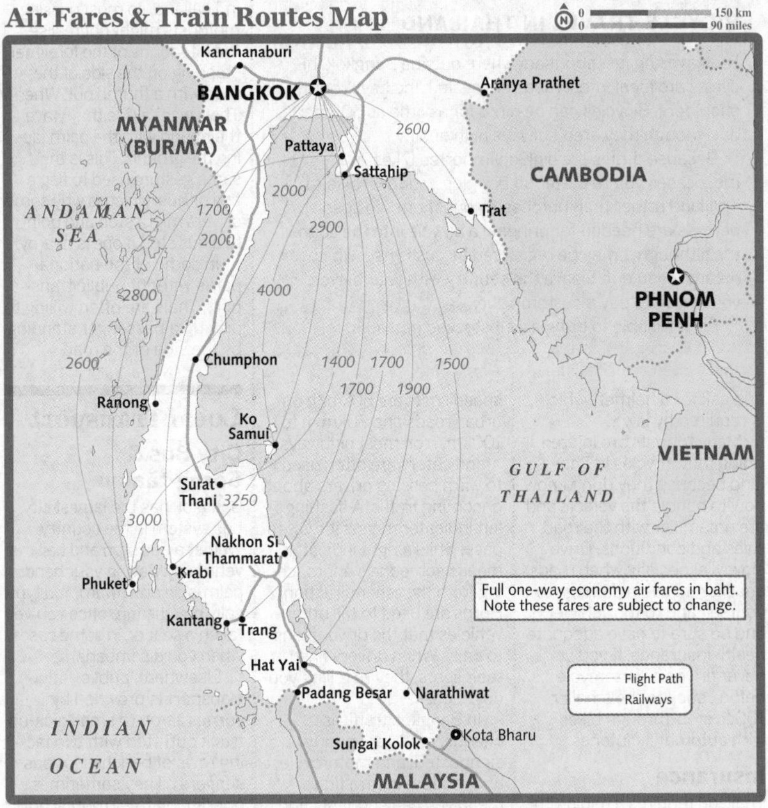

Full one-way economy air fares in baht. Note these fares are subject to change.

Flight Path
Railways

for 'midnight *kôw đôm*' (rice soup), when passengers are awakened for a meal.

Reservations

You can book air-con BKS buses at any BKS terminal. Ordinary (fan) buses cannot be booked in advance. Privately run buses can be booked through most hotels or any travel agency, but it's best to book directly through a bus office to be sure that you get what you pay for.

Car & Motorcycle

Driving Licence

Short-term visitors who wish to drive vehicles (including motorcycles) in Thailand need an International Driving Permit, though this requirement is not always enforced.

Fuel

Modern petrol (gasoline) stations are in plentiful supply all over Thailand wherever there are paved roads. In more-remote, off-road areas *ben·sin/nám·man rót yon* (petrol containing benzene) is usually available at small roadside or village stands. All fuel in Thailand is unleaded, and diesel is used by trucks and some passenger cars. Several alternative fuels, including gasohol (a blend of petrol and ethanol) and compressed natural gas, are used by taxis with bifuel capabilities. For updates about fuel options, see the website of **BKK Auto** (www.bkk.autos.com).

Hire

Cars, jeeps and vans can be rented in most major cities and airports from local companies as well as international chains. Local companies tend to have cheaper rates than the international chains, but their cars tend to be older and not as well maintained.

Motorcycles can be rented in major towns and many smaller tourist centres from guesthouses and small mum-and-dad businesses. Renting a motorcycle in Thailand is relatively easy and a great way to independently tour the countryside. For daily rentals, most businesses will ask that you leave your passport as a deposit. Before renting a motorcycle, check the vehicle's condition

BICYCLE TRAVEL IN THAILAND

For travelling just about anywhere outside Bangkok, bicycles are ideal; most roads are sealed and have roomy shoulders. Bicycles can be hired for as little as 50B per day, though they aren't always high quality.

Because duties are high on imported bikes, in most cases you're better off bringing your own bike to Thailand rather than purchasing one there. No special permits are needed for bringing a bicycle into the country, although it may be registered by customs – which means if you don't leave the country with your bicycle, you'll have to pay a customs duty.

It's advisable to bring a well-stocked repair kit.

and ask for a helmet (which is required by law).

Many tourists are injured riding motorcycles in Thailand because they don't know how to handle the vehicle and are unfamiliar with the road rules and conditions. Drive slowly, especially when roads are slick, to avoid damage to yourself and to the vehicle, and be sure to have adequate health insurance. If you've never driven a motorcycle before, stick to the smaller 100cc step-through bikes with automatic clutches.

Insurance

Thailand requires a minimum of liability insurance for all registered vehicles on the road. The better hire companies include comprehensive coverage for their vehicles. Always verify that a vehicle is insured for liability before signing a rental contract; you should also ask to see the dated insurance documents. If you have an accident while driving an uninsured vehicle, you're in for some major hassles.

Road Rules & Hazards

Thais drive on the left-hand side of the road (most of the time!). Other than that, just about anything goes, in spite of road signs and speed limits.

The main rule to be aware of is that right of way goes to the bigger vehicle; this is not what it says in Thai traffic law, but it's the reality. Maximum speed limits are 50km/h on urban roads and 80km/h to 100km/h on most highways.

Indicators are often used to warn passing drivers about oncoming traffic. A flashing left indicator means it's OK to pass, while a right indicator means someone's approaching from the other direction. Horns are used to tell other vehicles that the driver plans to pass. When drivers flash their lights, they're telling you not to pass.

In Bangkok traffic is chaotic, roads are poorly signposted, and motorcycles and random contra flows mean you can suddenly find yourself facing a wall of cars coming the other way.

Outside the capital, the principal hazard when driving in Thailand is having to contend with so many different types of vehicles on the same road – trucks, bicycles, túk-túk and motorcycles. This danger is often compounded by the lack of working lights. In village areas the vehicular traffic is lighter but you have to deal with stray chickens, dogs and water buffaloes.

Hitching

Hitching is never entirely safe in any country and we don't recommend it. Travellers who hitch should understand they are taking a small but potentially serious risk. Hitching is rarely seen these days in Thailand, so most passing motorists might not realise the intentions of the foreigner standing on the side of the road with a thumb out. When Thais want a ride they wave their hand with the palm facing the ground. This is the same gesture used to flag a taxi or bus, which is why some drivers might stop and point to a bus stop if one is nearby.

In some of the national parks without public transport, Thais are often willing to pick up a passenger standing by the side of the road.

Local Transport

City Bus & Sŏrng·tăa·ou

Bangkok has the largest city-bus system in the country. Wait at a bus stop and hail the vehicle by waving your hand palm-side downward. You typically pay the fare once you've taken a seat or, in some cases, when you disembark.

Elsewhere, public transport is provided by *sŏrng·tăa·ou* (a small pick-up truck outfitted with two facing rows of benches for passengers). They sometimes operate on fixed routes, but they may also run a share-taxi service where they pick up passengers going in the same general direction. In tourist centres, *sŏrng·tăa·ou* can be chartered just like a regular taxi, but you'll need to negotiate the fare beforehand. You can usually hail a *sŏrng·tăa·ou* anywhere along its route and pay the fare when you disembark.

Depending on the region, *sŏrng·tăa·ou* might also run a fixed route from the centre of town to outlying areas. Sometimes these vehicles are larger six-wheeled vehicles (sometimes called *rót hòk lór*).

Mass Transit

Bangkok is the only city in Thailand to have an above-ground and an underground light-rail public transport system. Known as the Skytrain and the Metro respectively, both systems have helped to alleviate the capital's notorious traffic jams.

Motorcycle Taxi

Many cities have *mor·đeu·sai ráp jâhng* (100cc to 125cc motorcycles) that can be hired, with a driver, for short distances. If you're empty-handed or travelling with a small bag, they can't be beaten for transport in a pinch.

In most cities, you'll find motorcycle taxis clustered near street intersections. Usually they wear numbered jerseys. Fares tend to run from 10B to 50B depending on distance; establish the price before climbing aboard.

Taxi

Bangkok has the most formal system of metered taxis. In other cities, a taxi can be a private vehicle with negotiable rates. You can also travel between cities by taxi but you'll need to negotiate a price as few taxi drivers will run a meter for intercity travel.

Train

Thailand's train system is most convenient as an alternative to buses for the long journey south. The 4500km rail network is operated by the **State Railway of Thailand** (SRT; ☎1690; www.railway.co.th) and covers four main lines: the northern, southern, northeastern and eastern lines. All long-distance trains originate from Bangkok's Hualamphong station.

Classes

The SRT operates passenger trains in three classes – 1st, 2nd and 3rd – but each class varies depending on whether you're on an ordinary, rapid or express train.

1st class In 1st class, passengers have private cabins, which are available only on rapid, express and special-express trains.

2nd class The seating arrangements in a 2nd-class, non-sleeper carriage are similar to those on a bus, with padded seats facing towards the front of the train. On 2nd-class sleeper cars, pairs of seats face one another and convert into two fold-down berths. The lower berth has more headroom than the upper berth and this is reflected in a higher fare. Children are always assigned a lower berth. There are air-con and fan 2nd-class carriages, and 2nd-class carriages are only found on rapid and express trains.

3rd class A typical 3rd-class carriage consists of two rows of bench seats divided into facing pairs. Each bench seat is designed to seat two or three passengers, but on a crowded rural line nobody seems to care.

Costs

Fares are determined by a base price with surcharges added for distance, class and train type (special-express, express, rapid, ordinary). Extra charges are added if the carriage has air-con and for sleeping berths (either upper or lower).

Reservations

Advance bookings can be made up to 60 days before your intended date of departure. You can make bookings in person from any train station. Train tickets can also be purchased at travel agencies, which usually add a service charge to the ticket price. If you are planning long-distance train travel from outside the country, you should email the State Railway of Thailand at least two weeks before your journey. You will receive an email confirming the booking. Pick up and pay for tickets an hour before leaving at the scheduled departure train station.

It is advisable to make advanced bookings for long-distance sleeper trains from Bangkok to Surat Thani, especially around Songkran in April and the peak tourist-season (December and January).

For short-distance trips, purchase your ticket at least a day in advance for seats (rather than sleepers).

Partial refunds on tickets are available depending on the number of days prior to your departure you arrange for a cancellation. Refunds can be handled at the train station booking office.

Station Services

All train stations have baggage-storage services (or cloak rooms). Most stations have a ticket window that will open between 15 and 30 minutes before train arrivals.

Most large train stations have printed timetables in English. Bangkok's Hualamphong station is a good spot to load up on timetables.

SĂHM·LÓR & TÚK-TÚK

Săhm·lór are three-wheeled pedicabs that are typically found in small towns where traffic is light.

The modern era's version of the human-powered săhm·lór is the motorised túk-túk (pronounced *'đúk đúk'*). They're small utility vehicles powered by screaming engines (usually LPG-powered).

With either form of transport the fare must be established by bargaining before departure. In tourist centres, túk-túk drivers often grossly overcharge foreigners so it's useful to have a sense of how much the fare should be before soliciting a ride. Hotel staff are helpful in providing reasonable fare suggestions.

Readers interested in pedicab lore may want to have a look at Lonely Planet's pictorial book *Chasing Rickshaws*, by Lonely Planet founder Tony Wheeler.

Health

Health risks and the quality of medical facilities vary depending on where and how you travel in Thailand. The majority of major cities and popular tourist areas are well developed with adequate and even excellent medical care. Travel to remote rural areas can expose you to some health risks and less adequate medical care.

Travellers tend to worry about contracting exotic infectious diseases when visiting the tropics, but such infections are far less common than problems with pre-existing medical conditions and accidental injury (especially as a result of traffic accidents).

Becoming ill in some way is common, however. Respiratory infections, diarrhoea and dengue fever are particular hazards in Thailand. Fortunately, most common illnesses can be prevented or are easily treated.

The following advice is a general guide and does not replace the advice of a doctor trained in travel medicine.

BEFORE YOU GO

Pack medications in clearly labelled original containers and obtain a signed and dated letter from your physician describing your medical conditions, medications and syringes or needles. If you have a heart condition, bring a copy of your electrocardiography (ECG) taken just prior to travelling.

If you take any regular medication bring double your needs. In Thailand you can buy many medications over the counter without a doctor's prescription, but it can be difficult to find the exact medication you are taking.

Insurance

Don't travel without health insurance – accidents *do* happen. You may require extra cover for adventure activities such as rock climbing or diving, as well as scooter/motorcycle riding. If your health insurance doesn't cover you for medical expenses abroad, ensure you get specific travel insurance. Most hospitals require an upfront guarantee of payment (from yourself or your insurer) prior to admission. Inquire before your trip about payment of medical charges and retain all documentation (medical reports, invoices etc) for claim purposes.

Vaccinations

Specialised travel-medicine clinics are your best source of information on which vaccinations you should consider taking. The **Centers for Disease Control** (CDC; www.cdc.gov) has a traveller's health section that contains recommendations for vaccinations. The only vaccine required in Thailand by international regulations is yellow fever. Proof of vaccination will only be required if you have visited a country in the yellow-fever zone (in Africa and South America only) within the six days prior to entering Thailand.

FURTHER READING

- **International Travel & Health** (www.who.int/ith) Health guide published by the World Health Organization (WHO).
- **Centers for Disease Control & Prevention** (CDC; www.cdc.gov) Country-specific advice.
- *Healthy Travel – Asia & India* (by Lonely Planet) Includes pretrip planning, emergency first aid, and immunisation and disease information.
- *Traveller's Health: How to Stay Healthy Abroad* (by Dr Richard Dawood) Considered the 'health bible' for international holidays.

IN TRANSIT

Deep Vein Thrombosis

Deep vein thrombosis (DVT) occurs when blood clots form in the legs during long trips such as flights, chiefly because of prolonged immobility. The longer the journey, the greater the risk. Though most blood clots are reabsorbed uneventfully, some may break off and travel through the blood vessels to the lungs, where they can cause life-threatening complications.

The chief symptom of DVT is swelling or pain of the foot, ankle or calf, usually, but not always, on one side. When a blood clot travels to the lungs, it may cause chest pain and difficulty in breathing. Travellers with any of these symptoms should immediately seek medical attention.

To prevent the development of DVT on long flights you should walk about the cabin, perform isometric compressions of the leg muscles (ie contract the leg muscles while sitting) and drink plenty of fluids (nonalcoholic). Those at higher risk should speak with a doctor about extra preventive measures.

MEDICAL CHECKLIST

Recommended items for a personal medical kit include:

- antifungal cream, eg Clotrimazole
- antibacterial cream, eg Muciprocin
- antibiotic for skin infections, eg Amoxicillin/Clavulanate or Cephalexin
- antibiotics for diarrhoea include Norfloxacin, Ciprofloxacin or Azithromycin for bacterial diarrhoea; for giardiasis or amoebic dysentery take Tinidazole
- antihistamine – there are many options, eg Cetrizine for daytime and Promethazine for night
- antiseptic, eg Betadine
- contraceptives
- decongestant
- DEET-based insect repellent
- oral rehydration solution for diarrhoea (eg Gastrolyte), diarrhoea 'stopper' (eg Loperamide) and antinausea medication (eg Prochlorperazine)
- first-aid items such as scissors, Elastoplasts, bandages, gauze, thermometer (but not one with mercury), sterile needles and syringes (with a doctor's letter), safety pins and tweezers
- hand gel (alcohol based) or alcohol-based hand wipes
- ibuprofen or another anti-inflammatory
- laxative, eg Coloxyl
- paracetamol
- steroid cream for allergic or itchy rashes, eg 1% to 2% hydrocortisone
- thrush (vaginal yeast infection) treatment, eg Clotrimazole pessaries or Diflucan tablet
- Ural or equivalent if you are prone to urine infections

Jet Lag & Motion Sickness

Jet lag results in insomnia, fatigue, malaise or nausea. To avoid jet lag try drinking plenty of fluids (nonalcoholic) and eating light meals. Upon arrival, seek exposure to natural sunlight and readjust your schedule.

Sedating antihistamines such as dimenhydrinate (Dramamine) and Prochlorperazine (Phenergan) are usually the first choice for treating motion sickness. Their main side effect is drowsiness. A herbal alternative is ginger. Scopolamine patches are considered the most effective prevention.

IN THAILAND

Availability & Cost of Health Care

Bangkok is considered the nearest centre of medical excellence for many countries in Southeast Asia. Private hospitals are more expensive than other medical facilities but offer a superior standard of care and English-speaking staff. The cost of health care is relatively cheap in Thailand compared to most Western countries.

Self-treatment may be appropriate if your problem is minor (eg traveller's diarrhoea), you are carrying the appropriate medication and you are unable to attend a recommended clinic or hospital.

Buying medication over the counter is not recommended, because fake medications and poorly stored or out-of-date drugs are common.

Infectious Diseases

Cutaneous Larva Migrans

This disease, caused by dog or cat hookworm, is particularly common on the beaches of Thailand. The rash starts as a small lump, and then slowly spreads like a winding line. It is intensely itchy, especially at night. It is easily treated with medications and should not be cut out or frozen.

Dengue Fever

This mosquito-borne disease is increasingly problematic throughout Southeast Asia, especially in cities. As there is no vaccine it can only be prevented by avoiding mosquito bites. The mosquito that carries dengue is a daytime biter, so use insect-avoidance measures at all times. Symptoms include high fever, severe headache (especially behind the eyes), nausea and body aches (dengue was previously known as 'breakbone fever'). Some people develop a rash (which can be very itchy) and experience diarrhoea. The southern islands of Thailand are particularly high-risk areas. There is no specific treatment, just rest and paracetamol – do not take aspirin or ibuprofen as they increase the risk of haemorrhaging. See a doctor to be diagnosed and monitored.

Dengue can progress to the more severe and life-threatening dengue haemorrhagic fever; however, this is very uncommon in tourists. The risk of this increases substantially if you have previously been infected with dengue and are then infected with a different serotype.

Hepatitis A

The risk in Bangkok is decreasing but there is still significant risk in most of the country. This food- and water-borne virus infects the liver, causing jaundice (yellow skin and eyes), nausea and lethargy. There is no specific treatment for hepatitis A. In rare instances, it can be fatal for those over the age of 40. All travellers to Thailand should be vaccinated against hepatitis A.

Hepatitis B

The only sexually transmitted disease (STD) that can be prevented by vaccination, hepatitis B is spread by body fluids, including sexual contact. In some parts of Thailand up to 20% of the population are carriers of hepatitis B, and usually are unaware of this. The long-term consequences can include liver cancer, cirrhosis and death.

HIV

HIV is now one of the most common causes of death in people under the age of 50 in Thailand. Always practise safe sex, and avoid getting tattoos or using unclean syringes.

Influenza

Present year-round in the tropics, flu is the most common vaccine-preventable disease contracted by travellers and everyone should consider vaccination. There is no specific treatment, just rest and paracetamol.

Leptospirosis

Leptospirosis is contracted from exposure to infected surface water – most commonly after river rafting or canyoning. Early symptoms are very similar to the flu and include headache and fever. It can vary from a very mild ailment to a fatal disease. Diagnosis is made through blood tests and it is easily treated with Doxycycline.

Malaria

Most parts of Thailand visited by tourists, particularly city and resort areas, have minimal to no risk of malaria, and the risk of side effects from taking antimalarial tablets is likely to outweigh the risk of getting the disease itself. If you are travelling to high-risk rural areas (unlikely for most visitors), seek medical advice on the right medication and dosage for you.

Malaria is caused by a parasite transmitted by the bite of an infected mosquito. The most significant symptom of malaria is fever, but general symptoms such as headache, diarrhoea, cough or chills may also occur – the same symptoms as many other infections. A diagnosis can only be made by taking a blood sample.

Measles

This highly contagious viral infection is spread through coughing and sneezing. Measles starts with a high fever and rash and can be complicated by pneumonia and brain disease. There is no specific treatment. Ensure you are fully vaccinated.

Rabies

This uniformly fatal disease is spread by the bite or lick of an infected animal – most commonly a dog or monkey. You should seek medical advice immediately after any animal bite and commence post-exposure treatment. Having a pre-travel vaccination means the post-bite treatment is greatly simplified.

If an animal bites you, gently wash the wound with soap and water, and apply iodine-based antiseptic. If you are not pre-vaccinated you will need to receive rabies immunoglobulin as soon as possible, followed by five shots of vaccine over 28 days. If pre-vaccinated you need just two shots of vaccine given three days apart.

STDs

The sexually transmitted diseases most common in Thailand include herpes, warts, syphilis, gonorrhoea and chlamydia. People carrying

RARE BUT BE AWARE

Avian Influenza Most of those infected have had close contact with sick or dead birds.

Filariasis A mosquito-borne disease that is common in the local population; practise mosquito-avoidance measures.

Hepatitis E Transmitted through contaminated food and water and has similar symptoms to hepatitis A; can be a severe problem in pregnant women. Follow safe eating and drinking guidelines.

Japanese B Encephalitis Viral disease transmitted by mosquitoes, typically occurring in rural areas; vaccination is recommended for travellers spending more than one month outside cities.

Meliodosis Contracted by skin contact with soil. The symptoms are very similar to tuberculosis (TB). There is no vaccine but it can be treated with medications.

Strongyloides A parasite transmitted by skin contact with soil; common in local populations. It is characterised by an unusual skin rash – a linear rash on the trunk that comes and goes. An overwhelming infection can follow. It can be treated with medications.

Tuberculosis The main symptoms are fever, cough, weight loss, night sweats and tiredness. Treatment is available with long-term multi-drug regimens.

Typhus Murine typhus is spread by the bite of a flea; scrub typhus is spread via a mite. Symptoms include fever, muscle pains and a rash. Following general insect-avoidance measures and taking Doxycycline will also prevent them.

these diseases often have no signs of infection. Condoms will prevent gonorrhoea and chlamydia but not warts or herpes. If after a sexual encounter you develop any rash, lumps, discharge or pain when passing urine seek immediate medical attention. If you have been sexually active during your travels, have an STD check on your return home.

Typhoid

This serious bacterial infection is spread through food and water. It gives a high and slowly progressive fever, severe headache, and may be accompanied by a dry cough and stomach pain. It is diagnosed by blood tests and treated with antibiotics. Vaccination is recommended for all travellers spending more than a week in Thailand, or travelling outside the major cities. Be aware that vaccination is not 100% effective so you must still be careful with what you eat and drink.

Traveller's Diarrhoea

Traveller's diarrhoea is by far the most common problem affecting travellers – up to 50% of people will suffer from some form of it within two weeks of starting their trip. In over 80% of cases, traveller's diarrhoea is caused by a bacteria (there are numerous potential culprits), and responds promptly to treatment with antibiotics.

Here we define traveller's diarrhoea as the passage of more than three watery bowel movements within 24 hours, plus at least one other symptom such as vomiting, fever, cramps, nausea or feeling generally unwell.

Treatment consists of staying well hydrated; rehydration solutions such as Gastrolyte are the best for this. Antibiotics such as Norfloxacin, Ciprofloxacin or Azithromycin will kill the bacteria quickly.

Loperamide is just a 'stopper' and doesn't get to the cause of the problem. It can be helpful, for example if you have to go on a long bus ride. Don't take Loperamide if you have a fever or blood in your stools. Seek medical attention quickly if you do not respond to an appropriate antibiotic.

Giardia lamblia is a parasite that is relatively common in travellers. Symptoms include nausea, bloating, excess gas, fatigue and intermittent diarrhoea. 'Eggy' burps are often attributed solely to giardiasis. The treatment of choice is Tinidazole, with Metronidazole being a second-line option.

Amoebic dysentery is very rare in travellers but may be misdiagnosed by poor-quality labs. Symptoms are similar to bacterial diarrhoea. You should always seek reliable medical care if you have blood in your diarrhoea. Treatment involves two drugs; Tinidazole or Metronidazole to kill the parasite in your gut and then a second drug to kill the cysts. If left untreated complications, such as liver abscesses, can occur.

Environmental Hazards

Food

Eating in restaurants is the biggest risk factor for contracting traveller's diarrhoea. Ways to avoid it include eating only freshly cooked food, and avoiding food that has been sitting around in buffets. Peel all fruit and cook vegetables. Eat in busy restaurants with a high turnover of customers.

Heat

Many parts of Thailand are hot and humid throughout the year. For most people it takes at least two weeks to adapt to the hot climate. Prevent swelling of the feet and ankles as well as muscle cramps caused by excessive sweating by avoiding dehydration and excessive activity in the hot hours of the day.

Heat stroke is a serious medical emergency and requires immediate medical treatment. Symptoms come on suddenly and include weakness, nausea, a hot dry body with a body temperature of over 41°C, dizziness, confusion, loss of coordination, fits and eventually collapse and loss of consciousness.

Insect Bites & Stings

Bedbugs live in the cracks of furniture and walls and then migrate to the bed at night to feed on you. You can treat the itch with an antihistamine. Lice inhabit various parts of your body but most commonly your head and pubic area. Transmission is via close contact with an infected person. They can be difficult to treat and you may need numerous applications of an anti-lice shampoo such as Permethrin. Pubic lice are usually contracted from sexual contact.

Ticks are contracted when walking in rural areas. They are commonly found behind the ears, on the belly and in armpits. If you have had a tick bite and experience symptoms such as a rash at the site of the bite or elsewhere, fever or muscle aches you should see a doctor. Doxycycline prevents tick-borne diseases.

Leeches are found in humid rainforest areas. They do not transmit any disease but their bites are often intensely itchy for weeks afterwards and can easily become infected. Apply an iodine-based antiseptic to any leech bite to help prevent infection.

Bee and wasp stings mainly cause problems for people who are allergic to them. Anyone with a serious allergy should carry an injection of adrenaline (eg an Epipen) for emergencies. For others, pain is the main problem – apply ice to the sting and take painkillers.

Parasites

The two rules to follow to avoid parasitic infections are to wear shoes and to avoid eating raw food, especially fish, pork and vegetables. A number of parasites are transmitted via the skin by walking barefoot, including strongyloides, hookworm and cutaneous *larva migrans*.

Skin Problems

Prickly heat is a common skin rash in the tropics, caused by sweat being trapped under the skin. Treat by taking cool showers and using powders.

Two fungal rashes commonly affect travellers. The first occurs in the groin, armpits and between the toes. It starts as a red patch that slowly spreads and is usually itchy. Treatment involves keeping the skin dry, avoiding

JELLYFISH STINGS

Box jellyfish stings range from minor to deadly. The jellyfish are generally found on sandy beaches near river mouths and mangroves during the warmer months.

The initial sting can seem minor; however severe symptoms such as back pain, nausea, vomiting, sweating, difficulty breathing and a feeling of impending doom can develop between five and 40 minutes later. Depending on the species of box jellyfish, stings are potentially fatal.

There are many other jellyfish in Thailand that cause irritating stings but no serious effects. The only way to prevent these stings is to wear protective clothing, which provides a barrier between human skin and the jellyfish.

First Aid for Severe Stings

Stay with the person, send someone to call for medical help, and start immediate CPR if they are unconscious. If the victim is conscious douse the stung area liberally with vinegar – simple household vinegar is fine – for 30 seconds. Some Thai beaches like Ko Kut and Ko Mak have installed vinegar stations on the beach. Pour vinegar onto the stung area as above; early application can make a huge difference. It is best to seek medical care quickly in case any other symptoms develop over the next 40 minutes.

chafing and using an antifungal cream such as Clotrimazole or Lamisil. The fungus *Tinea versicolor* causes small and light-coloured patches, most commonly on the back, chest and shoulders. Consult a doctor.

Cuts and scratches become easily infected in humid climates. Immediately wash all wounds in clean water and apply antiseptic. If you develop signs of infection, see a doctor. Coral cuts can easily become infected.

Snakes

Though snake bites are rare for travellers, there are over 85 species of venomous snakes in Thailand. Always wear boots and long pants if walking in an area that may have snakes. First aid in the event of a snake bite involves 'pressure immobilisation' using an elastic bandage firmly wrapped around the affected limb, starting at the hand or foot (depending on the limb bitten) and working up towards the chest. The bandage should not be so tight that the circulation is cut off, and the fingers or toes should be kept free so the circulation can be checked. Immobilise the limb with a splint and carry the victim to medical attention. It is very important that the victim stays immobile. Do not use tourniquets or try to suck the venom out.

The Thai Red Cross produces antivenom for many of the poisonous snakes in Thailand.

Sunburn

Even on a cloudy day sunburn can occur rapidly. Use a strong sunscreen (at least factor 30), making sure to reapply after a swim, and always wear a wide-brimmed hat and sunglasses outdoors. Avoid lying in the sun when the sun is at its highest in the sky (10am to 2pm). If you become sunburnt stay out of the sun until you have recovered, apply cool compresses and take painkillers for the discomfort. One per cent hydrocortisone cream applied twice daily is also helpful.

Travelling with Children

Thailand is relatively safe for children from a health point of view. A medical kit designed specifically for children may include paracetamol or Tylenol syrup for fevers, an antihistamine, itch cream, first-aid supplies, nappy-rash treatment, sunscreen and insect repellent. It's a good idea to carry a general antibiotic (best used under medical supervision) – Azithromycin is an ideal paediatric formula used to treat bacterial diarrhoea, as well as ear, chest and throat infections.

Good resources are the Lonely Planet publication *Travel with Children*; for those spending longer away Jane Wilson-Howarth's book *Your Child's Health Abroad* is excellent.

Women's Health

Pregnant women should receive specialised advice before travelling. The ideal time to travel is in the second trimester (16 and 28 weeks), when pregnancy-related risks are at their lowest. Most of all, ensure travel insurance covers all pregnancy-related possibilities, including premature labour.

Traveller's diarrhoea can quickly lead to dehydration and result in inadequate blood flow to the placenta. Many of the drugs used to treat various diarrhoea bugs are not recommended in pregnancy. Azithromycin is considered safe.

In Thailand's urban areas, supplies of sanitary products are readily available. Your personal birth-control option may not be available so bring adequate supplies. Heat, humidity and antibiotics can all contribute to thrush. Treatment of thrush is with antifungal creams and pessaries such as Clotrimazole. A practical alternative is one tablet of fluconazole (Diflucan). Urinary-tract infections can be precipitated by dehydration or long bus journeys without toilet stops; bring suitable antibiotics for treatment.

Language

Thailand's official language is effectively the dialect spoken and written in central Thailand, which has successfully become the lingua franca of all Thai and non-Thai ethnic groups in the kingdom.

In Thai the meaning of a single syllable may be altered by means of different tones. In standard Thai there are five: low tone, mid tone, falling tone, high tone and rising tone. The range of all five tones is relative to each speaker's vocal range, so there is no fixed 'pitch' intrinsic to the language.

➡ **low tone** – 'Flat' like the mid tone, but pronounced at the relative bottom of one's vocal range. It is low, level and has no inflection, eg bàht (baht – the Thai currency).

➡ **mid tone** – Pronounced 'flat', at the relative middle of the speaker's vocal range, eg dee (good). No tone mark is used.

➡ **falling tone** – Starting high and falling sharply, this tone is similar to the change in pitch in English when you are emphasising a word, or calling someone's name from afar, eg mâi (no/not).

➡ **high tone** – Usually the most difficult for non-Thai speakers. It's pronounced near the relative top of the vocal range, as level as possible, eg máh (horse).

➡ **rising tone** – Starting low and gradually rising, sounds like the inflection used by English speakers to imply a question – 'Yes?', eg săhm (three).

WANT MORE?

For in-depth language information and handy phrases, check out Lonely Planet's *Thai Phrasebook*. You'll find it at **shop.lonelyplanet.com**, or you can buy Lonely Planet's iPhone phrasebooks at the Apple App Store.

The Thai government has instituted the Royal Thai General Transcription System (RTGS) as a standard method of writing Thai using the Roman alphabet. It's used in official documents, road signs and on maps. However, local variations crop up on signs, menus etc. Generally, names in this book follow the most common practice.

In our coloured pronunciation guides, the hyphens indicate syllable breaks within words, and some syllables are further divided with a dot to help you pronounce compound vowels, eg mêu·a-rai (when).

The vowel a is pronounced as in 'about', aa as the 'a' in 'bad', ah as the 'a' in 'father', ai as in 'aisle', air as in 'flair' (without the 'r'), eu as the 'er' in 'her' (without the 'r'), ew as in 'new' (with rounded lips), oh as the 'o' in 'toe', or as in 'torn' (without the 'r') and ow as in 'now'.

Most consonants correspond to their English counterparts. The exceptions are b (a hard 'p' sound, almost like a 'b', eg in 'hip-bag'); đ (a hard 't' sound, like a sharp 'd', eg in 'mid-tone'); ng (as in 'singing'; in Thai it can occur at the start of a word) and r (as in 'run' but flapped; in everyday speech it's often pronounced like 'l').

BASICS

The social structure of Thai society demands different registers of speech depending on who you're talking to. To make things simple we've chosen the correct form of speech appropriate to the context of each phrase.

When being polite, the speaker ends his or her sentence with kráp (for men) or kâ (for women). It is the gender of the speaker that is being expressed here; it is also the common way to answer 'yes' to a question or show agreement.

The masculine and feminine forms of phrases in this chapter are indicated where relevant with 'm/f'.

Hello.	สวัสดี	sà-wàt-dee
Goodbye.	ลาก่อน	lah gòrn
Yes./No.	ใช่/ไม่	châi/mâi
Please.	ขอ	kŏr
Thank you.	ขอบคุณ	kòrp kun
You're welcome.	ยินดี	yin dee
Excuse me.	ขออภัย	kŏr à-pai
Sorry.	ขอโทษ	kŏr tôht

How are you?
สบายดีไหม — sà-bai dee măi

Fine. And you?
สบายดีครับ/ค่า แล้วคุณล่ะ — sà-bai dee kráp/kâ láa·ou kun lâ (m/f)

What's your name?
คุณชื่ออะไร — kun chêu à-rai

My name is ...
ผม/ดิฉันชื่อ... — pŏm/dì-chăn chêu ... (m/f)

Do you speak English?
คุณพูดภาษาอังกฤษได้ไหม — kun pôot pah-săh ang-grìt dâi măi

I don't understand.
ผม/ดิฉันไม่เข้าใจ — pŏm/dì-chăn mâi kôw jai (m/f)

ACCOMMODATION

Where's a ...?	... อยู่ที่ไหน	... yòo têe năi
campsite	ค่ายพักแรม	kâi pák raam
guesthouse	บ้านพัก	bâhn pák
hotel	โรงแรม	rohng raam
youth hostel	บ้านเยาวชน	bâhn yow-wá-chon

Do you have a ... room?	มีห้อง ... ไหม	mee hôrng ... măi
single	เดี่ยว	dèe·o
double	เตียงคู่	đee·ang kôo
twin	สองเตียง	sŏrng đee·ang

air-con	แอร์	aa
bathroom	ห้องน้ำ	hôrng nám
laundry	ห้องซักผ้า	hôrng sák pâh
mosquito net	มุ้ง	múng
window	หน้าต่าง	nâh đàhng

Question Words

What?	อะไร	à-rai
When?	เมื่อไร	mêu·a-rai
Where?	ที่ไหน	têe năi
Who?	ใคร	krai
Why?	ทำไม	tam-mai

DIRECTIONS

Where's ...?
... อยู่ที่ไหน — ... yòo têe năi

What's the address?
ที่อยู่คืออะไร — têe yòo keu à-rai

Could you please write it down?
เขียนลงให้ได้ไหม — kĕe·an long hâi dâi măi

Can you show me (on the map)?
ให้ดู (ในแผนที่) ได้ไหม — hâi doo (nai păan têe) dâi măi

Turn left/right.
เลี้ยวซ้าย/ขวา — lée·o sái/kwăh

It's ...	อยู่ ...	yòo ...
behind	ที่หลัง	têe lăng
in front of	ตรงหน้า	đrong nâh
next to	ข้างๆ	kâhng kâhng
straight ahead	ตรงไป	đrong bai

EATING & DRINKING

I'd like (the menu), please.
ขอ (รายการอาหาร) หน่อย — kŏr (rai gahn ah-hăhn) nòy

What would you recommend?
คุณแนะนำอะไรบ้าง — kun náa-nam à-rai bâhng

That was delicious!
อร่อยมาก — à-ròy mâhk

Cheers!
ไชโย — chai-yoh

Please bring the bill.
ขอบิลหน่อย — kŏr bin nòy

I don't eat ...	ผม/ดิฉันไม่กิน ...	pŏm/dì-chăn mâi gin ... (m/f)
eggs	ไข่	kài
fish	ปลา	blah
red meat	เนื้อแดง	néu·a daang
nuts	ถั่ว	tòo·a

Key Words

bar	บาร์	bah
bottle	ขวด	kòo·at
bowl	ชาม	chahm
breakfast	อาหารเช้า	ah-hăhn chów
cafe	ร้านกาแฟ	ráhn gah-faa
chopsticks	ไม้ตะเกียบ	mái đà-gèe·ap
cold	เย็น	yen
cup	ถ้วย	tôo·ay
dessert	ของหวาน	kŏrng wăhn
dinner	อาหารเย็น	ah-hăhn yen
drink list	รายการเครื่องดื่ม	rai gahn krêu·ang dèum
fork	ส้อม	sôrm
glass	แก้ว	gâa·ou
hot	ร้อน	rórn
knife	มีด	mêet
lunch	อาหารกลางวัน	ah-hăhn glahng wan
market	ตลาด	đà-làht
menu	รายการอาหาร	rai gahn ah-hăhn
plate	จาน	jahn
restaurant	ร้านอาหาร	ráhn ah-hăhn
spicy	เผ็ด	pèt
spoon	ช้อน	chórn
vegetarian (person)	คนกินเจ	kon gin jair

Signs

ทางเข้า	Entrance
ทางออก	Exit
เปิด	Open
ปิด	Closed
ที่ติดต่อสอบถาม	Information
ห้าม	Prohibited
ห้องสุขา	Toilets
ชาย	Men
หญิง	Women

with	มี	mee
without	ไม่มี	mâi mee

Meat & Fish

beef	เนื้อ	néu·a
chicken	ไก่	gài
crab	ปู	ɓoo
duck	เป็ด	ɓèt
fish	ปลา	ɓlah
meat	เนื้อ	néu·a
pork	หมู	mŏo
seafood	อาหารทะเล	ah-hăhn tá-lair
squid	ปลาหมึก	ɓlah mèuk

Fruit & Vegetables

banana	กล้วย	glôo·ay
beans	ถั่ว	tòo·a
coconut	มะพร้าว	má-prów
eggplant	มะเขือ	má-kĕu·a
fruit	ผลไม้	pŏn-lá-mái
guava	ฝรั่ง	fa-ràng
lime	มะนาว	má-now
mango	มะม่วง	má-môo·ang
mangosteen	มังคุด	mang-kút
mushrooms	เห็ด	hèt
nuts	ถั่ว	tòo·a
papaya	มะละกอ	má-lá-gor
potatoes	มันฝรั่ง	man fa-ràng
rambutan	เงาะ	ngó
tamarind	มะขาม	má-kăhm
tomatoes	มะเขือเทศ	má-kĕu·a têt
vegetables	ผัก	pàk
watermelon	แตงโม	đaang moh

Other

chilli	พริก	prík
egg	ไข่	kài
fish sauce	น้ำปลา	nám ɓlah
ice	น้ำแข็ง	nám kăang

noodles	เส้น	sên
oil	น้ำมัน	nám man
pepper	พริกไทย	prík tai
rice	ข้าว	kôw
salad	ผักสด	pàk sòt
salt	เกลือ	gleu·a
soup	น้ำซุป	nám súp
soy sauce	น้ำซีอิ๊ว	nám see-éw
sugar	น้ำตาล	nám đahn
tofu	เต้าหู้	đôw hôo

Drinks

beer	เบียร์	bee·a
coffee	กาแฟ	gah-faa
milk	นมจืด	nom jèut
orange juice	น้ำส้ม	nám sôm
soy milk	น้ำเต้าหู้	nám đôw hôo
sugarcane juice	น้ำอ้อย	nám ôy
tea	ชา	chah
water	น้ำดื่ม	nám dèum

EMERGENCIES

Help!	ช่วยด้วย	chôo·ay dôo·ay
Go away!	ไปให้พ้น	ɓai hâi pón

Call a doctor!
เรียกหมอหน่อย — rêe·ak mŏr nòy

Call the police!
เรียกตำรวจหน่อย — rêe·ak đam·ròo·at nòy

I'm ill.
ผม/ดิฉันป่วย — pŏm/dì-chăn ɓòo·ay (m/f)

I'm lost.
ผม/ดิฉัน หลงทาง — pŏm/dì-chăn lŏng tahng (m/f)

Where are the toilets?
ห้องน้ำอยู่ที่ไหน — hôrng nám yòo têe năi

SHOPPING & SERVICES

I'd like to buy ...
อยากจะซื้อ ... — yàhk jà séu ...

I'm just looking.
ดูเฉย ๆ — doo chĕu·i chĕu·i

Can I look at it?
ขอดูได้ไหม — kŏr doo dâi măi

How much is it?
เท่าไร — tôw-rai

That's too expensive.
แพงไป — paang ɓai

Can you lower the price?
ลดราคาได้ไหม — lót rah-kah dâi măi

There's a mistake in the bill.
บิลใบนี้ผิด นะครับ/ค่ะ — bin bai née pìt ná kráp/kâ (m/f)

TIME & DATES

What time is it?
กี่โมงแล้ว — gèe mohng láa·ou

morning	เช้า	chów
afternoon	บ่าย	bài
evening	เย็น	yen
yesterday	เมื่อวาน	mêu·a wahn
today	วันนี้	wan née
tomorrow	พรุ่งนี้	prûng née

Monday	วันจันทร์	wan jan
Tuesday	วันอังคาร	wan ang-kahn
Wednesday	วันพุธ	wan pút
Thursday	วันพฤหัสฯ	wan pá-réu-hàt
Friday	วันศุกร	wan sùk
Saturday	วันเสาร์	wan sŏw
Sunday	วันอาทิตย์	wan ah-tít

TRANSPORT

Public Transport

bicycle rickshaw	สามล้อ	săhm lór
boat	เรือ	reu·a
bus	รถเมล์	rót mair
car	รถเก๋ง	rót gĕng
motorcycle taxi	มอร์เตอร์ไซค์ รับจ้าง	mor-đeu-sai ráp jâhng
plane	เครื่องบิน	krêu·ang bin
train	รถไฟ	rót fai
túk-túk	ตุ๊ก ๆ	đúk đúk

Numbers

1	หนึ่ง	nèung
2	สอง	sŏrng
3	สาม	săhm
4	สี่	sèe
5	ห้า	hâh
6	หก	hòk
7	เจ็ด	jèt
8	แปด	Ƀaat
9	เก้า	gôw
10	สิบ	sìp
11	สิบเอ็ด	sìp-èt
20	ยี่สิบ	yêe-sìp
21	ยี่สิบเอ็ด	yêe-sìp-èt
30	สามสิบ	săhm-sìp
40	สี่สิบ	sèe-sìp
50	ห้าสิบ	hâh-sìp
60	หกสิบ	hòk-sìp
70	เจ็ดสิบ	jèt-sìp
80	แปดสิบ	Ƀaat-sìp
90	เก้าสิบ	gôw-sìp
100	หนึ่งร้อย	nèung róy
1000	หนึ่งพัน	nèung pan
10,000	หนึ่งหมื่น	nèung mèun
100,000	หนึ่งแสน	nèung săan
1,000,000	หนึ่งล้าน	nèung láhn

When's the ... bus?	รถเมล์คัน ... มาเมื่อไร	rót mair kan ... mah mêu·a rai
first	แรก	râak
last	สุดท้าย	sùt tái
next	ต่อไป	đòr Ƀai

A ... ticket, please.	ขอตั๋ว ...	kŏr đŏo·a ...
one-way	เที่ยวเดียว	têe·o dee·o
return	ไปกลับ	Ƀai glàp

I'd like a/an ... seat.	ต้องการ ที่นั่ง ...	đôrng gahn têe nâng ...
aisle	ติดทางเดิน	đìt tahng deun
window	ติดหน้าต่าง	đìt nâh đàhng

platform	ชานชาลา	chan-chah-lah
ticket window	ช่องขายตั๋ว	chôrng kăi đŏo·a
timetable	ตารางเวลา	đah-rahng wair-lah

What time does it get to (Chiang Mai)?
ถึง (เชียงใหม่) กี่โมง — tĕung (chee·ang mài) gèe mohng

Does it stop at (Saraburi)?
รถจอดที่ (สระบุรี) ไหม — rót jòrt têe (sà-rà-bù-ree) măi

Please tell me when we get to (Chiang Mai).
เมื่อถึง (เชียงใหม่) กรุณาบอกด้วย — mêu·a tĕung (chee·ang mài) gà-rú-nah bòrk dôo·ay

I'd like to get off at (Saraburi).
ขอลงที่(สระบุรี) — kŏr long têe (sà-rà-bù-ree)

Driving & Cycling

I'd like to hire a ...	อยากจะ เช่า ...	yàhk jà chôw ...
car	รถเก๋ง	rót gĕng
motorbike	รถ มอร์เตอร์ไซค์	rót mor-đeu-sai

I'd like ...	ต้องการ ...	đôrng gahn ...
my bicycle repaired	ซ่อมรถ จักรยาน	sôrm rót jàk-gà-yahn
to hire a bicycle	เช่ารถ จักรยาน	chôw rót jàk-gà-yahn

Is this the road to (Ban Bung Wai)?
ทางนี้ไป (บ้านบุ่งหวาย) ไหม — tahng née Ƀai (bâhn bùng wăi) măi

Where's a petrol station?
ปั๊มน้ำมันอยู่ที่ไหน — Ƀâm nám man yòo têe năi

Can I park here?
จอดที่นี่ได้ไหม — jòrt têe née dâi măi

How long can I park here?
จอดที่นี่ได้นานเท่าไร — jòrt têe née dâi nahn tôw-rai

I need a mechanic.
ต้องการช่างรถ — đôrng gahn châhng rót

I have a flat tyre.
ยางแบน — yahng baan

I've run out of petrol.
หมดน้ำมัน — mòt nám man

Do I need a helmet?
ต้องใช้หมวกกันน็อกไหม — đôrng chái mòo·ak gan nórk măi

GLOSSARY

ah·hăhn – food

ah·hăhn ɓàk đâi – southern Thai food

ao/ow – bay or gulf

bâhn/ban – house or village

bòht – central sanctuary or chapel in a Thai temple

BTS – Bangkok Mass Transit System (Skytrain)

chedi – stupa; monument erected to house a Buddha relic

chow lair/chao leh/chow nám – sea gypsies

đa·làht/talat – market

dhamma – right behaviour and truth according to Buddhist doctrine

đrùđ jeen – Chinese New Year

fa·ràng – foreigner of European descent; guava

ga·teu·i/kathoey – 'ladyboy'; transvestites and transsexuals

gò – see *ko*

hàht/hat – beach

hôrng/hong – room or chamber; island caves semisubmerged in the sea

Isan/isăhn – general term for northeastern Thailand

jataka – stories of the Buddha's previous lives

jeen – Chinese

kathoey – see *ga·teu·i*

khao/kŏw – hill or mountain

klorng/klong/khlong – canal

ko/koh/gò – island

Khun – honorific used before first name

laem/lăam – geographical cape

llongyi – Burmese sarong

masjid/mátsàyít – mosque

meu·ang/muang – city

moo·ay tai/muay·thai – Thai boxing

MRT – Metropolitan Rapid Transit (Metro); the underground railway in Bangkok

nám – water or juice

nám đòk – waterfall

nibbana – nirvana; the 'blowing out' or extinction of all desire and thus of all suffering

nóy/noi – small

ow – see *ao*

pak tai/ɓàk đâi – southern Thailand

Pali – language derived from Sanskrit, in which the Buddhist scriptures are written

prá/phra – monk or Buddha image

prang/ɓrang – Khmer-style tower on temples

ɓàk đâi – southern Thailand

ɓèe·pâht/pii-phâat – classical Thai orchestra

ɓrang – see *prang*

ráhn goh·ɓee – coffee shops (southern Thailand)

râi – an area of land measurement equal to 1600 sq m

Ramakian – Thai version of India's epic literary piece, the Ramayana

reu·a hăhng yow – long-tail taxi boat

reu·an tăa·ou – a longhouse

reu·sĕe – Hindu rishi or sage

rót aa – blue-and-white air-conditioned bus

rót tam·má·dah – ordinary bus (no air-con) or ordinary train (not rapid or express)

săh·lah/sala – open-sided, covered meeting hall or resting place

săhm·lór – three-wheeled pedicab

săhn jôw – Chinese shrine or joss house

sangha – brotherhood of Buddhist monks; temple inhabitants (monks and nuns)

sà·nùk – fun

soi – lane or small street

Songkran – Thai New Year, held in mid-April

sŏrng·tăa·ou – small pickup truck with two benches in the back, used as bus/taxi

SRT – State Railway of Thailand

stupa/chedi – domed edifice housing Buddhist relics

suttas – discourses of the Buddha

talat – see *đa·làht*

TAT – Tourism Authority of Thailand

tha/tâh – pier, landing

Thai ɓàk đâi – also *Thai Pak Tai;* southern Thais

tâm/tham – cave

thànŏn – street, road, avenue (we use the abbreviation 'Th' in this book)

đròrk/trok – alley, smaller than a soi

túk-túk – motorised *săhm·lór*

vipassana – Buddhist insight meditation

wâi – palms-together Thai greeting

wan prá – Buddhist holy days which coincide with the main phases of the moon (full, new and half) each month

wang – palace

wát – temple, monastery

wí·hăhn/wihan – counterpart to *bòht* in Thai temples, containing Buddha images but not circumscribed by sema stones

yài – big

Behind the Scenes

SEND US YOUR FEEDBACK

We love to hear from travellers – your comments keep us on our toes and help make our books better. Our well-travelled team reads every word on what you loved or loathed about this book. Although we cannot reply individually to postal submissions, we always guarantee that your feedback goes straight to the appropriate authors, in time for the next edition. Each person who sends us information is thanked in the next edition – the most useful submissions are rewarded with a selection of digital PDF chapters.

Visit **lonelyplanet.com/contact** to submit your updates and suggestions or to ask for help. Our award-winning website also features inspirational travel stories, news and discussions.

Note: We may edit, reproduce and incorporate your comments in Lonely Planet products such as guidebooks, websites and digital products, so let us know if you don't want your comments reproduced or your name acknowledged. For a copy of our privacy policy visit lonelyplanet.com/privacy.

OUR READERS

Many thanks to the travellers who used the last edition and wrote to us with helpful hints, useful advice and interesting anecdotes: Adeline, Aileen, Alice Hedger, Andrew Bustamante, Andrew Jennings, Barry Walden, Benno Bauchspiess, Bertrand, Brandon Hausmann, Cecilie Normand, Christopher Byrd, Daniel, Dinesh, Eveline Fortuin, Gordon Hague (Blacktip), Heather Johnson, Helen Macnee, Jan Mulder, Jihi Bustamante, Jilly MacPherson, Joana Correia, Jonathan Boyle, Kat, Katia Moretti, Liz McEwan, Luigi Huikeshoven, Marco Ooms, Mark Britowich, Mathias, Mehmet, Menard, Ms. Oy, Murat Mirata, Rachel Cooper, Robert Carter, Sara Forssell, Saskia Beijering, Sergio Sancho, Stefano Tirelli, Suwatchai Praesomboon,Theodore Gemmer, Thomas Stegemann, Tristan Fourcault, Ulla Pajanen, Yvonne Degen

AUTHOR THANKS

Celeste Brash

Thanks to Samui Steve, Johnny, Kirk Stucker, Rachel and Stephen and Nick Ray for help on Samui. On Ko Pha-Ngan a huge thanks to my friend Marissa Bright and to the folks at Chaloklam Diving who, despite going out of their way to help, never found out who I was. On Tao thanks to Heather and Andy Keeler, Chris and Pu, Gemma and Ed. Huge thanks to Brandon Presser for great base text and tips, and as always to my family for holding the fort at home without me.

Austin Bush

A massive shout out to LPers for Life Ilaria Walker and Bruce Evans, and huge thanks to coordinating author Celeste Brash and the kind folks on the ground in Thailand.

David Eimer

Much gratitude to Khun Morn for her Trat tips and islands advice. Thanks to China Williams and to Ilaria Walker, Bruce Evans, Diana Von Holdt and Lorna Goodyer at Lonely Planet. As ever, thanks to the many people who passed on information along the way, whether knowingly or unwittingly.

Adam Skolnick

As is always the case for me in Thailand, I received far too many friendly smiles and welcome insights to thank everyone appropriately. So allow me to give one giant hug to this fun, strange, spicy and soothing country that is so very easy to adore. I'd also like to thank Aleesha Wilson and Annie Lim for their assistance; Pak and James in Krabi; Chawalit 'Lek' Ratanachinakorn at Saneha; Wilai and family in Phuket Town; Nico, Diane, Scott and Chaini at my new Phuket home; Tony and Jo at Rum Jungle; Wan Phakawan, James Hembrow, Ja and Thanasin; and the wonderful Celine Masson, Claude Sauter and your sweet children for our continued, valued and deepening friendship. All is Love.

ACKNOWLEDGMENTS

Climate map data adapted from Peel MC, Finlayson BL & McMahon TA (2007) 'Updated World Map of the Köppen-Geiger Climate Classification', Hydrology and Earth System Sciences, 11, 1633–44.

Illustrations pp56-7 and pp62-3 by Michael Weldon.

Cover photograph: Hat Phra Nang, Krabi. © Chad Case/Alamy

THIS BOOK

This 9th edition of *Thailand's Islands & Beaches* was researched and written by Celeste Brash, Austin Bush, David Eimer and Adam Skolnick. The previous edition was written and researched by Celeste and Austin along with Brandon Presser. This guidebook was commissioned in Lonely Planet's Melbourne office, and produced by the following:

Commissioning Editor Ilaria Walker
Coordinating Editors Lorna Parkes, Luna Soo, Tracy Whitmey
Senior Cartographer Diana Von Holdt
Book Designer Clara Monitto
Assisting Editors Bruce Evans, Anne Mulvaney, Chris Pitts

Cover Research Naomi Parker
Language Content Branislava Vladisavljevic
Thanks to Elin Berglund, Ryan Evans, Larissa Frost, Errol Hunt, Genesys India, Jouve India, Anne Mason, Kate Mathews, Wayne Murphy, Martine Power, Angela Tinson

Index

Map Pages **000**
Photo Pages **000**

Map Pages **000**
Photo Pages **000**

L

M

Map Pages **000**
Photo Pages **000**

T

V

W

Y

Z

Map Legend

Sights
- Beach
- Bird Sanctuary
- Buddhist
- Castle/Palace
- Christian
- Confucian
- Hindu
- Islamic
- Jain
- Jewish
- Monument
- Museum/Gallery/Historic Building
- Ruin
- Sento Hot Baths/Onsen
- Shinto
- Sikh
- Taoist
- Winery/Vineyard
- Zoo/Wildlife Sanctuary
- Other Sight

Activities, Courses & Tours
- Bodysurfing
- Diving
- Canoeing/Kayaking
- Course/Tour
- Skiing
- Snorkelling
- Surfing
- Swimming/Pool
- Walking
- Windsurfing
- Other Activity

Sleeping
- Sleeping
- Camping

Eating
- Eating

Drinking & Nightlife
- Drinking & Nightlife
- Cafe

Entertainment
- Entertainment

Shopping
- Shopping

Information
- Bank
- Embassy/Consulate
- Hospital/Medical
- Internet
- Police
- Post Office
- Telephone
- Toilet
- Tourist Information
- Other Information

Geographic
- Beach
- Hut/Shelter
- Lighthouse
- Lookout
- Mountain/Volcano
- Oasis
- Park
- Pass
- Picnic Area
- Waterfall

Population
- Capital (National)
- Capital (State/Province)
- City/Large Town
- Town/Village

Transport
- Airport
- Border crossing
- Bus
- Cable car/Funicular
- Cycling
- Ferry
- Metro/MRT station
- Monorail
- Parking
- Petrol station
- Skytrain/Subway station
- Taxi
- Train station/Railway
- Tram
- Underground station
- Other Transport

Note: Not all symbols displayed above appear on the maps in this book

Routes
- Tollway
- Freeway
- Primary
- Secondary
- Tertiary
- Lane
- Unsealed road
- Road under construction
- Plaza/Mall
- Steps
- Tunnel
- Pedestrian overpass
- Walking Tour
- Walking Tour detour
- Path/Walking Trail

Boundaries
- International
- State/Province
- Disputed
- Regional/Suburb
- Marine Park
- Cliff
- Wall

Hydrography
- River, Creek
- Intermittent River
- Canal
- Water
- Dry/Salt/Intermittent Lake
- Reef

Areas
- Airport/Runway
- Beach/Desert
- Cemetery (Christian)
- Cemetery (Other)
- Glacier
- Mudflat
- Park/Forest
- Sight (Building)
- Sportsground
- Swamp/Mangrove

OUR STORY

A beat-up old car, a few dollars in the pocket and a sense of adventure. In 1972 that's all Tony and Maureen Wheeler needed for the trip of a lifetime – across Europe and Asia overland to Australia. It took several months, and at the end – broke but inspired – they sat at their kitchen table writing and stapling together their first travel guide, *Across Asia on the Cheap*. Within a week they'd sold 1500 copies. Lonely Planet was born.

Today, Lonely Planet has offices in Franklin, London, Melbourne, Oakland, Beijing and Delhi, with more than 600 staff and writers. We share Tony's belief that 'a great guidebook should do three things: inform, educate and amuse'.

OUR WRITERS

Celeste Brash

Coordinating Author, Ko Samui & the Lower Gulf Celeste first arrived in Thailand as a student of Thai language, history and culture at Chiang Mai University. She's come back countless times since and has run the gamut from wild nights on Ko Pha-Ngan to weeks of silence at a Buddhist wát. Her writing has appeared in publications ranging from *Islands* magazine to newspapers and anthologies. She's contributed to around 50 Lonely Planet guides but her heart is irrevocably stuck on Southeast Asia. When not in exotic places, she and her family live in Portland, Oregon. Find her on the web at www.celestebrash.com.

Austin Bush

Bangkok, Food & Drink, Food Spotter's Guide Austin Bush came to Thailand in 1999 as part of a language study programme hosted by Chiang Mai University. The lure of city life, employment and spicy food eventually led Austin to Bangkok. City life, employment and spicy food have managed to keep him there since. A native of Oregon, Austin is a writer and photographer who often focuses on food. Samples of his work can be seen at www.austinbushphotography.com.

David Eimer

Ko Chang & the Eastern Seaboard, Hua Hin & the Upper Gulf A decade of visiting Thailand in search of beaches and fine food prompted David to relocate to Bangkok in 2012. Since then, his work as a journalist for a variety of newspapers and magazines has taken him from the far south of Thailand to its northernmost extremities, with many stops in between. Originally from London, David spent seven years living in Beijing, and another five in LA, prior to moving to Bangkok. He has contributed to 11 Lonely Planet books.

Adam Skolnick

Phuket & the Northern Andaman Coast, Ko Phi-Phi & the Southern Andaman Coast Adam Skolnick writes about travel, culture, health, sports, human rights and the environment for Lonely Planet, *Outside*, *Travel & Leisure*, Salon.com, BBC.com and ESPN.com. He has co-authored more than 20 Lonely Planet guidebooks, and on this research trip he drove more than 3000 kilometres and hopped on more than 50 long-tails. His debut novel, *Middle of Somewhere*, is set to be published in 2014. You can read more of his work at www.adamskolnick.com. Find him on Twitter and Instagram (@adamskolnick).

Published by Lonely Planet Publications Pty Ltd
ABN 36 005 607 983
9th edition – July 2014
ISBN 978 1 74220 738 4

10 9 8 7 6 5 4 3 2 1
Printed in China